Infancy

Infant, Family, and Society

SECOND EDITION

SECOND EDITION

Infancy

Infant, Family, and Society

Alan Fogel

UNIVERSITY OF UTAH

WEST PUBLISHING COMPANY

Saint Paul   New York   Los Angeles   San Francisco

Production Credits

Copyediting: Marilynn Taylor
Artist: Rolin Graphics
Composition: The Clarinda Company
Cover/Interior Design: K. M. Weber
Cover Photo: The Image Bank, Michel Tchereykoff, photographer

Copyright © 1984 by West Publishing Company
Copyright © 1991 by West Publishing Company
50 W. Kellogg Boulevard
P.O. Box 64526
St. Paul, MN 55614–1003

Printed in the United States of America
98 97 96 95 94 93 92 91   8 7 6 5 4 3 2 1 0

Library of Congress Cataloging-in-Publication Data

Fogel, Alan.
   Infancy: infant, family, and society/Alan Fogel.—2nd ed.
      p.   cm.
   Includes bibliographical references and index.
   ISBN 0-314-79878-1 (soft)
   1. Infants.   2. Infants—Family relationships.   3. Child
development.   4. Parent and child.   5. Family.   I. Title.
HQ774.F63   1991
305.23'2—dc20   90-25156
                                                                  CIP

Photo Credits

vi Courtesy of Jacqueline Fogel; **6** The Bettmann Archive; **9** © Stuart Cohen/Comstock; **18** © Jeffrey Grosscup; **33** Courtesy of the University of Wisconsin Primate Laboratory; **43** © Bill Anderson/Monkmeyer; **55** © Suzanne Arms-Wimberley; **73 (left and right)** Courtesy of Dr. J. Aznar; **80** © Lennart Nilsson. Photo originally appeared in *A Child Is Born*, by Lennart Nilsson (New York: Dell Publishing Company) and *Behold Man*, by Lennart Nilsson (Boston: Little, Brown and Company). **81** © Lennart Nilsson. Photo originally appeared in *A Child Is Born*, by Lennart Nilsson (New York: Dell Publishing Company) and *Behold Man*, by Lennart Nilsson (Boston: Little, Brown and Company). **105** © Elizabeth Zuckerman/PhotoEdit; **108** © Alan Oddie/PhotoEdit; **119** © Suzanne Arms-Wimberley; **134** © Jeffrey Grosscup; **140** © Myrleen Ferguson/PhotoEdit; **145** © Suzanne Arms-Wimberley; **156 (top)** © Suzanne Arms-Wimberley; **156 (middle)** © Suzanne Arms-Wimberley; **156 (bottom)** © Elizabeth Crews; **181 (top, middle, and bottom)** Courtesy of D. Rosenstein and H. Oster, *Child Development* (1988); **185** From A. N. Meltzoff and M. K. Moore, *Science*, 1977, 198: 75–78 **191** Courtesy of Marianne Moody Jennings; **208** © Erika Stone/Photo Researchers, Inc.; **221** © Suzanne Arms-Wimberley **229** © Elizabeth Crews; **255** © Elizabeth Crews; **264** © Erika Stone/Photo Researchers, Inc.; **268** © Bill Aron/Photo Researchers, Inc.; **275** © Elizabeth Crews; **283** Courtesy of Richard Walk, whose granddaughter is in the photograph; **285** © Suzanne Szasz/Photo Researchers, Inc.; **328** © Robert Brenner/PhotoEdit; **331** © Jeffrey Grosscup; **334** © Robert Brenner/PhotoEdit; **346** © Ray Ellis/Photo Researchers, Inc.; **362** © Elizabeth Crews; **366** © Myrleen Ferguson/PhotoEdit; **385** © Barbara Ries/Photo Researchers, Inc.; **401** © Victor Englebert/Photo Researchers, Inc.; **404** © Myrleen Ferguson/PhotoEdit; **416** © Jeffrey Grosscup; **424** © Robert Brenner/PhotoEdit; **433** © Myrleen Ferguson/PhotoEdit

For my father and mother, Walter and Sherry Fogel

ABOUT THE AUTHOR

Alan Fogel is a Professor of Psychology at the University of Utah. Born in Miami, Florida, he earned his B.S. in physics at the University of Miami (Coral Gables, Florida), and his M.A. in Physics at Columbia University (New York, NY) where he was a Faculty Fellow. During his three-year term with the United States Peace Corps in Bogota, Colombia, Fogel taught physics and worked on developing physics curricula for high schools. Through this experience Fogel became interested in how young people learn, which led to his completion of a Ph.D. degree in education, with a focus on early childhood development, at the University of Chicago.

Dr. Fogel is active as a researcher and author. He has co-edited two books on research in child development: *Emotion and Early Interaction* (with Tiffany Field), and *Origins of Nurturance: Biological, Cultural and Developmental Perspectives on Caregiving* (with Gail F. Melson). He has also written an undergraduate text on child develpment, *Child Development: Individual, Family and Society* (with Gail F. Melson). Fogel has published scholarly papers on development in infancy. These include studies of emotional development, social and communicative development in relation to parents and to peers, and on topics of infant development of concern to health care providers and early childhood educators. This work is published in *Child Development, Developmental Psychology, Developmental Psychobiology, Infant Behavior and Development, Journal of Pediatric Psychology, International Journal of Behavioral Development,* and *Current Topics in Early Childhood Education.* Fogel has been supported in his research through grants from the National Science Foundation, The National Institutes of Health, the National March of Dimes Foundation, and the United States Development of Agriculture. He is a member of the national research honor society, Sigma Xi. He has lectured widely in the United States, Japan (where he spent the 1983–1984 academic year as a senior research scholar under a Fulbright Fellowship) and in Europe (where he was a Visiting Professor at the Free University in Amsterdam in 1990).

CONTENTS

■ CHAPTER 4

The Process of Childbirth   115

■ CHAPTER 5

The Psychology of the Newborn (the First Two Months)   153

■ CHAPTER 6

**Attention and Anticipation
(Two to Five Months)**   199

■ CHAPTER 7

The Origins of Initiative
(Six to Nine Months) 239

■ CHAPTER 10

Conflict, Doubt, and Power
(Eighteen to Twenty-Four Months)   343

■ CHAPTER 11

"I'm Not a Baby Anymore" (Twenty-Four to Thirty-Six Months)   379

■ CHAPTER 12

The Effects of the Infancy Period on the Formation of Individual Differences   415

■ APPENDICES

PREFACE

Babies evoke mixed feelings in almost everyone. Common descriptions of babies range from wonderful, cute, delightful, cuddly, soft, and warm on the positive side to noisy, smelly, demanding, and frustrating on the negative side. The way we feel about babies usually depends on how much experience we have had with them, how old we are, what kind of mood we happen to be in, and things we've heard from others about babies.

What is the real truth about babies? This book draws heavily on infancy research that has been conducted in the past twenty years and provides an authoritative, scientifically-based account of infant development. The research results reported in this book, combined with your own experience with infants, should lead you closer to a view of what babies are like.

This book is designed to report not only the facts about infants but also to convey the vitality of infants as developing human beings. This is accomplished by taking a chronological approach to infant development. The goal in each chapter is to construct a multifaceted picture of babies in a particular age period. Similar topics are covered in each chapter, with an eye toward distinguishing the developmental uniqueness of babies at each age. In most chapters, these topics include: motor and physical development, perceptual and cognitive development, and social and language development. I have also focused on research that describes what infants actually do, think, and feel and on how they behave in everyday contexts.

In reading the first edition, some students found it difficult to trace the continuity within topics across chapters. I have tried to make these links clearer. In addition, I try to cover some topics completely in a single chapter, even if the topic applies across a number of stages. Examples of this are differences in parental treatment of first-born and later-born children (Chapter 5), the transition to parenthood (Chapter 6), and sex differences in treatment of infants and sex-role identity (Chapters 11 and 12). These and other topics can be found with an active use of the table of contents and the index. Students should not be afraid to reread the same topics from an earlier chapter to help clarify how the infant has changed in a particular domain.

Instructors can encourage such integration by asking students in class, in study questions, on homework exercises, and on exams to explicitly differentiate, for example, the perceptual abilities of three- and seven-month-old infants.

Observational exercises, interviews with parents of babies of different ages, and films help to bring these developmental differences to life for students. The value of this text will be enhanced if these kinds of instructional supports can be included in the course.

For a shorter course, instructors can skip similar sections in each chapter. Instructors wishing to focus on the infant can skip the Family and Society and Applications sections. Those wishing a more applied course or a more socially oriented course could skip the sections on Motor Development and Perceptual Development. Another way to shorten the course is to drop whole chapters. Those that could be dropped without serious discontinuity are Chapter 2 (theory), Chapter 4 (birth), and Chapter 12 (early experience and individual differences).

The chronological approach is conceptually easier and more rewarding than trying to piece together a sense of the infant at a particular age across a large number of topics. Often, this cannot happen until the end of a course using a topically organized book. More often, topical books give developmental changes in such a broad sweep that the application of the topic to a particular age is not made explicit. A chapter on social development, for example, might focus on attachment at one year at the expense of detailed accounts of social behavior at other ages. This book strives to give students a sense of the infant's integrity at each age that they can continue to update as they read each new chapter.

In addition, one of the unique features of this text is that each chapter includes a section on the infant in the family and society. In this section, you will find such topics as the effects of infants on parental and care-giver development, father-mother differences, infant-sibling and infant-peer interactions, maternal employment, and social policies toward infants. Of particular importance is that this section in most chapters contains a significant discussion of cultural differences in infancy and infant care.

Each chapter also addresses a current issue in infant development, under the heading of "Applications." These issues include abortion, sudden infant death syndrome, day care, and child abuse. Finally, each chapter has a section entitled "Points of Contact." This section contains concrete suggestions for infant care and social interaction with infants. It is based on the research reviewed earlier in the chapter but written in an informal tone that could be applied immediately by care givers. Finally, each chapter has a summary and glossary of terms.

As in the first edition, this book contains a chapter covering the third year of life (Chapter 11). Few other books take infant development this far. This chapter provides the necessary concepts for students to imagine how infants become preschoolers. This transition, from prelanguage to language and from the concrete to the symbolic, is one of the more fascinating and difficult-to-understand developmental changes. It adds to the student's comprehension of where infants are going developmentally and leads naturally into a more detailed look at early and later childhood.

In addition to the chapters covering each stage of infant development, there are several topical chapters that cover broad issues. Chapter 1 provides a basic orientation to infancy in the twentieth century and includes a historical review of infancy. A new section in this edition, Methods of Research on Infant Development, gives an overview of some of the basic research techniques used in infant studies.

Chapter 2 acquaints the student with the current theories of infant and early childhood development. This theoretical review has been completely rewritten and updated in this edition. It now better reflects theoretical perspectives that are actively used by infancy researchers. After each theory is presented, it is critically evaluated. The chapter urges an eclectic approach to theorizing about infants, rather than a contest about which theory is best overall. In order to help the rest of the book stand alone without this chapter, I have referred to theory only sparingly elsewhere. Instructors who wish to teach a more theoretically based course should guide students in the theoretical interpretation of the research presented in each chapter.

Chapter 3 covers the area of prenatal development in an innovative manner that you will not find in any other text in this area. First, the chapter places the prenatal period in a developmental context. The emphasis is on the continuities between prenatal and postnatal development. Although most prenatal development is physical, the developmental processes are similar to those found later. A second unique feature of this chapter is that there is a strong emphasis on behavior and learning, missing from most treatments of prenatal development. Attention is devoted to behavioral developments and to the effects of prenatal motor and sensory experiences on later development. Traditional topics of genetic, chromosomal, and teratogenic influences are treated in depth.

Finally, Chapter 12 addresses the effects of the infancy experience on the formation of individual differences. Such topics as intelligence, sociability, and temperament are covered in detail. Although individual differences are addressed in each chapter, the larger problem of how individual differences are formed and maintained requires us to take a look back on the entire infancy period.

The Appendix contains standard growth charts for boys and girls, as well as a list of potential careers in the field of infancy. This is included because changes in our society have led to a new focus on the early childhood years. There is an increasing demand for quality day-care providers, and there is a growing professionalism to be found in careers working with infants. This benefits everyone. The parents of infants prefer to trust their babies to the care of professionals. Professionalism encourages higher pay and better working conditions for providers, as well as the establishment of standards of professional excellence.

This second edition reflects these developments. There are higher standards for the training and education of providers now than in 1984, when the first edition was published. This book, while remaining applied in focus, is more rigorous and research based. This edition also balances the earlier focus on social development in the family and society with a greater attention to the details of basic infant developmental changes, particularly in the motor, perceptual, and cognitive domains. The second edition has also been enhanced with more figures and tables illustrating the material.

I would like to thank the following persons for the contributions to this second addition. First, I found the insights of the following reviewers especially helpful: David Andrews, John Colombo, Martha Childers, Kathleen Elson, Rebecca Glover, Sue Martin, Pamm Mattick, Sharon McCluskey, Charles Nelson, Gregory Pettit, Mark Reimers, Sandra Twardosz, and M. Virginia Wyly. Second, I thank those members of the editorial staff at West Publishing who participated in this work: Seán Berres, Lynette D'Amico, Tom LaMarre, Jayne Lindesmith,

Kristen McCarthy, Melody Rotman, and Mary Schiller. Third, my work on this edition was assisted invaluably by research assistants Caroline Hampsey, Ava Phillips, Christa Pierce, and Kim Ward, and by editorial assistants Alison Smith, Sandra Sommer, and Cindy White. Finally, my family—Jacqueline, Menasheh, and Dan—were unbelievably supportive, although they may never let me write another book.

ONE

Basic Concepts of Infant Behavior and Development

———

CHAPTER OUTLINE

Have you ever wondered about the details of your own birth? Do you think it was painful or pleasurable? What must it have been like living inside your mother? Do you remember learning to crawl or to walk? What was the first word you ever said? If you know the answer to any of these questions, it is because you have asked or were told about it by someone who was an adult when you were a baby.

Infancy is mysterious to us because we have no direct memory of our own infancy, because we rely on the memory of others who were there, and because babies themselves cannot tell us what they feel, at least not in words. The mystery of the infant's mind has intrigued parents, philosophers, and theologians for thousands of years. In the twentieth century, the search for understanding infancy became a recognized field in the sciences. The twentieth century has also raised infancy to the status of a topic of fundamental importance to society.

■ INFANTS IN THE NEWS

When does life begin?
Congress debates the use of fetuses in research.
Fallout from nuclear plant contaminates human breast milk.
Diet and exercise is the secret to weight loss after childbirth.
Drought and war sentence Ethiopian infants to death by starvation.
You can teach your child to read before age two.
Is day care a basic human right, a privilege for the rich, or the end of early childhood as we know it?

If you read the newspapers or watch television news programs, you'll recognize some of these headlines and advertisement leads. At the end of the twentieth century, babies are big news and big business. Reports of abandoned infants, child abuse, and miracle survivals of the tiniest premature infants take as much time and space in local news media as automobile accidents and crimes.

Medical Miracles

Medical research has discovered remarkable new treatments for disorders of the prenatal and infancy periods. Parents can discover soon after conception if their infant carries a genetic disorder. In the most serious cases, parents may choose to terminate the pregnancy. In a growing number of cases, however, treatments given to fetuses directly can permanently eliminate the effects of such disorders (see Chapter 3). Premature infants are more likely to survive and live normal lives than ever before. Simple treatments for combatting infant death in the Third World are saving millions of lives (see Chapter 4).

If infants from a wealthy nation survive past birth, the chances that they will die from a serious disease are extremely small due to widespread immunizations and health care. Public health officials are beginning to make progress in reducing the largest cause of infant death in these countries: accidents. Parent education for infant health and safety, safer toys, better infant restraints for automobiles (more infants and children lose their lives in auto accidents in North America than from all other causes of death combined!) and better enforcement of seat belt laws are all helping to reduce injury and mortality (see Chapter 8).

Global Concerns

A growing number of charities are devoted to infancy and are collecting an increasing number of contributions from those who can afford to give. In North America, homelessness, teenage pregnancy, infants born with handicaps, infants with drug addiction and AIDS are getting our attention and our support. Private contributions combine with foreign aid from wealthy governments and United Nations funds to help rescue infants and young children in the Third World from disease, contaminated food and water, poverty, starvation, war, and natural disasters, such as floods and earthquakes. Many orphaned infants from the Third World are adopted by parents in Western countries.

Babies Play Starring Roles

Infancy is in. The "how to" articles, products, and books on childrearing, pregnancy, and childbirth are squeezing other items off store shelves. Most large supermarkets in Europe, Asia, and North America have an entire aisle devoted to baby products: diapers, oils, powders, foods, furniture, strollers and packs, books and magazines.

If the 1970s and early 1980s were the era when Hollywood discovered the coming of age of teenagers and the Vietnam War, the late 1980s and early 1990s must be the years of the baby movie. Three bachelors get handed a baby by one of their ex-girlfriends, and after initial struggles, all become devoted parents. A career-oriented woman who is left with a baby after a distant cousin dies first tries to keep her executive-level job, then quits it and rediscovers herself and the meaning of motherhood. A poor couple desperate to have children temporarily steal a baby from a wealthy family with many children. They care for, love, but later return the baby to its original home.

Why is there such a deep and growing interest in infancy in the world today? All of the issues and problems existed long before they were so frequently discussed and so recently brought into the international consciousness. To get some insight into the answer to this question, we can review some of the historical trends in society's interest in infants.

■ A BRIEF HISTORY OF BABIES

Among the topics mentioned in the last section are both positive and negative aspects of infancy. An infant born into today's world may experience poverty or wealth, love or abuse, health or disease. Was it always this way? In general, the answer to this question is "yes." In all periods of our history for which there are archeological or historical sources, we can find evidence of both kindness to and neglect of children.

Early Civilizations

In ancient Egypt and Greece, historians have found evidence of toys and games for children and written documents describing the need to love and protect infants (Greenleaf, 1978). A first-century B.C. Chinese text, *Liji* (*Record of Rituals*), states, "When training is premature, nothing is gained other than a great deal of work. Keep babies quiet, and do not stimulate them. Only after behavior emerges from inside can proper guidance begin" (Kojima, 1986b, p. 44). Unfortunately, this sensitivity to the needs of children was confined primarily to the educated and wealthy sectors of society. Slavery, ignorance, and disease robbed many children of life and love.

Middle Ages

A similar distinction between privilege and deprivation continued throughout recorded history. In the Middle Ages in Europe, the largely rural population began to move in large numbers to cities and towns. At the same time, there were frequent changes in the political boundaries as empires dissolved and local powers asserted themselves. These social changes contributed to an increasingly educated urban population on the one hand and to the growth of a class of urban poor who suffered from disease, malnutrition, pollution, and ignorance on the other. The unhealthy conditions of poor people in cities were much worse than for the poor in the countryside. Because of inadequate sanitation and other sources of urban pollution (pollution is not a new problem), infants of the urban poor were more likely to die or to suffer birth defects than those from rural areas. Because cities drew people away from family roots and because disease claimed the lives not only of infants but of mothers in childbirth, many orphaned children walked the streets as beggars, thieves, and prostitutes. As you can see, the story of childhood among the urban poor then is not too much different from today's.

It was not until the European Renaissance, beginning in the sixteenth century, that we began to see the emergence of written philosophies of child rearing. Infants and children appeared in paintings that showed them in religious settings, in stylized clothing, and with adult-like facial features and mannerisms. In one painting, Christ as an infant is shown making the Catholic gesture of benediction to a group of people kneeling before him.

Reason and Passion

By the eighteenth century, new ideas began to emerge about the value of human life, dignity, and freedom. In France, Jean Jacques Rousseau (1712–1778) argued that childhood was a time of special privilege, that children bring goodness into the world (not original sin), and that education should be sensitive to the needs and inclinations of the infant and young child. The social movement of which Rousseau was a part was called *romanticism.*

Its followers included the great English romantic poets, such as William Wordsworth (1770–1850), who wrote of childhood in idealized terms.

Behold the Child among his new-born blisses,
A six years' darling of pygmy size!
See, where 'mid work of his own hand he lies,
Fretted by sallies of his mother's kisses,
With light upon him from his father's eyes!
(From "Imitations of Immortality from Recollections of Early Childhood," in Williams, 1952, p. 263).

Compare, however, the words of William Blake (1757–1827), who recognized the need to educate and guide children, not simply to love and protect them. Blake's verses also reflect an awareness of the more painful and difficult paths down which one's life might lead without the proper guidance.

He who mocks the infant's faith.
Shall be mock'd in Age and Death.
He who shall teach the child to doubt
The rotting grave shall ne'er get out.
He who respects the infant's faith
Triumphs over Hell and Death.
The child's toys and the old man's reasons
Are the fruits of the two seasons.
(From "Auguries of Innocence," in Williams, 1952, p. 229).

Blake rejected the simple notions of innocence found in the romantics. In a poem called "The Scoffers," Blake suggested that the scientific achievements of Sir Isaac Newton were far more lasting intellectual milestones than the mocking voice of Rousseau. Charles Dickens was another author who rejected romanticism. Instead of depicting the childhood of nineteenth-century England as a time of happy contentment, in *Oliver Twist* and other famous stories he courageously exposed the effects of disease, poverty, child abuse, and child labor for all to see.

Also from England, the philosopher John Locke (1682–1704) accepted the importance of early education for children, but he believed that children needed more structure. Locke is known for his rational approach to education, decidedly not a romantic one, because he thought children needed specific guidance and discipline. Starting from a notion that the infant's mind is a *tabula rasa*, a blank tablet on which anything could be written, Locke argued that education should provide the skills to make rational choices. The philosophical movement to which he belonged has been called *empiricism*.

The romantic ideas of freedom and happiness combined with the empiricist ideas of reason and realism to create the philosophical foundations for the national revolutions in France and America. These ideas also led in the nineteenth century to the growth of social responsibility toward infants and children and the rise of the idea of the child as an integral part of the definition of the family. The "discovery" of the child was due to urban forces in Europe and North America that segregated the family from the workplace, defined the mother's role as major supervisor of the domestic scene, and allowed love or sentiment (rather than family inheritance or economic well-being) to be the bond holding the family together (Hareven, 1985).

It should be noted, however, that the development of the nuclear family and its privatization was at first confined to the white middle class. Families from other classes and ethnic and racial groups preserved the pre-industrial extended form in which love, work, and education all took place within the family. The changes in the family did not occur uniformly in all parts of American society, and these cultural patterns still account for many of the differences among families today (Hareven, 1982).

These social changes led to the growing awareness of the public's responsibility for the welfare and development of infants. Although the first English-language pediatric textbook appeared in 1545, welfare and medical institutions devoted exclusively to children did not open in Europe and the United States until the 1850s, around the same time as the rise of immunization and the pasteurization of milk. Maternal deaths were reduced in this period by the invention of anesthesia and procedures for sterilizing medical instruments (Greenleaf, 1978).

These medical advances further solidified the family by reducing infant mortality. As each child could be counted on to live a healthy life, families began to consciously reduce the number of children so as to invest more emotional energy in each child. By the middle of the nineteenth century, infancy and childhood had emerged in the public mind as a separate and valuable stage of life. Child rearing and family advice literature began to be published (Hareven, 1985). Manufactured baby dolls first appeared in Europe in 1825. The first public playground was developed in Boston in 1885 (a few heaps of sand dumped in a vacant lot), but by 1915, 430 U.S. cities had

A North American mother and her baby in 1913. The elegant carriage is matched by the fashionable clothing worn by both individuals. Well-educated parents probably were aware of the competing ideas of Watson's behaviorism and Gesell's maturationism.

well-planned public playgrounds (Blank & Klig, 1982; Greenleaf, 1978; Zietz, 1969).

Infants Enter the World of Science

The beginning of the twentieth century saw the rise of the scientific study of infant development. Earlier views of romanticism versus empiricism were replaced by the ideas of *nature* (genetic) versus *nurture* (environmental) contributions to development. Arnold Lucius Gesell (1880–1961) thought that the orderly changes seen in early development were specified by the genes. The genetic timetable for the patterning of development was called *maturation*. Gesell made a career out of the careful measurements of developmental changes in size, motor skill, and behavior in infants and young children. He was the first scientist to use a one-way mirror for unobtrusive observation and the first to use film to record behavior.

Contrary to Gesell, John B. Watson (1878–1958) believed that children could be trained to do almost anything, given the right kind of reinforcements. He did studies in which he taught small children to be afraid of cuddly animals by making loud noises whenever they touched the animals.

Because Gesell believed in genetic maturation, he cared little about individual differences, focusing instead on the "average" child. This created anxiety in parents who read his works and discovered that their own children walked or talked later than the average age at which Gesell said they would. Even today, to paraphrase the radio host Garrison Keillor, all parents want children who are above average.

Watson also left a lasting imprint on North American society. As waves of immigrants landed on the shores of the United States and Canada, each had to believe that they could make a new life for themselves and their children. The idea that anyone could succeed regardless of past history or genetic heritage sustained the hopes of many new arrivals. Watson also placed responsibility for child outcome directly on the shoulders of parents; if the child failed, it was the parent's fault. He encouraged parents to avoid kissing and holding their babies in order to make them independent individuals.

Sigmund Freud (1856–1939) presented strong counterarguments to Watson and Gesell. Freud (see Chapter 2) recognized that all infants experienced emotional highs and lows and that even infants felt the need for love and possessed powerful desires. Freud's daughter, Anna, devoted most of her life to bringing her father's insights out of the adult psychoanalytic session and into the real lives of parents and children. Anna Freud taught parents to hold and cuddle babies and to be patient while babies discovered and tried to manage their own desires in appropriate ways (A. Freud, 1965). Here too, parents were faulted for their children's developmental problems: in this case, for giving them too little attention and affection and for "selfishly" not understanding the situation from the child's point of view.

Infants Go Public

These scientific theories of infant care and infant development spread rapidly into Western culture in the nineteenth and twentieth centuries because of the rise of the mass media. Electronic communication brought these theories to many people. Urbanization and the automobile created an increasingly mobile and nuclear family separated from grandparents and having to rely on the advice of child-care experts. Thus, society created a demand for better trained and better supported behavioral scientists who could share their expertise with a public hungry for rational approaches to child rearing.

Let us return to the question raised at the end of the previous section. Why is infancy even more in the public mind today than it was twenty-five years ago? Although there is no single answer, I think it is a reaction to this rapid growth of rational and scientific approaches to psychology and human development since the 1950s.

The scientific revolution during these years in behavioral research on infancy was very much in the empiricist tradition. The research emphasis was on infant learning and cognitive development. The publication of *The Competent Infant* (Stone, Smith & Murphy, 1973) reflected a desire to discover ever earlier signs of intelligence in infants. Parents strived to train their infants to achieve the maximum potential at the earliest possible age, similar to the eighteenth-century empiricists.

More recently, however, romantic ideas of infancy have begun to return, as reflected in the late 1980s collection of baby movies. A very work-oriented, rational adult attempts to apply the latest scientific and detached methods to infant care. This always fails, and the adult gets frustrated, but in the process, the rational adult unexpectedly becomes emotionally attached to the baby in a big way. What happens next is pure romanticism. The hard edges melt away from the adult, letting the "more pure" instincts of love and affection guide her or him in the parenting role.

A bit of romanticism has also returned to the scientific studies of infant development. The 1980s have seen a rise in studies of parent-child relationships, emotional development and attachment, communication and language. Of course, the more rational approaches to infant development continue to grow in such fields as cognitive neuroscience and behavior genetics. We will be discussing these trends in developmental science and some of the findings from the research in later chapters. In the next few sections, we will review some of the research approaches that have been devised for the study of infant development.

■ WHAT IS AN INFANT?

How you define infancy depends on what you want to know about infants. If you are a painter, a poet, or a filmmaker, infants may serve as metaphors for divinity or for innocence. Scientists rely more on careful and repeatable direct observations of infants. They strive to understand infants in their own right, detached from our social and cultural conceptions of the nature of infancy. Although all scientists admit that they, as products of their own society and culture, can never rid themselves completely of bias, they make explicit attempts to reach this goal.

Topics in Infant Development

A large number of topics in infancy have been studied scientifically. Some of these topics are listed below:

Perceptual/Sensorial Skills. These involve the development of the infant's senses—vision, touch, hearing, smell, vestibular-proprioceptive movement and balance, and taste—and the way in which the infant uses these sensory modalities to acquire knowledge about the world. Perceptual skills are not fully developed at birth; in fact, the human infant has a relatively rudimentary perceptual system for the first months of life. The sensory modality that has received the most attention from developmental scientists is vision, probably because of the relative ease with which standardized visual materials can be created for the purpose of experimentation. Auditory perception ranks second in the number of research studies devoted to it.

What is an infant? More than a pretty face, an infant is a complex human being from the start. Infants have the ability to execute motor actions, solve problems, express feelings and communicate with other people.

Sensorimotor/Tool-Using. Movement is fundamental to all forms of developmental change. As infants make simple movements, such as turning their heads, the visual images on the retina change. These self-produced spontaneous movements allow the child to compare perceptual inputs and begin to construct a clearer view of the solidity of objects and spatial patterns. The development of motor skills usually is correlated with changes in other areas. Crawling and walking allow infants to access new parts of their world and enhance the awareness of the self as an independent agent. Infant motor skills progress from simple acts, such as turning over, to locomotor skills, to fine motor coordination of objects and tools, such as toys and crayons. Scientific interest in motor development declined after the 1930s, but the 1980s have seen a rapid increase in studies of motor development.

Conceptual/Thinking. Cognitive developmental studies chart changes in the infant's capacity to make sense of the world. For example, a major cognitive change occurs about the age of six months, when infants begin to form conceptual categories. Infants of this age have been shown to distinguish males from females and adults from children. By nine months, infants are beginning to develop an awareness of the fact that objects exist independently from the self. It is only in the latter part of the second year that infants behave as if they are actually thinking, reasoning, and planning actions mentally. Up until this time, the infant could execute a plan of action, but all of the trial and error of the attempt was acted out; there was no mental ability to preselect appropriate courses of action and eliminate others.

Representational/Symbolic. The crowning achievement of cognitive development in the first three years of life is the emergence of representational and symbolic thinking: the ability to grasp the idea that a sound or a picture (a spoken or a written word) can represent something entirely different. The written word for "dog" bears no visual similarity to a real canine, nor does the sound of the spoken word "dog." Children cannot grasp the relation between the symbol and the actual object until late in the second year of life. This achievement ushers in a rich new phase of the children's development: pretend play and shared meaning with others through language.

Communicative/Linguistic. Learning a first language in the short space of three years is an educational accomplishment of such magnitude that it would be hard to duplicate at any later point in life. There is more to language than just learning the meanings of words. It is also necessary to learn how words are used, when to speak and when to listen, and how to understand what others are saying. Language in this sense is really only one form of a broader intention to communicate, to share information, and to learn more about the world. Language, if we look at how it is used in everyday situations, is just as much a social skill as a cognitive skill.

Social/Interactive. Infants begin to learn social skills long before they ever acquire their first words. Some of the social skills that infants need to learn are so basic to human life as we know it that it is hard to believe that there was a time in our lives that we did not possess such capacities. One of these very basic social skills is the ability to take turns in a conversation. Although infants seem to be born with naturally occurring bursts and pauses in their behavior, any semblance of taking turns seems to be created by the adult partner who learns to insert smiles, coos, and words into the natural silences left by the infant. Although the infant does not initially intend to leave these spaces, the experience of having them filled by the adult eventually leads to a growing awareness that he or she is indeed a partner, one who can initiate, pause, speak, or act in concert with another. This ability does not appear before the age of five or six months.

Expressive/Emotive. An important part of the infant's social skills is the ability to experience certain kinds of emotional states as well as to express what is felt. Most of the research on infant emotional development seems to indicate that the kinds of emotions infants can feel change with age. It is generally agreed that infants do not know the feeling of fear before about eight months, and they cannot experience complex feelings, such as guilt, pride, or shame, until they are almost three years old. Even though most of the basic emotional expressions can be observed in newborns, infants develop the capacity to express mixed emotions and subtle shades of feeling as they mature. Infants also develop the ability to control the kinds of emotions they wish to express, but this does not happen until the second and third years of life.

Self-Regulatory/Coping. Most parents would probably be delighted to watch their babies develop each of the skills listed above. The development of self-regulatory skills is greeted by parents with a sense of relief that goes beyond delight. The ability of an infant to cope with the stresses of everyday life takes from the parent's shoulders a considerable burden. The hallmarks of successful self-regulation are sleeping through the night, waiting patiently while a meal is being prepared, handling the fear and distress of separation from parents, fighting assertively to retrieve a toy from a meddling sibling. All of these milestones, and many others that occur during the first three years of life, represent the growing autonomy of the child's functioning and therefore lead to a greater sense of freedom for the parents or care givers. Common to all these events is the ability to continue to function in the face of high levels of arousal. We shall see in later chapters that infants need to cope with high levels of negative arousal, but they must also learn to deal with high levels of positive arousal in situations where excitement and enjoyment threaten to become overwhelmingly intense.

When Does Infancy End?

Another aspect of defining infancy is the question of how long it lasts as a developmental period. Is infancy over when a child learns to talk or to walk? Is it over when the child herself, sometime between the second and third birthdays, begins to realize that she is a "big girl." Although there is no clear demarcation of the infancy period, this text will cover the period between conception and the third birthday, giving some perspective on development before birth and on the transition into the preschool years.

Stages of Infant Development

The definition of infancy also includes how we mark the important developmental transition points during the infancy period. In reality, infancy is a slow and continuous process of change. As far as the baby is concerned, it makes little difference how adults demarcate the important milestones of development.

The important divisions of an infant's life are viewed differently by each culture. The *Alor* people of Lesser Sundra Islands do not count the infant's age in months or days but rather as a series of stages of development. The first stage lasts from birth to the first smile, the second from smiling to sitting up alone or crawling, and another stage is marked from this point to the onset of walking. The *Chagga* of Tanganyika apply different names to infants depending upon their stage of development. A newborn is called *mnangu*, or "incomplete." A *mkoku* is "one who fills the lap," and a *mwana* is an infant before the age of three years (Mead & Newton, 1967). These linguistic labels are comparable to the terms *newborn, infant,* and *toddler* in English.

Parents and other infant care givers may use another type of division for the first three years. They may be more concerned about the ages at which infants become capable of independent play with other infants, the beginning of toilet training and the onset of bowel control, or the age at which infants become more relaxed when separated from their parents.

Developmental scientists tend to use milestones having to do with one of the areas mentioned in the last section. In making the decision about how to divide this book into chapters, Jean Piaget's sensorimotor substages (see Chapter 2) were chosen as the organizing unit. Piaget's work has received wide acclaim and acceptance. Although some do not agree with Piaget's explanations of development and others say he ignored important aspects of development, his three books on infancy (Piaget, 1952, 1954, 1962) provide one of the most detailed descriptions of infant skills.

Using Piaget's stages as a way to organize the book does not mean that the focus of each chapter is only on Piaget's ideas. On the contrary, a wide variety of research, theory, and applications that pertain to infants and their families at each of the age periods will be presented in each chapter. Thus, Piaget's theory will be used to organize infant development into stages, but we will not be limited to viewing infancy in these terms only.

What is Developmental Change?

The discussion of how and where to divide infant development raises a broader issue of how to define development. *Development* is ordered change. Not all changes that we observe in infants are developmental changes. A baby can change from being happy to being angry, but we wouldn't call such changes developmental since the child frequently changes between these two emotions.

Developmental changes are not reversible. Once we graduate to a new stage, we generally lose some of our earlier ideas or skills as we gain new ones.

Developmental changes are not temporary. Such changes persist over relatively long periods of weeks, months, or years.

Developmental changes are not haphazard. Development occurs in an orderly sequence that is similar across infants. Few infants speak in whole sentences without first passing through a period of one-word speech.

Using these ideas about development, we can describe developmental changes in each of the skill areas listed in the previous section. The motor skill progression—lying on the back, turning over, sitting up, standing and walking—represents nonreversible, permanent, and orderly change. Of course, infants who walk can still lie down and turn over, but older infants will never again experience a stage in which all they can do is lie down and turn over. The only exception would be in the case of neurological damage due to accident or disease. Similarly, in the area of language development the progression—crying, cooing, babbling, one-word speech, and multi-word speech—has all the required features of developmental change.

What is the Origin of Differences Between Infants?

A final issue in the definition of infancy is the way in which we describe the formation of *individual differences*. One part of the problem is the question of how to classify individuals into different groups. This depends on which of the particular areas of infant skill the research is most concerned with. For example, under the heading of "self-regulatory/coping skills," researchers have classified infants according to their ability to remain calm under stressful conditions. In the presence of a new toy, one that moves and makes noise, some infants will withdraw or act fearful. These infants are called "reactive." Nonreactive infants will be more likely either to ignore the toy or to approach it for exploration.

Another part of the problem of individual differences is understanding their cause. This usually means sorting out the relative influences of nature and nurture. Some recent research suggests that about 5 percent of all infants will remain extremely reactive over periods of up to several years (Kagan, 1989). Although the percentage is small, the *stability* of the reactive pattern over time and its early onset suggest that reactivity is in part genetically based. Nevertheless, not all infants who begin life with extreme reactivity remain reactive for a long time. If reactivity has a genetic basis, it must be open to some modifying influence of the environment such that infants can learn to cope with their high arousal and develop strategies for approaching new things.

Just as each culture has its own way of dividing the infant's life into stages, each culture, and perhaps each individual, has its own theory of the formation of individual differences. For example, the fourth-century Greeks believed that one could create a less reactive child by exposing the infant to a variety of fearful events early in life. Europeans in the nineteenth-century believed just the opposite; that reactivity could be lessened by protecting the child from fear-producing experiences (Kagan, Kearsley & Zelazo, 1978). Which of these "folk" theories is correct? How could you decide between them?

The position taken in this book is that while folk theories are important parts of people's beliefs and structure the way that people behave, scientific theories are more likely to uncover the actual processes that create developmental change and individual differences. The reason is that the scientist relies on many sources of evidence (individual folk theories may develop only from experience within one's own family), tries to separate what is repeatable and stable from what is coincidental (folk theories tend to infer general patterns from a small number of instances), and attempts to rid observations of bias (folk theories often embody what the observer hopes to see or believes should occur, rather than what actually does happen).

This does not mean that scientists always succeed in reaching these ideals. No scientific study is flawless, and all science is infused with the values of individuals and cultures. Nevertheless, because science has a set of codified and generally accepted procedures for acquiring and interpreting data, scientists can build on these procedures as they discover better, less biased methods. In the next section, we turn to a brief discussion of research methods in the study of infant development.

■ METHODS OF RESEARCH ON INFANT DEVELOPMENT

One of the earliest forms of systematic observation and recording of infant behavior is the daily diary kept by parents about their baby's life. These *baby biographies* began to appear in the sixteenth century. For example, the

German philosopher Dietrich Tiedemann (1748–1803) observed his infant son in such areas as motor skills, language, thinking abilities, and social behavior. Tiedemann described what we now call the *Moro reflex* (see Chapter 5) as follows:

. . . If he was held in arms and then suddenly lowered from a considerable height, he strove to hold himself with his hands, to save himself from falling; and he did not like to be lifted very high. Since he could not possibly have had any conception of falling, his fear was unquestionably a purely mechanical sensation, such as older persons feel at a steep and unaccustomed height, something akin to dizziness (Tiedemann, 1927, p. 216).

Another famous baby biographer was Charles Darwin. Here Darwin describes a startle reaction (Darwin uses the word "start") of his infant son William Erasmus. "Doddy," William's nickname, was born December 27, 1839.

When nine weeks and three days old—whilst lying on his back cooing and kicking very happily—I happened to sneeze—which made it start, frown, look frightened and cry rather badly—for an hour afterwards every noise made him start—he was nervous. I think he certainly has undefined instinctive fears—as for instance when stripped naked—I think also when peeping under dark doorways (Darwin, Notebook on Child Development, p. 6).

Longitudinal Versus Cross-Sectional

These baby biographies made important contributions to knowledge about infant development. All scientific fields have begun with a period in which people made extensive descriptions of natural phenomena. These diaries have preserved information in the form of a *longitudinal* record of the same children observed frequently over a long period of time.

In a *longitudinal study*, researchers can follow the same group of children as they get older. Longitudinal studies are important for determining how particular early experiences of individuals affect their later development. Change is measured against the individual's own record of growth. The disadvantage is that it requires the researcher to wait for the child to grow, although this takes less time for infants compared to older children.

Few researchers can find the research funding to support such long-term efforts. Another problem is *attrition,* which occurs when longitudinal subjects drop out of the research study before they complete the entire period of observation. Not only does attrition lower the number of subjects in a study, but researchers worry whether the subjects who remain are different from those that drop out.

One of the methods most commonly used today for the study of developmental change is a *cross-sectional study* in which the researcher selects children of different ages. Cross-sectional studies have the advantage of giving us a sense of age change in development without having to wait for the children to grow up. An additional advantage is that researchers who only observe children from two or three different age groups have more time to collect data from a large number of children, thus revealing patterns of between-individual variation in behavioral characteristics and age of attainment of developmental milestones. Thus, while cross-sectional studies allow us to make generalizations about groups of infants, they cannot tell us how individual infants develop over time, which is what the baby biographies did well.

Investigating Alternate Interpretations

The main problem with the baby biographies, however, was that the writers often failed to distinguish their own interpretations of and expectations about the infant's behavior from what the infant was actually doing. Thus, although Tiedemann and Darwin made accurate descriptions of their infants' behaviors, they also introduced their own ideas about what the behaviors meant—"a purely mechanical sensation" or "an instinctive fear."

These kinds of interpretations introduce one form of systematic *bias* into scientific studies. Researchers today try to prevent bias by being clear about the distinction between the child's actual behavior and their interpretation of the behavior. The accurate recording of the actual behavior becomes a problem in *assessment* or *measurement,* while the interpretation of the behavior becomes a *conceptual* or *theoretical* problem.

Researchers today work to verify their own theoretical interpretations of infant behavior. They do this, however, by trying to examine *alternate interpretations* for the same results. Alternate interpretations are examined by varying the conditions of observation in systematic ways and looking for changes in the infant's behavior. We refer to research that is designed to test alternate interpretations as *systematic research.*

Some of the first systematic studies were done with infants and young children in nursery schools, and they tended to focus on early social and emotional development. Bridges (1932), Buhler (1930), and Parten (1932) studied emotional development and peer interactions in nursery school settings. Other early work examined perceptual and physiological aspects of behavior. Holden and Bosse (1900) found that infants could distinguish between colors, Conel (1939, 1941) discovered major anatomical changes in the infant's brain during development, and Marquis (1931) found that human infants could be classically conditioned.

Jean Piaget (1896–1980) followed in the tradition of the baby biographers by making extensive written notes, often on a daily basis, about the behavior of his three infant children. The difference between Piaget and his predecessors is that he not only observed natural behavior, he tried out little experiments in order to test alternate interpretations of what the children could do. At one point, Piaget was trying to determine whether his 8-month-old daughter Jacqueline (J.) was capable of imitating mouth movements and sounds.

One of the problems of inferring the ability to imitate is that adults unwittingly do a lot of imitation of infants. During early social play, infants and adults appear to imitate each other's sounds or facial expressions over a long series of turns. In reality, the infant is capable of making a series of smiles. Adults insert their own smiles imitatively into the pauses naturally left between the infant's smiles, making the infant appear to have imitated the previous adult smile.

In this example, J. seemed to imitate her father's biting movements, or did she? Piaget wasn't sure whether J. only appeared to imitate because he had started out by imitating movements she could already make.

J. was moving her lips as she bit on her jaws. I did the same thing, and she stopped and watched me attentively. . . . J. began to imitate me an hour later. . . . In order to understand this new development, two circumstances must be noted. Firstly, for some days she had not merely imitated sounds for their own sake but had watched the mouth of the model with great attention. Secondly, as she moved her lips, J. began by making a slight noise with her saliva . . . and I had imitated this sound at the outset. Her interest in the movements of the mouth was thus clearly due to interest in the production of sound.

[Three days later] I resumed the experiment without making any sound and without J. herself having made the movement beforehand. She watched my lips moving and then distinctly imitated me three times, keeping her eyes fixed on my mouth (Piaget, 1962, pp. 30–31).

Experiments and Quasi-Experiments

In this example, Piaget combined naturalistic observation with an experiment. An *experiment* is a research study in which one aspect of the situation is manipulated while all other aspects are held constant or controlled. In this case, in order to discover J.'s ability to imitate mouth movements *on her own*, Piaget waited for a time when J. had not made the movement spontaneously for some time, and he did not produce any sound when he made the movements himself. The prior condition (the child makes no similar spontaneous movement and the adult does not imitate the child) and the presentation of the adult model (absence of sound) were controlled. The experimental manipulation is the presence or absence of a movement-only adult model.

In modern versions of Piaget's famous imitation experiment, many other aspects of the situation are controlled: the position in which the child is sitting, the behavior of the adult model, the familiarity of the adult to the infant, and the procedures of observation (see Chapter 5). The following are some of the procedures infant researchers have used to eliminate bias in their studies.

Control groups that do not receive any manipulation are compared to groups of infants who receive the experimental manipulation. Alternatively, different types of manipulations are compared using multiple *contrast* groups. In imitation research, different groups of infants are each presented with a different model (e.g., tongue protrusion, mouth movement, or a facial expression and a no-model control group). If imitation occurs, the frequency of tongue protrusion following the model should be the highest in the group having seen the tongue protrusion model. This procedure controls for the fact that most babies produce tongue protrusion spontaneously, such that there would be some tongue protrusion seen in all the groups.

Random assignment is used to determine which subjects belong to each experimental group. A flip of a coin or some other random process is used to assign subjects to groups. In some cases, it is unethical to use random assignment in a study. For example, suppose we want to compare the effects on language development of differences in mother's speech to infants. We obviously cannot randomly assign mothers to infants. We use instead the natural variations of maternal speech within the existing population of infants and mothers.

A study that relies on natural variations to create contrast groups rather than random assignment is called a *quasi-experimental* study. The problem with quasi-experiments is that the variable on which the groups are assigned (e.g., the amount of maternal speech) may also correlate with other factors (such as the amount of mother's overall social skills and general expressiveness). If this occurs, it is impossible to say which factor—speech, social skills, or expressiveness—is the cause of differences in infant language. In most cases involving human infancy, quasi-experiments are all we can do. As discussed later in this book, researchers have developed ways to examine the mutual influences of many potential causes that enter into a quasi-experiment.

Reducing Bias in Research

Reliability and *validity* procedures are other ways of attempting to reduce bias in research. *Reliability* is a measure of the consistency with which an assessment procedure is applied. If one is trying to measure an infant's preference for looking at her mother compared to an unfamiliar woman, observers may be asked to record the duration of infant looking at each adult. The extent of agreement between two independent observers about those durations is a measure of reliability.

Validity is the degree to which the procedure accurately measures what it is intended to measure. For example, one might ask if the duration of time looking at the mother versus the stranger is a valid measure of infant's preference for one or the other. A baby may look longer at an unfamiliar face because it is new and different from more familiar faces. In order to test whether looking duration reflects preference or merely curiosity, one would have to compare the looking duration measure with other measures of preference. These might include the time spent smiling at and vocalizing to each adult. Validity is measured by the extent to which multiple measures tend to correlate with each other.

A final means of lowering research bias is to protect the outcomes of a study from the unintended influence of the subjects or the experimenters. This is usually accomplished by assuring that both the subjects and the experimenters are *blind* to the specific purpose of the research and blind to the group assignment of the subjects. In a study on the relationship between infant language and mother's speech, experimenters who administer the tests of infant language should not be the same as those who observe mother's speech. The mothers should not be aware of the precise measures and relationships being tested, although they might be told that they are participating in a study on infant language development.

Research Ethics and Informed Consent

Research ethics adopted by most institutions in North America require that subjects should give their informed consent to participate in research. *Informed consent* is a voluntary agreement to participate in a research study (or for a minor to participate with the parent's consent) that must be based on accurate information about the purpose, procedures, risks, and benefits of the research study (Keith-Spiegel, 1983).

In order to meet the ethical guidelines as well as the scientific requirement that subjects be blind to the purpose of the research, researchers usually tell subjects about the general purpose of the study but not about the specific measures to be used. Subjects must be told about all the procedures to enhance their cooperation and to minimize anxiety, but they needn't be told

The electrodes used to record the brain's event related potentials are sewn into a comfortable headband. Physiological recording equipment used for infants cannot be intrusive or restrict the infant's movements too much.

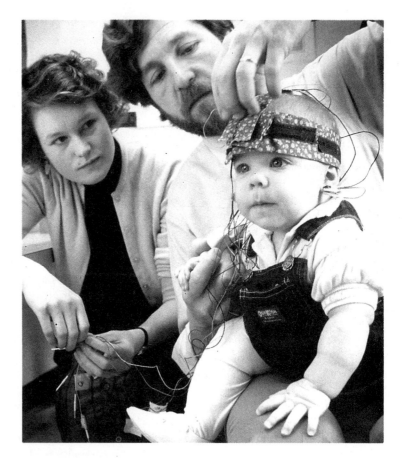

about the specific purpose of the procedures. Most researchers will provide a *debriefing* session for subjects following the completion of their participation. During the debriefing, more details are provided and all subject's questions should be answered frankly. In research using human subjects, researchers have the responsibility to design studies of lasting value to society and to respect the rights and dignity of the individuals who volunteer their time to participate.

So far, we have reviewed research methods that are common to all developmental studies at any age. Infants are not as easily studied as older children or adults. Infants cannot describe their inner states, take standardized written tests, or respond to interview questions. Because of the difficulty working with infants, special procedures have been devised to record their motor and social behavior and to learn more about their perceptual, cognitive, and emotional skills.

Physiological Recording

Automatic recording of *psychophysiological* activity is one method of studying infant behavior. The level of arousal in the autonomic nervous system (ANS) can be measured with a variety of techniques. *Heart rate* recordings tell us about the infant's level of physiological arousal associated with particular types of observed behavior and in different situations. An example of the use of heart rate in research is in the measurement of whether infants can perceive depth. Gibson and Walk (1960; see Chapter 8) discovered that infants older than 6 months would not proceed to crawl to their mothers if they suddenly saw a deep drop-off between themselves and the mother. The drop-off was created by a trough several feet deep that interrupted the surface on which the infant was crawling. To protect unwary infants from harm, the researchers covered the trough with plexiglass, creating the so-called *visual cliff* device.

Depth perception using infants under 6 months could not be studied with the visual cliff because it required infants to have the ability to crawl. When attached to heart rate monitors, however, infants as young as two months showed some changes in their heart rate indicating moderate arousal (though not fear) and thus perception of the depth (Campos, Langer & Krowitz, 1970). It was not until infants began to crawl that they showed heart rate changes similar to those measured during a fearful response. Thus, although 2-month-olds perceive the depth, they must have the experience of crawling around in the real world in order to appreciate the depth with an appropriate level of fear (Campos, 1976).

A number of techniques exist for the automatic recording of behavior. Gross motor activity has been recorded with a device called an *actometer*, which can be fixed to the infant's clothing or attached to a crib mattress. It records the number of position shifts of an infant as a function of time. Infant sounds can be studied with a *sound spectrograph* that shows the duration, pitch, and frequencies of vocalizations. Sucking, respiration, and changes in gaze direction can also be detected by electronic devices and recorded as a continuous function of time.

Central nervous system (CNS) activity has been measured with a variety of so-called "brain wave" techniques. Electrodes are fastened to the infant's scalp with a small amount of petroleum jelly. The electrodes detect the minute changes in electrical activity inside the brain without hurting the infant. Because the currents generated in the brain are small, infants must be presented with a particular stimulus—a sound or a visual object—many times and the electrical responses must be averaged by a computer in order to detect the existence of the "signal" of the response to the stimulus against the "noise" of normal spontaneous brain activity. The resulting averages are called averaged event-related potentials (ERPs). Although such techniques cannot be used to monitor an infant's ongoing mental state, they can tell us whether there is a general ability to detect a stimulus. ERP methods have also been used to diagnose brain disorders in the form of abnormal patterns of electrical activity or lack of predicted responses.

Although physiological recording devices can allow us to detect information we could not otherwise observe, they have important limitations. We can never be sure of the precise meaning of a change in a physiological measure. Many events other than emotion or perception could trigger a change in heart rate or brain activity. Second, physiological activity is itself a response. Just because the heart rate changes when the infant is afraid does not mean the heart is indeed the source of the emotion. All bodily systems are intimately linked together as a complex system such that small changes in one part of the system can have major repercussions throughout the entire system. There is no way to say when and where a response originates or is encoded in the body.

Standardized Experimental Procedures

Another approach to inferring what infants are experiencing is to examine systematic changes in their behavior under controlled conditions. One way to do this was mentioned earlier. In *paired-preference* methods, infants are shown two visual stimuli side by side, or else they hear sounds presented to one or to the other side of the head. During such procedures, infants are either held quietly by their mothers or sit in an infant seat in a darkened room to reduce competing sources of stimulation. There is usually a blank screen directly in front of the infant on which is mounted a display of flashing lights (see Figure 1.1).

A small peephole in this screen, invisible to the infant, allows an observer to look directly at the infant's face and judge where the infant is looking or for how long (Fantz, 1961). In a more sophisticated variant of this procedure, an invisible infrared light is reflected off the infant's cornea and the angle of reflection is detected by an electronic sensor. The angle of reflection can be translated electronically to determine the precise position of the infant's gaze (Haith, Bergman & Moore, 1977). The latter procedure has also been used to examine the developmental changes in the way infants scan visual objects (see Chapter 6).

At the beginning of an *experimental trial* (presentation of one pair of stimuli), the light display flashes to attract the infant's attention to the center. When the infant is judged to be looking at the center, the flashing lights are turned off and the paired visual display is presented, usually by a rear-screen

---

■ **FIGURE 1.1**
A Typical Infant Testing Apparatus Used in Perceptual Preference and Habituation Procedures

Stimuli are projected with computer-controlled slide projectors. The beam from one projector shows pictures on the right side of the screen; the beam from another shows pictures on the other side. The eye camera records where the infant is looking. (After M. M. Haith, C. Hazan, & G. S. Goodman. Expectation and anticipation of dynamic visual events by 3- to 5-month-old babies. *Child Development*, 1988, 59, 470. Copyright 1988 by the *Society for Research in Child Development*. By permission.)

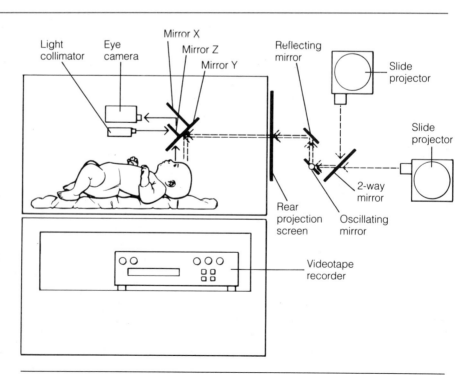

slide projector (for example, mother on left; stranger on right). Duration of looking left or right is recorded before the visual displays go off. On the next trial, the flashing lights are again used. After the infant looks to the center, the mother appears on the right and the stranger on the left. The order of presentation of the stimuli is *counterbalanced* across trials to eliminate any bias due to an infant's preference to turn to one side or another. Preference is determined by the average across trials of the infant's duration of looking to mother and to stranger.

A second procedure for the assessment of infant psychological experience uses repeated exposure to the same visual or auditory stimulus. Each time the stimulus is repeated is one trial. If a researcher repeatedly shows the same picture to a baby—say, a picture of a face with a sad expression—the baby spends less and less time looking at each new presentation of the picture, acting as though he was getting bored with the same old thing. The phenomenon of a gradual decline in looking time over repeated presentations of the same stimulus is known as *habituation*.

Researchers select some minimum amount of looking time as the criterion to decide when the baby has become habituated to a stimulus. For example, if the baby's initial looks at a facial expression last about thirty seconds, a reasonable habituation criterion for subsequent trials might be five seconds. Once the baby has reached the criterion looking time, researchers change the picture or sound—in our example, from the face with a sad expression to the same face with a happy expression. If the baby can't tell the difference between the two expressions, he or she will go on looking at the happy expression for durations shorter than the habituation criterion. However, if the baby can detect a change, the infant will begin to look longer at the happy face than at the last presentation of the sad face. This abrupt increase in looking time after a change in the stimulus is called *recovery*. A study by Field, Woodson, Greenberg, and Cohen (1982) used this technique with newborn infants to see if they could differentiate between happy, sad, and surprised facial expressions. Remarkably, newborns could differentiate the expressions.

A final standardized procedure we will review is called the *response contingent* procedure, which is used often in studies of auditory and taste perception. In this technique, infants are trained to change their behavior if they can detect certain features of the sounds or tastes. Once taught, infants will alter their behavior in order to hear their favorite sound or to receive their preferred taste.

DeCasper and Fifer (1980) used this technique with an automatic suck recorder. The suck recorder is a pacifier that is connected to a pressure transducer (which converts varying degrees of pressure into electrical impulses), which in turn is connected to recording equipment. Each infant in the study was equipped with a set of headphones and a suck recorder. After a two-minute adjustment period, the infant's sucking was recorded for five minutes with no sounds coming through the headphones. During this period, the experimenter computed the median duration of the pauses between sucking bouts (see Chapter 5).

In the experimental period, infants sucked as usual such that half of their pauses were below the median and half above. When the experimenters detected a pause that was longer than the median interval, they presented the infants with either the voice of their mother (through a recording of her segment of a Dr. Seuss story) or the recorded voice of a stranger (reading the same segment). Five of the infants were randomly assigned to a group that could evoke their mother's voice by pausing their sucking for longer than the median pause length and evoke the stranger's voice by pausing for less than the median pause interval. The other five infants had the reverse conditions.

Because the presentation of the adult voices was made *contingent* upon the duration of the sucking pause, infants quickly learned that by speeding up or slowing down their sucking, they could produce one or the other voice. If the infants had a preference for one or the other voice, they would systematically shift their pause length to "suck" for that voice. Eight of the ten infants showed a tendency to shift their pause length to produce their own mother's voice. Four of the infants were retested twenty-four hours later in a situation in which the criterion for obtaining the mother's voice was reversed from the previous day. All four continued to suck for their mother's voice.

The main problem with all these techniques is that the failure of an infant to respond does not necessarily mean the infant cannot respond. Thus, it is usually necessary to do repeated testing of the same infants and/or to use a relatively large sample of infants.

Methods of Observing Infant Behavior in Quasi-Experimental Settings

A large portion of research on infants involves the observation of their behavior in relatively natural circumstances. On the one hand, research ethics prohibit extensive manipulation of human subjects, and on the other hand, a great many important questions require direct observation of infants. These include observations of free play in social groups, exploratory play and actions on objects when the infant is alone or with others, the social communication between infants and other people, and the stability of behavior patterns over long periods of time.

Observing the ongoing behavior of infants is difficult because many things are happening at the same time. Imagine trying to write down everything that happens during a social interaction between two partners in the exact sequence in which it occurs, including not only what they say to each other, but all of the nonverbal social behaviors, such as looking, facial expressions, gestures, and body movements.

Researchers have developed a number of techniques to simplify the task. First of all, it is important to be selective in what you want to observe. Since you can't see everything, you should be guided in your choice by some concept and by defining in advance the kinds of behaviors that will be recorded. For example, suppose you wanted to observe how an infant interacted with her mother before and during the approach of an unfamiliar person. Specific behaviors that might be relevant to the child's relationship with her mother are approaching the mother, following the mother, and staying near the mother's side when the stranger is present. Older infants may also ask about the stranger or ask to be picked up and held.

After choosing a list of behavioral categories, the observer is trained to recognize each category until an acceptable level of inter-rater reliability can be obtained. *Coding* is the process by which observers record the presence or absence of the predefined categories as they are watching an infant. A number of coding strategies have been used.

One relatively easy coding strategy is suitable to pencil and paper recording of live observations. When any one of the categories is seen, it is checked off on a sheet of paper on which the categories have been listed. Observers will watch for a predetermined time period, such as fifteen seconds, and then during the next fifteen seconds, the observer checks off all the codes observed. Actual observations take place during alternate fifteen-second time blocks. This method is called *time sampling,* since only a portion of the time from the continuous stream of action is chosen for coding.

Time sampling is useful to get a general idea about the different types of behavior that occur in any situation, and it can be done with simple tools, such as a clipboard, a watch, and a pencil. This strategy does not produce a very accurate estimate of either the frequency or duration of behavior. In a fifteen-second time sample, a behavior that occurs more than once is only recorded as a single entry, without regard to its duration. A single continuous occurrence of a behavior that spans two observation intervals will actually be recorded twice (see Figure 1.2).

Audio and video recordings can improve the accuracy of observational data over time-sampling methods. Once behavior is recorded on tape, observers can replay the tape as often as necessary to code the entire period of observation. Replaying the tape allows for observers to check their errors.

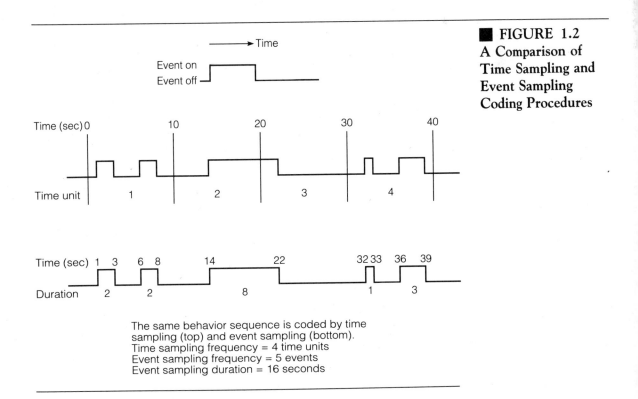

■ FIGURE 1.2
A Comparison of Time Sampling and Event Sampling Coding Procedures

The same behavior sequence is coded by time sampling (top) and event sampling (bottom).
Time sampling frequency = 4 time units
Event sampling frequency = 5 events
Event sampling duration = 16 seconds

Advocacy for Infants and Their Families

In this chapter, we learned that the twentieth century has been a period of increased public awareness about the development of infants. There is a strong perception that some proportion of tax revenues should be spent for the benefit of all infants. It was not always this way. The United States was founded on basic principles of self-reliance and upon the idea that parents had both the responsibility and the right to raise their children without undue intervention from the government. Legally, children are viewed as the possessions of their parents, and the government may only interfere with families in extreme circumstances of abuse and neglect. This legal concept, called *parens patriae,* was part of English common law originating in the fifteenth century.

The effects of *parens patriae* can be seen in the history of public welfare in the United States. The first nursery schools, day-care centers, and public health programs in the United States were established in the nineteenth century. The state Boards of Charity, begun in 1863, were the first government welfare institutions. They provided protection from abuse for children living in orphanages and working in factories but not for those living at home with parents. Two White House conferences on children, in 1909 and 1930,

led to the creation of the Social Security Acts of the 1930s that established a welfare system, aid to dependent children, and financial and rehabilitation services for needy children and their families.

Because of the ideals of self-reliance and *parens patriae,* the government confined its protective activities to the most needy segment of society, to children whose parents could not provide support for them. Receiving welfare and the protection of public funds—even if the funds protected infants from abuse and exploitation—was thought of as a social stigma.

Contrast these narrow ideas of the public interest in children with the infant and child-related discussions going on in the halls of state legislatures in the 1990s. At issue is proposed legislation to provide minimum standards for all day-care centers and day-care homes, whether attended by the rich or the poor. Surprisingly few states have such standards, and there is little national day-care policy. Under discussion is legislation to provide, as a basic right, liberal parental leave policies so that parents (men and women) with young infants might be given unpaid time off from work after their baby is born without threat of losing their jobs. No such national policy exists.

APPLICATIONS

Although there are few programs that provide direct benefits to families with infants, there are some indirect ways in which tax money is used. Corporations are given income tax deductions for providing on-site day-care centers. Parents can deduct the cost of child care from their incomes, thus reducing their overall income taxes. This, however, is not much of a help to families in which both parents have to work just to get by. They often cannot afford child care of good quality, and the lack of legal standards encourages the proliferation of poor quality for-profit day care.

In many ways, the United States is unique among the developed countries of the world in its reluctance to support infant development as a national policy. Infant health care, proper nutrition, clean and well-managed child care that is affordable, and parental leave policies have all been publicly supported by law with tax funds for many years in such countries as France, Sweden, the Soviet Union, China, and Japan.

In those countries, there is no argument that infants and children are in the national trust, that they are the most valuable resources a society has, and that all families with infants and children deserve encouragement and government support. In the United States, these are controversial issues because of the fear that government will take over the rights of individuals and families. In the United States, it seems that the damages done daily to the mental and physical health of millions of poor and homeless, and even some middle-income infants and children, is the price we seem willing to pay for our frontier-days notions of personal freedom and self-reliance.

Without a nationally recognized set of values in support of infants and children, groups that speak out for children's rights have begun to form. They operate at local, state, and national levels, mostly with volunteers and supported entirely by private funds.

Child and family advocacy has become an important part of the social and political fabric of the United States. Professional advocates—whose salaries are paid by the organizations—take their places with volunteers, parents, child-care professionals, and researchers to make phone calls, prepare position papers, and lobby lawmakers. Not all these advocacy groups have similar positions. Some want more funds for day-care centers, while others want tax breaks to allow parents to stay home and raise their own children.

In a complex society that contains many different cultures and many different value systems, advocacy will always be an essential part of democracy. It is important to realize that just because you believe in particular rights for infants, those rights probably are not currently guaranteed by law and are not likely to become so without the combined efforts of many concerned individuals.

Videotapes can be made with a digital clock image in the corner of the screen so that actual elapsed time between behavior onsets and offsets can be recorded more accurately than time sampling would allow.

Another way of recording is with the use of personal computers that have an internal clock. They can be programmed to remember the elapsed time every time a key is pressed. Different keys can represent different behavior categories as an observer watches either a live or a videotaped interaction. Because observers enter information only when a category of interest changes (rather than when a time interval changes), this approach is called *event sampling*. Hand-held electronic *event recorders* work on the same principle. In even more high-tech versions, computers are electronically interfaced with videotape players. A timing signal is recorded on one audio track of a stereo videotape and the computer can "read" the time. This frees the observer from having to watch the videotape with an electronic recorder whose clock is running at full speed so that the observer cannot stop to correct a mistake or add new information. The computer-video interface combines the convenience of electronic recording with the ability to stop frequently and replay the tape as often as necessary.

A final type of observation is called a *trait rating*. Unlike the other observational methods in which the ongoing behavior of an infant is recorded, in this method the observer watches a segment of the infant's behavior and makes a judgment about the infant's level of performance. The rating given to the infant is made by selecting a level that the infant best fits on some rating scale.

In the example used above, the coding categories were discrete behaviors: approaching, following, and staying near the mother when a stranger is present. In time and event sampling, the observer would record each category separately whenever it was observed to occur. A rating scale could be devised for the entire interaction that would eliminate the need for detailed behavior records. For example, after watching the entire observation session of the infant with mother and stranger, an observer might rate the child on a scale of one to five, where one is comfort with the stranger (not approaching or following the mother), three is maintaining a moderate distance from the mother, and five is extreme anxiety (clinging to mother and following closely).

Ratings are effective when the measure of interest to the research need not be equated to specific behaviors; in this case, only the overall level of comfort versus anxiety. Ratings are easier to do, but they often require more coder training since they are open to subjective interpretation. Behavior codes are often simpler to learn but require more coder time since they must be assessed continuously during an observation period. Time and event sampling are necessary when one is interested in the *dynamics* of behavior: how it unfolds over time.

Using a rating strategy, infant's social play can be assessed according to Mildred Parten's (1932) scale of mutual involvement in play (see Table 1.1). One could simply rate the highest level of play or count up the total number of instances children were observed in each level of play during a period of time. Bakeman and Brownlee (1980) observed three-year-old children in out-of-doors free play using coding categories similar to those of Parten.

**■ TABLE 1.1   Types of Play Between Young Children,
Adapted From Parten (1932)**

TYPE OF PLAY	DESCRIPTION
Solitary play	Child plays alone Example: Child sits alone in sandbox and fills pail with sand
Parallel play	Play in close proximity to other children but without interaction Example: Two children sit next to each other in a sandbox, each filling a pail
Associative play	Children respond to each other during play but maintain separate goals Example: Two children talk to each other while playing with sand in a sandbox
Cooperative play	Play is organized around joint activities Example: Two children work together to build a sand castle

---

Instead of rating, they recorded the presence or absence of each category of play during successive fifteen-second time intervals for about one hundred minutes.

Besides learning about the overall level of play in the children, Bakeman and Brownlee were interested in the sequences of play. For example, when did parallel play occur in relationship to group play? It could be that parallel play occurred during the first half of the observation, and then group play took over. However, they discovered that parallel play was sandwiched between episodes of group play. For children of this age, parallel play seemed to function as a "time out" from group play in which children could relax, work momentarily on their own, or observe other's behavior before reentering the mainstream of group activity.

■ SUMMARY

Infants in the News

■ Prenatal and infant development are frequent topics in the news, on television, and in the movies today.
■ Advances have been made in the treatment of prenatal disorders and in the care of premature and sick infants. ,

A Brief History of Babies

■ During all periods of recorded history, some infants and children have received love and care while others have been abused or neglected.
■ Urbanization, beginning in the middle ages, brought changes to the family and to the health and safety of infants.

■ The ideas of romanticism and empiricism in the eighteenth century marked the beginning of philosophical and educational efforts directed toward infants.
■ The development of the nuclear family and its privatization, along with advances in infant medical care, in the nineteenth century created the discovery of infancy as an important period in the life course.
■ Infants became the subjects of scientific study in the nineteenth and twentieth centuries, sparked by the debate over whether nature or nurture has the most influence over behavioral development.

What Is An Infant?

■ Infancy can be divided into topical areas, such as: perceptual/sensorial, sensorimotor/tool using, conceptual/thinking, representational/symbolic, communicative/linguistic, social/interactive, expressive/emotive, and self-regulatory/coping.
■ The division of infancy into stages of development is somewhat arbitrary and depends on the purposes of the culture or group.
■ Developmental changes are not reversible, not temporary, and not haphazard.
■ Individual differences between infants may or may not be stable over the course of infancy. Scientists are still trying to determine whether these differences are due to genetic or environmental factors.

Methods of Research on Infant Development

■ Longitudinal studies and cross-sectional studies have both strengths and weaknesses.
■ Systematic research tests for alternate interpretations of an observation.
■ Controlled experimental studies are desired for determining causes and effects, while quasi-experiments are useful for obtaining basic descriptive data on aspects of infant and family development.
■ Systematic research is marked by attention to reliability, validity, and observer bias.
■ Since infants cannot provide informed consent to participate in research, their parents must do so. Researchers need to observe ethical guidelines when using human subjects in research.
■ Automatic recording of behavior involves measurement of heart rate, respiration, brain activity, and aspects of behavior.
■ Paired preference tests, habituation procedures, and response contingent procedures are techniques for testing perception and cognition in infants.
■ Time sampling, event sampling, and rating scales are used for the direct observation of infant behavior.

Applications: Advocacy for Infants and Their Families

■ In a society based on *parens patriae*, public funds are typically allocated for only the most needy cases.
■ Current trends show increased public laws and funds to benefit all infants.
■ All individuals in a democratic society must participate in the process of changing local, state, and federal policies regarding infant and family development.

■ GLOSSARY

Attrition   The loss of subjects over time in longitudinal research studies.

Baby biography   A written detailed observation of the day-to-day changes in the behavior of a single infant; one of the first forms of scientific observations of infant behavior.

Coding   The process by which observers record the presence or absence of predefined behavioral categories as they are watching an individual or a group.

Control group   A group used in experimental studies that does not experience the intervention or manipulation received by the experimental groups; allows a test of the effects of the manipulation compared with no manipulation.

Counterbalancing   Presenting experimental trials in different orders across subjects in a research study; controls for order effects.

Cross-sectional study   A research study in which age differences are studied using different infants at each age.

Development   Change that is nonreversible, not temporary, and not haphazard.

Empiricism   An eighteenth-century philosophical idea that knowledge is derived from direct observation and that human problems can be solved with logical reasoning.

Event sampling   The process of coding behavior in which codes are recorded only when a preselected event actually occurs; usually the time of occurrence is also recorded.

Experiment   A research strategy in which some factors are manipulated by the experimenter, while others are controlled or held constant across groups.

Experimental trial   A time period during which a particular experimental manipulation occurs; experiments often include repeated trials in which the subjects are observed under varying conditions.

Habituation   The gradual decrease in looking time across repeated presentations of the same visual or auditory stimulus.

Informed consent   The principle that participation of human subjects in research should be by voluntary consent based on a complete description of the procedures, risks, and benefits of the research.

Longitudinal study   A research study in which developmental changes are followed in the same individual over time.

Maturation   Developmental change that is controlled by hereditary timing mechanisms.

Nature   Refers to the belief that behavior and development are controlled primarily by hereditary influences.

Nurture   Refers to the belief that behavior and development are controlled by environmental influences.

Paired-preference procedure   A research technique that relies on differences in infant looking time to assess perceptual preferences.

Quasi-experiment   A research strategy in which the experimenter does not manipulate the subjects but takes advantages of natural variations in the environment.

Random assignment   A procedure in which subjects are placed into experimental and control groups by the flip of a coin or some other nonbiased method.

Recovery   Increase in infant looking times in response to dishabituation.

Reliability   The extent to which multiple observers agree about the coding of ongoing behavior.

Response contingent procedure   A research technique in which different stimuli are made contingent upon different infant actions. Display of one or the other action by the infant usually means a preference for the contingently related stimulus.

Romanticism   An eighteenth-century philosophical idea that children are inherently good and have the ability to develop successfully with minimal guidance.

Stability   The extent to which an individual maintains the same ranking on some trait within the reference group at different ages.

Systematic research   Research that is designed to test alternative interpretations of the results.

Time sampling   A method of direct observation in which all events occurring within a preset time interval are recorded without noting the exact frequency or time of onset and offset.

Trait rating   A summary judgment about an infant's level of performance made after observing the infant in a particular situation.

Validity   The extent to which an assessment procedure accurately measures the concept or goal of the experimenter.

TWO

Theories of Infant Development

Each of the views of infant development that you read about in Chapter 1 —from different cultures and from different historical periods— were theories of how babies develop and about the importance of a baby's experiences. Each of us has our own theory about infants, but most of us have not articulated our theories. For many, our personal theories of infant development may only be revealed in the course of actually working with infants or in raising one of our own.

A *scientific theory* is a set of concepts that explain some aspects of the observable world with structures, processes, or mechanisms presumed to exist but unable to be observed directly. A scientific theory differs from the folk theories mentioned in Chapter 1 in several ways:

1. A scientific theory helps to organize observations derived from systematic research, using accepted methods of observation and assessment.
2. A scientific theory is phrased in terms of general principles that can be applied to specific research findings and applications.
3. A scientific theory should accurately predict future observations in a majority of cases. A theory whose predictions are not confirmed should be changed or abandoned.

Scientific theories applied to the study of human development focus on describing and predicting the ways in which children change over time. For example, what is the process or mechanism that explains the developmental transition from preverbal to verbal communication in infancy? Another task for theories of human development is how to explain the origins of individual differences. Why does one child become adept at language skills from an early age, while another is slow to pick up these abilities?

In this chapter, we shall examine a variety of theories of human development that have been applied to infancy: ethological, learning, cognition, emotion, and systems theories. The main principles and concepts of each theory are described, the historical trends within each theory are reviewed, and the contributions of the theory to contemporary research are outlined. Finally, the main limitations of the theory are critiqued.

■ ETHOLOGICAL THEORY

Ethology is the study of the influence of the evolution of the species on the types of behavior and the process of behavioral development found in that species. Ethological theory is based on the work of Charles Darwin, who set the stage for thinking about how our genetic *nature* contributes to the formation of species characteristics and between-individual variations. In Darwin's theory, plant and animal species evolve by *natural selection.* Each individual within the species carries a slightly different group of genes that will contribute to individual differences in appearance and behavior. Some inherited characteristics will allow the individual to adapt to the environment and ensure that the individual's genes are passed on to the next generation through reproduction. If individuals have genetic variations that make them unsuited to their environments, they may not survive long enough to reproduce, and their genes will be lost to future generations. Thus, the environment influences the range of natural genetic variations to select the fittest individuals (Darwin, 1859).

Species-Specific Innate Behaviors

Derived from Darwin's ideas, ethological theory suggests that all animal species have *species-specific innate behaviors* that have evolved by the process of natural selection. Species-specific behaviors are those that are seen only in one species, such as the song of a sparrow or human speech. Although these behaviors are species specific, both are examples of a more general function of communication. The selection of a specific form of communication in a species is presumably related to the survival of its members over many generations.

Another example of a cross-species behavior that is related to survival is a close relationship between mother and infant, seen in all mammalian species. Each species has a different set of species-specific patterns of behavior that reflect the attachment bonds between mother and infant. Mother cats lick and nuzzle their infants, but mother monkeys groom, cuddle, and carry their babies around. All mammals nurse their young, but the styles of nursing differ between species. In dogs, the mother lies on her side while her puppies nurse. The mother does not look at her babies, but she may lick them. In humans, nursing is done with the infant in the mother's arms, typically while the mother is looking at, talking to, and touching the infant.

The concept of species-typical innate behavior was applied to human infancy in John Bowlby's (1969) theory of attachment. Bowlby suggested that newborn infants were innately receptive to adult social stimulation (such as calming after being picked up) and that infants could emit signals to which adults were innately sensitive (feeling the need to respond when hearing a baby cry). Later, as infants develop more social skills, the attachment is expressed in new ways (such as through a smile or when a frightened child yells, "Mommy!").

Critical Periods

Another aspect of ethological theory is the prediction that species-specific behaviors are enhanced and modified in specific environments. Typically, in many animal species, the young seem more biologically susceptible to the acquisition of new behavior compared to older individuals. It often happens that there is a limited period of time in early life during which environmental input can make a difference in later behavior. This period of maximum susceptibility is called a critical period. A *critical period* is a relatively short period of time (compared to the individual's life span) in which learning can occur, and whatever the animal learns in this period has a permanent and irreversible effect.

For example, in some species of birds, attachment of the infant to an adult occurs only for a period of about two hours, just several days after hatching. If a gosling follows its mother around during the critical period, it will develop a preference for the mother over other adults and will stay close to the mother after the critical period ends and for a long time after. This learning of attachment preferences is called *imprinting.*

Konrad Lorenz (1965) found that goslings could become imprinted on a number of different objects during this period. Lorenz made goslings imprint on flashlights, electric trains, and even himself. He would walk near the goslings during the critical period, squatting and honking like a mother goose. In his description of these early studies, he wrote, "In the interest of science, I submitted myself literally for hours on end to this ordeal" (Lorenz, 1952, p. 42). For this and other work in ethology, Lorenz won a Nobel Prize in 1973, one of the few behavioral scientists to have received this honor.

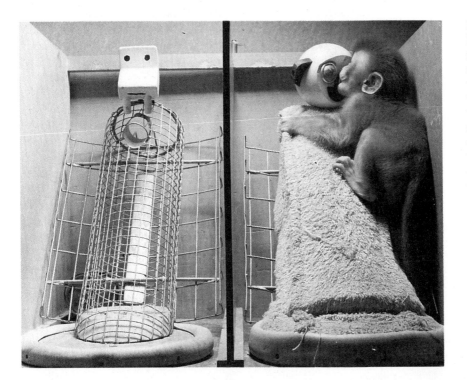

In research by the Harlows, infant monkeys preferred the substitute mother that was covered with a soft cloth, rather than the wire mother to which the food was attached. This study showed that attachment in monkeys is more related to contact comfort than to feeding. In humans, attachment is related to play and communication.

A large number of studies—mostly with mallard ducklings—have been done on imprinting since Lorenz's classic work. One of the main results is that imprinting occurs only after the ducklings leave the nest and only if they can follow a moving hen who is calling to them (Bateson, 1966; Hess, 1959). A recent study (Dyer, Lickliter, & Gottlieb, 1989) suggests that before imprinting, ducklings may be more sensitive to the visual images of their walking siblings than to the mother hen. Ducklings may leave the nest initially as they see other ducklings doing this. Once this happens, the ducklings will respond as a group to the hen's call, follow her as a group, and thus become imprinted.

The picture of imprinting that emerges from these recent studies is that a series of related events must be tied together: imprinting involves age-mates and locomotion and auditory perception and cannot be thought of as a simple photographic image of the mother printed on the duckling's brain. The concepts of imprinting and critical periods seem to be even more complex in humans, involving large numbers of complex interactions. Indeed, due to the complexity of human developmental processes, it is unlikely that simple notions of critical periods can apply.

For example, there does not seem to be anything akin to imprinting in humans. In the first place, there is no specific time during which exposure must occur in order for attachment to develop. Human infants can become attached to multiple care givers and to multiple objects at different times in their development and with both short and long exposure times (see Chapters 6 and 7). Toddlers can become attached to grandparents even if they see each other only once or twice a year. Infants who spend time in day care of good quality do not appear to be any less attached to their parents than those infants who are cared for at home by their parents (see Chapter 9).

Studies of infants reared without adult play and interaction in orphanages in Europe and the Middle East showed that these children developed severe symptoms of withdrawal, and monkeys reared without adults tend to show similar symptoms: rocking, head banging, extreme fear in the presence of strangers, and an inability to form relationships with other individuals (Harlow & Harlow, 1965; Spitz, 1965).

On the other hand, some of the early orphanage studies have been criticized for confusing the symptoms of malnutrition—common in those institutions—with those predicted for maternal deprivation. Follow-up studies on early mother-deprived monkeys showed that some social experiences—in particular, interactions between the deprived monkeys and monkeys younger than themselves—provided when the deprived monkeys were juveniles had the effect of partially reversing the social withdrawal (Suomi & Harlow, 1972). Gorilla infants who are raised by human mother surrogates develop more aggressive and antisocial behaviors compared to gorillas raised with their mothers. However, after spending time in a group of gorilla peers, human-reared juvenile gorillas will act more like those who were mother-reared (Meder, 1989).

Another potential example of a human critical period is the development of language in the first three years of life. Some confirmation of this view is found in the case of a girl named Genie who was found in 1970 at the age of thirteen after having been isolated in a small room since infancy. Her father, apparently a psychotic who hated children, forced Genie to remain in a closet and refused to let anyone speak to her. Susan Curtiss, a developmentalist who spent many years trying to help Genie recover, reported that Genie learned *some* language (Curtiss, 1982); after several years of practice, Genie could string up to three words together to make her intentions and thoughts known, but she never seemed to grasp the idea of grammar, and she never learned to ask questions. The problem with this single case study is that we have no way of knowing whether Genie suffered from some form of brain damage or other impairment early in life. Such an organic deficit might be the real cause of Genie's language retardation. Certainly we cannot do language deprivation experiments on groups of healthy children. Thus, there is no concrete evidence that critical periods exist for humans.

Kinship

Another branch of ethological theory is called sociobiology. In this view (Wilson, 1975), natural selection does not operate on individuals per se but on groups of individuals that constitute the basic social unit in that species. In a beehive, for example, only the queen can produce eggs. This suggests that the hive has been selected as a social group in which individuals specialize their roles. Workers and queens evolved together, in relation to each other, and not as individuals.

In human societies, such groups are defined by kinship ties, that is, genetically related individuals in the same family. Individuals can increase the chances of their genes surviving into the next generation not only by ensuring their own survival but also the survival of any other individual who shares some of their same genes. *Altruism* is the act of being helpful or caring toward others. If individual genes are "selfish," there can be no genetic basis for altruism. On the other hand, if I save a kin at the expense of sacrificing myself, I am still assuring that some of my genes get passed to the next generation. Sociobiology predicts that we will be more altruistic to those with whom we share a larger percentage of genes.

The best example of this is the investment in time and energy that parents give to their biological children, with whom they share 50 percent of their genes. (That is the highest percentage you can share with anyone, except an identical twin. Identical twins share 100 percent of their genes, while other siblings share only 25 percent). For example, there is a higher incidence of child abuse by stepparents compared to biological parents (Daly & Wilson, 1981; Lenington, 1981), and some adopted children feel the need to locate their biological parents (Triseliotis, 1973).

Also, to the extent that helping others and sharing in cooperative activities increase the chances of survival for themselves and their kin, people will behave altruistically toward others who are not kin. Hence, sociobiology predicts that cultural practices are genetically based and human infants are genetically predisposed to orient to the social environment.

Sociobiology has been criticized for its assumption that all human actions, including language and culture, are genetically based. It is difficult to disprove such a statement. Sociobiologists assume that there is a specific genetic mechanism for all behavior, and it is the role of theory and research to discover what those mechanisms are. Another problem is that sociobiologists make their statements based on the number of shared genes individuals possess and the ways in which genes are distributed in the species. They have little to say about individual variability or about individual patterns of developmental change. In the following section, we turn to an ethological theory that focuses on between-individual variability.

Heritability

A final issue that ethological theories have addressed is the concept that individual differences between members of a species are based in part on the natural genetic variability found in a population. A belief that heredity is the main factor in the determination of individual differences was common until the early twentieth century. One of the first research psychologists, Francis Galton (1822–1911), studied similarities and differences between fraternal and identical twins. In an 1874 book called *English Men of Science: Their Nature and Their Nurture,* Galton showed that many of the relatives of outstanding scientists of the time had achieved professional or intellectual success in their own fields. The tendency for high achievement to run in families, argued Galton, was evidence for a hereditary transmission of this trait.

Today, we have a large amount of evidence for the familial similarity of a number of behavioral characteristics, but we also know now that genetic transmission is only one way in which families pass on their characteristics to the next generation. The newly emerging theory of *behavior genetics* has relied on a number of techniques for differentiating the relative roles of genes and environments for the determination of individual differences.

It is not enough to compare the similarities and differences between fraternal and identical twins as Galton once did. Since identical twins look alike and are the same sex, they are more likely to be treated alike by parents than fraternal twins who are no more similar than any other two siblings in a family. Identical twins may be dressed alike and encouraged to spend more time together, creating opportunities for mutual imitation. Thus, for twins reared together, nurture cannot be sorted out from nature.

Behavior geneticists can only begin to examine the relative impact of genes and environment by studying identical twins who have been raised in separate families. If they resemble each other more than other children, it is evidence for the role of the genes. On the other hand, observing biologically unrelated children raised in the same families tells us something about the effects of a shared or common family environment independent of genetic influence (Loehlin, 1989).

Among humans, this kind of work is done with adoptive parents and children. In other animal species, researchers can experimentally create matches and mismatches between parental and infant characteristics using *cross-fostering* studies. In either case, researchers need relatively large samples of individuals in order to begin to see a pattern of influence that can be attributed to either the genes or to the shared family environment. Theoretical statements made from such data are *probabilistic.* That is, all we can conclude is that if you possess a particular set of genes, you are somewhat more likely to develop a particular kind of behavioral characteristic than a person without those same genes: the action of the genes is not *deterministic,* since there are environments that might lessen the impact of those genes on the behavioral outcome (Scarr & McCartney, 1983).

In order to understand the probabilistic character of genetic influence, behavior geneticists have outlined some of the ways in which the genes interact with the environment. The genetic code is a set of chemical instructions for producing proteins in the nucleus of a living cell (see Chapter 3). This raw genetic code is called the *genotype*. Through a complex set of chemical interactions between the genotype and the environment of the cell, particular types of proteins are produced. These interactions ultimately yield the neural and muscular tissues that underlie our mental and behavioral abilities. The farther away from the cell we get, the more complex the interactions and the environments that may affect the way the genes act.

The outcomes of the genotype-environment interactions are called the *phenotypes*. Phenotypes are resultant products—the tissues, behaviors, cognitions, and emotions. Thus, it is important to understand that *all* phenotypes are genetically determined—the result of a genotype-environment interaction. One way to think about this is that the genotype does not directly determine the phenotype, but rather that *the genotype determines the opportunities by which the environment may have an influence on the phenotype.* The theoretical issue is how much between-individual variability in the phenotype is related to variability in environments or variability in genotypes.

For example, some genetic predispositions may never appear in the phenotype because the genotype is never exposed to a "needed" environmental resource at a particular time in life. Thus, a gosling will never manifest its species-typical attachment behaviors if it is not exposed to an adult goose during the critical period for imprinting. This is an example of a genetic predisposition that is easily influenced by the environment. *Environmental variability would therefore have a larger probability of predicting individual phenotypes* compared to genetic variability. In fact, genetic variability usually accounts for only a small proportion of behavioral variability. Many genes, each with a small influence, rather than a single gene, usually are involved in influencing behavior (Plomin, 1990).

Other genotypes may be less susceptible to variations in the environment. For example, if a group of infants are genetically predisposed to blindness, variability across these infants in the amount of exposure to light and visual stimuli will have little influence on the phenotype for visual perception. In this case, *genetic variability between individuals (inheriting or not inheriting a blindness gene) will have a larger probability of predicting individual phenotypes* compared to environmental variability.

No genes and no environments are 100-percent deterministic. In some cases, genetic disorders can be eliminated in the phenotype through surgery, drug treatments, or by avoiding certain environmental factors (*e.g.*, controlling diabetes through diet). There is also the hope that some genetic disorders can be "cured" by as yet undiscovered techniques (see Chapter 3).

In some cases, genetic variability may predict variability in phenotypes early in life but not later. A stable pattern of temperamental withdrawal tends to be correlated with eye color (withdrawn infants are overrepresented in the group of blue-eyed infants than would be expected by chance) during the first three years of life. During the preschool period and later, there is no correlation between eye color and temperament (Kagan et al., 1987). These findings suggest that temperamental withdrawal may be genetically based, but after several years, the variability of that phenotype in the population is better predicted by environmental rather than genetic variability. The opposite could also be true: a genetically based skill at language might account for between-infant differences at age three, but not earlier in infancy, as shown by correlations between the onset of right- or left-handed preference and the emergence of language (Fagard & Jacquet, 1989; Ramsay, 1980).

Behavioral genetics can be criticized because in most human situations, it is extremely difficult to sort out the relative effects of genetic and environmental variability. It is difficult to find cases of identical twins reared apart. Even when this happens, it may be that the reasons for the twins' separation at birth may not make them representative of the rest of the population. Also, there is a tendency for adoptions to occur within similar racial, ethnic, and social class groupings, increasing the degree of shared environment that may account for the twins' similarity.

Behavior geneticists have hypothesized that genetic factors predispose individuals to choose certain kinds of environments. Thus, a genetically based phenotypic temperamentally withdrawn infant may seek social isolation and avoid stressful situations (Scarr & McCartney, 1983). Nevertheless, it is nearly impossible in human subjects to say whether the genes caused the individual to select a particular environment, whether the environment created the phenotype, or whether there is a complex interaction between genotype, phenotype, and environment.

Finally, ethological theory assumes that all behavior has an underlying genetic component. While this may seem clear for such species-specific universal behaviors as attachment and language, the genetic basis of the effects of television on infants or their preference for one story book over another is a more difficult theoretical problem. Because televisions and books were not in the environment in which the current pool of human genes was created, the important issue arises of exactly how the genes exert their influence on behavior. The complex genotype-environment interactions that influence the phenotype are typically not a concern of either sociobiologists or behavior geneticists.

■ LEARNING THEORY

Traditionally, learning theories have been contrasted with ethological theories as being on opposite sides in the nature versus nurture debate. Learning theories suggested that the environment was the prepotent influence, while ethological theories seemed to dwell on genetic influences. As we saw in the section on ethological theory, this simple characterization is not accurate. Ethologically oriented researchers see the genes as regulating the *kinds of learning and ages at which learning is possible* in a species. Often, their research methods are nearly identical to those of learning theorists: both are studying the conditions under which learning takes place. On the other hand, learning theorists are cognizant of species differences in learning, since the vast majority of work based on learning theory has been done with nonhuman species.

Learning theory researchers have contributed to our understanding of development in several ways. First, they have discovered simple yet powerful ways to enhance learning. Second, they have shown that with the proper kinds of environmental supports, individuals and species can be trained to achieve considerably more than what might have been expected from ethological models of species-typical behavior. We might say that learning researchers work at the upper end of a species' range of abilities, as they search for more optimal strategies to enhance learning skills.

Classical Conditioning

One of the first demonstrations that learning could occur under the influence of a systematic environmental manipulation was done by Ivan Pavlov (1849–1936) in Russia. Pavlov attempted to teach dogs to salivate on cue, not simply in the presence of food. He discovered that if a bell was rung every time a hungry dog was presented with food, the dog would later salivate at the sound of the bell without any food present. This process, called *classical conditioning*, or learning by association, is illustrated in Figure 2.1.

In classical conditioning, there must be an unconditioned stimulus that induces the unconditioned response. An example from human infancy is the fear (unconditioned response) induced by strangers in strange places (unconditioned stimulus). Learning occurs when the unconditioned stimulus occurs at the same time as some new conditioned stimulus. Following repeated exposure to this pairing of conditioned and unconditioned stimuli, the unconditioned response will occur in the presence of the conditioned stimulus. For example, if the child's doctor wears a white coat, the fear of the strangeness of the doctor's office may become associated with white coats. Thus, the infant may cry later at the sight of anyone—even a familiar person—wearing a white coat.

Operant Conditioning

In a later development of learning theory, B. F. Skinner (1939) was trying to condition birds. Since classical conditioning theory assumes that all unconditioned responses must be related to unconditioned stimuli, this presented Skinner with a problem. He could not discover the unconditioned stimuli for most of the animal's actions: behavior seemed to be emitted spontaneously

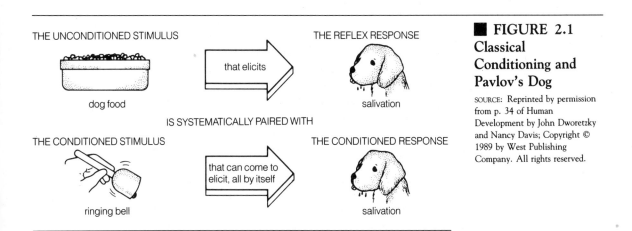

■ FIGURE 2.1 Classical Conditioning and Pavlov's Dog

SOURCE: Reprinted by permission from p. 34 of Human Development by John Dworetzky and Nancy Davis; Copyright © 1989 by West Publishing Company. All rights reserved.

from the animal without any obvious external stimulation. Skinner referred to these spontaneously emitted actions as *operants*. He was not interested in what caused the operants, and he accepted the fact each different species will have different types of operants. His goal was to change the way in which the animal emitted the operants.

Skinner discovered that the rate of emitted behavior could be controlled by the consequences of the behavior, that is, by what happened in the environment immediately following the operant's occurrence. In one experiment, a pigeon was placed in a cage with no food tray. On the side of the cage was a colored disk. As the pigeon in the cage emitted the operant of pecking, it pecked at all parts of the cage at random. When the bird happened to peck the colored disk, a small bit of food was dropped into the cage. Over time, the bird began to narrow down its pecking to the region of the cage containing the disk, and eventually it pecked exclusively at the disk: the animal discovered the contingency between its own operant, the disk, and the food. This is similar to our description of the response contingent method of infant research (see Chapter 1). The process by which the frequency of an operant is controlled by its consequences is called *operant conditioning*.

Consequences that increase the frequency of the preceding operant are called *reinforcers*. A *positive* reinforcer is an action or reward that follows the operant and increases its frequency. In some cases, the frequency of an operant is increased following the removal of an aversive stimulus. Thus, the absence of a consequence that increases the frequency of the operant is called a *negative* reinforcer.

Suppose an infant performs some action that the parents would like to encourage, such as drinking all his or her milk. Parents can increase the frequency of this happening with praise for the child after finishing the milk (a positive reinforcer). On the other hand, the child may increase the frequency of finishing the milk to avoid being scolded for *not* finishing it. The absence of scolding becomes a negative reinforcer.

There are several learning processes by which the frequency of a behavior can be decreased instead of increased. One way is by punishment, which is any consequence that reduces the frequency of an operant. In the above example, the scolding may act as a punishment to decrease the frequency of *not* finishing the milk.

Extinction is the process by which the frequency of an operant decreases when a reinforcing consequence is removed. In the first few months of life, it is important to respond promptly to an infant's crying. This response, however, may increase the frequency of infant crying (although the intensity and duration of crying may decline over time). When the infant is several months older, the child has more of an ability to tolerate distress, and parents may want the infant to calm down on his or her own. Parents can extinguish crying by not responding to it as frequently or as promptly as before.

Both classical and operant conditioning are able to explain particular learning phenomena in infancy, especially in situations in which there are repeated opportunities for exposure to similar environmental consequences. There are, however, developmental differences in an infant's susceptibility to conditioning and to the types of environmental stimuli and conditions that are most conducive to serve as reinforcers or punishers. Unfortunately, learning theory cannot explain how these individual differences and development changes are caused. That is, there is nothing in the theory about individual variability and the effects of the social context on the child's learning. We now turn to a more recent development that seems to take account of individual and developmental factors in learning.

Social Learning Theory

Researchers began to notice that simple conditioning was not enough to explain patterns of behavior seen in human infants and children. Several theoretical developments led to *social learning theory*. First of all, it was discovered that as infants change their behavior to adjust to the contingencies between their behavior and the environment, infants seek to change the environment to preserve or enhance the same pattern of contingencies. Thus, infants come to control not only their behavior but also the behavior of other people around them (Bijou & Baer, 1965).

For example, suppose a parent reinforces the child every time the child asks for help and ignores the child whenever the child whines or cries to get help. The child is likely to increase the frequency of verbal requests for help, but in addition, the child will come to *expect* help whenever it is asked for in the appropriate way. On the parent's side, when the child asks for help verbally and without whining, the parent is more likely to provide the assistance. Thus, the increase in the child's verbal requests will condition the parent to increase the frequency of giving help. As a result of this complex social process, the child's recognition of the contingency has ultimately changed that child's social environment.

A second theoretical development was the discovery that infants could change their behavior in ways that had nothing to do with conditioning. Entirely new behaviors could be acquired almost immediately through *observational learning* (Bandura, 1977). Just by watching an adult or peer model, an infant could imitate the behavior and incorporate that imitated act into the infant's own goals.

A final theoretical advance of social learning theory is the idea that infants are more likely to acquire new behaviors in some situations compared to others. Both conditioning and observational learning are more likely to occur if infants are motivated to pay attention to the consequences of their action or to the model. Thus, an infant's goals help to organize the way in which the infant picks up information from the environment. In a word, social learning theory introduced the self (including cognitions and motivations) as an intelligent actor and organizer of information (see Figure 2.2).

If the infant's experiences are contingent upon the infant's actions and if those actions subsequently change the behavior of others in ways that accord with the infant's goals, a feeling of self-efficacy emerges (Bandura, 1989). If on the other hand, the infant's goals are typically thwarted and the social environment behaves capriciously, feelings of helplessness and despair emerge (Seligman & Maier, 1967).

Social learning theory has been applied to a wide variety of issues in infant development. It suggests that environments can be structured in ways that are conducive to infant learning and to longer-term feelings of self-efficacy. The

■ **FIGURE 2.2**
Diagram of Triadic Reciprocality

The triadic relationship between behavior, cognition and personal factors, and environmental contexts determines social learning.

SOURCE: Adapted from A. Bandura. *Social foundations of thought and action: A social cognitive theory.* Englewood Cliffs, N.J.: Prentice-Hall, 1986, p. 24 (Reprinted by permission).

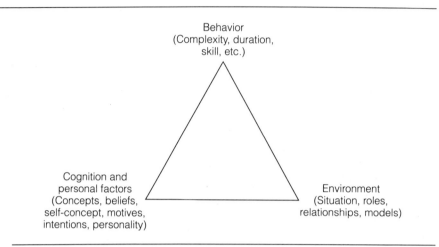

theory focuses on the immediate context of behavior and shows the importance of the environment being responsive to the infant's current goals and needs and not a mere mechanical producer of reinforcers.

As with ethological theory, it is difficult to apply learning theory to real-life processes. Although learning theory has had remarkable success at predicting infant behavior during controlled laboratory experiments, real-life environments are never so simple or so contingent. There may be many processes, including genetic contributions, that might influence the way in which behavior is acquired. Because learning theory focuses on the immediate conditions of learning, it appears to suggest that an infant at any age can acquire any behavior if the environmental and motivational conditions are right. Since this is clearly not the case, learning theory cannot explain the sequence and timing of developmental stages in infancy. Although learning theorists deny that stages exist—behavior is acquired gradually and cumulatively—the existence of universal developmental sequences cannot be denied. It is hard to imagine otherwise how such individualized, cumulative, and reciprocal parent-infant social learning processes could lead to such similar outcomes across infants.

A problem common to both ethological and learning theories is that they are not developmental: they describe processes that regulate behavior, and they assume that development occurs more or less automatically by a genetically controlled maturation. Although individuals at different ages are studied, the goal is not to explain how infants progress from one stage to the next.

In the remainder of this chapter, we review three theoretical approaches in which development is thought of as an active process—not merely the accumulation of learning experiences nor merely the unfolding of a genetically precoded developmental sequence. Cognitive theories assume the existence of an organizing mental process that propels development; emotion theories see feelings as central organizers of experience and change; and systems theories examine the mutual influences of all relevant aspects of the infant and the environment in the induction of developmental change.

■ COGNITIVE THEORY

Constructivist Approaches

One of the central theories of cognitive development is that of Jean Piaget (1896–1980), who was trained as an invertebrate biologist before he became interested in the study of human development. Biologists had studied development from the point of view of adaptation to the environment. An *adaptation* is a change in an individual's functioning that makes the individual better suited to survive in a particular environment. Piaget's contribution to cognitive development was to conceptualize human intelligence as a form of adaptation to the environment. In his view, even small infants can act in intelligent ways, not by thinking but through their physical actions on the environment to meet their own goals (Piaget, 1952).

For Piaget, an infant who is touching an object is developing an intelligent way of "knowing" that object. Knowledge, rather than being a static library of information, is conceived as an active process of engagement between the knower and what is to be known. All complex forms of knowing develop out of simpler actions found in infants, such as sucking, chewing, touching, and crawling.

Jean Piaget is known for his theoretical contributions and also for his empathic sensitivity with young children. His many experiments with his own three infants were sensitive and embedded into the infant's daily activities.

Piaget brought two principles of biological adaptation into his study of the development of intelligent action: assimilation and accommodation. *Assimilation* refers to the process by which an individual can relate to those aspects of the environment that are already suited to his or her needs or capacities. It is the application of what one already knows or does to the current situation. *Accommodation* is the alteration of existing abilities to better fit the requirements of the task or situation. Accommodation is more likely to occur if assimilation does not result in an effective adaptation to the environment.

Typically, most actions involve both assimilation and accommodation. Between the ages of six and twelve months, human infants must learn to eat solid foods. This is not an easy task, because the infant's tongue is not yet coordinated enough to keep food in the mouth. While sucking on a breast or a bottle, the baby's tongue moves in and out like a piston. When a baby is first given solid food on a spoon, the baby's response is to move the tongue in a sucking-like motion, which has the effect of expelling food from the mouth. Thus the infant assimilates the tongue and mouth actions of sucking to the eating of solids. Since this simple assimilation leaves the infant hungry, the child must accommodate mouth and tongue movements so they are better adapted to the shape of the spoon and the consistency of the solid foods.

Piaget's main goal was to apply his theory of intelligent adaptation to the development of human intelligence, and he looked for the origins of intelligence in human infancy. He referred to the first two years of life as the *sensorimotor stage*, involving individuals' growing awareness of their effect on the environment and their changing conceptualizations of space, time, and cause-effect relationships (Piaget & Inhelder, 1969). Piaget divided the sensorimotor stage into six substages, each of which we will describe in later chapters. Piaget also described a number of stages beyond the infancy period. These are summarized in Table 2.1.

The sensorimotor stage was thought to contain the seeds for the development of thought, language, social skills, and morality. According to

■ **TABLE 2.1 Piaget's Cognitive-Developmental Stages of Child Development**

APPROXIMATE AGE (YEARS)	STAGE	DESCRIPTION
0–2	Sensorimotor	Infants learn through direct experience of the senses and by handling objects and moving them around. They do not understand that things exist outside their own actions.
2–6 or 7	Preoperational	Ability to form mental representations, language, thinking as internalized action but centered on the self's perspective; in ability to think logically.
7–11 or 12	Concrete operational	Thinking takes the perspective of others and is logical with respect to concrete actions and objects, such as the rules of a game; inability to think about abstract things.
12–adult	Formal operational	Thinking nonconcrete, abstract things, ability to solve word problems, to form a coherent system of thought relating many ideas, and to think about future possibility.

SOURCE: Reprinted by permission from p. 39 of Child Development by Alan Fogel and Gail F. Melson; Copyright © 1988 by West Publishing Company. All rights reserved.

Piaget, the earliest forms of thinking, seen around the age of eighteen months, are "interiorized actions," the actions of the sensorimotor period. Three basic principles about human infants characterize Piaget's theory.

Individuals play an active role in their own development. The major motivation for developmental change comes from inside the individual in the form of the experience of a failure to reach an adaptation to the environment. This experience of failure, when accommodation and assimilation fall short of adaptation, is called *disequilibrium.* Since disequilibrium is defined in relation to what each individual wants to accomplish, it cannot be imposed from the outside: babies seek knowledge about those things that motivate their curiosity.

Infants develop knowledge by means of their own actions on the environment. The accommodation process literally changes the infant's view of the world since by altering his or her own actions, the child comes to "know" new uses for the same objects. Through action, individuals create knowledge. Since knowledge is an active process of creation, this theory is often referred to as *constructivist*: a theory in which knowledge is built up by doing rather than being imposed on the child from the outside.

Infants will learn better from experiences if those experiences can be assimilated to their current developmental level. The currently available set of skills and knowledge is known as the infant's *schemes.* Schemes can be either sensorimotor—that is, involving physical actions, such as reaching and chewing—or they can be conceptual—that is, ideas, concepts, or thoughts. In order for accommodation to occur, the infant has to assimilate the existing set of schemes to the environment. For this to happen, the environment should present challenges that are moderate, not overly difficult or beyond the infant's grasp. Thus, solid foods at first have to be soft in consistency (the infant does not have teeth yet) and given on a spoon that is small enough to fit in the infant's mouth. Adults have to hold the spoon at just the right angle and move it in and out of the infant's mouth at the appropriate time.

Piaget's original work on infancy was based on observations of his own three children. These observations are unrivaled in their clarity, accuracy, detail, and theoretical import (see Chapter 1). Many of the details of this work continue to be studied in ongoing research.

Piaget's work is clearly distinguished from learning theories and from ethological theories. Piaget believed that development is not imposed on the infant from the outside nor guided solely by maturational change. Adaptation suggests a more active, infant-centered perspective. Using genetically given sensory and motor systems and operating within the constraints imposed by the environment, each child can realize specific personal goals by finding the best adaptive match between sensorimotor skills and environmental constraints. Intelligence is precisely the deliberate harnessing of both nature and nurture to meet one's goals.

One problem with Piaget's theory is related to how Piaget decided to divide development into stages. As we discussed in the previous chapter, there is a certain arbitrariness in the particular behavioral milestone that we choose to mark the beginning or ending of a stage of development. Once you pick an indicator of a stage transition, then you do not expect to see that behavior appearing earlier or later in development. Unfortunately for stage theories, this often happens.

For example, research has found that certain behaviors may occur well before Piaget's stages suggest that they should appear. A good example is imitation. Piaget (1962) claimed that infants younger than nine months could not imitate movements, such as a facial expression, that they could not see themselves make. Yet there is current evidence that such imitation may be possible at birth (see Chapter 5). Early imitation is possible as long as the experimenter can find simple ways to present the task to the infant (Kaye & Marcus, 1978). Another example is that infants can comprehend whole sentences beginning at the end of the first year of life, but they are not able to produce similar sentences until almost one year later. Infants first learn to produce nouns and noun phrases in the second year of life, but it is not until the third year that they learn to produce verb phrases of similar complexity (see Chapters 9, 10, and 11).

Information Processing Theories of Cognitive Development

Imagine a toddler, about two years old, playing with her peers in a day-care center. The toddler playroom has glass windows that enclose it from the entrance foyer of the day-care building. Out of the corner of her eye, the toddler sees her mother come into the foyer. Her mother stops to speak with someone. The little girl gets up, walks to the door that opens onto the hall, walks down the hall, turns left, enters the foyer, and runs up to mommy with arms outstretched.

Piaget's explanation of this behavior, assuming this is not the first time it happened, would be simply "assimilation." Piaget might also place our toddler in the fifth or sixth stage of his scheme of development, since she was able to see her mother as a separate person, stop what she was doing, and walk around a barrier to reach her mother. A younger baby might recognize her mother but might try to walk directly to mom by going toward the glass wall.

Many developmentalists are dissatisfied with this kind of explanation because it leaves unspecified the mental processes that may be involved. Let's think about what they might be. First of all the child must be able to focus her *attention* on the person who walks in. Next, the jumble of colors, lines, and moving images must be organized into a coherent picture that has a meaning for the child; this is known as the *perceptual process*. Perception takes place partly in the sensory system (in this case, the retina and optic nerve) and partly in the brain (in this case, the visual cortex). The particular perception (and it should be clear that a perception is a mental event) is organized according to specific categories using the processes of *recognition* and *recall memory*. The child interprets this perception as one that she's seen before and she remembers what this perception means to her (mommy!). At this point she can invoke *thought processes* to make some decisions: Should I go see mommy? How can I get there? Should I go through the door or wave through the window?

Information processing theories attempt to specify the way in which the mind handles the information presented to it by the environment (see Figure 2.3). This type of cognitive theory does not run counter to Piagetian theory; it tries to provide a more specific picture of mental processes and their changes in the course of development. Research in information processing generally requires sophisticated technology to measure such things as visual fixation time, eye movement patterns, auditory sensitivities, etc. (See Chapter 1.)

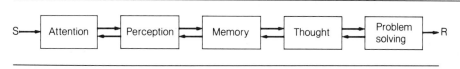

■ FIGURE 2.3
Components of
Information
Processing

Kagan's (1971) research showed how the amount of time the infant spent gazing at a stimulus was influenced by different factors as the infant matured. During the first few months, the baby prefers to look at the edges and borders of objects and at moving objects. This seems to be due to innate properties of the human visual system at birth. By the third month of life, the infant starts to look longer at things that resemble what he has seen in the past.

Kagan found that infants between two and ten months like to look at stimuli that are neither totally novel nor totally familiar. By the time they are eight months, mental abilities allow for the further processing of information. Instead of continuing to look at things merely because they are discrepant, infants look at things that are problematic, that raise questions, or that they are trying to understand or classify in some way. Kagan (1971) showed pictures to three-year-old children of a face in which the nose, eyes, ears, and mouth had been scrambled in a random order (see Figure 2.4). While younger children tended to ignore this face because it was too discrepant, the three-year-olds were confused. They asked questions like, "What happened to his nose?" or "Who hit him in the nose?" or "Who that, mommy? A monster?" Kagan referred to these kinds of questions as *hypotheses* and suggested that this accounted for the older infant's interest in particular stimuli.

One contribution of information processing theory is that it can be applied to problems in early education and in the treatment of handicapped infants. In Piaget's view, infants pass through major stages in which all of their capacities are integrated and centered around a single stage. Information processing views predict that infants may get off their cognitive developmental track if only one of their component processes is faulty. For example, an infant with poor perceptual skills may show signs of retardation even if

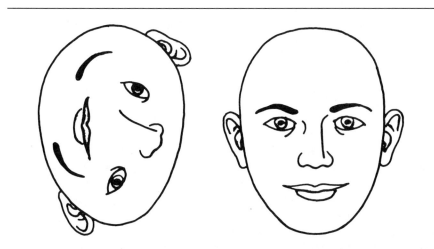

■ FIGURE 2.4
Scrambled Face

SOURCE: Kagan, 1971. Reprinted by permission of the author. Reprinted by permission from p. 168 of Child Development by Alan Fogel and Gail F. Melson; Copyright © 1988 by West Publishing Company. All rights reserved.

everything else about the infant is intact and healthy. Without perception, however, nothing else can operate well. Simple interventions to improve hearing or eyesight, for example, may be all that is necessary to drastically improve the developmental prognosis for some infants. Some premature infants have a hypersensitivity to touch. They can be easily overstimulated, leading to later mental retardation. When touch and other environmental factors are regulated, most premature infants will develop normally (see Chapter 5).

One problem with information processing theory is that it offers few clues about how each of the informational processing components develop. Each component—memory, perception, etc.—is presumed to change gradually, leading to overall improvements in cognition. On the one hand, this sounds like a genetically based maturational perspective. However, some experiments have shown (see Chapter 6) that babies can be trained to improve their memories. In any case, there is nothing in information processing theory that is akin to Piaget's notion of adaptation. Information processing is more a theory of how infants act and think than of how action and thought develop.

■ EMOTION THEORY

Just as cognitive theories view intelligent adaptations or information processing as playing the major organizing role in behavior and development, emotion theories make the same claim for motivational and feeling states. The distinction here is similar to the difference between the eighteenth-century empiricists and romantics (see Chapter 1). Although today's developmental theorists accept that both cognition and emotion are important, the cognitive theorists assume that we are ultimately ruled by reason, while the emotion theorists claim that passion guides us.

Psychoanalytic Theory

There are few things in human life that are more insistent and compelling than a baby's cry. Part of this has to do with the fact that adults are attuned to respond to signals of distress and pleasure from infants. But it is also due to the fact that small babies *are* demanding and insistent. When cold, hungry, wet, or tired, very young infants have no sense of social decorum; they want the unpleasantness stopped, and right away.

Babies are equally insistent about the things that please them. During the first few months of life, a hungry baby is almost animalistic in the consumption of milk at breast or bottle. Most babies take the milk in as if it were their first and last meal, and it is nearly impossible to interrupt their voracious attack on the nipple without provoking screams of distress.

This type of behavior is what Sigmund Freud (1903) referred to as *primary process* functioning. Primary processes involve the unfettered exhibition of feelings coupled with the relative inability to delay gratification of those feelings. The typical sequence of primary process functioning is as follows. Infants experience some kind of tension or need, which leads to a state of restlessness or fussiness. Lacking any means of gratifying themselves or even of searching for gratification, they become more and more upset and continue until another person comes along to provide them with what they need.

Freud labeled that part of the individual's personality ruled by the primary processes the *id*, and he believed that young infants were governed entirely by the id. The id can be thought of as all of the person's needs and desires but especially those desires that are irrational, overwhelmingly compelling, and not tolerant of any delay.

According to Freud, infants gradually learn to control some of these impulses. Their cries become less insistent, for example, and they develop the capacity to wait for gratification and even to satisfy themselves. The ability to tolerate discomfort and frustration and to moderate the pursuit of pleasure falls under the heading of the second system of personality functioning, which Freud called the *ego*. The ego refers to the *regulatory* functions of the person. In the earliest months, this involves delay of gratification, but in general, the ego is responsible for helping the individual meet his or her needs in the most effective way.

The ego, therefore, is the agency that directs the infant to goals, in spite of any barriers, detours, or other inhibitions along the way. As the infant gets older, the ego relies increasingly more on thought process, mental representation, problem solving, and rational approaches to the world. Since one usually cannot expect to get one's needs met immediately or even easily, the ego is said to operate within the constraints of reality using *secondary processes*, as opposed to the primary processes that are rooted in myths, dreams, fantasies, and unrealistic expectations.

The third part of the personality, as conceived by Freud, was the *superego*, which contained the cultural rules and moral values that the child learns through socialization. Since the superego was not thought to form until the third or fourth year of life, we shall not consider that aspect of the personality in this book.

How Did Freud View Infant Development?

At birth, there is only the id, and only later does the infant develop the regulatory mechanisms that comprise the ego. Beyond this general formulation, Freud also thought that both the id and the ego continue to develop over the life span, and he distinguished two major phases of development during the first three years of life: the *oral* stage and the *anal* stage.

The development of the id reflects changes in sensitivity of the body's erogenous zones. During the first year of life, the infant is particularly aware of sensations of pleasure and displeasure in the mouth region, through activities such as sucking, chewing, biting, and swallowing. This period is called the oral stage. During the oral stage, the infant tends to view the world from the point of view of consuming it. Freud felt that infants in this period believe that they can incorporate everything and everyone, that the world is centered upon their own gratification. Although Freud referred to this feeling as one of omnipotence, it is unlikely that infants experience the sense of being all-powerful, since they do not know that they are controlling anything, and they are not aware that they are dependent upon others (Baldwin, 1980). What they are more likely to feel is the expectation of being gratified when they need it, a kind of trust in the inevitability of satisfaction.

The anal stage begins sometime in the second year of life when the primary erogenous zone becomes the anal region of the body. Freud thought that children found pleasure in the distension of the bowel, the withholding of feces, and the elimination of feces. In the same way that the oral period was associated with the development of a sense of security, the anal period corresponds to the development of feelings of independence and autonomy. Gaining self-control over the bladder and bowel muscles is a major personal achievement, and the feelings associated with producing, owning, holding onto, and voluntarily giving up one's feces are thought to relate to the child's growing sense of self and personal autonomy.

The *phallic* stage, which begins in the fourth year of life, represents a increased interest in the genital area, an identification of one's own gender, and the onset of the Oedipus and Electra complexes, in which the preschooler tries to identify with the same-sex parent and feels possessiveness toward the parent of the opposite sex. The phallic stage and the latency and genital stages that follow take us beyond the scope of this text. These stages are outlined in Table 2.2.

What Can Go Wrong in Development?

Freud placed a great deal of emphasis on the infant's basic needs and on the ability of the parents to effectively gratify those needs. The mother was seen as the primary agent in the infant's continuing development. The infant becomes attached to the person who feeds him or her because, at first, the child associates the powerful urges of hunger satisfaction with the person providing the food. If the feeding is done by many different people, the infant will never develop a sense of attachment and will never learn to love.

Even when the mother is a permanent object in the child's life, she may fail to effectively gratify the infant in an appropriate or consistent way. Or, alternatively, she may continue to provide immediate gratification, thus never allowing the infant an opportunity to strengthen individual ego mechanisms.

To take one example of how Freud's theory might work, a child whose mother insists on early toilet training and cleanliness may be deprived of the opportunity to experience the pleasure of those first true possessions (the child's feces). Such a child could develop a possessive, "uptight," or stingy disposition in later life in an attempt to hold onto his or her possessions for fear they will be taken away again.

What Are Some of the Problems with Psychoanalytic Theory?

Most of the developmental predictions of Freud's theory, such as the one just discussed, have never been scientifically verified. In the last chapter of this book, we shall review some studies suggesting that specific or isolated experiences in infancy, whether traumatic or pleasurable, have no lasting psychological consequences.

Second, there is considerable evidence to suggest that feeding is not a crucial context for the infant's development of attachment. The classic studies of Harlow and Harlow (1965) on rhesus monkeys and the related work of Schaffer and Emerson (1964) on human mother-infant attachment definitively showed that infants became attached to individuals and objects that played little or no role in the day-to-day feeding and needs satisfaction of the infants. Instead, human infants seem to become attached to people with whom they can communicate through sharing and play.

■ TABLE 2.2 Psychoanalytic Stages of Development

APPROXIMATE AGE	ACCORDING TO FREUD	ACCORDING TO ERIKSON
0–1 1/2 years	*Oral stage*—Pleasure and experience gained from the mouth, sucking, and biting.	*Trust vs. mistrust*—Development of expectancy of gratification or frustration.
1 1/2–3 years	*Anal stage*—Pleasure from anal region through elimination and retention.	*Autonomy vs. shame/doubt*—Self-assertiveness and self-control or uncertainty and shame.
3–6 years	*Phallic or Oedipal stage*—Interest in own genitals, desire to possess parent of opposite sex.	*Initiative vs. guilt*—Taking initiatives and a sense of purpose or guilt about independent activity.
6–11 years	*Latency stage*—No overt sexual desires, interest in learning new skills.	*Industry vs. inferiority*—Interest in learning and skill development or sense of inadequacy and loss of motivation.
Adolescence	*Genital stage*—Adult sexual desires and the establishment of sexual relationships.	*Identity vs. role confusion*—Perception of self as a unique individual, development of personal values, or confusion about identity and role in life.
Young adulthood		*Intimacy vs. isolation*—Emotional commitment to other people, lasting relationships, or sense of loneliness and isolation.
Adulthood and middle age		*Generativity vs. stagnation*—Investment in the world of work and childrearing or inactivity and purposelessness.
Old age		*Integrity vs. despair*—Acceptance of one's life as the only life one could live, acceptance of death, or despair over failures, losses, and mistakes.

SOURCE: Reprinted by permission from p. 34 of Child Development by Alan Fogel and Gail F. Melson; Copyright © 1988 by West Publishing Company. All rights reserved.

One of the main problems with Freudian psychoanalytic theory is that it is a theory of adult mental life, memory processes, and inner experiences. Freud never formally observed infants; he instead developed his ideas on the basis of his patients' recollections during psychoanalysis. It would perhaps be more accurate to describe psychoanalytic theory as a representation of infancy and childhood as remembered by adults.

The very fact that psychoanalytic theory relies upon the inner feelings and thoughts of the person (the id and ego) makes it nearly impossible to study using the usual tools of behavioral research; the concepts are simply not operational definitions that can be used as a basis of scientific measurement. This very flaw, from the perspective of the behavioral scientist, can also be viewed as one of the strengths of the theory. Few theories of infant development have provided us with any attempt to conceptualize the mysterious infant psyche. Although we can't prove them, Freud's ideas have stimulated and intrigued scholars and lay persons for almost a century.

Although few infancy researchers base their work on Freud's theory, it is important today because of its influence on clinical work with infants and their families. In addition, Freud's placement of the emotions at the center of developmental change has had a lasting influence on the other emotion theories that we will now review.

Psychoanalytic Theory After Freud

Since Freud's writings, other psychoanalysts have considered the area of infant development and have found occasion to elaborate and expand the work of the master. One of the best-known of Freud's followers was Erik Erikson. Erikson (1950) accepted Freud's basic premise that changes in erogenous sensitivity from oral to anal to genital awareness form the core of the developing person. Erikson, however, placed more emphasis on the impact of the infant's family and society. He viewed each stage of development (eight stages in all across the entire life span) as a potential crisis of the personality. An individual might continue his or her forward progress in development, or the person might become side-tracked at any point.

Erikson's developmental stages in the first three years are given in Table 2.2. The first conflict of the life cycle was related to the development of a sense of *basic trust* in the environment. This trust developed if the mother was able to satisfy the infant's needs in such a way that the baby came to expect the environment to be friendly and helpful. *Mistrust* occurred when the mother (or other care giver) did not allow the infant to develop the expectancy that needs would be met adequately. The concept of trust involves not only an expectation that others will provide help when needed but also a sense of trust in self. That is, by sometime in the second year, infants should be able to tolerate a variety of stressful situations—hunger, cold, separation, conflict with others—by relying on their own resources for coping. This sense of trust in self was thought to derive from experiences of trusting in others.

In the second stage, the infant could either develop a sense of *purpose* and *autonomy* or else a sense of *shame* and *doubt*. This again depended upon the parent's ability to support the infant's desire to assert him- or herself and to reward and to share in the infant's personal achievements. If the parent chastises the infant for being assertive or fails to delight in the infant's accomplishments, the infant may feel ashamed and exposed and develop a sense of doubt about his or her abilities to be independent and assertive.

Although Erikson's theory goes further than Freud's in specifying the links between the infant and the social environment, it suffers from the same kinds of flaws as the former; its assertions are unverifiable since the key concepts of the theory are couched in terms of thought and feeling. Although Erikson worked with younger children than Freud did, he still lacked the direct experience and observation of infants that would be needed to construct a more objective account of infancy.

Somewhat later, psychoanalysts began to rely on observational data gathered from young infants. Citing evidence from scientific studies of infant development, Hartmann (1958) argued that there was a rudimentary ego even at the time of birth. Hartmann cited evidence showing that newborns possess self-protective mechanisms. If hungry or tired, they will not continue to cry forever; instead, their systems will automatically shut down, and they will go to sleep for a while. Newborns also have the ability to tune out unpleasant stimulation, and in general, they have higher thresholds for arousal than adults. Hartmann also cited the long list of newborn reflex behaviors (see Chapter 5) that newborns use, for example, to get food or to protect themselves from suffocation.

The issue of the growth of personal autonomy was later taken up by Margaret Mahler (1975), who developed a neo-psychoanalytic approach to understanding the development of a sense of self and individual autonomy. *Individuation*, according to Mahler, is reflected by the toddler's ability to cope with separation from the care giver, with feelings of loneliness and sadness, and by a realistic sense of what he or she needs to get from others compared to what the child can handle on his or her own.

The main contribution of psychoanalytic theories after Freud is that they have brought more specificity to an understanding of the infancy period than did Freud. While Freud never observed infants directly, Mahler made extensive observations on early development. Her work and that of others led to the refinement of the field of infant psychiatry and other clinical applications related to infant development. Because of the psychoanalytic emphasis on the parent-infant bond, most clinical interventions in infancy involve a large component of parent education and enrichment. When infants have severe feeding, toileting, emotional regulation, or autonomy problems, clinicians will most often work with the mother-infant dyad to help solve the problems.

Erikson's and Mahler's theories suffer from similar problems as Freud's. That is, they lack experimental confirmation and their constructs are too abstract and subjective for measurement. Few research studies today are based directly on these ideas.

Discrete Emotion Theory

A theory of emotional development that has generated a considerable body of recent research is discrete emotion theory. Whereas psychoanalytic theory postulated innate urges of the id, discrete emotion theory suggests that there is an innate set of basic human emotions, a position more similar to that of Darwin (1872) than that of Freud. These discrete emotions include interest, fear, anger, sadness, joy, surprise, excitement, and disgust.

Each emotion is a discretely different state from all the others, and each serves a different purpose in the individual's life and ultimate survival (Ekman, 1984; Izard, 1971; Plutchik, 1980; Tomkins, 1962). Evidence for the discreteness of these emotions comes from a number of related observations. First of all, most newborn infants possess the ability to execute the facial expressive movements necessary to produce each of the discrete emotions (Oster, 1978), and some of these newborn facial expressions are tied to specific adaptive functions at birth. For example, infants will try to expel bad-tasting substances from their mouths while making a disgust expression, and their crying seems to relate to identifiable sources of distress (Izard & Malatesta, 1987).

In general, each discrete emotion is thought to have not only a characteristic facial expression but also to relate to a unique function for the individual, to have a specific effect on other people, and to be accompanied by a particular motivational state. Anger, for example, has the characteristic expression of clenched and bared teeth, square mouth, and knit brows. Anger motivates a person to take direct action, it functions as a response to having one's goals blocked, and it signals to others that a confrontation is likely.

The discrete emotions represent a primary motivational system, believed to be genetically encoded and to develop by maturation. In this view, emotions are complex neurophysiological states that can affect the mind and the body to change thought processes and evoke action. In the first few months, infants are largely dependent upon the pushes and pulls of their emotions (similar to the notion of the dominance of the *id* in early life). Later, children are believed to develop the ability to self-regulate the discrete emotions through a process of social learning (Izard & Malatesta, 1987). Thus, because overt expressions of anger are not likely to be tolerated, infants must learn by both conditioning and imitation to channel their feelings into more socially acceptable forms.

Emotions can develop via both maturation and social learning in the following ways. Strong emotions become less frequent with age and are expressed in more socially appropriate forms (*e.g.*, saying "I'm really angry," as opposed to screaming and hitting). Emotions become more complicated as discrete emotions are mixed (*e.g.*, joy and anger mixed will become mischief). Emotional expressions can be modulated by active coping processes (*e.g.*, biting the lower lip to hold back crying). Finally, emotional states become detached from emotional experience (*e.g.*, trying to smile even though one is feeling sad). However, this latter achievement does not begin until after the infancy period.

Discrete emotion theory has contributed to our understanding of these processes of emotional development and especially of the interaction of the innate emotions with the social environment to produce developmental changes in emotion. Indeed, the idea that the emotions actually develop in the ways mentioned above is a relatively new one. Discrete emotions are relatively easy to research. Facial expressions can be coded, heart rate and other physiological measures can be used, and the process of emotion socialization between infants and adults can be readily observed in naturalistic situations.

A problem with discrete emotion theorists is that they tend to focus on facial expressions that fit into their list of discrete emotions and to ignore facial expressions that do not fit. Infant's faces are incredibly mobile, and they often make "odd" facial movements that are not recognizable as emotional states by adults. These unconventional movements include mouthing, asymmetrical expressions, eyebrow squiggles, nose wrinkles, and lip puckers.

Note the complexity of this facial expression of emotion. It includes lowered brows that are knit in the center, partially closed eyes, and a downturned mouth. What do you think the baby is feeling?

In addition, infants express emotions with their whole bodies and not just with their faces: consider arm stiffening, kicking, and back arching. These examples show that emotions may be expressed in a variety of ways by infants, not necessarily through the neurophysiological pathways to the face as hypothesized in discrete emotion theory (Fogel & Reimers, 1989).

It is quite likely that the emotional world of the infant is very different from that of the adult. Imposing the adult-conventional discrete emotions on infant experience is somewhat like imposing adult categories of communicative and linguistic meaning on the host of infant grunts, coos, squeals, frets, and other purely baby-like vocalizations. It may be that a unique baby-like emotional world that is not divided into a small number of discrete states evolves into the recognizable adult discrete emotions in the same way that early vocalizations evolve into conventional linguistic forms of communication.

Cognitive/Constructivist Theories of Emotion

Other theories of emotional development do not rely on the assumption of a neurophysiological set of discrete emotions early in life. Rather, they assume that emotion is intimately tied with cognitive processes.

A Piagetian, or cognitive, approach to emotional development has been offered by Alan Sroufe (1979). Sroufe showed how there were few true emotions in the early months of life and that emotions developed in close correspondence to cognitive milestones. The emotions of shame and pride, for example, do not appear in children until they have the cognitive ability to separate self from other, since shame is defined as the feeling of being exposed and that means exposed *in front of* some other person. To be able to feel shame, we must realize that other people have feelings and ideas and that others can see us as we see them. Similarly, pride is a sense of self-importance and self-satisfaction. A baby of twelve months can smile or laugh when he or she achieves a goal, but this is the pure enjoyment of assimilation rather than the warm glow of pride in oneself.

You can find a listing of Sroufe's stages of affective development in Table 2.3. We shall have occasion to elaborate upon these aspects of emotional development in Chapters 6 through 11.

Sroufe's theory falls somewhere midway between Piagetian and psychoanalytic theories in relation to its views about the developmental organizing force. Instead of saying, as Piaget might, that disequilibrium causes the organism to act in a certain manner, Sroufe felt that discrepancy was associated with frustration or disappointment and it was this emotion that led the child to act upon the environment.

To make a firm theoretical statement about whether thoughts are more important than feelings, or vice versa, is a little like the old chicken-and-egg debate. In reality, thoughts, perceptions, memories, and emotions are all facets of the same multifaceted phenomenon of human life and human consciousness. More often than not, thoughts and feelings interact and work together to help determine action. When the mother of an eighteen-month-old infant leaves him alone in a strange setting, the infant may initially feel distress and anger. If there are other people or toys in the room, the infant can often use them to occupy himself, and he can rely upon good memories of his mother and perhaps the expectation that she will return shortly. In other words, the baby's thoughts help to regulate and control the baby's feelings, while the feelings may evoke certain kinds of thoughts and not others.

Joseph Campos and Linda Barrett's (Barrett & Campos, 1987; Campos & Barrett, 1984) functional theory of the emotions holds that emotions serve to adapt the infant to the environment by providing a motivation to act in adaptive ways. Contrary to the discrete emotion perspective, Campos and Barrett postulate that emotional experiences are linked not to specific facial expressions but to a "family" of related movements and events. Emotions are complex combinations of vocalizations, physiological arousal, action tendencies, goals, and cognitions. This view provides for multiple pathways of expression and action. Anger, for example, may be expressed by the face, kicking, hitting, or screaming, in any combination. Anger would not be expressed by smiling or by cooing. Thus certain families of actions tend to be associated with any given emotion, but the specific form of the expression will vary on different occasions and across different individuals.

■ **TABLE 2.3   Developmental Sequence of the Emergence of Basic Human Emotions**

MONTH[a]	Pleasure-Joy	Wariness-Fear	Rage-Anger
0	Endogenous smile	Startle/pain	Distress due to covering the face,
1	Turning toward	Obligatory attention	physical restraint, extreme discomfort
2			
3	Pleasure		Rage (disappointment)
4			
	Delight Active laughter	Wariness	
5			
6			
7	Joy		Anger
8			
9		Fear (stranger aversion)	
10			
11			
12	Elation	Anxiety, immediate fear	Angry mood, petulance
18	Positive valuation of self affection	Shame	Defiance
24			Intentional hurting
36	Pride, love		Guilt

[a]The age specified is neither the first appearance of the affect in question nor its peak occurrence; it is the age when the literature suggests that the reaction is common.

SOURCE: L. A. Sroufe, Socioemotional development. In J. Osofsky (Ed.), *Handbook of infant development* New York: Wiley, 1979. Reprinted by permission.

The theories of Sroufe and Campos and Barrett all assume some kind of neurophysiological, cognitive, or emotional process by which emotions are linked to expressions and actions. Michael Lewis and Linda Michalson (1983) place less emphasis on neurophysiological components of emotion. They believe that in early infancy, there is not a primacy of emotions or cognitions but that both interact in complex ways. Through a process of social learning, infants come to identify particular feelings with particular expressions and verbal labels. In this view, infants have feelings that they do not understand or recognize. Through a process of parental labeling of their feelings (*e.g.*, saying things like "You must be angry" or "Why are you sad today?"), children learn to construct the social meaning of their emotions. Children also imitate adults' use of emotion expressions in particular situations. If adults are smiling, the infant will also smile. In the process, the infant comes to associate the inner feelings of enjoyment with the expression of smiling in others and with the typical situations in which such feelings tend to occur.

All of the constructivist theories of emotion emphasize an active learning process by which infants use their emotions in everyday life and adapt those emotions to the experiences around them. Constructivist theories allow for a broader range of emotion expression and for a more flexible linkage between emotions and expressions than the relatively small set of discrete emotions. In these views, emotions are not of central importance, but they act in concert with cognitions, actions, and social experiences to produce developmental change.

One problem with constructivist accounts is that they do not provide any insight into why particular expressions are more often associated with internal experiences than others. Discrete emotion theories assume that when a baby cries, that baby is indeed feeling distress. Constructivist views suggest that infant crying may not be directly associated with an inner experience of distress and that if crying is associated with an inner experience, the experience may be quite different from that of an adult with the same facial expression or body movement. There is considerable evidence that pain-producing stimuli, such as inoculations, can reliably evoke crying in infants, including vocalization, facial expression, and physiological arousal (Izard, Hembree, & Huebner, 1987). It is hard to imagine, given this convergent evidence, that infants are not experiencing something akin to pain.

These theories differ in the extent to which emotion is to be considered as a realm unto itself, whether emotions take priority over cognitions as the source of developmental change, or whether emotions and cognitions act in concert with social experiences to produce development. Unlike psychoanalytic theory, which has made more of a contribution to clinical practice, constructivist emotion theories and discrete emotion theories continue to inspire a considerable amount of research on infant development.

■ SYSTEMS THEORY

As suggested in the above analysis of the role of emotion in infant development, theories differ in the importance that they attach to emotion, cognitions, and social experiences for development. Systems theories share the view that *all* facets of the child and the environment are equally important and that development is a complex process by which outcomes are determined through the active interaction of these facets. Rather than focusing on one element, systems theories attempt to understand developmental change in its entirety: the whole child in the whole environment.

A *system* is a set of interdependent components in which each of the components affects the others in reciprocal fashion. Systems theories are those that recognize the mutual dependencies between the infant and the environment. An example is the system of interaction between emotions and cognitions discussed above. In the parent-infant interaction system, the behavior of a parent is likely to depend on the sociability of the infant. Infants who smile more and cry less are likely to have parents who are more relaxed and socially attentive to the infant. This parental social attentiveness will in turn affect the infant's continued sociability. In addition, a parent's relationship to the infant may also be affected by marital satisfaction, his or her relationship with other family members, the financial well-being of the family, his or her own job satisfaction, and even by society's attitudes about the parenting role. Conversely, the successful functioning of society depends on the patterns of interaction and socialization within the family, where infants and children are initially prepared for their roles in that society.

Ecological Systems Theory

Urie Bronfenbrenner has developed a conceptual framework for understanding the complex relationships between the infant, the family, and society. He views the society as part of the *ecology of human development*, "the study of the progressive, mutual accommodation, throughout the life span, between a growing human organism and the changing immediate environments in which it lives, as the process is affected by relations obtaining within and between those immediate settings, as well as the larger social contexts . . . in which the settings are embedded" (Bronfenbrenner, 1979). Bronfenbrenner defines the "ecological environment" as having four levels of functioning between persons.

Microsystem. This level is made up of all the relationships between the person and his or her environment in a particular setting. An example of a microsystem is all of the transactions that take place between the child and the physical and social environment of the family. Other settings in which children are typically found are schools, camps, hospitals, play groups, and churches or synagogues. Children are affected by many aspects of their immediate microsystem environment, including social interactions, housing, and nutrition (Melson, 1980). We shall deal with a number of these aspects in the course of this book.

Mesosystem. This system includes the interrelationships between the major settings in which children are found. An example would be the interaction between the family and the school. A child who is experiencing many difficulties in school is likely to force the parents into having more interactions with school officials—with developmentalists or counselors, for instance—and those family-school interactions should in turn have an effect on the child's functioning.

Exosystem. The exosystem is the extension of the mesosystem to include other social systems that do not contain the developing child but that have some effect on the child. The world of work, neighborhood institutions, the media, the government, the economy, transportation all affect the functioning of the family, the school, and the other social settings in which children are found. One would also hope that the needs of the developing person would be communicated to these other systems through the family and school.

Macrosystem. The macrosystem is that which contains all of the various subsystems that we have been discussing. It contains all of the general tenets, beliefs, and values of the culture or subculture, and it is made up of the written and unwritten principles that regulate everyone's behavior. These princi-ples—whether legal, economic, political, religious, or educational—endow individual life with meaning and value, and control the nature and scope of the interactions between the various levels of the total social system.

The idea of the macrosystem suggests that cultural values and practices have an effect on child-rearing practices and on the development of children and that children should also have an effect on cultural practices. Cross-cultural studies have shown that in populations having high infant mortality rates, health and safety of children is the main parental concern. These cultures have evolved practices that enhance the health of the infant and at the same time alleviate parental anxiety related to infant death (LeVine, 1977). Throughout this book, we shall cite examples of cross-cultural studies showing how culture affects children's development. Our brief look at systems thinking in this chapter was meant to introduce the idea that we need to look beyond the infant organism in order to more fully understand infant development. The relationships between these various subsystems are shown in Figure 2.5.

An example of ecological systems theory as applied to the family system suggests that infants may be influenced by and influence others either by direct effects or by mediated effects. A *direct effect* is one that occurs as part of a social relationship in which the child is an active participant: for example, the infant-parent, infant-peer, or infant-sibling relationship. A *mediated effect*

■ **FIGURE 2.5**
Ecological Systems Theory

The child is contained within a nested system of social relation-ships and institutions. Except for microsystems, children are not di-rect participants in any of the other social systems that may af-fect their lives.

SOURCE: Reprinted by permission from p. 50 of Child Development by Alan Fogel and Gail F. Melson; Copyright © 1988 by West Publishing Company. All rights reserved.

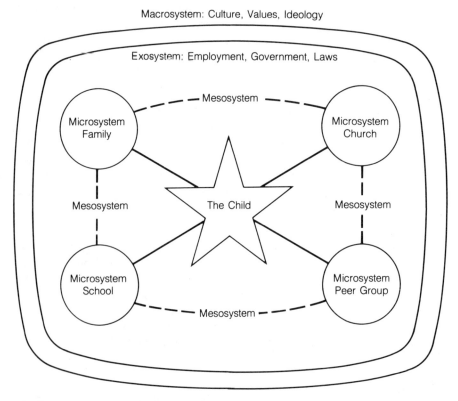

occurs when the infant affects or is affected by people with whom the child does not share an active relationship.

Mediated effects occur when the child's relationship to an individual is interpreted by the parent, such as when parents caution young children about talking to strangers. Another example concerns the child's relationship with grandparents. Though children in American society often spend little time with their grandparents, visiting perhaps only once or twice a year, they nevertheless seem to develop special relationships with their grandparents. This can be accounted for by parental mediation. Since the parent's relationship to their own parents is so important, this importance is transmitted to the child who then comes to think of grandma and grandpa as special people (Lewis & Feiring, 1978).

Belsky (1981) proposes a model of the family system that incorporates some of these ideas. His model is depicted in Figure 2.6. The parts of this model that have been studied the most are the parts marked by the lower two arrows representing the effects of infants on parents and vice versa. Belsky points out that this model differs from models of the two-person system or even models of mediated effects. With mediated effects, the acts of one individual affect another who then affects a third person. In this model are included the effects of one individual (for example, the infant) on the relationship between the parents, and conversely the effects of the marital relationship on the infant directly and indirectly as it affects each spouse's ability to parent. One other notable aspect of this model is that it includes the idea of systems. For example, the marriage may affect a spouse's ability to parent, which may affect the infant, whose subsequent behavior may affect the marital relationship. Thus in systems fashion, each component is capable of affecting every other component in a mutually influential manner.

Ecological system theory has contributed to research and applied work with infants. Since this theory's conception, a growing number of research studies have examined the infant in the context of the family or the school. In addition, we are becoming more aware of the effects of the larger social and cultural ecosystem on infants. Nuclear radiation and environmental toxins affect prenatal development and mother's milk. The effects of having two parents working outside the home—on both the infant and the parents—is a complex family and social issue. We are becoming aware that child abuse

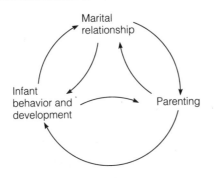

■ **FIGURE 2.6**
Model of Family System Functioning

SOURCE: J. Belsky, Early human experience: A family perspective. *Developmental Psychology*, 1981, 17, 3–23. Copyright 1981 by the American Psychological Association. Adapted by permission of the author.

and neglect are social ills caused in part by poverty, discrimination, drug use, and stress.

Ecological systems theory does not, however, specify the processes by which these effects might occur. For example, a disturbed parent-infant interaction may depend in part on the mother's drug use or the father's absence from the family. Precisely how the parent-infant interaction mediates these ecological factors is not explained by the theory. In addition, the theory does not provide any guidance with respect to which of the many ecological factors are most likely to affect a family and under what circumstances the family is or is not affected. In other words, the richness of the conceptualization of multiple interacting effects is not supported by enough detail to guide research or practice. For that reason, most research based on ecological systems theory is descriptive of the processes that occur under a variety of social conditions.

Another problem with ecological systems theory is that it is not developmental. Although the theory points to factors that might affect infants of different ages, it is not a theory about how infants develop from one age to the next. Because adults are the primary mediators of ecological factors on infants, other versions of systems theory focus on the infant-adult interaction in order to explain infant development. These theories deal with the process by which cultural skills—such as language—are transferred from parent to infant during social interaction.

Interactive Systems Theory

Up until the 1960s, the parent-infant relationship was viewed as a one-way process: parental behavior affects infant behavior; infant-care practices directly influence infant developmental outcomes. This was due to the general acceptance of psychoanalytic and learning theories, both of which view the parent as the primary socializer. In these theories, parents got all the credit for child-rearing success and all the blame for child-rearing failure. Cognitive theories had little to say about the role of the parent, making the assumption that cognitive development was the result of the individual's transactions with the physical environment.

In the early 1960s, an infant psychiatrist, Louis Sander, developed a theory of the early mother-infant relationship in which he explicitly recognized the reciprocal mutual influences rather than a one-way influence from mother to child (Sander, 1962). Sander's stages of development in the mother-infant interaction are given in Table 2.4. The importance of this theory is that it recognized that both parent and infant develop in relationship to each other over time.

A large body of research since then has confirmed the reciprocal nature of the parent-infant interaction (Schaffer, 1984). The evidence is so persuasive that most developmentalists today accept the idea of mutual influence in the parent-infant system as fact. This change in theoretical orientation toward the parent-infant relationship contributed in part to a revival of the forgotten work of Lev Semanovich Vygotsky (1896–1934), a Soviet educator who worked with parents and founded schools.

Vygotsky did most of his work in the early years after the Russian revolution. Following from the political theory of Marxism-Leninism that emphasized the cooperative nature of society, Vygotsky suggested that all

■ TABLE 2.4   Louis Sander's Stages of the Development of Mother-Infant Reciprocity

APPROXIMATE AGE (MONTHS)	STAGE	DESCRIPTION
0 to 3	Initial Regulation	The parent is concerned with helping the infant cope with biological function and the establishment of regular patterns of sleeping, feeding, arousal, and quieting. The infant begins to show differential responsiveness to the care giver.
4 to 6	Reciprocal Exchange	The beginnings of mutual play and reciprocal interactions can be seen. The parent and infant learn to anticipate signals from each other to coordinate feeding, playing, and caretaking activities.
7 to 9	Initiative	The infant begins to take the initiative in social exchanges and shows preferences for certain kinds of social activities over others. The infant experiences feelings of success or frustration in meeting goals.
10 to 13	Focalization	The infant makes directed demands on the mother and tries to test her availability. The parent is used as a secure base for exploration.
14 to 20	Self-assertion	Infants take their own initiatives in a wider variety of settings. Infants learn to achieve success and pleasure autonomously (apart from the mother).

SOURCE: L. W. Sander. Issues in early mother-child interaction. *Journal of the American Academy of Child Psychiatry,* 1962, *1,* 141–166.

individuals are defined by the social group and that their knowledge is an active social construction. Vygotsky suggested that adults do not directly socialize the child into the culture but rather follow the child's own motivations to learn. By careful observation of what the infant wants to understand, adults can introduce forms of guidance that allow the infant to realize his or her goals. According to Vygotsky, it is precisely when the infant is uncertain and looking for information that the infant is most susceptible to the adult's guidance.

Vygotsky referred to those aspects of the child's knowledge or skill that were in the process of developing but still in a state of uncertainty as the infant's *zone of proximal development.* When adults provide assistance and guidance in the child's zone of proximal development, they use culturally derived procedures. For example, suppose the child is trying to express his or her desire for an object using grunts. If the adult suggests more culturally appropriate ways of requesting (speech, pointing, etc.), the child will pick up the cultural skills because those skills best serve the child's motivation at that particular moment. If the adult models appropriate forms of requesting when the child is not interested in requesting, the adult's models will not have an impact on the child.

The concept of the zone of proximal development, therefore, suggests that children will acquire culturally acceptable practices but only if parents can adjust the timing and level of their actions to the ongoing motivational state of the children: mutual, cooperative interaction is at the heart of Vygotsky's theory. Because Vygotsky became ill and died at the young age of thirty-eight, he was not able to elaborate his theory. Developmentalists today are taking over where Vygotsky left off.

For example, Kenneth Kaye (1982) developed a theory of the development of the parent-infant social system that follows in the tradition of both Vygotsky and Sander. Kaye's stages of the parent-infant relationship are shown in Table 2.5. These stages chart the developmental changes in the infant's zone of proximal development. For example, in the stage of "shared intentions," infants become excited or fussy in relation to particular internal or external events. Quite often, infants in this period do not know what is actually causing their pleasure or unrest. Parents can provide the missing link by guiding the infants toward an understanding of the events that affect their lives. This process of interpreting the child's intentions and goals continues well beyond the infancy period. Even as adults, we need other people to help us sort out the causes of our thoughts or feelings. The guidance we receive from friends, parents, and mentors is not different in this regard from what infants receive from their parents and other adults.

Another theory derived from Vygotsky's work is that of Jerome Bruner (1983). Bruner suggests that language development arises out of earlier social-communicative routines between parents and infants. These routines must be ones in which the infant is an active participant. Bruner focuses on simple parent-infant social games, such as the one shown in Figure 2.7. The

■ TABLE 2.5   Kenneth Kaye's Stages of Individual Development in a Social Context

APPROXIMATE AGE (MONTHS)	STAGE	DESCRIPTION
0 to 3½	Shared rhythms	Parents use the inborn regularity in infant behavior—cycles of sucking and attention arousal—to build an "as if" dialogue. Parents provide frames to help the infant regulate arousal and attention.
2½ to 13	Shared intentions	Sharing begins as a responsibility of the parents, who guess the infant's intentions and attribute meaning to the infant's behavior in a "he says" manner. Parents also serve as an auxiliary memory bank for the infant, possessing information useful to the infant's continued functioning.
8 to 24 and over	Shared memory	The infant can anticipate the parents' intentions and remember shared experiences. The infant learns what to expect of others and what they expect of him or her. The infant recognizes gestures and words but does not know that others understand them.
15 and over	Shared language	Self-consciousness and the consciousness that others have selves develop. Symbols are used. The infant projects his or her own view of reality into the minds of others and internalizes the perspective of others. The infant understands that the meaning of symbols is understood by both partners and therefore can participate in true dialogue.

SOURCE: K. Kaye. *The mental and social life of babies.* Chicago: University of Chicago Press, 1982. © The Society for Research in Child Development, Inc.

■ FIGURE 2.7

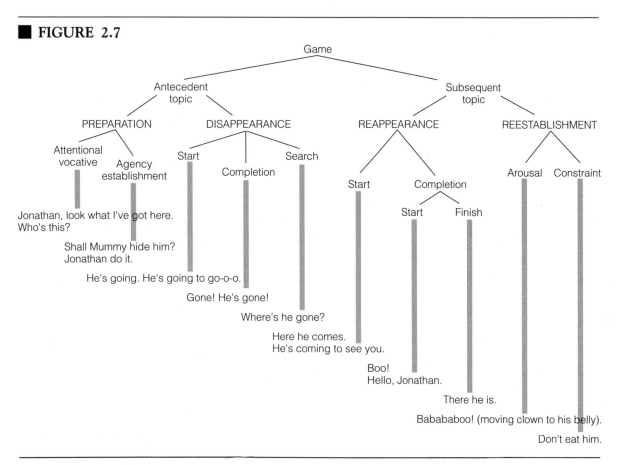

SOURCE: Bruner, J. *Child's Talk*. New York: W. W. Norton, 1983, p. 50. Used with permission.

infant's participation in the game is part of his or her zone of proximal development because parents not only create the game's structure, they also make sure the game is a challenge for the infant that goes slightly beyond what the infant is capable of doing. Because the infant wants to play, he or she is more attuned to learning about the rules of the game and the behavior necessary to play. In Bruner's examples, the necessary behavior is turn taking and language that the child learns as part of play in the company of an adult.

In these theoretical views based on Vygotsky's theory, there is still an emphasis on the transmission of culture from parent to child. Although these theories clearly show that the transmission occurs as part of a mutual interaction, the end result is that the child seems to learn culturally appropriate actions directly from the parent. The social interaction is necessary merely to assure that the child is motivated to learn. It is unlikely, however, that adults could ever demonstrate all the features of a culture or language to the child.

Another theoretical perspective called *dynamic systems theory* (Fogel, 1990a; Fogel & Thelen, 1987) suggests that the adult-infant interaction gets infants attuned to *some of* the relationships between their own actions and a *few* culturally relevant behaviors. Given this modest start, infants can be more informed observers of the social process or can work out the details of particular skills through their own explorations. For example, suppose someone points out a cultural rule to you that you never noticed before, such as, "It is not appropriate to wear blue jeans to work." From this simple statement, you begin to notice what people in your workplace are wearing, and you also begin to notice the situations in which people tend to wear blue jeans. You may try wearing jeans in different situations in order to judge other's reactions. Ultimately you may come to a complex understanding of dress codes, personal tastes, and your own personal style of dress. You may even relate dress styles to many other aspects of your personal and work life.

In dynamic systems theory, knowledge and action are not transmitted to you in their entirety by other people. Rather, knowledge and action are emergent discoveries that you make in the process of interacting with others. An *emergent* discovery is one in which a complex action or idea is assembled in a spontaneous and creative manner from simpler components. Infants can utter sentences they never heard before or develop their own style of playing a game, because their action is not a direct copy of a cultural standard but rather an emergent product of simple cultural rules interacting with personal abilities and motivations. Action and knowledge, therefore, are dynamically active constructions made up of bits and pieces of experience.

Action is dynamic because every time it is repeated, it is slightly different. Dynamic systems theory suggests that performing culturally appropriate actions on repeated occasions is like singing a song many times. Each time you sing the song it changes, and you learn something new about the words, the music, or your own ability to sing. Action is not a direct copy of what other people do; it is not like making a tape recording of a song and replaying the tape again and again.

Interactive systems theories have had a major impact on research and on practice. Even from Vygotsky's era, these ideas influenced early childhood education. Teachers in day-care centers and nursery schools have known for generations that education begins with the child's motivations and that it is the teacher's job to adapt to the skill level of the infants. Many parents do this intuitively, and most current child-rearing advice books encourage this behavior. Teaching young parents how to pay attention to the inclinations of their babies is a major component of parent-education classes for parents who are having difficulty with their babies, such as teenage parents, single parents living in poverty, parents with clinical depression, and parents who have a handicapped infant (see Chapter 9).

Simple, one-directional parent-to-child socialization theories would not be acceptable in developmental research journals today. Research based on interactive theories has given us detailed descriptive accounts of the ways in which parents and infants play games, come to understand each other, and develop over time.

Like ecological systems theories, interactive systems theories suffer from lack of specificity. Someone who wanted to do research on the parent-infant interaction would get little guidance from these theories about which behaviors are important. In addition, these theories are difficult to verify since one could never measure all of the relevant interactive processes. In the example of the blue jeans, it would be nearly impossible to follow the developmental implications of that process since it is embedded into the fabric of the person's daily life.

Another criticism of interactive systems theories is that they focus on small details of social experience without taking account of the broader issues, such as those raised in ecological systems theories. Many interaction theorists study primarily the *mother*-infant interaction and fail to consider the family systems processes described earlier, including the roles of the father and siblings.

As a general rule, no one theory can ever deal with the entire range of human developmental phenomena. Researchers, clinicians, and educators need to examine each of these theories in order to take what is most meaningful for any given application. These theories should not be seen as mutually exclusive but rather as complementary: each focusing on a different and interesting aspect of infant development.

■ SUMMARY

Ethological Theory

■ Ethology is the study of a species's evolved behavior characteristics.

■ Although certain survival functions are present across species, each species has a unique species-specific behavioral pattern.

■ Critical periods are less useful for explaining development in humans compared to that of other species of animals.

■ Sociobiology predicts that individuals will be more likely to help other people when they share the same genes, as between a parent and a child.

■ Behavior genetics studies the probabilities of predicting individual differences between phenotypes using either differences between environments, between genotypes, or both.

Learning Theory

■ Classical conditioning discovered learning by association that occurs when unconditioned and conditioned stimuli are paired during training.

■ Operant conditioning occurs when the frequency of behavior is controlled by its consequences: reinforcement, punishment, and extinction.

■ Social learning theory suggests that learning occurs when the individual has a motivation to attend to the consequences. Infants can also learn by observation and imitation.

Cognitive Theory

■ Constructivist approaches suggest that infants develop intelligence by means of their own explorations in the world. Infant intelligence is of a sensorimotor rather than a verbal-symbolic form.

■ Information processing theories break cognition down into a series of component processes, each of which can function independently of the others. Breakdowns in the cognitive system may occur if any of the components are not properly functioning.

Emotion Theory

■ Psychoanalytic theory states that development is organized around emotional tendencies and that parents play the major role in helping infants to resolve their emotional crises.

■ Discrete emotion theory assumes that there is an innate set of basic human emotional states that are present in the newborn. During development, infants learn how to regulate their emotions and express them in socially appropriate ways.

■ Constructivist theories of emotion suggest that there is an interaction between emotion and cognition, as emotional understanding is created in the process of interacting with others.

Systems Theory

■ Ecological systems theory suggests that infant development is related in direct and indirect ways to the family and to society and vice versa.

■ Interactive systems theory focuses on the process of communication between parents and infants and the ways in which that communication leads to developmental change in the infant.

■ GLOSSARY

Accommodation   A change in individual functioning and skill in order to meet new environmental demands.

Adaptation   The process of becoming better suited to survive and succeed in a particular environment.

Altruism   Behavior motivated by the desire to benefit another, even at a cost to the self.

Assimilation   The adaptive utilization of those aspects of the environment that are within the limits of our skills and biological processing capacities.

Association   The psychological linkage between a stimulus and a response that occurs in the environment at about the same time.

Behavior genetics   The study of between-individual variability in phenotypes as a result of variability in environments or in genotypes.

Classical conditioning   Learning by association; the linking together of a stimulus and a response occurring at the same time.

Critical period   A relative short, well-defined period in the life cycle when the individual is particularly receptive to certain kinds of environmental stimulation. If that stimulation is not received, the individual is not likely to profit from later exposure to similar stimuli and other normal developmental processes may be disrupted.

Cross-fostering   A research design in which children are reared with adoptive parents, rather than their biological parents.

Determinism   When the genes exert influence on the phenotype that is unmediated by the environment.

Direct effect   When any one factor exerts influence on another factor without any mediating effect.

Disequilibrium   The infant's experience during failures at adaptation. Disequilibrium is the motivational force that leads the infant to adapt by means of assimilation and accommodation.

Ecology of human development   Refers to the physical and social environments in which children develop.

Ego   The sum total of the regulatory functions of the person. It includes coping, information processing, and emotions. The ego mediates between the person's needs and the demands of the environment.

Emergent process   A process by which infants discover complex actions and knowledge in the course of elaborating the action beginning with a relatively simple starting point.

Equilibration   The process by which new schemes are formed; the balance between assimilation and accommodation in which challenges posed by the environment are effectively mastered and new skills are developed.

Ethology   The study of the context, function, and evolutionary origins of behavior.

Extinction   The elimination of learned behavior by ceasing to reinforce the behavior.

Genotype   The set of chemical messages within the DNA that direct the formation of protein within a cell nucleus. Also, an individual's genetic inheritance.

Hypotheses   Refers to the second stage of Kagan's information processing theory. A hypothesis is a question or a problem that is posed by the infant about a stimulus. The motivation to answer the question or solve the problem causes the infant to look longer at the stimulus than at nonproblematic stimuli.

Id   The individual's basic, biological needs. During infancy, these needs are centered primarily around the oral and anal erogenous zones.

Imprinting   A process in which the young of some animal species become attached to an object or person by means of a brief exposure to that object or person.

Individuation   The process by which the child becomes autonomous. It corresponds to the ability to cope with separation from the care giver and with a realistic sense of self.

Mediated effects   Factors that influence the direct relationship between other factors.

Natural selection   The theory of the evolution of species, proposed by Charles Darwin, in which genetic changes are explained by differential survival of offspring who have characteristics that are well-suited to the environment.

Negative reinforcement   A consequence of an action that reduces the frequency of that action.

Observational learning   Learning without reinforcement or association by watching how others perform in certain situations.

Operant conditioning   An increase in the likelihood that a particular response will occur following a reinforcement of that response.

Phenotype   The functioning organism; everything other than the DNA.

Positive reinforcement   A consequence of an action that increases the probability of that action in the future.

Primary process   The unfettered exhibition of needs, coupled with the relative inability to delay gratification of the needs. Refer to the direct expression of the id.

Probabilistic   Refers to the nondeterministic influence of the genotype over the phenotype. A particular genotype will not lead to a specific phenotype for all individuals.

Punishment   A consequence that decreases the frequency of the behavior that it follows.

Reinforcement   An environmental stimulus that, when appearing following a specific individual response, increases the likelihood that the response will occur again.

Scientific theory   A system of concepts that explains some features of the observable world with structures, processes, or mechanisms that are presumed to exist but cannot be observed directly.

Secondary processes   Mental representations, problem solving, rational behavior, inhibition, and realistic expectations; expression of the ego.

Sensorimotor stage   The first two years of life, according to Piaget, in which the child "understands" the world through action and sensation rather than through concepts and ideas.

Species specific innate behavior   Behavior patterns that occur only in one species and are the result of evolution by natural selection.

System   A set of interrelated components that are governed by feedback processes and that exchange information and material between themselves and between the environment and themselves.

Trust   The expectation that the environment will be able to meet one's needs and calm one's distress.

Zone of proximal development   Those infant skills that are in the process of developing and are the most uncertain.

THREE

Before Birth: Prenatal Behavior and Development

Although many people think of birth as the beginning of life, it is now known that much of what takes place before birth during the nine-month period of gestation has important effects on subsequent development. Although we know very little about the psychological and behavioral effects of prenatal life, we have a growing body of evidence that attests to the importance of the intrauterine environment for future health and physical growth. During prenatal development, all of the major organ systems of the body, including the brain, undergo rapid development, and it is just at the point of the most accelerated development of an organ that it is most susceptible to environmental influences.

As we shall see in this chapter, the womb—uterus and placenta—is not the impenetrable shield of nurturance and security that literature and mythology would have it be. The placenta functions as a link between mother and fetus. In some cases, the placenta becomes a wonderfully adept censor, keeping potentially unassimilable substances form crossing into the immature fetal circulatory system. Often, however, it does not filter harmful substances. The womb is an environment, albeit a very special and uniquely suitable environment, to which the fetus must adapt.

This chapter will cover the development of the fetus from conception until the last month of pregnancy. In the first sections, we discuss conception and heredity. The next section covers normal prenatal development. This is followed by a section on prenatal risk, including such topics as genetic and chromosomal disorders, teratology, and genetic counselling. The last section of the chapter addresses physical and psychological changes in the mother and the response of the rest of the family to her pregnancy.

■ DEVELOPMENTAL PROCESSES BEFORE BIRTH

Conception

Human development begins with the union of a female *ovum* and a male *spermatozoa*. During sexual intercourse, many millions of sperm cells enter the vagina. These cells are propelled through the uterus and into the Fallopian tubes, partly via the pumping action of the vaginal and uterine muscles and partly by the swimming movements of the spermatozoa. Only a few hundred sperm cells will reach the Fallopian tubes, and even those will die if they do not encounter an ovum within twenty-four to forty-eight hours.

Ova are produced in the ovaries, usually one for each menstrual cycle. Adult females will have about 350 ovulations over approximately thirty years of fertility. The ovum is covered with small hairlike appendages that can be dissolved by an enzyme secreted by the spermatozoa, and it eventually decomposes if not encountered by a sperm cell. For fertilization to take place, many spermatozoa must bind to the surface of the ovum, after which an opening is made at random for the entrance of a single sperm cell. Once that sperm cell enters the ovum, a chemical reaction occurs to prevent other sperm cells from entering. The fertilized ovum is called a *zygote*.

Spermatozoa and ova, collectively referred to as *gametes*, are produced inside the adult's body. Girls are born with a large number of immature ova in their ovaries. These remain inactive until puberty. Boys are not born with spermatozoa; rather, the onset of adolescence triggers the production of hormones in the male that stimulate the manufacture of about two million sperm cells per day for the rest of his life.

The Period of the Zygote

Given the beginning as a zygote, a single-celled organism, it is difficult to see how a fully developed human can emerge. At the start of development, several processes are important in inducing developmental change. One process comes from inside the cells themselves, and another relates to the cells' interactions with the environment inside the mother's body.

Within the cell nucleus, the genetic material is in the form of a spiral-shaped molecule called deoxyribonucleic acid (DNA). Inside this spiral are locations at which any one of a number of different types of smaller molecules—called bases—may be attached. The DNA is segmented into sections, each of which contains a different set of bases. Each segment is called a *gene*. The genes are arranged in long strings, much like beads on a necklace, into structures called *chromosomes*.

Chromosomes can be seen under a microscope, as shown in Figure 3.1. Most chromosomes look like the letter X. The X is made up of two strands that are joined near their middle. The genes can be seen in Figure 3.1 as

■ FIGURE 3.1
Human Chromosome Pairs before and after Karyotyping

Humans have twenty-three pairs of chromosomes, and in the karyotype, the pairs have been matched. One member of each pair is from the mother and one from the father. The X chromosome of the twenty-third pair is highlighted separately at the far right of the second row.

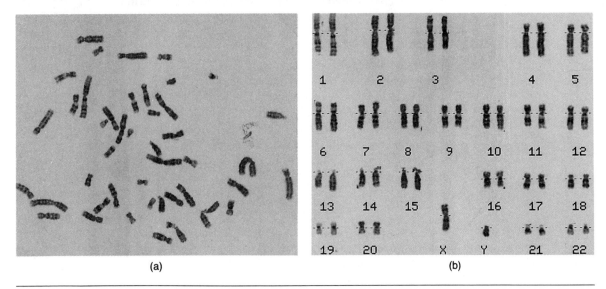

(a)   (b)

SOURCE: Courtesy of Dr. J. Aznar.

alternating bands of light and dark. Chromosomes come in matched pairs, as shown in the bottom part of Figure 3.1. This arrangement of chromosomes into pairs is achieved by cutting the upper photo and placing the chromosomes in order. The rearranged photo is called a karyotype. Note that chromosomes come in different sizes and that a single Y-shaped chromosome on the twenty-third pair contains the genetic code for a male.

Every cell in one's body, except for the gametes, contains forty-six chromosomes representing about one million bits of genetic information. Each of the body's cells contain the same set of genes and chromosomes. Each gamete normally contains only twenty-three chromosomes. The forty-six chromosomes in most body cells represent twenty-three pairs.

Individual cells develop by dividing into two identical daughter cells. During *mitosis*, each chromosome within the cell nucleus makes a copy of itself before cell division occurs. The original set of chromosomes and their identical copies don't get mixed up: each set pushes away from the other until they occupy opposite sides of the nucleus. The cell will divide into two only after this physical separation of the two identical sets of chromosomes occurs (McIntosh & Koonce, 1989).

Although every cell in an individual's body carries the same set of genes and chromosomes, every individual has a slightly different set. This genetic variability arises first during the creation of the gametes. In the special biological environment of the female ovaries and the male testicles, cells divide in the absence of the chromosome copying process that is characteristic of mitosis. In *meiosis*, each daughter cell contains only twenty-three chromosomes. When sperm and ovum unite during fertilization, the resulting zygote will have a unique combination of forty-six chromosomes, half from the mother and half from the father.

Since each individual gamete contains a slightly different set of chromosomes and genes and the particular pair that unite for fertilization is random, the number of genetically different individuals is enormous. This explains how siblings can be genetically different. Fraternal twins (dizygotic) are as different as any two siblings since they are the result of two ova produced and fertilized in the same reproductive cycle. Only identical twins (monozygotic) have exactly the same genetic material, since they result from a single zygote that splits into two identical zygotes after fertilization has taken place.

Every individual begins life as a zygote that progresses through the initial states of mitosis. As a result of mitosis, the number of cells in the developing organism grows rapidly, doubling every few hours. Because mitosis is an exact copying process, each of these cells has the same genetic material.

One of the great mysteries of early development is how, given identical genes in each cell, the different tissues and structures—muscles, blood, sensory receptors—can develop. The biologist Waddington expressed it thus:

". . . a simple lump of jelly that . . . eventually turns into a recognizable small plant or worm or insect or some other type of organism. Nothing else that one can see puts on a performance which is both so apparently simple and spontaneous and yet, when you think about it, so mysterious (Waddington, 1966, p. v)."

To find some solutions to this mystery, we have to go outside the cell and examine its environment.

Research on nonhuman prenatal development has shown that in almost all species of animals, the cells will form a sphere-like cluster (Sameroff, 1984). Because some of the cells are on the surface and some on the interior of the sphere, these different regions will be in contact with different environments. The interior cells will be next to other cells like themselves, while the exterior cells will have a different cellular environment on each side of the cell.

Each of these environments exposes the cell to different molecules that may be transported into the cell from the neighboring cells. In addition, physical forces on the cell will cause it to produce specific molecules in the cell's body. When these molecules enter the cell nucleus, they activate some of the cells genes and inhibit the action of other genes. When the genes are activated, they begin to send chemical messages back out to the main cell body, changing the cell's structural characteristics. In this way, the interior cells will begin to differ in their properties from the exterior cells.

As cell division proceeds, cells form groups in which distinct molecular processes occur. Boundaries are formed between the different groups that prevent the processes of one group from leaking into another (Trevarthen, 1973). Thus, the development of the phenotype—the cell's specific characteristic as neuron or muscle—is the result of a constant and dynamic interaction between the genotype and the intra- and extracellular environment (Antonelli, 1985).

The effect of the cell's environment has been shown in a series of experiments on nonhuman embryos. Early in the process of the formation of different regions, cells can be removed from one region and placed in an entirely different region. After a few cell divisions, the transplanted cells resemble the region in which they were placed, not the region that they came from (Spemann, 1938; Ebert & Sussex, 1970).

As cells begin to differentiate into distinct regions, physical structures begin to form. The most common type of embryonic structure is the formation of a tube. Figure 3.2 shows how this occurs. In the top part of the figure, cells on the top of the sheet have been genetically activated to reproduce cells with the ability to stretch. Cells on the bottom of the sheet have been genetically activated to produce contraction. As cells divide and there is increasing differential stretching and contracting, the sheet eventually curls into a tube. Tubes can also be formed when a ball of cells contracts in the center, eventually making a kind of donut shape. In vertebrate animals, one of the early forming tubular structures is the spinal cord and spine (see Figure 3.2, bottom).

It is usually assumed that development is a continuous series of acquisitions along the road to maturity. Prenatal development *does* show a number of aspects that are continuous, but there are also instances in which certain structures are formed only to disappear at a later point. Meredith (1975) catalogues the types of prenatal changes as follows.

Changes in Kind. One of the most noticeable changes of this sort is the gradual differentiation of multiple kinds of tissue from the relatively uniform zygote. There are also certain structures that emerge and disappear. For example, the pronephros, the precursor of the kidney, is only there for two weeks, gill arches are present for three weeks, an external tail appears and

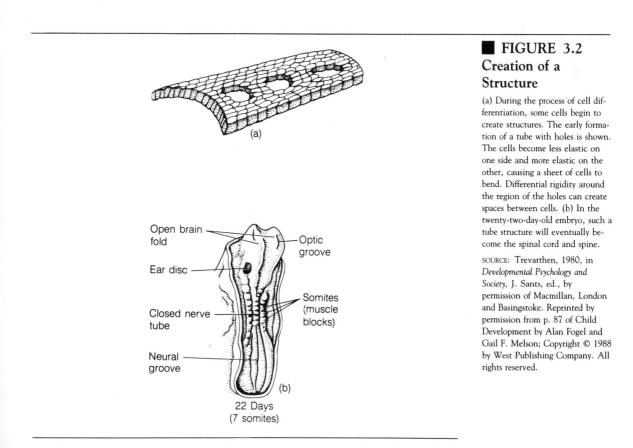

(a)

Open brain fold

Optic groove

Ear disc

Closed nerve tube

Somites (muscle blocks)

Neural groove

(b)

22 Days
(7 somites)

■ **FIGURE 3.2**
Creation of a Structure

(a) During the process of cell differentiation, some cells begin to create structures. The early formation of a tube with holes is shown. The cells become less elastic on one side and more elastic on the other, causing a sheet of cells to bend. Differential rigidity around the region of the holes can create spaces between cells. (b) In the twenty-two-day-old embryo, such a tube structure will eventually become the spinal cord and spine.

SOURCE: Trevarthen, 1980, in *Developmental Psychology and Society*, J. Sants, ed., by permission of Macmillan, London and Basingstoke. Reprinted by permission from p. 87 of Child Development by Alan Fogel and Gail F. Melson; Copyright © 1988 by West Publishing Company. All rights reserved.

disappears between the second and fourth months, and finger pads are seen between the third and fifth months.

Changes in Number. Depending upon the particular structure or organ, cell numbers increase and decrease over time. Obviously, the overall number of cells continues to increase.

Changes in Position. The fetus changes in the relative orientation and position of the organs. When the heart is formed, for example, it lies near what will become the face. Over time it will move lower, more toward the back, and it will rotate and tilt. Other organs and limbs undertake their own particular paths of migration.

Changes in Size. Size change varies with the time and location of the organ. During the second month, the head and neck regions grow faster (*cephalo-caudal* development), there is more growth near the spine than in the front (*dorsoventral* development), and the growth rate is higher near the shoulders and hips than near the extremities (*proximodistal* development). As development proceeds, these trends reverse themselves.

Changes in Shape. Immediately after fertilization, the organism has an oval shape. Several weeks later, its shape is elongated and is mostly head. There are also changes in the shape of cells and organs.

The prenatal period is usually divided into three parts: the zygote, the embryo, and the fetus. The *period of the zygote* begins at the time the ovum is fertilized and lasts about two weeks, or until the ovum is implanted in the uterine wall. The period of the *embryo* begins about two weeks after fertilization and extends until the beginning of the third month, at which time it is designated a *fetus*. This designation is applied when the organism begins to resemble a human in its external features and when the bones begin to harden into a more rigid skeletal structure.

The period of human gestation lasts about thirty-eight weeks, but this can vary from between thirty-six and forty weeks for a full-term infant. In the first half-week, the zygote divides to about twenty cells, and at the end of the week some differentiation can be noted. At the end of the second week, there is a clearly defined *embryonic disk* that lies between the *amniotic sac* and the *yolk sac*, which themselves have differentiated out of the original zygote. This organism is now called the *blastocyst*, and sometime during the third week, it implants itself in the lining of the uterus. The blastocyst, still only 1/125 of an inch long, triggers the secretion of hormones that inhibit menstruation. As the concentration of these hormones, known as *human chorionic gonadatropin* (HCG), increases, they can be detected in the urine and are used in laboratory pregnancy tests (see Figure 3.3)

The Period of the Embryo

From the structures of the blastocyst—the embryonic disk, the yolk sac, and the amniotic sac—further differentiation will occur. The embryonic disk differentiates into three layers. The *endoderm* eventually becomes part of the digestive, urinary, and respiratory systems. The *mesoderm* will become the muscles, bone, circulatory system, and reproductive system. The *ectoderm* will become the central nervous system and brain, the sense organs, and the skin, hair, nails, and teeth.

The yolk sac produces blood cells and becomes part of the liver, spleen, and bone marrow, all of which later produce blood cells. By the end of the embryonic period, the yolk sac has disappeared. The amniotic sac persists throughout gestation. It grows to cover the embryo and to contain the amniotic fluid that provides a cushion from sudden movements of the mother's body.

Surrounding all of these developments is a membrane called the *chorion*. The placenta forms from the outer surface of the chorion. The placenta functions as a link between the blood streams of mother and embryo, which are not directly connected. The placenta passes nutrients and oxygen from the mother's blood to the fetus's through the umbilical cord and serves to eliminate the fetal wastes via the mother's blood stream. The fetus is in the upright position throughout most of the pregnancy, so there is no danger of the cord choking the fetus because of its location, the effect of gravity, and the relative inflexibility of the cord from the pressure of the blood circulating in it (like a hose with the water turned on). There is an increased risk of choking at birth because the fetus has changed positions—head down for delivery—and the head may now come in contact with the cord.

By the third week, one can distinguish the head and primitive circulatory and skeletal systems. By the end of the first month, the heart is beating and there are cavities for the ears, nose, and mouth (see Figure 3.4). The head is large relative to the rest of the body and has gill arches, and the body has upper limb buds and a small tail. At this point the embryo may be between 3 mm and 5 mm (⅕ inch long).

Now development is occurring very rapidly. In the next two weeks, the beginnings of the eyes, nose, lungs, and liver grow, and bones begin to form. The gill structures become transformed into bones of the inner ear, the neck, and cartilage of the larynx, as well as the eustachian tubes, thyroid and thymus glands, and the trachea. By six weeks, the limbs are beginning to differentiate rapidly and fingers and toes will appear shortly. The tail is still present and may comprise 15 percent of the embryo's total length of 12 mm (½ inch). The total weight is about 2 grams (1/14 ounce). About half of the weight of an eight-week-old embryo is in its head. It has all of the major organs except genital organs. It has a skeleton, eyebrows, knees, fingers, toes, and buds for teeth.

The first evidence of prenatal behavior is seen during the embryonic period in the movements of the muscles of the heart. At first, the movements are jerky and spontaneous, but gradually they become more rhythmic as they pump blood cells between the heart, yolk sac, and chorion. The origins of these rhythmic movements are unknown since they occur before the embryo has developed its nervous system (Hofer, 1981).

By the thirty-second day of life, the human embryo has a rudimentary sensory system (see Figure 3.4), but these sense organs are not connected yet to any nerve fibers. The first nerve cells form between four and five weeks, and the first spontaneous movements of the body occur a week later. By seven weeks, the embryo is responsive to touch in the mouth region and will turn its head to the side (Trevarthen, 1973).

■ **FIGURE** 3.3
Early Stages of Prenatal Development

(a) Blastocyst stage: The fertilized egg (zygote) has made its way down the Fallopian tube and has undergone repeated cell division and multiplication on the way. It attaches to the uterine lining and begins to grow into the uterine wall in search of nutrients. (b) and (c) Cell division and differentiation continue at a rapid pace and specific structures begin to take shape. The developing organism is now a bulge on the uterine wall. (d) and (e) Embryo stage: Gradually the form of the embryo takes shape. By the end of the first month, the head and the arm and leg buds are visible, a primitive heart has started to pump, and other organs are beginning to develop. At this stage, the human embryo closely resembles the embryos of most other animals.

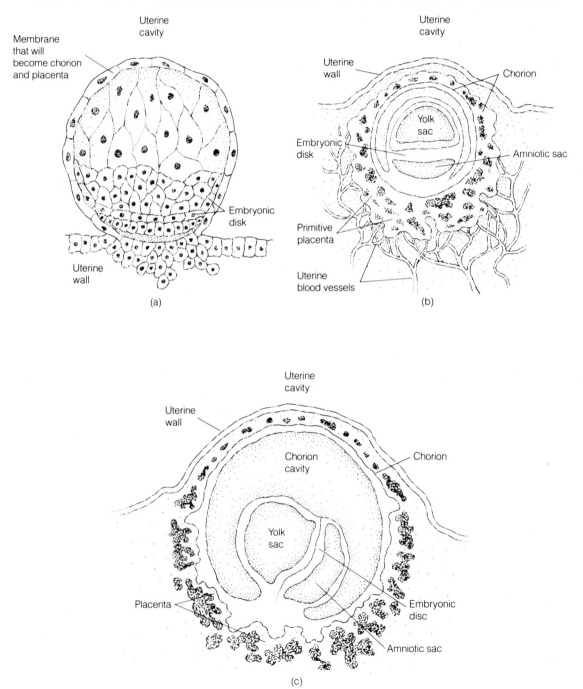

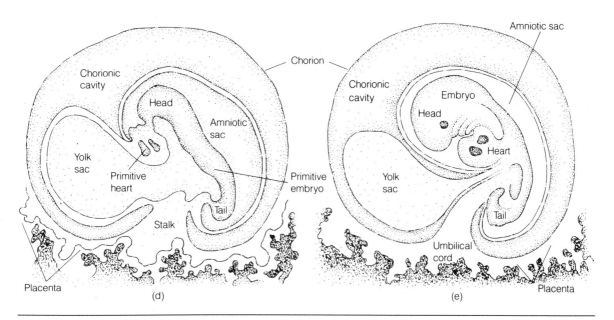

SOURCE: Mary J. Gander and Harry W. Gardiner, *Child and Adolescent Development*, p. 63. Copyright 1981 by Mary J. Gander and Harry W. Gardiner. Reprinted by permission of the publisher, Little, Brown and Company.

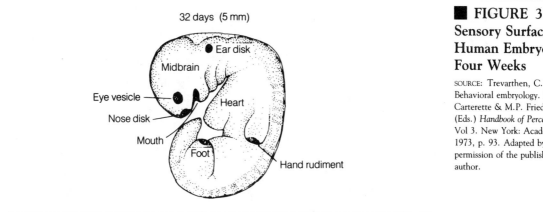

■ FIGURE 3.4
Sensory Surfaces of a Human Embryo at Four Weeks

SOURCE: Trevarthen, C. Behavioral embryology. In E.C. Carterette & M.P. Friedman (Eds.) *Handbook of Perception.* Vol 3. New York: Academic Press, 1973, p. 93. Adapted by permission of the publisher and author.

The Period of the Fetus: 7 to 16 Weeks

During the early part of the fetal period, a large number of spontaneous behaviors emerge, including mouth and limb movements. The fetus can also be stimulated to act by a number of occurrences. These include maternal muscle contractions, sounds, and alternation of maternal glucose and oxygen levels. Fetal behavior changes can be observed using *ultrasound* recording (see next section; Johnson et al., 1989). These behavior developments are shown in Table 3.1.

■ TABLE 3.1   Chronology of Fetal Behavior

AGE (WEEKS)	BEHAVIOR
8	Stroking the mouth region produces flexion of upper torso and neck and extension of arms at the shoulder.
9	Some spontaneous movements. More of the whole body responds when the mouth is stroked. Startle reflex.
10½	Stroking the palms of the hands leads to partial closing of the fingers. Hiccups.
11	Other parts of face and arms become sensitive. Head rotation.
11½	Sensitive area spreads to upper chest. Hand-face contact.
12½	Specific reflexes appear: lip closure, swallowing, Babinski (see Chapter 5), squinting, sucking.
14	Entire body is sensitive, with more specific reflexes, such as rooting, grasping, finger closing. Body stretching.
15	Can maintain closure of the fingers (grasp) with muscle tightening, muscle strengthening. Yawn.

SOURCE: Hooker, 1952; Johnson et al., 1989; Trevarthen, 1973.

The six-week-old embryo is less than an inch long. There is a heartbeat, eye patches, a rudimentary brain, and a stomach and liver. At this age there are no connections between the brain and the rest of the body.

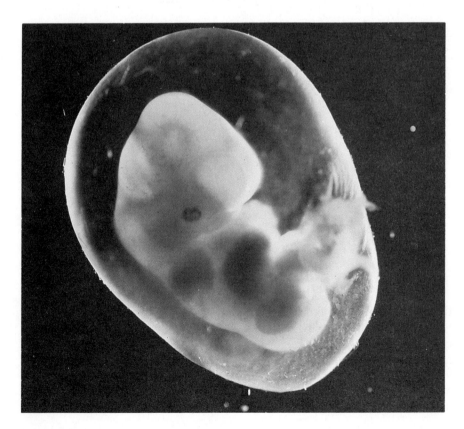

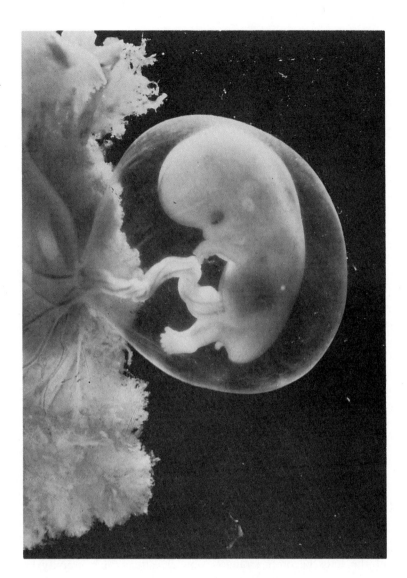

The fetus just after three months is about 2 and a half inches long and weighs 1/2 ounce. Most of the internal organs are formed, and fingers and toes can be seen. At this age the fetus is capable of reflexive movements such as sucking, swallowing, grasping, and stretching.

The purpose of these early fetal movements is not entirely clear. One experimental technique used in studies of nonhuman embryos is to prevent a fetal movement from occurring, either through severing the nerve connections or introducing a local anesthetic, and then to study the future development of the individual. For example, chick embryos that have been prevented from moving were unable to move later. The muscles and nerves of these chicks developed normally, but their joints had become frozen into bone (Drachman & Coulombre, 1962). In another study with mice, inability to move the tongue embryonically resulted in deformation of the soft palate (Walker & Quarles, 1976). The relatively high incidence of cleft palate in infants of alcoholic mothers may be due to the anesthetic effects of alcohol on fetal mouth movements (Hofer, 1981). Other experiments have shown that movement in the fetus helps to induce the development of nerve endings in the sensory receptors.

Again we have an example of a complex developmental dynamic. As tissues and structures form, spontaneous movements are produced. The movements induce further development in those same tissues and structures, which in turn strengthens the movement pattern, making it more responsive and predictable.

Aside from behavioral development, physical development is also occurring. By about 16 weeks, the fetus has become about 3 inches long and weighs about ½ ounce. During the period from 12 to 16 weeks, the external genitals form as a result of the interaction of the fetus' genes with the environment of the cells.

The genetic determination of sex occurs at conception. Females have two X-shaped chromosomes in the twenty-third pair, while males have one X- and one Y-shaped chromosome. All of the ova a woman produces have only X chromosomes. About half of the spermatozoa produced by men contain and X and the other half a Y chromosome in the twenty-third place. The genetic sex of the zygote will thus depend on which of the father's spermatozoa actually fertilizes the ovum. For reasons not fully understood, more males are conceived than females, in the ratio of 105 to 100. During the life span, an increasing number of females survive at every age so that by age 60, the ratio of males to females is 70 to 100.

Up until the third month after conception, genetic males and genetic females have similar external structures in the genital area. During the second month, the hormone testosterone is secreted in male fetuses, which activates particular genes that induce the development of the internal ducts that will later connect to male genitals. The continued action of testosterone causes the development of the external male genitals at around three months. Female genitals do not require any specific hormone to develop at this stage (Lamb & Bornstein, 1987).

The Period of the Fetus: 17 to 22 Weeks

Up until the sixteenth week, the list of spontaneous and stimulated fetal behavior continues to grow. Between seventeen and twenty-two weeks, however, the fetus becomes strangely quieter, after which activity begins again and lasts until birth. Research on fetal sleep has shown that the reduction of movement is due to the rapid development of the brain (Hofer, 1981).

You might think that the development of the brain would induce more movement, rather than less. Up until this time, the brain has stimulated large movements that involved the whole body, including arms and legs. During the period between 17 and 22 weeks, the brain is beginning to develop pathways to inhibit such uncontrolled, spasm-like movements. The result is that after 22 weeks, the movements of the fetus will be more specialized and controlled. After this point, for example, we begin to see the emergence of specific facial expressions and coordinated hand movements.

This period of prenatal development, therefore, is characterized by rapid brain development. As shown in Figure 3.5, the brain's weight and volume increase by a factor of 4 between four and six months of age. During the fetal period, the major process of brain growth is cell division and intercell connections in the nervous system. After six months, new brain cells

■ FIGURE 3.5
Development of the Human Brain

Upper set: Human brains at the same scale of magnification.
Lower set: Development of the corpus callosum linking the hemispheres and of the cerebellum.

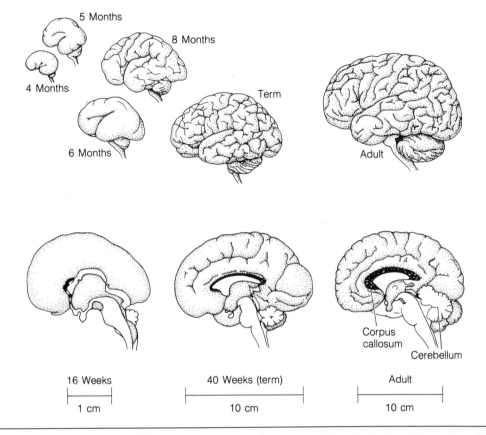

SOURCE: Trevarthen, 1980, in *Developmental Psychology and Society*, J. Sants, ed., by permission of Macmillan, London and Basingstoke, p. 71.

continue to be formed, but at a much slower rate. Following birth, the major process of brain development is an increase in intercell connections and in cell specialization. Thus, during the early fetal period, when the brain is growing the most rapidly, it is the most susceptible to influences from the environment.

During this period of development, the fetus is changing its physical characteristics. In the fourth month, a fine, long hair, *lanugo*, grows over most of the body. Coarser hair appears on the head in the fifth month, and eyebrows and eyelashes grow in the sixth month. During this period, the skin glands secrete a waxy substance, the *vernix caseosa*, that serves to protect the delicate skin. This period also marks the formation of fingernails and toenails, as well as the adult teeth buds.

The inhibition of movement by the brain makes sense from the point of view of physical development. The rapid increase in fetal size means that there is less space in which to move around. At six months, the fetus weighs about 900 grams (2 pounds). Most babies born at this age do not survive, and if a baby is less than 600 grams or less than twenty-four weeks, the chances of survival are exceedingly slim.

The Period of the Fetus: 22 to 36 Weeks

The beginning of this period is the time when mothers can first feel the fetus moving. By now, a doctor can detect the fetal heartbeat with a stethoscope. Based on data from infants born prematurely and also from ultrasound recordings of the fetus inside the womb, there is evidence for a large number of new patterns of movement that begin during this period.

The fetus has been observed to cry, grunt, and yawn. By the eighth month, the fetus can suck its thumb and open its eyes. Grasping and postural adjustment movements have also been observed. By this time, the fetus can see, hear, feel, and smell. Thus, by about the seventh month, most fetuses could survive if born, given appropriate intensive care (see Chapter 4).

One of the most remarkable achievements of the late fetal period is the development of clear-cut states of arousal (Hofer, 1981; Johnson et al., 1989). A *state* is an organized pattern of physical and physiological responding of an infant that is related to the internal level of arousal or activation. States are alternating periods of activation and quiesence. During the fourth and fifth months, periods of activation and quiet in the fetus are irregular, and transitions from quiet to active are sudden and jerky. By the sixth month, a clear and regular alternation between activity and rest occurs about once every forty minutes, based on data taken from sensors placed on the abdomens of sleeping women (Sterman & Hoppenbrouwers, 1971). This basic rhythm continues unchanged until after birth (Robertson, 1987).

These periods of activity and rest are the developmental precursors to waking and sleep states of the newborn. Fully developed sleep states appear in the fetus by 28 to 30 weeks. At this time, the rest period is divided into a period of quiet sleep and a period of active, or REM sleep. *REM* (rapid eye movement) sleep is characterized by short, jerky, vertical eye movements, spontaneous body movements, and irregular respiration. The 32-week-old fetus spends about three-quarters of its time in REM sleep.

The purpose of REM sleep is not fully understood. One hypothesis (Ruffwarg, Muzio & Dement, 1966; Vertes, 1986) is that it is a form of self-stimulation similar to earlier body movements. The last month of gestation is a period during which the fetus gains a considerable amount of weight. From 900 grams at 24 weeks, the fetus typically grows to about 3,500 grams at 36 weeks (about 7 pounds), most of which is in the development of subcutaneous fat tissues that will provide the newborn with insulation against the cold. Because of this weight gain, the fetus becomes too cramped to move its body. REM sleep may provide a less physically demanding source of movement stimulation to assist the development of the fetal brain and sensory organs.

Another remarkable achievement of the last few months of prenatal development is the emergence of the ability to learn. A number of people have speculated that fetuses may become imprinted to the heartbeat sounds of their mothers so that after birth, the sound of a heartbeat is comforting to the infants. Indeed, it has been found that a majority of adults hold infants on the left side of the adult's body, closer to the heart (Salk, 1973).

Using a response contingent procedure (see Chapter 2), DeCasper and Sigafoos (1983) found that newborn infants will change their rate of sucking to turn on the sound of a heartbeat. Although these studies do not prove that newborns recognize the specific heartbeat of their mothers, they seem to suggest that a general preference for heartbeat sounds may have been learned.

In another study (Panneton & DeCasper, 1986), researchers asked pregnant women to sing "Mary Had a Little Lamb" frequently during the period two weeks prior to their due dates. After birth, the newborns' preference for "Mary Had a Little Lamb" over the song "Love Somebody" was tested using the conditioned sucking procedure. The newborns could clearly perceive the difference between the two songs, and in addition, they preferred to listen to the song that they had heard prenatally. DeCasper and Spence (1986) found postnatal preferences for stories read prenatally.

There could be many explanations for these findings. Perhaps the newborn auditory system has a preferential bias for sounds and rhythms like heart-beats and nursery rhymes. One would have to sort out the effects of general auditory preferences from specific types of exposure to sounds, which is extremely difficult to do in human developmental research. Prenatal learning has been convincingly demonstrated in other animals. Rat pups who had been exposed prenatally to a mint smell after birth preferred to suck on mother's teats to which the same smell had been applied (Smotherman & Robinson, 1987).

In some cases, premature exposure to stimulation may interfere with later normal development. In many species, fetuses are exposed to sound before they are exposed to light stimulation. What happens if the fetus is exposed to light before the normal time of birth, as often happens with infants born prematurely? In one study, the normally closed eyes of fetal rats were surgically opened (Turkewitz & Kenny, 1985), which interfered with the normal development of the rats' auditory system.

In a similar procedure, mallard ducklings were given premature visual experience before they heard their mother's call during the normal imprinting period (Gottlieb, Tomlinson, & Radell, 1989). The ducklings that were prenatally exposed to light could not recognize the mother's call and failed to become imprinted. However, when prenatally light-exposed ducklings heard the mother's call *while in the dark*, they had no trouble recognizing her voice. Thus, the early exposure to light only interfered with later auditory learning if both sources of stimulation were present simultaneously. With respect to the sensory development of premature human infants, these results may suggest that overstimulation of immature sensory systems may be detrimental, while simpler stimuli that do not require multisensory processes may enhance development.

We have traced the early development of behavior, brain, and body in the prenatal period. The processes that were discussed apply generally to prenatal development. We now turn to a consideration of individual differences in fetal development, their causes, and their consequences.

■ INFLUENCES ON PRENATAL DEVELOPMENT

Fetuses are not only genetically different. Each fetus is exposed to an environment different from that of every other fetus. Thus, the relative importance of genetic and environmental influences on the development of individual differences in the phenotype can be studied prenatally as well as postnatally. Although all phenotypes are the result of a complex gene-environment interaction, particular phenotypes may be more associated with genetic or environmental variations than others. Thus, this section is divided into genetic, chromosomal, and environmental influences.

Genetic and Chromosomal Influences on Development

In Chapter 2, we discussed how behavior geneticists think about the origins of individual differences in the phenotype as being the result of individual differences in genotypes and/or environments. Individual variations in phenotypic characteristics that are closely correlated with individual characteristics in genotypes are less susceptible to variations in the environment. Physical characteristics, such as hair and eye color, baldness and height, fall into this category, although all of these phenotypes can be influenced by the environment to some extent. Let us examine some of these processes in more detail.

It is rare for genes to act alone in the determination of a phenotype. Most phenotypes are derived from *polygenic inheritance*, that is, they arise from the action of a combination of genes interacting with the environment. In most cases, at least two genes enter into the phenotype: one from the mother and one from the father. With a polygenic characteristic such as skin color, a number of genes from the mother combine with an equal number from the father, and the offspring's skin color is likely to be somewhere between the skin colors of the parents. Children in the same family may exhibit a range of skin colors.

Because chromosome pairs in an individual are made up of singles from each parent, genes that typically interact with each other to produce a phenotype are located at similar sites along the chromosome of each member of the pair. This is illustrated in Figure 3.6. Genes that act together to express a particular phenotype are called *alleles*.

In the past, it was believed that some phenotypic characteristics were inherited by a simple two-allele combination called *dominant-recessive inheritance*. Eye color is one example. The dominant allele (the one related to brown eyes) will always be expressed, even in the presense of a recessive mate (the allele for blue eyes). Thus, a person with brown eyes might actually carry a recessive allele for blue eyes, and two brown-eyed parents could produce a blue-eyed child if the zygote happens to contain two blue recessive alleles and no brown dominant allele. This simple dominant-recessive pattern rarely occurs, however. Eye color, like skin color, comes in many different shades and variations: the typical signature of polygenic inheritance.

Another pattern of inheritance relates to those characteristics that are displayed differentially between the sexes. *Sex-linked inheritance* relates to phenotypes that are tied to genes that appear on the twenty-third chromosome. Recall that genetic males have an X and a Y chromosome as their

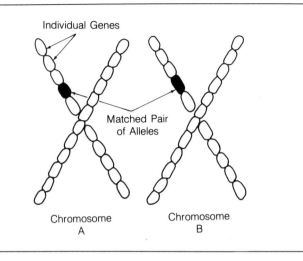

Individual Genes

Matched Pair
of Alleles

Chromosome
A

Chromosome
B

twenty-third pair. Not only is the Y chromosome missing one of its arms compared to the X chromosome, but the Y is also considerably smaller than the X. For this reason, one might think that women would have more sex-linked characteristics than men, but this isn't the case. For females, the alleles on the X chromosome will express themselves in interaction with their matched alleles on the other X chromosome of the twenty-third pair. For males, alleles on the X chromosome of the twenty-third pair will express themselves in the absence of an interaction with a mated allele.

Sex-linked inheritance produces primary (genitals) and secondary (facial hair, body shape, etc.) sexual characteristics in males and females. Other sex-linked characteristics are baldness, color blindness, and a disorder of blood clotting processes called hemophilia, all of which occur primarily in males.

In most cases, these latter sex-linked characteristics are caused by a recessive allele on the X chromosome. If the recessive allele is paired with a dominant allele on another X chromosome, that dominant allele can override the influence of the recessive gene. Females are thus less likely to display the phenotype for baldness because they can inherit both the dominant and the recessive allele. A male who inherits a recessive allele for baldness on his X chromosome will not have the corresponding dominant allele on his Y chromosome: there is no site for it to occupy (see Figure 3.7).

Because the X chromosome in the male's twenty-third pair always comes from his mother (Y chromosomes are only produced by males), women are the carriers of these sex-linked characteristics. A male is more likely to have a hairline like his maternal grandfather's than his own father's (McClearn, 1970).

In some cases, however, a woman will inherit two recessive alleles for a characteristic such as baldness. Some of these women will bald, while others will not. In addition, while most men who inherit a recessive baldness gene actually bald, some of these men retain their hair. How can this happen?

Much like the formation of the external genitals in the third month of prenatal development, baldness is a characteristic that is expressed in the

■ FIGURE 3.7
Sex-Linked
Inheritance

The male Y chromosome is missing dominant alleles that are found on the lower left-hand branch of the female's X chromosome.

SOURCE: Reprinted by permission from p. 94 of Child Development by Alan Fogel and Gail F. Melson; Copyright © 1988 by West Publishing Company. All rights reserved.

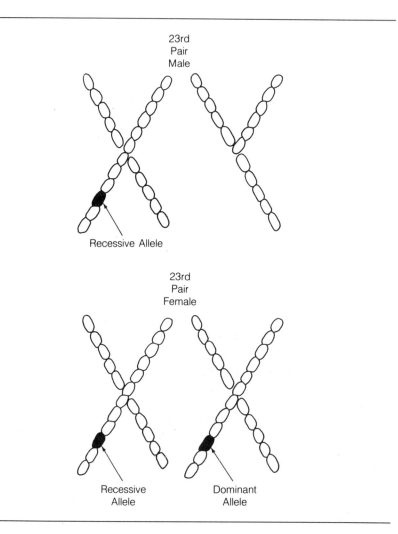

phenotype only when the gene for baldness interacts with the hormone testosterone. Because men typically have higher levels of circulating testosterone than females, their baldness gene will almost always be expressed. Men who don't bald are either not genetically predisposed to baldness or else they are but have low levels of circulating testosterone. Similarly, females who bald carry two recessive genes and have higher-than-average testosterone levels. Female baldness can be treated with estrogen (a female hormone) supplements, but these have undesired side effects, such as the prolongation of menstruation or the disruption of normal menopausal processes.

Genetically Based Disorders

Occasionally, problems more serious than baldness can be carried by the genes from one generation to the next. These genetically based disorders are not deterministic of a particular phenotype. Rather, if an individual carries a particular gene, the probability of acquiring its related disorder is increased.

In some cases, genetic disorders are so severe that the fetus will die. It has been estimated that two out of every three conceptions are spontaneously aborted in the early months of pregnancy. In a large majority of these cases, the embryo has genetic or chromosomal abnormalities. In addition, over 80 percent of newborn deaths can be accounted for by neural tube defects (15 percent) and chromosomal and genetic abnormalities (67 percent) (Roberts & Lowe, 1975; Strobino et al., 1987; Tharapel et al., 1985; Young et al., 1986). Thus, abortion and mortality of malformed fetuses seem to be natural biological functions to eliminate malformations. In other cases, infants stricken with a genetic disorder can live for several years or even longer, depending on available treatments.

Most of the evidence for genetic disorders is derived from genealogical studies in which the path of a disorder can be traced through a family tree. For example, manic-depressive disease occurs in a high incidence in the Old Order Amish community in Lancaster, Pennsylvania. Because the entire population of this Amish community is descended from fewer than one hundred people who settled there before 1750 and the community kept excellent genealogical, disease, and death records, researchers were able to study the chromosomes of hundreds of afflicted individuals. When this is done, the specific gene that causes the disorder can be detected because it is the only one that is identical in all cases. However, other characteristics also occur along with this gene, making it difficult to say what the gene actually causes.

When specific genes can be isolated, it gives hope for the early detection and possibly the treatment of the disorder. Of the three thousand known genetic disorders, researchers have only isolated the genes for about thirty of them. It is extremely difficult to do this kind of work. First, one needs good family genealogies, and second, it takes years to find the single gene or genes out of the many thousand genes carried by humans.

Consistent sex differences are also used as clues to the genetic origins of certain disorders. Sex-linked inheritance accounts for color blindness and hemophilia in males. Hemophilia is known as the disease of royalty, since the female descendants of England's Queen Victoria were carriers of the disease and many of the males in the family inherited it. Hemophilia can be treated today with various medications to aid in blood clotting. Other sex-linked disorders are color blindness and some forms of muscular dystrophy.

In some cases, a single recessive gene can cause multiple effects. Marfan's syndrome is one example. This disorder is associated with a weakened heart, mild bone structure deformities, long fingers, and eye lens problems. It is believed that Abraham Lincoln suffered from this disease. Phenylketonuria, or *PKU*, is a recessive disorder in which the person cannot properly metabolize phenylalanine, an essential amino acid found in most forms of protein. If detected early, the level of phenylalanine-containing foods can be lowered in the child's diet, thus reducing the chances that mental and nervous deficits will develop. PKU occurs in 1 in 25,000 births. It can be tested for at birth, and parents can be counseled about their baby's diet (Levy et al., 1970).

Some disorders afflict particular racial groups in which members are likely to intermarry, increasing the chances of having a child inherit two recessive genes. Among Jewish couples in which both members can trace their origins to European ancestry (Ashkenazic Jews), there is a 1 in 3,600 chance of producing a baby with *Tay-Sachs disease*, an enzyme deficiency that brings a steady deterioration of mental and physical abilities. Infants may become blind or deaf, have paralysis, and lose the ability to swallow. Few live past the age of five (Silver, 1985).

Black infants have a 1 in 400 chance of inheriting *sickle cell anemia*, a disorder of the red blood cells in which they tend to clot and block off blood vessels. People afflicted with sickle cell anemia may become mildly retarded or have heart and kidney problems. Unlike Tay-Sachs disease, sickle cell anemia can be partially treated, and its victims can live normal lives. The sickle cell gene is also associated with a positive side-effect. Those who have the disease as well as those who are merely carriers of the gene are partially immunized against the deadly disease of malaria. People with sickle cell genes are not good hosts for the malarial parasite, which spends part of its life cycle in the blood. Malarial protection is probably the reason why the sickle cell gene was maintained in the population.

Other genetic disorders are polygenic. Because these disorders take a combination of factors in order to occur, the incidence of them is less than the single gene sex-linked and recessive disorders. Polygenic disorders include cleft lip and cleft palate, spina bifida (exposed spinal cord), some forms of diabetes, and some forms of heart defects.

Chromosomal Disorders

During the process of meiosis, errors sometimes occur as chromosomes split and recombine. One gamete may wind up with too many chromosomes, another with too few. *Monosomies* are abnormalities of the twenty-third pair, the sex chromosomes. This occurs when one member of the pair is missing. In *Turner's syndrome*, a female has only one X chromosome. This is associated with a lack of complete sexual determination, other physical deformities, and mental retardation.

A *trisomy* is a chromosome pair that has an extra chromosome accidently attached to it. Trisomies can occur on the sex chromosomes, resulting, for example, in *Kleinfelter's syndrome* (XXY) in which the male has female characteristics and is mentally retarded. The most well known of the trisomies is trisomy 21, in which an extra chromosome is attached to the twenty-first pair. The resulting disorder is known as *Down's syndrome*, characterized by short stature, flabbiness, cardiac and glandular abnormalities, small mouth, mental retardation, and folds of skin over the eyes that has given the syndrome the alternative name of "mongolism."

It is known that Down's syndrome is more prevalent in infants born to mothers nearing the end of their fertility (see Table 3.2). For this reason, most women over the age of thirty-five are counseled to have amniocentesis (see below) to test for the presence of chromosomal abnormalities during pregnancy. It has recently been hypothesized that estrogen levels in the mother may explain Down's syndrome. Since estrogen production is highest between the ages of twenty and thirty-five, women older than this may be more likely to have a Down's baby than are women between those ages. Estrogen may enhance the process of meiotic cell division, and its lack may cause incomplete cell division (Crowley, Gulati, Hayden, Lopez, & Dyer, 1979).

■ TABLE 3.2   Risk of Down's Syndrome as a Function of
             Maternal Age

AGE OF MOTHER	PROPORTION OF BIRTHS
<30	1/1500
30–34	1/750
35–39	1/280
40–44	1/130
>45	1/65

SOURCE: Quienan, 1980.

Furthermore, there is an increased risk of Down's syndrome when fathers
are younger than twenty and older than fifty-five years, and errors in the
genetic material of sperm cells may account for as much as one-fourth of all
Down's cases (Arehart-Treichel, 1979).

Environmental Influence on Prenatal Development

The study of birth defects is known as *teratology*, for the Greek word *tera*
meaning monster—hardly a pleasant-sounding association. Teratology,
however, is an extremely valuable area of investigation, since it attempts to
find the causes of birth defects as a way to avoid them in the future. Up until
this century, birth defects were mysterious. They were often attributed to
magical, spiritual, or supernatural causes, or else they were read as omens or
signs. The ancient Babylonians considered birth defects an omen, since
according to their views, omens were taken to be any "unnatural" occurrence.
Many primitive societies today have some theories of the causes of birth
defects, but these are mostly superstitious beliefs, such as the admonition that
eating twisted or deformed plants may lead to birth deformities (Mead &
Newton, 1967).

If the birth defect arises because of some environmental cause rather than
a chromosomal or genetic abnormality, then the agent responsible for the
defect is known as a *teratogen*. Teratogens come in many different forms, from
viruses to chemicals to nuclear radiation, and their existence testifies to the
importance of environment-infant interactions even before birth.

The general public was made aware of the devastating effects of toxic agents
on fetal development through two drugs that were once widely prescribed for
pregnant women: *thalidomide* and *DES*. Thalidomide was a mild tranquilizer
that was available in Europe in the 1950s. It was taken by pregnant women
in the early months of pregnancy to help control nausea and insomnia. It was
discovered to be teratogenic after a number of physicians traced the presence
of heart defects and deformed or missing limbs to the mother's use of the drug
during pregnancy. It was found that the time in pregnancy at which the
mother had taken the drug determined the particular deformity. If she took it
just at the time when the arms were forming, for example, then the arms
suffered the most deformity.

Another way in which teratogenic agents may operate is illustrated by the
case of the drug diethystilbestrol (DES), a hormone given to pregnant women
between 1948 and 1969 to help prevent miscarriage. Between 500,000 and

two million women were believed to have taken this drug. In this case, however, the effects did not show up at birth but rather when the offspring of these women had reached adolescence. A rise in the number of cases of vaginal cancer in teenage girls, and sterility and other genital abnormalities in teenage boys, was eventually traced back to DES.

As a general rule, the effects of toxic agents on the fetus will depend upon a number of factors. Among these factors is the point in pregnancy at which the exposure occurs. Since two-thirds of all birth defects occur in the first trimester (Heinonen, Sloane, & Schapiro, 1976), the earlier in pregnancy one is exposed to a toxic agent, the greater the risk (see Figure 3.8). In reality, the first few days and weeks of fetal life allow for a minimum of susceptibility. The effect of the teratogenic agents increases and peaks during the period of the rapid differentiation of the organs and limbs and then declines again. If the exposure occurs during the time when organs are growing at a rapid rate, the result will likely be a structural defect. It if occurs after organ growth is mostly completed, the result will more likely be growth retardation or a functional disturbance (Kopp & Parmelee, 1979). Other factors include the

■ FIGURE 3.8
Stages of Prenatal Development and Birth Defects

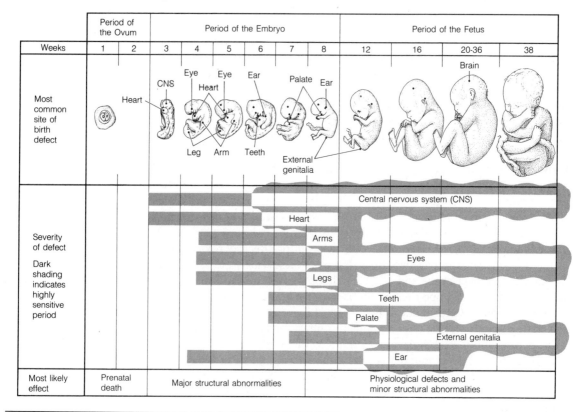

size of the dosage and the length of exposure, with longer, larger doses creating the greatest risk (Vorhees & Mollnow, 1987).

As more research has been done, the list of teratogenic agents has increased. Some of these are listed in Table 3.3. For some of these agents, the effects are well established in both animal and human studies. Agents that are listed as suspected may have been confirmed in animals but not in humans. One problem with isolating the effects of particular agents is that more than one factor may occur at the same time. For example, it is difficult to determine the effect of an antinausea drug apart from the condition that caused the severe nausea in the first place (Vorhees & Mollnow, 1987).

■ TABLE 3.3 Commonly Occurring Agents and Their Teratogenic Status

	FACTORS KNOWN TO CAUSE BIRTH DEFECTS IN HUMAN FETUSES	FACTORS SUSPECTED OF CAUSING BIRTH DEFECTS
Drugs	Tranquilizers and hypnotics Barbiturates, anesthetics, alcohol, narcotics (heroin, cocaine, marijuana), antinausea drugs, (thalidomide, bendectin)	Antidepressants
	Stimulants Amphetamines, tobacco (nicotine)	Caffeine
	Analgesics Aspirin	Antihistamines, diuretics, antiallergens, antacids
	Antibiotics Streptomycin, tetracycline, sulpha	
	Hormone supplements	
Chemicals and Radiation	Mercury, lead, PCB	Asbestos, agent orange, pesticides, cleaning fluids, paints
	Nuclear radiation	X rays, microwaves
Foods	Some vitamins (especially A), poor maternal nutrition	Additives and preservatives, dietary supplements
Diseases	Viral (rubella, influenza, AIDS, smallpox, chicken pox, polio), syphillis, herpes simplex, diabetes, toxoplasmosis, toxemia, obesity, hypertension	Vaccines
Other Maternal Factors	High stress, Rh incompatibility, age, multiple pregnancy, low income, poor prenatal care, injury	Moderate stress

SOURCES: Butler, 1974, Heinonen et al., 1976; Jacobson et al., 1985; Jones, 1975; Kopp & Parmelee, 1979; Lester & Dreher, 1989; Minkoff et al., 1987; O'Brien & McManus, 1978; Rubin et al., 1986; Smith, 1978; Taylor, 1989; Vorhees & Mollnow, 1987.

Perhaps the largest current area of research in teratology is the effects of maternal alcohol consumption. Discovered in 1973, *fetal alcohol syndrome* (FAS) is associated with some forms of mental retardation, facial abnormalities such as small narrow heads with widely spaced eyes and an underdeveloped jaw, hyperactivity, growth retardation, more premature births and miscarriages, lower birth weight, and heart defects (Blake & Scott, 1984; Jones, 1975; Smith, 1978). Currently, FAS occurs at an incidence of 1 to 3 per 1,000 births in the United States (Fifth Special Report to the U.S. Congress on Alcohol and Health, 1984).

These extreme effects occur in infants of women who are in the upper 5 to 10 percent of alcohol consumption. About 60 percent of American women drink alcohol, and 5 percent drink more than two drinks per day. The heaviest drinkers, those who consume more than five drinks per day on the average, have a 30-percent increase in risk of having an FAS child (Landesman-Dwyer, 1982; Rosett, 1980).

More recently, the focus of research has been on moderate drinking during pregnancy, one to two drinks per day. Infants born to these mothers are not likely to have physical deformities. However, follow-up studies show that by age 4, these children have mild to severe learning disabilities and slightly retarded physical growth. This pattern of outcomes has been called *fetal alcohol effects* (FAE) (Abel et al., 1983).

In many cases, women who consume alcohol during pregnancy also smoke cigarettes. Even after controlling for the effects of nicotine, research finds a dose-response relationship between the amount of alcohol consumed and the number of errors four-year-olds make on attention tasks (Streissguth et al., 1984). A *dose-response relationship* occurs when levels of the drug consumed are directly correlated with the strength of the outcome effect. The effects are relatively small for children whose mothers had one drink per day but increase rapidly for higher rates of consumption.

The evidence is not strong that low levels of alcohol consumption during pregnancy will have an effect. However, because the research in this area is relatively new, there may be unmeasured consequences of even low levels of alcohol. Pregnant women are best advised to eliminate all alcohol consumption until after their babies have been born. On the other hand, if you are currently pregnant and have been a light or occasional drinker since conception, the chances of this having an effect on your baby are relatively small. Nevertheless, you should terminate further alcohol consumption until after the birth of the baby.

Teratogenic research has expanded into many areas, more than can be reviewed here. In recent years, industrial products and wastes have been shown to cause lasting learning deficits. For example, PCB is a synthetic hydrocarbon used in plastics and electrical equipment. It leaked into the soil and water, affecting plants and fish. The problem was especially severe for fish in Lake Michigan. Although there is an official ban on the commercial use of fish caught in lower Lake Michigan, local fisherman catch and eat the fish. Pregnant women who ate PCB-contaminated fish were more likely to have children with mild to severe learning disabilities in a dose-response relationship (Jacobson et al., 1985).

Smoking both tobacco and marijuana has been shown to cause respiratory problems, birth complications and learning disabilities in early childhood

(Lester & Dreher, 1989; Moss et al, 1987; Richardson et al., 1989). Remarkably, the effect of cigarette smoking on reducing birth weight of the fetus is the same whether it is the mother or the father who smokes, and if both smoke the effect is doubled. As in related studies of older children and adults, the effects of passive smoking are just as severe as direct smoking, causing respiratory problems in those exposed (Rubin et al., 1986). In the case of smoking, both parents should abstain during pregnancy.

With cocaine and intravenous drug use on the rise, there is an increasing incidence of cocaine-addicted pregnant women, as well as women infected with the AIDS virus. Cocaine use by mothers reduces birth weight and creates circulatory, respiratory and urinary problems. It also increases the risk for Sudden Infant Death Syndrome (see Chapter 6), attentional difficulties and motor development lags (Bingol et al., 1986; Moore et al., 1986; Taylor, 1989). Having a mother with AIDS also reduces birth weight, and these children are considerably more likely to contract serious infectious diseases such as pneumonia later in the first year of life (Minkoff et al., 1987).

A problem with understanding and solving the problems of teratology is that so much of our modern environment is made up of potentially harmful chemicals, radiations, and pollutants. Some are harmful to people of all ages, causing cancer and other diseases. In some cases the fetus may be more susceptible than older children and adults.

Experts advise that pregnant women should take no drugs unless explicitly advised by a physician. Even a seemingly harmless drug like aspirin, especially when taken late in pregnancy, can cause problems with labor and delivery. With all prescription drugs, it is wise for the mother to question the physician about the availability of research on the drug's teratogenic effects. Women are counseled to avoid alcohol and cigarettes, X rays and microwaves, food containing preservatives, colorings and other artificial additives, and contact with people who have viral diseases and other infections. Consult with a physician before taking vitamins or using caffeine (note that many cola drinks contain caffeine). Use sodium bicarbonate (baking soda) as an antacid and natural fiber foods as a laxative. Literature on making pregnancy safe for the baby and mother is available from the March of Dimes Birth Defects Foundation, 1275 Mamaroneck Avenue, White Plains, New York 10605.

Teenage Pregnancies: The Problem That Won't Go Away?

The majority of infants with birth defects in the United States are born to teenage mothers. Births to girls under nineteen reached a peak in 1970, when 645,000 infants were born to teen mothers. By 1984, the figure had fallen to 470,000 births per year to girls under nineteen. This decline is a bit misleading, however, as you can see in Table 3.4 (Furstenberg, Brooks-Gunn, & Morgan, 1987).

The decline in births was primarily in the group of eighteen-to-nineteen-year-olds. For girls under seventeen, the birth rate has remained relatively unchanged at about 200,000 births per year since 1970. The teen pregnancy problem has not gone away since it is these younger girls who are most at risk for birth complications.

Teenage mothers tend to be at risk for all kinds of birth complications. The death rate for infants of teenage mothers is twice that of older mothers, and

■ **TABLE 3.4   Changes in Adolescent Fertility by Age and Race in the United States**

AGE / RACE	1970	1980	1983	1984
	Number of births (in thousands)			
Under 15 years				
White	4	4	4	4
Black	7	6	5	6
15–17 years				
White	144	128	110	105
Black	77	66	58	57
18–19 years				
White	320	260	229	216
Black	95	84	79	77
Total births	645	552	489	470

SOURCE: Furstenberg, Brooks-Gunn, & Morgan, 1987.

the incidence of low-birth-weight infants is much higher among infants born to teenagers. Is this associated solely with the age of the mother? The evidence suggests that there is nothing inherent in the age of the mother that would alone account for these problems. But teenage mothers seem to be at risk for childbearing because such a large proportion of teenage mothers come from low socioeconomic conditions with the attendant problems of poor nutrition, high stress, poor medical care, and poor family relationships (Gunter & LaBarbera, 1980; Phipps-Yonas, 1980). Teenage moms are *seven* times as likely to be poor before pregnancy as older mothers (Guttmacher Institute, 1981).

Thus the risks of adolescent pregnancy can be best understood from a social systems perspective. These studies show how the society has a direct impact on the developing infant and on the family. A family that is already stressed by economic factors is likely to view the pregnancy with apathy and resentment, leading to insufficient care during the prenatal months and after the infant is born.

The treatments for the teenage pregnancy problem are complex. They should involve the entire community and culture. In general, teenagers are caught in a web of conflicting cultural standards (Marecek, 1987). At home, they may receive the message that sex out of wedlock is prohibited. In school, there is peer pressure to engage in sexual behavior, and in the movies and on television, sexuality and sexual activity are glorified. Many movies and shows present macho and sexist themes in which men repress women (Gordon, 1982; Sprafkin & Silverman, 1982). Girls from impoverished homes or those who have suffered physical and sexual abuse may see pregnancy as a way to leave home or establish their own identity.

A Louis Harris poll taken in 1985 showed that 80 percent of a representative sample of American adults favored television messages about birth control, but major networks (except CNN) at the time refused to carry birth control advertisements because they were too "controversial" (Harris, 1985). This attitude has changed. Depending upon your point of view, at least one positive side-effect of the AIDS epidemic is a more open attitude in the United States toward discussing sexuality and taking appropriate precautions. With more information and support, teenagers have the opportunity to make positive choices in their lives.

In Sweden, for example, research has shown that the availability of contraceptives and information about sexuality actually reduced the rate of teenage pregnancy and abortion by half. Schools emphasize the social and emotional aspects of sex education, rather than the mechanical-physical aspects. Gynecological clinics are connected to most high schools, and girls can consult and receive services without cost and with confidentiality. Birth control devices are available for both girls and boys. However, premarital sexuality is not a strong moral issue in Sweden, and the population is more homogeneous than in the United States (Trost, 1985).

Can Birth Defects Be Prevented?

With respect to all forms of birth defects, there are two aspects to prevention: diagnosis and treatment. If parents suspect that they may be at risk for having children with genetic, chromosomal, or teratogenic disorders, they should consult with their physician. Usually, parents are referred for *genetic counseling*, a service that can help investigate family histories and prescribe certain kinds of diagnostic approaches.

Most chromosomal abnormalities and many genetic disorders can be detected in fetuses as young as sixteen weeks by *amniocentesis* (Nora & Fraser, 1974). During this procedure, a small amount of amniotic fluid is withdrawn from the mother's uterus through a long hollow needle inserted through the mother's abdomen. The fetal cells present in the fluid can be tested for the presence of over one hundred genetic or chromosomal abnormalities. The sex of the fetus can also be determined. Usually, amniocentesis is done only in circumstances where some problem is suspected—for example, if the mother is over the age of thirty-five or if there is a history of genetic disorders in the family—because there is some risk associated with the procedure. One or two out of every two hundred mothers will have a spontaneous abortion after the procedure, and four to six fetuses may receive minor injuries due to puncture wounds. In addition, the procedure increases in cost depending upon the number of laboratory tests that are needed to analyze the amniotic fluid.

Another procedure for diagnosing genetic abnormalities is called *ultrasound*. High-frequency sound waves can be bounced off the fetus's body to reveal the outline of the soft tissues. Thus gross abnormalities of the body can be seen and detected. It carries less risk than amniocentesis, but it is less able to detect genetic and chromosomal problems. Ultrasound has also been used during amniocentesis to help locate the position of the fetus's body before the needle is inserted. Ultrasound can detect the presence of multiple fetuses and the placement of the fetus (Barss, et al., 1985).

One problem with these methods is that they cannot be done until relatively late in the pregnancy, usually at the beginning of the second trimester. Tests on amniotic fluid often require up to four weeks. By that time, the parents' anxiety levels are likely to be high, and the decision to abort a malformed fetus is made more difficult because of the mother's growing emotional attachment to it and because an abortion will require more difficult surgical techniques. Physicians are attempting to develop tests that can be used during the first trimester.

A recently developed type of test is called *chorionic villus sampling* (CVS), in which a bit of the chorion is sampled. It has the advantage of diagnosing a wider range of disorders, and it can be done during the first trimester. It does not require that the physician puncture the amnion, and it is relatively painless since entrance is made to the uterus through the cervix rather than through the abdomen. Ultrasound may be used to guide the sampling procedure. Although recently developed, CVS has proved safe for mother and fetus, causes only minor discomfort to the mother, and has a 100-percent diagnostic success rate (Green et al., 1988; Von Hemel et al., 1986; Smidt-Jensen & Hahnemann, 1988).

Unfortunately, many types of disorders cannot be detected with any of these diagnostic procedures. In addition, each disorder requires a specific test, and each test can be quite costly. Thus, genetic counseling must be selective and done only with a thorough knowledge of the family history.

After such tests are made and a prenatal disorder is discovered, what can be done to treat the problem? There are currently three avenues for treatment: the fetus can be treated medically while inside the uterus, the doctor and family can make concrete plans for treatment following the birth, or the family can choose to abort the fetus.

Fetal medicine is one of the fastest growing fields of medicine. Doctors have had success treating certain disorders by giving vitamins to the mother. In other cases, tubes have been inserted into the fetus to draw blood or to drain harmful buildups of fluids from the head or the bladder. Ultrasound can be used to monitor the progress of the disease, the intervention, and the treatment (Forestier et al., 1988; Frigoletto et al., 1986). Following childbirth, there is also a growing number of advanced surgical and drug treatments for such disorders as heart defects, facial deformities (such as cleft palate), and PKU. Information on genetic counseling is also available from the March of Dimes Birth Defects Foundation.

Abortion as a Personal, Medical, and Social Issue

Abortion is a choice of last resort for pregnancies at risk for the mother and/or the fetus. What constitutes risk, however, is a matter of national debate. Abortion is practiced throughout the world for a variety of reasons: prevention of birth defects, to protect the life or health of the mother, in the cases of rape or incest, because of poverty, and as a means of family planning. The last two reasons—low income and birth control—account for most of the abortions.

Most Americans believe that abortion is justified to protect the mother's life or health, in the case of rape or incest, and to prevent birth defects (see Table 3.5), and these statistics have not changed in the last ten years. However, a declining number of Americans are willing to approve abortion for low-income women or as a means of birth control.

Contrary to the trends in these beliefs, the number of abortions is steadily increasing. In 1985, 1,588,550 abortions were performed, and women with family incomes below $11,000 accounted for one-third of these abortions. Nonwhites accounted for 31 percent of abortions, nearly double their representation in the population as a whole. Most of the women seeking abortion were under the age of twenty-five (Guttmacher Institute, 1989).

■ TABLE 3.5   Attitudes toward Abortion in the United States

"Please tell me whether you think abortions should or should not be legal under each of the following circumstances."

CIRCUMSTANCE	PERCENT APPROVAL BY YEAR	
	1978	1988
Mother's health endangered	88	84
Rape or incest	81	85
Birth defect	80	60
Can't afford child	45	19

SOURCES: Ebaugh & Haney, 1980; Gallup, 1988.

According to these statistics, the largest proportion of the population seeking abortion are young, lower-income black and Hispanic women. Of course, women of all ages and ethnic backgrounds seek abortions for a variety of reasons. It seems, however, that there is a conflict between those who believe that income and family planning should not play a role in abortion decisions and those who seek abortions for those reasons.

What Is the Controversy Over Abortion?

In reality, there are many abortion issues that are controversial. The one issue that receives the most attention is the right to life for the fetus versus the mother's right to make reproductive choices. The Constitution of the United States includes the right to privacy, and that right pertains especially to personal decisions made in the context of the home and the family. Thus, in their landmark *Roe v. Wade* decision, the justices on the 1973 U.S. Supreme Court concluded that the decision to terminate a pregnancy is part of a woman's right to privacy guaranteed by the Constitution. The Court's decision further divided pregnancy into three equal periods. In the first period (0 to 12 weeks) the decision to abort was up to the mother and her physician. In the second period (12 to 24 weeks), because abortion is more complicated, the health and safety of the mother was the main deciding factor. No limitations were placed on the reasons for abortion during these two periods. After 25 weeks, abortions were not permitted, except when the mother's life or health was in extreme danger.

In July 1989, in *Webster v. Reproductive Health Services*, the Supreme Court maintained a woman's right to privacy in seeking an abortion before 20 weeks. However, it also upheld Missouri laws requiring a fetal viability test before an abortion can be performed after 20 weeks and banning the performance of all abortions by public employees or in public buildings, except to save the life of the mother.

The *Webster* case opened the door for states to pass laws limiting abortions and mobilized antiabortion activists, such as the National Right to Life Committee (NRLC). In response, groups such as the National Abortion Rights Action League (NARAL) increased their efforts to represent the opposing view. While any law that completely prohibits abortions is likely to be ruled unconstitutional because of its conflict with a woman's right to privacy, abortion foes are seeking to make abortions more difficult to obtain.

They seek a ban on all abortions used for family planning or for sex selection. They want mothers to be informed about the possible risks of abortion, to be shown pictures of what their fetus might look like in its current stage of development, and to be told about alternatives like public assistance and adoption. They insist that abortions should not be obtainable except with the consent of both the mother and the father and that minors should have the consent of their parents before obtaining an abortion. Finally, they wish to prohibit public funds and public buildings from being used for abortions unless the mother's life is at risk (Agnew, 1990).

The legal question is whether these proposed policies are constitutional. There are too few court cases in which these issues have been tested. It is not only the woman's right to privacy that is at issue here. Some of these proposals may also conflict with constitutional guarantees for freedom from discrimination. Since the banning of public assistance affects primarily lower-income mothers and since most of these women are members of racial and ethnic minorities, such laws may be inherently discriminatory. The ultimate affect of these abortion restrictions may be that wealthy women will have access to medically safe abortions, while poor women will be forced to return to the backdoor clinic and self-inflicted injury.

What Does Scientific Research Have to Contribute to the Abortion Debate?

Central to both the *Roe v. Wade* and *Webster* cases is the issue of fetal viability. *Viability* refers to the ability of the fetus to survive on its own, without dependence on the mother. Medically speaking, a fetus is viable if after birth it can be sustained on life-support systems in a neonatal intensive care unit (see Chapter 4). Viability begins between 24 and 30 weeks (Grobstein, 1988). These medical findings are quite consistent with both the *Roe* and *Webster* decisions.

An entirely different issue is, "When does human life begin?" According to Dr. Lewis Thomas of the Memorial Sloan-Kettering Cancer Center in New York City, the question of when human life begins can be resolved "only in the domain of metaphysics. It can be argued by philosophers and theologians, but it lies beyond the reach of science". Taking the opposite view, Charles A. Gardner states, "There will always be arguments based on spiritual or ethical beliefs to convince an individual of the rightness or wrongness of abortion, but each person should first understand the biology to which those beliefs refer. . . . The benefit of that knowledge, more sophisticated, subtle and complete than ever before, has been notably missing from most public discussions of abortion and from all the legal decisions that have created so much recent publicity" (Gardner, 1989, pp. 557–559).

What is this biological knowledge to which Gardner refers? It is the research on prenatal development that we reviewed earlier in this chapter. It is often argued that the zygote at conception is human because it contains all of the necessary genetic instructions to make an individual human being. According to Jack Willke, 1989 NRLC president, "Contained within the single cell who I once was, was the totality of everything I am today" (as quoted in Gardner, 1989, p. 557).

However, as we saw earlier in the chapter, the zygote can only develop by a complex process of interaction with the environment. The location and biochemical environment of a cell, not only its genetic code, are what determines its later composition. There is no single way for that zygote to develop, since it is subject to a large number of factors, including what the mother eats, breathes, and touches. There is no preformed person residing in the zygote or even in the embryo: the person is a complex gene-environment interaction that takes a long time and the proper nutrients to grow.

Abortion foes suggest that one way to decrease the number of abortions due to family planning is simply to encourage more contraception. This idea has both merits and drawbacks (see "Applications: Family Planning" in this chapter). Another alternative to abortion is carrying the infant to term and placing the infant for adoption. However, if most abortions are performed on younger women living in poverty and subject to drug and alcohol abuse and poor prenatal care, removing abortion rights from these women increases the chances of teratogenic effects ranging from preterm birth at one extreme and retardation and deformity on the other. The costs to society (who will take care of these children and who will pay for their care?) and the ultimate quality of life for them (related to their particular ailments and due to the fact that handicapped children in foster care have a high probability of being subject to child abuse) must be taken into account in formulating public policies on adoption versus abortion.

Another argument in favor of the human individuality of the embryo and fetus can be found in the film, *The Silent Scream*, which shows a reflexive "withdrawal-like" movement of a 12-week-old fetus following an abortion. The argument is that the fetus intentionally withdraws and feels pain. Given the chronology of fetal behavior and development established by research (see Table 3.1), we can see that reflexes begin to appear at 12 weeks. Compare this development, however, to the development of the brain and nervous system (Figure 3.4). The 12-week-old fetus has an extremely rudimentary nervous system. Anything even closely resembling a human brain does not form until the twentieth week, and brain electrical activity (EEG) resembling that of adults does not begin until between 26 and 30 weeks. This age corresponds with other measures of viability, suggesting that a brain that is capable of behavioral regulation and intentional functioning develops only late in fetal life (Grobstein, 1988).

Should these scientifically based observations take precedence over moral and ethical considerations? Certainly they should not. However, as both Gardner and Grobstein have argued, it would be pointless to try to resolve the abortion issue in the absence of the scientific data.

As a constitutional democracy, the government of the United States cannot make laws that infringe the rights of individuals or groups, nor can laws be made that make religious beliefs into legal doctrines. The Constitution does not define whether the capacity for consciousness and intentional behavior is a criterion for human rights protections, and this is at the heart of the mother's versus the fetus' rights issue. Until that legal issue can be resolved, the abortion debate is likely to continue for some time.

■ FAMILY AND SOCIETY

In this section, we shall conclude our discussion of prenatal development by looking at the effect of the new baby on the family. Although new parenthood can be thought of as a "crisis," it is perhaps more appropriate to call it a major phase of adult development. It is a phase, not unlike infancy or adolescence, that requires a good deal of effort of adaptation. Parenthood has, like most other important developmental phases, its own pleasures and sorrows, rewards and misgivings, and memories both fond and painful.

For most people, the first step in becoming a parent is pregnancy, and the first issue that new parents must deal with is the physical changes that a woman's body undergoes during that nine-month period.

What are the physical changes associated with pregnancy?

What are the first signs of pregnancy? The failure to menstruate is usually considered to be the most reliable indicator, but it is not foolproof. A woman may menstruate for two or three months after she has conceived, and failure to menstruate may be due to such other causes as age, illness, or emotional upset. Breast changes may also be symptomatic of pregnancy. These may occur in the form of fullness, tingling, or hypersensitivity. About half of all women experience some nausea, usually in the morning, but this typically passes after eight weeks. "Morning sickness" is believed by some to relate to biochemical changes, while others think it is an adaptive mechanism that functions to provide a reason for the mother to get more sleep and rest.

Other symptoms of pregnancy are fatigue and frequency of urination. Conclusive diagnosis can only be obtained through laboratory tests, however. Pregnancy test kits are currently available for use at home, but they are not reliable in all cases.

During pregnancy, the uterus grows from about 2 ounces to 2 pounds, and the abdominal muscle fibers grow to about ten times their original length. Maternal uterine muscles are extremely important for a number of reasons. They will open the cervix at birth to provide a passage for the baby, they will contract to push the infant out, and they will continue to contract after birth to restrict the continued flow of blood to the uterus. The latter function is essential to avoid a major blood loss. The vaginal muscles also change during pregnancy. The vagina increases in length and capacity and more blood is supplied to the area. In addition, vaginal secretions increase in quantity and in bacteriological action.

Because of these secretions, sexual intercourse during pregnancy may be more satisfying to some women than it was before pregnancy. In general, sexual intercourse during pregnancy is not harmful. Consultation with one's physician is suggested since each woman is different and intercourse during late pregnancy may not be advisable.

Physicians who care for a mother's and fetus' health during pregnancy and who deliver babies are called *obstetricians/gynecologists*. Those who care for the baby immediately after birth and during childhood are called *pediatricians*. Women should be encouraged to discuss all aspects of their pregnancy and delivery with their obstetricians. Obstetricians differ in their willingness to answer questions and to allow a mother to make decisions about the course of her labor and delivery. To the extent possible, women should select an obstetrician whose beliefs and practices accord with their own.

As pregnancy procedes, the placenta forms within the uterus and secretes hormones that nurture the fetus and also prepare the mother's body for birth. The placenta is constructed to enhance the exchange of nutrients and other substances between the mother's and the fetus' blood supply (see Figure 3.9). As we saw earlier, the placenta filters some things and passes others.

In reality, because the fetus has genes from the father as well as the mother, it exists within her as a foreign body. Under most circumstances, such foreign cells would be attacked by a person's immune system. Why doesn't this happen to the fetus? Apparently, the cells in the uterus near the placenta are responsible for blocking the local production of the immune response system. Studies of how the uterus does this may have applications in cancer research (because cancerous tumors may block the immune system) and in organ transplants, where doctors would like to stop the normal process of rejection (Silberner, 1986).

The placental hormones also induce changes in the breasts as they become ready for lactation. They increase in size as fat is replaced by mammary gland tissue and more blood supply. A clear, yellowish liquid called *colostrum*, high in protein and antibodies, may be secreted by the fourth month of pregnancy. Colostrum is the first food of the breast-fed infant. It is gradually replaced by milk during the first few days after birth.

In general, the mother's body adapts itself to work harder. The mother's digestive and eliminative systems (kidneys, intestines, and sweat glands) must begin to take on the requirements of the developing fetus. These extra requirements are often accompanied by discomforts. Typical complaints of

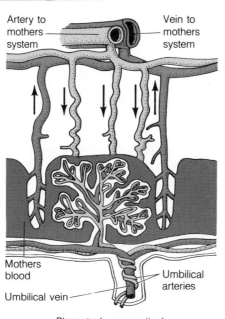

Artery to mothers system

Vein to mothers system

Mothers blood

Umbilical vein

Umbilical arteries

Placenta (cross section)

■ FIGURE 3.9
Changes in Maternal Circulatory System During Pregnancy

A detailed cross-section of the placenta is shown here. Note that there are two portions of the placenta—the embryo's portion and the mother's—and that they are interwoven. Those parts of the drawing that belong to the embryo are shown in light gray, those of the mother are in a darker gray. The gray umbilical vein and arteries carry the embryo's blood, exchanging nutrients, wastes, and so on, with the mother's blood—but the two blood supplies do not come in direct contact.

SOURCE: Reprinted by permission from p. 108 of Child Development by Alan Fogel and Gail F. Melson; Copyright © 1988 by West Publishing Company. All rights reserved.

pregnant women include leg cramps and varicose veins, temporary changes in skin pigmentation, stretch marks on the abdomen, shortness of breath and lethargy, indigestion and constipation, and moodiness. The severity of these symptoms depends upon a woman's body structure, nutritional status, fatigue, and psychological sense of well-being.

All of these facts show how the mother and fetus comprise a unique biological system in which feedback between them accounts for their mutual development. As the fetus changes, the mother's body changes in response, and continued changes in her body and its functioning provide the nourishment and biological support necessary for fetal growth and development. Both mother and fetus act as a system in their exchange of materials with the outside environment. One of the most important aspects of this interchange is the intake of food by the mother.

According to Guthrie (1979), the main purpose of good prenatal nutrition is to avoid depletion of maternal stores of nutrients and to allow the mother to produce sufficient milk for breast feeding. Malnutrition during pregnancy does more than simply deplete the mother's nutritional supplies; brain development can be severely hampered in the infant who has been born from a malnourished mother (Brown, 1966; Naeye, Dienera, & Dellinger, 1969; Werner, 1979). These authors argue that because the number of neuronal brain cells does not substantially increase after twenty weeks gestational age, the early months of pregnancy are a critical period for brain development, and the nutrition that the fetus receives from the mother will determine how many cells are produced.

The average weight gain for women in pregnancy is about 24 pounds, although this can range to as much as 40 pounds depending upon the size of the infant and the mother's constitution. Severe restrictions of calories during pregnancy is not recommended and may even be harmful. Adolescent girls require even more nutritional enrichment than adults because their bodies are still growing. Mothers are advised to eat a diet of balanced foods rather than taking vitamin and mineral supplements, since some vitamins may harm the fetus if taken in large quantities (Shank, 1970).

Aside from nutrients, the mother receives information from the social environment, and the feedback processes that govern this exchange may ultimately affect the health and development of the baby. One of the most important sources of interchange for the mother is her relationship to her family and her own psychological adjustment to the state of becoming a parent. Although this is most apparent in first-time parents, each new baby brings with it a continuing psychological adaptation within the mother and within each of the other family members.

How do adults make the transition into parenthood?

In her writing about this phase of adult development, Alice Rossi (1968) coined the term "transition to parenthood" as a way of capturing the developmental aspects of the change but avoiding any connotation of its being a major "crisis." She divided parenthood into four major stages— anticipatory, honeymoon, plateau, and disengagement-termination—the first two of which refer to the prenatal and infancy periods, respectively.

In many countries mothers must balance the demands of pregnancy with the world of work. This balancing act may create forms of psychological stress that is resolved in most cases by the time the infant is born.

According to Rossi, parenthood and not marriage is the major transition into adult life. The birth of an infant is both a physical and a psychological point of no return. Unlike marriage, birth is an irreversible process.

One of the reasons that pregnancy and childbirth are psychologically important is that they to some extent constitute a break from one's own childhood. Once one has a child of one's own, one loses the "innocence" of being only a child of one's parents. Ironically, pregnancy and childbirth often move women closer to their own mothers at the same time that they are moving apart from them. The new mother moves away from a previous sense of dependency on her own mother and moves toward a greater sense of identification with her mother. The mother's own parents may be encouraged to renew or readjust their feelings about their daughter by attempting to reestablish bonds that were strained or broken during adolescence or young adulthood.

Pregnancy, however, is not entirely free of difficulties. The stress of carrying the child and adapting to the physiological changes of one's body and the psychological conflicts attached to the awareness of inevitable, impending parenthood help contribute to the difficulty of the adaptation (Bibring, 1959; Grimm, 1967).

These states are typically transitory and often result from fatigue and other physical side-effects of pregnancy. In general, adaptation to pregnancy involves coping with these unexpected emotions and with the physical changes of one's body.

During the later stages of pregnancy, many women in North America become preoccupied with their weight gain. In our culture, a high value is placed on a slender and attractive female body. Even though some women enjoy the sense of being pregnant, most worry about their appearance in some way. Many women feel as though they are losing control over their own bodies; they feel conspicuous or embarrassed at times. In the last months, women begin to feel awkward and sexually less attractive, and some worry about losing their husbands to more attractive women (Leifer, 1980).

Women differ on how much these concerns worry them. Although there is little research in this area, one study finds that women who worried the least about their pregnancies were the most committed to becoming a parent and had the most involved husbands. The study also found that many mothers who were ambivalent about their pregnancies and who were concerned about their appearance and behavior eventually adapted to the parenting role (Leifer, 1980). Since there are no long-term follow-up studies, we cannot judge whether adaptation to pregnancy is related to later parenting.

What is the father's adaptation to pregnancy like?

The first-born child causes a major excitement for the entire family. The father is the most closely involved with this process, and the evidence suggests that he, too, undergoes some important developmental changes as well as some specific changes in mood and behavior during this period.

For the male, pregnancy may be seen as a sign of his masculine potency, but it may also be interpreted as a sign of bondage—an end to his fantasy of a life of adventure and freedom. Pregnancy can seem, at least initially, as either welcoming or threatening.

Many expectant fathers do not see themselves in merely a supportive role. They have a sense that they, like their mates, are experiencing an important development in their lives. Some cultures have traditions, called *couvade*, that encourage expectant fathers to identify with their mates and to act out the female role in a culturally approved manner. Cross-cultural studies have shown that *couvade* occurs primarily in societies in which females are salient and valued in their roles (Whiting, 1974). It may be that the increased involvement of fathers in the childbirth process in our own culture reflects our increasing recognition of the importance of women's contributions to the family and to society. For a father to take time off from work, to spend that time going to prenatal classes, to discuss feelings openly, to attend the delivery, and to actively share in the "woman's" world of childbearing is an open expression of the value and worth of that world.

How is *couvade* expressed in other societies? Fathers in the Ifugao tribe of the Philippines are not permitted to cut wood during their wives' pregnancy, as a form of identification with the changes in life-style associated with being pregnant. In the Easter Islands of the Pacific, the wife leans against the husband during labor and delivery. Among the Lepcha, both parents undergo a ceremonial cleansing in the fifth month of pregnancy (Mead & Newton, 1967).

There are many men who do not share these feelings, for whom the work of childbearing may be seen as less important or too threatening. The temptation to engage in extramarital sex increases during pregnancy, as does the incidence of wife beating (Gelles, 1978). No matter how fathers respond, there is no doubt that pregnancy is a family affair and that it affects the marital relationship, which in turn affects the well-being of the fetus and the newborn.

It is also clear that most fathers develop a psychological attachment to the fetus. Mothers' and fathers' attachment to the fetus was assessed in a sample of 218 women and 147 of their mates. The sample was randomly distributed among income, ethnic, and racial groups, and the pregnancies were developing normally. The parents rated their attachment to the fetus and other feelings as shown in Table 3.6. Both mothers and fathers were similar in their ratings, although fathers were more likely than mothers to be anticipating the birth, while mothers were somewhat more likely to express overt feelings of love for the fetus (Mercer et al., 1988).

How do siblings adapt to the mother's pregnancy?

Advice books for parents tend to recommend that the first child be prepared for the arrival of the baby, although there are differences of opinion about how much to say. An early study (Sewall, 1930) found that differences in preparation of the first child during pregnancy did not relate to the severity of the jealousy reactions of the child following the birth of the baby. More recent studies (Dunn & Kendrick, 1982; Trause et al., 1978) have also found no relationship between prenatal preparation and the later quality of the sibling relationship.

■ TABLE 3.6　Maternal and Paternal Responses of Feelings about the Unborn Baby

RESPONSE	PERCENTAGE OF WOMEN	PERCENTAGE OF MEN
Worry, anxiety, concern	8	4
Pleased, hopeful, positive	14	11
Talks to, loves, attached	18	8
Ambivalent, negative	13	12
Anticipating birth, curious	48	66

SOURCE: Mercer et al., 1988.

It seems that the first child, typically only three or four years old, is unlikely to understand the meaning of the mother's attempts at preparation. Even if they do understand, they are unlikely to anticipate the emotional experience that occurs when the new child arrives. Dunn & Kendrick (1982) found instead that in families having a high level of confrontation between mother and first child and in which the mother used prohibition and restraint, the first child was more likely to behave in an interfering or irritating manner toward the new baby. ■

Large families—like these children from India—are common in many places. Often, the older children are expected to care for the younger ones.

Family Planning

Family planning is the voluntary alteration of normal reproductive patterns. The type of family planning used, if it is used at all, depends on a complex network of social and cultural factors interacting with moral and interpersonal factors within the family. In wealthy countries, family planning is a matter of personal choice for middle- and upper-income families. Family planning becomes a critical issue when the population of a country exceeds the ability of the environment to provide for the health and welfare of all the people. The same is true for low-income families in the United States.

Countries can be divided into two groups of low versus high population growth rates. In the low growth-rate countries, the population increases by about 1 percent each year. The United States falls into this group. The high-growth countries can have as much as 3 percent per year increase, doubling their population every twenty-five years or so. India is such a country. It is one-third the area of the United States, but it has three times the population. Other high-growth countries are Brazil and Kenya.

In India, a significant proportion of the people are illiterate and live below the poverty level. They have inadequate food, shelter, and clothing. There is active resistance to family planning since these families depend on large numbers of children for their livelihood. In the 1970s, India passed a law requiring sterilization for all parents with two or more children who wanted to continue receiving welfare. Although the law was repealed in 1977, sterilization remains the most common form of birth control, and the voluntary use of contraception has increased (Blaikie, 1975) but not sufficiently.

China has been more successful in reducing its high birth rate. China is about the same size as the United States, but it has five times as many people. However, in the past ten years, the Chinese have reduced the birth rate to 1 percent per year by allowing only one child per family. This is done by granting those who comply more vacation time and more welfare benefits. Elderly women in each village, called "granny police," are charged with counseling and disciplining women who wish to have a second child (Galvin, 1989; New York Times, 12 May 1985).

In many African countries such as Kenya, women have as many as seven children apiece, and because of a lowering of the infant mortality rate, the population increases drastically. Women use birth control to space births rather than to reduce the number of children. In some African countries, oral contraceptives are believed to be harmful, and in others, religious taboos against touching one's own genitals prevent the use of condoms and diaphragms. On the other hand, new birth control devices are highly effective. One device is a skin implant that prevents conceptions for five years and has been well accepted in cultures that use skin scarification as a beauty practice. Injections of birth control hormones work in areas where people have come to associate injections with good health (Holden, 1988).

On the whole, it seems that culturally adapted interventions work the best and that education of the people is a necessary ingredient in a successful family planning program. The problem is particularly acute among the poor of all nations who lack education. For

continued at top of next page

APPLICATIONS

these women, abortion will continue to be the preferred method unless a considerable change in policy takes place to provide birth control education and birth control devices on a regular basis.

In the United States, this might mean making birth control education and devices readilyavailable to sexually active teenagers. Some of the religious values that are antiabortion may paradoxically prevent young people from seeking alternative methods of contraception because premarital sexuality is not condoned. The fact is, however, that sexual activity is occurring in this population, and society needs to respond to this reality in ways that respect and protect these youths, their families, and their children within the bounds of constitutional protections of rights and privacies.

The moral climate in the United States has also prevented research, testing, and distribution of birth control alternatives currently available in European and other countries. There are injectable contraceptives that last up to several months. The most controversial new product, RU 486, called the abortion pill because it terminates pregnancies after conception has taken place, is not permitted to be sold in the United States. As a result, about one-third of couples in the United States resort to voluntary sterilization, giving this country one of the highest sterilization rates in the world (Roberts, 1990).

■ SUMMARY

Developmental Processes Before Birth

■ Conception takes place when one spermatozoon enters the ovum, creating a zygote.

■ All cells in the body have the same set of genes and chromosomes, except the gametes.

■ Development of a cell depends as much on its location and chemical environment as on its genetic composition.

■ The period of the embryo begins when the zygote implants in the uterine wall.

■ Embryos display rudimentary behavior patterns, such as heartbeats, respiration, and whole-body jerky movements.

■ The period of the embryo ends when most of the major internal organs are formed.

■ During the period of the fetus, the major developments occur in the brain and nervous system. Later in fetal development, we see the beginnings of controlled movements, such as facial expressions and grasping. Fetuses after 28 weeks have states of arousal and REM sleep, and they can learn.

Influences on Prenatal Development

■ Genetic influences can occur through polygenic inheritance, dominant-recessive inheritance, or sex-linked inheritance.

■ The action of the genes, as well as the occurrence of genetic disorders, depends on the interaction of the genes with their environments.

■ Chromosomal disorders involve additions and deletions of chromosomes.

■ Teratogenic effects occur when the maternal environment transmits harmful substances to the fetus. Alcohol, drugs, and diseases are among the common teratogens that produce birth defects of varying severity.

■ The higher incidence of birth defects and mature births among teenage mothers can be attributed to the effects of poverty and poor prenatal care, rather than to the age of the mother alone.

■ Many birth defects can be diagnosed prenatally through genetic counseling. Treatments include fetal medicine, postnatal intensive care, and abortion.

■ Abortion is a controversial issue in the United States, especially if it is done because of low income or for family planning. The rights of a woman to privacy conflict with the possible rights of the fetus in most legal decisions. It is difficult to establish when human life begins, but scientific research can add important information to the debate.

Family and Society

■ Mothers must learn to cope psychologically with the physical changes in their bodies that occur during pregnancy.

■ Fathers often identify with their mates' changes and act in supportive roles, depending upon personality and cultural expectations.

■ Preparing a first child for the birth of the second child does not seem to affect the amount of later sibling rivalry.

Applications: Family Planning

■ The choice of family planning methods depends on personal and cultural values. Family planning is most needed in societies where the size of the population outstrips the ability of the economy and resources to provide for everyone's welfare.

■ GLOSSARY

Allele   A gene whose action depends upon at least one other gene, its allelic counterpart, to produce the phenotype. Usually alleles are at the same location on each chromosome of a pair.

Amniocentesis   Sampling a small amount of amniotic fluid for the purpose of determining the genetic and chromosomal makeup of the fetus.

Amniotic sac   A membrane that encloses the embryo and fetus and contains amniotic fluid in which the fetus floats, providing a natural cushion.

Blastocyst   A fertilized ovum during the first two weeks of prenatal development, before implantation in the uterus.

Cephalocaudal development   Growth that proceeds from the top of the body to the bottom.

Chorion   The inner lining of the placenta, separating the placenta from the amniotic sac.

Chorionic villus sampling   A test for birth defects in which a small amount of the chorion is sampled. It can be done earlier in pregnancy than amniocentesis.

Chromosome   An arrangement of about twenty thousand genes, aligned in a long string. Each cell in the body contains forty-six chromosomes, except for the gametes, which contain twenty-three chromosomes.

Colostrum   A clear, yellowish, high-protein liquid secreted by the breasts beginning in the fourth month of pregnancy and continuing until several days after birth.

Couvade   A father's attempt to experience the mother's feelings during pregnancy and delivery, seen in the form of culturally accepted rituals.

DNA (Deoxyribonucleic acid)   A molecule that contains a biochemical code for the production of body tissues. Genes are sections of DNA that control the development of specific characteristics of functions of the individual.

Dominant-recessive inheritance   A two-gene inheritance pattern in which the recessive gene appears in the phenotype only if no dominant gene is present.

Dorsoventral development   Growth begins at the spine and moves outward.

Dose-response relationship   A relationship between the drug's dosage and the drug's effects in which increasing dosages lead to stronger effects.

Ectoderm   One of the cell layers in the embryonic disk that will become the central nervous system, brain and sense organs, skin, hair, nails and teeth (see *endoderm* and *mesoderm*).

Embryo   The period of prenatal development beginning in the second week after conception and extending until the third month of pregnancy.

Embryonic disk   A layer of cells in the blastocyst that will eventually become the embryo's body.

Endoderm   A layer of cells in the embryonic disk that will become the digestive, respiratory, and urinary systems (see *extoderm* and *mesoderm*).

Fetus   The period from the third month of prenatal life until delivery of the newborn.

Gamete   Spermatozoa or ova: reproductive cells have twenty-three chromosomes each.

Gene   A section of the DNA molecule that comprises the smallest unit of the codes for inherited characteristics.

Genetic counseling   Assessing the parents' likelihood of producing a child with genetic or chromosomal abnormalities.

HCG (human chorionic gonadotrophin)   A hormone whose presence signals the onset of pregnancy.

Karyotyping   Photographing a micrograph of a set of chromosomes, and then cutting the photograph and arranging the chromosome pairs for easy examination.

Lanugo   Fine hair that grows over most of the fetus' body, beginning in the fourth month.

Meiosis   The process of cell division that produces gametes, resulting in only half the usual number of chromosomes.

Mesoderm   A layer of cells in the embryonic disk that leads to the development of muscles, bones, circulatory and reproductive systems (see *endoderm* and *ectoderm*).

Mitosis   The cell-division process by which each chromosome makes a copy of itself before cell division takes place.

Monosomy An abnormality of the twenty-third chromosome in which one member of the pair is missing.

Obstetrician A physician who specializes in prenatal care, delivery, and reproductive health.

Pediatrician A physician who specializes in the care of infants and children.

Plieotropy When a single gene is responsible for multiple phenotypic characteristics.

Polygenic inheritance When multiple genes are responsible for a single phenotypic characteristic.

Proximodistal development Parts of the body closer to the trunk develop faster than the extremities.

REM sleep Sleep in which rapid vertical eye movements are accompanied by irregular body and respiration movements.

Sex-linked inheritance Refers to those characteristics that are carried in the genes of the sex chromosomes.

State of arousal An organized system of physical and physiological responding that is related to the internal level of arousal, from sleep to waking.

Teratology The study of birth defects.

Trisomy A chromosome pair with an extra chromosome attached to it.

Ultrasound Obtaining an outline of the fetus by means of high-frequency sound wave reflections.

Vernix caseosa A white, cheesy coating that protects the fetal skin.

Viability The ability of the fetus to maintain its own life outside of the uterus.

Yolk sac A region of cells in the blastocyst that will eventually become the embryonic blood supply and internal organs.

Zygote A fertilized ovum.

The Process of Childbirth

——

This chapter covers the infant's transition from prenatal to postnatal life. Family members have been anticipating the moment of birth with both hope and concern, while the fetus is making movements that prepare for the next phase of its life. We shall discuss the process of birth and some of the birth complications that may affect the infant's development. We will review the physical features of the newborn infant and cover aspects of newborn health. We examine the causes and cures for infant mortality in the United States and in different parts of the world. Finally, we discuss the parents' psychological adaptation to the birth process, breast- versus bottle-feeding, and some cross-cultural differences in the management of birthing. In the next chapter, we cover newborn behavior, perception, and learning abilities.

■ THE CHILDBIRTH EXPERIENCE

The Stages of Labor

During the last several weeks of pregnancy, the muscles in the uterus begin to contract and expand at irregular intervals, sometimes days or weeks apart. These gentle muscle contractions, called *Braxton-Hicks contractions* or false labor, have two important effects. First, they help to widen the cervix to a width of 1 to 2 centimeters. The *cervix* is the opening between the uterus and the vagina. Normally closed during pregnancy, the cervix must expand to a width of about 10 centimeters (5 inches) in order for the fetus to pass from the uterus into the vagina.

Second, the Braxton-Hicks contractions may also help to move the fetus closer to the cervix in preparation for birth. In almost all cases, the fetus's head is oriented downward. About 4 percent of all births are *breech* presentations (with the buttocks first), and a small fraction are *transverse* presentations (the fetus is oriented on its side). These types of presentation are shown in Figure 4.1. Caesarean deliveries are usually recommended when there is a breech or transverse presentation since it is not possible to turn the fetus once it has descended into its prebirth position.

Labor begins when contractions start to appear at regular intervals spaced about ten to twenty minutes apart. Labor is usually divided into three stages (see Figure 4.2). The first stage lasts until the cervix is fully dilated to 10 centimeters. Contractions in this stage help to flatten and open the cervix. This is the longest stage of labor, and its duration may vary from a few minutes to a few days (Guttmacher, 1973). The mean duration of the first stage is about eight to fourteen hours for *primiparous* mothers (mothers giving birth for the first time) and about six hours for *multiparous* mothers (Danforth, 1977; Parfitt, 1977).

In the second stage of labor, the infant passes through the cervix and vagina. During this period, contractions serve to push the baby through the vagina. This stage usually lasts between one and two hours. The final stage of labor is the birth of the placenta, often called the afterbirth. This stage takes less than one hour in most cases.

If you ever wondered where the name *labor* comes from, it is because of the difficult muscular work involved. Although some women are fortunate to go through the entire three stages in a matter of several hours, other mothers may

■ FIGURE 4.1
Various Deviations from the Most Optimal Vertex Presentation

The first drawing on the left shows a minor deviation in which the head is first but is turned to the side. The next shows a prolapsed cord. The more extreme presentations are shown in the three drawings on the right.

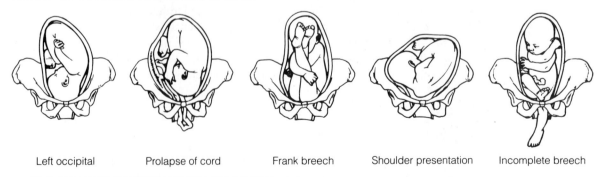

| Left occipital | Prolapse of cord | Frank breech | Shoulder presentation | Incomplete breech |

SOURCE: Rosenblith & Sims-Knight, 1985, p. 158.

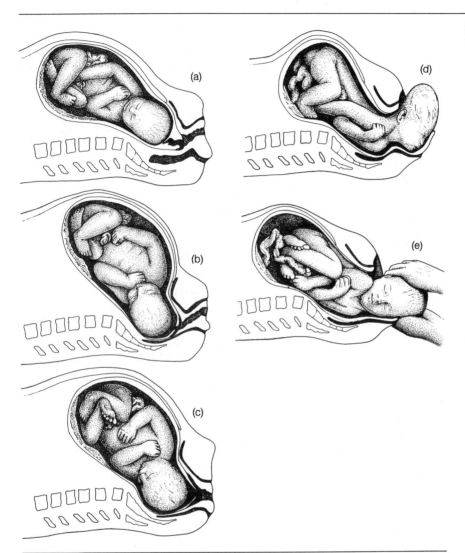

■ **FIGURE 4.2**
**Birth Process: Stage
1 and Part of Stage 2**

(a) End of the first stage of labor.
Baby's head is moving through the
cervix. (b) Transition. The baby's
head is moving through the birth
canal, the vagina. (c-e) The second stage of labor. The baby's
head is moving through the opening of the vagina (c), it emerges
completely (d), and the head is
then turned so that the rest of the
body slides out (e).

SOURCE: Reprinted by permission
from p. 116–117 of Child
Development by Alan Fogel and
Gail F. Melson; Copyright © 1988
by West Publishing Company. All
rights reserved.

be in labor for twenty or thirty hours, during which time they have little
chance to sleep or rest.

No one knows what signals the onset of the first stage of labor. Babies are
expected to be born about 280 days from the first day of the mother's last
menstrual period, but only about 4 percent of all births occur on their exact
due date. It is generally considered to be in the normal range for babies to be
born within two weeks before or after the due date (Guttmacher, 1973).

Caesarean Deliveries

Vaginal deliveries occur in about 84 percent of all births in the United States,
while the remainder are done by Caesarean section. In a *Caesarean section,* an
incision is made in the mother's abdomen and uterus while she is under a local

or a general anesthetic. The baby and placenta are both removed. Caesarean sections, also called C-sections, are used in the case of breech or transverse presentations. Some diseases that infect the mother's vagina, such as syphilis, herpes simplex, and AIDS, can be transmitted to the infant during delivery, and a C-section birth helps to prevent the transmission of this infection to the infant. C-sections are also recommended in multiple births (twins, triplets, etc.), with babies whose heads are too large for the mother's pelvis, when the fetus becomes dangerously entangled in the umbilical cord, and in the case of fetal distress.

Fetal distress is a sudden loss of oxygen or a change in the heart rate or respiration of the fetus, usually determined by fetal monitoring. Fetal monitoring is done by attaching monitoring electrodes to the mother's abdomen or, in extreme cases, directly to the fetus's head via the vagina and cervix. Fetal monitoring is advantageous if the baby is suspected of being at some risk for fetal distress. Ultrasound can also be used to determine the position and behavior of the fetus prior to birth.

Severe fetal distress can cause serious complications. For example, too much pressure on the fetal head during delivery can cause excess blood pressure and possibly bleeding inside the scalp, called intraventricular hemorrhage. Loss of oxygen, which sometimes happens in long and difficult labors, can lead to fetal brain damage. Using a fetal monitor, a physican can decide if the risk to the infant requires an emergency C-section.

C-sections have saved the lives and health of many mothers and infants. They are not without risk to the mother, however. Because it is a surgical procedure, the mother is at greater risk of infection and postoperative stress. In the past, it was thought that once a woman had a C-section, she could not have vaginal deliveries in the future. This practice is changing as an increasing number of C-section mothers are having vaginal deliveries of later-born children.

There has been an increase in the number of C-sections performed in the United States over the past twenty years, which is hard to account for since the proportion of breech and difficult labors has not changed. Some people have complained that obstetricians are too quick to perform C-sections as an attempt to avoid lawsuits against them if the baby or mother suffers during a vaginal delivery or because they could make more money by doing surgery compared to a routine delivery. It is difficult to prove these claims, however.

Other reasons for an increase in C-sections are better nutrition and therefore larger babies and more accurate fetal monitoring that allows a more sensitive and early detection of fetal distress. In addition, there is little evidence that a C-section has any lasting negative side-effects on mothers or on infants. Field and Widmayer (1980) found no differences in newborn behavior between C-section and vaginally delivered infants. At four- and eight-month follow-up observations, no consistent differences could be detected.

In another study (Hollenbeck et al., 1984), observations were made at 3 and 28 days on 62 vaginally-delivered and 35 Caesarean-delivered infants. No differences were found between the two groups in mother-infant interactive behaviors such as care giving, kissing, imitating, smiling, touching, vocalizing, fussing, and feeding. Overall, however, the fathers in the C-section groups were more involved with their infants than in the vaginal group.

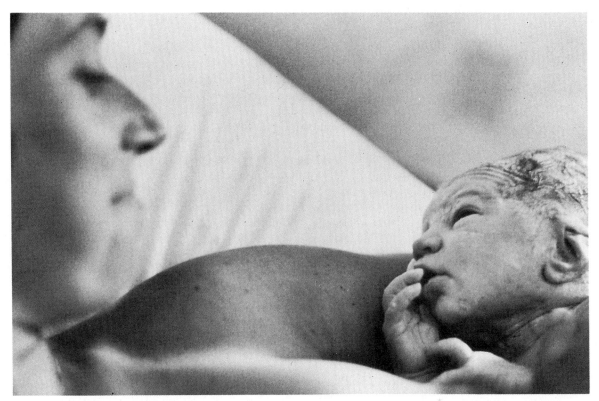

Childbirth can be an exceptionally moving experience for all members of the family. In many hospitals, fathers are encouraged to attend the childbirth, providing support for their mates and enhancing their own feelings of participation.

Fathers may be more involved with C-section infants because mother receive more medication and take longer to recover than in a vaginal delivery.

This positive effect of C-sections on parents was replicated in a long-term follow-up study of 58 C-section and 274 vaginal deliveries (Entwisle & Alexander, 1987). The children were studied as first-graders in 1982. There were no differences between the children's California Achievement Test scores, nor in tests of personality, temperament, and special problems. Parents of C-section children, however, believed that their children had a greater ability for schoolwork, and their children expected higher grades than other children.

In sum, although C-sections carry some increased risk for the mother due to complications of surgery, the health benefits to the mother and infant are enormous. Although C-section should only be used in emergency cases, follow-up studies show that there are no measured harmful effects to mother or infant resulting from the C-section experience. Probably because of the additional worry and expense of a C-section, parents, especially fathers, of babies born this way seem to have slightly more positive attitudes toward their babies than do parents of vaginally delivered infants.

Drugs and Delivery

In the case of either vaginal or Caesarean delivery, most mothers are given some type of medication to control pain and/or to regulate the course of labor.

According to Judeo-Christian tradition, women are supposed to suffer during childbirth as punishment for Eve's sins: "In sorrow thou shall bring forth children" (Genesis 3:16). This belief persisted until 1847, when a Scottish obstetrician, James Young Simpson, gave ether to a delivering mother to ease her pain. Simpson had to combat both medical practice and religious values to fight for the use of pain relievers in childbirth. He argued that the Hebrew word previously translated as "sorrow" should have been translated as "work" or "labor." Furthermore, he cited the "deep sleep" that God imposed on Adam when Eve was "delivered" from one of his ribs. Popular success of the painless childbirth spread rapidly, encouraged by the use of chloroform during Queen Victoria's two childbirths (Brackbill, 1979).

Today, the science of drug use during labor and delivery is complex. Perhaps because obstetricians who delivered babies were less concerned with the infant than with the mother, the development of *anesthesia* (loss of sensation) and *analgesia* (pain relief) has proceeded without much concern for the welfare of the infant, although this has recently been changing.

Drugs used during labor fall into three main classes: preanesthetic, general anesthetic, and local anesthetic. *Preanesthetic* drugs are given to induce labor (oxytocin and prostaglandin), to reduce discomfort or pain (narcotics), and to provide relaxation (sedatives and tranquilizers). *General anesthetics* are used when there is a need to speed delivery (during fetal distress, for example) or for a Caesarean section. In addition to the anesthetic agents, other drugs must be administered to relax muscles and reduce excess salivation and sweat secretions. *Local anesthesia* is administered at various sites along the spinal cord, depending upon how localized or widespread the area that must be anesthetized (Brackbill, 1979).

In most industrialized nations, the method most used for pain control is drugs. Although drugs are medically controlled and have been proved safe for the mother, it is by now well established that most general anesthetics administered to the mother cross the placenta during labor and delivery. Unfortunately for the neonate, those organ systems that are the most susceptible to chemical insult—the central nervous system primarily—and those that would be the most effective for drug clearance—the liver and kidneys—are the least well developed. Other organs of the newborn are better developed, such as the heart and lungs, but these systems have little or nothing to do with helping the system get rid of the drugs.

How long the drugs remain in the newborn's system will depend on the type of drug, the time during labor at which it was given, and the dosage given to the mother. Some drugs take a long time for the mother's body to process. If such drugs are given late in delivery, they may not enter the infant's blood stream before the cord is cut.

A considerable amount of research has been done to assess the effects on the infant of drugs used during delivery. It has proved difficult to establish the specific effects of drugs in part because of the large number of drugs that are available and the differences in dosage and timing. Since most women are given multiple drugs, one can't single out the effects of one or the other. Because only 5 percent of all deliveries done in hospitals in the United States are drug-free, it is hard to find a control group (Rosenblith & Sims-Knight, 1985; Stechler & Halton, 1982).

A more difficult methodological issue is that mothers are not assigned randomly to groups according to type of drugs used. Doctors prescribe drugs according to the characteristics of the mother during labor and delivery. Thus, differences in the newborns may be caused by the difficulties of delivery, rather than by the drugs used to alleviate those difficulties. Mothers who receive fewer drugs may be better educated, have more income, and receive better prenatal care. Finally, there is no standard outcome measure used to assess the effects on the child, and it is rare that research follows infants longitudinally to assess long-term effects (Rosenblith & Sims-Knight, 1985).

It is not surprising, therefore, the most studies of drug effects yield inconsistent findings. Some studies find positive and some negative effects for the same drugs. Low to moderate dosages of drugs do not have measurable effects; and when effects are found, they are small in magnitude and don't last beyond the newborn period. Only one drug, oxytocin, used to induce or to speed up the rate of contractions as a preanesthetic, has shown consistent effects on infant motor functioning and school achievement (Broman, 1981; Rosenblith & Sims-Knight, 1985).

One should not conclude from this review that most drugs are without impact. Even though no effects can be shown overall, some infants and mothers may show extreme but short-term reactions. Some drugs may impair a mother's ability to participate in her delivery by paralyzing muscles normally used to push the baby out, while others may make her drowsy. Many women seem to suffer from gaps in their memories of the childbirth experience. In one study (Affonso, 1977), 86 percent of the women interviewed could not remember some of the events of their childbirth and wanted to know more. They would ask the doctor and nurses; they had bad dreams and felt somewhat frustrated. Some mothers asked the same questions over and over. This problem seems to occur when labor is either extremely long or extremely short, in high-risk conditions, or when there is a high level of medication.

On the other hand, for some mothers anxiety and pain increase dramatically prior to and during labor and delivery (Westbrook, 1978). Drugs serve to calm these mothers and reduce their discomfort, making them better able to enjoy the birth of their infant (Field & Widmayer, 1980; Shnider, 1981).

The Management of Childbirth

Most childbirths in North America take place in hospital settings. From a medical perspective, the hospital environment allows for a large staff to assist in labor, delivery, and the care of the newborn. Hospitals also provide access to emergency medical care in the event of fetal distress or complications with labor.

At the turn of the century, most childbirths took place in the home. Once it became accepted practice to give birth in the hospital, the experience of childbirth for women and their families changed. In the home, the mother could be surrounded by familiar sights and sounds and have the support of other family members. In the early days of hospital care, mothers were left in bare-looking rooms for labor, and birth took place in a sterile operating chamber. Family members were prohibited from accompanying the mother. The babies were separated from the mothers for several days, bottle feeding was encouraged, and hospitals stays could last up to a week for normal deliveries.

Today, childbirth in hospitals has become more humane. There is a growing recognition of the need to treat childbirth less like a disease and more like a normal event. Labor and birthing rooms are comfortably furnished, and they can accommodate other family members. Because of a new awareness about the psychological benefits of early mother-infant and father-infant contact, babies are separated from parents only in the case of a medical complication. Otherwise, early and frequent contact is desirable. We'll return to the issue of early parent-newborn contact in the next chapter.

Early Discharge. In the case of normal deliveries, hospital stays can last from 1 to 3 days. Some hospitals allow discharge within 3 hours after the birth if the mother receives no analgesia or anesthesia and the infant is in good health. Under these conditions, there is no increased risk associated with early discharge (Mehl et al., 1976). More recently, early discharge is allowed on demand in consultation with the physician.

One study compared primiparous women who were discharged after a 12-to-24-hour stay with those discharged after a stay of 36 to 80 hours (Lemmer, 1986). Although both mothers and infants in the sample were healthy at the time of discharge, mothers in both groups received drugs during labor and delivery. At two months after birth, there were no differences between the two groups in medical, psychological, or behavioral concerns. The main difference between the two groups was that the women who elected early discharge felt that the home was a better and more supportive environment for comfort, recovery, and early adaptation to their babies. Indeed, the early-discharge mothers reported more social support in the home (availability of relatives and friends) and were more confident in their ability to manage on their own.

Lamaze and Childbirth Preparation. While the advantages of drugs are that they can be administered in controlled doses and that they are effective, there are a number of alternatives to speed labor and relieve pain.

Many diverse kinds of pain-relieving methods have been used throughout human history. Margaret Mead and Niles Newton (1967) have cataloged the most commonly used methods of pain relief in both Western and traditional cultures around the world today. One common practice, used by the Laotians, the Navaho, and the Cuna of Panama, among others, is the use of music during labor. Among the Comanche and Tewa Indian tribes, heat is applied to the abdomen.

Some groups believe that pain and ease of delivery are functions of the mother's body position during labor and delivery. Many cultures encourage women to give birth in a sitting position, usually by being held from behind by another woman. The Taureg of the Sahara insist that the laboring mother walk up and down small hills in order to allow the infant to become properly placed to facilitate delivery. They usually deliver from a kneeling position. In fact, most obstetrics textbooks in the United States at the turn of the century advocated an upright position during labor.

For some peoples, prevention is the best cure. The Ainu of Japan believe that maternal exercise will make the fetus small and encourage a shorter labor. (The Japanese value smaller newborns and are not pleased with multiple births because they are too animal-like.) In a number of other cultures, including the Hopi of the American Southwest, women are encouraged to exercise during pregnancy.

Nonchemical pain control during labor in developed Western countries today is likely to be achieved using the *Lamaze method.* Frederick Lamaze, in France, developed a system of exercise, breathing, and massage that was based on a theory of pain during labor developed by Grantly Dick-Read in Great Britain (Dick-Read, 1933/1972). According to Dick-Read, women become afraid during childbirth due to the pain that develops when muscles are contracted. He suggested that if women were to employ some commonly known methods of relaxation, their experience of pain would be lessened. Female animals naturally fall into panting and breathing patterns. Using these observations and the work of Dick-Read, Lamaze based his method on the use of rhythmic breathing as a mental distraction from pain and on relaxation methods to prevent it (Karmel, 1959).

Pain also has been associated with negative attitudes toward pregnancy and childbirth (Nettlebladt, Fagerstrom, & Udderberg, 1976) and with a lack of support from the husband. Women whose husbands were present during the labor and delivery, as well as those whose husbands stayed with them for longer periods, perceived childbirth as less painful (Davenport-Slack & Boylan, 1974; Nettlebladt et al., 1976). It could be, however, that women who were more likely to view childbirth as less painful were those who requested their husbands' presence for longer periods during the delivery. In addition, people who choose such approaches are a self-selected group whose positive attitudes about labor and delivery might help them, even under adverse conditions.

There is some debate, though little concrete data, on how childbirth preparation affects women (Wideman & Singer, 1984). Some suggest that the effect is due to education and the ability to anticipate fearful events. Some think it is due to the relaxation techniques and/or the social support provided by the Lamaze approach, while others think the effect is related to positive images about the childbirth experience (Nichols & Humenick, 1988). Here are some examples of imagery techniques that have been used (Jones, 1987):

"Imagine that you and your baby are breathing in harmony. Now imagine that you are inside the womb, face-to-face with your unborn child, who is comfortable and secure in a private sea of crystal-clear water" (p. 87).

"Imagine yourself opening. Envision the baby's head against the cervix and the cervix widening to let it pass. At that time, mentally say yes to the contractions as they come and fade away" (p. 145).

Some research has shown, however, that relaxation techniques may be superior to this approach since these images tend to be transitory, while breathing and massage can be sustained for longer periods (Geden et al., 1984).

Upright Postures. In traditional hospital labors and deliveries, women have been confined to a supine position for most of the time. There is a growing recognition that upright postures may be beneficial both to mother and infant. Anatomically, when mothers are upright the pelvis widens, there is a more easy access to the birth canal for the fetus, and pushing is more effective with the assistance of gravity. Upright postures also seem to improve the blood circulation to the mother's abdominal muscles and increase the oxygen supply to the fetus (Cottrell & Shannahan, 1987).

Research is somewhat inconclusive about the benefits of upright postures. Some studies find effects—such as fewer birth complications, shortening of labor, less backache pain, and more ease of pushing—although other studies find no effects. In general, it can be concluded that upright postures do not have negative effects and that, in some cases, they may relieve discomfort (Gardosi et al., 1989; Holland & Smith, 1989; Lupe & Gross, 1986).

Upright postures can be achieved in a number of ways. During labor, some women find it helpful to get up and walk around, to stand, or to squat. Just changing positions sometimes relieves discomfort. During the actual delivery, some hospitals use a birthing chair (see Figure 4.3), although there is some evidence that a squatting cushion (Figure 4.4) is more effective and more practical (Gardosi et al., 1989).

Home Births. Another alternative to hospital delivery is the modern practice of birth at home. Home births are standard practice in some countries, such as the Netherlands and most of Scandinavia. These births are assisted by professional midwives, and the incidence of infant mortality is lower in these countries than in the United States. On closer examination, this effect is not due to home birth itself but to other factors. There is a relatively high level of education in these countries and a low incidence of poverty. In addition, women who are at risk are not allowed to have home births. This includes

■ FIGURE 4.3
Birthing Chair

A modern birthing chair can be adjusted for both vertical and horizontal delivery positions according to the comfort of the mother.

SOURCE: Adapted from *In the Beginning: Development in the First Two Years,* by J. F. Rosenblith and J. E. Sims-Knight, p. 180. Copyright © 1985 by Wadsworth, Inc. Reprinted by permission of Brooks/Cole Publishing Company, Monterey, California 93940.

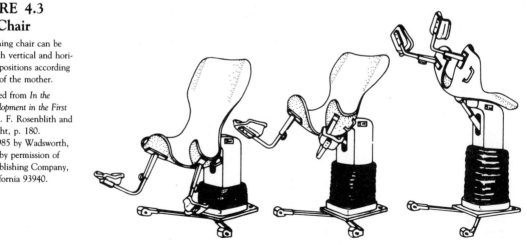

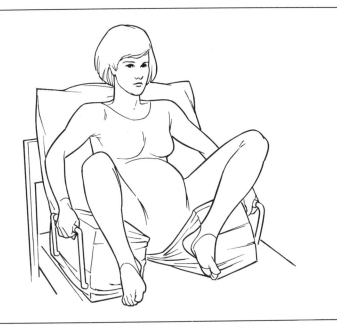

■ FIGURE 4.4
**Supported Squatting
on the Birth Cushion**

SOURCE: Gardosi, J., Hutson, N.,
& Lynch, C. Randomized,
controlled trial of squatting in the
second stage of labor. *The Lancet,
2*, 1989, p. 75.

cases of very young or very old mothers, unmarried women, low-income women, or those with medical risks (Rosenblith & Sims-Knight, 1985).

In the United States, home deliveries are often not attended by a physician or even a midwife, and they may not be screened for risk. On the other hand, when there is a trained professional in attendance, screening, and a nearby hospital in case of emergency, home births in the United States are no more risky than hospital births (Cohen, 1981; Hazell, 1975). Although these findings are encouraging for those who are thinking about the home birth option, it is important to point out that these research studies are not conclusive evidence for the safety of home birth. First, it is hard to know if the success of home birth is due to the type of person who chooses this option. Since studies are done on women who have chosen home birth on their own, there is no way of knowing how such practices might affect other women who do not make this choice. Second, most midwives or physicians will not admit into their home birth practice any woman who does not have a clean prenatal bill of health and a low risk of pregnancy or delivery disorders. Therefore, the home birth sample is likely to have fewer problems than the general population of women giving birth.

The Leboyer Method: Birth without Violence. Before leaving this section, we should discuss alternatives for the infant. Frederick Leboyer (1975) suggests that some hospital routines are traumatic for the infant: holding the infant upside down in the cold air, placing the baby on a cold metal scale, putting silver nitrate in the eyes, separating the infant from the mother, putting the baby under bright lights and exposing him or her to loud sounds, and prematurely cutting the umbilical cord. The *Leboyer method* suggests that the delivery room be quiet and dimly lit and that the infant be placed on the mother's warm abdomen right after birth until the umbilical cord stops pulsing. After the cord is cut, the infant should be placed in a warm water bath. Leboyer reports that infants so treated tend to be more relaxed and alert than other infants. Leboyer is not questioning the reasons for hospital procedures. He is simply saying that we have the power to make the birth experience more sensually pleasant and less aversive for the neonate without compromising medical imperatives. Why should newborn infants be treated with any less respect for their needs for comfort and pleasure than anyone else?

Leboyer's claims that such procedures increase the newborn's alertness have not been verified scientifically. Most studies reporting positive effects were biased by the observer's preference for the method and the lack of a control group (for example, Rappoport, 1976). One well-controlled study (Nelson et al., 1980) found no difference in alertness between Leboyer and non-Leboyer babies, nor were there any differences in developmental test scores between the two groups at 8 months. Furthermore, half of the Leboyer babies reacted to the warm water bath following birth with irritable crying. As with upright postures and childbirth preparation classes, it is difficult to establish a conclusive effect for these practices. On the positive side, most of the practices discussed here cannot be shown to have any harmful side-effects.

In the next section, we look more closely at the infant following birth. First, we examine the physical characteristics of the normal newborn infant, and later we discuss newborns who are at risk.

■ THE BABY AT BIRTH: HEALTH AND RISK

The transition from an essentially aquatic existence to a world of air, light, and gravity is one of the most abrupt and remarkable developmental shifts in the human life span. Much of what we can observe in the human newborn is related to making this difficult adaptation to extrauterine life. Some of the souvenirs of their prior home will stay with the infants as they make this change.

As you might imagine, the newborn's lungs are filled with mucus and amniotic fluid, making initial attempts at breathing difficult. As the mucus gradually drains over the first few weeks of life, the infant's breathing becomes more regular and quieter. Just about any kind of stimulation can induce respiration, even the mere exposure to air. Breathing also can be stimulated by a sneeze, cough, yawn, or cry. Some alternative birthing methods use massage or dipping the infant into warm water as a stimulus to start breathing. Slapping the baby is not necessary.

Another major adaptation of the newborn to extrauterine existence is the loss of the umbilical connection to the mother. Immediately after birth, the abdominal muscles surrounding the umbilical vessels contract to inhibit the circulation of blood in the cord. Once the cord has been cut, the navel opening usually heals within a week, and the dried remains of the cord fall off in another few days.

Once the umbilical cord has been severed and respiration has begun, it takes about thirty hours for the oxygen level of the blood to reach nearly normal levels. The blood pH balance needs about one week to become established, and it takes about ten days for blood pressure to reach normal levels.

Just after birth, infants are wet with amniotic fluid, and their skin may still be coated with the white, cheesy vernix caseosa. The color of the skin may be pale to pink, or it may be slightly yellowish due to *normal physiological jaundice*. Jaundice is caused by unbalanced liver function. It can be treated by placing the baby under special lamps.

Almost all babies are born with smoky blue eyes, which do not develop their true color until later in the first year. Even black neonates may have light skin and blue eyes for the first few days of life, since eye and skin pigments depend on white light for further development.

At birth, the newborn retains some of the physical characteristics of the fetus. The newborn's head is about one-fourth its total length, and the infant's legs are about one-third. Newborns have virtually no voluntary control over their head, although if their head is cradled, they can turn it from side to side. The newborn has somewhat bowed legs, with the feet bent inward at the ankles so that the soles of the feet are almost parallel. The typical "baby face" includes a very short neck, no chin, and a flattened nose. Newborns' heads are often temporarily misshapen from the pressures of the birth process. This gradually disappears by the end of the second week of life. Some fetal hair may remain on the infant's head, eyebrows, and back (the lanugo). This hair usually is replaced by more permanent hair within the first few months.

Newborns have six soft spots on the top of their heads, called *fontanels*. These openings provide some room for the various bones of the skull to move during the birth process, and they allow for the growth of the brain during the first years of life. They do not fully close until about eighteen months. The closure of the fontanels is shown in Figure 4.5. The time of the fontanel closure is unrelated to infant sex, race, birth measurements, or later growth measurements; slowly closing fontanels are not a sign of abnormal development (Kataria et al., 1988).

At birth, virtually all the nerve cells in the brain are present, but they have not developed very far. During the first year, the brain doubles in size (from

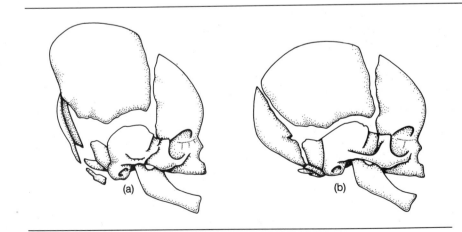

(a)   (b)

■ FIGURE 4.5
Skull of a Newborn

(a) Molding of the bones of the baby's head during passage through the birth canal. (b) By the third day of life, the bones return to their normal position.

350 to 750 cubic centimeters), and it doubles again by the sixth year. Most of the postnatal brain growth is accounted for by the increase in *myelinization*, the development of a protective sheath around the nerve pathways, as well as by an increase in the volume and density of *dendritic* connections between the cells. Dendrites are the branchlike filaments that connect the nerve cells and transmit nerve impulses between the cells.

While these processes of brain development are occurring, the cells that receive fewer inputs and connections will eventually die. Thus, postnatal experience tends to actively select certain areas and cells in the brain for further development. Those areas and cells that are not used will eventually be lost (Greenough et al., 1987). We will return to the topic of brain development in Chapter 7.

Other important changes are occurring in other parts of the newborn's body. At birth, the newborn's genitals appear large and prominent. Both sexes may have slightly enlarged breasts that may excrete a white, milklike substance, and females may have a brief "menstrual flow." These phenomena are caused by the massive infusion of maternal hormones during the birth process, and the effects disappear quickly. The newborn may also look withered, since there is very little body fat except in the cheeks, where it is needed for sucking. This withered look is even worse for premature infants, since their fat pads in the cheeks are underdeveloped.

Each baby's body has a characteristic "feel" to it, depending on the infant's muscle tone and response to tactile stimulation. There are wide individual differences in the way newborns feel when held. Some are cuddly: they will mold into the arms of the care giver and curl up when held. Others are tense and tight; some squirm and some sprawl. An adult can almost hold the entire infant in one hand.

Taking in food through the mouth is not an entirely new experience to a newborn, since babies suck in the uterus. Nevertheless, one of the major prenatal-to-postnatal transitions involves the handling of nutrients. Before birth, nutrient intake and waste matter both pass through the umbilical cord. After birth, the newborn's digestive system must take over those functions. Filling the intestines of the newborn is a greenish-black substance called *meconium,* which consists of digested bits of mucus, amniotic fluid, shed skin, and hair that was ingested prenatally. Due to the excretion of meconium and also because the mother's milk does not develop before the first few days, there is typically a weight loss during the first week that is rapidly regained. The fluid that is excreted by the breasts in the first few days is called *colostrum* (see the section on feeding in this chapter).

Some babies may suffer from a gastrointestinal disorder, *colic,* which appears to have no cure and no known cause. The gastric pain causes a considerable amount of distress for the infant and worry for the parent, but most cases of colic clear up by about three months of age.

The process of keeping physiological signs at a steady level is known as *homeostasis.* At birth, temperature homeostasis is not fully functioning, and infants easily can become chilled if not wrapped. Infants also can become easily overheated if they are too heavily clothed. Infants should not be overdressed; as a general rule; they should wear the same number of layers of clothing as the adults in the some room. Infants need to be exposed to cold as well as warmth to help them develop their own capacity to regulate their body temperature. This will not fully develop until after one month of age, when the sweat glands become more fully functional.

In the next section, we discuss methods of assessing the health status and behavioral abilities of the newborn infant. Following that, we consider risks to the newborn.

Assessing the Infant's Status at Birth

Once a baby is born, a series of assessments may be done to determine whether there are any complications or whether this infant is in need of special attention. Assessments are divided into three basic groups. *Screening* assessments give an indication of the newborn's ability to survive and whether there are any immediate medical needs. *Neurological* assessments test for problems in the newborn's central and peripheral nervous system, such as major brain, spinal cord, or sensory damage. *Behavioral* assessments are used to rate the presence and strength of behavioral responses to stimulation and spontaneous activity. Some of the more common newborn assessment procedures are listed in Table 4.1.

One of the most common newborn screening tests was developed by Virginia Apgar (1953) and is known as the *Apgar score*. The test is relatively easy to do and takes only a few seconds. The rating usually is made at one minute and again at five minutes after birth. Table 4.2 shows the categories of the Apgar rating and the possible score an infant may receive in each of five areas: respiration, heart rate, muscle tone, color, and reflex irritability. The infant's total score is summed over each of the five areas. A total score of 7 or greater usually indicates that the infant is in no immediate danger, whereas less than 7 indicates some kind of severe risk to life. If the rating is less than 4, the infant is in critical condition.

■ TABLE 4.1   Newborn Assessment Tests

TYPE OF TEST	NAME OF TEST	DESCRIPTION OF TEST
Screening	Apgar	Heart rate, respiration, and other vital signs.
Neurological	Dubowitz Assessment of Gestational Age	Differentiation of small-for-dates, from appropriate weight for gestational age.
	Neurological Examination of Prechtl and Beintema	Test of reflexes, posture, and motor development.
Behavioral	Graham-Rosenblith Tests	Responses to physical objects, strength of grasp, and response to covering the nose and mouth.
	Brazelton Neonatal Assessment	Reflexes, responses to social and physical stimuli, response to covering nose and mouth, time spent in different states, and number of changes between states.

■ TABLE 4.2   The Apgar Rating Scale

	SCORE		
AREA	0	1	2
Heart rate	Absent	Slow (<100)	Rapid (>100)
Respiration	Absent	Irregular	Good, infant crying
Muscle tone	Flaccid	Weak	Strong, well flexed
Color	Blue, pale	Body pink, extremities blue	All pink
Reflex irritability:			
Nasal tickle	No response	Grimace	Cough, sneeze
Heel prick	No response	Mild response	Foot withdrawal, cry

SOURCE: Apgar, 1953.

The reason for making two ratings is to encourage hospital staff to continue to monitor the newborn over several minutes. Often staff members are distracted by other events and may miss the possible deterioration of the infant's condition. In addition to the Apgar, the infant can be screened on the basis of its physical appearance, color, and the presence of any obvious deformities (Judd, 1985; Olds et al., 1984; Sardana, 1985).

Apgar scores have been found to relate to a variety of prenatal and birth complications. On the other hand, Apgar scores are less likely to predict later outcomes of the infant, probably due to the fact that low scores indicate immediate treatment that may alleviate the problem (Francis, Self, & Horowitz, 1987). On the other hand, low Apgar scores are strongly correlated with infant mortality, especially if the scores decreased between the two testings (Atkinson, 1983; Lipsitt et al., 1979; Naeye, 1979; Serunian & Broman, 1975).

Although the Apgar score is useful for determining the infant's viability, it is a relatively crude assessment scale. It tells us little about the actual complications the infant may have. Pediatricians and developmentalists began searching for an assessment procedure that would help identify early the various behavioral and functional disorders that occur in later childhood. They thought that if such problems could be detected in the newborn, medicine and psychology could more effectively concentrate its efforts on prevention, rather than simply treat problems after they had appeared. A number of neurological and behavioral examinations of the newborn infant can be used for specific diagnoses. Each of these examinations has its specific limitations and range of usefulness (Self & Horowitz, 1979).

Among the neurological tests, the Dubowitz scale tests for the gestational age of the infant at birth. The *gestational age* is the number of weeks of age since conception. Gestation is another word for pregnancy. To check the gestational age, raters use the infant's muscular control, physical size measurements, skin texture and color, amount of lanugo, and the size and development of the ear, breasts, and genitals. If the test is administered by a trained examiner and the infant is not grossly abnormal or in severe distress, the Dubowitz can predict the gestational age within a few days (Dubowitz et al., 1970; Jaroszewicz & Boyd, 1973). The neurological test of Prechtl and Beintema examines all of the newborn's basic reflexes. It is related to the short-term status of the newborn, but like the Apgar, less clearly to long-term outcomes (Francis et al., 1987).

Both the Graham-Rosenblith and Brazelton behavioral assessments use similar types of procedures. For example, infants' heads are placed face down on a mattress. Most normal infants will turn their heads to one side to free the nasal passages. A similar test is done with a cloth placed gently over the face. In another test, infants are pulled by the arms into a sitting position to check for head control and muscle tone. A flashlight and a bell are moved from side to side to see if the infants can localize the stimulus by turning their heads. Faces and voices are also used in the Brazelton test. In addition, observations are made about the infant's ability to control distress and maintain an awake state.

Because the Brazelton test involves a larger range of newborn behavior, it is the most frequently used. The Brazelton test has been studied extensively. It relates well to other newborn tests, such as the Prechtl and Beintema test. The test finds reliable individual differences between normal infants and can also be used to diagnose the behavioral difficulties of high-risk infants (Brazelton et al., 1987; Francis et al.; 1987).

Another use of the Brazelton test is as an intervention. Research has found that mothers and fathers increased their knowledge of and responsivity to the baby if they observed their baby while it was undergoing the Brazelton test, especially if the examiner explained the test and responded to the parents' questions (Liptak et al., 1983; Myers, 1982; Worobey & Belsky, 1982).

The field of newborn assessment is rapidly improving as researchers determine the most reliable indicators of long-term problems. Improved scoring procedures and statistics and a large number of longitudinal follow-up studies have also contributed to the development of better assessments. In the last chapter of this book, we will return to the issue of the long-term persistence of individual differences between infants.

Birth Complications

For the purpose of discussion, the infant's early history is usually divided into three main phases: the *prenatal,* the *perinatal* (the period from one month before birth to about one month after), and the *neonatal.* Although the leading cause of severe impairment stems from prenatal problems (Kopp & Parmelee, 1979), most of these problems do not show up until the perinatal period. In addition, a number of complications of the perinatal period are due to the process of birth itself. About 3 to 5 children in 1,000 show severe developmental problems before entering school, and about 85 percent of these problems can be attributed to prenatal and perinatal causes. Compared with the effect of prenatal and perinatal causes on later development, the contribution of neonatal problems—illness, disease, and accidents—is relatively small (Kopp & Parmelee, 1979).

According to Kopp and Parmelee, perinatal problems usually derive from the following causes: disorders of delivery, perinatal infections, asphyxia, hypoglycemia (low blood sugar levels), prematurity, and cardiac and respiratory difficulties. Many of these problems appear to be caused by prenatal factors, many of which we discussed in the last chapter. There is considerable evidence that many of the complications of the perinatal period can be overcome if the infant is exposed to a supportive social and physical environment. Infants who are raised in inadequate social and economic conditions are more likely to develop more permanent deficits as a result of a perinatal complication (Kopp & Parmelee, 1979; Sameroff & Chandler, 1975). We will discuss the developmental outcomes of early deficits in the last chapter.

One birth complication, low birth weight, has been receiving a good deal of recent attention from psychologists, parents, and physicians. Much of this interest has to do with modern improvements in perinatal intensive care that have permitted more low-birth-weight infants to survive without serious complications.

What is Prematurity?

There is some confusion surrounding the labeling of various classes of premature infants. In general, there a number of factors that can vary in the determination of an infant's status. These are the birth weight, the gestational age, and the relationship between these two things. Table 4.3 lists some of these classifications.

About 9 percent of all births in the United States are considered premature. In 1975, about 40 percent of preterm infants developed intellectual and neurological deficits. Due to improvements in medical technology and knowledge about the preterm infant, the percentage of later deficits continues to decrease. Infants are normal today who would have been severely handicapped a generation ago, had they even survived. Today, only about 5 to 15 percent of preterm infants develop deficits (Kopp & Parmelee, 1979). These improvements in care relate to the development of the neonatal intensive care nursery. Better ways have been found to increase nutritive intake, since the premature infant has a relatively immature sucking and swallowing pattern. Temperature control and the monitoring of critical signs also have been improved, and we are learning more about the sensory needs of the premature infant.

The youngest and smallest babies run the most risk of complications and death. Babies under 1,000 grams or less than 32 weeks gestational age are currently considered to be at the most risk. Although more of these babies are saved each year, more babies with handicaps will be likely to survive from this group.

■ TABLE 4.3 Forms of Prematurity

CLASSIFICATION FACTOR	PREMATURE CATEGORY
Birth weight	
Less than 2,500 grams	Low birth weight
More than 2,500 grams	Normal birth weight
Gestational age	
Less than 37 weeks	Preterm birth
More than 37 weeks	Full-term birth
Weight less than expected for gestational age	Small for dates
Weight appropriate for gestational age	See weight and term classification above

In the previous chapter, we looked at a variety of genetic, chromosomal, and teratogenic agents that may lead to premature birth. For example, lower birthweight usually results from such factors as smoking and alcohol use and poor maternal health or nutrition. Exceptional stress and persistent family discord during the pregnancy period has also been associated with low birth weight (Ramsey et al., 1986; Reeb et al., 1987; Stein et al., 1987).

Problems of Premature and Low-Birth-Weight Babies

Short-Term Effects. Because of their early birth and/or low birth weight, prematures are often at a disadvantage in getting a good start on adaptation to the real world. They suffer more from a lack of oxygen during the birth process, they are more likely to have jaundice and to suffer physical and mental impairments as a result of the birth process, and about one-fourth to one-third of them will die, depending upon the severity of their complications (Kitchen & Murton, 1985).

A problem with making generalizations about the abilities of premature infants is that there is a large variation in their weight and gestational age, prematurity has many different causes, and the quality of neonatal care is highly variable. Researchers today categorize infants into experimental groups on the basis of weight, gestational age, and on whether they have medical complications in addition to the prematurity. In follow-up studies of the effects of prematurity, researchers compare normal infants with premature infants of the same gestational age, rather than with the natal age of the premature. For example, a 3-month-old normal infant might be compared with a 4-month-old premature infant, both of whom were conceived about the same time.

In addition, gestational age is the best indicator of developmental status. Many premature infants cannot suck from a bottle successfully until they are about 35 weeks gestational age, about the age of a full-term newborn (Brake et al., 1988). Typical patterns of full-term sleep and waking do not begin until 34 weeks gestational age, before which the preterm infants spend considerably more time sleeping than waking (Korner et al., 1988).

Thirty-four weeks appears to be the age at which preterm infants show a marked increase in their ability to respond appropriately to external stimulation. Before that age, it takes a considerable effort on the part of an adult to keep the baby still and alert in the presence of a new tactile, auditory, or visual stimulus (Als et al., 1988).

Long-Term Effects. The long-term effects of any particular event or risk factor in early infancy are particularly difficult to assess. In Chapter 12, we will return to the general problem of how to determine the effects of early experiences. For now, you should keep in mind that the effects of prematurity independent of other factors cannot be determined. This is because many premature infants have other complications and we cannot assign infants randomly to experimental groups based on prematurity and health status. In addition, many premature and sick infants receive a variety of short-term and long-term interventions—including special attention from their families— that may alleviate their conditions. It would be unethical to withhold

Premature infants often spend weeks in intensive care units. With appropriately gentle medical intervention and sensitive handling, most of these infants will develop normally into adulthood.

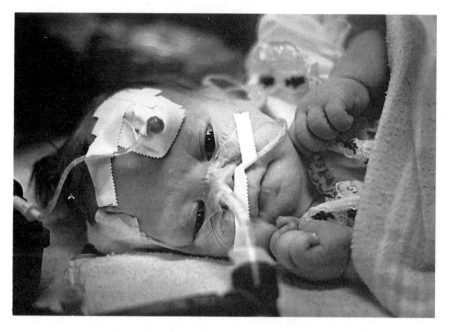

intervention or family support just in order to observe how a baby would develop without these resources.

Perhaps the only consistent outcome of prematurity is a continued history of being small in size (Kopp & Parmelee, 1979). On the other hand, babies who are small at birth often show remarkable catch-up growth if they receive appropriate care and nutrition (Pena et al., 1987). *Catch-up growth* refers to a more rapid growth rate than for normal infants early in life and a more normal growth rate once the infant reaches a weight that is appropriate for his or her gestational age. For most prematures, catch-up growth is the most rapid during the first year of life (Pena et al., 1987). Catch-up growth may occur at any point in childhood if the individual suffers a deprivation, accident, or illness and is later restored to normal functioning (Barrett et al., 1982; Tanner, 1970).

The effects of prematurity on intelligence, motor skills, perceptual skills, and emotion is considerably more variable across studies. The complexity of the outcomes can be illustrated with the following results. In one study, a group of premature infants was classified according to health status at birth: high-, moderate-, and low-risk groups were formed according to respiratory problems in the hospital. At 12 and 18 months of age, the high-risk premature infants had considerably more difficulty coping with stressful situations, and once they became distressed, they were more difficult to soothe (Stiefel et al., 1987). This study shows that health risk, when added to prematurity, has a significantly greater impact on emotional regulation than prematurity alone.

In another study, infants who experienced intraventricular hemorrhage (IVH) were assessed on motor and behavioral measures at 1 and 2 years (Sostek et al., 1987). The infants were grouped according to severity of IVH and birth weight. Birth weight and IVH had a minor correlation with outcome at 1 year and no relationship at age 2. This study suggests that the central nervous system has a remarkable ability to recover from early trauma. Although recovery is not immediate, by age 2, there is no noticeable effect on motor and behavior skills. This behavioral recovery is called *self-righting* and is comparable to catch-up growth for physical size.

For factors related to the parent-infant relationship, we find in some cases no differences between full-term and very-low-birth-weight infants (less than 1,500 grams) in mother- and father-infant attachment at 1 year when the comparison is made at equivalent gestational ages (Easterbrooks, 1989). Other research shows that parents of premature infants are more active and stimulating than parents of full-term babies, at least during the first year. Preterm infants during the first year receive more holding, vocalizing, and care taking, even though these infants are less attentive and less likely to play and vocalize than full-term babies. About the time the preterms catch up with the full terms, their parents also show more normal levels of behavior toward them (Branchfeld et al, 1980; Crawford, 1982). It may be that these parental actions are used to compensate for a less active infant, and they may actually help the infant to recover.

For some parents, however, dealing with a preterm leads to lasting difficulties in the relationship. Preterms become easily overwhelmed with stimulation, and parents may experience them as unrewarding. Some parents experience burnout in their role (Barnard et al., 1984), and there is a higher than expected percentage of premature infants among children who are later abused or neglected (Hunter et al., 1978). Some prematures have deficits that last until early and middle childhood. These deficits are in such areas as emotional maturity, language skill, perceptual and motor function, serious illnesses, and mental retardation (Blackman et al., 1987; Grigoroiu-Serbanescu, 1981; Lefebvre et al., 1988; Skeoch et al., 1987).

In general, researchers are more likely to see such long-term effects of perinatal risk only for the most extreme cases of illness or very low birth weight. This is probably because these conditions are less likely to be alleviated than the less severe conditions. Remember also that if a study does not find any differences between premature and full-term infants in later life, it does not mean that life has been normal or easy for the prematures. Their improved status in later life may have been the result of persistent, difficult, and costly interventions on the part of parents and professionals. In the next section we will discuss some of these intervention procedures.

Interventions for Premature Infants

Medical Procedures in the Hospital. In a modern neonatal intensive care unit (NICU), there are an increasing number of procedures that are adapted to the special needs of premature infants. The smallest infants need high levels of oxygen, warm temperatures, bedding that does not bruise their thin and delicate skin, and nutrients. In the past, providing these needs produced more complications for the infants who were exposed to dangerously high levels of noise and light inside of incubator boxes, bruised from touch, and scarred from needle pricks. Blindness resulted from too much oxygen and sensory loss from too much noise.

Today, premature infants are on open beds in a nursery that has higher concentrations of oxygen in the air. They are warmed with low intensity lights, and their bedding is extremely soft. Some hospitals use sheepskins or water beds. The babies are touched gently and as little as possible, sound and light are kept at moderate levels, and the oxygen content of the blood can be monitored continuously by a probe attached to the skin surface, reducing the need for blood sampling (Korner, 1987).

Behavioral Procedures in the Hospital. A variety of approaches have been used either to compensate for missing intrauterine experiences or to try to enhance catch-up growth. Certainly, one important form of stimulation that a preterm lacks is whole body movement, called *vestibular-proprioceptive stimulation*. Full-term fetuses of the same gestational age would experience the movements of the mother's body while in the uterus. Preterm infants have received rocking stimulation by adults, in hammocks, and on oscillating waterbeds. To the extent that these movements match the temporal patterning of maternal biological activity rhythms, they seem to increase weight gain (Hofer, 1975; Korner, 1987).

Although prematures, especially the smallest ones, cannot ingest fluids, they can suck readily on a pacifier, called *nonnutritive sucking* (NNS). Fetuses of the same gestational age inside the uterus also suck regularly. In several studies, premature infants who were provided with pacifiers on a regular basis required fewer tube feedings, started bottle feeding earlier, slept better, gained more weight, and were discharged earlier from the hospital (Anderson et al., 1983; Field et al., 1982; Woodson et al., 1985). More recently, it has been found that NNS reduces the infant's average heart rate, thus allowing the infant the opportunity to use its energy resources for growth instead of life maintenance (Woodson & Hamilton, 1988).

Another form of behavioral intervention is stroking and handling. It appears that for very-low-birth-weight infants (less than 1,500 grams), stroking can actually be detrimental due to the extreme sensitivity of the infant's skin. In one study of this group of infants, talking helped to bring the infants into an attentive state, while talking plus touching caused the infant to withdraw (Oehler & Eckerman, 1988). For babies between 1,500 and 2,500 grams, stroking in the form of back massage, neck rubbing, and movement of arms and legs had remarkable effects. In a 12-day test period, the prematures who received the stroking had a 50-percent increase of weight compared to prematures who did not receive stroking. The stimulated infants had larger heads and fewer complications (Field & Sostek, 1983). Studies of animal infants has shown that touch stimulates hormones that regulate the action and development of the brain (Schanberg et al., 1987). These studies clearly show that the overall amount of stimulation is not important. Rather, some specific forms of stimulation work better than others, and the most effective stimulation will depend on the infant's gestational age and weight.

Finally, interventions can be made with the parents to educate them about the special needs of the premature infant. Parental visitation to the NICU gives the infant more opportunities for stimulation and aids in the parents' positive perceptions of their infants. Both mothers and fathers benefit from frequent visitations (Levy-Shiff et al., 1989), and infants who are visited more frequently by parents are released sooner from the hospital (Zeskind & Iacino, 1984). Since most mothers of preterms are low-income teenagers, educational interventions directed at making mothers more aware of their responsibilities and setting more realistic goals are effective in improving the outcomes for their babies (Field et al., 1980; Zeskind & Iacino, 1987).

The cost to society of premature infants born to low-income mothers is enormous. The cost of care of such infants is borne by government assistance such as Medicaid and by increased health insurance premiums for everyone. A single day in an NICU can cost thousands of dollars. In the long-term, continuing deficits bring additional costs to society with remediation and special education programs, long-term health care, and the social costs of delinquency and criminal behavior that may result from early brain damage and later deprivation.

Prevention costs considerably less. Good prenatal care for low-income women could reduce prematurity and complications radically and cost less than a thousand dollars per child. Simple hospital interventions such as those described here also have long-term benefits to society. Unfortunately, low-income women find it difficult to obtain good prenatal care, Medicaid places limits on the number of allowable prenatal visits, and it takes a long time to process claims. Ultimately, the prevention of birth defects will require radical changes in our society, including the elimination of poverty and prejudice.

■ PERINATAL MORTALITY

Similar to prematurity and health risk, infant mortality is greatest in areas where income is low and health care is inadequate. Most of the causes of perinatal death can be found in poor prenatal care and ill health or malnutrition of the mother during pregnancy. A similar picture can be drawn for maternal mortality. Table 4.4 presents infant and maternal mortality for

■ TABLE 4.4   Infant and Maternal Mortality*

COUNTRY	MATERNAL MORTALITY		INFANT MORTALITY	
	1971	1985	1971	1985
Mexico	146.4	90.5[b]	63.3	53.0
United States	20.6	8.0[b]	19.1	10.4[d]
Canada	18.3	3.2[c]	17.5	7.9
Venezuela	92.1	58.9[b]	50.2	26.1
Chile	132.1	35.5[c]	77.8	19.5
Sweden	7.9	5.1	11.1	5.9[d]
England	16.9	8.2[c]	17.9	9.4
Egypt	95.9	78.5[a]	103.3	70.5[a]
Singapore	20.8	4.7	19.7	9.1[c]
Japan	44.8	15.8	12.4	5.5

*Less than one year of age. Maternal deaths per 100,000 live births; infant deaths per 1,000 live births
[a]1982
[b]1983
[c]1984
[d]1986

SOURCE: United Nations. *Demographic Yearbook*, 1986.

some selected countries around the world. It can be seen that the most deaths occur in less developed countries.

One general trend that seems to hold across all nations is the steady decline in the mortality for both mothers and infants. It is important to note when reading Table 4.4 that maternal mortality is expressed as a rate per 100,000 live births, whereas the infant mortality is expressed per 1,000 live births. Clearly, infants are more likely to die than mothers, and the causes of maternal mortality are very different from the causes of infant mortality.

Apparently the trend of decreasing mortality over time has been going on since records began to be kept in 1750. Balog (1976) traced the changes in mortality over the last two hundred years in the United States and found that there were no obvious dips in the rate after major medical advances, such as drugs and sterilization procedures. He concluded that changes in mortality rates reflect trends in general economic growth, a higher standard of living, and better education—in short, social and economic factors.

In the United States, even though mortality has fallen for both whites and nonwhites, nonwhite mortality remained almost ten years behind white mortality in 1986 (Information Please Almanac, 1987). A closer look at the causes of death shows that nonwhites tended to succumb to conditions that are indicative of poor prenatal care. Homicides, birth injuries, and congenital abnormalities were nearly the same in both groups. These categories have little to do with the quality of prenatal care, health, or nutrition. For all the other categories, whites fared more favorably. The most common causes of neonatal mortality among the poor in the United States and in the developing nations are respiratory problems and diarrhea. They derive from an inability of the immature system to cope with normal bacterial infections and physical insults, and they stem largely from deficits acquired prenatally. Studies have shown, for example, that adequate nutritional supplementation during pregnancy can cut the infant death rate by as much as half (Werner, 1979).

Nonwhite babies were most afflicted by respiratory problems. They also tended to be born more prematurely than whites. The evidence supports a socioeconomic difference between the two groups rather than a racial explanation.

Apparently malnutrition, poverty, and ill health act as a system: one feeds upon the other to worsen or maintain high death and disease rates. In many countries, people who cannot make a living on farms move into the cities to join an increasingly large inner-city poor population. They move into slums with poor sanitation; they have little food and no money. Urban employment places special burdens on the mother for travel away from home, and there are seldom adequate child-care facilities. Lack of energy from malnutrition contributes to the inability to cope with these enormous problems.

The prevention and elimination of these problems depend on intervention in the cycle of poverty and ill health. Community-based clinics providing medical care during pregnancy, simple disease screening procedures, immunizations, nutrition education, fertility advice, upgrading of parental competence, improved sanitation, and the effective management of diarrhea already are being implemented in many less developed countries (Puffer & Serrano, 1973; WHO, 1976).

Supplemental nutrition given to mothers has a greater effect on mortality than on infant birth weight. In a study done in Bogota, Colombia, supplemental food for malnourished mothers increased birth weight by only 77 grams but decreased the neonatal death rate from 42 per 1,000 to 23 per 1,000 births. Food availability for pregnant mothers in the Third World can be increased by higher contributions from rich nations, reducing pressures to use land for cash crops (such as coffee and cocoa) in order to allow local farmers to grow their own food, supporting local health care, and breast-feeding (Falkner, 1985).

The United Nations has developed and tested a successful health education program called GOBI, which stands for Growth charts, Oral rehydration, Breast-feeding, and Immunization (Werner, 1986). By comparing their own infant's development to standard growth charts, parents can detect failure-to-thrive. *Failure-to-thrive* is a condition in which infants fail to respond to the environment and continue to deteriorate even when intervention is available. Oral rehydration—providing fluids—is the primary treatment for infantile diarrhea. Breast-feeding provides adequate and sanitary nourishment as well as natural immunization (see the section on breast-feeding in this chapter). Immunization protects children from many infectious diseases.

An alternative explanation of the reduction in infant mortality is that it may be associated with a decreasing number of pregnancies a woman will have. In the 1700s, a woman might expect to carry ten to fifteen conceptions to term, and this would mean an increased probability of mortality for each infant. The age of the mother, the spacing between pregnancies, and the number of pregnancies all account for a portion of the risk of infant death.

Changes in socioeconomic conditions, even in the United States, can affect maternal and infant health. In inner-city Detroit, during the 1982 recession and the slowdown in the automobile industry, the infant death rate was the highest in the nation: 33 deaths per 1,000 live births (Michigan Department of Public Health, reported by Associated Press, 20 November 1982).

Age and sex are also important factors in determining the probability of death. The highest probability of death is when an infant is less than twenty-four hours old. In fact, if a baby survives beyond the first day, the odds of mortality are extremely low, about 1 per 1,000 or less. With regard to sex, males tend to have a higher death rate all through their life spans. More males are conceived, but more are miscarried or spontaneously aborted.

These raw statistics are sobering, but they do little to make us aware that each time an infant dies, the family feels a major loss. The next sections will try to give you insight into the human element behind the mortality tables.

How Does the Family Respond to the Death of an Infant?

The loss parents feel when a newborn dies may not be the same feeling as when an older child or some other close relative dies, but neonatal death can deeply affect parents. Unfortunately, society has failed to see the importance of neonatal death for the parents (Helmrath & Steinitz, 1978). If parents are not encouraged to successfully mourn the loss and deal with the painful feelings and memories, the incomplete bereavement may lead to disturbed perceptions and inappropriate behavior with later children (Drotar & Irvin, 1979).

The normal sequence of emotions parents experience after neonatal death is similar to other kinds of grief reactions. Upon hearing the news that their baby has died or will soon die, parents experience shock and denial. They think a mistake has been made and wonder if it can be corrected. The next phase is feelings of sadness and loss mixed with anger. This anger may be directed at others, such as the obstetrician, or it may be directed at themselves in the form of self-blame. Gradually, parents come to accept the death and readjust the reality to their lives. This can often take several years. Having healthy children later on helps this process, but parents continue to fear that something will go wrong with the next child and wonder what their lost child might have been like.

A number of practitioners have argued that the loss of the newborn should be treated like any other death in the family. As it turns out, many hospitals simply dispose of the body without allowing the parents any option to view it. Parents often are concerned about the actual disposition of the infant's body. They may have painful and frightening fantasies: Perhaps the infant did not

Medical checkups and nutrition during pregnancy have lowered the world-wide infant mortality rate, but even modern medicine cannot remove the painful feelings of loss that parents face following the death of an infant.

die naturally but was used for some strange experiment. Perhaps they have the child's body on display in a jar for medical students to look at. Was the infant cremated or just thrown away? As unlikely as these fantasies are, they are quite common among such parents. Even more surprising is that most obstetrics and pediatrics personnel know virtually nothing about what happens to an infant's body after death (Cohen et al., 1978).

In one experimental program (Cohen et al., 1978), parents are offered the option to view the body. If they elect to do this, a nurse brings the infant wrapped in a blanket. The blanket is tucked to hide any abnormalities. At the sight of the deceased infant, mothers are less afraid than expected. In all cases in this program, infants are given appropriate religious services and burials.

Between life and death there are some gray areas. Infants may be born viable but suffer from gross deformities or other conditions that would impair later functioning. The issues faced by parents and doctors in these situations are not unlike those faced by the families of persons in comas or with terminal and painful diseases or by those close to the elderly and infirm. *Euthanasia* is the act of causing a painless death or of letting someone die naturally without trying to prolong life with "heroic" medical procedures. As you can imagine, the idea of euthanasia cuts across some serious and difficult religious, ethical, legal, medical, and personal issues that are not easily resolved. With the advent of sophisticated neonatal intensive care, parents and pediatricians are facing these issues more and more (see "Applications: The Case of Baby Doe" in this chapter).

Some hospitals take photographs of sick infants at birth. Because parents are distressed to hear that their infant is ill and may die, the hospital photo may be the only one that is taken. Many states now have support groups for parents following perinatal death. For a list of such groups, see Estok and Lehman (1983). Similar grief reactions are seen in cases of miscarriage, especially in instances of repeated miscarriage, and in sudden infant death syndrome, in which death occurs unexpectedly between 1 and 6 months of age (see Chapter 6). In all cases, factual and frank discussions with medical personnel, the availability of the autopsy report, and funeral services all help the parents cope (Dyregrov & Matthiesen, 1987; Kotch & Cohen, 1986).

What are the attitudes and emotions of women following childbirth?

As with every other major event in life, we would expect childbirth to have a lasting impact on the individual and to be the source of a good deal of psychological adjustment in the days and weeks that follow. Westbrook (1987) asked women to remember their feelings during pregnancy, labor, during the hospital stay, and upon returning home. Of the two hundred women interviewed in Sydney, Australia, most reported high levels of positive feelings all the way through. In discussing their anxieties and worries, however, changes were noted depending on the stage in the process. For example, during pregnancy and labor, women experienced the highest levels of total anxiety, fears of death, and fears of mutilation. Most of these severe anxieties were reduced right after the birth.

One emotional change that can occur after birth is *postpartum blues*, which seem to occur in some form in about two-thirds of all women after childbirth

■ FAMILY AND SOCIETY

APPLICATIONS:

The Case of Baby Doe

On April 9, 1982, a baby was born in Bloomington, Indiana, who was given little chance to survive. The baby had Down's syndrome and multiple complications, such as a blocked esophagus and an enlarged heart. In this case, the physicians agreed that surgery would not be worth doing because it had a limited chance of success and it would only prolong the infant's life for a few weeks, increasing the suffering of both the infant and the family.

The medical decision, agreed upon by the parents, was to withhold treatment for the infant. Because of the infant's state of health, this decision was an act of euthanasia: making the infant comfortable and well-fed while waiting for an inevitable death.

This baby continued to live longer than the doctors expected, and the case caught the at-

tention of the county prosecutor, who charged the parents and physicians with criminal neglect. Two county judges agreed with the parent's decision, but the prosecutor eventually asked the Indiana Supreme Court to issue an order to provide treatment for the infant, who later became known as Baby Doe.

The issues in the Baby Doe case are similar to the issues in the abortion debate. On the one side are those who feel that newborns should have a constitutional right to treatment even without the consent of their parents, and on the other side are those who argue for the newborn's right to die peacefully in cases where the quality of life outweighs the preservation of life.

Because of Baby Doe and other similar cases, in 1984, the U.S. Senate amended the

(Yalom, 1968). These "blues" usually take the form of brief episodes of crying or mild depression that seem to begin and end suddenly and without warning. Postpartum blues should be distinguished from the more serious and infrequent occurrence of clinical postpartum depression.

In a sample of 129 women in Australia, only sixteen were severely depressed and only fifteen showed no mood changes following childbirth. The rest of the sample experienced one or more brief episodes of crying (Meares, Grimwalde, & Wood, 1976). In general, however, the moods of women after childbirth are relatively stable and positive (Murai, Murai, & Takahashi, 1978). After all, childbirth is, and should be, a rewarding and fulfilling experience for both mother and father. How childbirth is experienced, however, is dictated in large measure by the cultural beliefs of the society.

What are some cultural differences in childbirth and infant care practices?

Not all societies greet the event of birth in the same way. Some peoples consider it as an illness or an abnormality, whereas others view it as part of the fabric of everyday affairs. The Cuna of Panama consider birth to be a secret event. In the United States, birth is considered a private affair with only

APPLICATIONS:

Child Abuse and Prevention Act of 1974. The amendment states that "withholding of medically indicated treatment from disabled infants with life-threatening conditions" could be considered a form of child abuse and neglect. However, the amendment lists three exceptions to this rule, exceptions that specify when euthanasia is permitted:

1. The infant is chronically ill and irreversibly comatose.
2. The provision of such treatment would merely prolong dying and would not be effective in ameliorating or correcting the infant's life-threatening condition.
3. The provision of such treatment would be virtually futile in terms of the survival of the infant, and the treatment under such circumstances would be inhumane.

While many accepted this legislation, it was not endorsed by the American Medical Association because the amendment does not mention issues related to the quality of life. Suppose, for example, that the infant would survive with an appropriate medical intervention. The law clearly states that such an intervention must be provided. But what if the infants who survive are so deformed, sick, or handicapped that their lives would be ones of constant pain, discomfort, and severe restriction of movement? It is this quality-of-life issue that doctors would like to have the freedom to consider in making recommendations to parents.

The Baby Doe case raises important questions about how society is to decide what is in the best interests of children. Is life worth preserving at any cost? Is the best intervention in some cases not to intervene? How should quality of life and stress—emotional and financial—on the family be weighed in decisions about the rights of children? As our technology advances, we can do extraordinary things, such as save the life of an extremely fragile newborn. Unfortunately, individuals and governments are not able to cope with the complex ethical and legal issues that this technology raises.

---

medical personnel and a few family members in attendance. Some cultures on the extreme end of the isolation viewpoint consider birth to be defiling and insist that women give birth in a separate area, which often is reserved for such things as childbirth, menstruation, and excrement (Mead & Newton, 1967).

At the other extreme, the Jahara of South America give birth under a shelter in full view of everyone in the village—even small children—and a number of Pacific Island communities regard the birth of a child as an event of interest to the entire community.

To illustrate the cultural influences on childbirth and child care practices in the newborn period, a portrait of three cultures from widely different parts of the globe will be presented: a group of Zinancantecan Indians from Mexico, originally of Mayan descent, a village in the south of Italy, and the Japanese.

During labor among the Zinancantecans, no drugs are used. The mother is supported and encouraged by an ever-present midwife. After birth, the newborn is placed naked before a fire. The midwife is still in attendance and begins to say prayers asking the gods to look kindly upon this child. A long skirt made of heavy fabric is brought out and put on the infant. Extending beyond the feet, the skirt is worn by both males and females throughout the first year of life. For fear of losing parts of the soul, the newborn is wrapped snugly in several layers of blankets, and even the face is covered, except during feedings. This practice is believed to ward off evil spirits and illnesses during the first few months of life (Brazelton, 1977).

On the other side of the Atlantic, birth in a small village in southern Italy usually takes place in a hospital, attended by a midwife. Just after the birth, as in Mexico, the newborn is dressed in clothing and ceremonial linens the family has provided. When the infant is dressed and usually within about ten minutes of the birth, the midwife goes into the hall where the mother's entire immediate and extended family has been waiting. They all accompany the midwife back to the mother's room, where everyone takes a turn congratulating, kissing, and fondling both the mother and the baby.

The family then provides a party of pastries and liquors to share with one another and with those who attended the birth. During the labor, the mother was never left alone, and she will continue to be supported by rituals like this one. The mother will be visited by many of her friends and relatives for some time after the birth. These visits have the effect of recognizing the contribution the mother has made to the community. This social support system is embodied in the role of the mother-in-law; from a few days before until about one month after birth, she feeds the mother ritual foods of broth, marsala, and fresh cheeses. All mothers breast-feed their infants, and the infant usually sleeps in the same bed as the mother or in a nearby cradle (Schreiber, 1977).

Finally, in traditional Japanese society, interdependent relationships between people are viewed as extremely important. Children are valued and loved, and their development is celebrated by a number of community rituals. These rituals begin about the fifth month of pregnancy when the woman begins to wear a special belt (called an *iwata-obi*) around her abdomen under the kimono. This ritual is believed to establish the child's first tie to the community. After birth, the umbilical cord is dried and saved in an ornamental box, reminding the mother and child of their once close physical bond. From birth until late childhood, children sleep with their parents since it is believed that sleeping alone breaks the family psychological bonds.

On the day of birth and on the third and seventh day of life, elaborate feasts are celebrated among all the relatives. Since these three days were thought critical to the infant's survival, the feast insured health for the baby. A special naming ceremony is performed on the seventh day, and at one month, the baby is taken to the Shinto shrine for blessing. At the age of one-hundred days, the infant is given a grain of rice as its first token solid food (Kojima, 1986). Although some of these traditional practices are changing due to the urbanization of Japan, the basic commitment to the infant's value remains.

Newborn feeding practices

In the United States, breast-feeding was the general practice until the turn of the century. In 1900, only 38 percent of mothers breast-fed, and this declined until 1966, when only 18 percent were breast-feeding. The number of women breast-feeding took a major turn upward in the 1970s, so that by 1976, about half of all mothers were breast-feeding at the time of discharge from the hospital. The incidence of breast-feeding in the United States varies with class and education. In one study done in Boston, 70 percent of women

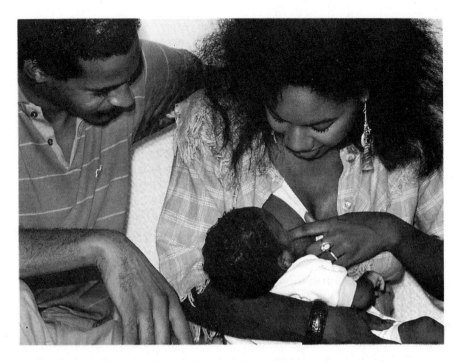

Breast-feeding can be a great source of pleasure for the mother and infant, especially in quiet family times. For some mothers, breast-feeding is inconvenient and difficult. Each family should choose the feeding option that best suits their lifestyle.

married to students, 40 percent of upper-class women, and 14 percent of lower-class women were breast-feeding (Guthrie, 1979).

The major factor for predicting success in breast-feeding is the desire of the mother to do so. The evidence suggests that mothers will automatically produce milk after birth. Milk will be produced even under conditions of maternal malnutrition. In such cases, the milk will be made in less quantity, but it will have the same nutrient quality as that of well-nourished mothers (Guthrie, 1979). This quality is usually maintained at the expense of the mother's reserve stores of nutrients.

Because breast-feeding is being encouraged as a way to prevent infant death in Third World countries, this presents a conflict for the mother who is undernourished. The World Health Organization recommends teaching mothers when and how to supplement the diets of breast-fed babies with foods prepared from locally available products (WHO, 1985).

Some women can even breast-feed without having given birth, as reports from around the world show. In one study of mothers who nursed adopted babies, the sample consisted of eighteen women who had never been pregnant, seven who had been pregnant but had never lactated, and forty who had previously lactated. All were able to nurse their adopted infants, and their success seemed to depend on factors such as the support of the husband and family, preparation by either hand pumping the breast or nursing another infant at least one month in advance, having an infant as young as possible, and nursing a great deal at first. Apparently sucking stimulation is more effective than hormone treatments in inducing lactation (Hormann, 1977).

Sucking stimulation can maintain the supply of breast milk even if the infant is feeding only once a day. This kind of minimal breast-feeding is often used by mothers who work outside the home, when weaning a baby from the breast, and using breast-feeding for "comfort" nursing for older infants. It is not necessary to mechanically express milk to maintain the supply during periods of minimal breast-feeding (Michaelson et al., 1988).

The nutritive demands of the lactating mother are far in excess of the demands made during prenatal life because of the accelerated weight gain of the infant just after birth. The milk secreted in just one month represents more calories than the net energy cost of pregnancy (Guthrie, 1979). This increased nutrient need can be met by the mother's eating the equivalent of an additional meal of five hundred kilocalories each day.

The composition of human milk differs from cow's milk, and human milk composition changes over the first few weeks of life (see Table 4.5).

Colostrum, the clear, yellowish liquid that is present in the first few days, is relatively high in protein. It also has enzymes that inhibit the growth of bacteria, microorganisms *(Lactobacillus bifidus)* that depress the growth of pathogens, and large "eating" cells (microphages) that protect against bacteria and some viruses (Guthrie, 1979). The higher composition of protein and calcium in cow's milk reflects the differential growth rate between calves and human infants: calves grow almost twice as fast.

To make cow's milk more similar in composition to human milk, most commercial infant formulas modify the cow's milk. The protein content is lowered, and the milk is treated to make it more easily digested. Butterfat is removed and replaced by vegetable oils. Lactose and other carbohydrates are added, and the calcium level is reduced. Finally, vitamins A, D, and C, and sometimes iron, are added to fortify the formula (Robinson, 1978). Today, formula and breast milk have the same nutrient values.

The effects of breast- and bottle-feeding on mother and infant

Because of the nutritional equivalence of breast milk and formula, there does not seem to be any reason to prefer one method over the other. Research has shown, however, that both breast- and bottle-feeding appear to have unique benefits as well as drawbacks. The choice of the best feeding method should be the result of careful consideration of these alternatives.

■ TABLE 4.5   Composition of Breast Milk Compared with Cow's Milk (per 100 milliliters of milk)

FACTOR	COLOSTRUM (1 TO 5 DAYS)	TRANSITIONAL (6 TO 10 DAYS)	MATURE	MATURE COW
Energy (kilocalories)	58.0	74.0	71.0	69.0
Fat (grams)	2.9	3.6	3.8	3.7
Lactose (grams)	5.3	6.6	7.0	4.8
Protein (grams)	2.3	1.6	1.2	3.3
Calcium (milligrams)	31.0	34.0	33.0	125.0
Casein (grams)	1.2	0.7	0.4	2.8

SOURCE: Adapted from Guthrie, 1979.

One advantage of breast-feeding is that it serves as a natural way to help mothers recover from childbirth. The sucking stimulation from the infant triggers the release of several maternal hormones, in particular oxytocin and prolactin. Oxytocin, as you may recall, is used as a drug to speed up contractions during labor. Oxytocin is essential following the third stage of labor since continued uterine contractions are necessary to shrink the uterus to normal size and prevent uterine hemorrhage. The oxytocin released from sucking does this naturally. If mothers do not breast-feed, they must be given oxytocin. Oxytocin also stimulates the breast to deliver milk only when sucking occurs and not otherwise. Prolactin stimulates the mammary glands to produce more milk.

There is some evidence that breast-feeding has a long-term effect on mothers, in particular the partial prevention of breast cancer. Women who breast-fed their firstborn infants longer than one month had a significantly lower risk of developing breast cancer, at least during the period before the onset of menopause (Byers et al., 1985; Siskind et al., 1989).

There are also health benefits to the infant. Mother's milk contains immunizing agents that protect against a variety of infections (Jelliffe & Jelliffe, 1988). The immunologic effect of human milk derives from the protein called secretory IgA, or SIgA. This protein coats the inner lining of the baby's intestines, acting to trap and kill harmful bacteria. SIgA also enters the lungs and breathing passages whenever the infant gurgles and blows milk bubbles and thus may protect against respiratory diseases. If a mother has a bacterial infection, her milk contains higher levels of SIgA that help to further protect the infant from catching the mother's infection (Pollitt et al., 1984).

Breast-feeding more than six months significantly reduces the risk of childhood cancer, especially lymphomas. Nonbreast-fed children are five times more likely to get lymphomas, a form of cancer that is higher in children with immune deficiencies (Smigel, 1988).

Behavioral differences between breast- and bottle-fed infants have been found. In a study of 100 healthy, full-term, vaginally delivered newborns, it was found that breast-fed infants are more irritably fussy than bottle-fed infants (DiPietro et al., 1987). This irritability, however, was associated with a more optimal physiological functioning, such as a slower heart rate, compared to bottle-fed infants. The higher irritability of breast-fed infants is not due to a less optimal mother-infant interaction. Some research has shown, on the contrary, that breast-fed infants get talked to, smiled at, and rocked more by their mothers (Dunn, 1975) during feeding, although no long-term behavioral differences have been found. Nor is the effect due to the fact that breast-fed babies get hungrier than bottle-fed infants (DiPietro et al., 1987).

Rather, DiPietro and associates propose that "the irritability of breast-fed neonates be regarded as the norm of neonatal behavior. Formula may have a depressant effect on behavior" (p. 472). This may be due to the differences in the specific types of proteins and sugars that constitute the two types of milk. If more irritability is the norm, these authors argue that it serves two purposes. The first is to enhance physiological functioning by giving the infant experience with varying degrees of arousal. The other is that crying may serve to stimulate more mother-infant interaction and provide more opportunities for feeding (Hunziker & Barr, 1986).

Taken together, the benefits of breast-feeding appear to be immunological and physiological, rather than behavioral or psychological. Since formula and drugs can nearly substitute for these effects, there seems to be little reason to choose one method of feeding over another.

In the end, the choice comes down to one of life-style and convenience. Mothers who work outside the home may need to opt for bottle-feeding. Personal preferences and cultural norms may also influence the process. Confidence in the natural versus medical approaches to uterine contractions and immunizations may further contribute to the decision. The lack of family resources may play an important role. In poor countries with little sanitation and contaminated water, bottle-feeding becomes a high-risk venture leading often to infant sickness and death (WHO, 1985). As in many other aspects of life, women in wealthy nations have more choices available than women in poor nations.

Finally, the wishes of other family members may play a role in the choice. Some fathers have feelings of jealousy, uselessness, and sexual frustration associated with their mates' breast-feeding. Some men may also experience feelings of ambivalence about the breast: who does it "belong" to? Who and what is it for? One study showed that these feelings can be alleviated somewhat by enhancing the father's participation in the birth experience and by improving father-mother communication on such issues as infant care and sexual fulfillment (Waletzky, 1979). ■

■ SUMMARY

The Childbirth Experience

■ Labor occurs in three stages: the opening of the cervix, the passage of the infant through the vagina, and the birth of the placenta.

■ About 16 percent of births are done by Caesarean section. There seem to be no ill effects of C-sections, compared to vaginal deliveries.

■ Drugs are used to speed labor and ease pain. Drugs can be safe if used sparingly. Short-term effects are common, but few long-term effects can be demonstrated.

■ Normal hospital childbirth was compared with a number of alternatives, including early discharge, Lamaze childbirth, upright postures, home births, and the Leboyer technique. These practices are all effective and safe for those who choose to use them, if they are implemented properly.

The Baby at Birth: Health and Risk

■ The newborn has unique physical characteristics, most of which disappear after a few weeks of life. These characteristics are the remnants of prenatal life and the effects of the birth process.

■ The art of newborn assessment is rapidly improving. Reliable and valid tests exist to determine the newborn's risk for survival, neurological problems, gestational age, and behavioral status.

■ Perinatal problems account for a large proportion of later deficits.

■ Prematurity is the largest single category of birth complication and seems to be caused by a variety of prenatal factors.

■ Premature infants are likely to be smaller, sicker, and behaviorally lagging, compared to full-term infants.

■ Long-term deficits occur mostly for very-low-birth-weight infants, under 1,500 grams. Most infants between 1,500 and 2,500 grams tend to recover eventually and lead normal lives.

■ The type of intervention that improves the long-term outcome for premature infants depends on the infant's gestational age and health. Medical interventions are improving and becoming less invasive. Behavioral procedures are extremely effective in improving health and weight gain at low cost. Parent education is also an effective strategy.

Perinatal Mortality

■ Poverty and disease are the biggest causes of infant mortality worldwide.

■ Supplemental maternal and infant nutrition, breast-feeding, growth monitoring, rehydration, and immunization can prevent many perinatal deaths.

■ Parents who lose an infant can be expected to grieve in the usual manner and thus should be helped through this process by medical personnel and family.

■ Euthanasia for newborns is a controversial topic that involves social, psychological, legal, and moral issues.

Family and Society

■ Most women adjust to the birth of their children rapidly and without long-term psychological effects.

■ Each society has its own unique way of welcoming newborns into the world. This involves a variety of rituals that ensure the health of the newborn and mother and carry a blessing for a happy life.

■ There are positive and negative aspects of both breast- and bottle-feeding. Each case must be examined individually to determine the best feeding method for the mother, the infant, and the family.

■ GLOSSARY

Analgesia   Pain-relieving drugs.

Anesthesia   Drugs used to mask the sensation of pain.

Apgar score   A screening test used to rate the infant's current health status and likelihood of crisis, rated at one and five minutes after birth.

Behavioral assessments   Tests used to measure the newborn's behavioral status, including reflexes, orientation to external stimuli, and state control.

Braxton-Hicks contractions   Also called false labor, these contractions serve to move the fetus into its prebirth position.

Breech presentation   The fetus is aligned with buttocks first against the cervix.

Catch-up growth   The higher rate of physical development seen in some cases of early deprivation or birth complications, compared to the normal growth rate.

Cervix   The membrane that separates the uterus from the vagina.

Caesarean section   Delivery of the fetus by making an incision in the mother's abdomen and uterus.

Colic   A condition of the infant in which distress persists without any detectable physical disorders, probably caused by gastrointestinal immaturity.

Colostrum   Clear, yellowish liquid that is secreted by the mother's breasts for several days after birth and before the onset of milk production.

Dendrites   Fibers that extend outward from nerve cells that enhance the connections to neighboring cells.

Euthanasia   Letting an individual die naturally without medical intervention, except to relieve pain.

Failure-to-thrive   The slow deterioration of an infant's condition and lack of responsiveness to intervention seen in cases of malnutrition and disease.

Fetal distress   A sudden loss of oxygen to the fetal brain caused by respiratory or heart problems or a restriction of the blood supply through the umbilical cord.

Fontanel   Spaces between the bones of the newborn's skull, which can be felt as soft spots on the scalp.

Gestational age   The age of the infant since the date of conception.

Homeostasis   The maintenance of biological functions within normal levels, for example, the regulation of body temperature.

Labor   Muscle contractions leading to the birth of the fetus and placenta.

Lamaze method   Pain relief during labor which uses breathing and relaxation techniques.

Leboyer method   An approach to delivery in which the newborn is kept warm in a water bath and under low levels of sound and light.

Meconium   The contents of the newborn's intestines; a greenish-black substance containing digested amniotic fluid and particles of hair and skin.

Multiparous   Mothers who have given birth more than once.

Myelinization   Protective coating over nerve conduction pathways that improves transmission of information.

Neonatal   The period immediately following birth.

Neurological assessment   Testing of newborn reflexes and postures to determine the intactness of the brain and nervous system.

Nonnutritive sucking   Sucking in the absence of fluids, including spontaneous sucking and sucking on a pacifier.

Normal physiological jaundice   A slight yellowing of the skin caused by immature functioning of the liver.

Perinatal   The period of about two weeks before and two weeks after birth.

Primiparous   A mother who is giving birth for the first time.

Postpartum blues   Sudden, transitory episodes of sadness or emotional lows, not related to pathological depression.

Screening assessment   Tests of newborn functioning used to predict the need for medical interventions.

Self-righting   The rapid behavioral and psychological development often seen in infants who are recovering from birth complications.

Toxemia   A disease of pregnancy associated with high blood pressure, swelling, and convulsions.

Vestibular-proprioceptive stimulation   The movement of the infant's body, usually accomplished by carrying and rocking.

FIVE

The Psychology of the Newborn

(THE FIRST TWO MONTHS)

─────

At birth, the baby must adapt to the physical changes needed to breathe air, to obtain nutrients orally, and to self-regulate body temperature. Birth also introduces a vast array of lights, sounds, touches, tastes, and smells that challenge the newborn's senses. What must the first taste of milk be like or the first look at a human face? Do these things have any meaning for the newborn infant?

From another perspective, birth is not a major developmental change for the infant. As we saw in Chapter 3, studies of preterm infants and ultrasound studies of fetuses show that many of the motor and perceptual systems of the newborn are already developed by thirty-six weeks gestational age. By this age or before, the fetus can suck, make movements like breathing and crying, has developed receptors and neural pathways for all the sensory systems, and has a distinct pattern of sleeping and waking states. So even though the newborn has never tasted milk, the infant has experienced the sensation of taste.

The abilities of the newborn infant have been the subject of a great many speculations and investigations by scholars. For thousands of years, philosophers have built theories of the human mind based on what is presumed to be acquired by experience and what is already endowed at birth. In the last 150 years, the sciences have taken up the investigation of newborn abilities, as psychologists, biologists, physicians, and nurses have tried to answer questions related to their own areas of interest.

Just in the past twenty years alone, the amount of information collected on the newborn would fill a small encyclopedia! Studies have been done on such diverse topics as treating newborn diseases, finding the best way to soothe a crying baby, understanding the development of sleeping and waking states, and the ability of the newborn to recognize his or her mother.

In the last chapter, we covered the physical features of the newborn and the initial adaptations to postnatal life. In this chapter, we cover some of the motor and behavioral abilities of the newborn and how they change over the next six or eight weeks. We'll look at some of the perceptual and cognitive aspects of newborn behavior and at the newborn's initial social interactions with adults. The issue of the role of early contact on the formation of attachment bonds will be covered in the "Applications" section. This chapter contains the first "Points of Contact" section, a regular feature of this and the following chapters, which describes some ways to enjoy the company of newborns and to provide them with developmentally appropriate stimulation.

■ PHYSICAL AND MOTOR DEVELOPMENT

States of Rest and Activity

During the fetal period, distinct periods of rest and activity begin to emerge at about 26 to 28 weeks gestational age. These primitive patterns of activity and quiescence change cyclically about once every 40 minutes. By 32 weeks, both rest and activity are more complex, divided into distinct states. As defined in Chapter 3, a state is an organized pattern of physical and physiological responding that is related to the infant's level of activation or arousal. At least two sleep states are present at 32 weeks, rapid eye movement sleep (called REM sleep or active sleep), and non-REM sleep (called NREM sleep or quiet sleep).

By 36 weeks or full-term gestational age, several other sleep states are present, including periodic sleep (a combination of REM and NREM sleep) and drowsiness (a transitional state between sleep and waking). These states are described in Table 5.1, along with the waking states of the normal full-term newborn infant.

Sleep States

How much time a newborn spends sleeping and when during the day or night that the baby sleeps are issues of great concern to parents. How much time does the typical baby sleep? A study of 100 newborns, with equal numbers of breast- and bottle-fed infants equally divided between boys and girls, found that newborns sleep an average of 16 to 17 hours per day, although this can vary between 11 and 21 hours (Parmelee et al., 1961).

Of course, this sleep does not occur as one continuous period. Sleep periods vary from 2 to 10 hours. For the first few weeks after birth, these periods can occur almost anytime during the 24-hour day, to the dismay of sleepless

■ TABLE 5.1   Newborn States of Arousal

STATE NAME	DESCRIPTION
Quiet sleep (NREM)	Respiration is regular, eyes are closed and not moving, and the baby is relatively motionless
Active sleep (REM)	Muscles are more tense than in quiet sleep, the eyes may be still or display REMs, breathing is irregular, and spontaneous startles, sucks, and body movements occur in rhythmic bursts
Drowsiness	Opening and closing of the eyes, increased activity, more rapid and regular breathing, and occasional smiling
Quiet alert	Eyes are open and the environment is being scanned, the body is still and respiration is more rapid than in sleep
Active alert	Awake with body and limb movements, although infants are less likely to attend to external stimulation and focus their eyes less often than in the quiet alert state
Crying	Elevated activity and respiration rate, cry vocalization, and facial expression of distress

parents. By 3 or 4 months of age, infants regularly sleep more at night than during the day, but night wakings are common thoughout infancy and early childhood (Kleitman, 1963). Changes in sleep patterns occur in part because sleep periods become longer and because they become synchronized with the day-night cycle.

If the average newborn sleeps 17 hours a day, what happens to the rest of the time? On the average, about 3 hours are spent in quiet alert, 2 hours in active alert, and 3 hours in crying. Of course, some babies are awake more than 3 hours and some less. Some babies cry for as much as 10 hours per day and others as little as one hour. Not much is known about the origins of these differences, but there is some evidence that they may be persistent, at least for several days or weeks (Colombo et al., 1989).

Waking States

Waking states are important for the processing of stimulation from the environment, processing that will lead to perceptual and cognitive development. Newborn infants have two basic modes of response to stimulation: orienting and defense. The *orienting response* is a heightened alertness of the individual that includes behavioral localization toward the source of the stimulation (a head turn to the source of a sound), changes in activation of the central nervous system (CNS), and changes in activation of the autonomic nervous system (ANS). A *defensive response* is a behavioral action that involves withdrawal from the source of stimulation and is characterized by CNS and ANS changes.

Changes in the CNS are typically measured by detecting electrical responses in the brain using event-related potentials, or ERPs (see Chapter 1).

Three newborn states:
Sleeping, alert inactivity,
and crying.

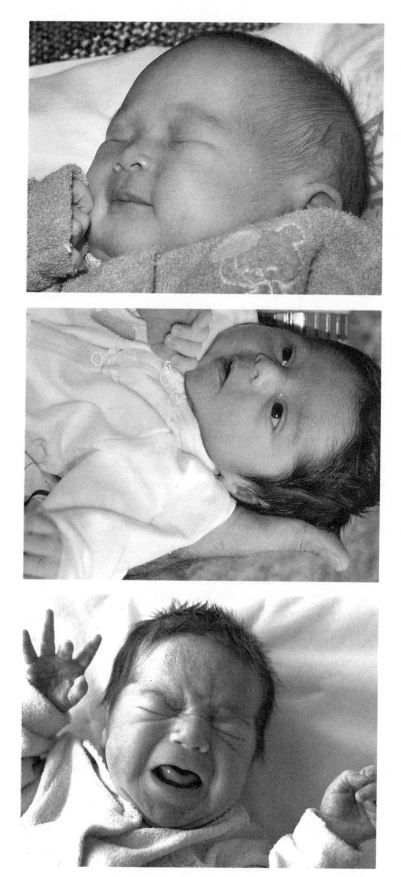

In preterm and full-term newborns, an increase of brain electrical activity shows a delay of between 0.5 and 0.8 seconds after the presentation of the stimulus, and the brain remains active for up to 1 second following the stimulus (Berg & Berg, 1987; Karrer et al., 1989). By 40 weeks gestational age (about one month old for a full-term infant), the ERP profile looks more adult-like. The initial orienting begins about 0.2 seconds after the stimulus and the processing phase occurs from about 0.3 to 0.5 seconds (see Figure 5.1). These findings suggest that newborns are able to orient toward and process information, but they are relatively slow.

Another indication of the newborn's orienting is from measures of the ANS, particularly changes in heart rate (see Chapter 1). It has been shown that heart rate deceleration is associated with orienting and attention, while heart rate acceleration is associated with defensive responses (Berg & Berg, 1987; Graham, Anthony, & Zeigler, 1984; Graham & Clifton, 1966).

Stimulation that is moderate in intensity will elicit decelerative orienting responses: soft talking, moderate light levels, holding and rocking can enhance alertness in the newborn. Stimulation that is intense and sharp produces defensive reactions. A sudden change in light level, a loud noise, a sudden change in body position will produce cardiac acceleration accompanied by a blink or a startle response. If the intense stimulus continues, newborns will turn away, grimace, or cry (Berg & Berg, 1987). Low-intensity stimulation, such as gentle rocking or whispering, may not produce any reaction in the newborn.

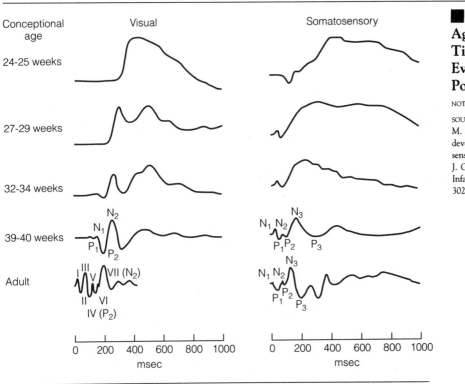

■ FIGURE 5.1
Age Changes in the Time Course of Event-Related Potentials

NOTE: msec = 1/1000 second

SOURCE: Berg, W. K. and Berg, K. M. Psychophysicological development in infancy; state, sensory function and attention. In J. Osofsky (ed.) Handbook on Infant Development, 1979, p. 302. New York: Wiley.

As infants develop, they seem to be able to orient to a wider range of both low- and high-intensity stimulation (Field, 1981b; Krafchuk, Tronick, & Clifton, 1983). It is as though the newborn were looking at the world through a very small window centered on the moderate range of stimulation. Developmental changes expand the size of the window to include both lower and higher intensities of stimulation so that the older infant is more sensitive to subtle cues and less sensitive to intensity (Berg, 1975).

How long or short the orienting or defensive response continues depends on the complexity and duration of the stimulus, rather than on its intensity. One type of experiment involves showing infants black-and-white checkerboard patterns of increasing complexity, starting with a 2-by-2-square checkerboard and going up to 32-by-32-square checkerboards. Newborns and one-month-olds show longer orientation to checkerboards with an intermediate complexity of 24-by-24 squares (Karmel & Maisel, 1975; Keen, 1974), suggesting that too much complexity can have a negative effect on orienting. Similar research has shown a preference among newborns for moderate complexity in patterns of lights or in sequences of musical tones (Clarkson & Berg, 1983; Turkewitz et al., 1972).

How long a baby orients to a stimulus will also depend on the baby's state. Transient orienting and defensive responses are more likely to occur in sleep and active alert states, while longer orienting and attention occur in quiet alert states lasting at least 10 minutes (Clifton & Nelson, 1976). Infants will also attend longer if they are being held upright or semireclining, compared to lying down (Gregg et al., 1976).

In summary, short-term orienting and defensive reactions can occur in any state, but longer orienting reactions require a waking state and an upright posture. Stimulation that is of moderate intensity and moderate complexity is the most conducive to sustained orienting. These results are summarized in Table 5.2.

■ TABLE 5.2   Factors Affecting Orienting and Defensive Reactions in the Newborn Infant

| | STIMULUS INTENSITY | |
	MODERATE	HIGH
Transient response	Eye opening, head turn	Startle, blink
	Heart rate deceleration Occurs in sleep and waking	Heart rate acceleration Occurs in sleep and waking
Sustained response	Continued orienting	Defensive withdrawal
	Heart rate deceleration Occurs in waking only	Heart rate acceleration Occurs in sleep and waking

SOURCES: Berg & Berg, 1987; Graham et al., 1984.

Developmental Change in States Is Related to Brain Development

During the first few months of life, infants become more tolerant of a wider range of stimulus intensity and complexity, and they are less likely to withdraw from potentially interesting sources of information. How does this developmental change occur? Recent research suggests that experience with moderately intense and moderately complex stimuli can have a profound effect on the development of the brain, which in turn allows for more sustained attention and less withdrawal.

To understand how this works, it is necessary to take a look at the structure of the neuron. *Neurons* are the information storage and transfer components of the central nervous system. The anatomy of the neuron is shown in Figure 5.2. Neurons code and transmit information in the form of electrochemical currents, called action potentials, that travel from the cell body along the axons to the axon terminals. Information is transmitted to the next cell at a junction called the *synapse* by chemicals called neurotransmitters. The

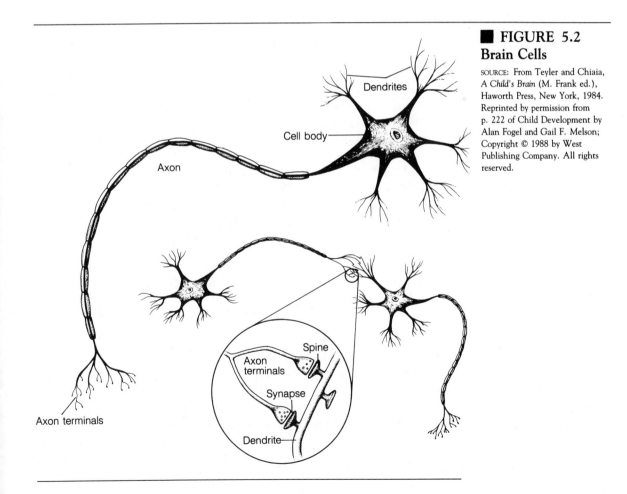

■ **FIGURE 5.2**
Brain Cells

SOURCE: From Teyler and Chiaia, *A Child's Brain* (M. Frank ed.), Haworth Press, New York, 1984. Reprinted by permission from p. 222 of Child Development by Alan Fogel and Gail F. Melson; Copyright © 1988 by West Publishing Company. All rights reserved.

synapse connects the axon terminals of the transmitting cell to the dendrites of the receiving cell, as shown in the figure.

The brain develops by four basic processes:

1. The creation of new cells via mitosis. This occurs almost entirely during the prenatal period of development.

2. The axons lengthen and the cells migrate to form distinctly different regions of the brain that are connected to different sensory systems. Brain development is from the inside out, as cells destined to become part of the visual cortex, for example, send out axons and connections that eventually meet the visual receptors in the optic nerve (Greenough et al., 1987). Neuronal growth and migration is guided by the glial cells, which are the structural cells in the brain that hold the neurons in their place. This process is usually completed by the seventh prenatal month.

In addition to lengthening, the axons also become more efficient conductors by developing a kind of insulation called *myelin.* Myelination improves the speed of information flow along the axon by a factor of about 3. Since myelination occurs most rapidly during the end of gestation and the first few postnatal months, we can better understand the results of the ERP studies (Figure 5.1). One-month-olds process information about three times faster than newborns.

3. The cells become more complex, growing more dendrites and axon terminals and making an increasing number of synaptic connections. By the age of 2 years, a single neuron may have as many as 10,000 different connections to other cells (Adinolfi, 1971). These new connections are thought responsible for the rapid behavioral and cognitive developments during the infancy period.

4. A final process of brain development is the specialization of cells and regions of cells. At the end of the prenatal period the human brain appears to have connections that allow newborns to perform their basic survival and adaptive functions: sucking, crying, states, reflexes, orienting and defensive reactions. These neuromotor pathways are called *experience expectant* pathways, because they seem to prepare the individual for surviving in a specific type of environment for which those behavioral skills are best adapted.

On the other hand, many areas of the brain at birth do not have a specialized function. Cells and synapses have developed prenatally whose only purpose seem to be to await the input of information that defines the particular individual's experiences. These cells and connections are called *experience dependent.* These cells respond to sensory experiences, and as particular sights and sounds are repeated in early development, specific synapses and cells are used more than others. The synapses that are used the most become strengthened, while those that are used the least eventually die (Greenough et al., 1987).

The developmental changes in numbers of synapses follow a similar course in each of the major areas of the cortex, the most advanced part of the brain that controls voluntary actions, including motor skills, perception, and emotion regulation. The number of synapses increases rapidly until birth and then decreases gradually, stabilizing at about the age of three years (Goldman-Rakic, 1987).

In summary, these changes in cell and synapse development show that the brain is highly dependent on experiences of the individual in order to develop. After birth, the brain's construction tailors its development to the experiences of its owner. These CNS developmental processes help us to understand how birth defects occur. Alcohol that the mother ingests during pregnancy limits the production of new axons and dendrites (Dow & Reoppelli, 1985), while lead exposure destroys myelin (Lampert & Schochet, 1968). These conditions limit the number of experience dependent connections and create slow information processing, making for a less adaptive, less intelligent individual.

These results, and others like them, demonstrate the systematic linkages between brain, experience, and behavior. And during the first few months, as infants experience stimuli of increasing intensity and complexity, connections favoring those types of stimuli will be strengthened. Ultimately, the window of sustained attention will widen. As sustained attention allows for the infant to inspect and explore specific stimuli, the brain will correspondingly create connections that make those specific events more easily recognized on subsequent occasions (Fischer, 1987; Goldman-Rakic, 1987; Hebb, 1949).

Developmental changes in the brain affect not only waking states but sleeping and crying as well. In the next section, we turn to an examination of crying and its development.

Crying State

Crying appears to be a highly organized behavior. Mothers have long noticed that infants have different kinds of cries that seem to be associated with different kinds of distress. Wolff (1966) found that cries have four phases: expiratory (exhaling, the actual creation of the cry sound), a rest period, an inspiratory period (inhaling), and another rest period. He found that the different types of infant cries could be distinguished on the basis of the length of each of these phases. Table 5.3 reports Wolff's findings.

One of the main features of the neonatal pain cry, for example, is an exceptionally long expiration followed by a long rest phase. It gives the listener the feeling that the baby has stopped breathing, and this long silence no doubt accounts for the salience of this cry to an adult. The pain cry also has a long expiration phase, much like the cry evoked when the infant is teased by having a pacifier pulled out of his or her mouth repeatedly. The

■ **TABLE 5.3   Properties of Neonatal Cries**

CRY PHASE	BASIC CRY	ANGRY CRY	PAIN CRY	BEING TEASED CRY
		TIME (IN SECONDS)		
Expiratory	0.62	0.69	3.83	2.67
Rest	0.08	0.20	3.99	0.07
Inspiratory	0.04	0.05	0.18	0.13
Rest	0.20	0.11	0.16	0.13

SOURCE: Wolff, 1966, pp. 202–204.

teased cry, however, does not have a long rest following expiration. These cry patterns repeat themselves over and over to form a crying bout.

Neonatal crying is symptomatic of a range of "normal" internal states, as we have seen, but it also may reflect a number of abnormal conditions. It has long been supposed that certain congenital disorders were associated with characteristic disturbances of the cry. The *cri du chat* syndrome is a serious neurological impairment that is associated with a cry that sounds much like that of a cat.

A series of studies reported by Lester and Zeskind (Lester, 1976; Lester & Zeskind, 1978; Zeskind & Lester, 1978, 1981) has examined variations in neonatal cry patterns under various conditions of mild to severe abnormalities. Cries were elicited by snapping a rubber band against the sole of the infant's foot. The cry sounds were recorded on a sound spectrograph. In general, infants with more complications required higher levels of stimulation to initiate the cry, took a longer time before they started to cry, had a shorter first cry expiration, cried less total time, and had cries of a higher pitch than infants with few or no complications.

The implications of these studies are several. Crying can be used by adults to "read" an infant's internal state, and it can be used by professionals to diagnose potential abnormalities. The studies by Zeskind and Lester showed that an abnormal cry is not always associated with a serious or permanent underlying abnormality. Such a cry merely may indicate that the infant was born under conditions of some stress. Many of the birth complications they studied had no lasting effects, and the cries later returned to normal. Crying, then, just like your grandmother could have told you, is a fairly reliable indicator of a newborn's degree of discomfort or stress.

Thus, there are general relationships that exist between crying and internal states suggesting that crying is an important avenue by which an infant's level of pain and discomfort can be made salient to an adult. This built-in communication mechanism is probably essential because the maintenance of waking states so crucial for the development of attention and the brain can only occur when the infant's distress has been reduced to tolerable levels. The wide range of physiological conditions among newborns also leads to a wide range of cry types and cry durations. How do these individual differences in infant crying affect adults?

The Effects of Crying on Adults

You might think that infants who cry a great deal or who have especially irritating cries are more at risk for insensitive or abusive parental treatment. This seems to be the case only when irritable crying is also associated with abnormal behavioral tendencies typical of infants with mental and motor perinatal defects and prematurity (Field et al., 1980) or when mothers have a preexisting negative attitude toward their infants that in part contributes to the high levels of infant distress (Crockenberg & Acredolo, 1983; Crockenberg & Smith, 1982).

Within the group of normally functioning infants, some can be classified as particularly *difficult* based on their irritability and responsiveness to adults. Infants who are rated by their parents as difficult in early infancy can remain difficult for periods up to several years, although the majority of infants rated as difficult early in life do not remain difficult for more than a few months (Lee & Bates, 1985; Swets-Gronert, 1984).

Research has shown that there are few consistent effects of difficultness on normal parent-infant relationships. Difficultness is not related to measures of maternal warmth or responsiveness (Bates et al., 1982; Daniels et al., 1984; Olson et al., 1984; Wachs & Gandour, 1981). Some studies have actually found increased maternal attention directed to infants rated as difficult (Bates et al., 1982; Pettit & Bates, 1984).

In the short-term, infant crying does affect adults in important ways. Adult women clearly perceive differences between basic cries and pain cries, whether they are mothers or not (Gustafson & Harris, 1990). These same women, however, when observed with an infant mannequin that emitted either a pain or a basic cry, showed no differences in their responses to each type of cry. Regardless of the type of cry, the women rocked, talked to, touched, held, distracted, and checked the diaper of the mannequin when asked to pretend to take care of it. They first tried actions to soothe the infant (such as holding and rocking) and later attempted to relieve the source of distress (by diapering or feeding). Even though cries were perceived as different, these women did not respond differently to the different types of cries, using the cry instead as a general indicator of infant distress.

Nonparents appear to be about as responsive to crying as parents (Zeskind, 1980), and generally equal levels of physiological arousal and responsiveness have been found for men and women (Frodi et al., 1978a). On the other hand, Frodi and Lamb (1980) found that child abusers had greater physiological arousal and expressed more annoyance at cries than nonabusers.

Other research has shown that particular aspects of the cry are more likely to affect how adults perceive the cry. Adults rate cries as urgent and irritable when the cries are of high pitch and of long duration, while cries are rated as signs of infant sickness if they are of variable pitch (Gustafson & Green, 1989; Zeskind & Marshall, 1988).

In summary, most adults find crying to be arousing, and they reliably can perceive differences between crying. Adults also respond to crying infants in an attempt to soothe the cry and relieve the source of the discomfort. Since most adults use similar means of trying to relieve infant distress, it is important to examine what research has shown about the effectiveness of these soothing techniques.

What Are the Best Ways to Soothe a Crying Baby?

Many calming techniques have been developed over the centuries of human existence: sucking, swaddling, rocking, and singing. Do they really work? Under what conditions does one technique work and not another?

Sucking on A Pacifier. Whether sucking pacifiers is harmful or beneficial is a question of practical concern to parents. Sucking on a pacifier, or nonnutritive sucking, occurs in many forms throughout the infancy period. If we count any incidence of nonnutritive sucking—on pacifiers, toys, fingers, thumbs, and adults' fingers—about 60 to 90 percent of all infants will do it. Nonnutritive sucking usually stops at the end of the first year of life. It may continue to occur, however, until four to seven years of age when a child is hungry, tired, or unhappy. A small proportion of children suck their thumbs until adolescence. In infants, thumb sucking appears primarily during sleep after the age of four months (Kessen et al., 1970).

It would appear from these statistics that nonnutritive sucking is not an unusual occurrence in infancy and early childhood. It may serve some important functions for the infant. We will deal with thumb sucking and the issue of self-calming and pacification in a later chapter. Here we will merely note that a number of hypotheses have been advanced about why newborn infants suck nonnutritively.

Pacification is one reason why infants suck. Sucking is an activity that immediately induces a state of calm in the infant, whether it is associated with nutritive intake or not. Another reason for nonnutritive sucking is that it feels good. This could come about because sucking is genetically associated with pleasure or because the infant develops a conditioned association between the sucking response and the pleasurable intake of nutrient. Sucking could have an inhibitory effect on other states or behavior. Regardless of the particular reason, nonnutritive sucking appears to be a spontaneous behavior that has some important benefits to the newborn and the older infant.

In a recent research study on infants at two weeks and two months of age (Campos, 1989), the effects of pacifiers on calming during routine medical exams was examined. At two weeks, the infants received a heel prick to draw blood, and at two months, they received an injection. Pacifiers were almost immediately effective in reducing crying and heart rate acceleration in response to the pain at both ages. A problem with the pacifier emerged, however, when it was removed or fell from the infant's mouth. In almost all cases, the infant returned immediately to the distress state. The only case in which the loss of a pacifier did not lead to distress is if the infant fell asleep before the pacifier was removed.

Swaddling. The same research study (Campos, 1989) also looked at the effects of swaddling at two weeks and at two months. Swaddling, or wrapping the infant in a blanket, tends to reduce motor movement and spontaneous startles. In this study, swaddling was less effective than the pacifier in reducing pain-elicited distress in two-week-olds, although it did lower their heart rate. Crying was reduced in 87 percent of the two-month-old infants. This may have been due to increased experience with swaddling for the older infants. If an infant did calm down when swaddled, he or she did not return to the distress state when the swaddling was removed. Thus, swaddling may be more effective than sucking for some infants since its effects continue after the baby is unwrapped, while infants who lose pacifiers may begin to cry all over again.

Massage is a technique related to swaddling in that the whole body is stimulated and its movements controlled. Massage, in addition to rocking and talking, has been shown to increase weight gain in premature infants (see Chapter 3), and it is used regularly in a variety of cultures, for example in India and in Guatemala. Unfortunately, there is no systematic research on the effects of massage on calming.

Rocking. The effects of *rocking* were studied in a group of thirty-six crying infants who were offered either vertical (on the adult's shoulder) or horizontal (supine) rocking to calm them. In general, rocking in any form helped calm the infants. The best form of rocking to calm a distressed infant turned out to be rocking intermittently (rather than continuously) in the vertical plane. The best form of rocking for putting the infant to sleep was continuous rocking in the horizontal plane (Byrne & Horowitz, 1979).

Sound. *Sound,* too, has a calming effect on the baby, but apparently not all types of sound work. Brackbill (1970) found that intermittent sound tended to increase infant arousal, whereas continuous sound led to an arousal decrease. In a later study, Brackbill (1975) explored the effects of varying the intensity of a continuous sound. She found that arousal decreased more when sound was presented continuously at eighty decibels (loud singing) than when presented at sixty decibels (normal singing). She also found that if the infant had experienced some stress—circumcised males in particular—the calming effect of continuous sound stimulation was even more pronounced.

Other studies have shown that the calming effect is more pronounced for lower frequencies of sound (one hundred to two hundred hertz) (Friedman & Jacobs, 1981; Hazelwood, 1977). A moderately low-pitched sound in the human vocal range is between one hundred and two hundred hertz. This also corresponds to the range of the octave below middle C. It appears, then, that the frequency range of a humming adult is appropriate for calming, whereas the high-pitched sounds of the voice can be used to alert the infant or attract his or her attention.

According to Brackbill (1971), the effects of continuous stimulation are not limited to sound: any stimulus that is continuous can work. Perhaps all the soothing techniques discussed derive their effectiveness from the property of continuity over time. Sucking, rocking, swaddling, and humming are all forms of continuous stimulation. Some evidence suggests that if more than one of these measures are applied, the effect is cumulative (Brackbill, 1971). There is also a wide range of individual differences. Some infants are better soothed by one method than another method, and some infants appear to be more easily consoled than others, regardless of the particular method used (Birns, Blank & Bridger, 1966).

Developmental changes also affect what best soothes the baby. While any kind of continuous auditory stimulation soothes in the first two months, the mother's voice is more effective by three months (Kopp, 1982). Visual stimulation becomes increasingly effective by three months, as does stimulation from objects to touch and hold (Kopp, 1982; Wolff, 1966).

In summary, state is important for the newborn infant for a number of reasons. First, the body needs periods of rest in order to consolidate resources for growth. Second, the infant's attention to the environment is dependent upon a state of quiet alertness. Finally, state regulates the types of interactions newborns have with their adult care givers.

Motor Coordinations of the Newborn: Reflexes

The basic rest-activity cycle that is characteristic of states is believed to originate in primitive areas of the brain that are responsible for autonomic activities, such as respiration, heart rate, body temperature, and sucking. This area of the brain is at the lower back of the head and is referred to variously as the brain stem, medulla, or hindbrain. At the next higher level, called the midbrain, which is located more or less in the very center of the head, such processes as attention, sleeping, waking, and elmination are regulated. At birth, these two areas are the most functional. Although all the cells of the external surface of the brain, the cortex, have developed, their connections with other cortical and subcortical (hindbrain and midbrain) regions are not yet developed.

Aside from state and temperature regulation, newborns also possess a variety of semiautomatic patterns of behavior—such as grasping, head turning, and sucking—that actually began to function prenatally. These semiautomatic behaviors are called reflexes. *Reflexes* are triggered only by specific elicitors, such as the presence of fluid in the mouth or an object in the palm, and they look about the same every time that they are triggered. Once triggered, a reflex must run its course without stopping.

The actual brain location that controls the reflexes is not known. They are presumed to originate in subcortical areas since they do not show evidence of any voluntary control. Voluntary control is shown when behavior can be adjusted, modified, or stopped to suit the demands of the environment. Voluntary control over behavior has its source in the cortex. The cortex also contains most of the sources of sensation, perception, language, and cognition and is considerably larger in humans than in other animals.

Reflexes associated with different parts of the body are listed in Table 5.4. Some of these reflexes reflect primitive forms of orienting behavior, including rooting, sucking, and grasping. Other ιreflexes are primitive defensive reactions, including the Moro reflex and the reaction to a cloth on the face or the head placed face down. Other reflexes seem to contain the elementary coordinations needed for later adaptive and voluntary movements. These include the stepping, standing, crawling, and swimmer's reflexes. Other reflexes do not seem to have a clear function, such as the Babinski reflex; however, the lack of a Babinski response may indicate neurological disorder.

In spite of the semiautomatic structure of reflexes, there is a wide variability in their display. In the same infant tested on different occasions, a reflex might be present at one time and not later. Some reflexes become more prominent in the days following birth, having been absent immediately after birth due to birth recovery processes. Some reflexes are easier to elicit in sleep states and others in waking states. There is also a difference in the strength and clarity of response between infants. After their cheeks are stroked to elicit rooting, one baby may barely turn his or her head to that side, while another may make a strong head turn, open the mouth, and begin to suck. Other factors that affect the strength and quality of a reflex response are age, time since last feeding, and the number of repeated attempts to evoke the reflex (Kessen et al., 1970; Prechtl, 1977).

These observations suggest that reflexes may be partly controlled by the cortex because they are more variable than the midbrain and hindbrain autonomic responses, such as sucking, breathing, and heart rate. Another explanation is that reflexes are only partly specified by neural circuitry. It is not only the brain that is developing, but the body as well. A reflex, or any behavior for that matter, could not happen without the particular muscles, bones, joints, and body proportions that are part of the baby's physical development. It may be that slowness to respond to stimulation is the result of poor motor coordination rather than slow brain processing.

■ TABLE 5.4   Newborn Reflexes

BODY PART	NAME	DESCRIPTION
Head and face	Head turning	Place baby face down on a mattress. Baby will turn head to side to free breathing passages.
	Rooting	Stroke baby's cheek gently near the mouth. Baby will turn head to the side that is being stroked.
	Sucking	Place a nipple-sized object in baby's mouth. Baby will start sucking movements.
	Defensive reaction	Cover the baby's nose and mouth with a cloth. Baby will turn head and move arms in an attempt to free breathing passages.
Arms	Tonic neck reflex	Turn the baby's head to one side or the other. The baby's arm will extend in the direction in which the head is turned, and the other arm will flex upward. This is also called the fencer's reflex.
	Moro reflex	Drop the baby's head slightly but abruptly. The baby's arms and legs will spread open and make an embracing movement, as if to grasp hold of something. This is a kind of startle reaction.
Hands	Palmer reflex	Lightly touch the baby's palm, and the fingers will clamp into a fist.
Torso	Swimmer's reflex	While baby is lying on its stomach, gently tap the back along the side and above the waist. The baby will twist its lower extremities toward the side that was touched.
	Crawling	Push against the soles of the baby's feet while the baby is lying on the stomach, and rudimentary crawling movements will result.
Legs	Standing reflex	Hold the baby gently under the arms while the feet touch a table. As you release support slowly, the baby will begin to show some resistance to the weight by stretching the muscles of the legs.
	Walking reflex	Hold the baby under the arms with the baby's feet touching a table and move the baby forward, keeping contact between table and feet. The baby will take "steps."
Feet	Plantar reflex	Similar to the Palmer reflex. The toes will curl inward when the instep is lightly touched.
	Babinski reflex	Gently stroke the outer side of the bottom of the baby's foot. The toes will curl outward like a fan.

SOURCE: Reprinted by permission from p. 133 of Child Development by Alan Fogel and Gail F. Melson; Copyright © 1988 by West Publishing Company. All rights reserved.

Each reflex has its own developmental course starting at different gestational ages. Some reflexes persist throughout life—such as startle and blinking—while others disappear in early infancy. Since the reflexes that disappear do so between three and six months of age, traditional explanations have assumed that the disappearance is the result of the development of the motor cortex, whose ability to regulate voluntary movement supresses the semiautomatic signals from the hindbrain (Firoentin, 1981; Illingworth, 1966; Molnar, 1978; Peiper, 1963). When adults receive damage to the motor cortex, some of these primtive reflexes reappear (Paulson & Gottlieb, 1968).

If motor and physical factors might account for the variability of expression of reflexes, could they also account for the developmental disappearance of reflexes? Thelen and her colleagues (1984) examined such factors in connection with the disappearance of the newborn stepping reflex.

Stepping is elicited in the newborn when an infant is held upright while the child's foot touches a flat surface gently. When the foot touches the surface, the newborn will pick up the foot by bending the leg at the knee in a kind of march-step movement. Remarkably, newborns do not pick up both legs at the same time: they alternate steps in the manner of later walking.

Thelen and colleagues found that stepping disappeared earlier in infants who had the most rapid weight gain. This could have happened either because the weight gain made the baby's legs too heavy to lift (a physical factor) or the gain was correlated with neurological development. Heavier babies might have more mature brains and thus more cortex to interfere with primitive reflexes (a neurological factor).

In a second experiment, the same researchers studied four-week-olds who could still step reflexively. They added weights to the babies' legs in an amount predicted to reflect the possible weight gain of the legs in the next few weeks. These weights practically eliminated stepping. In a third experiment, four-week-olds were tested for stepping while their legs were submerged under water and then again on dry land. The step rate was much higher underwater, again suggesting that weight and gravity contribute to the disappearance of stepping, rather than brain development alone. Thelen and associates (1981) also found that stepping movements could be seen in the form of kicking in any age infant when the infant was lying on his or her back.

In this experiment, it was not the effect of weight gain alone. Rather, the decline of stepping is the result of the fact that after birth, fat grows faster than muscle. This means that babies' legs simply became too heavy for them to lift on their own! Zelazo (1976) found that if babies were given stepping exercises every day, stepping did not disappear. This workout program may have built their tiny muscles to be capable of lifting more than those of the average baby of a particular age.

Asynchronous Growth

You shouldn't take these findings to mean that one-month-olds should go on diets, exercise their legs, and do weight training. First of all, the added stepping exercises did not make the babies walk any sooner than babies who did not receive the training (Zelazo, 1976). Second, there is a good reason why babies of this age need to grow fat rapidly: to keep warm and protect their muscles against shocks. Fat gain is kept at a minimum prenatally to make birth easier and because most of the fetal energy resources go into brain development. Muscles get stronger later in the first year.

This shows that infants do not grow "all at once." Different body regions grow faster at different times, that is, asynchronously. This is shown in Figure

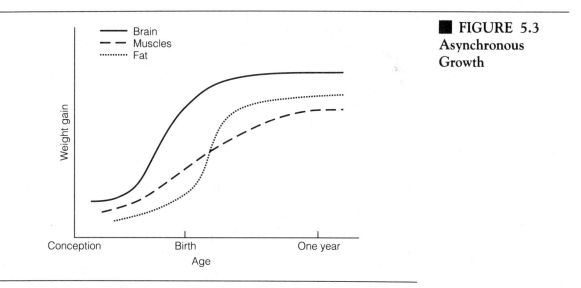

■ FIGURE 5.3
Asynchronous
Growth

5.3. Because physical growth relies on the body's ability to metabolize nutrients to create energy to support the growth, the body conserves its growth resources to at most a few domains at any one time.

What determines which areas should turn on their growth spurt and which ones should temporarily turn off? This is difficult to determine, but it may be genetically controlled in part. Human infants invest most of their fetal resources to develop the brain and perceptual systems. Because we can rely on the care of adults, we do not need strong and able muscles early in life. On the contrary, chimpanzees have to be strong enough to cling to their moving and swinging mothers from the day of birth. Their survival depends more on physical strength and speed than on reasoning, logic, and culture.

A comparison of chimpanzee and human newborns' scores on selected items of the Brazelton newborn assessment test (Table 5.5) confirms this

■ TABLE 5.5   Comparison of One-Month-Old Chimpanzees with One-Month-Old Humans on the Brazelton Newborn Assessment Scale

SCALE ITEM	CHIMPANZEE	HUMAN
Orientation—inanimate visual*	3.00	7.00
Orientation—inanimate auditory*	4.71	7.55
Orientation—animate visual*	5.28	7.33
Orientation—animate auditory*	4.14	7.77
Alertness	6.42	6.44
Cuddliness	4.42	5.55
Tremulousness*	0.71	4.11
Irritability*	6.71	3.44
Pull-to-sit*	8.28	5.44

*Represents items for which the differences between chimpanzees and humans are statistically significant.

SOURCE: Hallock et al., 1989.

(Hallock et al., 1989). Chimpanzees score about the same as human newborns on state control and alertness and higher on motor skills in the pull-to-sit task and on irritability. Human newborns score higher on orienting to stimuli and on tremulousness (tremors or shaking of the limbs), an index of motor immaturity.

Sucking

One reflex that is clearly part of the lower brain system is sucking, perhaps because of its crucial importance to survival. Sucking is an example of a reflex that begins prenatally and does not disappear. This, however, is a bit misleading since sucking becomes more voluntary and changes form and mode of expression in later infancy. Sucking is accomplished through the combined action of three sets of sucking pads: the lips, the gums, and the fat pads inside the cheeks. It is the gums—not the lips—that form a closed pressure seal around the nipple while the cheek pads prevent a collapse of the oral cavity from the negative pressure created (Kessen et al., 1970).

Sucking is a two-phase process. In the first phase, the lower jaw drops to create a *negative pressure* in the mouth. This method works because of the closed seal around the nipple formed by the gums. This method differs from that used by an adult, who creates negative pressure by breathing in. In the second phase of sucking, that of *milk expression*, the newborn's tongue presses the nipple against the hard palate while moving from the front to the back of the mouth. Finally, the swallowing reflex is triggered by the presence of fluid in the mouth. Apparently the newborn sucks and swallows in a single-action pattern in which the tongue moves in and out while the baby swallows. This explains why young infants have trouble eating solids and drinking from a cup: the pushing action of their tongues tends to expel more material from their mouths than they are able to successfully ingest. The ability to separate the expressing and swallowing movements does not occur until late in the first year.

Sucking, like crying, tends to occur in a rhythmic pattern. While the infant is actually sucking, there are usually about two sucks per second. Typically, infants suck in a burst-pause pattern: bursts of successive sucks separated by pauses between them. The bursts usually last from anywhere between five and twenty-four sucks. Like the other reflexes, the sucking rate depends primarily on the state of arousal rather than factors related to hunger. The amount of pausing is primarily determined by the milk flow. If the flow is too fast, pauses disappear and only occur again when the flow is reduced (see Figure 5.4). Pauses do not appear to be associated with fatigue, since infants seem to be able to suck without pausing for long periods under high milk-flow conditions (Kessen et al., 1970).

We discussed earlier in the chapter how nonnutritive sucking provided a source of pacification for the newborn infant. It would seem natural that infants under two months, who cry more than older infants, would use their own hands and fingers as sources of sucking stimulation. In fact, hand-to-mouth behavior is a relatively rare occurrence at this age, but it does happen under some conditions. For example, it occurs in newborns when the arms are

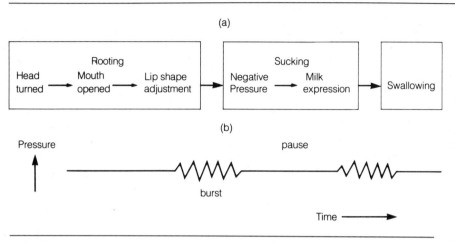

■ FIGURE 5.4
Organization of
Sucking Behavior

(a) Sequence of acts comprising sucking behavior, from initial orientation to the nipple until swallowing has occurred.
(b) Changes in sucking pressure with time, showing the characteristic "burst-pause" pattern.

flexed and the hands come near the mouth when the baby begins to cry (Hopkins et al., 1988), if the infant is given sweetened water when upset (Blass et al., 1989; Rochat et al., 1988), or if the infant's hand is held near the mouth by an adult (Fogel, 1985), as shown in Figure 5.5. Apparently, infants do not do this intentionally until about four months of age. Before then, the meeting of the hand and the mouth is a happy accident from which the infant can take temporary comfort (Fogel, 1985; Hopkins et al., 1988).

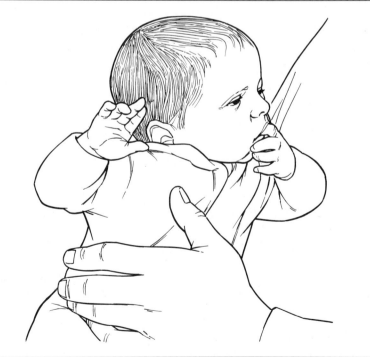

■ FIGURE 5.5
Hand-to-Mouth
Contact During
Distress at Two
Months

Hand is "found by accident" when baby turns head to the side. Hand cannot be pulled to midline for sucking.

SOURCE; Thelen, E. and Fogel, A. Towards an action-based theory of infant development. In J. Lockman and N. Hazen (eds.) *Action in a social context: perspectives on early development.* New York: Plenum, 1989, p. 51.

Summary of Physical and Motor Development

In many ways, the newborn infant is a highly organized individual. In a sense, we are more tightly organized and predictable as newborns than at any later time in life. These babies cycle regularly through a series of states of rest and activity. Although parents cannot predict exactly when a baby will wake up or fall asleep, they have a pretty good idea of how much their baby sleeps and how alert he or she can be and under what conditions.

Ethological theories suggest that the regularities of the newborn's behavior—states, state changes, and reflexes—can be explained by genetic programming in which the sources of these behaviors lie in precise locations in the brain. The argument is that the newborn needs to suck, cry, calm, sleep, and self-stimulate in order to survive and develop.

Dynamic systems theory, on the other hand, suggests that all behavior is the result of a complex interaction among a large number of related factors. We suggested that not even prenatal development is under the direct control of the genotype: a series of events in the environment of the cell and in the uterine environment of the mother must be present in order for a gene to express its message on the phenotype.

Similarly, whether we observe a strong or a weak reflex or no reflex at all is explained by a combination of factors, including whatever genetic codes exist for giving the newborn's body its particular structure, whether the baby has had time to unstretch its prenatally flexed arms, the rate of development of fat versus muscle, and whether or not the baby has something in its mouth at the moment.

While ethological theories predict that these combinations of events are already coordinated by some genetic program, both systems theory and cognitive theory predict that the baby is not really aware of making these things happen: they happen sometimes by chance. The baby then discovers that a particular combination of things works to solve an immediate problem. In some cases, the baby will recognize the value of this discovery and try to make it happen more often. In other cases, these combinations continue to occur by chance and eventually disappear. As we'll see in the next sections, perceptual and cognitive development show similar patterns of adaptability to current conditions and experiences.

■ PERCEPTUAL DEVELOPMENT

The sensory world of the newborn infant is not as sharply focused or as discriminating as that of the adult. Nevertheless, newborns have the ability to see, hear, taste, smell, and feel. There has been a great deal of research on the topic of the newborn's perceptual abilities, especially in the area of vision and audition. We'll review the research on all the senses. Following this, we will look at the newborn's cognitive skills. These include a variety of information processing abilities, learning, imitation, and memory.

The Visual World of the Newborn

Oculomotor skills refer to the movements that the eye must make in order to bring objects into focus, follow moving objects, and adjust for objects at different distances. The lens of the eye is responsible for bringing objects into focus on the retina. Visual *acuity* is a measure of the len's ability to focus on the retina, as well as the retina's ability to decode the light. A common measure of acuity is the Snellen chart, with the large letter E on the top and successively smaller letters below. An acuity rating of 20/20 is given to a person who can see a particular line on the chart clearly at 20 feet. A person with 20/50 vision is able to see at 20 feet with the same clarity as a person with 20/20 vision can see at 50 feet.

Newborns' visual acuity is tested by their ability to see stripes of decreasing thinness in comparison to an all-gray stimulus, using a pattern preference test (see Chapter 1). Although the estimates vary between studies, a newborn's visual acuity is between 20/300 and 20/800, with an average of about 20/500 (Aslin, 1987). This low level of visual acuity in newborns is not related to an inability of the lens to focus. Rather, it seems to be the result of the immaturity of the dendrites and axons of the neurons in the retina and optic nerve and the relative lack of myelination (Cohen et al., 1979; Salapatek & Banks, 1978). By six months, visual acuity improves to nearly 20/20 in most infants.

Another important oculomotor skill is the ability to track the path of moving objects. Newborns' tracking is a bit jerky, and they are able to follow only relatively slowly moving objects. More adult-like following begins between six and eight weeks (Aslin, 1981; Kremenitzer et al., 1979).

Scanning occurs as the eye traces a path across a visual stimulus. Since the eye cannot see an entire image all at once, it must make small, rapid movements to move from one point of fixation to the next. One-month-olds tend to scan small, localized regions of a figure, usually around its edges, while by three months, infants spend more time scanning finer details of a figure (see Figure 5.6).

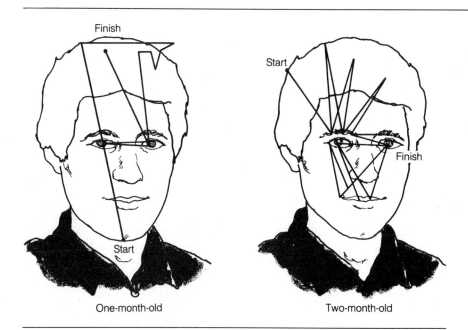

One-month-old   Two-month-old

■ **FIGURE 5.6**
Facial Scanning Patterns

The superimposed lines show where a baby will look at a face. One-month-olds look mostly around the outside, while older babies look at the inner details, especially at the eyes.

SOURCE: Reprinted by permission from p. 158 of Child Development by Alan Fogel and Gail F. Melson; Copyright © 1988 by West Publishing Company. All rights reserved.

A final aspect of oculomotor control is the ability to adjust the eyes to see objects at different distances. The ability to judge the relative distances between two objects and whether objects are close or far is called depth perception. The sensation of depth derives from the fact that each of our eyes sees something different. Try looking at an object nearby with one eye and then the other to see for yourself.

The comparison of the retinal images on each eye is called *stereopsis*. Experiments on stereopsis are done by presenting the infant with a visual image that can only be seen with both eyes. This is usually a display of dots that look random when seen with one eye but reveal a particular figure in a region of the field when seen with both eyes. Infants under two months were not able to perceive the figure, showing that they did not have stereopsis (Fox et al., 1980; Held et al., 1980). The ability to compare the differences between the two retinal images emerges slowly between three and six months.

Another way the eyes can work together to perceive depth is by moving toward each other (convergence) when objects approach and away from each other when objects recede (divergence). Again, infants under two months of age are not able consistently to converge or diverge as objects change their distances.

Thus, until about two to three months of age, infants have functional but limited oculomotor skills. However, in spite of these limitations, infants can use their vision in a variety of ways and may even be able to recognize visual patterns after repeated exposure.

Pattern vision refers to the ability to detect an overall pattern, to make sense out of an otherwise complex jumble of lines, depths, and colors. We know from a number of studies that newborns can detect differences between visual images and seem to prefer some images more than others. As we have already mentioned, by one month, infants prefer stimuli with moderate levels of intensity and complexity, as shown from studies of checkerboards with different numbers of squares. Researchers have also used vertical and horizontal lines of different thicknesses and densities.

Newborns also prefer to look at objects with clearly marked edges that are outlined in high-contrast black and white rather than shades of grey. They also seem to prefer circular patterns rather than straight lines (Fantz et al., 1975). Newborns like to look at the external contours of a figure, especially if the edges are sharp; their gaze tends to follow along these lines, and once on a line, they rarely break out to scan other regions of a figure (Haith, 1980; Maurer & Salapatek, 1976; Milewski, 1976).

These pattern preferences in newborns seem to match their relatively poor visual acuity, while allowing them to actively explore objects with their eyes. As we saw in the fetus, active sensory and motor exploration seems to be a form of self-stimulation that is necesasry to maintain continued development of the CNS and the associated motor skills. In this view, the patterns the newborn prefers are not necessarily meaningful: they merely serve to help the visual system develop at three months to a point at which the infant can see the world more clearly and pick out enough details to make meaningful distinctions, such as between a familiar and an unfamiliar person.

This perspective suggests that infants need experience with the perceptual world before they can make sense out of it. Starting with some simple preferences for physical features of a stimulus, the infant later comes to attach particular features with other sources of information. Thus the sounds, smells, and touches that an infant has come to understand as "mother" will only match up with the visual recognition of her at three months.

This view is similar to that of Piaget, who held that infants gradually build up representations of the world by means of repeated encounters, each compared with the others. In this way, the infant constructs perceptions by active engagement and experience.

An alternative view is that infants should have at least some meaningful forms of pattern perception at birth. Related to ethological theory, this view suggests that particular patterns are preferred because they have a meaningful survival value for the infant (J. J. Gibson, 1966). Thus, the curved lines and circles and the levels of complexity that infants seem to prefer are very similar to the curves, lines, and details of the human face. Some early research suggested that infants preferred faces to other visual stimuli, but once the stimuli were controlled for equal amounts of sharp outlines and circles, infants showed no preference for faces (Sherrod, 1979). Clear preference for faces emerges around two to three months of age (Maurer, 1985). Differences between facial expressions are not perceived until at least three months, and this ability improves gradually over the first year (Nelson, 1985). These findings are quite consistent with the developments in the oculomotor system discussed earlier and with the Piagetian constructivist view of perception.

Another area of pattern perception research in newborns has not led to such a clear preference for the Piagetian constructivist theory over Gibson's ethological perspective. This is the case of the visual perception of looming objects. A looming object is one that appears to approach on a direct collision course. A zooming object is one that appears to recede.

The Puzzling Case of Looming-Object Perception

Gibson's theory predicts that newborns ought to be able to perceive looming objects meaningfully, that is, the perception should be accompanied by appropriate defensive reactions of avoidance of the impending collision. Piaget's theory predicts that the looming object should be perceived as would any moving edge pattern but the infant would not interpret this image as a threat. We also know that newborns lack the stereopsis and the convergence necessary for accurate depth perception that might be required to detect a looming object.

The research on looming perception is a good example of how experimental evidence complements theoretical prediction and ultimately leads to the formulation of new questions. When looming was first studied in the late 1800s, it was found that infants under two months did not blink at the approach of the looming objects. This failure to blink was interpreted as a lack of response to the object. Later studies did not measure blinking but found what appeared to be an organized defensive reaction using behavioral measures, including widening of the eyes, raising the arms, and moving the head backwards (Ball & Tronick, 1971; Bower et al., 1971). These studies suggested that there is an innate defensive reaction to looming (see Figure 5.7).

A series of studies by Yonas and others (Yonas et al., 1977; Yonas et al., 1979; Yonas et al., 1980) repeated the looming experiments in more detail.

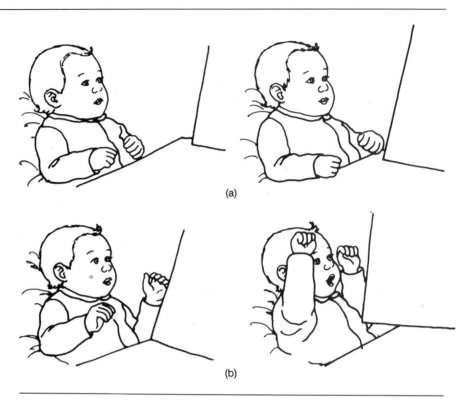

(a)

(b)

They studied infants at both one and three months of age, they showed the infants both looming and zooming stimuli to compare the responses, and they used not only body movements but eye blinks as well. They found blinking at three but not at one month.

They did find that one-month-olds moved their heads backwards and lifted up their arms in the looming situation; however, they offered an alternative interpretation. Assume that the one-month-old does not perceive the object meaningfully as on a collision course and that there is no depth perception. All the one-month-old can do is look preferentially at strongly contrasted outlines. Now imagine looking at a looming object if all you can see and understand is its outline. What you see is a square (if that's the shape of the object) getting larger and larger. In addition, since the newborn focuses only on one part of a stimulus, he or she is likely to scan just the top edge of the square. As the square expands, the top edge gets longer, but it also gets higher in the visual field. In order to keep watching this attractive-looking edge, the baby has to tip his or her head up. At some point, the baby loses motor control over the head and it falls backward, bringing the arms up with it.

To further test this hypothesis, the Yonas group presented a looming object that moved on a trajectory such that the top edge remained at the same height in the visual field. In this situation, the infants did not move their heads backward. They concluded that newborn infants do not have an organized defensive reaction based on vision.

A final contribution to this literature comes from a study by Nanez (1988). He also measured blinks and body movements, zooming and looming objects, with one-month-old infants. Furthermore, Nanez measured when the blinking and head movement occurred in relation to how close the object appeared to be on the screen. He also measured at what part of the screen the baby looked, for example, at the top edge of the object or elsewhere. In addition to a zooming and looming object, this study also had a zooming and looming window of the same size. The object was created by a rear-screen projection display of a dark shape expanding on a light background. The window was created by a light shape expanding on a dark background. If the response is a true defensive reaction, infants should respond only in the object and not in the window condition.

This in fact happened. In the object condition, the infants moved their heads backward at the same speed at which the object approached. They blinked, but just immediately prior to the anticipated collision, which may be why others have not noticed blinking in one-month-olds. In addition, even though the infants' heads moved backwards, they were actually focused on the center of the visual display and not on the upper edge. None of these reactions occurred in the window condition.

Finally, to control for possible differences in the amount of light intensity in the object and window displays, infants were tested for differences in response to changes in screen illumination without a loom or a zoom (the screen went from light to dark and from dark to light). Infants blinked more when the screen went from dark to light, and no head movements occurred in either illumination condition. In terms of blinking, this is just the opposite of the infants' response to the increase of illumination in the window condition, at which they did not blink.

These results strongly support the view that the infants perceive looming meaningfully as impending collision. The author suggests that the Yonas findings may be flawed because in order to record on videotape the infant's head movements and blinking, they had to shine a spotlight on the infant, which may have impaired the infant's ability to see the screen. In the Nanez study, low room-light levels were used with a highly sensitive low-light video camera.

The details of this research on looming objects reveal the complexities of doing research on young infants and the creativity of scientists in designing new experiments that delve into issues raised by previous studies. Other issues still remain, however. Even if we may be convinced that there is a meaningful defensive reaction to looming objects, how can we explain the apparent lack of meaning that the newborn attaches to the face and to facial expressions?

It could be that only some visual patterns are innately meaningful, while others must be constructed by experiences in the world. Perhaps those that are innately meaningful are those that are the most immediately threatening for survival. From a systems perspective, however, we must remember that vision is only one sense modality. Research on auditory perception and olfactory (smell) perception shows that infants can distinguish human sounds and smells and can use sound and smell to recognize their mothers almost immediately after birth. Thus, even though vision is relatively slow to develop, meaning may be found in other senses that develop at an earlier age.

Auditory Perception

We will not go into the same detail about the other senses as we did about vision, because there is considerably more research on visual perception and the studies illustrate the more general developmental theories that are important for you to understand. Thus, we report the main findings in these areas. You can be sure, however, that in any area of perception research, there are many controversies that are still unresolved due to the inherent difficulty of the work.

Auditory perception does not require the same motor components as vision. Thus, developments in the sensitivity of the ears are likely to depend on the maturation of the auditory nerve and the components of the ear's anatomy. These factors appear to be more mature at birth than those associated with vision. The auditory nerve is almost completely myelinated, and the bones of the middle ear are almost adult size at birth. After birth, most development occurs in the expansion of the auditory canal and the ear drum and the articulation of the auditory cortex in the brain. These processes reach adult levels by about one year, which is the same time that speech begins (Eilers & Gavin, 1981).

Auditory Sensitivity. There are two basic aspects of sensitivity to sounds: loudness and pitch. Loudness is usually measured in decibels (dB). Loud thunder is about 120 dB, 70 dB is a noisy street corner, 60 dB is a normal conversation, and 40 dB is a whisper. Pitch is the frequency of the sound wave and is usually measured in hertz (Hz). One Hz is one cycle per second. A high C note on a piano is 3951.07 Hz, and the low C note is 65.41 Hz. This range of notes also corresponds to the frequency range of the human voice.

How loud does a sound have to be before a baby can hear it? Sensitivity to sounds is measured by either a change in heart rate, a blink response, a head turn, ERP recordings, or using a conditioned head turning or conditioned sucking procedure (see Chapter 1). The softest sounds a newborn baby can hear are in the range of 40 dB to 60 dB (Berg & Berg, 1979), although sounds from 50 dB to 70 dB are necessary to awaken a sleeping infant (Wedenberg, 1956). In general, the research shows that while most adults can hear sounds as low as 0 dB to 5 dB, the most sensitive newborn cannot hear below about 20 dB (Schulman-Galambos & Galambos, 1979), although this improves over the first year.

This research is complicated by the fact that the ability to detect a sound of a particular level of loudness depends on the frequency of the sound and also the duration of the sound. For example, infants seem to be unable to detect sounds of short duration. A sound needs to be at least twenty seconds long, or if it is short, it should be repeated very frequently for a baby to orient toward the sound (Clarkson, 1989; Muir & Field, 1979). Babies are more sensitive to sounds in the middle range of the piano's notes, although they tend to prefer higher to lower pitched sounds (Kessen et al., 1970). Finally, babies prefer sounds made up of more than one note, a sound made up of a wide band of frequencies (Eisenberg, 1976).

If we put together all the characteristics of sounds that are most easily heard, and in fact preferred by newborns, the most common source of such sounds is an adult female voice either talking or singing. Although newborns are sensitive to a wide range of sounds and will orient to men who raise the pitch of their voice, researchers have speculated that prenatal experience with the sound of the mother's voice may have attuned infants to sounds of that level of loudness and mixture of pitches. In addition, it has been hypothesized that newborns recognize their own mothers' voices from those of other adult females.

Recognition of Mother's Voice. We saw in Chapter 3 on prenatal development that newborns preferred to listen to a song or story that their mothers sang or read aloud two weeks prior to birth compared to a song they had not heard and that newborns seem to prefer heartbeat sounds similar to those they must have heard prenatally. Other research seems to support the view that infants can distinguish their own mothers' voices from those of other women.

Recall the study described in Chapter 1 in which newborn infants recognized their own mother's voice compared to the voice of an unfamiliar female. The striking thing about this study is that all the infants were reared in the hospital nursery between birth and the time of testing one day later, and they therefore had minimal contact with their mother's voice, at least outside the womb. It is not clear what such a discovery means. Although it could be interpreted as a precursor to later mother-infant attachment, it also could reflect a conditioned response to a prenatal association between infant activity and maternal speech sounds. In any case, newborns are already on the path to developing a special tie to their mothers.

Recognition of Speech Sounds. If newborns recognize their mother's voice, and they can distinguish between different songs and stories that they heard prenatally, how do they accomplish this? They might detect overall patterns of rhythm and pitch that differentiate one person from another. In addition, infants might be able to hear differences among syllables that give them cues about a speaker's uniqueness.

A now classic study by Eimas and colleagues (1971) found that one-month-olds could distinguish between two very closely related speech sounds: "p" having the sound "puh", and "b" having the sound "buh." By two months, babies can recognize not only consonant differences but also vowel differences in sounds (Kuhl, 1981; Swoboda et al., 1978). Finally, Fifer (1987) found that two-day-old infants preferred their mothers' voices over those of other women even when the infants heard the adults speaking only a single syllable.

It seems that newborns not only recognize the broad category of speech compared to nonspeech and mother compared to nonmother, they can also distinguish between some of the finer aspects of speech sounds. These results suggest that there is a unique match between the infant's auditory capabilities and the types of sounds adults make when speaking.

Ethological theory suggests that this match is genetically based and may be necessary to ensure the survival of the human newborn who is totally dependent on adults. We also learned earlier in this chapter that adults are especially sensitive to the newborn's cry sounds. This combination of mutual sensitivities sets the stage for more complex parent-infant interactions as we'll see later in this chapter.

On the other hand, learning theory suggests that the newborn constructs a preference for human voices as a result of hearing these voices prenatally. This early exposure to sound shapes the development of the auditory components of the CNS and predisposes the infant to similar sounds in the future. It may be that the reason newborns can recognize their mothers by sound, but not by sight, is that they had no prenatal exposure to patterned visual stimulation.

Taste, Smell, and Touch

Taste perception has been studied using ANS measures, such as heart rate and respiration, brain ERP, body movement, changes in facial expression, sucking and tongue movements. Newborns appear to be able to distinguish the four basic tastes: sweet, salt, sour, and bitter. Babies clearly prefer sweet tastes to all the others.

We saw earlier how a sweet solution helped to calm a crying baby. Infants will consume more of a sweeter solution than a less sweet one, although they will stop sucking if the solution gets too sweet (Crook, 1978; Desor et al., 1973). Sweet fluids seem to relax infants, as shown by the sequence of facial actions in Figure 5.8. At first, babies show a negative expression, followed by relaxation and sucking (Rosenstein & Oster, 1988; Steiner, 1973).

In response to sour and bitter tastes, newborns show more consistently negative expressions, especially upper lip raising (as in disgust) and nose wrinkling. They also become more restless and stop sucking (Rosenstein & Oster, 1988; Steiner, 1973). Crook (1978) found that newborns do not like salty solutions. They will suck less the more salty the solution. Rosenstein & Oster (1988) found similar negative facial expressions for salt as for bitter and sour. However, other studies (Beauchamp & Maller, 1977; Desor et al., 1975) failed to find variations in sucking rates in relation to the saltiness of the solution. Sensitivity to saltiness may develop slowly over the first two years of life (Beauchamp et al., 1986).

Research on odor sensitivity has been done in ways similar to that of taste. Some of the same facial expressions have been seen in response to smells as described above for tastes (Steiner, 1977). Lipsitt and others (1963) found that newborns could differentiate between such odors as vinegar, licorice, and alcohol. In response to unpleasant odors, newborns will make disgust-like faces. They will turn away from unpleasant odors and turn towards pleasant ones.

Odors may be another way, besides sound, that infants recognize their mothers. Infants older than six days tend to turn their heads more often to a pad containing their own mother's breast milk than to a pad containing the milk of another woman (MacFarlane, 1975). In a study using similar methodology, breast-fed infants were able to recognize pads containing their own mother's underarm odor compared to pads worn by unfamiliar women, although bottle-fed babies showed no evidence of recognition (Cernoch & Porter, 1985). These differences between breast- and bottle-fed infants are probably due to the fact that breast-fed babies spend a longer time in direct contact with their mothers' bare skin than bottle-fed babies.

Interestingly, new mothers—whether their deliveries were vaginal or Caesarean—were able to recognize their own infant's odors (Porter et al., 1983; Russell et al., 1983). Similar to what we found for auditory perception,

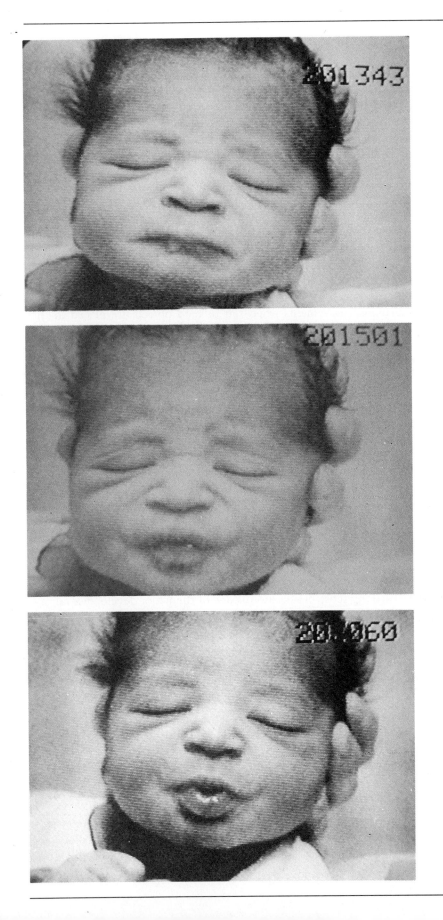

■ **FIGURE 5.8**
Facial Expressions Elicited by the Sweet Solution

Initial negative facial actions are followed by relaxation and sucking.

SOURCE: Rosenstein, D. & Oster, H., *Child Development*, 1988.

there seems to be a mutual olfactory (odor) sensitivity between infants and mothers. Thus, infants and mothers have a number of alternative and complementary channels of communication that ensure the beginnings of an emotional bond.

Olfactory and taste responses are probably not mediated by the cortex at this age. Both normal infants and deformed infants born without a cortex were able to detect odors and tastes (Steiner, 1977). This suggests that these perceptions are linked to the midbrain and hindbrain survival functions related to sucking and feeding.

Finally, newborn infants seem highly sensitive to tactile stimulation. The presence of the newborn reflexes bears witness to this fact. In addition, researchers have found changes in behavior and heart rate when infants are stimulated with touch or with an air puff to various regions of the body (Bell & Costello, 1964; Rose et al., 1976). Infants' mouths and hands are especially sensitive, and even in the first few weeks of life, they make different kinds of hand and mouth movements when soft or hard objects are placed in their hands or mouths (Rochat, 1987). Although is is possible that infants use touch to recognize their mothers, no studies have been done on this topic.

Newborns also appear to feel pain. In response to normal medical procedures, such as injections and circumcision, infants show increased distress and may exhibit disturbances of sleep for the next few days (Emde et al., 1976). The sensitivity to painful stimulation increases during the first week of life (Lipsitt & Levy, 1959).

In summary, infants are able to perceive with all their senses, and their sensitivity improves rapidly over the first few weeks and months of life. Certainly this improvement is due in part to changes in the brain. On the other hand, the changes in the brain depend closely on the kinds of experiences the infant has during this period. There is also evidence that newborns recognize some forms of stimulation as meaningful, that is, they associate the stimulation with adaptive behavior: they seem to defend against looming objects, and they cry in response to pain. It is also true that many forms of stimulation have no particular meaning for the infant: a face may be perceived simply as a series of lines, a melody as a sequence of sounds. The process of making sense of sensation is one of the major developmental tasks of infancy, and we shouldn't expect infants to come into the world with an understanding of more than a few simple things. In the next section, we take up the issue of the newborn's ability to understand, learn, and feel.

■ COGNITIVE DEVELOPMENT

Although newborns have not yet acquired the capacity for deliberate thought, they possess a number of ways to process information that are collectively referred to as cognition. These processes include learning and memory, orienting and habituation, and imitation.

Can Newborns Learn?

The answer to this question is clearly yes. We have already reported that in late pregnancy, the fetus seems capable of learning sound patterns and voices well enough to distinguish between them after birth. This means the fetuses learned not only to distinguish the sounds, but also they remembered the differences when heard weeks later, after they were born.

However, newborns have important limitations on their learning ability. Perhaps a better way to ask the question of whether newborns can learn is to ask under what conditions they are most likely to learn.

In spite of a great deal of effort, it has been very difficult to demonstrate classical conditioning in newborns, that is, the learning of an association between an unconditioned stimulus and a conditioned stimulus (see Chapter 2 for a review of learning theory). In one of the few convincing demonstrations of classical conditioning, researchers used the unconditioned response of rooting and sucking to the unconditioned stimulus (UCS) of a sweet fluid in the mouth. The presentation of the sweet fluid was paired during training with a light stroking of the infant's head (the conditioned stimulus, or CS). After training, the infants rooted and sucked to the stroking stimulus in the absence of the sweet fluid. In addition, when the sweet fluid was removed entirely, the babies rooted and sucked to the stroking, but they also cried showing that they had learned a connection between the stroking (CS) and the sweet taste (UCS) (Blass, Ganchrow & Steiner, 1984). Classical conditioning may be possible when the UCS evokes a powerfully rewarding natural response.

Operant conditioning is much easier to demonstrate in the newborn. Indeed, operant conditioning is so reliable that it is the basis for one of the more common infant perception tests. Recall that the conditioned sucking procedure (Chapter 1) involves conditioning infants to alter their sucking rate in the presence of particular sounds or pictures (DeCasper & Fifer, 1980) or syllables (Jusczyk, 1985). Head turning can also be conditioned successfully (Papousek, 1967). Once the infants learn the connection between their behavior and the reinforcement, they can signal their preferences with the "correct" sucking rate or head turn direction.

These studies of operant conditioning clearly show that newborns can remember the link between their behavior and its consequence long enough to complete the experiment on that day. Suppose, however, that you trained a week-old infant to suck for the sound of her mother's voice by increasing her sucking rate. Now, if you bring the same baby back to the laboratory on the following day and put her in the experimental setting with no further training, will she remember the training and begin to suck at a fast rate?

This kind of procedure is the basis for most studies searching for infant memories that last longer than twenty-four hours. Do babies under two months of age remember what they learned twenty-four hours ago? It is very likely that they may remember under certain conditions, although not enough research has been done on this age group. Babies of this age seem to remember the sound of their mother's voice and some of her characteristic odors. When a group of mothers was asked to repeat the same word sixty times a day each day to their babies who were between two and four weeks of age, the infants recognized the word after delays of between fifteen and forty-two hours (Ungerer et al., 1978). Perhaps the key to establishing a long-term memory in the newborn is a great deal of repetition, rather than a single exposure. In the next chapter, we'll review research showing that by three months of age, infants can remember things, even from brief exposures, up to two weeks later.

Habituation

Another form of infant learning and short-term memory is habituation. Like conditioned sucking, habituation is a reliable response that is used as the basis of a number of infant testing procedures (see Chapter 1). Recall that habituation is the gradual decline in the strength of a response following repeated presentations of the same stimulus. For example, if you live on a noisy street, you eventually habituate to the noise, that is, you no longer notice it on a regular basis. If some new element is added to the noise, for example, a siren or the screech of brakes, this is enough to renew your interest in the street noise. This renewal of interest is called dishabituation.

Researchers have found evidence of habituation in motor and heart rate responses in newborns to auditory stimuli (Zelazo et al., 1984), visual stimuli (Slater et al., 1984) and tactile stimuli (Kisilevsky & Muir, 1984). In addition, habituation can be shown in premature newborns (Field et al., 1979). In one study, infants born without a brain cortex (anencephalic) did not habituate to noise (Brackbill, 1971), while other studies have found heart rate response habituation to an auditory stimulus in such infants (Graham et al., 1978).

In summary, studies of learning and habituation in newborns show that some simple forms of learning take place at preterm gestational ages and continue until about two months of age. These rudimentary learning abilities may be mediated by the cortex, but they also could be built into the lower structures of the brain as basic survival mechanisms.

Clearly some simple learning is fundamental to the survival of newborns. The recognition of maternal sounds and smells orients the newborns to their primary resource for survival. Learning how to orient to and approach sources of food (sweet fluids and milk) and how to avoid noxious smells and tastes on future exposures seems so fundamental to survival that a brain stem mediation of such responses is quite plausible. More sophisticated forms of learning and cognition—complex associations, long-term memory, categorization, and inference—must await the further development of the brain's cortical connections and the enhanced acuity of the senses.

Newborn Imitation

A final area of newborn cognition that we will discuss is imitation. Piaget believed that newborns lacked the cognitive skills to imitate a gesture they could see with one of their own they could not see. He thought this ability began only at eight or nine months of age. Recent studies have shown that infants appear to possess this capability in the first month of life. Meltzoff and Moore (1977) studied twelve- to twenty-one-day-old infants' abilities to match tongue protrusion, lip protrusion, mouth opening, hand opening, and hand closing. In their study, each infant was shown a series of gestures made by the same adult. In the infant could reliably produce the same gesture following the adult's display of that gesture, as compared with following the adult's display of another gesture, imitation could be inferred. The researchers found that infants were much more likely to demonstrate a particular gesture following the modeling of that gesture than at any other time (see Figure 5.9).

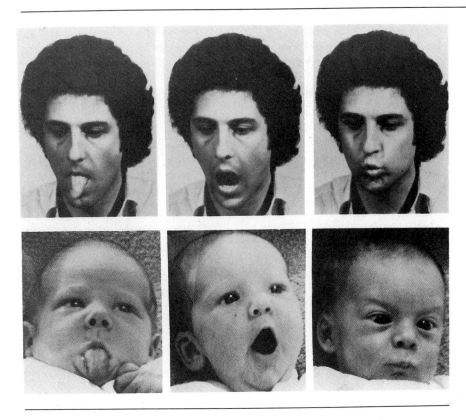

■ FIGURE 5.9
Imitation of Facial Expressions in Newborns

Sample photographs from videotape recordings of two- to three-week-old infants imitating (a) tongue protrusion, (b) mouth opening, and (c) lip protrusion demonstrated by an adult experimenter.

SOURCE: A. Meltzoff and W. Moore. Imitation of facial and manual gestures by human neonates. *Science*, 1977, *198*, 7578. Copyright 1977 by the American Association for the Advancement of Science. Reprinted by permission of the publisher and the author.

A number of replications of the Meltzoff and Moore study have been successful in producing correct matching of gestures in very young infants. Jacobson (1979) found correct matching of tongue protrusion and hand-opening models, but she also found that other stimuli could evoke the same responses in the newborns. Moving a ballpoint pen toward and away from the infant's face in the same manner as a tongue might move in and out was also successful in eliciting tongue protrusion in infants. A dangling ring elicited hand opening and closing. Jacobson concluded that the infants were not imitating a particular gesture as much as they were imitating a movement pattern or responding with some oral behavior.

Each of these studies used relatively few subjects and rather simple gestures. Field, Woodson, Greenberg, and Cohen (1982) used seventy-four neonates (an average of thirty-six hours old), and instead of simple gestures they used a set of complex facial expressions: happy, sad, and surprised.

The results show that infants match expressions. During the demonstration of the surprise face, newborns showed more wide eyes and wide mouth opening. During the demonstration of the sad face, they had tight mouths, protruded lips, and furrowed brows; during the happy face demonstation, infants had more wide-lip expressions. Matching was more likely to occur during the middle trials, suggesting that it is not due to the immediate arousal of the visual display, nor is it a reflexive response. These possibilities could be true only if the infants imitated on the first few trials.

Other replications of this work have been reported by Meltzoff and Moore (1989) using head movement, by Reissland (1988) using lip widening and lip pursing with a sample of Nepalese newborns, and by Heimann (1989) using tongue protrusion and mouth opening. Heimann also found that infants who imitated more at birth gazed away less from their mothers during social interaction at three months, suggesting that early imitation reflects a possible social receptivity.

On the other hand, some teams of researchers have failed to replicate the findings (Koepke et al., 1983; McKenzie & Over, 1983). Others have argued that although there is a slightly elevated probability of the baby displaying the modeled gesture, in fact all babies display a wide variety of gestures following the model and there are wide individual differences between babies (Anisfeld, 1979).

Thus, although the evidence is in favor of some form of newborn imitation, it is at best a fleeting and hard-to-detect response. Its occurrence in any form reflects a rather remarkable capacity of the immature human brain and perceptual system to process information and reflect it back to the outside world. Like learning and habituation, even occasional imitative responses are likely to orient the care giver in a positive way toward the infant and enhance the probability of an early parent-infant attachment. We will return to this topic in a later section.

■ EMOTIONAL DEVELOPMENT

Emotion can be examined from the perspective of an individual's internal feelings and how they are related to facial and bodily movements thought to express such feelings. Another aspect of emotion is how it is communicated. Certainly the newborn's expressions communicate messages to adults, as we saw in the case of crying. Recognition and understanding of other's emotions takes place later in development, as we will see in later chapters.

The baby at birth has a rather wide expressive range. From the perspective of discrete emotion theory (see Chapter 2), there are a small number of basic human emotions, and these emotions are associated with specific facial expressions. Some studies (Oster, 1978; Rosenstein & Oster, 1988) find that newborns show most of the adult discrete emotions, including smiling during drowsy states. In addition, the expressions made (as we saw earlier in the chapter for responses to tastes and smells) are appropriate to the stimulation in the sense that an adult would respond in a similar way to the same stimulus.

On the other hand, newborns have a wide variety of movements that appear to be expressive but are not facial expressions. For example, reddening of the entire body, kicking and thrashing, contorted arm movements, and stiffening of the body. These movements may be related to internal feelings, according to constructivist theories of emotion (Campos & Barrett, 1984). In this view, emotion can be expressed in a variety of behavioral, vocal, and physiological ways.

One of the more interesting demonstrations of the existence of newborn feelings was the result of an accidental discovery. A group of researchers at Brown University were studying the newborn's ability to learn and also exploring the range of newborn sensitivity to taste and to smell (see earlier sections of this chapter). While investigating newborn preferences for sweet fluids, Lipsitt (1979b) and Crook (1978) found that the babies sucked in longer bursts with shorter pauses between bursts. Within a sucking burst, the interval between sucks is higher for sweetened water compared to plain water, and while sucking the sweet water, the newborn's heart rate increases. Thus the babies were sucking for longer periods and holding the sweet liquid longer in their mouths before swallowing. The researchers concluded that the babies were "savoring" the pleasurable sensation of the sweet taste. In addition, when plain water was given following the sweet water, the babies showed aversive reactions.

In the end, however, we have only circumstantial evidence for newborn feelings. Most developmental scientists are willing to make the assumption that newborns have genuine feelings. The arguments between the different camps of scholars are over the quality of the newborn's feeling (do newborns feel only simple emotions, such as pleasure and displeasure, or are they capable of more subtle gradations of feeling?) and whether all potentially expressive movements are actually associated with a feeling (does a newborn smile show happiness, or is it merely a reflexive twitch?). In later chapters, we'll return to these issues.

As a care giver, it seems wise to make the assumption that infants of all ages have feelings, since it helps us to understand their needs. The interventions that we make that are consonant with our interpretations of infant emotions often seem to have the intended effect. We pick up a crying baby to soothe what we believe to be the child's pain or discomfort as much as to stop the crying, and the subsequent relaxation of the infant confirms our belief about his or her inner states of feeling. We now turn to a discussion of infant-care giver interactions.

Early adult-infant interaction: the beginnings of emotional ties

As we saw in the last chapter and earlier in this one, adults and infants have sensitivities and responses that seem to make a good mutual fit. Newborn sucking responses are perfectly suited to obtain milk from the breast; the newborn's appearance, sound, and smell are powerful attractors of adult attention and care; the newborn seems primed to recognize the primary care giver by smell, sound, and possibly touch.

According to ethological theories, especially that of John Bowlby (1969), in the early weeks and months of life, we share a common heritage with most other mammals who nurse and show a good deal of solicitude toward their young. Not every order of animals behaves this way. Reptiles give birth to eggs and usually leave the young to fend for themselves after hatching. Bird species do not nurse their young, nor do they give birth to live infants; however, they do show a good deal of parental care-giving behavior.

After the domestic cat gives birth, the mother lies on her side to expose her nipples. The mother licks the kittens, which are blind at birth, and the licking helps orient them to her body, nuzzle into her fur, and begin to search for the nipple. After only a few days, each kitten has a preferred nipple, and there is a rapid improvement in the speed with which a kitten can find its nipple (Rosenblatt, 1972).

■ FAMILY AND SOCIETY

The example of the domestic cat illustrates the idea that there is a complex series of behavioral exchanges between mother and infant by which each learns to adjust to the other. Over time, the initial trial-and-error response is reduced, and nursing and other forms of interpersonal interaction become more efficient. In this case the mother, no less than the infant, is subject to the tug of powerful evolved forces that insure the survival of the young.

From the very start, the human adult-infant interaction involves more than just a streamlining of the behaviors necessary for feeding and caretaking. There is also a social-psychological component that may form the basis of later interpersonal communication between adults and infants. Mothers and infants were observed on the day after birth and again at two weeks of age during breast- or bottle-feeding while the mother jiggled the infant (Kaye, 1977; Kaye & Wells, 1980). Jiggles were anything the mother did to stimulate sucking, such as shaking the infant or gently moving the nipple in and out of the mouth. Jiggles rarely occurred, but when they did, they tended to occur during pauses in sucking, and mothers claimed they were using the jiggling to get the infant to start sucking again. To test whether this was effective, Kaye checked the duration of the pauses without jiggles in relation to the duration of the pauses containing a jiggle. He found that when the mother jiggles during a pause, the jiggling actually lengthened the pause. The mother's intervention tended to delay the onset of the next burst of sucks by about two seconds. This pattern held true so long as the mother continued to jiggle the infant.

If, however, she jiggled momentarily and then stopped, the infant was more likely to begin a burst of sucks than in either the no jiggle or the continuous jiggle conditions. Kaye believes that the pattern that develops—suck-pause, jiggle-stop, suck-pause, jiggle-stop, and so on—is the precursor to later forms of social discourse. The pattern looks very much like a dialogue in which there is an exchange of turns: baby, mother, baby, mother.

This turn-taking situation is still rather one-sided. Although the infant can adjust the timing of the onset of the burst of sucking within a limited range, he or she cannot change the pattern altogether. The mother, on the other hand, is quite capable of changing her behavior to fit the situation. She is able to choose what to do and when to do it. It is almost as if the pauses in sucking serve as "slots" or "spaces" into which the mother can insert her interventions. Although the whole thing has the appearance of turn taking, that seems to be an illusion created entirely by the mother's ability to adapt to the infant.

Most of the studies of early parent-infant interaction have been done with the infants' mothers; it was only recently that investigators began to look at the father-newborn interaction. Some of these findings are summarized in the next section.

Are fathers capable of interacting with newborns?

Controversy surrounds the questions of whether fathers are capable of caring for newborns. Some studies have found that fathers spend very little time interacting with their newborns; other have found that fathers would like to spend more time with their babies; and still others have shown that when fathers actually do spend time with newborns, they can be just as competent as mothers in administering care and affection. In reality, there is no contradiction between these studies: they all could be true and probably are true to a certain extent. They merely represent different aspects of the fathering role. Although we will discuss the father's role and behavior in more detail later, in this chapter we will confine our discussion to studies of fathers and newborns.

Perhaps the most often quoted study of fathers was done by Rebelsky and Hanks (1971). They attached a microphone to infants' cribs and recorded all the sounds heard there for twenty-four hours a day over a two-week period, starting at two weeks of age. The subjects were ten normal, middle-class white infants and their families. They found that fathers' vocalizations were heard an average of only 37.7 seconds per day. The most time a father was heard near the crib in a day was 1,370 seconds, or about 20 minutes, and the least was 0 seconds.

These findings often are interpreted to mean that middle-class white American fathers spend almost no time at all with their newborns. Unfortunately, this generalization is not justified from the data. First of all, only vocalizations were recorded. Fathers may have been more inhibited than mothers in talking to the infants, especially in the presence of the microphone. Second, the microphone was attached to the crib and not elsewhere. Fathers could have spent a considerable amount of time with their infants in other parts of the house, and they may have been less likely to put the baby to bed.

More recent studies of large-scale national samples of parents and infants are considerably more generous in their view of fathers' participation in infant care. Fathers appear to spend between 20 and 35 percent as much time as mothers in direct participation in infant care. Clearly, however, most of the burden falls on the mothers' shoulders. Mothers appear to take the primary responsibility, while fathers take the role of helpers and baby-sitters (Lamb et al., 1987; Pleck, 1983).

Fein (1976) found that fathers have a strong desire to share in the experience of parenting but need a good deal of support to do so. Men's ability to participate in parenting tasks depended on the amount of social support they received. Men who adjusted better to parenthood had more knowledge about children and better relationships with their wives than men who had trouble adjusting to being fathers. This is in contrast to the factors predicting parental adjustment in women, which include self-esteem, identification with mothering role, and adaptation to the pregnancy experience (Entwisle & Doering, 1981; Feldman & Nash, 1986; Wente & Crockenberg, 1976).

In a series of studies by Ross Parke (Parke & Sawin, 1980; Parke & Tinsley, 1981; Sawin & Parke, 1979), infants were observed with mothers and fathers in a maternity ward of a hospital. During feeding and other care-taking tasks, fathers were at least as active as mothers and with similar levels of sensitivity and affection. A more recent study found that new fathers' heart rates and blood pressures were elevated while holding their newborns compared to when they were not holding the babies, suggesting heightened arousal (Jones & Thomas, 1989). On the whole, however, mothers spend more time caretaking during this period than the fathers.

On the other hand, Sawin and Parke (1979) also found that the involvement of the father in care-giving affected the mother-infant relationship. From the perspective of family systems theory, families in which the fathers were more involved had mothers who showed more interest and affection toward the neonate. Of course, this result could be explained the other way around: interested, affectionate mothers may be more adept at encouraging fathers to take part in the care of the infant.

Fathers do play an important role, even in the newborn period. They may not do as much as mothers overall, but they seem to be able to learn to become competent care givers with some encouragement and training.

Do firstborns have different interactions with mothers than later borns?

Another factor influencing the family system at this period of time is whether the parents have had prior experience with an infant. As a general rule, newborns who are firstborn receive more care-giving interaction (Kilbride, Johnson, & Streissguth, 1977). Perhaps because of the novelty of the experience, parents devote more time and energy to the care of the firstborn than to infants born later. One study examined family photo albums and found considerably more photographs of firstborn children than of children born later (Titus, 1976).

One of the reasons for this is that *primiparous* mothers (women who have given birth for the first time) receive more obstetrical medication than *multiparous* mothers (mothers who have given birth more than once), which may lead to an infant who is somewhat slower to respond to stimulation. Brown, Bakeman, Snyder, Frederickson, Morgan, and Hepler (1975) found that mothers spend more time with their firstborns, but they also found that the firstborns in their sample were more passive and nonresponsive than babies born later. Could it be that mothers have to spend more time simply to get the infant sufficiently aroused to feed?

Another explanation of the difference is that the mothers of firstborns are less skilled as care givers. Do they spend more time because they are less efficient at getting the normal care-giving tasks accomplished? Thoman and her colleagues (Thoman, Barnett, & Leiderman, 1971; Thoman, Leiderman, & Olson, 1972) found that primiparous mothers spend more time in nonfeeding activity during a feeding session. They were more likely to change activity frequently, such as shifting the infants' posture, providing more stimulation, and talking more to the newborns. Their infants spend less time on the nipple and did less sucking when attached than infants born later. These mothers could be spending more time because they are more uncertain about how to handle the infants or because they are more excited by the infants and wish to touch, explore, and talk to the infants. The number of changes of activity decreased over the first three days for primiparous mothers, suggesting that it doesn't take them very long to get down to the business of feeding during the feeding period.

Another explanation is that first-time mothers are simply more anxious than other mothers. An anxious mood is likely to be caused by lack of security in the childrearing role, and it may be enhanced by such factors as separation from the infant due to prematurity and illness. Anxiety in first-time mothers at birth is correlated with anxiety at one month but not at later follow-up observations (Fleming & Orpen, 1986; Fleming et al., 1990), suggesting that

In keeping with its commitment to
affirmative action,

The firm of

Jennings & Jennings

is pleased to announce the addition

of its first male associate

Samuel Clark Jennings

7 lbs. 12 1/2 oz.

Effective November 21, 1990

Partners   Associates
Terry H. Jennings   Sarah A. Jennings
Marianne M. Jennings   Claire E. Jennings

New parents are proud of babies regardless of gender or birth order. Birth announcement cards or notices printed in the newspaper are ways that parents communicate this special event to others.

most early insecurities that might influence behavior are reduced after a few months' experience.

In summary, adults and infants seem ready to interact with each other and have feelings and behaviors that mutually complement. Under the right conditions, any adult can interact successfully with a newborn and with enough exposure to the baby can develop a lasting attachment. The emotional tie between adults and infants does not seem to depend on a particular experience or a particular starting time (see the Applications section below). Rather, emotional bonds develop slowly and in a variety of ways. Many senses and behaviors can be involved, and if one pathway is absent (the parents do not have the opportunity for early contact, for example), other pathways are available to enhance the adult-infant communication process. ■

Parent-Infant Bonding

Bonding has become synonymous with the ideal of good mothering. It is a word that is on the lips of nurses, physicians, and psychologists, and it is a notion that has begun to pervade the columns of *Redbook, Ladies' Home Journal,* and the local newspaper. If any mother still believes that the development of her baby will not be hampered seriously if she has not been able to bond properly with the infant, she is probably out of touch with the mainstream of the U.S. public. Early bonding—the dos and don'ts, the pros and cons, the facts and myths—has come into its own as a media event, with all the attendant distortions and exaggerations media events so often bring with them.

What is bonding?

Bonding has a number of definitions. Some use the word to signify the relationship of attachment between infant and mother. People speak of a relationship as "bonded" or "not bonded." Bonding also has been used to refer to the events that take place during the first few hours after the birth of an infant, when mother and infant are placed alone together and in skin-to-skin contact. Finally, some people refer to bonding as the process that translates the latter experience into the former. These individuals presume or try to prove that skin-to-skin contact in the first hours after birth will predispose the mother-infant pair to a closer, more affectionate, warmer relationship later.

How has bonding been studied?

The concept of bonding grew out of the pioneering work of Marshall Klaus and John Kennel of Case Western Reserve University.

Their first reports detailed an apparently universal pattern of behavior seen in mothers presented with their naked newborns immediatly after birth. The mothers in their study first began to touch the neonates' fingers and toes. This phase usually lasted between four and eight minutes. After this, the mothers began to move inward, touching the infants' limbs, and ended their exploration by an encompassing palm contact with the infants' abdomens, accompanied by massaging movements (Klaus, Kennell, Plumb, & Zuehlke, 1970). In the same study, it was found that mothers of premature infants progressed through the same phases but took longer.

Since then, the pattern of maternal behavior at first contact with the neonate has been replicated on many occasions and in a wide variety of settings. It has been shown that fathers, when given the same opportunity to lie next to their newborn children, progress through the same sequence of phases (McDonald, 1978; Rodholm & Larsson, 1979). There appears to be a pattern of adult behavior on first contact with the infant, the universality of which suggests a genetically determined response to the young on the part of the adult. In this sense, the adult response to the first contact with the newborn is not unlike adult responses to the cry, the smile, and the facial configuration of the neonate.

What are the long-term effects of early contact?

Although few doubt the validity of the first contact behavior pattern, controversy arises over the relative importance of this behavior, or the lack of it, for the infant's development. Not long after the first-contact phenomenon had been reported, Klaus and colleagues published a study showing that mothers who had

APPLICATIONS

early contact with their infants in the new-born period were more likely to spend more time holding their infants in an *en face* position. The *en face* position is one in which the mother holds the infant so that they can maintain eye contact with one another. The study had twenty-eight primiparous mothers of low-income families who did not plan to breastfeed. The experimental group had one hour of extra contact at birth and another five hours of extra contact each afternoon while in the hospital. The observers at one month were not aware of the group identity of the mothers (Klaus, Jerauld, Kreger, McAlpine, Steffa, & Kennell, 1972).

Since that report appeared, many studies have been done, and the results have been inconsistent. The goal of this review is not to present all the studies that have been done on the effects of early contact but to provide a representative sampling of the types of findings that have appeared.

One study used a sample of middle-class white infants from Canada who had normal deliveries. The experimental group had one hour of extra contact beginning at forty-five minutes after birth. In follow-up observations at one and three months, the mothers who had had extra contact did more smiling, sing-ing, holding of the babies in the *en face* posi-tion, and playing without the use of a toy than the mothers in the control group. There were no differences between the groups in the amount of touching behavior. This study was somewhat flawed, since only one of the two observers at the one- and two-month sessions was unaware of the mothers' group identity. We have no way of knowing in what way the informed observer might have had an influ-ence over the naive observer (Kontos, 1978). Another study using a similar sample and schedule of observations as the Kontos study (Curry, 1979) but using blind observers failed to find any differences at thirty-six hours and at three months in the amounts of holding;

encompassing, affectionate close contact; *en face* holding; smiling; or kissing of the infant.

In a well-controlled study done in Sweden, Schaller, Carlsson, and Larsson (1979) found evidence of higher levels of proximal contact in the extended contact mothers (rubs, pats, kisses, and touches) at two and four days, but they found no differences at forty-two days. A replication study by the same group of investi-gators (Carlsson, Fagerberg, Horneman, Hwang, Larsson, Rodholm, Schaller, Daniels-son, & Gundewall, 1979) yielded similar find-ings: differences in the first few days but no differences one month later.

DeChateau (1980; 1987) reported some differences between extended and control groups at thirty-six hours but only in the posi-tion in which the mothers sat to hold their infants while feeding them. A three-year fol-low-up, also from Sweden, reported no differ-ences.

A number of other studies have also failed to support the claims of the importance of early contact (Goldberg, 1983; Lamb, 1982; Myers, 1987). Furthermore, similar research on the effects of early contact on fathers has failed to turn up any lasting effects (Palkovitz, 1985). The important factor in paternal in-volvement with newborns is an ongoing inter-active relationship, no matter whether this starts at birth or several days or weeks later.

Although it is impossible to prove that early contact has no long-term effects, these studies, done in different countries and under many different conditions, seem to suggest that any differences due to extended or early contact are at best transitory, lasting no more that a few days or months. It is also extremely important to note that all the studies, without exception, have focused on maternal attach-ment or changes in maternal behavior follow-ing the experience of early contact. There is absolutely no evidence that any of these ma-

continued at top of next page

nipulations have any effect on the baby's future attachment to the mother, in spite of media claims to the contrary.

There is some evidence that early contact has effects on mothers from low-income groups or on mothers at high risk for attachment problems. In these cases, the additional contact seems to be an important boost to get the mother-infant system started. In ordinary cases, however, the mother-infant relationship has a number of alternative feedback systems that enable it to maintain its course without the benefit of early contact.

What are the implications of these findings?

The implication of this research is that mothers who do not have the opportunity for early contact need not worry about the well-being of their infants. Indeed, there are many situations in which early contact is impossible, such as with premature infants, sick infants, sick mothers, or adopted infants. In these cases, it is especially important for the parents to not worry about what may have been lost and to concentrate on developing their relationship with their babies.

We will discuss some of these issues again in the final chapter, when we ponder the effects of early experience. To set the stage for that chapter, consider that the human species would be severely limited in its adaptive flexibility if the future well-being of its individual members depended on a few short minutes

following birth. These studies also teach us something about how systems function. A complex system usually has multiple possible paths to the same end point, the more alternatives found in the system, the more adaptive the system can become.

None of this is meant to deny the fact that it may be extremely satisfying for parents to have the opportunity to have early contact with their babies, rather than be artificially isolated from them by hospital rules and regulations. We have already described how early discharge and immediate contact during home births have demonstrated that there are no ill effects of such alternatives as rooming-in.

A much more solid argument for early and extended contact would be based on the immediate satisfaction of the parents or on insuring that each parent get the fullest possible enjoyment from the childbirth experience, rather than on any lasting impact of that early contact on the infant.

The search for the effects of early contact perhaps reflects our society's more general need to justify everything in terms of its ultimate usefulness or its payoff down the road. This social value has made the path to changing childbirth practice a rocky one, and it is because of this prevailing attitude that the failure to replicate the effects of early contact may disappoint many well-intentioned individuals. It makes more sense to search for realistic reasons to justify allowing parents a choice in the amount of access they can have to their newborn infants.

A baby's first attempts to gaze at people and objects may be brief. If infants are shown an object while they are alert, they may learn to look for longer periods. For newborns, objects should be brightly colored with simple shapes, such as a striped ball, a mirror, a shiny bracelet, or a white paper plate with a face painted in thick black lines.

Hold objects about 8 to 10 inches from the baby's face. This distance is where the infant can best focus his or her vision. Hold the object steady or move it slowly from side to side. Some newborns show a clear preference for looking at certain objects. Watch to see which ones the baby seems to prefer.

An infant may enjoy looking at objects from different points of view and from different positions, such as while being cradled in mother's arm, lying on his or her back, or sitting in an infant seat. A baby's attention may be attracted by objects that make noise or music. Baby's attention is especially attracted to the high-pitched voices of care givers.

If the infant becomes overstimulated when watching objects, try showing just one at a time and moving the object more slowly in the baby's visual field. If the baby still appears to be overstimulated (turning away, crying, sucking a fist, etc.), the game should be put aside until a later time.

Although true eye contact does not begin until about six weeks, infants will look in the direction of your eyes and face. This is encouraged by gentle talking while holding the baby up near your face. Cutting down on outside sources of stimulation will also help encourage the baby to focus on the care giver. If a baby will not look at your face, cut back on the level of stimulation and allow the baby a chance to look at you.

You can follow the baby's direction of gaze with your face until the baby is looking at you and then give the baby a big smile while saying "Hi!" Newborns like to hear soft whispers and humming sounds. After the baby is looking at you, smiles can sometimes be elicited by quiet, high-pitched voices, gentle tummy strokes, and smiling faces.

Thus, even though newborns have only a limited capacity for attention and interaction, with some gentleness and patience, the care giver can be rewarded with a responsive infant.

POINTS OF CONTACT

■ SUMMARY

Physical and Motor Development

■ The fetal states of rest and activity develop into sleeping and waking states.

■ Newborns sleep about seventeen hours per day.

■ Responsiveness to the environment is related to orienting and defensive responses. Newborns will orient to stimuli of moderate intensity and complexity.

■ Brain development depends on experience with the environment. Part of the brain is experience expectant, while other parts are experience dependent. Brain growth involves cell loss as well as increases in connections.

■ Crying is an organized rhythmic activity that has reliable effects on adults. Infants who cry a great deal are not necessarily at risk for problems in parent-infant attachment.

■ Each method of soothing infants has advantages and disadvantages.
■ Reflexes are highly variable within and between infants. Many disappear by about six months, while others remain with us for life. Both brain and motor factors may contribute to the disappearance of reflexes.
■ The infant does not grow all at once; different parts of the body grow at different rates and at different times.
■ Sucking is a complex activity that can be adapted to the environment.

Perceptual Development

■ Newborn visual acuity and visual processing is poor but improves rapidly during the first three months.
■ Infants can perceive some meaningful patterns, but in most cases, they do not attach meanings to their perceptions.
■ Hearing, smell, and taste are more acute at birth than vision, perhaps due to prenatal experiences. Infants can recognize their mothers by sound and by smell.

Cognitive Development

■ Newborns are susceptible to operant conditioning but less so to classical conditioning.
■ Habituation and conditioning reflect rudimentary memory processes as infants need to compare current with past experiences. Most newborn memories seem to last no more than a few hours, unless the stimulus is repeated often.
■ Newborns appear to be able to imitate simple gestures they themselves can make. Imitation is irregular and not especially salient to a casual observer.

Emotional Development

■ Newborns have a large repertoire of facial expressions and body movements possibly related to emotion expression.
■ There is some evidence that newborns can feel basic states of pleasure and displeasure but not sophisticated gradations of emotion.

Family and Society

■ Adults and infants seem to have mutually complementary communications that get their interaction started and set the stage for later emotional ties.
■ There are many alternate pathways for adult-infant communication and recognition, suggesting that the deprivation of early contact is not crucial for the formation of attachments.
■ First-time parents are somewhat more hesitant with their babies than other parents, but this difference disappears after several months.

■ GLOSSARY

Acuity   The ability of a perceptual system to resolve the incoming information into a sharp focus.

Asynchronous growth   Refers to the fact that growth occurs in different regions of the body at different times and different rates.

Bonding   The feelings of attachment the care giver derives from close physical contact with the baby.

Burst-pause pattern   The pattern of sucking behavior in which the baby sucks for a few minutes, stops, and resumes sucking.

Defensive reaction   Avoidance or aversive response to noxious or potentially threating stimuli.

Experience dependent   Brain regions and pathways that are not fully formed and must await environmental input for their development.

Experience expectant   Brain regions and pathways that are more or less fully developed at birth, allowing the infant to adapt to particular types of environmental stimuli related to basic survival.

Milk expression   The second phase of sucking, in which the infant presses the nipple against the roof of the mouth with the tongue to force milk out.

Myelin   A protective coating over nerve cells that aids the conduction of action potentials.

Negative pressure   The first phase of sucking, in which the gums create a seal around the nipple and the jaw drops to create a suction inside the mouth.

Neuron   A conductive cell in the central nervous system.

Oculomotor skill   Refers to the movements of the eye, including lens focusing, convergence and divergence, scanning, and tracking.

Orienting response   Direction of attention and action toward an attractive stimulus.

Pattern vision   The ability to detect meaningful patterns amidst the jumble of visual stimuli at any moment.

Reflex   A semiautomatic response to a specific stimulus that, once elicited, must run its course.

Stereopsis   The ability to compare the different images coming from each eye.

Synapse   The connection between axons and dendrites by which action potentials are transmitted between neurons.

SIX

Attention and Anticipation

TWO TO FIVE MONTHS

———

CHAPTER OUTLINE

During the first few months, babies seem to be in a world of their own. They sleep a great deal, they have few means of communication other than crying, and their movements seem self-contained and repetitive. We have seen how these newborn behavior patterns are organized and highly adaptive for the initial tasks of postnatal survival.

About the age of two months, most babies experience their first major developmental transition since birth. Their motor movements seem to become more purposeful and deliberate, a change from the earlier cyclical and reflexive movements. Their perceptual systems, especially vision, become acute, while waking time and attention span increase rapidly. Adults first notice this as infants seem to be able to establish and maintain eye-to-eye contact between six and eight weeks. Around this time, demanding crying wanes and is replaced by other forms of emotional communication, especially by smiling in response to other people. These changes lead to more prolonged and satisfying adult-infant social interactions and the beginnings of social play.

As the quality of the infant's attention becomes more focused, the infant begins to have a memory of experiences. This memory forms the basis of the infant's anticipation of enjoyment in the company of particular other people and the ability to anticipate regularly recurring routines, such as meals and baths. Thus, the beginning of social and psychological development occurs between two and five months.

■ PHYSICAL AND MOTOR DEVELOPMENT

Physical Development

In infancy and early childhood, a natural accompaniment to psychological development is physical development. Physical development is usually measured in terms of height and weight. Additional indices include the circumference of the head, the fat-to-muscle ratio, the emergence of baby teeth, and bone growth. Standard charts for height and weight for boys and girls from birth to thirty-six months are given in the Appendix.

At birth, most infants are 19 to 21 inches in length and weigh between 7 and 8 pounds. Boys are slightly longer and heavier than girls and remain so, on the average, throughout life. The period of most rapid growth in both height and weight occurs in the first six months of life. By this age, height grows by a factor of 1.5, while weight grows by a factor of 2. This is a lot of growth in a short period. Imagine a teenager (the other period of life in which rapid growth occurs) growing half again his height in 6 months (say from 5 feet to 7.5 feet!).

Individual differences in birth height and weight are relatively small, since they are limited by the constraints of fitting through the mother's pelvis and vagina during birth. Individual differences become larger with age (there is a wider range of heights and weights among two-year-olds than among one-year-olds). In addition, as the infants get older, their height becomes a better predictor of their adult height. Infant weight is not a very good predictor of adult weight since weight is more variable than height and more dependent upon environmental factors. As we saw in Chapter 3, weight gain in premature infants can be influenced not only by diet but also by age-appropriate stimulation. In Chapter 7, we'll return to the topic of infant nutrition and its effects on growth.

Also, keep in mind that growth is asynchronous (see Chapter 5). Different parts of the body grow at different rates, and growth spurts occur at different times in each body region. Before birth, the head grows faster than the rest of the body, while after birth, the body begins to grow faster. The process in which head growth precedes body growth is called cephalocaudal development. Growth also proceeds outward, first centered on the body and later on the developing limbs in a process called proximodistal development. This is why it takes almost a year for infants to begin standing and walking. These growth processes are illustrated in Figure 6.1.

Motor Development

Aside from physical growth of the body, the infant is also becoming more skilled at a variety of motor movements. In the realm of motor development, we consider the control over posture, over locomotion, and over the

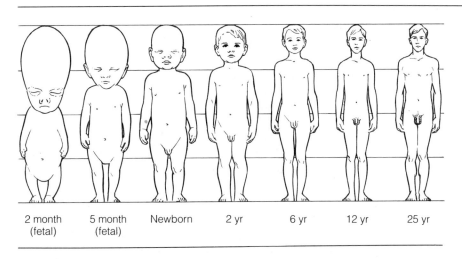

■ FIGURE 6.1
Developmental
Changes in Body
Proportion

The very different proportions of
body length accounted for by the
head, trunk, and legs at different
ages or stages of development. The
disproportion is greatest in fetal
life: The head decreases from 50%
of total body length at 2 months
post conception to only 25% at
birth and 12% in adulthood.

SOURCE: Rosenblith, J. & Sims-
Knight, J. *In the beginning:
Development in the first two years.*
Brooks-Cole/Wadsworth: Belmont,
CA, 1985, p. 296.

| 2 month (fetal) | 5 month (fetal) | Newborn | 2 yr | 6 yr | 12 yr | 25 yr |

movements of the hands and arms. Motor development was studied
extensively in the early part of the twentieth century (Gesell, 1928; McGraw,
1935; Shirley, 1931).

The infant's level of motor development can be assessed today using a
variety of standardized testing situations derived from the early work in this
area. Some of the more commonly used motor developmental assessment tests
are listed in Table 6.1. Based on using the test with many infants, both the
average age of achievement of a skill as well as the range of ages seen in
normal infants can be reported. The age norms for the achievement of body

■ TABLE 6.1   Commonly Used Infant Development Tests

NAME OF TEST	AREAS OF COMPETENCY ASSESSED
Gesell Scales (Gesell, 1925)	Motor behavior, language behavior, adaptive behavior, and personal-social behavior.
Bayley Scales of Infant Development (Bayley, 1969)	Motor area (gross body coordination) and mental area (adaptability, learning, sensory acuity, and fine motor coordination).
Denver Developmental Screening Test (Frankenburg, Dodd, Fandal, Kuzak, & Cohrs, 1975)	Personal-social behavior, fine motor-adaptive behavior, language behavior, and gross motor coordination.
Einstein Scales of Sensorimotor Development (Escalona & Corman, 1969)	Prehension, object permanence, and space (detour behavior and perspective taking).
Infant Psychological Development Scales (Uzgiris & Hunt, 1975)	Object permanence, development of means, development of imitation, development of causality, development of objects in space, and development of schemes for relating to objects.

SOURCE: Reprinted by permission from p. 150 of Child Development by Alan Fogel and Gail F. Melson;
Copyright © 1988 by West Publishing Company. All rights reserved.

postures and hand and arm control between 2 and 5 months of age are given in Table 6.2 using the standard scores from the Bayley test.

These assessment procedures are useful for diagnosing retardation and motor deficits in infants, but they only work well under specific conditions. First, the test norms only apply to infants in a particular cultural and economic group. Second, the test is only applicable if it is administered in precisely the same manner for each infant. The ability to grasp a cube is supposed to be assessed when the infant is supported in a sitting position. What if, instead, you presented the cube while the baby was lying supine? How might such a postural change affect the infant's hand motor skills? Do you think two-month-olds could manipulate a cube better with their hands or with their mouths?

The assessment tests do not take these kinds of differences into account because they assume, based on the earlier studies, that motor development is largely under genetic control and that improvements in motor skill could be related directly to the development of the brain. As we saw in the last chapter, for the disappearance of the stepping reflex, this simple theory of genetic control cannot be correct. Physical exercise and environmental support for motor skill also enhance the infant's ability to achieve motor coordinations.

As a simple case, consider how an infant seat, a high chair, and an infant walker provide postural support so that the baby can execute manual and locomotor movements. Similarly, the positions in which adults hold infants also influence the range of motor skills that the infants can display. In general, the ability of a baby to perform a motor skill depends in part on brain development, on the difficulty of the task, and on the supports and resources present in the environment in which the task is carried out.

■ TABLE 6.2 Norms for the Development of Motor Behavior Patterns in North America

TEST ITEM	AVERAGE AGE	NORMAL AGE RANGE
A. *Head and Body Control*		
Holds head erect when upright	7 weeks	3 weeks–4 months
Holds head steady when upright	2.5 months	1 month–5 months
Elevates chest and head in prone position	2.2 months	3 weeks–5 months
Thrusts arms and legs in supine position	1 month	1 week–2 months
Turns from side to back	2 months	3 weeks–5 months
Turns from back to side	2.5 months	2 months–7 months
Sits with support	2.2 months	1 month–5 months
Sits with slight support	3.7 months	2 months–6 months
Sits alone momentarily	5.2 months	4 months–8 months
Pulls self to sitting	5.7 months	4 months–8 months
B. *Hand and arm control*		
Holds onto large ring in supine position	1 month	3 weeks–4 months
Grasps 1-inch cube with palm	3.7 months	2 months–7 months
Grasps cube with partial use of thumb	5 months	4 months–8 months
Reaches with one hand	5.5 months	4 months–8 months

SOURCE: Bayley Infant Development Tests, as reported in Rosenblith and Sims-Knight, 1985.

Task Complexity. We saw in the last chapter that the motor movements of stepping were not present between two and six months if the infant is held upright with the feet placed on a surface. On the other hand, when the same infant's legs are under water, stepping becomes easier. The task is also made easier when the infant is placed supine, where kicking shows the same alternating pattern of leg movements as seen in stepping. These kicking movements are actually very coordinated. Leg alternation is preserved even if one leg is weighted experimentally: the babies increase the kick rate in the unweighted leg as the weighted leg slows down (Thelen et al., 1987).

Similar results have been shown for fine motor skills, such as manipulating objects. Between the ages of two and five months, objects like balls and cubes are more difficult for the infant to handle than objects that have graspable appendages, such as a cube with holes in which the baby can insert his or her fingers or a ring with a hole in the middle. If the object can be grasped, infants show better manipulatory abilities between two and five months.

At first, babies will grasp an object and move it directly to their mouths without even looking at it. Beginning about four months, babies will alternate putting the object in their mouths and looking at it. At this age also, infants will hold the object in one hand while looking at it and fingering the object with the other hand (Rochat, 1989). This means that exploration is confined at first to grasping and mouthing and later to fingering, mouthing, and looking. The older baby uses more motor actions and more perceptual systems in exploring the environment.

Even more sophisticated hand movements can be seen when infants do not actually make hand contact with objects. Without an object, infants in this age period can move their hands and fingers to make grasping and fingering movements, their fingers can move in graceful and rhythmic patterns, and they can point and make pincher grasp movements. These movements are different depending on whether the babies are looking at an object or a person (Trevarthen, 1977), and they also differ according to the babies' emotional states as observed during social interaction with adults (Fogel, 1981; Hannan, 1987; Papousek & Papousek, 1977; Trevarthen, 1977) (See Figure 6.2).

In my own studies, Tom Hannan and I found that two- and three-month-old infants were more likely to point if they were alert and attentive. Typically, the pointing movements were not even directed at the object of the infant's attention: pointing was more like an expression of interest than a direct communication about the object at this age (Fogel & Hannan, 1985; Thelen & Fogel, 1989) (see Figure 6.3).

Under four months, infants therefore appear more sophisticated in their motor skills if the task is simplified and made easier. This, of course, would be true at any age. A beginner can ride a bike, for example, if the task is made easier with training wheels. With experience, infants become capable of doing the motor movements under a wider variety of conditions.

Consider the development of reaching for objects. Before three months, infants will reach for objects without coming into contact with the objects. During these prereaching movements, the infant's hand is actually in a fist, as the arms seem to swipe in the direction of the object. In many cases, the infant is not even looking at the object very intently. Around three months, the infant will watch the object during the entire reach. Furthermore, the

■ FIGURE 6.2
State-Dependent Hand and Arm Expressions

The position of hands in different behavioral states of infants: (a) alert waking state; (b) closed fists in uncomfortable or distressing situations; (c) passive waking state; (d) transitional states to sleep; (e) sleep.

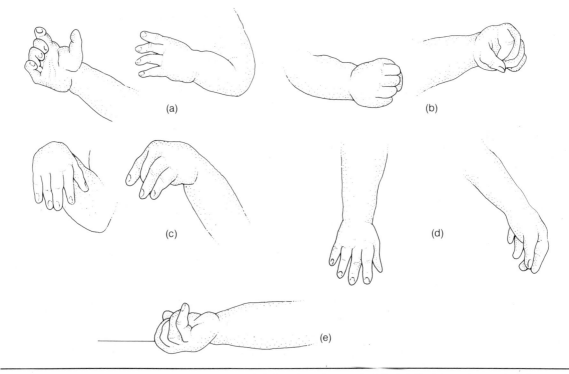

SOURCE: Papousek, H. Mothering and the cognitive head start: Psychobiological considerations. In H. R. Schaffer (Ed.), *Studies in mother-infant interaction.* p. 71. Copyright 1977. Academic Press, Inc. (London) Ltd.

■ FIGURE 6.3
Development of Pointing

(a) Point at 2 months during face-to-face interaction with mother. Index finger extends while arms are flexed and does not indicate direction of gaze. (b) Point at 9 months during free play with mother. Both arm and finger are extended in direction of object of interest.

SOURCE: Thelen, E. and Fogel, A. Towards an action-based theory of infant development. In J. Lockman and N. Hazen (eds.) Action in a social context: perspectives on early development. New York: Plenum, 1989, p. 53.

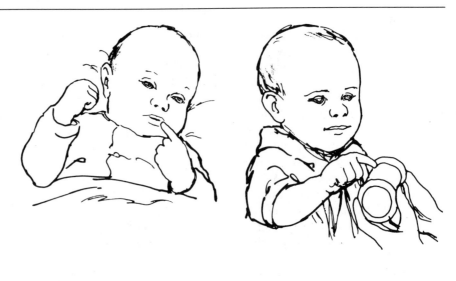

hand begins to open, adjusting to the perceived size of the object, and stays open until contact is made (von Hofsten, 1984).

Supports and Resources. The developments in muscle strength, manipulation using the fingers, and open-handed reaching make the infant less dependent upon the difficulty of the task. In other words, the infant becomes more able to achieve the goal in a wider variety of situations. How do these changes come about? What is the cause of motor development?

We have already suggested that brain development is not enough to explain changes in motor skill. The infant also has to have practice making movements in easy situations in order for the brain to develop. Since human infants have such a limited ability to move around the environment or to think about how to make tasks easier, they need social partners to do this for them. It is usually the infant's care giver who creates situations in which object manipulation and motor movements are made easy.

During simple social play with objects, adults help infants to practice their budding motor skills (Lyra, 1987). In a study that I did with Lisa West, we found developmental changes in the types of supports mothers provided for object play (Fogel, 1990b; West & Fogel, 1990). At first, when infants are unable to reach, adults will show objects to babies and demonstrate the object's properties (shaking a rattle or squeezing a soft toy). During this period, adults may also place the objects into the infants' hands, allowing the infants to grasp and hold the objects or bring the objects to their mouths. After the infants acquired the ability to reach for objects, mothers stopped showing and placing and began to hold the objects steady and within reach of the babies, apparently to give the babies the opportunity to practice reaching. Once reaching was mastered, mothers began to challenge the babies with more complex objects and with two objects at one time.

Another way in which adults provide supports for motor skills is by holding the infants in postures that are most conducive to the execution of those skills. For example, when infants first are learning to sit, they need to balance their bodies with one hand. This detracts from their ability to reach for things with two hands (Rochat, 1990). Adults can hold babies upright and free both their hands. We have found that upright babies are more attentive to the physical environment, while supine babies are more likely to look at their mothers (Fogel, Dedo, & McEwen, 1990).

The effects of the adult on motor development in infants is nowhere more salient than in some African cultures. One study done in Mali (Bril et al., 1986) found that mothers put babies through some active workout routines. The babies were given postural control exercises starting from birth, including training in sitting and standing. Mothers also stretched the babies' muscles and suspended the babies by their arms and legs (see Figure 6.4).

As a result of this practice, many African babies have advanced motor coordination compared to Caucasian North American babies. In addition, because their limbs are exercised frequently, certain reflexes such as stepping do not disappear after two months, as found in North American infants (Super, 1976). On the opposite end of the spectrum are Navaho infants, who spend many hours on cradle boards. Their motor development is slower than the other groups (Chisholm, 1983). Eventually, however, all babies achieve the important motor milestones. Differences in experience seem to influence the age at which the motor skill is first acquired.

■ FIGURE 6.4
Postural Manipulations by Adults

STRETCHING

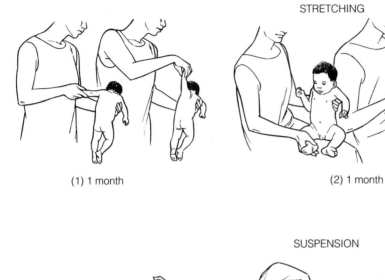

(1) 1 month   (2) 1 month   (3) 1 month

SUSPENSION

(4) 1 month   (5) 1 month   (6) 1 month

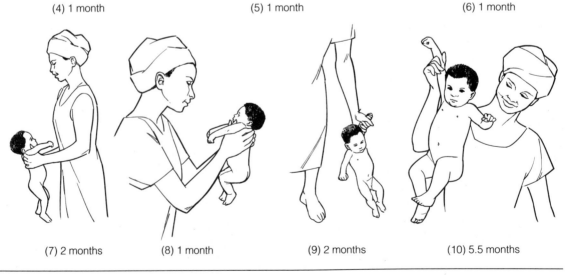

(7) 2 months   (8) 1 month   (9) 2 months   (10) 5.5 months

SOURCE: Bril, B. and Sabatier, C. The cultural context of motor development: Postural manipulations in the daily life of Bambara babies (Mali). *International Journal of Behavior Development*, 9, 1986, p. 445. Elsevier: North-Holland.

■ PERCEPTUAL DEVELOPMENT

As we saw in the last chapter, perceptual development is also influenced by the kinds of experiences the child encounters. Lack of exposure to sensory information can impede the articulation of brain pathways that ultimately improve the acuity and information processing abilities of the senses.

The period from two to five months represents a major shift in perceptual development. During the first two months, infants can see, hear, smell, taste, and feel. Infants have clear preferences for certain types of perceptual experiences, such as looking at sharp and bold outlines of figures or listening to high pitched voices. In some cases, infants under two months can recognize particular patterns that seem to have a meaning to them—looming objects, their mothers' voices and smells—but pattern detection is the exception rather than the rule.

In general, infants under two months are attracted to particular physical qualities of stimulation: intensity, sharpness, and complexity. Between two and four months, infants recognize and prefer meaningful patterned stimuli and will respond to recognizable patterns (a smiling face, for example) regardless of its level of intensity, complexity, or sharpness. Much of this can be accounted for by the improved visual acuity and oculomotor control discussed in Chapter 5.

During this same age period, infants show the ability to discriminate between the basic colors and show the same range of color vision as adults (Aslin 1987; Bornstein, 1981). While newborns prefer colored to black-and-white stimuli, it is not until three months that infants show a preference between colors: they look longer at red and yellow (Adams, 1987). Adults prefer red and blue, on the average. It is not clear whether this represents a developmental change in color preference. While adults can be asked what colors are most pleasant, longer looking times in infants could either mean a preference, or they could reflect increased interest in an unfamiliar stimulus.

Visual Pattern Perception

Ability to perceive whole patterns, rather than unconnected lines and shapes, has been demonstrated in infants as young as three months. The technique involves showing infants a picture of a figure—usually two-dimensional—during a familiarization period. Then, using habituation procedures, the familiar figure is replaced with either an unfamiliar one or the same figure rotated into different orientations or seen from different angles. Generally, by three months, infants will dishabituate when a totally novel figure is introduced but not when a different view of the familiar figure is shown (Bornstein et al., 1986; Caron et al., 1979; Fagan, 1979; Gibson et al., 1979; McKenzie et al., 1980).

Another procedure is to observe scanning movements made by infants looking at pictures of simple figures, such as circles and squares, drawn with dashed or dotted lines. Infants older than three months will scan these figures as if they were drawn with a solid line. If one of the dashed-line elements is drawn at an unexpected orientation, infants will scan this element more than the other elements that appear to them to be part of a pattern (Van Giffen & Haith, 1984).

Visual perception develops by seeing the same object from a number of different perspectives. Colorful mobiles with varied shapes are particularly interesting. Research using mobiles has found that babies of this age can tell the difference between a familiar mobile and the same one with only a single piece removed.

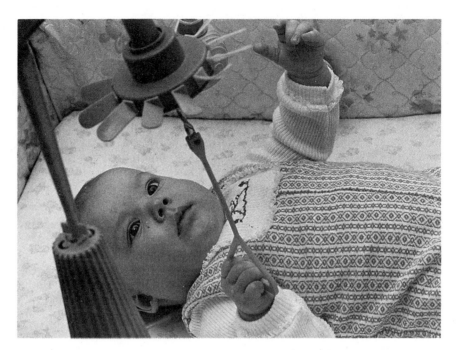

By three months, infants are able to visually differentiate familiar from unfamiliar faces from a variety of live and photographed faces of mothers compared to unfamiliar women (Barrera & Maurer, 1981; Kurzweil, 1988). Infants of this age seem to prefer looking at faces compared to nonface stimuli that have been carefully constructed to have exactly the same complexity, brightness, and black-and-white contrasts (Dannemiller & Stephens, 1988) (see Figure 6.5). Remarkably, both three-month-olds and six-month-olds prefer to look longer at faces that adults have judged as attractive compared to faces adults judged as less attractive (Langlois et al., 1987).

Why should infants prefer faces over other types of visual stimuli? Faces do have clear outlines and moderate complexity. They are composed of closed circular shapes that babies like to look at. Babies seem to prefer shapes that are symmetrical (shapes in which one side is the mirror image of the other side). Faces have vertical symmetry, and three-month-olds prefer vertical symmetry to horizontal symmetry (Bornstein & Krinsky, 1985; Fisher et al., 1981).

Is it a fortunate coincidence that faces happen to have just those elements that make them attractive to babies? Or is the visual system designed in such a way that its first preferences direct it toward social objects? It could be that both things are true. We share similar visual systems with other vertebrate species, and most vertebrates have symmetrical faces. Perhaps both faces and visual systems evolved together in relation to each other.

Preference for faces continues to develop throughout the first year of life (Maurer, 1985). Three-month-olds can perceive some facial expressions. They are best at recognizing a smile, particularly if it is a wide, open-mouth smile and if their mothers encourage attention to faces (Kuchuk et al., 1986). However, it is not until six months that infants become competent at recognition of a variety of specific facial expressions and emotions.

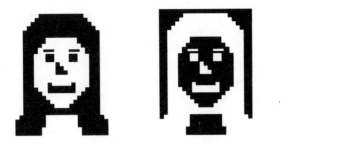

(a)   (b)

(c)   (d)

■ **FIGURE 6.5**
Stimuli Used in Face
Preference Studies
SOURCE: Dannemiller, J. and
Stephens, B. A critical test of
infant pattern preference models.
Child Development, 1988, p. 212.
Society for Research in Child
Development.

Perception of Moving Objects

One problem with the research presented so far is that most of the test stimuli
are drawings or photographs, in other words, static and two-dimensional
representations. You might think that babies would be more familiar with
moving three-dimensional objects and faces, and thus they might recognize
differences between moving objects better than stationary ones.

This seems to be true. Infants at this age look longer at dynamic faces and
moving patterns than at static ones (Kaufmann & Kaufmann, 1980; Samuels,
1985). Infants habituated to a moving object do not dishabituate to the same
object presented from different stationary views (Kellman, 1984; Kellman &
Spelke, 1983), and infants habituated to a rigid object making one type of
movement do not dishabituate to the same object making different types of
movements (Gibson et al., 1979).

In addition, by three or four months, infants perceive moving objects as
whole units. Infants appear to use object movements to detect whether an
object is two- or three-dimensional (Yonas et al., 1987). If part of a moving
rigid rod is blocked from the infants' view by a screen, the infants still
recognize the object when the screen is removed (Kellman & Spelke, 1983),
and by five months, infants will reach for small moving objects that appear to
be in front of larger stationary objects, but do not reach for small moving
objects that are behind the larger object (Von Hofsten & Spelke, 1985).

By using movement cues, four-month-old infants are also aware that objects
are solid and that they take up their own space. In one study, a platform like

210   Infancy ■ Infant, Family, and Society

a drawbridge was rotated back until it hit the top of an object projected on a screen, at which point the platform stopped. In another condition, the platform kept rotating as if it was passing directly through the solid object. Babies looked longer at the second event, suggesting that they were puzzled by this spatial impossibility (Baillargeon, 1987).

Finally, infants appear to detect complex patterns of motion. Using a "point light display" technique (Figure 6.6), the movements of a human body during walking can be represented by a series of moving lights on the joints. Using a computer, this light display can be inverted, or the lights can be moved to create displays that would not be biologically possible (joints in incorrect locations and body parts moving in opposite ways). Between three and five months, infants prefer to look at normal walkers or runners compared to inverted ones or biologically impossible ones (Bertenthal, Proffitt, & Cutting, 1984; 1987; Fox & McDaniels, 1982).

As with the infant's preference for faces, it appears that the perceptual system early in life is disposed to detect real-world information. Infants appear to be able to see not only patterns but also whole objects. They are better at detecting relevant information (such as whether the object can be reached and grasped or whether the object is familiar) if they are able to see the object from multiple perspectives and in motion.

From a continuous inspection of a moving object, infants can detect what is similar about the object seen from different perspectives. Some have suggested that the perception "this is a whole object" is derived from detecting the object's invariant properties as seen from different perspectives (Ruff, 1978; 1985). *Invariance* refers to those aspects of the object that remain the same regardless of how the object is moved. There is some controversy over

■ **FIGURE 6.6**
Motion Perception Stimuli

Panel A shows the canonical display of 11 point-lights moving as if attached to the head and major joints of a person walking. The motion vectors drawn through each point represent the perceived motions of the display. Panel B depicts the scrambled walker display, which is identical to the canonical display except that the relative locations of the point-lights are scrambled. Correspondingly numbered points in the two displays undergo identical motions.

SOURCE: Bertenthal, B., Proffitt, D., & Cutting, J. Infant sensitivity to figural coherence in biomechanical motions. *Journal of Experimental Child Psychology*, 1984, p. 217, American Psychological Association.

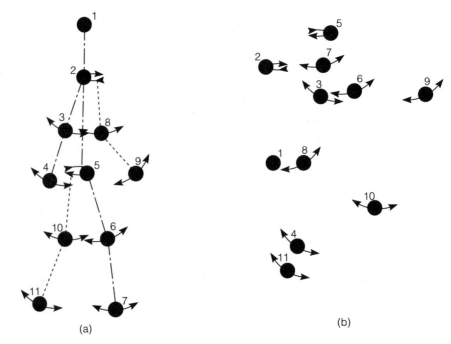
(a) (b)

exactly how infants detect invariances (do they compare angles, distances, overall shapes, or what?), but there is no doubt that infants like to seek out invariant properties of objects at a very early age.

Other Perceptual Developments

We saw in the last chapter that infant auditory perception is rather good during the first two months of life. Infants recognize and prefer their mothers' voices at birth, for example. By four months, infants prefer human speech to nonspeech sounds (Fernald, 1985).

Infants appear to be able to detect different emotions expressed in the voice earlier than they can see differences between facial expressions. Five-month-old infants listened longer to positive compared to negative vocalizations, and they displayed appropriate facial expressions when hearing these two types of sounds. There was more smiling to voices expressing approval and more frowns to voices expressing disapproval (Fernald, in press). Since the babies could not have understood the content of the speech, they must have detected the emotional information from the auditory cues alone: pitch, timing, and intensity.

Infants can discriminate between different speech sounds at birth, and by four months, they can recognize invariant aspects of sounds. Thus, infants detect the similarities between syllables all of which begin or end with the same vowel or the same consonant sounds (Jusczyk & Derrah, 1987).

Speed of auditory processing also improves. At birth, infants can recognize sounds and locate sound sources, but only if the sound is repeated many times or if the sound is heard for at least twenty seconds. By three to four months, sounds can be recognized after shorter exposures, and infants can localize the source of briefly heard sound at wider angles from the midline of the body than they could at birth (Aslin, 1987; Morrongiello et al., 1990).

Sound localization is improved by three months if the infant has visual cues about the sound source, compared to a sound heard in the dark or made from behind a screen (Morrongiello & Rocca, 1987). Infants also seem to detect relationships between sights and sounds at this age. There is a preference for hearing a film soundtrack that is synchronized with the visual object's movements and sound compared to a soundtrack that has been altered (Bahrick, 1988). Babies prefer to look at visual objects that make a noise compared to silent objects (Lawson & Ruff, 1984).

These results and other similar research (Broerse et al., 1983; Spelke & Owsley, 1979) suggest that infants perceive objects cross-modally. *Cross-modal perception* is the ability to integrate information coming from at least two sensory modalities. Infants appear to expect sights and sounds to "go together" after about four months of age. Indeed, they seem to treat information from one sense modality as equivalent to another modality. Infants habituated to an auditory rhythm did not dishabituate to seeing a visual object move to the same beat and vice-versa (Mendelson & Ferland, 1982).

Cross-modal transfer of information between vision and touch occurs at about four to six months, a bit later than visual-auditory transfer, probably because infants do not have exposure to handling objects much before this age (Rose & Ruff, 1987; Streri & Spelke, 1989). There is one study, reported above in the section on motor development, that found there is transfer earlier between vision and touch if infants are able to explore the object with their mouths (Rochat, 1989). More studies need to be done in this relatively underexplored area of perceptual development.

■ COGNITIVE DEVELOPMENT

Cognition involves the processing of perceived information. Cognition includes learning and memory and the ability to mentally compare different situations in order to evaluate their similarities and differences. In actuality, since perception involves memory and comparison in the detection of the familiar and of invariant properties of objects and sounds, it is often difficult to separate one from the other.

Thus far, we have discussed cognition in terms of different information processing steps: perceiving, habituating, learning, and remembering. A number of important developmental changes take place in these areas during the period of two to five months. Another way to think about cognition is not as separate information processing steps but as a unified approach to understanding and acting in the environment. This approach is more typical of Piaget's theory of cognitive development in infants (refer to Chapter 2). In this section, we'll first discuss the developments in individual aspects of information processing and then describe Piaget's views about infants of this age.

Habituation

During the period from two to five months, infants improve in their speed of information processing, due in part to rapid changes in myelination and the formation of synapses and in part to an increasing ability to focus attention on familiar types of tasks. While a newborn could take as long as 5 or 10 minutes to habituate to a repeated stimulus, by three months of age, infants typically habituate within 1.5 to 2 minutes. By six months, this time drops to half a minute (Bornstein, 1985). Like all cognitive and perceptual tasks, the speed of information processing will also depend on the complexity and difficulty of the stimulus and on the infant's alertness at the time of testing.

There are individual differences in the speed of habituation. Infants who are fast habituators at three months are more likely to be fast habituators at six months (Colombo et al., 1987; Mayes & Keesen, 1989). Infants who are faster habituators tend to have parents who stimulate their abilty to focus visual attention (Bornstein & Benasich, 1986). Speed of habituation is also correlated with perinatal risk factors, illness, nutrition, and poor state control (Bornstein, 1985; Moss et al., 1988) and thus may be used as an early index of cognitive differences. Unfortunately, although these individual differences seem fairly good predictors over a period of four or five months, they are not likely to predict long-term differences in cognitive development.

Long-Term Memory

We saw in the last chapter that infants have short-term memories lasting several hours or days right from birth. Research done in the 1970s showed that long-term memories lasting several weeks were present in five-month-old infants. Researchers used a standard habituation procedure to get infants familiar with a set of face stimuli. They were tested on the same day and dishabituated to a novel face not contained in the group of familiar faces to which they had been exposed. After several days or weeks, the infants were returned to the same laboratory and shown a few of the familiar and a few novel faces. They looked more at the novel faces, even without being "reminded" about the total group of previously familiarized faces (Cornell, 1979; Fagan, 1979).

Other studies have shown such memories in three-month-olds using a contingent learning procedure (Sullivan et al., 1979). Babies were placed supine in cribs with brightly colored mobiles suspended overhead. Experimenters decided beforehand that they would move the mobile if the baby kicked with either the right or the left foot (but not with both feet). The mobile actually moved more the harder the infant kicked, thus increasing the speed of conditioning. On the initial training day, the babies were given about fifteen to twenty minutes of training. Then the babies were brought back to the same laboratory a few days later and placed in cribs without any further training.

Infants who were tested less than two weeks after training managed to repeat the same leg movements they learned during training, although the longer the delay between training and testing, the longer it took the infants to remember to kick in a particular way. After a delay of longer than two weeks, infants behaved as if they had never seen the mobile. If they were retrained at intervals shorter than two weeks, infants could reactivate the memory for an indefinite period (Rovee-Collier et al., 1981).

Even at three months, infants rely on visual cues about their immediate surroundings that help them remember how to kick as trained. When babies were retested in different cribs, in the same cribs with different colored bumpers, or with different mobiles, they were less likely to remember the event (Butler & Rovee-Collier, 1989). Some studies have shown that infants even remember the individual components of the mobile. If components of different colors or shapes are substituted, even several weeks later, the infants can notice this (Hayne et al., 1987). These findings suggest that familiar, routine environments may be important for infants of this age as they begin to develop a sense of permanence and stability of the world and what to expect from it.

On the other hand, lack of stability in the environment may have negative consequences for cognitive development. Crying and the negative emotion associated with it seems to create a kind of amnesia for experiences associated with the crying (Fagen et al., 1989). Using a similar mobile-kicking contingent procedure, during training the experimenters changed the mobile from one with ten components to one with only two components. Some of the infants cried as a result of this change. Other did not. The infants who cried were not able to reactivate the kicking technique to the ten component mobile even one week later. The infants who did not cry when the mobile was changed could easily reactivate the kicking.

Apparently, the emotion associated with a learning situation becomes part of the memory, as do the specific sights and sounds of the surrounding environment in which the training takes place. These studies are providing a much richer view of infant experience and development than a strict information-processing perspective. They suggest that learning and development occur in an integrated way that involves the whole infant, as well as the situation in which the learning occurs.

Piagetian Perspectives on Cognitive Development

This integrated view of development is similar to that of Jean Piaget (refer to Chapter 2). Piaget viewed infant actions as adaptations to the environment, adaptations that involve the whole infant; motor, cognitive, and emotional aspects are interconnected. During the newborn period, the majority of the infant's actions are in the form of mostly automatic reflexes. The infant uses reflexes to adapt to the environment (such as with rooting, sucking, and grasping), but it cannot be said that the infant is conscious of his or her own activity or that the infant uses the reflexes in a purposeful way. Nevertheless, reflexes are not rigid and mechanical. We saw in the last chapter that even reflexes can be accommodated to the particular situation, as in sucking on different-shaped nipples or displaying stepping movements only when lying supine.

During the period from about one to about five months, infants begin to act somewhat more purposefully. They are able to recognize the connections between their behavior and events in the environment, as we saw in the research related to making mobiles move when kicking. We know from some studies that even newborns can recognize the connections between their behavior and the environment. For example, infants can be trained using conditioned sucking techniques to suck in a particular way to hear their own mother's voice. However, it takes a long time to train newborns to do this, and the training is not always successful.

By two to three months, the ability to recognize simple connections between behavior and its effect is very well established and can be seen in almost everything the baby does. Piaget noticed this in each of his own three children—Laurent, Lucienne, and Jacqueline—as he saw them discover the relationship between their behavior and its effects and then repeat the same behavior many times and often with great delight. The observations in the box, taken directly from Piaget's observation notes, describe how Laurent at two months and twenty-one days of age repeatedly bends his head back to look at his crib. At about the same age, Lucienne repeatedly coughs for the "fun" of it.

■ OBSERVATION: Stage II Behavior (Piaget, 1952, pp. 70, 79)

At 0;2(21), in the morning, Laurent spontaneously bends his head backward and surveys the end of the bassinet from this position. Then he smiles, returns to his normal position and then begins again. . . .

In certain special cases the tendency to repeat, by circular reactions, sounds discovered by pure chance, may be observed. Thus at 0;2(12) Lucienne, after coughing, recommences several times for fun and smiles. Laurent puffs out his breath, producing an indefinite sound. At 0;2(26) he reproduces the peals of his voice which ordinarily accompany his laughter, but without laughing and out of pure phonetic interest. At 0;2(15) Lucienne uses her voice in similar circumstances.

Piaget called these repetitive movements *circular reactions*. During sensorimotor Stage II, the circular reactions described in the box are called *primary
circular reactions*. Primary circular reactions are repetitive movements in
which the infant focuses on his or her own actions. In some cases, the actions
involve other objects (like kicking to get a mobile to move), and in other
cases, they involve the infant's own body. The infants at this stage do not
appear to be interested in the object for its own sake. Their actions are not
intended to explore the object's properties but rather to experience their own
behavior and its effects.

Later during Stage II, infants are beginning to combine different primary
circular reaction schemes into more unified behavior patterns. An example of
this is the development of visually guided reaching at about four months.
Piaget viewed this as the integration of vision, arm, and hand actions: the
baby somehow makes the connection between seen objects and his or her own
actions. During the next stage, secondary circular reactions are more focused
on repeated attempts to explore the properties of objects (such as repeated
banging or repeated fingering of a toy).

The Stage II baby is apparently not making a conscious distinction between
the movements of the mobile and the movements of his or her own body.
Babies of this age probably exist in a world in which what they perceive is
directly linked to what they feel. It is a bit like young children who believe
that the world disappears when they close their eyes or that other people exist
only to meet their needs.

The primary circular reactions create powerful motivations for babies to
become engaged in the environment, especially if adults create highly
ritualized and repetitive situations as in feeding, playing, bathing, and
diapering. During this period of development, babies begin to notice the
regularity in these routines. They smile and show other signs of pleasure when
involved in such routines. A limitation of babies of this age is that they don't
enjoy deviations from the routines, which makes it difficult for them to
quickly adapt to new care givers. This seems to be related to the infant's
perception of contingent relationships between his or her behavior and its
effects.

One of the most important elements in early learning and memory
development is the experience of contingency (see Chapter 5). Two-month-
olds are capable of discovering contingencies, and one study has shown that
the babies enjoy it. The movements of a mobile were linked to infants' head
presses on an automatic pillow in a study done by Watson (1973). If the
infants discovered that the mobile would move with respect to their head
presses, they usually smiled and cooed. In contrast, if the pillow was
"capricious" and inconsistently rewarded head presses, infants became
frustrated and distressed.

These findings have implications for the kinds of experiences adults should
provide for infants during Piaget's Stage II. If babies realize that their
environment is controllable—that their own actions will produce predictable
responses in the people and objects around them—they will show increasing
positive involvement with the world. If the environment is capricious, infants
will become distressed, angry, and withdrawn or simply uninterested
(Watson, 1973). It is important, therefore, for adults to adapt their behavior
to be responsive to infants so the infants will gain a sense of efficacy that will

lead to further exploration. In early infancy, exploration, cognition, and motor behavior are all part of the same underlying developmental process.

Another area in which we see a transition between reflexive action and primary circular reactions is infant vocalization.

During the first two months of life, infants' vocalizations are of three sorts: cry, discomfort, and "vegetative" (Stark et al., 1975). The cry is used to express acute distress, whereas discomfort sounds are associated with distress that is not as severe; they are more like fussing or complaining than crying. The infant's vegetative repertoire includes a series of biological noises, such as the cough, burp, sneeze, hiccup, suck, snort, grunt, and sigh. These sounds are all so basic to the biological necessities of the infant organism that there is very little individual variation across infants, nor do they change much in sound characteristics over time.

Somewhere between five and eight weeks, most infants begin to "coo." As distinguished from the other sounds already in the infant's repertoire, cooing is primarily an expression of comfort. If all the infant's sounds are analyzed with sophisticated sound recording and frequency amplitude-resolving equipment, it is found that all the auditory properties of cooing can be found in the more primitive forms of sound making. According to Stark (1978), these findings suggest that infants are beginning to take the sounds they made reflexively and recombine them in the form of exploratory vocal activity. Recalling Lucienne's coughing for fun, we see that infants begin to use their voicing in repetitive ways reminiscent of other motor circular reactions.

Cognition refers in part to the process by which we come to understand the environment and in part to the way we store and retrieve that information. For the young infant, the process of knowing involves action upon the environment. According to Piaget, *the meaning of a particular object or person to the infant is the very motor action the child is able to perform on it.*

For example, a rattle *means* "graspable, seeable, suckable." During this stage of sensorimotor development, the rattle is not yet "an *object* to be grasped, seen, or sucked," for that kind of conceptualization of the rattle as object would require that the infant understand the separateness of the object as a physical entity, which does not begin until eight months of age. In Stage II, the "object" is "known" simply by the actions that can be performed on it.

Much of what goes on in Stage II, then, is a systematic exploration of the infant's own body. The repetitious play with reaching, tapping, cooing, banging, and other behaviors is a self-contained curriculum in the workings of the muscles and other voluntarily controlled body parts. All the while, the infants are expanding their minds and increasing their store of remembered experiences and lists of pleasurable and noxious situations. These will come in handy as they expand into the next stage of development.

In the section of this chapter on perception, we saw that the infant's ability to perceive object solidity, distance, and depth seems more sophisticated than what the infant can actually do with the objects, causing some to question Piaget's strict view that cognition is directly related to action. It could be that Piaget overlooked some basic cognitive ability of the four-month-old to form a concept of objects and space without direct experience (Baillargeon, 1987).

Another interpretation derives from a dynamic systems perspective in which we consider not only the babies' abilities but also the fact that babies of this age are growing up in a social context. Because of the presence of adult care givers, babies have the experience of being moved around in space, even though they cannot move themselves. Even before infants can reach for and manipulate objects, adults bring objects into view, manipulate the objects in appropriate ways (like shaking a rattle and turning a ball around), and place them into the babies' hands (see earlier discussion of supports and resources for motor development in this chapter). Thus, even though Piaget thought to integrate motor, perceptual, cognitive, and emotional aspects of the infant, he failed to recognize the role of adults in supporting infant development.

■ EMOTIONAL DEVELOPMENT

One of Piaget's main contributions was the recognition that cognition and perception do not occur in a vacuum: all of the infant's experiences are connected to feelings. The studies of contingency learning clearly show that motivation to explore can be heightened or dampened by changing the contingency of the child's experiences. Before we deal directly with the topic of emotional development, we introduce some basic terminology.

Emotional development is a concept that takes account of a number of related aspects of an individual's functioning. The development of emotional *expression* concerns the study of the behavioral manifestations of inner experience. Emotional development also concerns changes in that inner world of feelings as the infant matures. This branch of the study of emotional development is often referred to as *affective* development. Still another part to the puzzle of emotional development is the way in which the infant learns self-control over affective states. This part of the study of emotion is referred to by many different names, depending on theoretical and methodological orientation. Synonymns for self-control are self-regulation, coping skills, arousal tolerance, and ego functions (see Chapter 2).

These three areas of emotional development—expression, affect, and self-regulation—will concern us throughout this book. There are many other areas of interest under the general heading of emotional development. These include people's verbal expression of their affective states, their ability to conceptualize their own affective state, and their ability to perceive another person's affective state (Fogel, 1982c). These abilities mostly apply to the older infant and young child, and the later chapters of this book will touch on them.

Changes in Emotional Expression

It is said that infants have all the basic emotional expressions at birth (Peiper, 1963), but these are reflexes that disappear after several weeks. There are only a relatively small number of functional expressions in a one-month-old infant, and these primarily are related to the affect of distress. The expression involves frowning (knit brows with the mouth turned down at the corners). It usually is accompanied by crying, generally with the eyes closed. Younger infants often may exhibit a trembling of the lips during crying, as well as a reddening of the face if the cry is intense enough. Chapter 5 described the different auditory characteristics of the types of crying seen in young infants.

During waking states, infants of one month may exhibit a range of expression between alertness and drowsiness. When infants are alert, their eyes are wide and bright, and their brows and mouth may alternate between movement and stillness. During obligatory attention episodes, infants may stare motionless for long periods.

Infants of this age often fade into brief periods of "dulling." Their eyes, although open and fixed, take on a glazed or dull quality. Smiles usually are not seen during alert states until about six weeks of age.

At one month, infants' faces seem to be able to register only levels of attention and arousal, plus degrees of distress. The number of distress expressions significantly decreases during the next few months, at the same time giving way to the appearance of more complex expressions. The form of the distress expression changes.

About the age of three months, the intensity of infant distress lessens. Infants develop a brief negative sounding vocalization, usually called fussing as distinguished from crying, that accompanies a distress facial expression. Fussing babies usually vocalize for a brief period, then become silent or coo for a while, and then return to fussing (Hopkins & von Wulfften Palthe, 1987).

By four months, infants may still exhibit intense distress cries, but now they often cry with their eyes open. Crying also may be accompanied by directed actions such as kicking, pulling, or pushing, and it may have few or no tears. These types of cries signal a new kind of expression: anger. Fear, another reaction related to distress, does not appear until later in the first year, but infants at four months can show "wary" or hesitant expressions. Infants of this age are capable of turning their heads or looking away from an unpleasant or confusing situation. Their wary or ambivalent expressions consist of an increased rate of gazing away from and looking back at the situation, combined with a reduction of expressions of positive affect (Bronson, 1972; Sroufe, 1979).

States of contentment and alertness are still present, but now the infant can express positive emotion through smiling and cooing. Smiling is probably one of the most studied of all the expressions; consequently, we know a good deal about its development. When presented with a motionless face, infants will spontaneously smile once they are older than two months. The amount of smiling to a motionless face reaches a peak at about four months, followed by a gradual decline over the first year. Studies done on institutionalized infants who receive less stimulation than infants raised at home have shown a similar pattern for the development of the smile, but the institutional infant's smiling first appears about one month later than the infants raised at home and reaches its peak a month later as well (Ambrose, 1961; Gewirtz, 1965). The similar patterns of development suggest that there is a strong maturational component in the development of smiling but that environmental stimulation may speed or slow the processes.

Smiling was observed in the context of social interaction, and similar developmental patterns were observed (Fogel, 1982a). It was found that beginning at three months, during social interactions, smiling occurred in clusters. The infant would smile four or five times in rapid succession, followed by a relative pause of twenty or thirty seconds, after which a new bout of smiles would begin. Evidently the continued development of the infant's cognitive capacities and the increased experience with faces make a dynamic and contingent adult face a better elicitor of smiling after four months than a motionless face.

The smiling response can be seen in blind infants at this age (Freedman, 1974). The first smiles of a blind infant are like those of other babies: they appear about one month of age and are fleeting. They can be evoked using a gentle touch or a soft sound and have a certain reflexive quality. The blind infant, however, continues to exhibit this type of smiling until six or seven months of age, when the smiles again take on the same character as those of sighted six-month-olds. Apparently, vision plays some role in the manifestation of prolonged social smiling seen in sighted infants between the ages of two and six months, but somehow the blind infants manage to develop a full-fledged smile even without the aid of vision (Freedman, 1974).

Development of Emotion Regulation

Emotion regulation (ER) gradually emerges over the first four months of life, as shown by the following transitions: a decrease in the overall amount of crying, a reduction in the force of obligatory attention, and the mastery of continuous and repeated bouts of smiling.

ER, if it works well, allows the individual to control the negative or overwhelming aspects of a situation without losing touch with the situation totally. Although looking away is a total break with something, it is only a momentary one, allowing the baby enough time to regroup his or her emotional forces for a new assault on the environment. ER is shown not merely by looking away but by the overall pattern of looking away and then back in a repeated fashion.

A second important ER skill that develops in the infant's third month is the smile itself. Studies on the relationship between heart rate changes and the occurrence of smiling have shown that smiles occur neither when heart rate is increasing nor when it is at its peak but rather when heart rate is on the decline (Sroufe & Waters, 1976). Smiling is a relaxation response, and it seems to be a way of reducing arousal without turning away from the situation.

When infants are developing new ways to maintain attention during periods of emotional arousal, they also are widening the range of arousal levels they can tolerate. At the upper end of arousal, the one-month-old is able to tolerate stimulation only if it is gentle and slowly changing, whereas the three-month-old can handle a wider variety of stimulation with more abrupt changes, such as a highly animated, talking adult.

A final contribution to ER is the baby's developing sensorimotor skills. During this period, the ability of infants to regulate their own distress improves as they can reach for objects and hold them without dropping them (Kopp, 1989). In relation to hand-to-mouth activity, discussed in the last chapter, infants can calm themselves down after four months, when they can reliably get the hand to the mouth and keep it there while engaged in other activities, as shown in Figure 6.7 (Thelen & Fogel, 1989; Toda & Fogel, 1989).

Researchers are gradually beginning to recognize that young infants use their whole bodies in emotion expressions and emotion regulations. ER

■ FIGURE 6.7
**Hand-to-Mouth
Activity**

SOURCE: Thelen & Fogel, 1989.

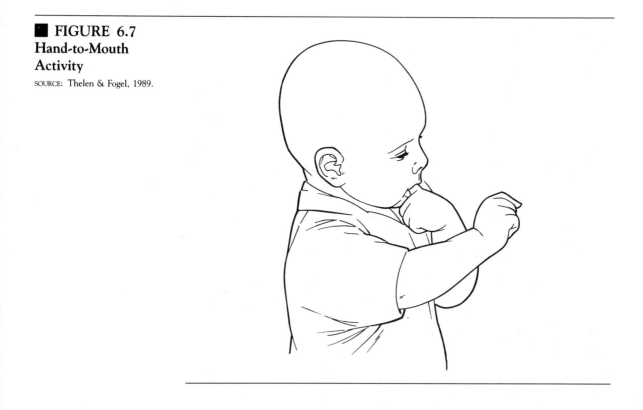

derives from the use of some nonemotional action pattern (like reaching for objects) to help the baby calm down when upset (Campos et al., 1989; Kopp, 1989). On the other hand, reaching for objects and other sensorimotor skills bring the infant into contact with situations never before encountered. The ability to reach generates new pleasures and also new sources of frustration. In this sense, emotion and emotion regulation do not reflect mere responses to the situation but also the baby's goals in the situation (Campos et al., 1989).

Suppose, for example, that the baby expresses anger because an adult is teasing and not giving the baby a toy. On the one hand, this means the baby is angry as a response to the situation, but the anger is defined in terms of some future desired state of affairs (getting the object). Thus, by about four or five months, emotions and how they are regulated are future-oriented and thus depend in part on motivations, memories, and cognitive expectancies.

The role of the adults should not be forgotten. Often, care givers can provide just the right supports that, when combined with the infant's own abilities, result in a spontaneous relaxation. Adults can also introduce new objects or challenge the baby to learn new social routines and games. These then become part of the baby's future orientation. We can better understand, in this case, why a baby is happy when a familiar game is repeated many times and why a baby gets upset if adults fail to play by the rules. Thus, when we take account not only facial expression but also other infant actions, cognitions, and the actions of adults, we may see more clearly the conditions conducive to ER (Fogel & Thelen, 1987).

Adults use exaggerated facial expressions and vocalizations when playing with infants between 2 and 6 months of age.

■ SOCIAL DEVELOPMENT

It is primarily in the company of adult care givers that infants of this age show the widest range of emotion expressions. In the company of infants, adults act in ways that engage the infants' attention and activate their emotions. By the age of two months, infants make distinctly different actions toward adults compared to other animate stimuli. For example, infants are more likely to smile, vocalize, and make relaxed arm movements with responsive adults compared to peers (Fogel, 1979b), to inanimate faces (Field, 1979), and to animate and inanimate toys (Legerstee et al., 1987).

First, we'll examine the types of behavior adults use with infants and some cultural differences in adult behavior. Next, we'll discuss how adult-infant interactions may be related to individual differences in infant development.

Adult Behavior with Infants

Exaggeration. In the company of young infants, adults tend to exaggerate particular aspects of their speech and body movement. Facial expressions are made larger than usual, as in mock surprise and mock sadness. Adults shake and nod their heads in deliberate movements. In speech, adults raise the pitch of their voices and have wider variations in pitch than when speaking to other adults. This tendency to exaggerate speech and in particular to widen the range of pitch has been found in a large number of different cultures (Fernald & Kuhl, 1987; Fernald & Simon, 1984; Jacobson et al., 1983; Papousek et al., 1985; Stern et al., 1983). Even in languages in which the pitch of a syllable conveys linguistic meaning—in tonal languages such as Mandarin Chinese—researchers have found overall increases of pitch when adults talk to babies compared to other adults (Grieser & Kuhl, 1988).

Slowing Down and Simplification. A second aspect of adult behavior with young infants is the tendency to slow down and simplify behavior. Each action, such as a head nod or a facial expression, is held for a longer period with an infant than with another adult. In addition, when talking to infants, adults leave longer pauses between their individual actions (Fernald & Simon, 1984; Papousek et al., 1985; Snow, 1977; Stern, 1977). Adults will prolong particular syllables and speak more slowly overall, giving their speech a melodic or sing-song quality (Papousek & Papousek, 1981). Similarly, adults reduce the complexity of their behavior and their speech when talking to infants, using single words instead of sentences or simple actions, such as a single head nod and a wide smile.

Rhythm and Repetition. Adults also use highly repetitive and rhythmic activities. They might say the same word or phrase many times with minor variations or make a series of exaggerated head nods punctuated with a clap or a vocalization. Different rhythms are used depending upon the purpose of the behavior (soothing versus attention getting) and depending upon the baby's responsiveness to the adult (Fogel, 1977; Koester, 1987; Papousek & Papousek, 1987).

When applied to speech, exaggeration, slowing down, rhythm, and melody make up a package that investigators have called *motherese.* Not only does it appear to occur in many different languages, but babies actually prefer to listen to motherese compared to normal adult speech (Fernald, 1985).

Matching and Attunement. A large share of adult behavior is used for matching or imitating the infant's behavior. Although infants can imitate adults, adults imitate babies much more. This imitation may involve matching infant vocal sounds, pitches, rhythms, facial expressions, body movements, and so on (Malatesta & Haviland, 1982; Moran et al., 1987; Papousek & Papousek, 1987). A concept related to matching is *attunement* (Stern, 1985), in which the adult's behavior is similar to an infant's but not an exact copy. For example, an infant may shake his or her arm up and down in a rhythmical motion. The parent may respond in a different modality, such as vocalizing "yea-yea-yea-yea" in exactly the same rhythm as the baby's arm movements.

Turn Taking. Finally, adults engage in turn-taking behavior with babies. In the early months, infants do not yet have a concept of turn taking. Adults fill in the natural pauses of the infant's actions with their own actions, creating the appearance of turn taking (Brazelton et al., 1974; Cohn & Tronick, 1988; Fogel, 1977; Trevarthen, 1977). This adult-controlled pattern of turn taking has been called *protoconversation* (Bateson, 1975). During this early period, adults will often overlap their vocalizations and actions with those of the infant, creating a sense of shared emotion, as when adults vocalize at the same time the baby is cooing (Ginsburg & Kilbourne, 1988; Stern et al., 1975).

Between the ages of four to six months, infants begin to shift to a more interactive mode of behavior: they learn to wait until the adult pauses before beginning their own actions. Infants appear to take the initiative more often by looking in the mother's direction and waiting until she responds before smiling or vocalizing (Cohn & Tronick, 1988; Kaye & Fogel, 1980). By about five months, then, infants are beginning to become true social partners rather than merely appreciative audiences for the display of motherese.

Cultural Differences in Adult Behavior toward Infants

We have already mentioned that some aspects of motherese may be universally seen in all cultures. In general, because babies are similar around the world, we can expect them to elicit similar sorts of behavior from adults. On the other hand, there are interesting cultural differences in the styles of interactions with infants.

Although virtually all mothers speak to their babies and use motherese when they do speak, Western mothers (Europe and North America) tend to rely more heavily on speech as a primary modality of stimulation for babies of this age. Other cultures use nonvocal forms of stimulation.

We have already seen how some African mothers interact with their babies using a very large variety of postural manipulations and motor exercise. In a study of infant development in Nigeria, Eluama infants (native language, Igbo) were compared to a group of infants in Oxford, England (Whiten & Milner, 1986). At three months of age, Eluama infants spend almost all their time, whether awake or asleep, in physical contact with an adult or within three feet of the adult. When the Elauma infants cried, they were responded to more often and more quickly than were the English babies, and the response from the adult was more likely to be physical rather than verbal. The Eluama infant is more a part of the mother's everyday life. She carries the baby around with her, and babies often ride on the mothers' backs or sit in their laps while the mothers go about their daily chores. The babies sleep next to their mothers. The pattern of close physical contact and rapid response to crying is common among hunting and gathering cultures worldwide (Konner, 1977).

Although Eluama babies receive as much stimulation with objects, they do not receive as much motherese-type behavior as the Western babies. On the other hand, Nigerian parents believe that a baby embodies the soul of a dead ancestor. Adults sometimes talk to the baby as if the baby were the lost relative (Nwokah & Fogel, in press).

Japanese mothers also react in different ways to their babies than North American mothers, and they respond less to their babies' vocalizations (Caudill & Weinstein, 1969; Fogel, Toda, & Kawai, 1988). However, the Japanese are not similar to the African mothers in other respects. They actually spend less time in physical contact with their babies than American mothers when the babies are awake, although Japanese babies sleep with their mothers at night. American mothers hold, rock, bounce, touch, and kiss their babies considerably more than Japanese, and when interacting with babies, American mothers hold their faces closer to the babies (Fogel et al., 1988; Otaki et al., 1986; Shand & Kosawa, 1985).

When they verbalize to babies, Japanese and American mothers are quite different. Over the course of an entire day, the Japanese mothers tend to use more negative vocalizations, such as prohibitions and expressions of negative feelings. When actually engaged in a playful interaction with their babies, Japanese mothers use more nonsense sounds and more baby talk, as shown in Table 6.3, while American mothers use more complete sentences and more recognizable adult words. When an American mother might use vocalizations to get her baby's attention, a Japanese mother either uses vocal noises or makes noise with her hands, like clapping and finger snapping (Toda, Fogel, & Kawai, 1990; Fogel, Toda & Kawai; 1988).

The overall impression of the Japanese mother as being somewhat less expressive and less active and more physically distant from the baby is also seen in some Native American cultures. The Navaho rarely talk to infants, although they are responsive to the babies' cries and touch the babies a great deal. Traditional Navaho keep babies more physically distant from their mothers with the use of cradleboards (Chisholm, 1983; Callaghan, 1981). Similar patterns of behavior have been observed among the Mayan Indians of Mexico (Brazelton, 1977).

In the Japanese and Native American cultures, adults believe that infants are precious and innocent beings, near to God, and that the infants should be kept generally quiet and not influenced by adults until they begin to make some of their own initiatives, around the age of six months. This "hands off" respect for the infant's autonomy and individuality is not found in the West, where we try to influence sleeping, feeding, and interactive social behavior from an early age. We want our babies to be scheduled, to smile at us, and not to cry (Fogel, Stevenson, & Messinger, in press).

The oriental philosophy of childrearing is summed up in the elaborate rituals performed for infants in Hindu culture in India (see Table 6.4). Although the Indian mothers talk to and touch their babies more than the

■ TABLE 6.3 Examples of Baby Talk Used by Japanese Mothers

ENGLISH EQUIVALENT	ADULT SPEECH	BABY TALK	EXPLANATION
Are you hungry?	Onaka suita?	Onaka shuita	Phonological change
Let's play	Asobimashoo	Achobimachoo	Phonological change
Please	Doozo	Doojo	Phonological change
Eye	Me	Meme	Duplication
It hurts	Itai	Itai-tai	Duplication
Get up	Okiru	Okki	Shortening
Hiccup	Shakkuri	Hikku hikku	Mimic sound of action
Lamp	Denki	Denki-san	Use of honorific
Dirty	Katanai	Batchii	Entirely new word

SOURCE: Toda, Fogel, & Kawai 1990.

■ TABLE 6.4   Hindu Beliefs About the Stages of Infancy and
             Childhood

STAGE	MODE OF RELATIONSHIP	RITUAL PERFORMED AT THE END OF THE STAGE
Garbha (fetus)	Symbolic	Jatakama: Birthing ritual
Ksheerda (infancy)	Dyadic intimacy (0–1 month)	Namakarana: Naming ceremony, the child meets father and siblings for the first time
	Dyad in family (1–4 months)	Nishakarmana: First outing, first look at the sun and the moon
	Dyad in world (4–8 months)	Annaprasana: Introduction to solid foods, weaning from the breast
Ksheerannada (early childhood)	Dyad dissolution (8 months–3 years)	Chudakarana: First ritual cutting of the hair

SOURCE: Sharan, 1988.

Japanese, they tend to keep the babies quiet and provide a very gradual introduction of the babies to the world, which does not begin in earnest until six to nine months, when in India early childhood is considered to begin.

Effects of Adult Behaviors on Infants

We don't know to what extent the parent's use of motherese and related verbal and nonverbal baby-directed communication actually contributes to infant social and emotional development. A large number of studies have documented correlations between mother behavior during social interaction and infant behavior at the same age and also at later ages. The more responsive the mother, in general, the less responsive the baby (Dunham et al., 1989; Symons & Moran, 1987; Tronick & Cohn, 1989). Unfortunately, it is impossible to determine whether these correlations result from the effects of the parents on the infants or from differences between infants that may affect the way the parents behave.

Types of Individual Differences Between Infants. Even at birth, babies are different from each other in their emotional responsivity and social behavior. Some babies are highly expressive in their facial and body movements, and others are relatively poker-faced, or inexpressive (Field, Greenberg, Woodson, Cohen, & Garcia, 1984; Fox, 1985; Lipsitt, 1981) and such differences can be found throughout the first year of life (Stifter, Fox, & Porges, 1989).

Some research has shown that the infants who are less expressive are actually more aroused by stimulation than the more expressive infants. The low-expressive infants tend to have higher overall heart rates, higher cortisol (a hormone related to arousal), and higher muscle tension (Field, 1987; Fox & Davidson, 1988; Kagan et al., 1987). Thus, these children have been referred to as inhibited, because they are physiologically predisposed to be highly responsive to stimulation, but they tend to withdraw from stimulation rather than express signs of engagement or enjoyment. Very similar patterns of individual differences have been observed in infant monkeys (Suomi, 1987).

There are many ways in which such individual differences may be created and preserved. One possibility is that they are genetically based. In part, this might be the case since identical twins are somewhat more likely to be similar in emotional reactivity than fraternal twins. On the other hand, these patterns may result from prenatal and perinatal causes, such as poor health and prematurity (Field, 1987). Finally, these differences may be due to how their mothers interact with the babies and respond to their emotional expressions.

It is clear that babies make some contribution to how others respond to them. A baby who is easily aroused is likely to withdraw from social interaction rather quickly. Adults often overreact to this withdrawal by trying even more aggressively to get the baby's attention, which in turn causes the baby to withdraw even more (Field, 1987; Gianino & Tronick, 1988). Under most circumstances, adults are highly attuned to baby's responses. Most adults, regardless of age or parenting experience, are able to correctly identify an infant's state just by hearing the sounds the baby makes in each state (Papousek, 1989).

On the other hand, babies beginning at two months of age seem highly sensitive to how others interact with them. This conclusion derives from studies of differences in young infants' responses to mothers, fathers, and unfamiliar persons (Dixon et al., 1984; Fogel, 1979a; 1979b; Parke, 1979). There is also a series of studies in which mothers are asked to modify their normal behavior with their infants so that the effect of such changes on the infants can be assessed.

Experimental Disturbances of Interactions. In one type of study procedure used with babies between two and five months, the mother is asked to play with and talk to her baby as she might do at home. After several minutes of positively toned play, the experimenter asks the mother to cease talking and hold her face in a neutral, nonexpressive pose. This is called the *still-face* procedure. In other studies, mothers are asked to simulate depression. Essentially, these procedures interfere with the mother's normally contingent responsiveness to her baby's expressions and vocalizations.

What do babies do when confronted with this unexpectedly unresponsive mother? Some babies continue to smile and look at the mother for a few seconds, after which they stop smiling and look away from the mother for increasingly longer periods of time. If the distorted mother behavior goes on for more than a few minutes, the babies becomes increasingly distressed and withdrawn. When mothers are asked to resume their normal interactions, most of the infants begin to cry if they had not cried already, perhaps with the intent to communicate the prior distress (Cohn & Tronick, 1983; Cohn & Elmore, 1988; Fogel et al., 1983; Toda & Fogel, 1989; Tronick et al., 1978). At the age of three to four months, infants are more distressed at the still face than at separation from the mother (Field et al., 1986; Fogel, 1979b). Babies get equally upset if the still face is posed by the live mother or an image of the mother over closed-circuit TV, but there is no change in the infants' behavior if the TV mother continues to be expressive while the sound is turned off (Gusella et al., 1988). Apparently, it is the sight of the unresponsive mother, rather than the absence of the mother, that is upsetting to the babies.

The Effects of Maternal Depression on Infants. A clearer case of the effects of lasting maternal nonresponsiveness on infants is that of maternal depression. Compared to normal psychological states and to other psychological problems, depression has the strongest effect on infants since its main symptom is a lack of emotionality. Depressed people are not merely sad; rather they are characterized by a flat emotional tone and preoccupation with themselves. These factors make depressed mothers less responsive as parents, which can be a major problem since severe depression occurs in 10 to 12 percent of women following childbirth (Field, 1987).

With infants under six months of age, depressed mothers do not use motherese-type speech (Bettes, 1988), they are less affectionate (Fleming et al., 1988), they are not often contingently responsive to their babies (Bettes, 1988; Field et al., 1985), or they alternate between disengagement and intrusiveness (Cohn et al., 1986). Depressed mothers have trouble tracking the activities of their infants and may fail to protect them from potential dangers by letting the babies fall off their laps, for example, or letting them get into electrical equipment (Gelfand & Teti, in press). Infants of depressed mothers are more likely to be fussy, have low levels of physical activity, and to be withdrawn. These patterns can be seen even when these infants interact with nondepressed adults (Cohn et al., 1986; Cohn et al., 1990; Field et al., 1985; Field et al., 1988; Field et al., 1989).

Unfortunately, the causes of depression are not well-understood, and treatments are slow and not always successful. Research has shown that about half of all mothers experience some mild forms of depression, called *postpartum blues,* that may last for several hours or days (O'Hara et al., 1989). These effects are due primarily to fatigue and stress. Postpartum blues are a normal part of the transition to motherhood and do not present a risk factor for the infant. Clinical depression, on the other hand, has no higher rate of occurrence for postpartum women than for nonchildbearing women. Depression can occur for a variety of reasons, most of which are poorly understood. Since infants and children of depressed mothers are at increased risk, these mothers should be under some form of psychological or psychiatric treatment. Other intervention programs are available that teach depressed mothers to focus on child-care tasks and to pay attention to the needs of the infants (Field et al., 1985; Gelfand & Teti, in press).

In summary, we cannot typically assess the effects of variations of maternal behavior on infants as long as both mother and infant are functioning normally. This is because each is responsive to the other, and through their interaction, they mutually define how the other behaves. This does not mean that the process is intentional or deliberate. While the mother may have particular goals (make the baby smile or reach for a toy), and so does the infant (maintaining a pleasant state, retrieving a toy), the means by which these goals get worked out in interaction is a constant process of mutual negotiation. As a result of this process, both the adult and the baby come to know each other and develop feelings of closeness toward each other. In the next section, we turn to a discussion of the factors affecting the infant's parents.

■ FAMILY AND SOCIETY

Chapter 2 reviewed some of the current theories about the nature of the family interaction. Family systems theory suggests that each member of the family is part of a feedback system with every other family member. In addition, when families have three or more members, the relationship between two of them can affect the third and vice versa (Belsky, 1981). From this perspective, we might predict that the birth of a baby would bring major changes for a family. If it is a first birth, the married couple must adjust to becoming a three-person system. In a three-person family, a new baby creates a new disequilibrium and necessitates an adjustment by each of the other family members.

In addition, developmental changes occur in all members of a family, including the adults and older siblings. In this section, we consider how adults develop through the transition to parenthood that occurs after the birth of the baby.

Developmental tasks of early parenthood

After a child is born, parents must learn to cope with a variety of new conditions, including a total alteration of life-style, lack of sleep, and the adjustment of the marital relationship to include new family members. In general, there are four types of problems new parents must address (Sollie & Miller, 1980).

First, there are the energy demands associated with infant care, such as loss of sleep and extra work resulting in fatigue. Mothers, if they are the primary care givers, must continue with the ordinary household tasks while trying to keep up with the baby. Second, new parenthood places stress on the marital relationship. This includes less time spent together and perhaps jealousy of the baby for taking time away from the marriage. It may take many months for sexual relationships to return to normal and more time before the couple is free to go out alone.

Third, parents begin to feel the responsibility of caring for and rearing a child. No matter how psychologically prepared one is before, the reality of the child's presence brings home the lifelong commitment. Parents may have doubts about their ability to manage this responsibility and to be good parents for their child. Finally, parents must cope with the additional costs of raising a child, in the form of food, clothing, and education. Just going to see a movie might cost double what it did before the child by the time one adds the costs of a baby-sitter. Whatever income a working mother might earn will be lessened by the cost of the child's daytime care. In addition, parents worry about day-to-day problems, such as infant health and sickness, crying, nutrition, and how to resolve conflicts (McKim, 1987; Wilkie & Ames, 1986).

Predictors of success in the transition to parenthood

In general, the degree to which parents will adopt the parenting role depends on both developmental factors in the life of the adult and on concurrent

Family times together can have a special meaning for a couple with a new baby. It is important for families to take time out from work and chores in order to play and relax together.

factors inside and outside the family system. Developmental factors include the adults' relationships with their own parents, their experience with child care, their self-esteem, and their readiness to have children. Concurrent factors include the marital relationship, other family members, the amount of social support available to the parents, and nonfamily factors, such as income and job satisfaction.

One of the key issues in the transition to parenthood is the effect of the infant on the marriage. Having a baby does not seem to alter existing marital relationships. Couples who had the most conflicts prenatally also have the most postnatally (Cowan & Cowan, 1981). The equality versus inequality of role relationships before childbirth tends to predict the amount of marital satisfaction after birth. In general, couples who are more likely to share responsibilities report higher marital satisfaction after childbirth than more traditional couples (Cowan & Cowan, 1981). Other factors found to increase marital satisfaction following childbirth are a positive and warm relationship with one's own parents (Belsky & Isabella, 1985) and a postbirth experience that is not more difficult than anticipated (Belsky et al., 1986). The latter difficulty affects women more than men, since women, even in nontraditional marriages, are more likely to have most of the burden of care in addition to the fatigue following childbirth.

Marital quality itself is strongly associated with both men's and women's involvement in the parenting role. For mothers, a high level of marital satisfaction is related to warmth and sensitivity toward infants, and the amount of father involvement in the marriage plays a major role in the long-term ability of mothers to cope with child rearing. For fathers, marital

APPLICATIONS

Unexpected Death in Infancy

What are some causes of unexpected death in infancy?

Chapter 4 discussed some of the causes of infant death during the newborn period. We saw then that the vast majority of infant deaths occur during the first few days of life. After the first month, the primary causes of infant death may be labeled "unexpected," since in most industrial societies, fatal infant diseases have all but been eliminated through the use of vaccines and preventive care.

One of the major causes of unexpected death in the first year of life is accidents. These may be traffic accidents or home accidents, such as suffocation, burns, poisoning, and drowning. Another major cause of unexpected death is homicide, including maltreatment, infanticide, sexual offenses, kidnapping, and killing accompanied by parental suicide (Hartmann & Molz, 1979).

The most frequent cause of unexpected death in the first year of life is *sudden infant death syndrome* (SIDS), also called *crib death.*

Figure 6.8 on page 234 shows the incidence of SIDS compared with all other causes of infant death in the United States.

What causes SIDS?

One of the problems in diagnosing and preventing SIDS is that there is no single disorder that seems to account for all the cases. The only thing they have in common is the manner of death. The SIDS diagnosis is applied if parents discover that their baby has died, perhaps at night or during a nap, and there is no apparent cause of death. Sometimes a non-SIDS cause of death may be determined following an investigation. Other causes of death that appear to be SIDS-related but are not are accidental asphyxiation, overheating, and infant abuse (Bass et al., 1986).

In the past, a case of SIDS might have brought the parents under suspicion of murder

satisfaction is associated with more positive attitudes toward the parenting role and with more time spent with the infant (Cox et al., 1989; Feldman & Nash, 1986; Heinecke, 1984).

Personality factors also affect adaptation to parenthood. Men who have had a good relationship with their own fathers and who have some personality traits associated with femininity (warmth, nurturance) make better parents. Fathers who are more invested in their careers and who are in mid-life are less likely to show warmth toward infants, although they are more involved in the practical and financial aspects of child care since they make more money than younger fathers (Feldman & Nash, 1986; Parke & Tinsley, 1987).

Interestingly, a very different set of personality factors are associated with parenting for women. Women who have higher self-esteem and a less egocentric orientation, that is, away from their own needs and toward the

APPLICATIONS

by suffocation. The threat of this insinuation, plus the shock, grief, and guilt brought on by the loss of the baby, placed an unusually heavy burden on the parents, many of whom wondered if they indeed had been the cause.

The fact that many SIDS cases seemed to be associated with colds or some mild respiratory problem led some researchers to study the relationship between respiration and SIDS. Very young infants often cease breathing for brief periods. These pauses in breathing, or *apneic pauses*, almost always occur during sleep (Baker & McGinty, 1979). Since most crib deaths occur during sleep, researchers have attempted to establish some connection between apnea and SIDS.

One study found that infants who had a higher frequency of apneic pauses had lower developmental scores for sensorimotor development at nine months of age (Black, Steinschneider, & Sheehe, 1979). This suggests that apnea is associated with sensorimotor skill in some way. Before an apneic episode, infants have been observed to make large motor movements, and during the episode, movement occurs and is accompanied by heart rate changes (Baker & McGinty, 1979; Hoppenbrouwers et al., 1978).

Lipsitt has speculated that the problem with the SIDS infant may not be the apnea, since all infants have apneic episodes, but that it may be related to some sensorimotor deficit that prevents the infant from making the correct movements and heart rate changes that will assist in recovery from the apnea (Lipsitt, 1979a; Lipsitt, Sturges, & Burke, 1979). Some of the sensorimotor deficits that may prevent recovery from apnea during the first year may have been caused by loss of oxygen during the perinatal period, by other inadequacies in the perinatal environment, or by genetic factors associated with low motor control over breathing. There is some evidence that all three factors may cause respiratory weakness (Black et al., 1979; Lipsitt, 1979a; Naeye, 1980; Schiffman, Westlake, Santiago, & Edelman, 1980).

Around the age of two to three months, infants are beginning to exert voluntary control over respiration as they produce vocal sounds, such as cooing, and in order to inhibit crying. Because this developmental change coincides with the onset of SIDS, it also suggests a sensorimotor or neuromotor deficit (McKenna, 1988).

continued at top of next page

needs of others, show more nurturance toward their children. Unlike men, women who have children later in life show higher care-giving responsibility and more satisfaction with parenthood. Older primiparous mothers are more confident of their skills and may interact more successfully with their babies than younger primiparous mothers (Feldman & Nash, 1986; Parke & Tinsely, 1987; Ragozin et al., 1982).

While men's involvement in infant care depends primarily on social factors, such as marriage, job, and social acceptability of parenting, women are more likely to be involved parents without such social supports. On the other hand, women's parenting suffers most when their self-esteem is low or when they experience depressed moods (Belsky, 1984; Feldman & Nash, 1986; Fleming et al., 1988). In an earlier section, we discussed the serious nature of maternal depression for infants. ■

APPLICATIONS

What are some other possible causes of SIDS?

A number of other possible causes have been found to be associated with SIDS. One possible cause, infant botulism, is caused by a toxin that comes from a spore. It affects the nervous system and results in paralysis; infants are known to be very susceptible to it (Marx, 1978). Botulism spores can be airborne, and they also are found on raw fruits and vegetables and especially honey. It is recommended that infants under twelve months not be fed these foods, and they should not put unwashed objects into their mouths (Marx, 1978). This is especially true for infants who are suspected to be at risk for SIDS.

Heat is another suspected cause of SIDS, and SIDS victims show symptoms similar to those of heat stroke. Some victims of SIDS were found to be excessively covered or dressed at the time of death (Stanton, Scott, & Downhan, 1980).

The inability to cope with relatively mild stresses, such as heat, apnea, or even mild toxicity, may result from some other systemic weakness. Oxygen deprivation in the perinatal period may be one cause. Another may be vitamin deficiency. Some researchers have suggested that SIDS victims, at least some of them, are deficient in a B complex vitamin, biotin.

Another possible cause is hormonal imbalance. A recent series of studies suggests that SIDS victims have an abundance of the hormone triiodothyronine (T_3), which is believed to play an important role in the development of the central nervous system. The concentration of T_3 was about three times as high in the blood of SIDS victims as in the blood of infants who died of other causes or of healthy infants (Chacon & Tildon, 1981). It is not known whether the increase in T_3 is a possible cause of SIDS or simply a side effect of the condition.

Although no one symptom can predict SIDS in all cases, SIDS infants have some of the following symptoms: difficulties in waking, shrill crying, few movements during sleep, poor oxygenation of the blood, pneumonia, and repeated hospitalization (Einspieler et al., 1988; Golding & Peters, 1985).

Can SIDS be prevented?

There is currently no foolproof method to prevent SIDS. Some infants may be identified at birth as being at risk for SIDS. Infants from deprived socioeconomic settings, who suffered oxygen deprivation, who have a high apnea rate, who have biotin or hormonal imbalances, or who have siblings who died or nearly died of SIDS are all at risk for SIDS.

There is no current medical treatment for the problem. About the only thing a parent can do is use a home apnea monitor, which emits an alarm if the infant stops breathing during sleep. This system has both advantages and disadvantages for use in the home. Monitor use caused extreme anxiety for the first month and led to a restricted social life for the parents. However, once they got over their initial anxiety, parents felt that home monitoring had beneficial effects; it caused few marital problems, and few parents resented the extra burden involved (Cain, Kelly, & Shannon, 1980).

APPLICATIONS

If SIDS is caused by a basic impairment in sensorimotor development, it may be possible to train infants to exert more effective control over breathing failures. One possibility is to artificially block the infant's flow of air for brief periods. Those infants who respond appropriately would be rewarded. Reinforcement of successful responses to air flow blockage may help the infant face a genuine respiratory problem (Lipsitt, 1980).

Another possibility is to encourage parents to let their babies sleep with them until the risk period for SIDS is past. On the one hand, this may provide closer parental monitoring of the infants. More important, it could be that if a baby is likely to make errors in respiratory control, exposure to parental breathing can have a significant effect on the regularity of the infant's breathing by creating a rhythmic cue to which the infant can become entrained (McKenna, 1987).

How can the SIDS victim's parents and family be helped?

Bereavement over SIDS victims shows a similar pattern over time as that for neonatal death: negativism, anger, shock, disbelief, and guilt (see Chapter 4 of this book and Mandell, McAnulty, & Reece, 1980; Smialek, 1978). In many ways, however, SIDS parents are in a unique situation because of the unexpected nature of the death, the fact that the cause is unknown, and the social myths and stereotypes that may accompany such a death (Markusen, Owen, Fulton, & Bendiksen, 1977).

Following the death of the infant, wives may become more dependent on their husbands for support. This, combined with the possibility that a husband may secretly resent or blame his wife for the death, may cause marital discord (Gruen, 1987). Siblings in the family may also be affected, both because of a sense of loss and because parental preoccupation may detract from the parents' relationships with the older children.

The more knowledgeable the parents' community, friends, relatives, and physicians are, the easier it will be for the parents to cope with the loss. Perhaps the best source of possible comfort and assistance is the family's pediatrician. Often, however, the pediatrician is either unwilling to help or, because of ignorance, unable to help. In such cases, parents may contact one of several national groups that have been organized by parents of SIDS victims, such as the National Foundation for Sudden Infant Death, Inc. (1501 Broadway, New York, NY 10036) or the International Council for Infant Survival (1515 Reisterstown Road, Baltimore, MD 21208). These groups are dedicated to medical research, providing support for survivors, public education, and informing the parents of their right to an autopsy (Aadalen, 1980). Autopsy is considered an essential element in relieving parents' guilt (Terjesen & Wilkins, 1979), although there are often delays and difficulties in dealing with local coroners and medical committees (Bluglass & Hassall, 1979).

For these reasons, parents of SIDS victims would benefit from contact with such groups and other knowledgeable individuals in the community, particularly other families of SIDS victims. Legal, social, and psychological assistance are all part of a complete intervention package to help parents fully recover.

■ FIGURE 6.8
Infant Deaths in the United States

The solid curve shows infant deaths from the sudden infant death syndrome. All other causes of infant deaths are charted by the dashed curve. The gray curve indicates the total numbers of deaths between the ages of ten weeks and twelve months. The syndrome is the most frequent cause of death between the ages of one month and one year, and at one age, it exceeds all other causes.

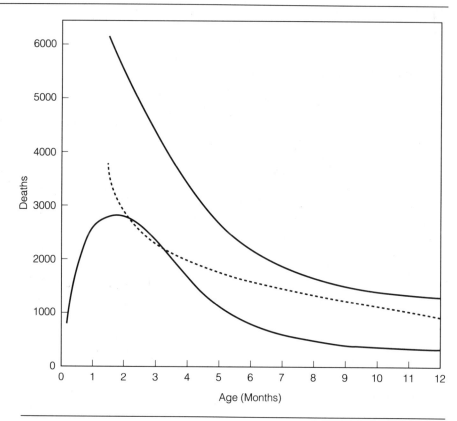

POINTS OF CONTACT

At one to four months, infants still have no awareness of self as perceiver or thinker, but rudimentary recognitions establish some of the first signposts. You might think of infants as amnesiacs, who must find their way back to themselves by first recognizing a few familiar things from which they may go on to build a mental image of who they are. Of course, amnesiacs know they are searching for themselves. Infants aren't searching for anything except some interesting contingencies, but they find themselves anyway.

You can help a baby find his or her way by encouraging circular reactions, providing contingent experiences, and playing games involving much repetition with variations. In the first month or two, you can gently talk to the baby each time you feed, diaper, or bathe him or her. The infant will come to recognize a particular voice in a particular place, thus contributing to a sense of predictability and encouraging positive feelings associated with recognition.

Don't just exercise the ears, though. Move the baby's arms and legs up and down and in and out gently, playing an "exercise" game. Gently touch the baby's cheeks and other skin surfaces, or blow softly and repeatedly on the arms and abdomen. Remember that at this age, the baby has a limited range of arousal toler-

continued at top of next page

ance and cannot handle too much stimulation. You have to be sensitive to cues for termination: head turning, avoidance reactions, crying, and spitting up are common responses to overstimulation. Don't be discouraged if this happens; use the experience to adjust your behavior the next time you play.

We have already talked about appropriate kinds of face-to-face play as the baby approaches two to three months. Remember to imitate, to use themes and variations, and to make your responses contingent upon the baby's responses. You also can buy or design toys that are contingent: mobiles, objects that dangle and can be swiped at, and so on. You can place a rattle in the infant's hand so the child can have the experience of "making" it make noise or let the

baby bang a pot with a spoon. Don't try to force the infant into a play situation; just be available to support the infant when he or she wants to get involved.

In general, your job is to encourage the baby to move, see, feel, and hear in a way that is safe and understandable. That's why the key to providing stimulation and enjoyment at this age is repetition and contingent responding. For this reason, too, toys are less important now than they will be later, because it is very hard to construct a toy that will be as contingent or as interesting as an adult. And don't forget that all babies are different. Whereas one can seemingly take as much stimulation as you care to offer, another may be slow to warm up and require a much more relaxed and gentle pace.

■ SUMMARY

Physical and Motor Development

■ The most rapid period of physical growth in human life occurs between birth and six months.
■ Some developmental disorders may be detected from standardized tests of infant motor skill.
■ Motor performance depends on the level of brain development, on the complexity of the task, and on the types of supports and resources available in the environment, especially from adults.

Perceptual Development

■ Acuity and speed of information processing improves in all perceptual modalities between two and five months.
■ Infants can detect color differences and a wide variety of patterns. They can perceive the solidity of objects and can recognize them from different points of view and using different sense modalities.
■ Infants have a strong preference for looking at faces and at moving objects and are better able to perceive differences between objects if they are moving.

Cognitive Development

■ The time taken for habituation decreases, and the infant's attention span increases.

■ Infants have memories for up to two weeks, but reminders make the memories longer. Memory is dependent upon emotional and contextual cues present at the time of the learning.

■ The main form of adaptation is primary circular reactions, in which the infants are exploring the effects of their own body movements and vocalizations.

Emotional Development

■ A distinction can be made between emotional expression, emotional feelings, and emotional understanding.

■ The infant's emotional expression becomes more complex and varied. Infants can use their whole bodies for emotional expression.

■ Improvements in emotional regulation are seen, but new challenges create new sources of frustration for babies.

Social Development

■ Adults display characteristic patterns of behavior with infants that include motherese-type vocalizations and actions.

■ Some aspects of motherese are universal, but cultures differ in the amount and type of verbal versus nonverbal behavior that is directed toward infants.

■ Research shows that adults are affected by their infants' behavior, and infants are affected by adult behavior, making the origins of individual differences hard to determine in most cases.

■ Infants are at risk when mothers have emotional disorders, such as depression.

Family and Society

■ Parents must adapt to a number of new challenges during the transition to parenthood.

■ Different factors predict the success of adaptation to parenthood for men and women.

Applications: Unexpected Death in Infancy

■ SIDS does not have a known cause but is believed to be linked to sensorimotor difficulties of respiration.

■ There are some prevention methods to use with infants at risk for SIDS, but none is foolproof.

■ Parents who lose a baby to SIDS need special counseling and understanding from relatives and their community.

■ GLOSSARY

Affective   Refers to the feeling aspects of emotion.

Attunement   Cross-modal matching of infant behavior by the mother or vice versa.

Apnea   Short cessation of respiratory movements.

Cross-modal perception   Integration of information across more than one perceptual modality.

Invariance   Detection of what is similar about an object in spite of variations in the conditions under which it is perceived; the basis of recognizing the same object from different perspectives.

Motherese   Changes in speech patterns involving exaggeration of pitch, higher pitch, use of rhythm and melody, slowing down, and simplification.

Postpartum blues   Transitory depressive feelings resulting from stress and fatigue following childbirth.

Primary circular reactions   Repetitive movements of the infant's body that are discovered by chance and repeated for fun.

Protoconversation   Initial form of turn-taking in adult-infant interaction in which the parent fills in the natural pauses in the infant's behavior but the infant does not take any social initiatives.

SIDS   Sudden infant death syndrome; a cause of death of unknown origins believed to be associated with errors in respiratory regulation, especially during sleep.

Still-face   An experimental manipulation in which mothers are asked to hold their faces in a neutral pose and cease talking to or otherwise interacting with their infants.

SEVEN

The Origins of Initiative

(SIX TO NINE MONTHS)

CHAPTER OUTLINE

Between the ages of four and six months, infants grow more adventurous. They leave the relatively protected world of close interactions with the care giver and move out to make contact with the world beyond the dyad. The subject of this chapter is the period from about six to nine months: Piaget's third stage of sensorimotor development. This development is physical, in that babies can creep or crawl, at least for short distances, on their own. It is also mental, since the infants begin to take a more serious interest in the object world and in other people besides the parents. Social interaction becomes more complex, and the first true social games, in which the infants play an active, participatory role, begin to appear in this stage.

■ PHYSICAL AND MOTOR DEVELOPMENT

By the age of five months, infants can sit supported and reach and grasp objects that are not too large or too small. Between six and nine months, improvements in posture lead to independent sitting and to supported standing. Muscle strength improvements allow babies to turn over and to move their bodies by creeping or by crawling. By nine months, infants can take a few steps while holding onto furniture or an adult hand. Their grasp improves in precision so that by nine months, infants can pick up small objects such as peas or carrot slices using just the tips of the thumb and index finger. These developments are listed in Table 7.1.

Do Infants Use a Preferred Hand?

One of the distinguishing features of the human brain is that the left and right hemispheres seem to serve different functions. Although researchers disagree about the precise allocation of functions to each side of the brain, the right hemisphere is believed to control spatial patterns and nonlinguistic information processing, while the left hemisphere is more sensitive to sequential processing of the sort used in the understanding of language. These left-right brain differences are found in right-handed people, while in left-handed people the hemisphere functions are reversed.

Because brain hemisphere specialization is linked to *handedness*, the preference for the use of one hand over another, the emergence in infancy of a preferred hand is thought to be related to milestones in the development of the brain. If there is a hand-use preference in early infancy, it might suggest that the left and right cortex of the infant's brain are already functioning differently.

At first glance, there is good evidence for left-right differences. Beginning at about two months of age, at the time when visually guided reaching begins, infants exhibit a hand preference. Like adults, more infants preferentially

■ TABLE 7.1   Norms for the Development of Motor Behavior Patterns in North America

TEST ITEM	AVERAGE AGE	NORMAL AGE RANGE
A. *Body control*		
Sits alone steadily	6.5 months	5 months– 9 months
Pulls self to sitting	8.2 months	6 months–11 months
Pulls self to standing	8.5 months	6 months–12 months
B. *Locomotion*		
Stepping movements while standing	8.7 months	6 months–12 months
Walks with help	9.5 months	7 months–12 months
Sits down	9.5 months	7 months–14 months
C. *Hand and arm control*		
Can scoop small pellet	5.5 months	4 months– 8 months
Finger-to-thumb grasp of cube	7 months	5 months– 9 months
Finger-to-thumb grasp of pellet	9 months	7 months–10 months
Rotates wrist while holding cube	5.7 months	4 months– 8 months
Combines objects at midline	8.5 months	6 months–10 months
Pat-a-cake at midline	9.7 months	7 months–15 months

SOURCE: Bayley Infant Development Tests, as reported in Rosenblith and Sims-Knight, 1985.

reach with their right compared to their left hands. Furthermore, this hand preference is relatively stable within babies over the first year of life (McDonnell et al., 1983; Young et al., 1983).

However, these left-right differences are not the same as those found in adults. About 90 percent of adults in all cultures are right-handed. However, for infants under one year, only about 30 to 50 percent show a preference for the right hand in reaching, while 10 to 30 percent have a left-hand preference. The remaining infants show no hand preference. In adults, hand preference is correlated with the hand preference of one's parents, but this is not true for infants (McCormick & Maurer, 1988). Thus, it seems that infants do have a right-side bias, but it is not nearly as strong nor as stable as adults'. In other words, the majority of infants show a hand preference at any age, but the preferred hand may change as the infants get older.

If infant hand-use preference is not linked to heredity, as is the case for most adults, what determines infant hand preference? According to one perspective, hand preference may develop out of earlier postural preferences. Most newborns, for example, prefer to turn their heads to the right side. It could be that the right-hand preference develops because that is the hand infants can see the most if their heads are turned to the side (Michel & Harkins, 1986). Adults may also have an effect on which hand is used by presenting objects preferentially to the infant's right or left side (Fogel, Karns, & Kawai, 1990; Harkins & Michel, 1988). More permanent hand preferences in infants do not emerge until the second year of life, perhaps as an interaction between heredity and environmental influences.

Effects of Hand Preference on Infant Motor Development

Why should we prefer to use one hand more than the other? Because the sides of our brains are specialized, perhaps handedness is a mere reflection of the brain structure. Actually, handedness does not mean that we use one hand and not the other; it means that each of our hands may be doing different things. When a baby explores an object, the hand that is doing the grasping and manipulating is no less important than the hand that is holding the object steady. Perhaps handedness evolved in order to allow each hand to perform a different but complementary function (Fagard & Jacquet, 1989).

When infants first begin to reach for objects, they use two hands and reach symmetrically toward the midline of the body. More mature reaching, beginning at around six months, involves reaching with a single hand for the object. What happens to the nonreaching hand at this time? The babies, who by six months are just learning to sit without support, extend the nonreaching hand backward in order to balance their upper bodies as the reaching hand moves forward (Rochat & Senders, 1990). Single-handed reaches would be impossible for babies without the postural counterbalance provided by the other hand and arm.

Being able to extend one arm independently of the other is also believed to be important for the development of crawling. In one research study, infants were observed going through the early stages of locomotor development (see Table 7.2). As long as babies were still reaching with two hands at the same time (showing no hand preference), they either creeped or rocked. They began to crawl as soon as they could reach with one hand, probably because

■ TABLE 7.2   Operational Definitions of Locomotor Stages

Pivot	Arms alternately flex and extend, one after the other, causing the trunk to pivot on the abdomen. Symmetrical leg extension is followed by forward flexion of one knee, in adduction. Head lifts.
Low creep	Both arms are flexed symmetrically, extended symmetrically, or one is flexed while the other is extended. Legs flex, one at a time. Face is lifted, but chest and abdomen contact supporting surface.
High creep	Both arms are extended, and both legs are flexed symmetrically. Knees are forward under trunk in adduction, lifting abdomen and chest from supporting surface. Head is well up from floor, and eyes look ahead.
Rocking	Arms extend symmetrically, and both legs are flexed symmetrically. Knees are forward under trunk, lifting abdomen and chest from supporting surface. Infant rocks back and forth, remaining in one location.
Crawling	Both arms extend downward from shoulder, then extend forward, alternately. Legs flex forward alternately. Arm and leg on opposite sides of body move simultaneously.

Note. These definitions were modified from Gesell and Ames (1940).

SOURCE: Goldfield, 1989.

crawling requires the extension of one hand and leg and then the other (Goldfield, 1989).

How Motor Skills Develop

The research on crawling shows that even though infants could get up on their hands and knees in a crawling posture, they still could not crawl because they lack a necessary component of crawling: alternate extension of the arms. This is similar to the younger infants, discussed in the last chapter, who could not step because they lacked the strength in their leg muscles to lift the legs. Dynamic systems theory predicts that new motor skills develop by adding additional components to existing skills.

A similar analysis could be applied to the development of walking. In the age period of this chapter, six to nine months, infants can stand and take a few steps, but they can't yet walk. Why not? Nine-month-old infants seem to possess the prerequisites of walking. They can pull themselves into a standing position, can take steps while holding onto something, and can alternate their leg movements. What they lack, however, is the ability to control balance.

This was discovered in research using a "moving-room" technique (see Figure 7.1). A standing baby is placed in a situation in which the floor is stationary, but the walls and ceiling of a miniature room are moved either toward the baby or away from the baby. Infants under one year will fall in the direction that the walls appear to be moving. Infants older than one year may sway but are less likely to lose their balance (Bertenthal & Bai, 1989). The

■ FIGURE 7.1

Schematic Drawing of Moving-Room Apparatus

Depicted inside the room is a child falling backward as a function of the room moving toward the child. This compensatory response would occur if the child perceived the optical flow produced by the room movement as specifying a forward sway rather than a movement of the walls.

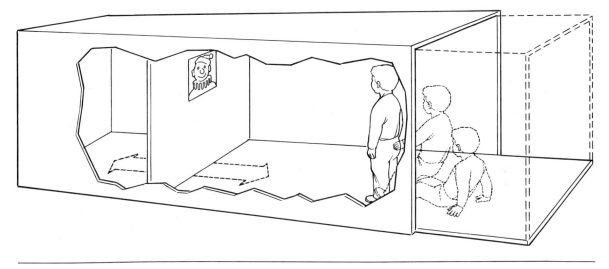

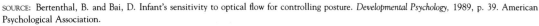

SOURCE: Bertenthal, B. and Bai, D. Infant's sensitivity to optical flow for controlling posture. *Developmental Psychology*, 1989, p. 39. American Psychological Association.

moving room recreates the visual experience of moving, without asking the baby to take steps at the same time. It is this visual experience of the room seeming to flow past the eyes that appears to cause babies to lose their balance.

This research suggests that perception of one's own movement in space is a key ingredient in controlling the posture necessary for locomotor development. Thus, not only is motor development a complex systems product of the different parts of the motor system (legs, trunk, and arms) but also includes the perceptual system and the type of environment in which the child is moving.

■ PERCEPTUAL DEVELOPMENT

New Developments in the Recognition of Objects and Depth

In the last chapter, we saw that by four months, infants are able to recognize that objects look the same from different orientations. Infants perceive objects as being solid, because they will become puzzled if one solid object appears to pass through another solid object. Infants can also perceive differences in distances between objects and will reach preferentially to objects they perceive as nearer to them. For infants of this age, however, object recognition and depth perception are easier if the objects are moving and if real objects, rather than pictures of objects, are presented.

After six months, however, infants can infer object properties and depth merely from visual cues alone. Another way to say this is that by six months, infants can "see" three dimensions when they are shown objects in two dimensions, as in a drawing or a photograph. Suppose identical pictures of an object, such as a car, are drawn in different sizes and placed next to each other. Adults looking at the pictures with one eye (monocular) would assume that the smaller car is farther away. Looking with two eyes, adults can easily see that the two cars are at the same distance but drawn to different sizes. These perceptual conclusions must be based only on the relative sizes of the pictures and not on the movements of one car away from the other or the movements of the perceiver in a three dimensional space.

By about seven months of age, infants with a patch over one eye will reach toward the larger of two identical pictures of a face, apparently perceiving it as closer (Yonas et al., 1982). If a small and a large checkerboard is used, the infants do not reach more for the larger one, since checkerboards have no standard size. If the infants are allowed to reach while looking with both eyes, they do not show a preference for the larger object, either the car or the checkerboard. Thus, by seven months, infants use visual cues, such as size, to judge depth.

By the same age, infants can use other visual cues to judge depth. If one object partially blocks the view of another, the blocked object is perceived as farther away (Granrud & Yonas, 1984), and relative shading in a drawing depicting a bump or a depression caused seven-month-olds, but not five-month-olds, to reach for the object shaded like a bump (Granrud et al., 1985). Both five- and seven-month-olds reached for actual bumps. Finally, by seven months, when objects are presented in a perspective drawing, infants appear to use the perspective information to reach for the object that is apparently nearer to them (Arterberry et al., 1989).

These studies show that infants can recognize objects in a wider range of situations. Recognizing objects in two dimensions is especially important for the understanding of pictures in a book or on television. Thus, we might expect an increased interest in picture books around the age of seven or eight months.

Other Perceptual Developments

Besides recognizing pictures in books, infants in this age period can also recognize differences between simple melodies. Six-month-olds can discriminate between six-note melodies differing by only one note (Trehub et al., 1984), and they can discriminate between melodies in which the pauses between notes are varied (Thorpe et al., 1989). By this age, therefore, babies can recognize some nursery rhymes and simple melodies heard in songs.

By this age also, there is continuing evidence of cross-modal perception. Thus, infants are sensitive to distortions in the sound track of a film showing a rattle shaking at a particular rhythm. If the sound is faster or slower than the rattle's movements, the babies notice the difference (Bahrick, 1987). As the visual and auditory display becomes more complicated, however, infants preferentially process the sound but not the vision, reflecting the fact that even at six months, auditory perception is more advanced than visual perception (Lewkowicz, 1988).

Infants of this age who are familiarized with an object only by touch can recognize the object by sight alone (Ruff & Kohler, 1978), and infants will alternatively look at, touch, and put objects into their mouths while exploring objects (Ruff, 1984). Furthermore, if babies hear a sound in the dark, they will reach for the object in the correct direction (Perris & Clifton, 1988). Finally, infants were given sweet and tart foods in cups of different colors. On subsequent color choice trials, the infants consistently picked the color that had been paired with the sweet food (Reardon & Bushnell, 1988).

In summary, these studies of perception show that by the middle of the first year of life, infants can use subtle cues to infer regularities in their perceptual world. They can now learn from pictures in books and on television. They can pick up relationships between different senses in order to pay attention to aspects of their environment that most interest them, such as the color of the baby food jar that contains their favorite flavor. On the other hand, these perceptual abilities lead to clear preferences, as we'll see later in the chapter. Babies begin to take the initiative in expressing their desires for particular pictures, objects, and tastes.

■ COGNITIVE DEVELOPMENT

During the period from six to nine months, the infant's brain continues to develop. Decreases in the speed of habituation and increases in the ability to visually attend to stimuli are correlated with developmental changes in the onset times of peaks in ERP (event-related potentials, see Chapter 1) curves (Karrer & Ackles, 1988). During these three months, infants increase in their looking time at novel stimuli and require less time to process familiar stimuli (Rose & Feldman, 1987). Studies using kicking to make mobiles move have shown that infant memory during this period is similar to memory at three months. However, while three-month-olds can remember how to produce mobile movements for up to fourteen days, seven-month-olds can remember for as long as twenty-one days (Hill et al., 1988).

Increasing Use of Concepts to Organize and Process Information

Thus, in terms of processing time and duration of memory, babies make small but important improvements in their abilities. More important, however, is that by six months, infants are more active in their processing of information. They seem to be able to group different stimuli into higher-order conceptual categories.

Using a habituation procedure, researchers showed babies a series of pictures of the same face taken from different poses. During the test trial, the infants dishabituated to an unfamiliar face but not to the same face in a different pose. This shows that the babies had organized all the different poses they saw into a higher-order concept of a particular face. Seven-month-olds, but not five-month-olds, were able to do this (Cohen & Strauss, 1979). In a similar type of study, seven-month-old infants were habituated to different faces having the same facial expression (a smile). They dishabituated to a different face with a nonsmile expression but not to a different face with a smile expression (Caron et al., 1982).

In an interesting variant of this procedure, infants were familiarized with somewhat distorted versions of a prototype figure (Younger & Gotlieb, 1988; see Figure 7.2). A *prototype* figure is one that is the clearest example of the form being represented. If infants are actively organizing the images of the distorted figures into a category, then they should prefer to look at a related prototype, compared to an unrelated prototype in a test trial in which both are available to look at. Infants who were familiarized with the "plus sign" distortions preferred the "plus sign" prototype at ages three, five, and seven months. Only seven-month-olds could recognize the prototype from the distorted versions of the odd-shaped figure shown in the lower part of Figure 7.2. This suggests that infants can more easily categorize more familiar looking patterns, but by seven months, infants try to categorize just about everything that they see.

Piaget's Third Sensorimotor Stage: Secondary Circular Reactions

Beginning at about four months and continuing until about eight or nine months, infants pass through Piaget's third stage of sensorimotor development: the stage of *secondary circular reactions*. This stage is a natural extension of the preceding one. Instead of only repeating actions that infants discover by chance on their own bodies (the primary circular reaction), they soon begin to repeat actions that, by chance, produce some effect on the external environment. The idea of *chance*—the fortuitous discovery of some interest-

■ **FIGURE 7.2**
Prototypes and Variations

Prototypical patterns shown with examples of corresponding low, medium, and high level distortions.

SOURCE: Younger, B. and Gotlieb, S. Development of categorization skills, *Developmental Psychology*, 24, 1988, p. 614. American Psychological Association.

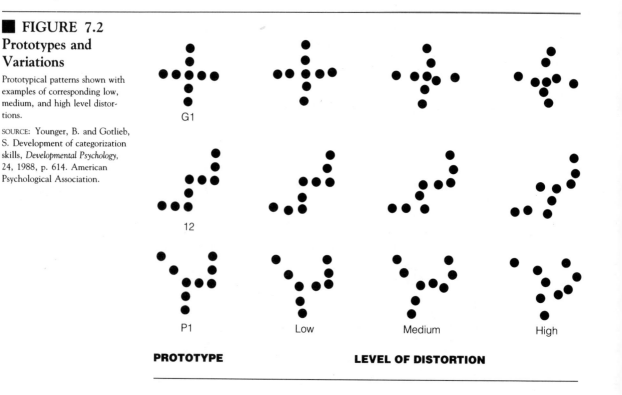

PROTOTYPE   LEVEL OF DISTORTION

ing result—is what distinguishes this stage from the ones that follow. Compared to the prior stage, primary circular reactions, a secondary circular reaction is a deliberate attempt to make something happen.

In a primary circular reaction, babies repeat a movement of their own bodies, but do not seem to make the connection between that movement and its effect. The movement creates a good feeling (a sound or a sight), but the babies seem focused on the efforts of their own bodies. In secondary circular reactions, babies are focused more on the events in the environment. They not only repeat actions that produce events, they vary the actions in order to explore changes in the effect. Piaget (1952) suggested that infants are trying to "make interesting sights last."

Babies will drop objects off the edge of their highchairs, perhaps listening for different sounds or looking at different movements when the objects hit the floor. They shake objects in different ways to notice the effect or repeatedly dump things out of containers (such as their food). Infants develop motor categorizations for objects, grouping them into things shakeable, drinkable, squeezable, and so on.

Infants in this period tend to apply the movements they use for a particular object as a way of representing or referring to the object. When Piaget shakes his son's rattles, Laurent at four and one-half months is too busily engaged in playing with the toy he is holding to actually strike his rattle. He seems to indicate the potential action by making a striking movement in the air. Instead of saying verbally "those are my rattles," Laurent expresses himself through a motor movement that has the exact form of his previous interactions with that object (see the Box, Observation 1).

At the same time, repeated occurrences in the environment take on meaning for the baby. By seven months, Laurent knew that he would be fed shortly after he heard his mother's bed creak. Earlier in his life, he would cry with hunger as soon as he woke up. Now he cries in relation to certain environmental events that have come to have a meaning for him. Like the act of "pretend" striking, the cry is a motor way of saying. "That's the sound of my food!" (see the Box, Observation 2).

These results show that infants in this period seem to believe that objects and events are connected to particular actions that they, or someone else,

---

■ OBSERVATIONS: Stage III Behavior (Piaget, 1952, pp. 187, 195)

Observation 1

Laurent . . . at 0;4(21) has an object in his hands when, in order to distract him, I shake the hanging rattles which he is in the habit of striking. He then looks at the rattles without relinquishing his toy and outlines with his right hand the movement of "striking."

Observation 2

At 0;7(10) Laurent cries in the morning as soon as he hears his mother's bed creak. Until then, although awake, he did not show his hunger. But, at the slightest creak, he moans and thus demands his bottle.

performs. Because of this action-object linkage, Piaget believed that infants will not be able to remain aware of an object after it can no longer be seen, heard, or otherwise operated upon by action.

One controversy that has occupied the attention of some behavioral scientists is the age at which infants develop *object permanence*: the ability to remain aware of an object even after it has gone out of sight. Piaget showed that infants will not search for an object that has been hidden until nine months, during Stage IV. Could it be that this searching for a hidden object must await the maturation of locomotor and motor skills that do not appear before nine months? Would infants at a younger age be able to keep track of a hidden object with their eyes in a setting that does not require the use of the motor skills that Stage III infants do not have?

In a study by Bower, Broughton, and Moore (1970), twenty-week-old infants watched a toy train moving back and forth on a horizontal track. A screen at the center of the track hid the train from the infants' view for a short time. These researchers claimed that twenty-week-olds possessed a concept of object permanence based on the following results of their study. Infants could follow the train's movements with their eyes. After the train went behind the screen, the infants would look at the side of the screen opposite the side at which the train disappeared, as if to anticipate its reappearance. Sometimes the experimenters tried to trick the babies by making a different object appear from the other side of the screen. When they did this, the babies looked confused, and their visual tracking of the object was disrupted.

This evidence seems to suggest that infants are "aware" of the train after it disappears, because they look for it on the other side of the screen and they know when a different object emerges. However, there may be other reasons why babies might disrupt their tracking of the object if a new object appears. It could be that the presence of the screen disrupts tracking, regardless of whether the object changes or not. Muller and Aslin (1978) found that tracking was disrupted just as often on object-change trials as on no-change trials. Furthermore, they showed that sometimes infants continued to move their eyes along the path of movement, even if the train stopped in plain view or if the train stopped behind the screen and did not reemerge. This latter finding suggests that infants do not really anticipate the appearance of the object from behind the screen. Their behavior could be explained by a simple continuation of the head motion in the same direction: a secondary circular reaction.

In another study, Meicler and Gratch (1980) found that infants were not really looking at the edge of the screen when the object reemerged after it disappeared: many five-month-olds did not even look at the screen after the object disappeared. If they continued to track the object after it reappeared, it was because they happened to catch sight of it again. Nine-month-old infants in their study, in contrast, were able to identify visually the screen as the possible hiding place of the object, and they appeared genuinely puzzled by the object-change trials.

Given what we know about the memory of infants under nine months, however, it seems quite likely that they should be able to remember objects when they can no longer see them. A more recent study examined object permanence in a situation that did not involve reaching or visual tracking (Baillargeon & Graber, 1988). Infants aged seven to eight months saw an

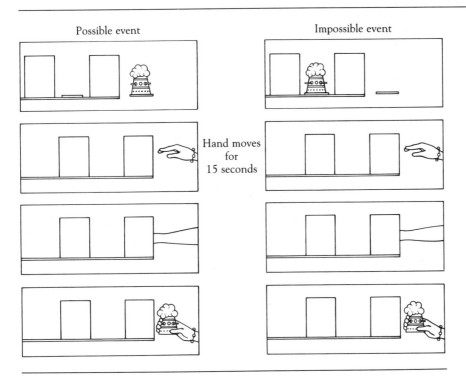

Possible event   Impossible event

Hand moves
for
15 seconds

■ FIGURE 7.3
**Sequence of Events
Used in an Object
Permanence task**

SOURCE: Baillargeon, R. and
Graber, M. Evidence of location
memory in 8-month-old infants in
a nonsearch AB task.
Developmental Psychology, 24,
1988, p. 505. American
Psychological Association.

object sitting on one of two red placemats that were placed 8.5 inches apart (21.5 cm). Next, two purple screens big enough to hide the object were slid in front of the placemats (see Figure 7.3). A hand then reached behind the screen and reappeared holding the object in both a possible situation or an impossible situation (Figure 7.3). Infants looked longer at the hand following the impossible situation compared to the possible one, showing that they remembered the object's location and were surprised when the object appeared from behind the opposite screen from which they had seen it placed.

Why do the infants seem to remember the object's location in this task but not in a task where they have to reach for an object or to track the path of a moving object? It could be that infant memory for locations can only be revealed in cases where action (reaching or tracking) is not required. Infants can remember situations at three months, and they can reach for objects by four months. Thus, one of the developmental achievements of Piaget's Stage IV (see next chapter) is the integration of what the baby knows with what the baby can do.

■ EMOTIONAL DEVELOPMENT

The Development of Negative Emotions

Until the beginnings of Piaget's Stage III, babies have basically one response to a negative experience: they cry. With the onset of secondary circular reactions, infants become more "aware" that they can cause things to happen.

When they cannot succeed at being an effective causal agent—when they can't get a toy they want, for example—a new source of negative experience enters their lives: *anger.*

Anger is a direct result of infants' having their motives disrupted. Although crying accompanies it, anger's facial expression is quite different from distress, as is the underlying feeling of the baby (Izard, 1981; Sroufe, 1979). In one study, infants' reactions to inoculations were observed at two, four, and seven months. At two and four months, infants reacted with physical distress, a direct response to pain. Distress is expressed by crying with tightly shut eyes. By seven months, the babies responded with more angry expressions, crying with open, vigilant eyes (Izard, 1981; Izard et al., 1987).

Separation from the mother is another situation that causes negative emotions. During Piaget's first and second stages, infants cry with distress, particularly if their mothers leave in the middle of a feeding or play session. The distress arises from the cessation of the pleasurable interaction. At this age, infants respond to maternal separation with some anger, especially if the mother happens to be a part of one of the infant's active secondary circular reactions when she leaves (Izard, 1981). Other research shows expressions of anger in seven-month-olds when a teething biscuit is removed from their mouths or when their arms are restrained (Stenberg et al., 1983).

Another negatively toned emotion seen at this age is *wariness.* Infants may become quiet and stare at a stranger or a strange situation, they may knit their brows and become momentarily sober, and they may look away (Bronson, 1972). In general, as babies get older, their helpless infantile fussiness practically disappears (Emde, Gaensbauer, & Harmon, 1976; Fogel, 1982; Malatesta et al., 1986). Helpless fussing gives way to demanding crying, anger, and wariness. Each of these forms of negative emotional expression is considerably more adaptive from the infant's point of view, and these developments reflect some significant advances in the infant's ability to cope with negative situations. It is certainly more adaptive to cry with open eyes. Wariness allows for even more prolonged inspection of the potentially worrisome stimulus. We might say that the increasing sophistication in the realm of negative responding, as its end result, brings the infant back into a positive engagement with the environment.

The Development of Laughter

Although the first laughs could be seen in the previous stage, primarily as a result of tickling and other vigorous stimulation, by six months babies will laugh at your jokes. They will laugh when you play tug with them, when they see you suck on their pacifiers or bottles, and when they try to pull the bottles out of your mouth (Sroufe, 1979).

Babies also laugh at very abrupt and highly arousing stimuli. They may laugh at things that once made them cry, such as a loud noise or the loss of balance. The laugh will sometimes follow a very serious or wary expression, almost as if the babies were trying to make up their minds about whether to get upset or enjoy the situation. In one study, Stage III babies watched while someone wearing a scary mask approached them. When the mask was worn by a stranger, the babies cried. When it was worn by their mothers, the babies laughed (Sroufe & Wunsch, 1972). This experiment suggests that by this age, the infant is beginning to use cognition *to decide what to feel*. This active involvement and *appraisal* marks the beginnings of adultlike emotional experiences in the infant. This growing awareness of the relationship between external events and internal experience allows the infants to sit back and enjoy being able to cause things to happen by their own actions (Sroufe, 1979).

Recognition of Emotional Expressions

Research on the infant's ability to recognize and discriminate different emotional expressions shows increases between six and nine months. Babies seem the most capable of recognizing smiles compared to other expressions. They have a concept of smile as determined from a study in which infants were familiarized to more versus less intense smiles. Later, they dishabituated only to nonsmile expressions (Ludemann & Nelson, 1988). Their ability to distinguish between other expressions, such as fear and anger, is relatively poor (Nelson, 1987).

On the other hand, as we saw in the last chapter, infants recognize emotion in the voice earlier than emotion in the face. When facial expressions of emotions are combined with voices expressing those emotions, seven-month-olds improve considerably in their ability to distinguish between emotions (Caron, Caron, & McLean, 1988; Phillips et al., 1990). Except for a happy expression, to which infants will respond with a smile, there is little evidence that infants view facial expressions as meaningful emotion signals (Nelson, 1987). The ability to extract meaning from viewing another person's face is extremely slow to develop, but we'll see the beginnings of this skill in the next stage (see Chapter 8).

■ SOCIAL DEVELOPMENT

Babbling: A Prerequisite for Later Vocal Communication

When infants are somewhere between four and six months of age, their vocal tracts begin to undergo major anatomical changes, bringing them closer to the vocal apparatus of the adult. At birth, the infants' tongues fill most of their oral cavities, and the tongue can only execute some primitive thrusting movements designed to help in sucking and swallowing (see Chapter 5).

Figure 7.4 shows how the vocal tract of the adult differs from that of the very young infant. Besides the differences between infant and adult tongues, note that the infant's epiglottis is in contact with the palate. This covers over the air tube from the lungs (the larynx) and helps prevent choking and inhaling of food particles. Beginning at four months, the oral cavity and vocal tract widen and lengthen, and the epiglottis begins to move away from the palate. This has the net effect of better allowing air to be taken in and pushed out through the infant's mouth (Kent, 1981).

Before the age of four months, infants can't breathe well through their mouths. This is why it is important to keep the very young baby's nasal passages clear of mucus. After four months, oral breathing allows the infant a much greater latitude for making new types of sounds.

■ FIGURE 7.4
Comparison of Infant and Adult Vocal Tracts

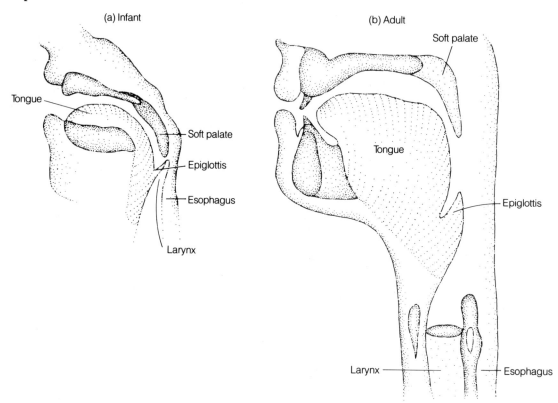

(a) Infant

(b) Adult

SOURCE: Reprinted by permission of the publisher from "Articulatory-acoustic perspectives on speech development," by R. D. Kent, in R. Stark (Ed.) *Language development in infancy and early childhood*, p. 109. Copyright 1981 by Elsevier Science Publishing Co., Inc.

After six months, infants use their ability to vary the direction of air flow, the pitch of the sound, its loudness, and the ability to abruptly stop air flow with the epiglottis to explore sound production (Zlatin, 1973). We can compare the manual manipulation of objects to the oral and laryngeal manipulation of air flow. The goos and gahs that result, or *babbling*, sound as though the babies are almost talking to themselves as they roll off a string of related vowel and consonant sounds to accompany their eating or playing.

There are two types of babbling that infants produce (Oller, 1980). The first type is called *expansion* babbling, which includes syllables containing mostly vowel sounds, such as raspberries, squealing, and growling. Expansion babbling occurs between four and six months. Between seven and ten months, infants produce what is called *canonical babbling*. Canonical babbling is composed of syllables having both a consonant and a vowel sound, such as "bah" or "pah." During canonical babbling, infants will repeat the same sound many times (called reduplication).

Many parents report that babbling sounds a lot like speech. Although infants of this age are not imitating the words of speech, there is evidence that babbling imitates the intonation contours (the rising and falling pitches) of sentences (Nakazima, 1972). Indeed, the intonation contours of babbling match quite well the contours of the speech spoken in the infant's home, in a study done in French-, Chinese- and Arabic-speaking homes (de Boysson-Bardies et al., 1984).

It has been thought, however, that the actual sounds made by infants when they babble are not language-specific. In fact, early observations of babbling suggested that even deaf babies babble in ways similar to hearing babies up until about nine months of age (Lenneberg, 1969). Recent research suggests that this is not the case, as shown in a careful descriptive analysis of babbling in deaf infants (Oller & Eilers, 1988). First of all, deaf infants show a substantial delay in the onset of canonical babbling, in some cases between six and eighteen months later than hearing infants. Second, the deaf infants produce considerably fewer well-formed consonant-vowel syllables. Although this study does not show that hearing infants copy the speech sounds of adults at this age, it does show that the ability to hear oneself vocalize contributes to the development of vocalization.

Indeed, the development of auditory perception seems to parallel the development of sound production in hearing infants. While younger infants are capable of distinguishing sounds of different pitch and intensity from each other, infants between six and nine months are beginning to organize sounds, especially speech sounds, into conceptual categories. Recall that in research on visual perception, after being familiarized with a set of somewhat distorted figures, infants preferred to look at the prototype figure that best fit the series of distorted figures seen before. A similar study done with distorted versions of speech syllable prototypes yielded very similar results (Grieser & Kuhl, 1989). The auditory stimuli were syllables in which the vowel sound was subtly altered in pitch using a computer simulation.

Infants of this age can distinguish between a wide variety of speech sound contrasts but are less sensitive than adults (Aslin, 1987). Their ability to distinguish between sounds improves when the test sounds are embedded in a series of familiar speech sounds (Karzon, 1985) or when embedded in sentences in which adults are speaking motherese (Fernald, 1985).

Infants can apparently distinguish between the intonation patterns of different languages. Some infants from monolingual English-speaking homes and some from bilingual Spanish-speaking homes were familiarized with a video display of a woman reciting a passage in either English or Spanish. In the test condition, infants dishabituated if the woman recited a passage in the language they had not heard during familiarization but not to a different passage read in the same language to which they had been familiarized (Bahrick & Pickens, 1988).

Overall, these results show that by the second half of the first year of life, infants would not be considered to be speaking or understanding language. However, infants are beginning to recognize and produce some of the characteristics of language as a system of sounds, apparently without any sense that those sounds have a meaning. When infants babble, therefore, they may sound to adults as if they are trying to talk, but it is more appropriate to view them as exploring the making of sounds rather than as trying to be communicative with sounds.

Nonverbal Communication and Attachment

Even though we cannot say that babies of this age are using language, they are making progress toward becoming more active communicative partners.

After six months, as the baby becomes more adept at manipulating objects and at exploring and manipulating the surroundings, the parent will begin to *interpret the infant's intentions.* Assuming that the parent has made a correct interpretation, the next step is usually to *help the infant carry out the intended acts.* In addition, parents often *create new intentions* that were not there in the first place. Instead of simply helping infants get objects they see, parents may hold out an object to get babies interested, or they may make sounds or movements to try to get babies to imitate them.

The parent creates, interprets, and completes intentions even though the infant may not be fully aware of these intentions. The situation is much like the study of music or language, for example, in which teachers require that their pupils learn simple exercises. The student has little notion of the purpose of learning scales, arpeggios, parts of speech, or conjugations. Nevertheless, the instructor understands the relationship of the exercises to the final skilled performance.

■ OBSERVATIONS:
Early Communicative
Interactions Rely on
Adult Interpretations
(Lock, 1980)

OBSERVATION 3

Mary; age 7(10): A spoonful of food has just been placed in Mary's mouth when the telephone rings. Mother takes Mary's left hand and wraps it round the spoon handle, which is sticking from Mary's mouth.
Mother: You take it while Mummy answers the phone.
Mary pulls the spoon from her mouth and while eating waves it about. While still holding the spoon, she pushes her hand around in her dinner and then starts licking her hand. While she is doing this mother returns.
Mother: There's a clever girl, are you feeding yourself? Here, let's wipe you, you're ever so mucky.
She takes the spoon from Mary to wipe her. Mary cries and struggles, then reaches out towards spoon.
Mother: All right, here you are. Let me show you.
She gives Mary the spoon and then guiding her hand, places it into the dish and then to Mary's mouth.
Mother: Oh, aren't we clever! Aren't we clever!

OBSERVATION 4

Mary; age 7(27): Mary is in her chair, having finished her afternoon meal.
Mother comes in through the door with a packet of biscuits in her hand. The door is behind Mary and out of her view. As mother comes in, Mary coos and smiles, turning round to see mother.
Mother: Yes, you heard me coming, didn't you?
She enters Mary's field of view, and Mary reaches out towards her mother's hand; her whole body straining in the chair.
Mother: Yes, they're your favourites, aren't they?

Some examples of these kinds of interpretive interactions involving a seven-month-old baby are given in the observation box.

As for the attachment process, infants during this period are becoming more selective with respect to adults than during the previous period. Babies between six and nine months will smile and laugh more toward familiar and trusted adults than toward unfamiliar adults. They may show some wariness in response to unfamiliar persons, but this has not blossomed into the more severe fearful reactions to strangers seen in some infants after the age of ten months.

Although infants are not yet taking a strong initiative to be in the presence of familiar persons, the kinds of interpretive interactions we described in the observation box clearly suggest that babies are aware of the care giver's actions with respect to the baby's needs. The infant's initiatives at this age seem to be situation specific in relation to the particular things done with the care giver, such as during play and feeding. In the next stage, infants develop a concept of their attachment figures that goes beyond any particular situation and creates a more general set of emotions of attachment and dependency with respect to those adults.

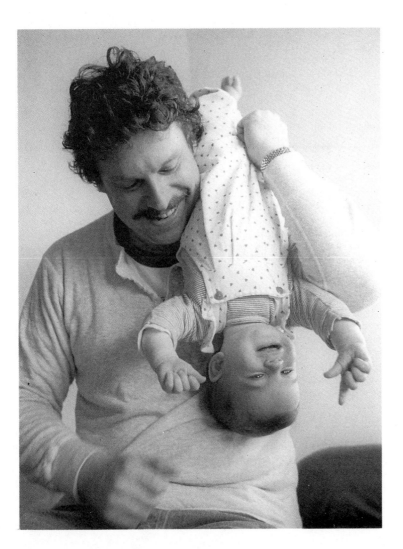

Fathers' games are typically more physically active than mothers'. These different styles of play are both important to infant development.

Parent-Infant Games

By six months, the infant is becoming more of an active social participant. By now, the infant is much more likely to take the initiative in play situations rather than simply respond to the care giver (Gustafson, Green, & West, 1979; Kaye & Fogel, 1980). Social play is now more frequent and more spirited, with laughter and squealing in the sound track.

Table 7.3 describes the typical games found in parent-infant play during the second half-year of life. Figure 7.5 shows the relative frequency of each game

---

■ TABLE 7.3   Descriptions of Conventional Games

Gonna get you: Mother repeatedly tickles, grabs, jostles, or provides other tactual/kinesthetic stimulation to the infant. Often includes a repeated vocalization such as "I'm gonna get you" or "Ahhhhhhh-boom!" which terminates just as physical contact is made. (Active participation by an infant could include fleeing when approached or attempting to "get" the mother.)

Patacake: Primary components are the mother's saying "patacake" and clapping or banging performed by either the mother or the infant. (Active participation by the infant would include beginning to clap only after the mother said "patacake" or patting the mother's hands.)

Horsie: Primary component is the mother's bouncing the infant, who is sitting on her knees or foot. The mother's verbalizations include "Want to play horsie?" or "Ride the horsie." (Active participation by the infant involves initiating the game or trying to prolong it by continuing to bounce after the mother has stopped.)

Peekaboo: One member of the dyad is hidden and reappears. Hiding is typically accompanied by mother's calling to the child (if the mother is hidden) or by her asking "Where's   ?" (if the child is hidden). Reappearance is typically accompanied by verbalizations such as "Peekaboo," "Peepeye," or "There he/she is!" (Mother may control all the hiding and uncovering, or the infant may actively perform some of these activities.)

Ball: Involves the infant's repeatedly receiving and losing the ball. (Mother may hold up both ends of the game by tossing the ball to the infant and then taking it away, or the infant may actively participate by presenting or returning the ball to the mother.)

Vocal game: Minimal requirement is that the mother be attempting to elicit a word or vocalization from the infant. In expanded form, these interactions are verbal or vocal-verbal "conversations."

Build tower-knock down: One member of the dyad builds a tower of blocks, and the other knocks the tower over. The sequence may be repeated many times. (Active participation by the infant is typically limited to knocking the towers down.)

Give and take: Involves repeated giving and receiving of objects. Receiving by the mother is often accompanied by a carefully articulated "Thank you." Typically, the infant gives and the mother receives, although mother often returns the object to the infant.

Point and name: One member of the dyad (usually the infant) repeatedly points to objects, each time waiting for a vocalization by the other (usually the mother, in the form of naming the object), before pointing to the next object. Pointing is sometimes accompanied by a questioning vocalization or by the query "What's this?"

Miscellaneous: Any traditional infant game that occurs very infrequently at a particular age. Included are the game "Overboard," in which the mother repeatedly turns the infant upside down and says "Little girl overboard," and the game "So Big," in which the mother says "How big are you?" and the infant stretches his or her arms out while the mother says "So big." Also included are sequences with a toy telephone in which the receiver is put to the infant's ear and the mother says "Hello," and interactions in which one or both members of the pair were waving or saying "Bye-Bye."

SOURCE: From Gustafson, Green, & West, 1979, p. 304. Reprinted by permission of Ablex Publishing Co.

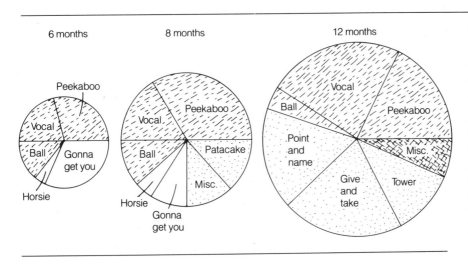

6 months   8 months   12 months

■ FIGURE 7.5
**Relative Frequency
of Parent-Infant
Games**

Dotted areas represent games in
which the infant's role is explicitly
active; blank areas represent games
in which the infant's role is typically passive. Hatched areas repre-·
sent games played at all ages.
Cross-hatched areas represent both
active and passive games.

SOURCE: From Gustafson, Green,
& West, 1979. Reprinted by
permission of Ablex Publishing
Co.

at six, eight, and twelve months of age. As infants get older, they learn to play
an increasing number of new games, such as "point and name" and "give and
take" at twelve months. In playing those games that are played at every
age—such as "ball," vocal games, and peekaboo—infants take an increasingly active role as they get older. Games like "gonna get you" and "horsie,"
in which the six-month-old played a relatively passive role, occur only rarely
at twelve months (Gustafson, Green, & West, 1979).

Note that these games are typical of middle-class white North American
populations and do not necessarily represent what parents and infants do in
other cultures. Furthermore, even in this particular population, games were
played in only about 10 percent of all social interaction episodes.

Cultural Differences in Parent-Infant Interaction

As infants get older, their mothers tend to spend less time with them. When
mothers do spend time with babies, the proportion of their time devoted to
games and play over simple caretaking increases with the babies' age. One
cross-cultural study found that the infants' rate of receiving social stimulation
does not appreciably change with age, but there is a decline in the proportion
of time the mother is represented. Evidently infants receive an increasing
amount of stimulation from other sources, such as relatives and peers
(Landau, 1976).

There are wide differences between cultures in the amount of time mothers
spend with babies, as well as in the types of activities they perform when with
the babies. When we look as worldwide differences in child-rearing patterns,
climate accounts for a significant proportion of cultural differences. In warm
countries, infants tend to be carried by their care givers, to remain in close
physical contact throughout most of the day and night, and to be breast-fed
until they are older than infants reared in cold climates. Infants in cold
climates are more likely to be separated from their mothers at an earlier age.
They sleep in cradles, are carried in strollers and buggies, and are kept at a
distance from the parents through the use of infant seats and playpens
(Angiobu-Kemmer, 1986; Whiten & Milner, 1986; Whiting, 1981).

These differences are believed to come about because of the need to wrap babies in cold climates against the cold (see Figure 7.6). Since both the adult and infant must wear many layers of protective clothing, parent-infant skin contact is very difficult. Over many centuries, child-rearing practices have evolved to adapt to this fundamental ecological constraint (Whiting, 1981).

There are also cultural differences in the type of play that occurs between infants and adults, although these differences are not always attributable to climate. In more technical and industrial societies, mother-infant play is embedded in a matrix of communication and warmth. In these societies— including for example, Japan, Europe, and North America— mothers guide play by interpreting infant goals, fitting into the infant's level of play, supporting the infant's intentions, and creating new possibilities for the infant to take initiatives (Kaye, 1982; Lock, 1980; Rogoff, 1990).

By contrast, in nontechnical, agricultural, and gathering communities, adults are more directive and ritualistic in their interactions with infants (Whiten & Milner, 1986). Among the Gusii, an agricultural community in Kenya, when mothers taught children to do a task, they used a lot of repetition, direct demonstration of the whole task (they did not break it into simpler components), they pulled on the infants' hands to encourage participation, they used very little vocalization and little praise or reinforcement (Dixon et al., 1984). Chomorro mothers, from a fishing community on

■ **FIGURE 7.6**
Infant Carrying Practices

In warm climates, infants spend more time in skin-to-skin contact with adults. Infants in cold climates must wear protective clothing, making them more difficult to carry for long periods.

SOURCE: Reprinted by permission from p. 187 of Child Development by Alan Fogel and Gail F. Melson; Copyright © 1988 by West Publishing Company. All rights reserved.

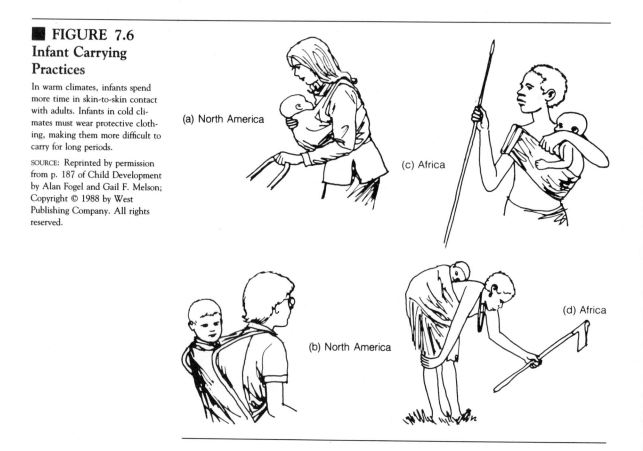

(a) North America

(c) Africa

(b) North America

(d) Africa

the Pacific island of Guam, were highly directive when interacting with infants; they talked quickly, dominated the interactions, were highly repetitive, and showed abrupt shifts of activity suited more to their own pace than to the infants' (Carlile & Holstrum, 1989).

One interesting aspect of the Chomorro study was that the researchers observed both Chomorro mothers and fathers and Caucasian parents in the United States playing with infants. They found no differences in the interaction styles between the Chomorro mothers, the Chomorro fathers, and the Caucasian fathers: they all differed from the Caucasian mothers.

What might explain these differences? Because the directive style of interaction is so prevalent worldwide, we should not be too quick to label it as "insensitive." One possibility is that this style of interaction—direct and insistent—is important for infants to experience, as it forces infants to be other-directed. We'll return to this perspective in our discussion of fathers below. This makes sense if the infant is also getting exposure to the kind of warm, sensitive interactions typical of the Caucasian mothers. Where might this come from in Chomorro, if both mothers and fathers are similar in their directive styles? Probably from infant interactions with extended family members, such as grandmothers and great aunts (Carlile & Holstrum, 1989).

Do you think there would be much difference in mother-infant interaction between middle-class families in two different European countries? One study that compared mother-infant interaction in English and Dutch families may provide an answer (Snow, DeBlauw, & VanRoosmalen, 1979).

In terms of general parameters of physical contact, the English mothers breast-fed their babies longer than the Dutch, and they spent more time interacting with their babies than the Dutch. By six months, two thirds of the English sample was still breast-feeding, whereas most Dutch mothers had stopped by six weeks. Virtually the entire Dutch sample used playpens at six months, whereas none of English mothers did (Snow et al., 1979). Mothers from both countries played about as much with their babies. The English mothers, however, played a greater variety of games with their infants.

In spite of these differences, there were some similarities, the most important of which was the use of verbalizations during game sequences. These verbalizations were quite structured in relation to the game, and they even occurred in games that were primarily physical. Snow et al. give the example of a "tickling verse":

Round and round the garden
Like a teddy bear, (said while tickling the baby's palm in a circular motion)
One step, two step, (walking fingers toward stomach or underarm)
Tickle you there! (said very fast, while tickling vigorously)
(Snow et al., 1979, p. 283)

Talking to babies happens relatively rarely on a worldwide basis. Many peoples believe that there is no reason to talk to prelinguistic infants, and they are probably correct from a purely semantic point of view. As we saw in the section on perception in this chapter, however, infants are quite sensitive to pitch, timing, and other melodic elements of the human voice, and during Stage III they are beginning to associate tonal patterns in the adult's voice with specific behavioral sequences. We will explore how the infant acquires verbal meaning in more detail in the later chapters.

Lest we leave this topic thinking that English mothers are more "sensitive" to their babies than Dutch mothers, note that the Dutch mothers vocalized more to their babies. This seemed to happen because they spent more time in the same room with the infant and less time engaged in other activities while with the infant. Thus it seems that Dutch mothers make up in vocalizations what they lack (relative to the English) in close physical contact. Also note that in spite of their relative geographical proximity, England and Holland have noticeably different climates. The shores of England are bathed with the warm waters of the gulf Stream, which keeps winter temperatures above freezing so it rarely snows in England in spite of the fact that it is farther north than the northernmost city of the continental United States. Holland, on the other hand, has a climate closer to that of its Scandinavian neighbors.

■ FAMILY AND SOCIETY

In the previous section, we looked at styles of mother-infant interaction in different cultures. We saw that how mothers interact with infants may depend on the presence or absence of other individuals in the family and on ecological factors, such as climate. In addition, ecological systems theory predicts that social factors external to the family may influence the style of mother- or father-infant interaction. In this section, we will take a look at maternal employment as one ecological factor that affects the family. We'll also examine the roles of fathers and siblings.

Maternal employment and its effects on infants

Since 1950, the number of working mothers has increased by 70 percent in the United States. In 1984, 46 percent of mothers with children under one year of age were working full-time, 53 percent with children under two years, and 58 percent with children under three years. This group of mothers is the largest growing segment of the work force (Yale Bush Center, 1985). One of the consequences of this increase in the number of working mothers is the problem of how to provide adequate care for their infants. We'll return to this problem in the next chapter.

In this chapter, we discuss how the maternal work role has impacted on the American family and especially how it has affected fathers and infants. First of all, how does maternal employment affect the mother's relationship with her infant and the infant's development? In general, infant-mother attachment is not seriously altered by maternal employment (Easterbrooks & Goldberg, 1985; Vaughn et al., 1980). On the other hand, if attachment is going to be affected, it is most likely to decline between mothers and their infant sons (Chase-Lansdale & Owen, 1987).

Why are boys most affected? It may be that boys are perceived as more independent and as requiring less parental nurturance and attention than girls, who are seen as more vulnerable (Parke & Sawin, 1980). Thus, when mothers are under extra stress and time pressures from their jobs, they may spend less time with their sons compared to their daughters. Other research suggests that there is a correlation between a son's insecure attachment and a mother's perceived level of stress. Mothers who felt more stressed by their jobs and the demands of family life had less securely attached sons (Benn, 1986).

The result of the effects of stress is compounded in low-income mothers whose employment may affect attachment in both sons and daughters (Barglow et al., 1987).

These results suggest that the impact of maternal work on infant-mother attachment is mediated by the mother's adjustment to the work role. Better psychological adjustment will lead to more sensitive infant care. Thus, researchers have asked what factors promote maternal adjustment to employment. A number of studies find that the important variable is the mother's desire to work, not the mere fact of working. Mothers who are well adjusted are those who are doing what they prefer: either working or staying at home with their children. On the other hand, there are adverse affects on adjustment if the mother does not want to work but has to for economic reasons or if the mother would like to return to work but feels she should stay home with her children (Alvarez, 1985; DeMeis et al., 1986; Pistrang, 1984).

Whether mothers work by choice or because of necessity, they typically end the day fatigued because of a phenomenon called role overload. *Role overload* occurs when the demands of a role are more than an individual can easily cope with or when the same person is required to perform too many roles. After a full day at work, many women come home to traditional conceptions of the wife role and the mother role. Women often continue to do most of the infant care and most of the housework, compared to men, even if they are working as many hours outside the home as the men (Scarr, 1984). Role overload is inevitable for single parents. Even though fathers with working wives do more infant care and housework than husbands of women who are not employed outside the home, men with working wives increased their contribution to family work by only an average of fifteen minutes per day (Crouter et al., 1987; Pleck & Rustad, 1980).

Lest you think this is entirely the fault of the men, research shows that men do proportionately more work at home if their wives have a less traditional attitude toward the male role. Thus, it may be the mother's own perception of her central family role and her failure to strongly encourage the husband's participation in the family that leads to low levels of father involvement. Women may be trying too hard to be "supermoms" (Barnett & Baruch, 1987; Palkovitz, 1984; Scarr, 1984), contributing to role overload.

Parental leave policies

Unfortunately, the amount of work a person does outside the home is only partially defined by the individual. Much has to do with the cultural demands placed on workers by society and by employers. Most work situations in the United States take little account of a person's obligations to family. An inflexible daily work schedule leaves little time or opportunity for parents to be involved in the day-to-day workings of the family. Corporations often have a policy of moving their employees from city to city as part of a training and advancement program.

Some alternatives exist, but they are not widespread. More flexible work schedules (*flextime*) began to be instituted in Europe in the early 1960s. Workers can take time off to take a child to the doctor, watch a baseball game, or whatever they desire.

After a child is born, Swedish workers are legally entitled to maternity and paternity leaves. Some employers allow husbands and wives to share the same jobs. That way they can both work and both spend time at home. Another help could be better pay and benefits for part-time work. Many employers only provide medical insurance, unemployment compensation, and other benefits to full-time employees. A parent who would like to spend more time at home is caught between the demands of the family and the very real needs to be covered by those benefit provisions.

The opportunity to take infant care leave of some type, without suffering loss of income or profession, is mandated by law in at least seventy-five nations, which include all the industrial societies in the world with one exception: the United States. Many employers in the United States feel that commitment to family is a luxury, and many women who hold senior positions in companies may be forced out of their jobs due to pregnancy and child rearing. This not only creates a work environment that is indifferent to family needs but adds to the stress of working parents (Magid & McKelvey, 1987; Scarr, 1984). The United States is also one of the few countries that does not have a national policy for child care (see next chapter).

A number of bills have come before the U.S. Congress in the hope of providing minimal national standards for parental leave and child care. They are typically defeated, usually with the help of strong lobbying efforts from the business and corporate community. On the positive side, due to the growing majority of working parents, such policies will become more politically advantageous to legislators in the near future. Nothing less than a major change in national value orientations is required: away from economic considerations and toward a recognition of the intrinsic value of supporting children and families, no matter what the cost.

Age and sex differences in nurturance toward infants

As the results of research on maternal employment suggest, infant care is thought to be part of women's work. Implicit in this belief is that nurturance is part of the female biological heritage and that women should be able to do this under any circumstances and without support. In actuality, these beliefs are simply not true. Research has shown that the interest and ability to care for babies is present in both males and females early in life and will continue in both genders if fostered by the social environment. In the following sections, we review age and sex differences in responses to infants.

Preschool-age. One study that used a single female infant placed in a playpen in a nursery school found that girls approached the baby more than did boys; once they were nearby, however, both boys and girls spoke to, reached out for, and touched the baby equally as much (Berman, Monda, & Merscough, 1977). Another study used both male and female infants in a waiting room situation. Preschool children were asked to wait in a laboratory room with a baby and mother for ten minutes. In this rather unusual situation, many children did not approach the baby. When they did, both boys and girls approached in equal numbers, and there were no differences in the types of interaction attempted by male and female children. They usually sat down on the floor, handed the baby toys, or showed the baby his image in a mirror (Melson & Fogel, 1982).

Melson and Fogel also found that the children almost never talked to the baby. If they wanted to find something out or make a comment, they would talk to the baby's mother about the baby. In addition, they found a same-sex effect for these unfamiliar infant-preschooler pairs similar to that found by Dunn and Kendrick (1982) for sibling pairs. At the ages of two and three years in the Melson and Fogel study, boys were more likely to approach male babies, and girls were more likely to approach female babies.

One interesting twist in this study was that by the time children were four to five years old, there were still no overall sex differences in the amount of time males and females interacted with the baby. However, both the males and the females preferred to interact with female babies. Perhaps the older boys no longer identify with the babies. By the time the boys were five years old, being a boy and being a baby were no longer compatible.

In more recent work, Melson and I found that if adults encouraged children to become involved with unfamiliar infants, both boys and girls increased their amount of interaction with the babies, and both boys and girls asked the adults many questions about the babies (Fogel, Melson, Toda, & Mistry, 1987). When we interviewed children in kindergarten and second grade about babies, we found both equal interest and equal knowledge about infant care on the part of boys and girls (Melson, Fogel, & Toda, 1986). In general, the research suggests that few sex differences are found among children in their attitudes, knowledge about, and behavior toward infants if they are exposed to infants with adult guidance (Melson & Fogel, 1988). For most children, this occurs in the context of the family, with baby brothers or sisters.

Siblings. Similar types of sex differences have been observed among siblings, that is, same-sex dyads tend to be more positive in their interactions than mixed-sex dyads (Dunn & Kendrick, 1982; Lamb, 1978b). On the other hand, preschool-age children talk to their younger siblings more than to unfamiliar infants. When preschool children talk to infants, both boys and girls modify their speech to make it sound more like motherese (Dunn & Kendrick, 1982; Sachs & Devin, 1976; Shatz & Gelman, 1973).

This speech by children includes simple utterances, repetition, and high pitch as in the following example taken from a four-year-old talking to her younger brother: "Harry! Harry! Have my camera! Have my camera!. Naughty boy. You . . . aah! Aah! No!" (Dunn & Kendrick, 1982, 124). In some cases, the preschoolers used repetition twice as often as their mothers when talking to the babies. About 25 percent of the preschool-age children were observed to use endearing terms toward the baby and to ask soliciting questions (Are you hungry? Are you getting frustrated?). On the other hand, the majority of the preschoolers rarely asked questions of the baby, whereas question asking is a major form of adult speech to infants (Dunn & Kendrick, 1982).

Sibling care givers are common in African-American families, and also in families with large numbers of children. Siblings who provide infant care are more nurturant and socially competent than siblings who do not have this opportunity.

Later childhood. Responses to infants by children in middle childhood and early adolescence were studied by Frodi and Lamb (1978). For children aged eight to fourteen years, girls interacted more with and ignored the baby less than boys. Interestingly, however, there were no sex differences in blood pressure, skin conductance, and heart rate: both boys and girls got equally aroused or unaroused by the sight of the infant. Girls, it would seem, made the choice to interact, whereas boys did not. A similar study of U.S. black children also found that girls were more likely to look at the babies than were boys (Berman, Goodman, Sloan, & Fernandez, 1978).

These differences in male versus female interest in babies continue through high school (Feldman & Nash, 1979a), but they seem to vanish for college students and for young adults (Feldman & Nash, 1978, 1979a; Frodi, Lamb, Leavitt, & Donovan, 1978). Some studies with adults have compared the responses of parents to babies with those of nonparents. The most responsive group is usually new mothers. Men's child-rearing status does not affect their responsiveness to babies (Feldman & Nash, 1978; Sagi, 1981). Mothers tend to be more accurate in their identification of the type of cry (pain, distress, and so on) than fathers, but both mothers and fathers can identify their own infant's cry compared with cries of unfamiliar infants (Wiesenfield, Malatesta, & DeLoach, 1981).

Parenthood: Mothers versus fathers. In most comparisons of fathers' and mothers' styles of interaction with infants, fathers appear to be more physical and active with infants than mothers. Fathers are also less contingently responsive with infants, have a style of play and interaction that is more directive and characterized by abrupt changes of activity. By contrast, mothers' games are quieter and more likely to depend on the pace set by the infant. Mothers also engage in proportionately more care giving than fathers (Belsky, 1979; Lamb et al., 1982; Parke & Sawin, 1980; Pedersen et al., 1980; Ricks, 1985; Sagi, 1982). These differences are seen as important for infants. While contingent responsiveness fosters infants' understanding of the connections between their own actions and those of others, the more directive and unexpected styles of father-infant play may lead infants to develop adaptive responses to challenges as they strive to keep up with the father's expectations.

Grandparents. Finally, Feldman and Nash (1979b) studied the responsiveness to babies of thirty parents of adolescents, twenty-eight parents whose grown children had left home, and twenty-six grandparents of infants. As you might have guessed, grandparents were the most responsive to babies compared with the other two groups. Grandmothers were more responsive than grandfathers, but grandfathers were more responsive than men at other ages, who tended to be less responsive to babies than their wives.

It seems that differences in male versus female responsiveness to infants appear in middle childhood and late adolescence and again in middle age. Young boys, men of child-rearing age, and grandfathers seem about equally responsive to babies as their female counterparts. These studies suggest that sex differences in interest in babies may be related to society's expectations of how males and females should behave rather than to some underlying biological predisposition favoring females. Males' interest in babies seems to correspond to the times in the life cycle when men are exposed to babies and are expected to take an interest in them. Women are more likely to be expected to be interested in babies all through their lives. ■

Infant Nutrition

Coincidences are common in human development. For example, the depletion of fetal supplies of iron coincides with the beginning of the teething period; the ability to make fine motor movements with the hands to grasp and pick up objects; and the decline of the extrusion reflex of the tongue, in which most things placed in the mouth are pushed out.

Just at the time when the infant's body is beginning to need a supplementation of nutrients (mother's milk has little iron), the baby begins to develop the ability to handle food, chew it, and swallow it. Is this more than a coincidence? We'll probably never really know, but it all works out nicely for the baby, who seems to develop the skill to consume solid foods at just the time when he or she needs them.

The American Academy of Pediatrics recommends that infants do not need supplementary foods until four to six months, (American Academy of Pediatrics, Committee on Nutrition, 1981; Anderson, Purvis, & Chopra, 1979; Barness, 1981). By six months, the baby has certain abilities that will help in the processing of solid foods. These include enzymes to digest carbohydrates, chewing and swallowing skills, and the ability to express satiety by head shaking (Stewart, 1981). Data indicate no relationship between the early introduction of solid foods or the amount of food the baby eats and whether the baby will sleep through the night. Thus no clear benefits can be gained from the early introduction of solid feedings (Chubet, 1988; Grunwaldt, Bates, & Guthrie, 1960).

Can the early introduction of solid foods do any harm?

There are some hazards associated with the early introduction of solid foods. The best source of nutrition for infants under six months is milk—preferably human. Any solid food is inferior nutritionally, so proportionately more is required to satisfy nutritional needs. This will lead to less consumption of milk and to a tendency to distend or overtax the stomach, resulting in the short term in gastrointestinal upset and in the long term in possible obesity. Early feeding of solids also has been associated with the development of food allergies, kidney malfunction, and the increased likelihood of developing strong food dislikes (Guthrie, 1979; Pipes, 1985, Robinson, 1978; Weir & Feldman, 1975).

How should solids be introduced?

By the age of five months, the digestive systems of most babies develop the enzymes to digest most proteins, and saliva production increases to lubricate swallowing. Drooling begins about this time, since the production of saliva exceeds the baby's ability to keep it under control. Furthermore, chewing, swallowing, and teeth pushing under the gums all make it easier to handle the demands of eating solids (Guthrie, 1979; Pipes, 1985; Sheppard & Mysak, 1984).

The first teeth do not typically erupt through the gums until about eight months, although individual infants may vary from the average dates of tooth eruption by as much as six months before or after (Lunt & Law, 1974; McDonald & Avery, 1983). In response to teething, some babies become fussy, while others don't seem to notice, although most babies like to bite semisoft objects as their teeth are coming in. This could present a problem if mothers are still nursing at this time. Biscuits may be given to chew on for infants under a year, and large carrot sticks may be given to babies older than one year.

General guidelines for how to introduce solid foods are available from a number of sources. Because of the possibility of food allergies, most experts recommend introducing one food at a time—for at least a week or two—before trying another. New foods should be offered in small amounts at first, and care givers should never force infants to take a food they do not like. Food should be lightly seasoned or not seasoned at all. Salts and sugars are not harmful in small quantities, but there is no need for them. They seem to be more important for the feeder than for the baby (Guthrie, 1979; Robinson, 1978).

The order in which solid foods usually are introduced to babies follows: cereals (one at a time), strained fruit or juice (except orange), vegetables, proteins (meat and cheese), egg yolk (not until eight months), and egg white (not until ten to twelve months) (Guthrie, 1979; Robinson, 1978). The order has to do with a number of developmental factors, such as production of digestive enzymes, consistency of food and the ability to chew, and the possibility of an allergic reaction (egg whites are one of the biggest troublemakers in this regard).

Up until one year, food should be mashed or chopped until it is fine enough that it won't cause choking. Finger foods are good for six-month-olds, and by nine to twelve months, infants can begin to feed themselves with a spoon. Until about eighteen months, spilling and messing food is quite common. Why shouldn't babies explore food just as they do everything else? A good recommendation is for the feeder to come armed with a towel, a sponge, and a sense of humor.

If infants persist in spilling food as part of a game or to get the care giver's attention, care givers can remove the food temporarily, while firmly stating that food is for eating. It is usually not necessary to coax infants to eat: they will eventually eat to satisfy their hunger. Thus, intake in any one meal is not so important. Care givers may wish to insist on proper mealtime behavior (within the limits of the infant's motor abilities and allowing for a little bit of fun), but it is generally not recommended to insist that the infant eat particular foods and particular amounts of foods. Babies

may avoid food because of its taste or because they are not hungry.

At the end of the first year, babies who are teething like to chew on carrots or dry toast, but these things are mangled more than consumed. Babies often go on food jags, refusing to eat more than one or two different kinds of things. Babies can be erratic in their appetites and seem to have strong ideas about when and what to eat (Pipes, 1985).

How to eat is also a big concern for most babies. They may only eat something if it is presented in a ritualized way—cut or arranged a certain way or served on a certain dish. There's not too much the care giver can do except live with these things, accepting them with good humor and the recognition that preferences are part of being human. Some people like their hamburgers with catsup and others, with mustard; some people like grits with their breakfast, and others eat bagels.

For a baby, a meal is more than food intake. It is an occasion of play, learning, and socializing: mealtimes are an important part of the infant's social, cognitive, and emotional development, not just a refueling for physical growth. Parents should try not to rush meals and should cut down on stimulation, such as the television, that might compete with the social aspects of feeding the baby.

As shown from the examples in the observation box related to communication, mealtimes contain complex sequences of social interaction. Issues of control arise often. The baby wants to hold the spoon, for example, but is doing more banging than eating. The mother takes the spoon and begins to feed the baby, who starts to protest and refuses to eat. Mother eventually returns the spoon to the baby. The best solution is to allow the baby as much time as needed to complete the meal. When this is not possible, care givers do need to model more appropriate eating habits but without undue domination. In eating as in other aspects of development, infants will never learn independent behavior unless they are allowed to develop their own sense of control and achievement in this realm. Patience and praise are the best teaching tools.

Self-feeding requires more coordination than most infants can manage. Parents need to give infants foods that are easily handled.

POINTS OF CONTACT

At the beginning of this stage, babies are just beginning to reach out and grasp things with some success. Over these four to five months, babies get better at grasping and holding onto objects, and they get better at locomotion. Any kind of play in which objects are handed to or taken from the baby is most appealing in this stage. As the baby gets good at moving around, you can play a kind of "catch and fetch" game by rolling a ball across the floor and letting the baby retrieve it. Babies have their own version of this game. They love to push toys off tables or throw them down, and they expect the care giver to rush to pick them up, put them back, and wait for the next round of pushing and throwing. You can guess who gets tired of this game first.

Toward the end of this period, babies really get the idea of listening to words. Their favorite words are often names: their own names, of course, and names like "Mommy" and "Daddy." Try to punctuate all your games with words. Babies quickly learn to associate tonal patterns with behavioral sequences.

This is the stage in which the baby perfects the art of anticipa-

continued at top of next page

tion. Games that have a set pattern and a "punch line" the baby can look forward to are perfect. A good example is singing "Pop Goes the Weasel." Chase games, like "I'm gonna get you" and the classic peekaboo, are just right for babies of this age group. Although the baby does not understand the words of the sentences you say to him, he or she can use differences in tonal patterns as a way of sensing the significance of your words. Games that ask questions of the baby begin to work in this stage. Questions have a pattern of rising intonation near the end of the sentence that a baby can recognize as being different from other kinds of statements. This rising pitch creates a sense of anticipation. Of course, you have to answer the questions yourself, but your answer gives the baby a sense of completeness and therefore delight. Examples are "How big is the baby?" and "Where is the baby?" (a variant on peekaboo).

Babies of this age know when things are about to happen. They watch out the window as their parents leave for work, and they look for them when they hear the door opening, or footsteps ringing in the hall. The babies also learn the sounds and sights of siblings and friends and usually get excited when they see or hear them approach.

It is important to exercise babies' bodies, as well as their minds. Helping babies stand, holding their arms to let them "walk," and picking them up are good ways to do this. Stage III babies like vigorous games, such as being tickled or being tossed up in the air and swung around. Gentleness and care are important, since babies' bodies are somewhat weak and it is easy to dislocate an arm by not being careful.

Babies of this age develop their own motor games. They will rock themselves, bounce on their legs, bang on things, and crawl and climb around the house to the extent of their ability. In general, these motor games and rhythmical movements are essential for normal motor and mental development. However, the care giver must be on the alert for potentially dangerous situations. Make sure the things babies like to hold onto to pull themselves up are secure, as well as that there are no dangerous objects—too heavy, too sharp, or too small—that might be in their normal path of movement.

■ SUMMARY

Physical and Motor Development

■ During this period, infants learn to locomote by crawling; they can sit alone and pull themselves up to standing. Grasping and reaching are well-coordinated.

■ Infants have a preferred hand, but their hand preference may change during the first year of life. Hand preference leads to the development of different uses of each hand that are necessary for the acquisition of unimanual reaching and crawling.

■ Walking develops after infants gain postural control.

Perceptual Development

■ Infants can now perceive objects from visual cues alone, allowing them to process information in pictures and on television.
■ Infants can recognize melodies and relate sound patterns to visual patterns.

Cognitive Development

■ Infant memory improves in duration, and infants can process information faster than in the previous stage.
■ Infants now try to form concepts out of their perceptual experiences. Concept formation appears to be organized around prototypes.
■ Using secondary circular reactions, infants discover relationships between their actions and the environment, and they will vary their actions to observe the effects.
■ Infants of this age can remember object locations, so long as they do not have to act on the objects.

Emotional Development

■ Anger and wariness are two new negative emotions seen during this period.
■ Laughter emerges as a new positive emotion.
■ Infants can recognize positive facial expression better than negative expression, however, they do not seem to attribute meaning to those expressions.

Social Development

■ Canonical babbling mimics the intonation patterns of speech and develops in conjunction with auditory perception of speech sounds. However, infants are not using babbling to express themselves in a meaningful, linguistic manner.
■ Infants can communicate nonverbally through action, however, they do not seem to fully understand the meaning of their own behavior. Adults are required to interpret the infant's meaning, which ultimately contributes to the infant's understanding of communication.
■ Parent-infant games are elaborated during this period. There are cultural differences in the amount of play versus care giving that are related in part to ecological factors.

Family and Society

■ Typically, maternal employment does not affect the attachment between mothers and infants. The important factor is whether the mother desires to return to work, in which case her adjustment is more successful.
■ Parental leave policy is lacking in the United States. It is necessary to help in the initial adjustment of the family to a new baby.
■ At all ages, boys and girls seem equally responsive to and knowledgeable about babies. Differences arise in social situations in which individuals are encouraged toward or away from nurturing roles.
■ Preschool-age siblings are capable of adapting their speech and behavior to the needs of the baby.
■ Fathers have a more directing and abrupt style of interaction compared to mothers.

Applications: Infant Nutrition

■ The age of starting solid foods coincides with changes in the infant's physical and motor development that make eating solids possible.
■ Foods should be introduced one at a time to allow for babies to express possible allergies.
■ Younger babies need food that is ground or mashed.
■ Eating is a social experience, and parents should allow plenty of time for meals.

■ GLOSSARY

Appraisal The process by which an individual uses cognitive judgments to regulate emotional experiences.

Canonical babbling Vocal behavior that includes reduplication (repetition) of consonant-vowel syllables.

Expansion babbling Vocal behavior composed of syllable-like vowel sounds, such as raspberries and squeals.

Flextime The policy of allowing flexible work schedules for working parents.

Handedness The preferential use of one hand over the other. Also refers to the use of each hand to do different things.

Object permanence The ability to remember the location of objects that are out of sight.

Prototype The clearest example of a particular form or sound. Prototypes also represent the average of all exemplars across all relevant dimensions.

Role overload When one person tries to fill too many roles or faces excessive demands from a single role.

Secondary circular reaction Repetition of a chance association between an action and its effect. In this case, each repetition is a slight variation of the one before in which the infant is exploring different ways to create effects.

Wariness A quieting or sobering of an infant, usually in response to a novel situation. Wariness is believed to be a precursor to fear.

EIGHT

Becoming a Cause and Becoming Vulnerable

(TEN TO TWELVE MONTHS)

CHAPTER OUTLINE

Physical and Motor Development
Perceptual and Cognitive
   Development
Emotional Development
Social and Language Development

Family and Society
Applications: Infant Health and
   Safety
Points of Contact
Summary
Glossary

The period from about nine to about twelve months encompasses Stage IV of Piaget's sensorimotor phase of development. As the title of this chapter indicates, infants discover two things about themselves: they can cause things to happen, and they are vulnerable to things happening to them. The awareness of themselves as agents and as recipients brings a whole new approach to life, as we will soon see. Babies in this stage know that things exist outside their field of vision or audition, and they feel uncertain in the presence of unfamiliar people or situations. These events signal an increased cognitive sophistication and a growing awareness of the possibilities—both good and bad—that the world has to offer.

■ PHYSICAL AND MOTOR DEVELOPMENT

By the age of one year, infant growth rates have leveled off (see growth charts in the Appendix). Most year-old boys are between 28 1/4 inches to 32 inches in length, and girls are between 27 1/2 and 31 1/4 inches. Both boys and girls will continue to grow at a rate of about 4 to 5 inches per year for the next several years. Boys weigh between 18 1/2 and 26 1/2 pounds, while girls at one year weigh between 17 1/4 and 24 3/4 pounds. By the twelfth month, most babies are eating a variety of solid foods, including table foods that are cut up for them. Most infants are holding their own spoons and can drink from a cup with both hands. By this period, almost all infants will experience teething pains and will have several teeth to help them chew their food.

With respect to motor developments, eleven months is the average age at which infants can stand alone (the range is 9 to 16 months), and at 11 3/4 months, the average baby can walk alone (the range is 9 to 17 months). By one year, most infants can sit down from a standing position, and most can climb up and down stairs by crawling. Negotiating stairs by walking alone takes almost another year for most babies.

The first months of independent walking initiate what some refer to as the toddler period of infant development. The label "toddler" seems to derive from the characteristic gait of the child who has not fully mastered the skill of walking. The earliest forms of childhood bipedalism have a distinct resemblance to a duck out for a jog—a sight that never fails to produce humorous delight in most care givers.

What accounts for this precarious-looking form of locomotion? When adults walk, both legs are moving at the same time: while one is moving forward, the other moves backward relative to the body. This kind of movement is called symmetrical gait. In the gait of toddlers, many steps are symmetrical, but many are also unsymmetrical. This happens because the toddlers often plant one foot and then seem to fall forward onto the other foot in a robot-like walk. Thus, while adult walkers are smoothly making every step symmetrical, toddlers have much more variability in their steps. Smoothness of gait reaches nearly adult levels about six months after the infant begins walking, regardless of the age at which the infant started taking steps (Clark et al., 1988). If infants are given support by an adult, their variability reduces, and they seem to be better coordinated walkers. This suggests that balance, not the timing of the limb movements, is the limiting factor (Clark et al., 1988).

Locomotion seems to have benefits other than the ability to move from place to place. After beginning to walk, ten-month-old infants increase their frequency and duration of social contacts. This is true whether the walking is supported or unsupported. It appears that an upright infant is more likely to be able to look, vocalize, and smile at adults (Gustafson, 1984).

Even more surprising is that locomotor experience seems to enhance cognitive development. As we'll see in the next section, one of the tests typically used to assess cognitive knowledge is the ability to search for hidden objects. Infants with more locomotor experience, who are apparently more accustomed to moving around in the environment, are the most likely to persist in searches for hidden objects. The locomotor experience could be either crawling or assisted walking (Bertenthal, Campos, & Barrett, 1984; Kermoian & Campos, 1988).

Fine motor development also seems to be intimately linked to cognitive and perceptual development. In one research study (Ruff, 1984), infants at six,

The infant's delight at mastering walking is not hard to decipher. Coordinated walking takes about 6 months to develop after the infant's first independent steps.

nine, and twelve months were observed while playing with objects that differed in weight, shape, or texture. Infants were handed one object to explore and then given another differing only in one property (for example, two cubes of the same size and weight, one with a bumpy and the other a smooth texture). Between six and twelve months, there was a decrease in mouthing and an increase in fingering of the objects. The twelve-month-olds also used more actions that were specific to the properties of the object. If the object's texture only was changed, babies increased the amount of looking at and fingering of the object. If the shape only was changed, looking at and fingering increased, but so did rotating the object and transferring it between both hands. Weight changes did not evoke a differential response.

Related research has shown that by twelve months, infants seem to use touching, listening, watching, and mouthing as alternative sources of information gathering. This is more than intersensory coordination; it is the coordination of different types of motor skills in the service of directed exploration of objects (Bushnell, 1982; Gottfried, Rose, & Bridger, 1977; Ruff, 1982).

This research shows that infants are using specific actions by twelve months, actions that are adapted to the type of object they are holding. Motor skill improvements and improvements in the ability to relate information cross-modally (between vision and touch) are essential in fostering cognitive development because they put infants into direct contact with more aspects of their world.

■ PERCEPTUAL AND COGNITIVE DEVELOPMENT

Concepts Become Integrated with Actions

By the age of seven months, infants are just beginning to categorize objects on the basis of their conceptual similarities. Between ten and twelve months, infants combine their ability to form concepts with the ability to use motor skills in a directed way. This can be seen in the development of relational play.

Relational play is action that demonstrates a knowledge of the relationships between two objects, for example, putting lids on pots, cups on saucers, spoons in cups (Fenson et al., 1976). The more perceptually distinct the two objects, the more likely it is that babies will combine them correctly (Bates et al., 1980). For example, if a box and its lid are different colors, infants will be more likely to see how they go together. Also, if the adult places the lid of the box on a table positioned near the top of the box, rather than near the bottom, babies are more likely to put the lid on the box in an appropriate manner.

The relationship between concept and action is also shown in studies in which infants were placed in front of a tray containing different groups of identical objects, for example, four identical human figures, four balls of the same color, and four identical toy cars. Six-month-olds pick up the objects in random sequence, even though they can visually distinguish the different types of objects in a standard habituation procedure. By twelve months, infants will pick up three or four identical objects in a row before going on to pick up other objects. About 40 percent of twelve-month-olds will take those identical objects and place them in a new pile by themselves (Starkey, 1981).

The Emergence of Intentional Action

The impression one gets from these observations is that infants are becoming deliberate in their actions on objects. They are not just discovering relationships between their own actions and their effects on objects; rather they are acting as if they have particular goals for their object play, such as combining objects together in a meaningful way.

This deliberate combination of different actions into a unified pattern of behavior is what Piaget (1952) called the coordination of secondary circular reactions. In the "Observations: Stage IV Behavior" below, Jacqueline's pushing away of her parent's hand shows how the infant can combine different actions with each hand to achieve a goal.

OBSERVATION 1

At 0;8(8) Jacqueline tries to grasp her celluloid duck but I also grasp it at the same time she does. Then she firmly holds the toy in her right hand and pushes my hand away with her left.

OBSERVATION 2

At 0;8(17) after taking a first spoonful of medicine, she pushes away her mother's hand which extends to her a second one.

Searching for Hidden Objects

A similar type of relational behavior is needed when infants search for hidden objects. In order to find an object that infants see being hidden behind a barrier or a cover, they have to move the barrier with one hand and grasp the uncovered object with the other hand. We saw in the last chapter that younger infants do appear to remember the hidden object's location, although they do not reach for the object once it is out of sight. Piaget found that by ten months, infants will readily search for the hidden object and they seem delighted to find it under the cover.

Now suppose you have two identical handkerchief-sized pieces of colored cloth on a table at which you are sitting opposite from the infant. You engage the infant with an attractive toy, such as a set of colored keys, and then you hide the keys under one of the pieces of cloth. Infants older than ten months will lift the cloth to retrieve the keys. Now suppose you take the keys back from the baby and hide them under the other piece of cloth. Infants younger than about fifteen months typically will look under the first piece of cloth, and they will not persist in looking under the second piece of cloth to find the object even though it was hidden in plain view of them! This is an easy demonstration to do with a year-old infant, if you want to convince yourself that babies could actually make such an obvious error.

This mistaken search for the missing object is called the A$\bar{B}$ error (pronounced "A, not B") by infancy researchers. The infants who find the object at location A, the first location, cannot find the object at location B, the second location. The explanation for this error has captured the curiosity of many infant researchers. Why does it happen?

According to Piaget, the infants act as if part of their definition of the object includes its location. In other words, infants do not yet conceive of a whole independent object as you and I might. Rather, infants define the object as the "keys-under-the-cloth," or the "ball-under-the-chair." This is similar to something that happens to adults. Most of us have had the experience of meeting someone briefly, say at a party, but not recognizing the same person seen in another location, such as at the grocery store. If we went back to another party at the same place and that person were again present, we would have no trouble recognizing the individual.

Following Piaget's elegant first experiments and his contextual explanation, there have been a number of seemingly contradictory results. First of all, it should be noted that by nine months, infants are almost 100 percent correct in reaching for objects at the A location (Wellman et al., 1986). Second, if objects are displaced at several different locations without being hidden or if objects are hidden under transparent covers, so long as the infants are first familiarized with the covers and objects, they are almost 100 percent correct in reaching for the object in any location, A or B (Butterworth, 1977; Yates & Bremner, 1988). The only case for which this is not true is if the object or the infant is moved along complex paths with many twists and turns (Landau & Spelke, 1988). This suggests that following the path of a moving object in space is not limiting the infant's search when the objects are hidden.

Memory of the hidden object cannot be a problem for nine-month-olds, as shown by the studies of Baillargeon, discussed earlier, in which eight-month-old infants remembered an object's location so long as they did not have to act on it. It appears, then, that infants of this age already have a concept of objects as existing when out of sight, and they do not appear to associate objects with particular locations since they will directly search for the object in multiple locations so long as they can see the object. Piaget's explanation may not be correct.

The AB̄ error is made most frequently when the object is out of sight, but even then, infants succeed under the following conditions. If there is no delay between the hiding and the opportunity to search for the object, they can find it. Errors are increased if infants are restrained for at least three seconds after the object is hidden at B (Diamond, 1988; Diamond & Doar, 1989). If the infants are allowed to lean their bodies in the direction of the hidden object, they can sometimes find it even after a delay by following the direction of their lean (Diamond & Doar, 1989). If the objects are hidden under covers that are perceptually very different, it is easier for the infants than if the objects are hidden under identical covers (Bremner, 1978).

Explanation Based on Inhibition of Direct Search. Currently, there are two major explanations for these findings, neither of which is related to Piaget's context memory perspective. Both explanations assume the infant has a concept of objects that is independent of visual contact and that the infant's preferred strategy is a direct search for the object. In the first explanation (Diamond, 1988; Diamond & Doar, 1989), the crucial finding is that errors increase when there is a delayed response. The delay causes two problems. First, infants lose their attention for the task at hand after a delay. Second, they cannot inhibit the desire for a direct search. Thus, after attention wanes and the infant can no longer see the object anywhere, memory for the direct path that the object took is lost if there is more than one hiding place.

This perspective is based on findings of infant brain development. In both monkeys and in humans, direct searches at A coincide with a spurt in the development of synapses in the prefrontal cortex. Gradually over the next year in humans, the number of synapses are reduced following selective experiences. The initial increase in the number of synapses creates a unique situation in which spatial memory is enhanced and direct searching occurs. However, this direct search occurs without inhibition. In this view, the infants make errors because they are too impulsive. Inhibition of a direct search—necessary if the object is hidden and there is a delay requiring alternate search strategies—derives from the reduction of synapses over time.

Explanation Based on Two Types of Search: Direct and Indirect. The second explanation, like the first, assumes that infants prefer and are usually successful using a direct search strategy. This explanation also assumes that the cognitive achievement of Piaget's Stage IV is the development of another kind of search strategy, an inferred location search (Wellman et al., 1986). Suppose you drop a coin and you see it roll under a chair. Using a direct search strategy, you look under the chair first, but the coin is not there. You then think about the path on which the coin was rolling, and you continue your search beyond the chair. In other words, you infer the probable location of the coin based on what you know.

Do ten-month-olds do this in the AB̄ task? Yes, it sometimes happens if there is a delay and if the covers are perceptually distinct. But in most cases, a delay in searching following hiding causes more errors. Shouldn't the delay allow the infants to reflect on the problem and use an inferred location search instead of a direct search? Suppose this is exactly what happens. When a delay is imposed, the infants abandon the direct search plan and therefore fail to watch or to remember where the object was last seen. Instead, the infants opt for the inferred search strategy, assuming that they can locate the object based on its prior location. Thus, when allowed to search, they look again at location A, try to imagine the object's probable path, and don't have enough information to find it.

This means that the AB̄ error is actually a manifestation of a new but rudimentary cognitive ability, in which the infants put too much faith. Let's return to our example of seeing a person in the grocery store and suppose that the person actually looks familiar but you can't remember where you met the individual. You use the current situation to trigger your memory using inferential reasoning. Perhaps you wonder if you saw the person in this grocery store or some other grocery store in the past. Reasoning in this way, you may never remember the original encounter at the party. Inference fails when the information you have is faulty.

Currently, there is no way to resolve this controversy. The second explanation is interesting because there are other developmental phenomena that are similar. Infants are always keen to try out new abilities even if they are not fully developed. Toddling is a good example. Standing and alternating leg movements work, and balance is most recently available but faulty. The result is a lot of errors, in the form of falling, but also an occasional graceful stride.

Imitation

During this age period, infants become more proficient at imitating actions that they see for the first time or that they have not done before. The imitations of newborns occur only for acts that they can already do. The observation of an adult doing the same types of acts increases the probability of the newborn's selecting a similar act. However, newborn imitation is slow and does not happen for all infants. Six-month-olds can imitate actions that they have not done before, but only if you give them many demonstrations and allow them plenty of time to process the information (Kaye & Marcus, 1978).

Piaget observed that Stage IV infants can imitate novel actions almost immediately. Typically, babies are better at imitating actions that are close to what they can already do. A recent study has found that nine-month-old infants can imitate simple actions on objects such as opening a box, shaking a toy egg-shaped rattle, and pushing a button. In addition, when the same babies were shown the objects twenty-four hours later, they reproduced the actions that were modeled the previous way (Meltzoff, 1988). Imitation that occurs following a delay from the time the action is seen modeled is called *deferred imitation*. Although this result would be predicted on the basis of our current knowledge of infant memory, Piaget did not observe deferred imitation until eighteen months.

Trying to get his children to imitate sounds was how Piaget discovered that they had a sense of quantity at eleven months of age (Piaget, 1952, p. 241). If Piaget said "papa," Laurent replied with "papa." If Piaget said "pa," so did Laurent. By adding more "pa" syllables, Piaget discovered that Laurent had trouble with more than three. Saying "papapapapapa" only got a "papapa" in return. Strauss and Curtis (1981) found that ten- to twelve-month-olds easily could discriminate visual arrays that differed only in number, particularly for one versus two objects, one versus three objects, and two versus three objects. They had a harder time with four versus three objects and no luck at all discriminating four from five objects.

Individual Differences in Cognition and Attention

The basic trends in cognitive development discussed in this chapter have been found to occur at about the same ages in different cultures around the world (Agiobu-Kemmer, 1986). On the other hand, within any group there are individual differences in the age of attainment of cognitive milestones and in the quality of cognitive abilities.

One important component of cognition is the ability to attend to objects for a long enough time to remember their locations, watch their paths of movements, or learn about their properties during exploratory play. Individual differences in the duration of sustained attention to objects have been found at age one year (Power et al., 1985). Infants who can sustain attention for longer periods engage in higher levels of exploratory play (Fenson et al., 1974) and score higher on developmental tests (Kopp & Vaughn, 1982; Ruff et al., 1990).

What factors account for individual differences in attention? To some extent, these differences may be related to differential development of the brain and may be partly constitutional (Kagan, 1990; Rothbart & Posner, 1985). We'll return to evaluate this explanation in the last chapter. On the other hand, differences in the care-giving environment have been shown to influence the quality of infant attention.

When mothers are trained to enhance their object-related behaviors during social play with infants — by demonstrating object properties, pointing to and naming objects, and questioning — infants' level of complexity of exploratory play is enhanced (Belsky et al., 1980). Actually, this effect seems to work the best for infants who have short attention spans. Their duration of attention increased following an intervention in which adults worked to point out object properties and refocus the infants after a loss of attention, while the duration of attention for high-attending infants did not change following the intervention (Parrinello & Ruff, 1988).

Another approach to the study of individual differences in cognitive ability is the assessment of infant's mastery motivation. *Mastery motivation* is an inherent motivation to be competent in a particular situation, and its measurement involves persistence in solving problems. At twelve months of age, persistent goal-directed actions on objects are typically followed by the expression of smiling or laughter by infants (McTurk et al., 1987), suggesting that persistence is in fact motivated by a goal and the achievement of the goal results in positive feelings of efficacy.

Similar to the study of adults' effects on infant attention, adult object-related behavior increased the level of mastery motivation only for twelve-month-olds who were rated as being temperamentally low in activity. For infants who were highly active, parental intervention had no effect or an interfering effect on the infants' mastery (Wachs, 1987). Thus, more active infants seem to be less in need of adult encouragement and intervention in their play than less active infants.

These studies suggest that adults can play important roles in the cognitive development of infants, particularly if their actions are designed to enhance the infants' attention to objects and their properties. This is not so much teaching or reinforcing but rather supporting the infants' own initiatives and helping infants to regulate their limited attention spans. These results also suggest that adult behavior needs to be adapted to the individual infant. Babies who are less active and poor attenders may need a more involved adult to help organize their own play. Babies who are more active and attentive may have different needs for adults, perhaps as an appreciative audience for showing off the infants' self-directed achievements.

■ EMOTIONAL DEVELOPMENT

As the sections on cognitive and motor development suggest, there is an increasing amount of integration in the infant's life. Motor skills create the tools with which the infant can operate on the environment to achieve goals, and goals increasingly structure the way in which the infant behaves. Earlier, infants became upset when someone caused them pain or if some expected event did not happen. Between the ages of ten and twelve months, infants become upset if their goals are blocked, and they become pleased if they can achieve an intended goal. Therefore, intelligent action is intimately bound up with the child's motivations and emotions.

The Development of Anger

Anger is the emotion most frequently elicited in infants when their goals have been disrupted. An angry expression has the following characteristics. The mouth is open with a squarish shape that is angled downward toward the back of the mouth. The brows are lowered and the eyes are opened and intense (see Figure 8.1). The expression of distress is similar for the mouth, except that the eyes are usually closed or partially closed (Figure 8.1).

If the infant is crying at the same time as making the anger expression, it represents a more intense state of emotion. When anger expressions were

■ FIGURE 8.1
Infant Expressions

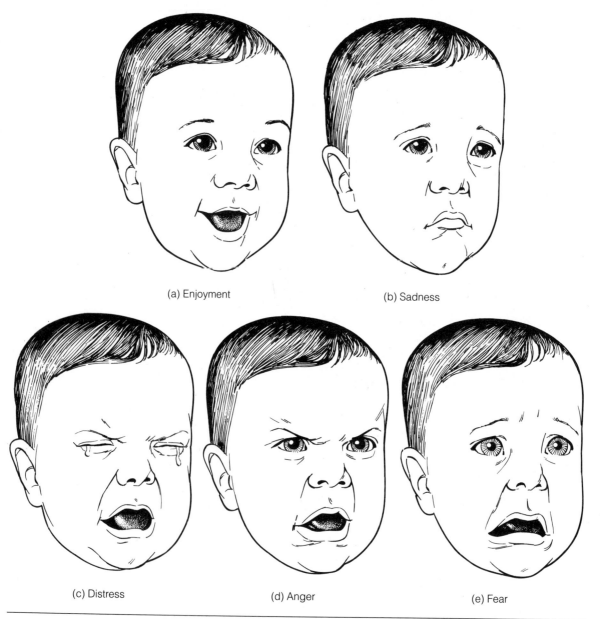

(a) Enjoyment

(b) Sadness

(c) Distress

(d) Anger

(e) Fear

SOURCE: Izard, C. The maximally discriminative facial movement coding system. Instructional Resources Center, University of Delaware, Newark, Delaware, January 1983. pp. 93, 95-98.

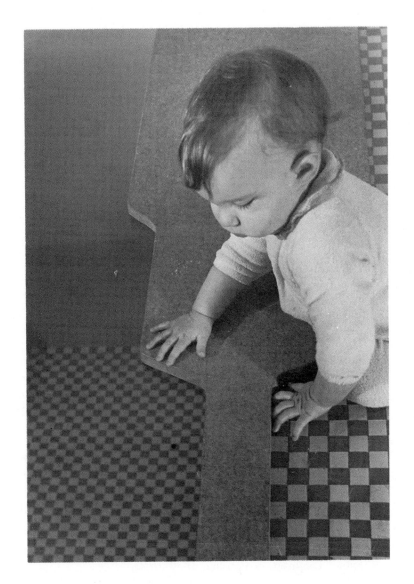

An infant approaches the visual cliff (photo courtesy of Richard Walk, whose grand-daughter is pictured here).

observed without crying, EEG recordings from the infants' scalps showed heightened activity in the left frontal region. When the infants were angry and crying, there was more activity in the right frontal region. The right frontal area is believed to be associated with more intense states of negative emotions. This suggests that low levels of anger, without crying, are probably adaptive and maintain the infants' orientation toward the environment (Fox & Davidson, 1988).

The emotion of anger began in the previous stage as a more vigilant and intense form of distress. Between ten and twelve months, anger becomes more purposeful and directed. Infants do such things as stomp their feet, hit away objects or interfering hands, or slap and kick (Sroufe, 1979). These expressions have the quality of outbursts, and they coincide with the development of goal-directed behavior seen in other realms of infant functioning during this period. Such overt expressions of anger are rarely seen in the natural environment (Demos, 1982), although care givers need to see only a single temper tantrum for the experience to linger in their minds for a long time.

The Development of Wariness and Fear

Around the age of six months, infants develop a wary look that may involve a raised brow furrowing above the nose and a relatively relaxed mouth. Wariness is related to the emotion of fear, since both involve an inhibition of action and may reflect a tendency for the individual to withdraw from the situation. The expression of fear involves the raised and furrowed brow of wariness and the retraction of the mouth corners straight back (Figure 8.1).

True fear expressions are rare in infancy, but they first appear around the age of ten months (Demos, 1982). Fear expressions may appear briefly and then change to anger or sadness (see Figure 8.1). Fear may also be shown by behavioral inhibition in the absence of a facial expression. Infants may stop their movements or actively avoid approaching the source of the fear. Infants feel fear when unexpected or threatening events occur. The following are some of the situations of which year-old infants are sometimes afraid.

Heights. Fear of heights has been assessed using the *visual cliff* situation. A piece of hard, clear plastic is extended over a box having a shallow and a deep side. Beginning at nine months of age, infants show fear in approaching the deep side of the cliff (Gibson & Walk, 1960; Schwartz, Campos, & Baisel, 1973).

Unpredictable Objects and Movements. Infants will show fear responses to any objects—either people or inanimate moving objects—that loom unexpectedly in front of them (Bronson, 1972; Cicchetti & Mans, 1976). Surprising events, like the popping up of a jack-in-the-box, may also cause fear (Ricciuti & Poresky, 1972). Unpredictable, noisy mechanical toys can cause fear. However, in one study, infants were given control over the movements of such toys. When the infants were in control, the toys were significantly less fearful (Gunnar, Leighton, & Peleaux, 1984).

■ OBSERVATION:
Stage IV Behavior
(Piaget, 1952, p. 249)

OBSERVATION 3

At 1;1(10) she [Jacqueline] has a slight scratch which is disinfected with alcohol. She cries, chiefly from fear. Subsequently, as soon as she again sees the bottle of alcohol she recommences to cry, knowing what is in store for her. Two days later, same reaction, as soon as she sees the bottle and even before it is opened.

Acquired Fears. Infants may become fearful of an otherwise benign situation because it reminds them of something they found stressful, fearful, or painful in the past. These fears can be said to arise from a conditioned association.

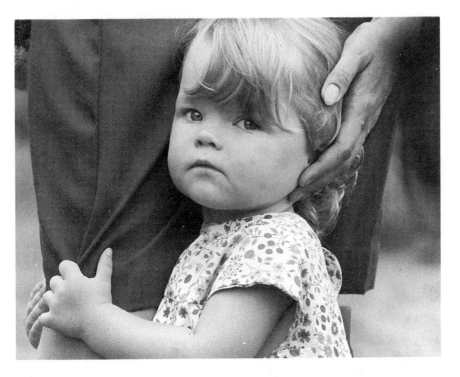

Infants of this age are naturally wary of new situations. They find great comfort in the company of familiar care givers.

They are different from fears of such things as heights or looming objects, which may be universal. Acquired fears are learned. Examples are fear of particular people, of doctor's offices, or of certain kinds of sounds, such as a dog's bark (Bronson, 1972; see "Observations: Stage IV Behavior").

Strangers. Fear of strangers takes two forms. One is a response to particular people or people wearing a particular kind of clothing or hairstyle. This is an acquired fear, or a *categorical stranger reaction* (Bronson, 1972). The other is a general wariness of the unfamiliar that appears in most infants from every culture beginning about eight months of age.

Although infants' reactions to strangers are usually different from their responses to their mothers, infants are not always afraid of strangers. The recent research indicates that infants fear strangers the most when the strangers' presence contains any of the elements of the unconditioned fear responses mentioned above. Factors such as the height of the strangers, the familiarity of setting, and whether the strangers loom in rapidly all play a part in the babies' appraisal of the situation.

Infants show more positive reactions if the strangers approach them slowly (Kaltenbach, Weinraub, & Fullard, 1980; Trause, 1977); if their mothers are present when the strangers approach (Eckerman & Whatley, 1975; Ricciuti, 1974; Trause, 1977); if they are with familiar care givers, such as baby-sitters or child-care providers (Fox, 1977; Ricciuti, 1974); if the strangers are midgets or children (Bigelow et al., 1990; Brooks & Lewis, 1976); if the strangers do not tower over the infants (Weinraub & Putney, 1978); and if the infants are in an unfamiliar setting, such as a laboratory, compared to a home (Brookhart & Hock, 1976; Skarin, 1977).

You might expect a baby to be less fearful at home than in a strange place. In strange places, infants seem to expect to see unusual or unfamiliar things. When the stranger intrudes on the familiar and predictable setting of the home, however, the infant gets disturbed. In fact, mothers bring their babies to many places, such as doctors' offices and grocery stores, and the babies are rarely upset by the many unfamiliar people they meet in those situations.

Recently, it has been discovered that infants are less fearful of attractive than of unattractive strangers (Langlois et al., 1990). An adult stranger wore a mask showing either an attractive or an unattractive face to a baby. The adult stranger was an attractive female. A professional mask maker made a cast of the woman's face and then created two lifelike masks. One was essentially a replica of the woman's face, and the other had been altered according to previous research on attractiveness. To make the mask unattractive, the eyes were narrowed and moved closer together, the eyebrows were lowered, and the nose was lengthened. These changes did not make the mask look abnormal or deformed. The experimenters placed a mask over the woman's face and asked her to interact with infants. She was not told which mask she was wearing and she was asked to behave as much as possible the same way every time she interacted with an infant.

When the stranger wore the attractive mask, infants showed more positive expressions and less withdrawal and got more involved in play with the stranger, compared to when she wore the unattractive mask. The results can only be explained by the infants' preference for attractiveness, since the stranger was unaware of which mask she was wearing. The same experimenters gave infants attractive and unattractive dolls to play with. Infants played longer with the attractive doll. There is currently no accepted explanation for this effect. It is important to point out that these behavioral differences showing a preference for attractiveness are short-term. Infants become attached to their care givers regardless of the level of attractiveness.

A number of studies have shown that babies can engage in positive and rewarding social interaction soon after meeting a new person. If the stranger proves acceptable to the baby, the baby often will spend more time playing with this interesting visitor than with his or her own mother (Klein & Durfee, 1976; Ross & Goldman, 1977b).

In contrast, if the stranger approaches too quickly, looms, towers, or otherwise violates the infants' personal space, fearful reactions easily can be evoked. However, would an adult react any differently? In one study (Kaltenbach, Weinraub, & Fullard, 1980), mothers and their eight-month-old infants sat side by side as unfamiliar female adults approached them quickly. The mothers showed more quizzical looks, frowns, and gaze aversions as the stranger got closer than did their infants. This suggests that "stranger fear" is not a stage of development that all babies go through. It may represent a growing awareness of situations that all humans fear—a step toward becoming more adult. Hesitancy toward strangers—especially intrusive ones—is something that stays with people throughout their lives.

If you want to make friends with a baby, the rules are not so different than with anyone else: go slowly, be sensitive to signs of withdrawal or wariness, let the baby get to know you on his or her own terms, and make sure the baby is properly chaperoned by his or her mother or care giver before you make any serious proposals. Finally, don't forget that year-old babies develop acquired fears. If the baby screams in terror at the mere sight of you, it could be that you remind the baby of a negative encounter. Even though it's hard to keep from feeling downright insulted, it's probably not your fault. It may take some extra sensitivity on your part to help the baby learn to like you for yourself.

The Development of Sadness

The emotion of sadness differs from anger and from fear in its expression. During sadness, the brows are raised at the center and drop at the sides, and the mouth corners are drawn back and down (see Figure 8.1). As we reported for anger, sadness without crying is less intense, showing left-frontal brain activity. With crying, sadness is accompanied by right-brain activation. Sadness in the earlier months accompanied disappointment when an expected event failed to happen. For example, when the baby expects to receive a treat or a hug and does not get it. By nine or ten months, sadness accompanies a feeling of loss. Because infants can now connect their memory of absent objects with some concrete action on the objects, infants may become sad if an object disappears and they cannot find it after a search.

In some cases, but not all, sadness accompanies separation from care givers. This emotion is sometimes called separation distress. Research has shown, however, that if mothers leave their babies behind in the company of the regular care giver (the grandmother, baby-sitter, father, and so on), there is little or no separation distress (Ricciuti, 1974; Stayton, Ainsworth, & Main, 1973; Suwalsky & Klein, 1980). One study of children admitted to residential care found that if they were admitted with a sibling, they showed less separation distress than if admitted by themselves, even if the sibling were not old enough to take care of the infant (Heinicke & Westheimer, 1966). Another study found that infants left with a total stranger cope significantly better with separation than infants left completely alone (Ricciuti, 1974).

Infants respond more positively to separation from their mothers if they are left with any other person, particularly a familiar one; if they are left with toys of any kind and if they can see or hear their mothers in an adjoining room (Corter, 1977); and if they are left with their own pacifiers (Halonen & Passman, 1978; Hong & Townes, 1976). If the mothers said "bye-bye" or made some other parting gestures before they left, it had no effect on one-year-olds (Corter, 1977). These parting gestures do seem to help older infants, however. In general, the longer parents take to say good-bye, the harder it is for the babies to initially adjust to the new situation (Field, Gewirtz, Cohen, Garcia, Greenberg, & Collins, 1984; Weinraub & Lewis, 1977). Babies who go to a new preschool or day-care center or who must be hospitalized show less distress if accompanied by peer friends or by siblings (Field, Vega-Lahr, & Jagadish, 1984; Robertson & Robertson; 1971).

If infants are separated from parents and are not provided with adequate substitute care givers, more serious depression and withdrawal can result, including both behavior and physiological changes (Reite et al., 1989; Tizard & Tizard, 1971). These effects can be ameliorated once the infants are restored to stable adult care, either with their biological parents or with adoptive parents (Reite et al., 1989; Suomi & Harlow, 1972; Tizard & Tizard, 1971). The effects on infants of substitute care by nonparental care givers is an important topic to which we will return in the next chapter.

The Development of Enjoyment and Affection

In the earlier months, infants showed positive responses to their care givers. The smile of recognition appears at two months, and the enjoyment of laughter during social play appears at five months. At ten months, the infant has a deeper and more lasting type of positive feeling that has been called affection (Sroufe, 1979). Affection has a characteristic expression that is similar to a simple smile in the mouth region accompanied by a widening of the eyes (see Figure 8.1). Such smiles occur at the approach of familiar care givers and are accompanied by right-brain activation. When infants smile at strangers, it is usually without the wide-eye component, and such smiles activate the left side of the brain (Fox & Davidson, 1988).

After a brief separation, infants often feel genuinely happy to see the care giver. This is a positive emotion that goes beyond the particular situation and expresses a lasting bond. Infants express these feelings not only to care givers but also to favorite toys and to siblings.

Differential responsiveness to people on reunion is probably one of the earliest and most reliable ways of telling who are the most important people in a baby's life (Stayton et al., 1973). In a stressful situation, if both the mother and another care giver are present, infants will approach the mother (Klein & Durfee, 1978). Even when infants spend more hours of the day in the company of care givers, such as on an Israeli kibbutz, they show more positive responses when reunited with their mothers after a brief separation than when reunited with the *metapelets*, or care givers (Fox, 1977).

These findings suggest that babies have a growing awareness of the specialness of certain people and respond to them in ways that communicate the depth of their feelings.

The Development of Mixed Emotions

Before leaving the topic of emotions, it is necessary to touch on the subject of mixed emotional expressions. By experimentally presenting different objects to babies, Ricciuti and Poresky (1972) showed that infants of twelve months had mixed emotional reactions, even to dolls and teddy bears: the babies alternately reached out toward the objects and pulled their arms back. Lest we think this sort of ambivalence was merely an artifact of testing infants in an unfamiliar laboratory setting, another study found evidence for mixed emotions by naturalistic observation in the infants' homes. This study found that pure expressions of joy, anger, distress, excitement, or fear occur only about half the time. The other half of the time more than one emotion is expressed on the infants' faces (Demos, 1982).

Enjoyment, for example, often is expressed with elements of excitement, surprise, or disgust. One fairly common expression among year-old infants is a smile combined with a "jaw-drop," producing a wide-open, smiling mouth. This usually occurs in situations such as a peekaboo game just before the mother appears and when she's saying, "Where's Mommy?" This mixed expression is believed to show a kind of pleasurable suspense (Demos, 1982). Try it on yourself and see if you can feel that emotion. Smiles also have been observed to occur with nose wrinkles, blinks, blows, and waves; each combination expresses a slight variation in the meaning of the enjoyment. Try each one out and see if you can figure out what they might mean.

In the next stage, distress will be combined with biting or stiffening the lip, showing that the baby is trying to control the crying. One-year-old babies do not do this, but they often alternate between distress and enjoyment, showing that they are able to maintain interest in a toy or in social interaction even though they may be tired or frustrated. The care giver can provide encouragement for the infant's efforts to gain control over frustration, teaching the baby the capacity to persist. The baby can learn that feeling distressed and frustrated do not necessarily mean the end of the game — that these "negative" affects are both tolerable and manageable (Demos, 1982).

Individual Differences in Emotion Regulation

One of the more important aspects of emotional development is the ability to regulate one's emotions: to maintain some self-control in the face of highly arousing (either exciting or distressing) situations. At this age, infants show differences in how they use people or objects to regulate emotions.

Heart rate measures have shown that even if infants do not cry during maternal separation, they do get aroused. We may observe an extended glance at the door, perhaps a sad expression, and then a concerted effort to become involved with the toys. It is almost as if the babies were using the toys to prevent feeling sad and lonely. Conversely, other infants who may ignore their mothers when they return from a separation also show elevated heart rates. These babies are coping with their ambivalent feelings about their mothers in relation to the feeling of loss they must have experienced when they were out of the room. The manner in which they cope with these feelings is not necessarily adaptive, since it effectively removes them from the only source of comfort they might receive: their mothers (Sroufe, 1979).

Some infants appear to be temperamentally more fearful, and they are more likely to become fearful or sad in stressful situations, such as during separations and in the presence of strangers. This kind of emotional reactivity may persist in some infants for a year or more (Campos et al., 1975; Connell, 1985; Kagan, 1990; Thompson et al., 1988). These differences in emotionality are associated with individual differences in brain asymmetry. That is, infants who become easily distressed to the point of crying by a maternal separation have more marked differences between left- and right-brain activity in the frontal area (Fox & Davidson, 1987). We'll discuss the possible origins of such differences in the final chapter.

Developments in the Infant's Ability to Use Emotional Information Expressed by Other People

In the last chapter, we reported research showing that by six or seven months, infants are capable of perceptually differentiating happy from fearful or sad expressions. At this age, however, infants do not seem to be affected by these differences. By nine or ten months, however, infants are beginning to use the emotional information displayed by others in a meaningful manner. There are at least three ways in which this can occur.

Affective sharing occurs when infants wish to communicate their feelings to another person or to confirm their feelings with another person. An example would be when a baby discovers an interesting relationship (like how a lid goes onto a pot), smiles, and then looks to the care giver. In this case, the infant is expecting a smile in return.

Social referencing occurs when infants face an uncertain situation. In this case, they look to another person's emotional expressions in order to help them decide what to do in this situation. When infants are presented with a noisy, unpredictable toy, they may look around to see how adults are responding to the toy. Positive responses from the adults may encourage the infants to approach the toy.

Underlying both affective sharing and social referencing is the development of the ability to delay an immediate emotional reaction to a situation and to evaluate how one is going to feel about the situation. *Appraisal* is the ability to use cognitive comparisons of alternate interpretations in order to regulate one's emotions. In affective sharing, the infant has a spontaneous reaction (such as a smile) and looks at others to appraise that reaction. A confirmation leads to continued smiling. In social referencing, the infant may be unable to appraise a situation and uses information from others to decide whether the uncertain event (a strange toy) should be greeted with delight or with wariness.

Between six and twelve months of age, affective sharing is the most common response in social situations, and this tends almost always to involve positive emotions (Hornick & Gunnar, 1988; Klinnert, 1984; Walden & Ogan, 1988). When infants of these ages are given novel toys or a rabbit in a cage, they tend to focus mostly on those objects and look at the care giver for confirmation, primarily when the care giver displays a positive expression.

Between ten and twelve months, infants begin to use social referencing systematically, although social referencing does not occur as frequently as affective sharing in naturalistic situations (Hornick & Gunnar, 1988; Nelson, 1985). Social referencing occurs when infants look at adults in an uncertain situation, when infants look as much at negative as at positive adult expressions, and when infants change their behavior (or at least pause before acting) as a result of the emotional information in the adults' faces.

Thus, by ten months, if mothers display a negative expression, some infants will avoid crossing a visual cliff, and avoid playing with toys or approaching a rabbit in a cage, and they will show more aversive responses to strangers to whom the mothers show negative expressions. Opposite patterns of behavior can be seen if the mothers display positive expressions in these situations, although negative expressions seem to have a more powerful effect on regulating infant behavior at this age (Gunnar & Stone, 1984; Hornick et al., 1987; Feiring et al., 1984; Sorce et al., 1985; Zarbatany & Lamb, 1985). Infants will reference almost any available adult, showing equal responsiveness to mothers, fathers, and strangers (Dickstein & Parke, 1988; Klinnert et al., 1986).

In addition to this directed referencing in uncertain situations, infants seem to be influenced by adults' emotions. During a play period, mothers were instructed to use facial and vocal expressions of either joy or sadness. In the joy condition, infants expressed more joy and looked more at their mothers while engaging in higher-level play behavior. In the sadness condition, infants expressed more negative emotions, looked less at their mothers, and played less (Termine & Izard, 1988). It is interesting to note that the mothers in this study had trouble maintaining the emotions as instructed. Sadness was often confused with expressions of anger, and it was hard for them to hold back an occasional smile during the sadness condition.

These studies show that by the second half of the first year of life, emotion is no longer a private experience. Perhaps without intending to do so, infants nevertheless begin to alter their own emotions according to what others are expressing. It would not be correct to infer that infants understand the feelings of others at this age or even that infants can differentiate their own feelings from those of others. These developments begin almost a year later. A more appropriate explanation is that infants want to be a part of the life around them, and they want to maintain positive feelings whenever possible. Coupled with new perceptual and cognitive skills, infants probably discover that particular types of facial expression are related to actions that either enhance or interrupt their own activities. Thus, by the end of the first year, those facial expressions of adults have become part of the means by which infants regulate their own actions. From the adult's perspective, the infants are becoming more socially responsive and are entering into more meaningful social communications.

■ SOCIAL AND LANGUAGE DEVELOPMENT

In this section, we cover new developments in the infants' communication with adults, including the beginnings of spoken language. Following that, we discuss care giver-infant attachment. Finally, we'll look at the beginnings of infant-peer relationships.

Developments in Infant Perception of Adult Speech

Before the age of about ten months, infants are capable of perceiving differences in melodic and intonation patterns, which allow them to recognize differences between melodies and between passages of speech. We also described how babbling seems to reflect the intonation patterns of speech but not the meaning of speech.

In speech to year-old children, adults continue to raise the overall pitch and to exaggerate the intonation contours of sentences. In one study, adults were recorded while talking to one-year-olds and to other adults about the following topics: attention getting, approval, prohibition, comfort, and play. Then the tapes were synthetically modified to remove all speech content while preserving the intonation. These modified tapes were played to other adults who were asked to judge the content of the speech. The judges were significantly likely to be more correct about the original content of the speech when they heard the modified speech to babies compared to the modified speech to adults (Fernald, 1989).

Thus, the exaggerated speech to year-old infants seems to emphasize the meaningful aspects of the intonation patterns of speech, making it easier to recognize meaning from the intonation alone. In related work, speech to year-old infants was sampled in France, Italy, Germany, Japan, Britain, and the United States. In all cases, the speech had similar exaggerated intonation contours, although the American mothers did the most exaggeration (Fernald et al., 1989). There is no doubt that infants at this age, as well as adults, can differentiate between these different speech intonation patterns (Ferland & Mendelson, 1989; Trehub et al., 1987). Thus, the capacity to recognize meaningfully different speech intonation patterns is well established by age one year. In addition, these patterns are fairly universal across languages.

There is some evidence that adult care givers actually make their speech more exaggerated and simpler for year-old infants than they did earlier in the first year. When the baby was three months old, the parents mostly were content to comment on the baby's condition or state or make some general inferences about their relationship to the baby (see Chapter 6). By the time the baby is eight months old, parents tend to use more commanding and directive language in relationship to specific aspects of their baby's behavior. Compared with parents' speech to four-month-olds, their speech to eight-month-olds is more related to what the child is doing; it is somewhat simpler in structure, almost as if the parents are simplifying their sentences because they think the infant is now listening (Davis, 1978; Sherrod, Crawley, Peterson, & Bennett, 1978; Sherrod, Friedman, Crawley, Drake, & Dervieux, 1977).

The parents begin to make specific responses to infant activity, which enhances the infant's ability to make connections between action and speech. Parents also provide the infant with some very detailed utterances. They not only name objects; they name small details of the objects, such as color, texture, response properties, and the infant's familiarity with the object. They make the object more real, such as making a toy cow moo or a stuffed dog bark.

Infants are treated to pop quizzes: "What does a cow say?" The mother corrects the baby's pronunciations and gives little compliments when things are done correctly. She instructs the child on how to play with a toy or how to behave, and she uses polite expressions, such as "please" and "thank you" (West & Rheingold, 1978).

Parents often do not correct infants, and they seem to enjoy the verbal mistakes infants make. The Marquesas Islanders enjoy their infants' incomplete development. They try to get the babies to perform their incomplete movements or to make verbal mistakes. These are humorous and enjoyable moments for the family (Martini & Kirkpatrick, 1981).

Perhaps because of these adult simplification techniques, during the period from ten to twelve months, infants develop a special sensitivity for both listening to and producing sounds from the language spoken in their home. Before the age of nine months, infants seem to be universal language perceivers, that is, they can distinguish important sound contrasts from many different languages. For example, African infants were able to distinguish between syllables in their native Kikuyu language, as well as between syllables found in English but not in Kikuyu (Streeter, 1976). In another study, babies born into Spanish-speaking homes can distinguish between both Spanish and English syllables, but the results were less conclusive for infants born into English-speaking homes (Eilers, Gavin, & Wilson, 1979).

A developmental study (Werker & Tees, 1984) looked at infants at four-to-six and at ten-to-twelve months from three different language groups: English, Salish (a native Canadian language), and Hindi. Babies from each group were tested with syllable contrasts from each language. Syllables were chosen in such a way that a native speaker could hear the differences between them, but a nonnative speaker could not. An example of this is the English contrast between *ra* and *la*. Japanese speakers cannot distinguish perceptually between these two syllables and often get them mixed up when they try to speak English. English speakers have a similarly difficult time distinguishing between the Japanese syllables *ki* and *kii*, as in *kite* (come) and *kiite* (listen). In the second syllable, the *ii* sound (pronounced like the "e" in "be") is held just slightly longer than the *i* sound in the first syllable; otherwise, the two sounds are identical.

The results of the Werker and Tees' study showed that the younger infants could distinguish the syllable contrasts from all the languages, but the older infants could only distinguish between the contrasts of the language heard in the home. A later study replicated these findings using computer-simulated sound contrasts similar to those found in English and in Hindi (Werker & Lalonde, 1988). Thus, by the age of ten months or so, infants lose a perceptual sensitivity that they had at an earlier age.

This may be accounted for by the selective processes of brain development discussed in Chapter 6. At first, synapses are overproduced, and later some are selected and strengthened, while others disappear. In the prefrontal area responsible for the ability to search for hidden objects, overproduction of synapses is just beginning at ten months of age, while in the auditory cortex, the overproduction occurs earlier, and by ten months, the number of synapses has started to drop (Goldman-Rakic, 1987).

In addition to becoming perceptually attuned to the speech spoken in the home, infants are beginning to grasp the meanings of some words and gestures. For example, around nine months, infants will make the appropriate action when parents say things like "play pat-a-cake" or "wave bye-bye to Daddy." It doesn't take much longer for parents to begin spelling out words like "bottle" or "candy" when speaking to each other in the baby's presence, so as not to get the baby interested at that moment (Bates et al., 1987).

Speech and Gestural Production by Infants

Between nine and twelve months, infants make a variety of sounds that attentive care givers recognize as words or word-like utterances. The sounds are used repeatedly in similar situations and not in other situations. Table 8.1 shows the first seven "words" in a child's vocabulary recorded in one of the early studies of language development.

Researchers disagree over whether these sounds are true words or true names for things since they are arbitary and idiosyncratic, rather than conventional. Instead, they seem like accompaniments to action, like saying "brrroom" when moving a toy car or grunting when exerting physical effort (Bates et al., 1987; McCune, 1989). These early word-like sounds don't appear to be communicative before twelve months of age, except in rare circumstances.

The meaning of such sounds, as well as of many of the infant's gestures, still depends on the interpretive activity of the care giver who recognizes a relationship between the sound or gesture and the situation in which the child uses it (Adamson et al., 1987; Lock, 1980). In the Observation Box below are some examples of care giver interpretations of infant acts, both verbal and nonverbal, at this age.

■ **TABLE 8.1   The First Seven "Words" in One Child's Vocabulary**

UTTERANCE	AGE (MONTHS)	MEANING
eh	8	Said to people, distant objects, and toys.
dididi	9	Disapproval (loud) or comfort (soft).
mama	10	Refers to food; also means tastes good and hungry.
nenene	10	Scolding.
tt!	10	Used to call squirrels.
piti	10	Always used with a gesture and always whispered; means that's interesting.
duh	10	Used with same gesture as for piti; seems to be a comment on ongoing action.

SOURCE: From W. Leopold, *Speech Development of a Bilingual Child* (Chicago: Northwestern University Press, 1949). Copyright 1949 by Northwestern University Press. Also reprinted by permission from p. 177 of Child Development by Alan Fogel and Gail F. Melson; Copyright © 1988 by West Publishing Company. All rights reserved.

■ **OBSERVATIONS: Communicative Behavior (Lock, 1980)**

OBSERVATION 4

Mary; age 12(20): (1) Mary turns around in her chair and tries to pick up an apple from behind her. (2) She fails and turns back to her mother, who has been watching her, and cries.
(3) Mother: What do you want?
(4) Mary gesturally reaches toward the apple. Mother then gives it to her.

OBSERVATION 5

Mary; age 11(5): Mary is sitting in her high chair with mother next to her. She has finished eating. Some of her toys are on the table in front of her. Mother picks up a squeaky duck and shows it to Mary. Mother: Who's this? (squeak squeak) Who is it? Is it the duck? What does the duck say?
Mary: ugh.
Mother: He doesn't say "ugh." He says "quack, quack, quack, quack" . . . "quack, quack, quack, quack." Ooh, and who's this? It's the doggie isn't it? And what does the doggie say? What does the doggie say? Mary? . . . Oh he doesn't yawn . . . What does the doggie say? "Woof, woof, woof, woof, woof," "Woof, woof, woof, woof, woof." Don't you want the doggie? Oh, you say it, "woof, woof, woof, woof, woof." Mary say it, "Woof, woof, woof, woof, woof." And who's this? Who's this? It's Teddy, isn't it? and Teddy says "aah." It's Teddy, isn't it? Aah, love Teddy. Ah, is it Teddy? Aah.
Mary picks up the dog.
Mother: Oh, is that your doggie? What does the doggie say? What does the doggie say? What does the doggie say? "Woof, woof, woof, woof, woof." "Woof, woof, woof, woof, woof." Doesn't he?

At this same age, infants are becoming more intentional in their communication using gestures. At three to five months, pointing is a spontaneous display of attention or interest (Fogel & Hannan, 1985); after five months, pointing is used instrumentally to touch or tap objects while exploring (Bates et al., 1987; Fogel & Thelen, 1987), but it is not until about ten months that infants use pointing in communicative ways (see Figure 8.2). We can say that infants use pointing and other gestures to intentionally communicate if they look between the adult and the object alternately and if they keep trying to communicate when the initial attempt does not succeed (Bates et al., 1987; Lock, 1980; see Figure 8.3).

In a recent study done in my laboratory (Messinger & Fogel, 1990), we examined the development of infant offering of objects. Before ten months, infants hand objects to their mothers in the course of exploratory play with

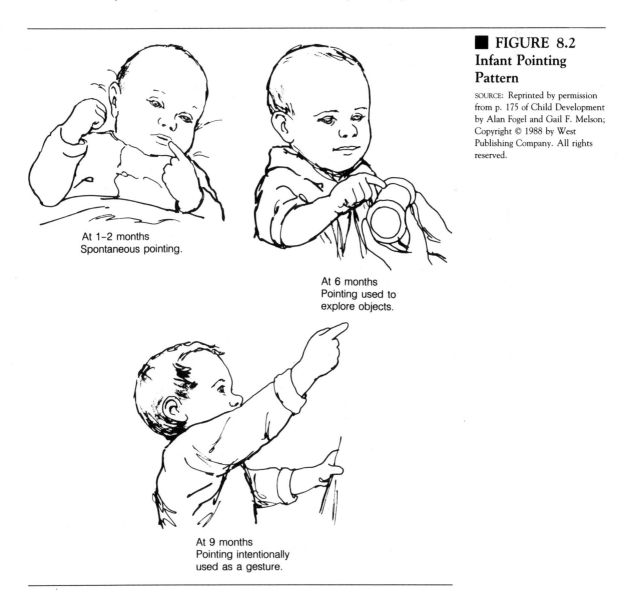

At 1–2 months
Spontaneous pointing.

At 6 months
Pointing used to
explore objects.

At 9 months
Pointing intentionally
used as a gesture.

■ FIGURE 8.2
Infant Pointing
Pattern

SOURCE: Reprinted by permission from p. 175 of Child Development by Alan Fogel and Gail F. Melson; Copyright © 1988 by West Publishing Company. All rights reserved.

■ **FIGURE 8.3**
Gestural
Communication
at One Year

SOURCE: Lock, A. The guided reinvention of language. London:
Academic Press, 1980, p. 98.

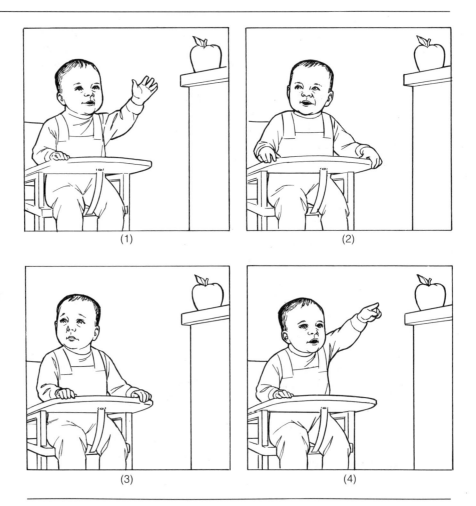

(1)   (2)

(3)   (4)

the objects. When this happens, the infants never take their eyes off the object. They look at the object as their mothers take it and then hand it back. If mothers playfully keep the object, the infants become frustrated. Beginning at ten months, infants alternate gaze between mother and object during the offering. We also found that in these cases, the infant initiates the object exchange. When the mother requests an object, the infant doesn't look at her during the offer. Finally, and importantly, when infants initiate offers and alternate gaze, they are likely to smile or laugh when the offer is completed.

This combination of communication and emotion has also been discovered in relation to the use of first words. When infants actually utter a word, they tend to have a neutral facial expression. Immediately following the word, their expression changes, typically to a positive expression (Bloom & Beckwith, 1989). These findings are consistent with the results on right-hemisphere specialization for mild and positive emotions (Fox & Davidson, 1988) and right-hemisphere specialization for language and communication. From the brain's point of view, language and positive emotion should be likely to co-occur.

As in our discussion of social referencing, it seems that by ten or twelve months, infants are becoming aware that they can more effectively meet their own goals if they use information gained from other people and if they signal their intentions in order to obtain adult assistance. We don't have to assume that infants have an awareness of the adult's point of view at this age.

Finally, from the adult's perspective, less time is spent in the kinds of purely social games (like horsie and peek-a-boo) described in the last chapter. Instead, infants are becoming more interested in their own explorations of toys and other objects. Thus, care givers spend more time involved in object-related play. This includes coordinating their activities using objects with those of the infant, such as playing an object manipulation game by building with blocks or feeding a baby doll. In addition, care givers are using words more deliberately as part of the actions on objects. An example would be describing in words what the baby is doing, requesting objects, offering objects, and saying "Here's the baby's bottle." (Bakeman & Adamson, 1984; Hodapp et al., 1984; Hunter et al., 1987).

The Development of Attachment

Our discussion of the role of emotion in interpersonal communication leads us to the topic of adult-infant attachment. *Attachment* refers to a lasting emotional tie between people such that the individual strives to maintain closeness to the object of attachment and acts to ensure that the relationship continues. The process by which infants develop lasting, affectionate emotional ties to adults over the first few years of life has been the subject of a great deal of scientific research. Before reviewing the findings of these studies, let's first look at some of the theoretical perspectives on how attachment develops.

Psychoanalytic theory suggests that attachment is the normal resolution of the oral stage of development (refer to Chapter 2). If the id's oral urges are gratified regularly during the first few months of life, the baby will develop the expectation that needs can be met and that distress will not continue for long without some relief.

After the baby is two or three months old, parents begin to notice that the baby's cry is a little less urgent when the baby is hungry or tired. At this time, psychoanalytic theory prescribes that the parents should wait a short time before responding to the baby. If the baby calms down, the parents have allowed the baby to meet this small crisis with his or her own resources. Not only do these minor frustrations lead the baby toward self-control, but they also make the baby aware of the person who is responsible for satisfying the oral needs. This awareness gradually expands into a dependency on that particular person and later into affection, attachment, and trust.

Learning theory has focused not on the feelings or concepts of the infant but on the behaviors observed when care givers and infants are together. Care givers seek positive reinforcements from their infants. For example, when parents pick up a baby, they expect the baby to become calm or to smile. When parents feed the baby, they expect the baby to coo and gurgle. When these positive reinforcements occur, the frequency of the same parental actions is increased on future occasions, which in turn reinforces the calming down, smiling, cooing, and gurgling of the baby. Learning theory, therefore, predicts that attachment behaviors develop by a complex process of mutual reinforcements (Cairns, 1979; Gewirtz, 1972).

Ethological theory suggests that adults have inherited some kinds of care-giving responses that are triggered in the presence of infants and young children and that infants are innately drawn to particular aspects of the care giver. In a classic study of the maternal-infant feedback system in infant monkeys (Harlow & Harlow, 1965), the babies were provided one "mother" made of wire mesh and a milk bottle attached and another "mother" of the same size made of wire covered with a soft cloth. The monkeys took food from the wire mother but spent almost all of the rest of their time with the softer mother substitute. In fearful situations, the monkeys clung to the soft mother and, when they got older, were even seen to carry the cloth mother around as a security object.

For monkeys, contrary to the predictions of psychoanalytic theory, physical contact with the mother is more important than food in the formation of attachments. Contrary to the predictions of learning theory, infant monkeys become attached to soft objects—an innate preference—and not to the object that gave positive reinforcement—the food-giving wire mother.

Studies of human infants in Great Britain (Schaffer & Emerson, 1964) have shown that the infants are most attached to the people who play and interact with them. Some babies who lived in extended families with many siblings and who had mothers who concentrated primarily on care-taking tasks such as feeding and diapering were less attached to the mother than to any aunt, uncle, or older sibling who spent the most time playing with the baby. This suggests that attachment in humans is based more on social interaction and communication than on feeding or physical contact as predicted by the psychoanalytic theory.

It was a dissatisfaction with the psychoanalytic and learning theory accounts of attachment that led John Bowlby (1969) to develop an ethological theory of attachment in humans. Bowlby suggested that mutual responsiveness and attraction between adults and infants resulted not because of mutual reinforcements but because the physical appearance and behavior of the adult and the infant each innately attracts the other.

Such behaviors were discussed in Chapters 6 and 7. The newborn and small infants' physical appearance, called babyishness, elicits protective responses from adults. Babies also have a host of behaviors, such as crying, sucking, smiling, looking at the care giver preferentially, following the adult around, and becoming distressed when the adult leaves that have the net effect of orienting the care giver to the infant and increasing the time that the infant spends in proximity to the care giver.

Bowlby suggests that as the infant develops cognitively, attachment shifts from its reliance on innate responses to any adult to the identification and recognition of a particular adult, to seeking that adult in an intentional, goal-oriented manner. The baby establishes a goal of maintaining proximity to the parent and uses information about the parent's present and past movements, the baby's locomotor skills, and current needs to keep the parent within view or to seek contact when needed.

By eight or nine months of age, infants begin to develop some of the same kinds of emotional feelings of closeness to the parents that the parents had felt for the infants since before the birth. We know this because infants of this age begin to display affectionate responses to the parents. During reunions after brief separations, one-year-olds feel genuinely happy to see the parent and may approach briefly for a hug or kiss (Sroufe, 1979). Infants will follow the parent and may be distressed at separation.

Bowlby's theory has been refined and expanded upon by others. Mary Ainsworth, who studied attachment in Uganda and North America (Ainsworth, 1979), suggests that there is a distinction between the *attachment system* (the network of feelings and cognitions related to the object of attachment) and *attachment behavior* (the overt signals such as crying and following that bring the parent and child in close proximity). She points out that each child's attachment system would be expressed through behavior in a unique way. For example, just because a baby does not get upset when his or her mother leaves does not indicate a lack of attachment. Rather, it may indicate the infant's relative feelings of security to carry on temporarily without the mother present.

Ainsworth believes that virtually all infants are attached to their parents but differ in the sense of security they feel in relation to the adult. The ease with which a distressed infant feels comforted by a care giver is called the *quality of attachment*, which has three basic patterns: securely attached, insecurely attached-resistant, and insecurely attached-avoidant (Ainsworth, Bell, & Stayton, 1971; Ainsworth et al., 1978).

Attachment quality is assessed in the Ainsworth Strange Situation Test, in which infants are observed with their care givers in an unfamiliar playroom (Ainsworth & Bell, 1970). The test consists of eight episodes:

1. Parent and infant are brought to the observation room by the observer.
2. Parent and infant play together for several minutes.
3. Parent and infant play with an unfamiliar adult.
4. The mother leaves the baby with the stranger for three minutes.
5. The stranger leaves, and the mother returns.
6. The mother leaves the baby alone.
7. The stranger returns without the mother.
8. The stranger leaves, and the mother is reunited with her baby.

An infant who is *securely attached* will seek comfort from the care giver during the reunion (episode 8) and once comforted will return to independent play. Securely attached infants show interest in objects and the stranger and will get acquainted with the unfamiliar setting by making brief forays, always returning to the adult's side, and using the care giver as a *secure base* from which to explore. Such infants will feel comfortable and secure in most situations.

There are two types of insecure attachments. *Insecurely attached-resistant* infants have a more difficult time feeling comfortable in a strange situation. They will vacillate between mother and an interesting object, but once near the object, they will not explore as freely as will the securely attached infants. The resistant infant is more wary of strangers and tends to get more upset when the mother leaves the room. During the reunion, such infants show ambivalent responses to the mother, first approaching her and then pushing her away.

Insecurely attached-avoidant babies tend not to be upset when left with an unfamiliar person or in a strange setting. During the reunion episode, they may avoid approaching care givers for comfort and may actively resist any attempts to be comforted by turning away and squirming to get down if picked up.

The Ainsworth Strange Situation Test and the three types of attachment quality by which infants can be classified have been shown to be highly reliable and valid. Test-retest reliability has been found in middle-class samples (Waters, 1983). This means that a baby who is classified as securely attached at one age will generally remain so at later ages. Those babies whose security classification changes over time come from homes in which there is a high level of social and economic stress, such as divorce, job changes, and poverty (Vaughn, Egeland, Sroufe & Waters, 1979).

Stability of security classification does not mean that the children display the same kinds of behavior in the strange situation at different ages. Recall Ainsworth's distinction between the attachment system and attachment behavior. Sroufe and Waters have contributed to attachment theory by specifying the ways in which different kinds of behavior can be organized into a pattern that indicates a secure or an insecure attachment system (Sroufe, 1979). For example, in the study by Waters (1983), infants were observed in the Strange Situation test at 12 and 18 months. A baby may have been classified as avoidant at 12 months because he turned his head away from the mother when she picked him up, while at 18 months, the same baby's avoidance might be expressed by arching his back and pushing away from the mother.

Antecedents of Attachment

What determines the quality of attachment at one year of age? There are two possible explanations: failure of the mother during the first year to create a warm and sensitive relationship with her baby and behavior problems that reside in the child that no maternal response can alleviate.

Some studies have shown that the more responsive the mother is to the infant's needs at three months, such as during face-to-face play or in responding relatively soon to the infant's cries, the more likely the baby is to be securely attached at one year (Ainsworth et al., 1971; Belsky et al., 1984; Blehar, Leiberman, & Ainsworth, 1977; Grossman et al., 1985). Related research has revealed similar maternal factors during the first year that are associated with attachment at twelve months. For example, Grossman and others (1985) found a relationship between secure attachment and maternal tender style, including a moderate tempo of speech, expressions of quiet pleasure, few directives, no impatience, an even attentiveness, and prompt soothing. Isabella and Belsky (1989) found that a general responsiveness to all types of infant behavior and reciprocal and mutually rewarding social interactions were antecedent to secure attachments. Smith and Pederson (1988) found a relationship between insufficient or intrusive mothering and later insecure attachment. Finally, mothers who perceive themselves as having little control over their children's behavior and who suffer from depressed moods are more likely to have insecurely attached infants (Donovan & Leavitt, 1989).

One danger in the interpretation of these studies is that they seem to assign the mother with full responsibility for the security or insecurity of attachment.

There are several reasons to believe otherwise. First, infant temperament may contribute to maternal responsiveness or lack of responsiveness. It is possible that a mother who has a fussy baby might respond to the baby less often simply because she has learned that her interventions are not always effective. Lack of security of attachment may therefore reflect an inborn inability to regulate distress and a heightened feeling of anxiety or wariness. The evidence for infant effects on adults is mixed, with some studies showing such effects and others not (Bretherton, 1985).

Some studies suggest that infant temperament is a strong predictor of attachment. For example, temperamental fearfulness is related to resistant behavior in the strange situation (Thompson et al., 1988). Children who at three months were less sociable and preferred play with toys to play with people were more likely to be scored as avoidant at twelve months (Lewis & Feiring, 1989).

It is unlikely, however, that either the mother or the infant is the sole determiner of attachment quality. There are other cases, for example, in which three-month-olds cry more because their mothers are not responsive to their needs (Belsky et al., 1984), thus setting up a negative cycle of infant fussiness countered by maternal insensitivity leading to a lack of security of attachment at one year.

In an even more complex pattern of findings, if young infants were highly active and intense, they became securely attached so long as their mothers did not try to pick them up and cuddle them often. On the other hand, active and intense infants became avoidant in the strange situation if they had mothers who insisted on a great deal of physical contact (Bohlin et al., 1989).

A final layer of complexity is added when we consider social and ecological factors that influence the mother. Insecure attachments at twelve months were predicted by newborn fussiness, but only for those mothers who were not responsive to the infant's cries at three months and who had few opportunities for social support (Crockenberg, 1981). In addition, parents who are at risk for failures of attachment—teenage mothers, adoptive mothers, or single parents—can often inspire babies toward secure attachments. It is only when these parental risk factors are compounded by lack of support networks, poverty, or a history of psychiatric disorders that insecure attachments develop (Allen, Affleck, McGrade, & McQueeney, 1984; Brooks-Gunn & Furstenberg, 1986; Sameroff & Seifer, 1983; Singer et al., 1985). Thus, insecure attachment can be explained by ecological systems theory as a complex combination of infant, parent, family, and social factors.

The Validity of the Ainsworth Strange Situation Test

These findings lead to another possible explanation of the results: a failure of the Ainsworth Strange Situation Test to be sensitive to possible differences in infants and families. When using a psychological test, one has to be careful in attributing a characteristic measured on the test to the individual. Do infants who test as insecure really feel insecure, or is it something about the testing situation that makes them act insecure in that situation but not elsewhere?

One indication that this might be a problem is that the test has not traveled well to other cultures. Usually, in North America, about two-thirds of the infants are classified as securely attached. This has not been true in other countries (see Table 8.2). In general, avoidant classifications are more frequent in North America and Europe, while resistant classifications are more frequent in Japan and Israel (Van IJsendoorn & Kroonenberg, 1988).

Takahashi (1986) has suggested that the strange situation test is too stressful for Japanese infants, who are rarely separated from their mothers and exposed to strangers during their first years of life. The higher percentage of resistant infants in the Japanese sample may be the result of infants' becoming overstressed and thus resisting attempts by the mother at comforting. Thus, cultural differences in child-rearing practices and culture specificity of the test may contribute to differences in outcome. More research is needed on this topic, however.

A related issue concerns the security of attachment of infants who spend a good deal of time in day care from early ages. Although the results are mixed, with many studies finding no differences in attachment between day-care and home-care infants, some studies find that day-care infants are more avoidant than home-care infants (see Chapter 9 for a fuller discussion). If we think the Ainsworth test is valid, then we might conclude that early day care jeopardizes the mother-infant relationship. On the other hand, infants who are used to daily separations from mother may not be disturbed by the series of separations and strangers in the Ainsworth test, and they may not greet their mothers when they return. Such babies may be classified as avoidant due to a lack of validity in the testing procedure.

Another approach to validity is to see whether the infant's attachment classification at twelve months is related to later behavioral outcomes. There have been a number of studies showing such a relationship. For example, securely attached children at one year were found during later infancy and early childhood to be more sociable with peers (Arend et al., 1979; Park & Waters, 1989; Slade, 1987b) and unfamiliar adults (Main & Weston, 1981; Thompson & Lamb, 1982) and to be more securely attached to their mothers at six years of age (Main & Cassidy, 1988). Securely attached infants are also more likely to be better problem solvers in preschool and kindergarten, to be more persistent and enthusiastic, to be more socially competent, and to have fewer behavioral problems (Bates et al., 1985; Block & Block, 1980; Erikson et al., 1985; Sroufe, 1983).

■ TABLE 8.2   Percentage of Infants Classified into Three Categories of Security of Attachment in Four Countries

COUNTRY	ATTACHMENT CLASSIFICATION		
	SECURE	RESISTANT	AVOIDANT
Israel	37.5	50.0	12.5
Japan	72.0	28.0	0.0
United States	62.0	15.0	23.0
West Germany	32.7	12.2	49.0

SOURCE: From Grossman et al., 1985; Miyake et al., 1985; Sagi et al., 1985. Also reprinted by permission from p. 194 of Child Development by Alan Fogel and Gail F. Melson; Copyright © 1988 by West Publishing Company. All rights reserved.

What Accounts for These Cross-Age Relationships?

In most of the studies reported in the last section, the investigators who measured the child's behavior in preschool were unaware of the child's classification rating on the Ainsworth Strange Situation Test. Thus the results cannot be accounted for by observer bias. On the other hand, these patterns of findings are correlational, and therefore, they only show a pattern of association rather than cause and effect.

We are still left with the question of how these early ratings are maintained over time and get translated into a variety of behavioral competencies. One simple model is that attachment security is a personality trait of the infant that gets generalized to many different behaviors. Equally plausible, however, is that the security of attachment as well as the child's later behavior is maintained by an interaction between the child and the care givers. In other words, perhaps attachment is not "in" the child but rather "in" the relationship.

Attachment researchers have recently begun thinking about a third model of attachment originally proposed by Bowlby (1969; 1980), called the internal working model. An *internal working model* is a sense of self and of other people that allows one to anticipate future behavior, react to new situations in a competent manner, and appraise the likelihood of success for action. For example, based on past experiences with the mother, the infant constructs a model of her as the person from whom particular types of support are likely to be received. As the infant's internal working model becomes solidified through experiences with the mother, actual behavioral monitoring of the mother becomes less necessary, and the infant is able to tolerate separations and react favorably to reunions.

Thus, the internal working model is relatively stable and gets updated gradually. The model is determined in part by interactive experiences, but eventually the model comes to affect interactions. Thus, a baby who has been disappointed by the mother many times in the past is not likely to accept changes in the mother's behavior if at a later time she desires more closeness to the baby (Bretherton, 1985). The notion of internal working model is related to a number of cognitive and emotional theories that postulate the existence of generalized representation of the individual's history of interpersonal experiences between self and other (Bretherton, 1987; Stern, 1985).

These ideas may have potential for explaining some of the long-term correlations of child behavior with earlier attachment classification, especially if we take account of the fact that care givers also have internal working models of themselves and their infants. The long-term stability of interaction patterns between mothers and infants may be maintained by stable internal working models in both mother and infant, which may enhance or inhibit interpersonal closeness over a long period of time (Main et al., 1985). The problem is that it is very difficult to get empirical measures of this type of intrapsychic construct, especially for the infants.

Infant-Peer Relationships

At the beginning of the first year of life, infants make different responses to peers than to their parents. At three months of age, infants are more likely to look at a peer for long periods and to make abrupt, jerky movements of the body while watching the peer. Their behavior toward their mothers is much smoother, with more smiling and vocalizing (Fogel, 1979). Field (1979b) found more vocalizing, reaching, and squirming to a peer compared with the infant's own mirror image.

At six months, infants are more likely to look at and vocalize to a peer but more likely to touch their mothers. As they get older, touching mothers increases and touching peers decreases, although by the end of the first year, infants are taking initiatives that will bring them into proximity with the peer (Vandell, 1980).

From six to twelve months, peer play is more likely in the absence of objects (Eckerman & Whatley, 1977; Jacobson, 1981; Vandell, Wilson, & Buchanan, 1980). When babies get together, they explore each other with mutual touches, they smile and gesture at each other, and they imitate each other. By the age of one year, peer play in the absence of objects begins to take on the quality of a dialogue, with mutual exchanges of tickling, touching, and laughing at each other (Ross & Goldman, 1977a). However, by twelve months, toys are becoming more important to the maintenance of the social interaction (Jacobson, 1981; Vandell et al., 1980). Games with toys have the same reciprocal quality as purely social games. There is mutual giving and taking of objects, offering and receiving, rolling and throwing balls back and forth, and so on. By this age, taking turns is such an essential part of peer play that interactions usually are disrupted if one child fails to take his or her turn (Ross & Goldman, 1977a). In comparison, infants at twelve months express a wider range of emotions in their interactions with their mothers and take more turns with them, perhaps due to the mothers' attempts to create dialogues through active structuring of the interaction (Adamson & Bakeman, 1985; Vandell & Wilson, 1987).

■ FAMILY AND SOCIETY

Since this chapter introduces attachment and its development, in this section, we will discuss attachments to other family members besides the traditional attachment figure—the infant's mother. We discuss differences and similarities of infant attachment to mothers versus fathers and then discuss the role of grandparents in infants' lives.

Are infants more attached to mothers or fathers?

On the whole, there are few differences between attachment to mother and father. This does not mean that infants have the same kind of relationship with each, but only that they can be adequately comforted in a stressful situation by either parent. Some research has shown that if their mothers and fathers are both present in a stressful situation, infants will choose the mothers (Bridges et al., 1988; Cohen & Campos, 1974). However, other work shows that infants would *much* rather be with one of their parents than with a stranger (Lamb, 1977).

Other research has shown that there are differences among families. Although most infants develop roughly equal preferences for their mothers and fathers, some will be more attached to one than the other (not necessarily the mothers), and a few infants will be insecurely attached to both parents (Lamb, 1978b; Main & Weston, 1981). These findings suggest that the kind of relationship an infant forms with someone is the result of a history of the child's past encounters with that person. Failure to become securely attached to one person does not preclude becoming attached to another. Main and Weston (1981) found that if an infant were securely attached to *either* the mother *or* the father, the baby would be significantly less wary of strangers than an infant who was not securely attached to either parent. In general, the more time fathers spend with infants, the more likely the fathers and infants will share a secure attachment and mutual communication (Pedersen et al., 1987).

Grandparents and their infant grandchildren

There are very few empirical studies of grandparents and grandchildren and no more than a handful on grandparent-infant relationships. With the decline of the extended family living under one roof, developmentalists have not taken much interest in grandparents as a source of influence on infants. In many cases, grandparents do not live near their children, and the once-a-year contact with the family is hardly enough to make much of an impression on an infant.

There are big differences in how involved grandparents are in infant care. In some families, grandparents have daily contacts with the infants and participate in care giving as well as play. In others, there may be little or no contact. This may be due to the fact that adults can become grandparents as young as thirty years of age or as old as ninety. The younger grandparents are still employed and have little time for infant care (Cohler & Grunebaum, 1981; Kornhaber & Woodward, 1981; Tinsley & Parke, 1984).

A few studies have been done on grandmother-infant attachment at one year. Subjects were white, primarily middle-class families in which the grandmother lived nearby and had relatively frequent contact with the infant. This research shows that mothers and grandmothers are nearly interchangeable as attachment figures: infants approach both in times of stress. The more time a grandmother spends with the baby, the more secure the attachment relationship (Myers, Jarvis, & Creasey, 1987; Schaffer & Emerson, 1964).

Some studies have shown that grandmothers in black families are considerably more involved with their infant grandchildren than in white families. The grandparents tend to live close by their grown children and devote much of their free time to the infants of their children (Cherlin & Furstenberg, 1986; Pearson et al., 1990; Wilson, 1986). Compared to white parents, black parents of infants have more frequent contact with kin—including grandmothers—and respect the advice of relatives, showing a concern for what the relative thinks is important (Wilson, 1986).

This strong network of ties between relatives was carried to the Americas from traditional African societies, and research has shown that this extended family system is important in the reduction of family stress from low income and teenage and single parenthood. It is typically found that the grandmothers are more patient and more warm with the infants than are the infants'

Infant Health and Safety

During this stage of development, the baby begins to crawl and toddle around the house, leading to potentially dangerous situations. Beginning at this age and continuing into early childhood, infants need to be protected from some of the obvious dangers their environments present.

What kinds of safety precautions should be taken?

Safety for young infants involves the following: avoiding falls and collisions, avoiding poisons, and preventing choking on small objects, burns, and drowning.

Collisions and falls

The biggest cause of injury and death among infants is automobile accidents. About 1,100 children under four years of age die every year in such accidents, and 7,000 infants per year suffer injuries. The tragedy is that most of these could be prevented by using well-designed car seats and seat belts, since most injuries occur when infants are riding in the front seat of a car on someone's lap. Even though every state has a safety restraint law for infants, less than half of infants are safely strapped in. Safety restraints are highly effective, and the number of deaths per year has been dropping in the past ten years under the new safety belt laws (Davis, 1985; National Safety Council, 1987).

Buy an infant car seat that is easy to install correctly. The seat should be in the center of the back seat. Be firm with the baby and don't let him or her out of the seat even if the child fusses. Don't let the child eat lollipops or hold sharp or pointed objects while the car is moving, and don't put loose items like groceries in the back seat (Chubet, 1988).

At home, falls and collisions can be prevented by taking simple precautions. Never leave a baby unattended on a table or a bed, block off access to stairs, and keep the baby's high chair away from a table or wall that could be used as leverage to push the chair over. Even though babies at this age have developed a wariness of the deep side of a visual cliff (see "Emotional Development" section earlier in this chapter), most infants do not have sufficient control over their locomotor skills at this age to prevent a fall. All infants suffer minor tumbles and shocks as they try to expand their motor skills. These are generally not serious, except if there is some suspicion of a broken bone or a severe head injury. A number of excellent books are available for parents and other care givers on the diagnosis of medical problems in infants and children. Be sure to read about the signs of concussion, and know what to do if you see one.

Falls can also occur from cribs, high chairs, walkers, windows, and grocery carts. Cribs should be checked for sturdiness, and they

continued at top of next page

teenage mothers. In addition to providing a buffer against the effects of mothers who have too many of their own problems to cope with their babies, the grandmothers serve as valuable sources of advice and instruction about parenthood for their own daughters. With the support of their mothers, many of these adolescent and at-risk parents are able to continue in their education and eventually become economically self-supporting and caring parents

APPLICATIONS

should have a mattress that can be lowered as the baby grows. There should be no more than 2 3/8 inches between the posts or slats to prevent infants from getting their heads stuck. Be sure that mobiles are securely fastened and will not fall if the baby grabs them. Don't use plastic bags to cover the mattress, and don't allow any strings within reach of the baby. Do not tie pacifiers to strings as the baby can easily become entangled or choke (Chubet, 1988).

Highchairs should not have sharp edges, springs that catch the baby's skin, or straps in which the baby can become entangled. The seat should not be slippery enough to make the baby slide down. It should be extremely easy to remove the tray without hurting the baby. Walkers are safe if the wheel base is wider than the seat and grip area and if they are not used near stairs or near furniture with sharp edges. Always strap infants into grocery carts, and never allow children to stand in a cart. For highchairs, walkers, jumpers, grocery carts, and changing tables, the most important rule is *under no circumstances leave the baby unattended!* If the phone rings, either ignore it or take the baby with you to answer it.

Finally, if you live in a building with more than one story, don't trust screens to keep an active toddler from falling out a window. Windows can be blocked so that they can open only enough for ventilation but not wide enough for a baby to fit through. Safety gates are recommended near stairs or to block off rooms that hold dangers for the baby. Buy gates that won't pinch a baby and that are easy for adults to open and close (otherwise, they will stay open).

Poisoning

Modern households are filled with lethal poisons, and most of them are kept within easy reach of an inquisitive infant. The cabinets under the kitchen and bathroom sinks are the most likely repositories of poisonous substances in the house: soaps, detergents, cleaning fluids, cosmetics, insecticides, and other toxic substances. It is wise to keep all such substances completely out of the infant's reach, since parental discipline is often not effective at this age in totally keeping the infant away from these dangers. Cabinets should be locked or "childproofed," or these substances should be moved well out of the infant's reach. Even if most things have child-proof caps, the caps and outer surfaces of the containers may contain enough toxin to make the infants ill if they should put them in their mouths. Child-care providers and parents should learn some of the common poisons and their antidotes. A poison antidote chart is available from most hospitals and pediatricians and should be posted in the kitchen or bathroom, where it can be readily consulted in an emergency.

Other potential sources of poisonous material include the leaves and flowers of house plants and lead and lead-based paints. Never allow babies to be in rooms where there are paint flakes and plaster dust. Like plaster dust, baby powders can be toxic as well, since they are so fine and can easily clog immature lung passages. Breathing can also be obstructed by plastic bags, and uninflated or broken balloon pieces are especially dangerous (although inflated balloons are not). Finally, infants—like fetuses—are affected by passive smoking; for

(Colletta & Lee, 1983; Furstenberg & Brooks-Gunn, 1987; Stevens, 1984).

These studies suggest that involvement between infants and grandmothers is dependent on social ecological factors, including ethnicity, race, and patterns of residence. These factors also determine the amount of mutual reliance and mutual trust between family members, both of which impact on the quality of the social network of kinship in which the child develops. ■

APPLICATIONS

infants, the danger lies in inhaling the smoke from burning cigarettes or the exhalations of smokers.

Swallowing small objects

If a small object becomes lodged in an infant's throat, it can disrupt breathing or cause choking. Like poisons, any object that can easily fit into an infant's mouth should be removed from the child's reach. Beads, coins, uncooked grains, paper clips, and so on are candidates for chokers. Be sure the button eyes of stuffed toys are sewn on securely and that rattles (with beads inside) are not cracked. As the infant learns to stand while holding furniture, small objects on the tops of tables and desks are vulnerable to the infant's reach. Make sure they are on high shelves or in childproofed drawers. Foods that are cut too small for babies before they can chew effectively can also be dangerous.

Burns and drowning

Infants suffer more from home fires and smoke inhalation than older children and adults. They are less mature and have more sensitive skin and lungs. They are also less able to escape on their own. Many burns also occur from overly hot bath water, from stove tops, splashing grease, and radiators. Be sure the child knows the meaning of the word "hot," keep the infant away from sources of heat, and always test the bath water before putting the baby in.

Baths are also dangerous because of slipping and/or drowning. Be sure to use nonslip pads in the bottom of the sink or tub. You can also buy a molded sponge in which the baby can sit. Keep infants away from pools and keep toilet seats down. Never leave a baby unattended near or in water.

Other dangers

One other category of common dangerous objects is sharp and pointed ones. Pencils, pens, and screwdrivers should never be given to infants of this age. If they want to scribble, let them use a nontoxic crayon (not a felt-tipped marker). Heavy objects, especially those infants can pull down on top of themselves, are also potential dangers. Keep the baby away from ropes or cords (such as venetian blind pulls), and avoid clothing that ties around the neck. The best prevention of many dangers is to crawl and walk around and look at the house from the point of view of someone who is two feet tall, curious, and clumsy.

Finally, toys are potentially dangerous. They should have no small parts, such as buttons, that are detachable, and small objects such as marbles should not be used. Toys should have no sharp edges, small holes, or openings that can cut, trap, or pinch fingers or tongues. Toys should be sturdy. Plastic is always better than glass, which can break or shatter. Toys should not contain any strings, elastic bands, or ropes longer than ten or twelve inches. Stuffed toys should not be so soft that the baby can suffocate, and they should be easy to wash.

continued at top of next page

APPLICATIONS

Emergency procedures

Even with the best attempts at prevention, infants will sometimes face life-threatening accidents or injuries. It is recommended that parents and care givers be familiar with the basics of first aid and cardiopulmonary resuscitation (CPR). A number of excellent infant health books are available, and first aid classes can be found through local health organizations. CPR is useful in cases of shock or drowning to resume breathing and provide heart massage. Simple but specific techniques should be learned to control bleeding, treat burns, stop choking, stop electrical shock, and treat poisoning (Chubet, 1988).

What are some important health considerations?

Most of the serious diseases of infancy and early childhood have been eliminated due to immunization procedures. Babies should be given a series of inoculations during the first two years of life as recommended by the American Academy of Pediatrics. These are shown in Table 8.3.

Most of the common diseases of infancy involve gastrointestinal or respiratory problems. Symptoms of the former include vomiting, stomach pains, diarrhea, and constipation. The latter is shown by runny nose, sore throat, coughing or wheezing, and trouble breathing. A fever is also a sign of illness. Consult medical care manuals. These generally give advice about when to call a doctor and what can be treated at home.

Although some illnesses are caused by viral or bacterial infections, repeated occurrences of particular symptoms should be taken as warning signs. The infant may be exposed to infectious or unsanitary conditions, or the illness may be a symptom of an allergic reaction. In the latter case, the physician should work with the family to isolate the possible source of the allergy.

■ **TABLE 8.3   Immunization Schedule for Infants**

AGE (MONTHS)	IMMUNIZATION
2	Diptheria, tetanus, pertussis (DPT), polio
4	DPT, polio
6	DPT, polio
12	Tuberculosis test
12 - 15	Measles, mumps, rubella (MMR)
18	DPT, polio
4 - 6 years	DPT, polio

SOURCE: Chubet, 1988; Immunization Practices Advisory Committee, 1983.

POINTS OF CONTACT

The year-old infant is awake and aware. There's not too much you can do that the baby won't notice. This will give you the sense that the baby has become more of an equal participant in play and love. At this age, babies begin to develop affectionate ties, and they begin to develop some of the human frailties that plague us all: vulnerability to loss and separation from loved ones, irrational fears, and insatiable curiosity.

There are some limits to this. Babies of this age do not suffer from self-doubt or pride. These particularly human vulnerabilities need at least another year before they begin to flower. The year-old is still cocky and assured, generally quite happy, and easily delighted by small surprises, like finding a hidden object or the mother's face behind a blanket. The ability to do things for themselves—things they have done with help in the past or that have been done for them—is a great source of amusement for babies. Letting babies hide things, such as their own faces or their mothers' during peekaboo games, is one example. Self-feeding is another, as is letting babies get their own diapers, hold the pins (if they're closed), or wash themselves in the bath. Needless to say, all these babyish attempts at self-care are as much a delight to the care givers as to the infants.

Don't let the first birthday pass without an appropriate celebration. Babies can really join in the festive spirit, although they have no idea what it is all about and have no conception of themselves as the objects of all the attention. At age one, babies are just going along with everyone else's fun. They will imitate when their fathers try to blow out the candles, they will clap along with everyone else, and they will have a great time pulling off the wrapping paper. Grandma should not be surprised when the wrapping gets more attention than the gift. For the baby, each is just an interesting object to explore. The ideas of gifts, giving, gratitude, and politeness are still a long way down the developmental path.

Here are a few games you can play with the baby. Hiding is a popular one; be sure to try all the variations of hiding objects and people, as well as let the baby do some of the hiding. Babies of this age like to be picked up, thrown, and swung around (carefully and gently, of course). They like to have cross-modal experiences. Make a book with different colors, shapes, and textures; let them smell and touch flowers or soaps of different colors. Sounds and sights can be combined with nursery rhymes acted out with the hands and face (for example, "eensy-weensy-spider"). Add some bouncing on the knee or tickling to complete the experience. Dancing with the baby to music combines all these experiences with physical closeness. This closeness also can be achieved by taking the baby into the bath with you if you have the opportunity.

Babies like to play with their own images in mirrors, although they do not yet recognize the images as themselves. Do not leave a baby alone with a breakable mirror. Read books with the baby, and name pictures in them. Ask the baby if he or she can recognize the pictures from the words you say.

There are many other things to do with babies of this age: consult child-care books and your own imagination. The main thing to keep in mind is that play is a form of learning—one that affects the whole child. A knee-bouncing nursery rhyme has cognitive, perceptual, linguistic, motor, and social elements. It is also important to encourage the baby's efforts by showing your enthusiasm for accomplishments, as well as by encouraging the effort involved in the attempts. Most important of all, plan to give the baby at least some "quality" time during the day. This is a time when you are not distracted by other chores or worries and you can devote your full attention to the baby. This may be during play, bathing, or feeding: the baby needs to bask in the warm light of total attention, love, and approval, at least for some part of the day. The baby also needs to learn how to control his or her needs, how to wait when you are busy, how to defer gratification, and other socialization tasks. You will find these easier to teach the baby if you provide enough pure and simple indulgence at other times. We'll have more to say about socialization and discipline in later chapters. At age one, the main message is, Enjoy!

■ SUMMARY

Physical and Motor Development

■ During this period, infants begin to walk. Balance is the limiting factor in their stability and regularity of steps.
■ The onset of independent locomotions enhances both cognitive and social development.
■ Infants' exploratory actions are more coordinated and adapted to the properties of objects.

Perceptual and Cognitive Development

■ By this age, the level of infants' actions is more consistent with their memory and conceptual ability.
■ Infants can perceive and act on relationships between objects, such as between cups and saucers, between causes and effects, between objects and their hiding places, and between the actions of others and their own actions.
■ Infants act in deliberate and intentional ways, persisting until a goal is achieved.
■ Although infants can find hidden objects in some circumstances, they still get puzzled by complicated paths of movement and multiple hiding places.
■ Infants can now imitate actions that they have never done before and can reproduce acts even after a twenty-four hour delay.
■ Individual differences in cognition result from an interaction between infant temperament and attentional skills and adult intervention.

Emotional Development

■ New forms of expression of anger, fear, sadness, and joy all develop at this age.
■ Infants can now express mixed emotions and ambivalence.
■ Affective sharing and social referencing both enhance infants' ability to use information about other people's emotional expressions, although infants do not yet understand that others have emotions.

Social Development

■ Infants become more selective in their perception of speech, losing their ability to recognize sound contrasts from languages other than the one heard in the home.

■ Intentional communication begins at this age, with gestures more so than with words. Most gestures are related to infants' interactions with objects.

■ Specific attachments develop. The quality of attachment can be assessed using the Ainsworth Strange Situation Test.

■ This test has both advantages and disadvantages. The results about a particular infant may reflect the infant as much as the infant-care giver relationship. Results should be used with caution and evaluated on a case-by-case basis.

■ At this age, genuine turn-taking exchanges with peers begin. Infant-peer relationships evolve around different themes than infant-adult relationships.

Family and Society

■ Infants are able to form attachments equally with mothers and fathers, although the type of attachment with each parent varies across families and depends on time spent and quality of interaction.

■ Grandmothers and infants also form attachments. Grandmothers are more likely to be involved with their infant grandchildren in black families, compared to white families.

Applications: Infant Health and Safety

■ Care givers need to be aware of the common sources of danger and accidents for infants.

■ Care givers should learn emergency treatment techniques to handle a variety of potential hazards.

■ Health care and immunization is essential for normal development.

■ GLOSSARY

AB error   An error in finding hidden objects that occurs when objects are hidden first in one place (A) and then in another place (B). The child finds the object at A but not at B.

Affective sharing   Occurs when the child seeks confirmation from others for his or her own felt emotion.

Appraisal   The ability to evaluate a situation and its circumstances before making an emotional response.

Categorical stranger reaction   An acquired fear of a particular type of stranger.

Internal working model   A set of mental representations and expectations one has about attachment figures.
Mastery motivation   The desire to become competent in a particular goal.

Metapelet   A substitute care giver, found on an Israeli kibbutz.

Relational play   The ability to combine two or more objects appropriately, according to their function.

Social referencing   A form of appraisal in which infants use the emotional expressions of others in order to regulate their own emotional reactions.

Visual cliff   An experimental apparatus used to determine the nature of an infant's fear of heights.

NINE

Expression, Exploration, and Experimentation

(TWELVE TO EIGHTEEN MONTHS)

The title of this chapter contains the key words for understanding the twelve-to eighteen-month-old baby: expression, exploration, and experimentation. Another *E word* that sums it all up is energy, one resource that seems to abound at this age. Babies start getting into everything, or so it seems. Because of their almost constant activity and because newfound mobility leads them into forbidden or dangerous areas, babies of this age require much more supervision than was necessary in earlier stages.

This chapter will trace the beginnings of spoken language. Language acquisition began at earlier ages in the form of nonverbal, prelinguistic social exchanges between the infant and the parent or care giver. Between the ages of nine and twelve months, some infants develop a rudimentary vocabulary. In this chapter, we will see how these prelinguistic interactions lead naturally into linguistic communication. This chapter also will cover the concurrent emotional and social developments in the first half of the second year of life.

In addition, we will be taking a close look at some very special families—those with a handicapped infant—and we will discuss society's impact on child care in the 1990s.

■ PHYSICAL AND MOTOR DEVELOPMENT

As we saw in the last chapter, balance is the limiting factor in the emergence of stable walking. A complete sense of balance takes a long time to develop. Walking tends to smooth out, with less of an unstable toddler look to it, about six months after the infant begins to walk (Clark et al., 1988). Around this time, infants will begin to show the ability to stand on one foot with help and to walk up and down stairs with help. These skills emerge at about 16 months for the average baby (a range of 12 to 23 months) (Rosenblith & Sims-Knight, 1985).

A recent area of research on walking is looking at how infants adjust their behavior to the type of surface on which they walk. If you are jogging, for example, you will run slower and adjust your steps more carefully as you change from a smooth surface to a bumpy or rocky surface. You don't have to wait until you step on the rocks to slow down. Instead, you use perceptual information about the surface to adjust your steps before you get to the rocks. Do walking infants have the same kind of link between their perception and action?

Several studies suggest that infants can perceive what different types of surface afford for their locomotor actions. Infants prefer to walk on matte compared to shiny surfaces. If the matte surface looks like it's moving in waves (the researchers used a water bed), infants shift to crawling (Gibson et al., 1987). In another study (Adolph et al., 1990), fourteen-month-old infants were encouraged to walk on either up-sloping or down-sloping surfaces. Infants were able to walk uphill on slopes from 10 to 40 degrees. They adjusted their bodies by leaning forward in the same way a mature walker would do. Fewer infants attempted to walk downhill. They stopped to touch the slope or stood on the brink and rocked on their feet. If the slope was perceived as too steep, they sat and slid down.

These studies show that an awareness of the surface on which one is acting is an essential ingredient of advanced motor skills. The same holds true for fine motor skills. During explorations of different types of toys, year-old infants were placed either at a foam or a hard table. At the foam table, infants did more mouthing and held the object with both hands. At the hard table, infants used each hand differently (one for support and the other for object manipulation, or each hand held a different object), and they used the table to explore the objects by scooting and banging (Palmer, 1989). It seems that babies of this age are beginning to discover what properties of the environment are best suited to support their motor actions. This matching of motor action with the type of surface is essential for operating safely and successfully.

As infants progress in their ability to adapt their skills to the properties of objects and surfaces, they are more able to use objects as means toward goals rather than as goals in themselves. Thus, at the beginning of the first year, we see the emergence of deliberate tool usage in infants.

A practical tool infants need to use is the spoon. One research team in England has charted the development of spoon use in the second year of life in painstaking detail (Connolly & Dalgleish, 1989). The result of their work is a fascinating story about the developmental unfolding of a skill. They classified different types of spoon grips (Figure 9.1), different heights at which

■ FIGURE 9.1
Grip Patterns

Clenched transverse digital grip (ulnar)

Transverse digital grip (ulnar)

Clenched transverse digital grip (radial)

Digital palmar grip

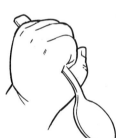

Transverse palmar grip (radial)

Transverse digital grip (radial)

Adult grip

Inter-digital grip

Transverse palmar grip (ulnar)

Adult clenched grip

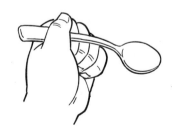

Ventral clenched grip

SOURCE: Connolly & Dalgleish, 1989.

the spoon was lifted between bowl and mouth, different paths the spoon takes between the bowl and the mouth, and different uses of the opposite hand. Their findings are summarized in the diagrams shown in Figure 9.2.

In the first stage, infants take the spoon in and out of their mouths or in and out of their dishes, but these two repetitive cycles are not connected. No food actually makes it from the dish to the mouth. In the second stage, we have the outlines of the complete action sequence, but babies are not paying attention to how much food gets onto the spoon. Often the only taste the babies get is what food manages to cling to the outer surface of the spoon. The movements

■ FIGURE 9.2
Principal Stages in Developing Skill in Using a Spoon

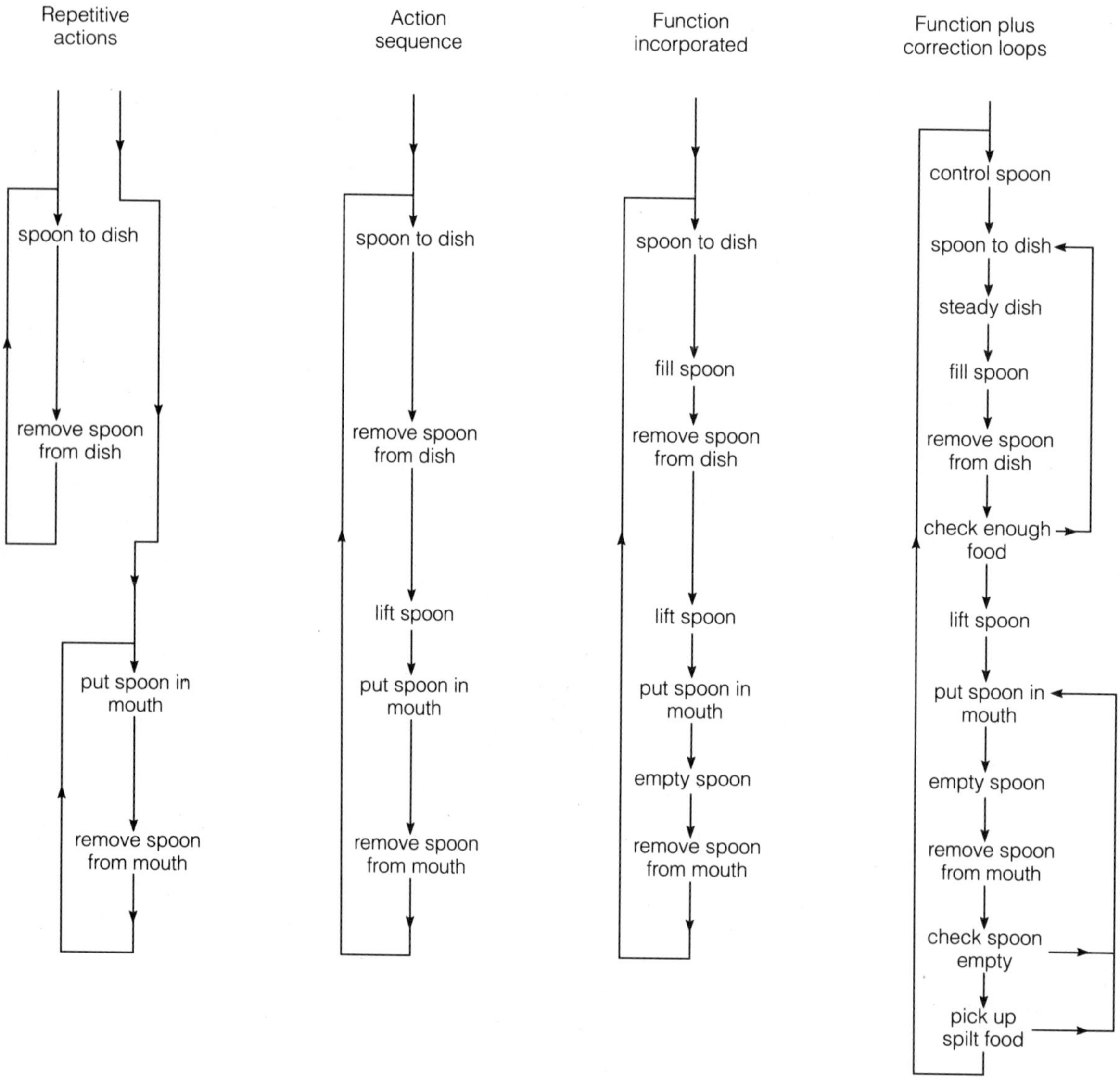

SOURCE: Connolly & Dalgleish, 1989.

from the dish to the mouth are jerky, and the spoon is not held in a grip that affords containing the food. During these two stages, care givers need to help feed infants.

By stage three, the action sequence of moving the spoon from the dish to the mouth now incorporates the function of moving the food. Although still not very efficient, at least the babies seem to be getting somewhere. In the final stage, not only is the action sequence functional, but it is correcting itself for errors. Thus, the babies will keep dipping the spoon into the dish until they are satisfied that it is holding enough food. They will also hold the dish steady. Similarly, at the mouth, the infants will continue to put the spoon into their mouths until it is clean.

This study shows how the spoon use can be a complicated motor challenge for a baby. The developments shown in Figure 9.2 take six to eight months from the onset of spoon use. Successful tool use involves not only making all the right moves at the right time but also the ability to adjust the movement to correct errors that occur in the process. In mature eating, few errors are made, and if they occur, they are adjusted very quickly.

■ COGNITIVE DEVELOPMENT

As the examples in "Observations: Stage V Behavior" show, infants in Piaget's Stage V are not merely using familiar means to achieve their goals: they are inventing new means. This is the stage of the *tertiary circular reactions*, or the beginnings of active experimentation and the search for novelty. In the previous stages, infants were most comfortable in familiar settings and were most likely to use the means they had discovered—largely by chance—to handle situations that arose. In Stage V, children become able to adapt themselves to brand-new situations, both by using tried and true

---

■ OBSERVATION:
**Stage V Behavior
(Piaget, 1952, pp. 269
and 285)**

OBSERVATION 1

At 0;10(11) Laurent . . . grasps in succession a celluloid swan, a box, etc., stretches out his arm and lets them fall. He distinctly varies the position of the fall. Sometimes he stretches out his arm vertically, sometimes he holds it obliquely, in front of or behind his eyes, etc. When the object falls in a new position (for example on his pillow), he lets it fall two or three more times in the same place, as though to study the spatial relation; then he modifies the situation.

OBSERVATION 2

. . .at 0;10(27). . . seated on her bed Lucienne tried to grasp a distant toy when, having by chance moved the folded sheet she saw the object sway slightly. She at once grasped the sheet, noticed the object shake again and pulled the whole thing toward her.

methods and by seeking out and discovering new methods of acting upon the environment. Stage V sometimes is called the stage of trial-and-error behavior, since infants attempt new combinations of action schemes until they find the one that will solve the problem.

A characteristic behavior at this age is experimenting to discover new ways of doing things. Infants discover that a distant object can be retrieved by pulling the blanket on which the object sits, or they find new ways to open containers. They try to figure out which objects best fit into particular containers. Unlike in the previous stage in which infants tried out new means to reach a single goal, babies in this stage seem to have multiple goals, and they examine which of the techniques available are best suited to the particular goal they have in mind at the moment and which other techniques are better suited to other goals.

In the previous stage, the infant was able to find a hidden object if the adult showed the baby where the object was being hidden. The baby often was fooled, however, if the adult moved the object in plain view to a new location. The Stage V infant is no longer so easily tricked. So long as the object can be seen moving from one place to another, the baby can follow the path of the object and find its hiding place, even after a long series of moves. This accomplishment implies that the infant has an increased awareness of space and a increased cognitive ability to comprehend longer periods of time.

In the area of imitation, the infant is able to model acts that are completely different from those seen before. This flexibility allows the toddler to become a very good copycat. The baby will try to imitate complicated actions done by an older sibling or a peer without having much understanding of the reason for those actions. Infants will remember such acts and will demonstrate deferred imitation up to a week after seeing the original model (Meltzoff, 1988). These are the origins of role play and dramatic play, both of which will take on increased significance in Stage VI, when the infant will begin to understand what it means to play a role and get vicarious experience by so doing. Stage V babies simply are having fun copying. Often the Stage V baby will copy to get a laugh out of the person being copied rather than because of trying on a role for size (see the later discussion of this).

Finally, infants develop more advanced categorization skills during this period. Recall that in the first year, infants could learn the relationships of particular examples to a simple category, such as faces, birds, or geometric figures of a certain prototypical shape. A simple categorization task is to recognize different sizes and shapes of birds as belonging to the category *bird*. A higher-order task is to be able to group birds, fish, lions, cats, and dogs into an *animal* category. Experiments have shown that by fifteen months, infants can correctly form higher-order categories for familiar objects. They can classify animals together, but they will not classify cars among the animals (Roberts & Cuff, 1989).

These two sections on motor and cognitive development are briefer than in previous chapters. This is not because twelve- to eighteen-month-olds are less interesting. Rather, it is because very little research has been done on the motor and cognitive aspects of infants this age, perhaps because the more salient developmental change at this age is the rapid growth of language, a topic to which we will return after a review of emotional developments during this period.

■ EMOTIONAL DEVELOPMENT

In this stage, the infant gains a new sense of self-awareness and control over emotional expressions. In the previous stage, infants learned to use the adults around them to regulate their own level of arousal. Through social referencing the infant could determine the appropriate way to react to a situation simply by watching a nearby adult. Infants also learned how to approach an adult care giver when they needed comfort, and they used the care giver as a secure base from which to explore the environment.

After twelve months, infants still rely on adults to a large extent, but now we can see the signs of a beginning attempt to control their own affective state. This happens both for pleasurable and nonpleasurable states.

How Do Infants Control Their Good Feelings?

In the previous stages, infants might smile at their care givers or laugh at a "joke," but these emotions were direct responses to the environmental events that provoked the emotion. Now infants can remain happy over a long period without the continuation of the stimulating event. This prolonged feeling of enjoyment has been called elation (Sroufe, 1979). Infants also may create situations in which happiness is produced and maintained. Babies of this age "show off" to provoke repeated laughs from the care giver. A baby can self-consciously exaggerate facial expressions and even do a bit of mugging for an especially receptive audience (Demos, 1982).

By thirteen months, infants have been observed to tease adults. The baby might get the attention of the adult, then walk over and reach toward a forbidden object, stopping just short of touching the object. The baby will wait until the adult cries "no" and then will smile or laugh (Bretherton & Bates, 1979). This is a complicated social maneuver in which the baby not only must know how to get another's attention but also can imagine the adult's response to his or her own behavior. This is very similar to a tertiary circular reaction in which the child is trying out different ways to make things happen. By eighteen or twenty months, babies and mothers play emotion games in which the children slap their mothers lightly, for example, the mothers pretend to cry, and then the children comfort them (Bretherton et al., 1986).

Finally, infants show delight in their own achievements (Sroufe, 1979). Because they are becoming aware of their own abilities to act on the environment, to create new means, and to experiment, they appreciate the sense of accomplishment that mastery over a new task brings. Babies' taking obvious delight in their first steps and in finding a toy they have been searching for are examples of this new sense of self-appreciation.

Babies continue to show their affection for the special people in their lives. These expressions may change from physical contact to expressions from a distance, such as a smile and a wave. In one study of infants' behavior upon reunion with their mothers after a brief separation, eleven-month-olds approached their mothers and sought physical contact immediately. Fourteen-month-olds, in contrast, were less likely to approach the mothers upon their return and more likely to use some form of signaling from a distance: crying, whining, or raising their arms as if to ask to be picked up. By nineteen months, the babies rarely even used this form of signaling. When their mothers returned, the babies were content merely to look at them before resuming their play (Serifica, 1978).

How Do Babies Control Their Fear and Distress?

In the previous stages, situations of stress tended to evoke fear or distress from the infant almost immediately. During an episode of separation from the mother, for example, infants were likely to cry or approach another friendly adult for comfort. After twelve months, infants visibly fight back tears (Sroufe, 1979). Since these babies are not overwhelmed with the distress, they search more for their mothers (Serifica, 1978). When their mothers are out of the room, infants often alternate between pouting and frowning (Sroufe, 1979) or biting their lower lips to control distress (Demos, 1982). As previously mentioned, the baby who so successfully fought back the tears during separation almost certainly will burst into tears upon the mother's return. Studies done in the United States and in the Gusii agricultural society in Kenya have also shown a relative reduction of attachment behavior during the period between twelve and eighteen months, that is, fewer approaches to the mother and fewer bids for attention and support (Reed & Leiderman, 1981).

There are limits to this ability for self-control, even in the mother's presence. Brooks and Lewis (1974) found that the longer an infant was in a freeplay situation with the mother present, the more likely the baby would approach, touch, and vocalize to the mother. Apparently babies can cope well on their own only for six to ten minutes before they begin to feel the need for attention and comfort.

■ SOCIAL AND LANGUAGE DEVELOPMENT

Since this stage is important in the development of language and since we already have hinted at the importance of spoken language for human behavior and development, this section will introduce some of the basic concepts of language development used in the next three chapters.

What Are the Basic Properties of Languages?

There are hundreds of spoken languages in the world, as well as countless dialects. Some languages, such as American Sign Language for the deaf, are not spoken at all. All human languages—no matter where or how they are used (spoken, signed, or written)—share important properties that distinguish them from other kinds of communication systems such as those found among other animals or those used for specific purposes, such as computer languages.

Roger Brown (1973) has defined three properties of human language. The first, *semanticity*, is the capacity of a language to carry meaning for both speaker and listener. Human adults are geared to find meaning in words and in all forms of social behavior. It is not unusual for an adult to try to interpret a gesture or a phrase made by someone else, whether that person intended it as meaningful or not. We have already discussed how adults try to find meaning in the more or less automatic behavioral expressions of very young infants. It is not until the last quarter of the first year that infants begin to use words and gestures in meaningful ways.

Productivity, Brown's second property, refers to the ability of a speaker to express many different meanings with a relatively small number of words simply by rearranging them into novel combinations. This is particularly helpful to young infants who are just beginning to use words. Although their rate of vocabulary growth is relatively slow, the number of things about which they can communicate increases rapidly over the second year of life.

Displacement is the property of language by which distant or absent objects, as well as abstract notions such as peace and justice, can be communicated. Displacement allows speakers to discuss past, present, and future; to learn; and to educate.

Aside from these three properties, language has a characteristic structure and function that sets it apart from other systems of communication. The structure of language, called grammar or *syntax*, refers to the fact that out of all possible combinations of word order, only a small number are meaningful to the native speaker. The function of language everywhere is to communicate. The study of a language's social and communicative function is called *pragmatics*. Pragmatics is more concerned with why people say something than how they say it. Theorizing on children's language acquisition has shifted from its prior focus on the acquisition of syntax to a functional view that the infants' natural inclinations to express themselves in a social context lead to linguistic competence (Nelson, 1973).

What Are the Theories of Language Acquisition?

From a historical perspective, developmental psychologists and developmental psycholinguists of this century first viewed language development in behavioral terms. Like any other behavior, speech can be conditioned and imitated. Although children must use imitation and reinforcement to learn the speech patterns of their own linguistic community, developmentalists differ over the extent to which these processes can account for how children acquire a language's syntax and how they come to use language productively. Learning theorists explain these accomplishments with concepts like "delayed imitation" and "generalization" of learned responses (Bandura, 1977; Bijou & Baer, 1965; Whitehurst & Vasta, 1975).

Nevertheless, learning theory cannot fully account for the fact that sentences have a very similar structure all over the world (subject, verb, and object, but not necessarily in that order). Imitation and reinforcement may help explain the learning of specific words and phrases but not the presence of linguistic universals of syntax. Another problem with the learning theory perspective is that it cannot explain why language is learned at the particular time in the infant's life that it is. Why does it happen right at the end of the first year and coincident with Piaget's Stages IV and V? If learning were the only mechanism available, we might expect to see a much wider range of ages for the onset and termination of language acquisition than we now see.

Theories based more on biological factors arose to try to explain these two problems with learning theory. As for the complaint that all language has essentially the same structure, Noam Chomsky (1975) reasoned that each infant is born with a rudimentary notion of syntactic structure—an innate universal grammar. According to Chomsky, this is the only way to explain how infants barely a year old can take sounds they have learned and organize them into meaningful sentences. Careful scrutiny of children's one-word productions and the incipient word order found in early two- and three-word utterances led to the construction of infantile grammars (McNeill, 1970). The results have been disappointing. Martin Braine (1976) has concluded that rather than expressing some underlying universal grammar, the child's "first productive structures are formulae of limited scope for realizing specific kinds of meanings" (p. 4). Language acquisition, according to Braine, is better understood from the point of view of pragmatics—what the child is trying to say and why—rather than from a syntactic, or structural, perspective.

As a response to the deficiencies in both learning and biological theories, functional theories of language acquisition have attempted to study language development in its natural context: the parent-infant interaction. In contrast to purely psychological, or individual-oriented, theories, the functional approach attempts to study language development in relation to the social system in which it naturally occurs. As we will see, the key milestones of the functional theory of language acquisition are not individual achievements (such as babbling, single word utterances, and multiword sentences) but achievements of the parent-infant dyad, such as taking turns; paying joint attention to an external object; and sharing meaning of particular gestures, words, and phrases.

How Do the Adult and Infant Know They Are Talking about the Same Thing?

Adults sense that their responses have meaning for the year-old baby, and they attempt to interpret the baby's meanings. *Joint attention* is one way adults make sure their messages are being received by the infant. The adults follow the infant's line of visual regard and confine their verbalizations and other responses to the objects at which the infant is looking. In this phase of development, joint attention is achieved by adults alone by looking back and forth between the object and the infant's face or by moving the object into the infant's field of vision and making it salient to the infant. In this way, adults can create a new focus of joint regard.

This phase of communication skills, in which infants are not aware of their roles in the process , has been termed *perlocutionary* by Bates (Bates, Camaioni, & Volterra, 1975). This phase of development also has been incorporated into Kaye's theory of the early parent-infant system. Kaye (1982) referred to this as the apprentice stage.

At the beginning of the second year, infants begin to take the initiative in creating joint frames of reference. Infants develop the ability to follow their mothers' line of vision (Butterworth & Cochran, 1980; Collis & Schaffer, 1975; Scaife & Bruner, 1975). Infants begin to use pointing to direct their mothers' interest to something they want (Leung & Rheingold, 1981; Murphy, 1978).

The ability to search for new means to reach goals imparts this kind of intentional or directed quality to the infants' communicative attempts. If infants do not get what they want by pointing or reaching for it, they are likely to look at their mothers, pull on them, point or reach for something, and look back at their mothers until they get what is needed (Harding & Golinkoff, 1979; Lock, 1980). This task persistence reflects a growing infant awareness that adults can perform certain functions and that the infant is capable of making them happen. This stage of intentional communication has been called *illocutionary* (Bates, Benigni, Bretherton, Camaioni, & Volterra, 1978; Bates, Camaioni, & Volterra, 1975).

In the last chapter, we saw the emergence of simple intentional gestures, such as pointing and offering. The child persists until a desired result is obtained but tends to repeat the same gesture. After twelve months, infants begin to use gestures in combinations to communicate more complex meanings (Lock, 1980), as shown in Observation 3 in the Observations Box below. In this example, the child first cries intentionally, and then after the mother arrives, the child points.

OBSERVATION 3

Peter; age 13(13): (a) Mother is putting Peter's slippers on.
Peter reaches upwards, laughs and shrieks "Lieee."
Mother: Yes, it's the light.
Peter: Dieee.
Mother: That's right, light, light.
(b) I am talking to Mother. Peter comes up to me and touches my wrist.
Peter: Dik do.
Andy: Yes, it's a tick tock.
I continue talking to mother, the above occurring without intruding into our conversation.

OBSERVATION 4

Paul; age 13(27): Paul is playing with his football, which becomes stuck among chair legs. He tries to free it but is unable to. He starts crying while on his hands and knees, then moves to a sitting position and continues wailing. Mother comes in.
Mother: What's the matter? What's the matter?
Paul continues crying but also points in the direction of the chair.
Mother: Oh, have you got it stuck again? I think you do it on purpose some times, and she gives him the ball.
Paul continues crying but less and less vigorously, until he stops.

■ OBSERVATION:
Communicative
Behavior
(Lock, 1980)

After one year, infants also develop symbolic gestures that refer to a particular activity (Acredolo & Goodwin, 1985; McCune-Nicolich, 1981). For example, a child who wants her hair combed will hold a comb and pretend to comb her hair. Pretending to drink from a cup might signal the need for a drink. In the example cited in the section on emotional development, the infant's stopping just short of touching a forbidden object is a meaningful symbolic gesture. Such gestures may refer to the past or the future and to objects that are out of sight. Thus, they have the character of words that are used to name objects and events.

The Onset of Intentional Naming

As explained in the last chapter, infants' first words are uttered in the context of their own activities. They are perlocutionary, that is, spoken as an accompaniment to action and not with a communicative intent. Saying or humming "mmmmm" while eating is an example of this kind of primitive speech.

For most infants, sometimes between ten and sixteen months, they begin to use words in an illocutionary manner, that is, to communicate some intention. One manifestation of this developmental change is the onset of naming. Naming is when a gesture or a word is used intentionally to refer to a specific object or event.

Carlotta, one of the infants whose speech development has been reported in the literature (Bates et al., 1975; Bates et al., 1987), used the sound "bam" in a perlocutionary manner when knocking over a tower of blocks. Several weeks later, Carlotta was sitting silently among her toys. She stopped, looked up, and said "bam," and then she turned and started to bang on her toy piano. What has changed here? The word "bam" has been removed from its original context as an accompaniment to action and is now being said in advance of the action, to stand symbolically for the action that is about to occur. Another example of naming is given in Observation 3 of the Observation Box.

Around the same time, Carlotta began to do other naming procedures. When asked during the reading of a book, "How does the doggie go?" Carlotta consistently replied, "Woowoo." She also used "woowoo" when seeing a dog in real life or when hearing a dog barking. At the same age, she was rapidly developing names for toys, foods, and clothing.

When children first learn a word or first make one up, a considerable period of time passes before that word is used in the same way adults use it. Infants make many errors in the application of words. One type of error is called *overextension*, meaning the child uses the word for instances not included in the adult's definition. An example is a child who uses the word "car" for a wide range of vehicles, including motorcycles, bicycles, trucks, and planes. Does this mean the child does not really understand the true meaning of the word "car"? Or does it mean that the child has a faulty concept of cars, believing that all vehicles are cars?

Nelson and others (1978) believe that children's overextending while naming an object reflects their active attempt to try to categorize objects. By naming all vehicles "cars," children "elaborate for themselves the similarities among things" (Nelson et al., 1978, p. 964). Bowerman (1978) reported that her daughter Eva first used the word "moon" to describe the real thing and then extended the word's use to such things as a half of a grapefruit, lemon slices, and steer horns—anything she saw having a crescent shape.

According to Nelson and others (1978), the child does not appear to be saying that "a car *is* a plane" or "a lemon slice *is* a moon." They think the child is saying that "a car *is like* a plane" or "a lemon slice *is like* a moon," much like an older child might say, "Look, it's round" or "It looks like a car."

Generally, adults have three choices when infants overextend their word use. They can accept the children's own version of the word; they can say that the children are not correct; or they can provide the correct label for the object (Gruendel, 1977). However, even though the adult says something like "That's not a cookie" in response to the child's overextension of the word "cookie" to refer to a hamburger, the child might not understand or hear the negation. The child's failure to understand the word "not" may lead to the child's taking the adult's response to mean "It's okay to call that a cookie. Mommy said it, too" (Gruendel, 1977). Gruendel's data suggest that as soon as the adult stops referring to the object with the child's overextension and uses only the adult word for it, the child soon learns the correct name.

Relationship of Production to Comprehension

The same child who used the word "car" to describe many different vehicles was able to readily point out the correct vehicle when asked a question like "Where's the truck?" In another case, a child could correctly point out strawberries when asked but insisted on calling them "apple." Research has shown that thirteen-month-olds could understand about fifty words, but they could not speak fifty words until they were about nineteen months of age. Thus the comprehension of a word takes place considerably earlier than the production of a word.

The earliest instances of word comprehension have been found at the age of ten months for objects that are both salient and very familiar. At that age, however, it takes great effort to teach infants to understand a word, and they may rely more on the adult's tone of voice and gesture in pointing out the correct object. By seventeen months, however, infants can learn word meanings easily—sometimes after a single exposure (Oviatt, 1978).

Not all children have such noticeable lags between comprehension and production; in fact, some children can understand far more than they produce, while for others production is much more closely related to comprehension. How can this be? Some children who produce little but understand a great deal may suffer from a speech or hearing disorder, but this accounts for only a small percentage. Some children may be overly cautious about speaking out until they are certain that they understand how to use the word. This may be related to a temperamental propensity to shyness (Bates et al., 1989). Lags in production may also be related to the amount of explicit naming done by care givers (Vibbert & Bornstein, 1989). Currently, there is no complete explanation of what accounts for these individual differences.

On the other hand, those children who have high linguistic comprehension show high levels of gestural production. Thus, even though they hesitate to communicate with words, they have articulated a rich array of symbolic gestures (Bates et al., 1990). This can be seen clearly in deaf children who develop a large number of communicative gestures at ages similar to when hearing children develop linguistic names (Petitto, 1985; Reilly et al., 1985).

Thus, virtually all children at this age try to make themselves understood in one way or another.

The lag between comprehension and production suggests that children in the second year know more than their verbal behavior would indicate and that their efforts to speak are not crude gropings reflecting incomplete understanding but active efforts to make sense out of a complex world of objects and people. The work of Nelson and others should caution us about making too many inferences about the meaning expressed in children's single-word utterances. The young child's speech may be an important part of the process of concept formation, rather than a mere comment upon a concept the child already has attained. At least one study has shown that after adults label novel objects for infants, the infants pay closer attention to those objects (Baldwin & Markman, 1989). Thus, in complex ways, the learning of language may place the infant on a fast track toward conceptual and cognitive development.

Interfaces Between Language, Play, and Cognition

One of the settings in which children are acquiring and using language is play. Linguistic performance and play do not always go together, however. First of all, in the domain of adult-infant play, some situations call for language use and others do not. When infants are in an object exploratory mode, they are less communicative, and maternal intervention is not related to infant language development. However, when play is symbolic— playing with a doll, having a tea party, and so on—the adult's level of language use, the specific instruction of objects and their uses and names, has a greater impact on the child's language development (Tamis-LeMonda & Bornstein, 1990).

Second, play with peers involves much less language and gesture than play with adult care givers. With peers, infants of this age tend to focus more on direct actions on objects. With mother, compared to with peers or being alone, infants use significantly more words and gestures, and their play is more symbolic and relational (Turkheimer, 1989; Zukow, 1986). A similar finding has been reported comparing parent-infant and older sibling-infant interactions (Teti et al., 1988). During experimental manipulations when mothers are asked to temporarily cease being responsive during play, infants increase their requests for assistance from the mothers (Ross & Lollis, 1987).

Do Infants Show Any Intentional Communicative Behavior with Peers at This Age?

There is an increasing attempt on the part of peers to show contingent responses to one another (Mueller & Lucas, 1975). One example is sharing behavior, which begins in this stage (Rheingold, Hay, & West, 1976). In response to a verbal request or a visual regard on the part of one infant, a peer will show or give an object to the infant who requests it. Although this does not happen all the time, there is an increasing tendency for peers to focus their attention jointly on the same object of interest (Eckerman, Whatley, & Kutz, 1975). In general, however, this happens much less at this age during peer, compared to adult play (Turkheimer, 1989).

Between peers, toys have a different role than between adults and infants. With adults, toys can be objects of a request or an offer, or the subject of naming and labelling routines. Toys are just part of a more complex interaction involving many levels of meaning. On the other hand, with peers, toys become the major focus of attention and serve as vehicles for the initiation and maintenance of social interactions. If someone else in the room is touching or manipulating a toy, the infant is likely to approach that person and make contact with the toy. Intentional communication—unlike a single-minded interest in the toy itself—requires that the infant not only touch the toy but also look at the other person and verbalize to that person about the object. Eleven- to thirteen-month-olds were likely to smile, vocalize, and gesture to an adult just before and just after making contact with the toy the adult was touching, but this happens less often between peers (Eckerman et al., 1979; Turkheimer et al., 1989). In one study, a novel toy was introduced into play between adults and infants and between infant peers (Marcos & Verba, 1990). In the infant-adult interaction, the infants pointed to the toy and looked at the mother, requesting its name and wanting to use it. When the same toy was introduced between two peers, they just looked at each other and laughed.

Does the Mother's Presence Affect the Way an Infant Plays with Peers?

Because of this newfound awareness of persons as potential communicators, we might expect the parent's presence to affect peer interaction. Infants still approach peers for different reasons than they approach parents. In general, given the simultaneous presence of both mother and peer, a child is more likely to initiate play with a peer (Vandell, 1979). With their mothers, children are more likely to seek physical contact and show negative emotions like distress and anger.

To answer the question posed at the beginning of this section, however, we need to compare the infant's behavior to peers when the mother is present with when she is absent. In a familiar setting—a parent co-op nursery school—ten- and fourteen-month-olds were found to be more social and less negative to peers when their mothers were out of the room (Field, 1979a). The main difference between mothers present and mothers absent was that the infants did more toy snatching and more crying when the mothers were present, even when the infants were playing with peers. Field believes that these behaviors may serve as signals to the mothers of the infants' relative discontent about something.

What Other Situational Constraints Affect Peer Relationships?

The mother's presence during a peer interaction is referred to as a *situational constraint*—an aspect of the environment that affects the nature of the peer relationship. We saw in Chapter 2 how factors outside a social system can affect the functioning of that system. The presence of a third person is one such constraint. Others include the infant's familiarity with the peer and each infant's level of peer experience.

Toddler friendships are genuine and important. Sharing and contingent responses are just beginning at this age.

Familiarity has been shown to affect how one-year-olds play together. Friends are more likely to interact together than nonfriends, even under controlled laboratory situations in which friend and nonfriend pairs are formed artificially and allowed to play by themselves for a short period of time (Becker, 1977; Young & Lewis, 1979). Lewis, Young, Brooks, and Michalson (1975) found that friends were more likely than nonfriends to touch and lean on each other, more likely to initiate interactions with each other, and more likely to show positive affect with each other.

Apparently, then, friendship can be shown to exist as early as twelve months of age. Although it is not clear from these studies whether infants at this age have the same kind of attachment to their friends as older children and adults do, infants seem more comfortable and expressive in the company of familiars.

The amount of experience an infant has had with peers is not as strong a situational constraint as peer familiarity. Some evidence suggests that experienced toddlers are more active in peer encounters than relatively inexperienced toddlers, as well as that the experienced toddlers are more likely to show more complex social behaviors (Mueller & Brenner, 1977; Vandell, 1979). Nevertheless, infants seem to need little prior exposure to other infants to act competently in their company, and infants seem to learn the ins and outs of peer play very quickly.

In this section, we discuss two important topics. First, we look at how handicapped infants affect families and their functioning, a topic that does not fit neatly into a single age period. Second, because many mothers are returning to work by the time their infants are one year old, we discuss the issue of how infant development is affected by nonparental care givers. In relation to this, the Applications section of this chapter covers the role of society in providing day care for all families who need it. When an infant has a long-term or permanent abnormality—a handicap, deformity, or special weakness—a family systems approach predicts that this infant will affect the entire family and that the family's response to the infant will affect the infant's own development. This section will explore these possibilities. You might want to go back and read the section in Chapter 3 on teratology, as well as the sections in Chapter 4 on euthanasia for handicapped neonates and on birth complications. Because the infant will affect every member of the family for a long time, the issues discussed in this section should be a part of any decision regarding life, death, or institutionalization for these infants at the time of birth.

How does a handicapped infant affect the family?

A handicapped infant creates an emotional trauma for most families at all levels of family systems functioning.

Individual responses. Parents, siblings, and other relatives go through a series of difficult feelings. There is almost always a chronic sorrow or depression—a feeling that the child will never fit into their lives or dreams. Individuals around the handicapped infant feel an emotional rejection of the infant that may result, in part, from a lack of knowledge about the handicapping condition. Family members also experience difficulty adapting—even to everyday demands—and they find most of their interpersonal relationships strained (Blake, Stewart, & Turcan, 1975; Brooks-Gunn & Lewis, 1982; Rapoport, Rapoport, & Strelitz, 1977).

Parents may be highly emotionally aroused much of the time. The shame and guilt they feel at being the "cause" of the problem is coupled with the extra difficulties of caring for the handicapped child. These may include extra visits to doctors and hospitals, special difficulties (such as soiling and wetting), special housing or equipment needs, financial difficulties, special care arrangements, special clothing, and special transportation (Rapoport et al., 1977). In the course of all of this, a parent may swing between the extreme attitudes of either wanting to abandon the child or trying to overprotect the child.

Siblings have unique individual responses to the situation. They may have trouble with peer relationships, become restless and disobedient, display temper tantrums, or live in a state of emotional misery. Part of the difficulty for siblings is that the added stress on the parents reduces the amount of parental time and emotional energy available to give them.

Handicapped infants even affect their grandparents. In one study (Davis, 1967), maternal grandmothers were less supportive of their daughters if the daughters had handicapped compared with normal infants. The feedback a

■ FAMILY AND SOCIETY

mother receives from her own mother may make her feel less supported and therefore affect her ability to care for the baby. If the grandmother senses that her daughter is not doing her job, the grandmother may withdraw even further. These mutual feedback effects show how the family system can work against the benefit of the infant. However, mutually supportive feedback can lead to a strengthening of the family to the ultimate benefit of the infant.

Effect on the marital relationship. Most of the research on the effect of a handicapped child on marital discord has shown that there is little or no effect. If couples separated or divorced after having a handicapped child, it was because of some problem in the marriage that existed before the child was born (Howard, 1978). Marital discord that can be directly traced to the child amounts to only 4 percent of the cases studied in a sample of 243 rubella birth defect children (Korn, Chess, & Fernandez, 1978).

Effects on the family. In contrast, the handicapped child has a definite impact on family interaction patterns. These may include changes in family routines, lack of vacations and other out-of-home visits, a limited social life, and parents' neglect of other children. These problems only occurred in about one-fourth of the sample of 243 rubella defect children (Korn et al., 1978), but some of these families had experienced similar disruptions even before the infants' births.

In general, most families who are provided with adequate social, economic, and psychological supports come to an effective resolution of these issues, although it may take a long time. A resolution usually means a realistic assessment of the child's abilities and limitations, continued feelings of sadness—but about the child rather than about the effect on the parents— and a recovery of the parents' self-esteem (Mintzer et al., 1985).

How do handicaps affect the parent-infant interaction?

Most evidence suggests that interactions are adversely affected by a child's handicaps. For example, premature infants who were delayed in smiling were smiled to less by their mothers (Field, 1982; Malatesta et al., 1986). Parents of blind infants feel less attached and are likely to interact less with their infants (Fraiberg, 1974). Children with cerebral palsy are likely to receive less maternal warmth if they are not walking by three years of age than if they walk earlier (Korn et al., 1978). Parents tend to interrupt their Down's syndrome infants' vocalizations more than their normal infants', even though the Down's infants vocalize less (Berger & Cunningham, 1983). Finally, parents of infants with an unattractive craniofacial deformity appear to be less nurturant than parents of normal children during the early part of the first year (Barden et al., 1989). In the second year, parents of infants with any kind of physical handicap are both more reinforcing of what the child actually can do and more likely to ignore the larger number of difficulties experienced by the child than parents of normal infants (Wasserman et al., 1985).

The amount of disruption of the parent-infant interaction depends on the severity of the handicap (Landry et al., 1986). Perhaps the mildest effects are seen in premature infants. Mothers of these infants are often overindulgent and overstimulating during the first year (Field, 1981a); these differences tend

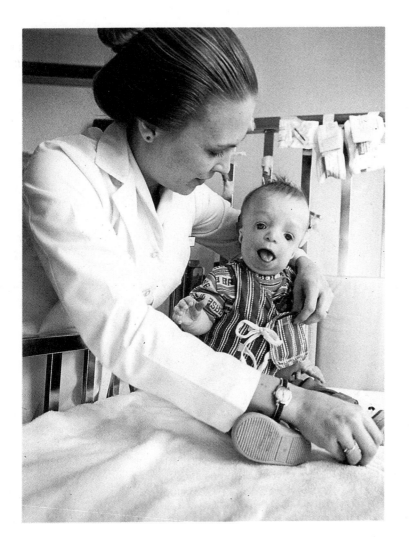

Many handicapped infants are capable of social relationships. Some require regular medical interventions. All such infants demand special care and attention from their families.

to disappear after the first year, perhaps because the preterm infants gradually catch up with full-term infants (Branchfeld, Goldberg, & Sloman, 1980; Crawford, 1982).

Even though preterm infants showed less vocalization, play, and attentive behavior than full-term infants in interaction with their mothers at six, eight, and ten months, most of these differences were no longer significant at twelve months. In addition, the extra holding and caretaking that preterm infants received during the first year, compared with full-term infants, was no longer apparent at twelve months (Crawford, 1982). Even though the differences between preterm and normal groups were lessened by one year for these behavioral indicators, other studies have shown that more subtle effects of prematurity may persist until early and middle childhood in such areas as emotional maturity, language skills, and perceptual-motor functioning (Grigoroiu-Serbanescu, 1981; Taub, Goldstein, & Caputo, 1977).

In general, however, by age three years, differences between preterm and full-term groups are typically absent. In preterm groups, as for full-terms, individual differences are best predicted by security of attachment at one year (Plunkett et al., 1988), by the severity of birth complications independent of prematurity (Landry et al., 1986), and by the infant's history of illness during the first years of life (Jarvis et al., 1989). Thus, the factors that complicate preterm birth have a longer-lasting impact than the prematurity itself.

Lasting interactive deficits are seen in more serious disorders. One study of 110 handicapped infants (with Down's syndrome, cerebral palsy, and developmental delay) found that the handicapped infants smiled and vocalized less than the matched sample of normal infants (Brooks-Gunn & Lewis, 1982). In fact, one-third of the handicapped infants never smiled in the first two years of life, although by age three, 80 percent had smiled. These babies cried more at older ages than the controls.

Other studies have shown that Down's syndrome babies have a very different pattern of sociability. Although most four-month-old infants when presented with a maternal "still-face" during social interaction (see Chapter 6) will cease smiling and gaze away, Down's infants actually gaze longer and may even smile (Legerstee & Bowman, 1989). This suggests that Down's babies may be overstimulated by social interaction and find it easier to express themselves when mothers are relatively quiet. Other research has shown that maternal attention-directing strategies during object play are usually less successful with Down's babies (Landry & Chapiesky, 1989). In response to these actions, mothers of Down's babies are likely to respond less and to attempt new interactions less than mothers of normal infants (Brooks-Gunn & Lewis, 1982; Jones, 1977).

Some research has shown that the developmental prognosis is better for handicapped infants whose social interactions with their mothers were more like those of normal infants. Cohen and Beckwith (1979) found that the frequency of social interaction in the early part of the first year of life predicted a child's competence at age two on the Gesell Developmental Schedule, the Bayley Scales of Infant Development, and a language development scale. This suggests that the more parents try to treat their infants as if they were normal children with "special" problems rather than as abnormal or problem children, the better off the children are in the long run. Several studies have shown that if maternal question-asking, which is found at high frequency for normal infants, is maintained at a high level for handicapped and language-disordered infants, it can have a marked effect on their social and communicative development (Leifer & Lewis, 1983; Yoder, 1989).

One part of the problem is that parents often may not understand the nature of their child's disorder. Another problem is that parents have trouble being happy and playing with a baby that is relatively less responsive. Even when the baby makes an occasional response, the parent often is unprepared and is not able to anticipate an appropriate answer. We might think that if a handicapped baby smiled less, the parents would be much more responsive to the few smiles the baby was capable of showing. One explanation offered by Fogel (1982b) is that parents adjust their responses partly on the basis of the timing of a baby's responses. Most babies smile at their parents at the very start of an interaction session, and then they smile regularly during the session. Parents seem to learn that if the baby does not smile at the beginning of an interaction episode, the baby is not likely to smile during that episode (Fogel, 1982b). Perhaps handicapped infants' smiles occur at random during an interaction, or perhaps they produce so few smiles that the parents are not able to discern an expectable pattern in their timing. In this way, a relative paucity of smiles can lead to parents' lack of responsiveness simply because they have not learned to anticipate when the smiles are likely to occur.

What can be done to help parents help their handicapped children?

Intervention programs designed to educate parents about their children's handicaps, to provide emotional support and the supportive network of a system of peers (other parents with similar problems), and to teach parents how to respond to and anticipate the needs of their individual children seem to have a significant success rate. Mothers in such intervention programs seem to learn to enjoy and respond more to their infants (Bromwich & Parmalee, 1979; Field, 1981a; Fraiberg, 1974).

In addition, local and state governments provide support services for handicapped children through day-care and school systems, as well as in hospital programs. Federal funds are available through such programs as Developmental Disabilities, Early Periodic Screening Diagnosis and Treatment, Head Start, Education of the Handicapped (PL 94-142), Title XX Social Services, and the National Institute for Mental Health. Most of these programs make funds available through community and state education and welfare agencies (McPherson, 1983).

John D. McKee was born in 1919 with cerebral palsy. Today, he writes articles and books about what it is like to grow up as a handicapped individual. In his autobiography, he writes eloquently about his life and family (McKee, 1955). His views seem to capture the ideas that modern scientific research is only beginning to discover: that knowledge burns brighter than ignorance, that all children need love and a chance to make it on their own, and that a sense of humor is one of the best shields against depression and guilt. McKee wrote the following:

At home with my family, I was perfectly relaxed. If I spilled something at the table, it was only as if one of my brothers spilled his milk or dropped his bread butter-side-down on the floor. Once in a while, if I was having a particularly tough time and was spreading my food around the dining room with a lavish hand, Mother would say, "Why don't you sit on the floor, Jack? Anything that falls up, we'll hand down to you." In the laugh that followed, the tension was broken, and I could usually finish my meal with a minimum of spilling. (McKee, 1955, p. 201).

In the next section, we turn to the topic of the effects of alternate and multiple care givers on infant development.

The effects of nonparental care on infants and parents

In the first edition of this book, published in 1984, I reviewed research on the effects of out-of-home care for infants. There were relatively few studies, and most showed no harmful effects, so long as the infants were left in high-quality care. Since 1984, there has been an explosion of new research, new findings, and especially, new public interest in the question of child care. The answers are no longer clear.

The effects of child care still depend on the quality of that care. Most researchers agree that child care after the age of twelve to eighteen months is not harmful and might even be beneficial to the child. Compared to

334 Infancy ■ Infant, Family, and Society

The effects of non-parental day care on infants depends on the conditions of the day care setting, the infant's age, and the parent-infant relationship. Only a small percentage of infants in the United States are able to attend a high-quality day care facility.

home-reared infants, day-care infants are more cognitively and socially advanced and are more likely to show independence in compliance to rules (Caldwell, 1986; Clarke-Stewart, 1984; Siegal & Storey, 1985). However, some researchers conclude that nonparental child care under the age of one year is potentially harmful.

The controversy is the result of a series of research studies reporting that the proportion of infants with insecure attachments increases if the infants have been in child care for at least four months beginning before the first birthday and for more than twenty hours per week, that is, children whose mothers are employed more than half-time (Belsky & Rovine, 1988; Barglow, 1987a; Schwartz, 1983; Vaughn et al., 1980). In samples of infants in the United States whose mothers do not work outside the home, the proportion of secure attachments is about 65 to 75 percent. In these samples of early child-care infants, the proportion of secure attachments, across all studies, is 57 percent (Belsky & Rovine, 1988). The difference in security between early child-care and home-care infants is small but statistically significant. In all these studies, the dependent measure is attachment security as assessed by the Ainsworth Strange Situation Test.

How should we interpret these findings? First of all, the majority of the early child-care infants are securely attached to their mothers and thus do not appear to be at risk. What accounts for those who develop insecure attachments? The infants most at risk for insecure attachments tend to be boys who are rated as difficult and/or fussy and whose mothers had strong career orientations, worked full-time, and expressed less anxiety about being separated from their infants (Barglow, 1987a; Belsky & Rovine, 1988; Chase-Lansdale & Owen, 1987).

One must be very careful in interpreting these results. It is *not true* that all boys in early child care have insecure attachments. It is *not true* that all career-oriented women have less securely attached children. It is a particular combination of these factors that seems to have the most impact: career-orientation combined with low concern over separation from the child and less sensitivity to the emotional needs of their sons.

Indeed, one study found sons of mothers who were highly sensitive to their emotional needs and who returned to full-time work early in the first year were securely attached to their mothers at eighteen months (Benn, 1986). Other research has shown that women who return to work out of economic necessity rather than out of career orientation express greater anxiety about working and have higher role conflict and lower life satisfaction (Alvarez, 1985; DeMeis, 1986). It seems there is no easy way to generalize from these findings to all cases. Rather, the research might point up some areas of potential risk for both mothers and infants that might assist families in coping with the daily separations of the day-care experience.

Another consideration in interpreting these findings is the meaning of attachment security as an outcome measure assessing the risk of early child-care experiences. As we mentioned in the last chapter, the Ainsworth Strange Situation Test appears to have a cultural bias. We also suggested that it may be biased against infants who have extensive nonmaternal care experiences. Resistance or avoidance of the mother on reunion may reflect the infant's relative independence of her. Perhaps one way to interpret the above results is that boys whose mothers are relatively independent themselves display more independence from the mother. On the other hand, since this increase of insecure attachments *does not* show up in boys or girls placed in child care after the age of one year, we still have to worry about why child-care experience under a year causes such a reaction in infants.

Another possible interpretation of the results is that the effects are temporary adjustments to child care. Most of the attachment assessments of the infants in early child care were done between the ages of one and two years. Can a lasting impact be detected in these infants? Research shows that the security of the early child-care infant's attachment to *mother* does not predict social and emotional competence in preschool; rather, the security of attachment to the substitute *care giver* and/or the quality of the early care setting is the best predictor of social and emotional competence in preschool (Howes, 1988; Howes, 1990; Howes & Stewart, 1987; Oppenheim et al., 1988; Phillips et al., 1987; Schindler et al., 1987; Vaughn et al., 1985). These relationships were found for infants in the United States in day-care centers or family day-care homes and on Israeli kibbutzim in which the child's primary attachment is with the *metapelet*. For infants reared at home primarily, as we saw in the last chapter, it is the child's attachment to *mother* that is the best predictor of preschool social behavior. These results are summarized in Table 9.1.

■ **TABLE 9.1   Relationships between Attachments in the First Year and Social and Emotional Competence in Preschool**

These results are for infants who experience more than half-time child care outside the home (child-care infants) under the age of one year. YES = security of attachment (and/or quality of child care) in the first year is correlated with preschool social competence. NO = security of attachment (and/or quality of child care) in the first year is not correlated with preschool competence.

PRIMARY TYPE OF CARE	ATTACHMENT FIGURE	
	MOTHER	CARE GIVER
Mother: in home	Yes	No (or unknown)
Child care: out of home	No	Yes

APPLICATIONS

Social Policy And Day Care

ITEM: In 1978, the nation's total investment in day care was $10 billion—$6 billion of which was paid directly by parents, with the remaining $4 billion coming from national, state, and local governments. Children under the age of three accounted for 11 percent of these costs.

ITEM: The U.S. Department of Health, Education and Welfare published minimum requirements for day care in 1968. Referred to as the Federal Interagency Day Care Requirements (FIDCR), they were never implemented because of political controversies within the federal government over which agency would best administer them, whether they could be enforced at all, and whether the government could afford to maintain its own standards.

ITEM: The FIDCR were revised in 1972 by a noted Yale psychologist, Edward Zigler. He included in-home care in the regulations, specified meal requirements and minimum wages, and set child-to-adult ratios: zero to eighteen months, 3:1; and nineteen to thirty-eight months, 4:1. The 1968 regulations did not set ratios for children under three years of age. Because of the low child-to-staff ratios and the minimum wages, the revised regulations could not be enforced (since very few facilities could comply).

ITEM: Two years later, Congress put day care in the hands of the states under the Title XX amendment to the Social Security Act. In 1975, the Department of Health, Education, and Welfare published new staffing ratios as follows: zero to six weeks, 1:1; six weeks to eighteen months, 1:3; eighteen to thirty-six months, 1:4. Congresspeople, state administrators, and care givers launched a tide of protest. The requirements were never enforced.

ITEM: In 1987, new federal child-care legislation began to be drafted in Congress, in collaboration with a number of child advocacy groups, including the Children's Defense Fund, the Society for Research in Child Development, the American Psychological Association, the American Academy of Pediatrics, and the American Federation of Teachers. Called the ABC bill (Act for Better Childcare), it is designed to provide child care for low- to moderate-income families and to provide incentives for states to improve the quality of care in centers and in family day care. In late 1990, however, Congress enacted the ABC child-care bill, but not a parental leave bill also under consideration.

ITEM: Although we are one of the world's wealthiest nations, we are subsidizing child care for less than 10 percent of our children under six years, compared to 100 percent in Sweden, 90 percent in France, and 50 percent in Israel and Hungary.

ITEM: More than half of young children in the United States are in second-rate child-care situations, with substandard facilities, poor staff training, and high staff turnover.

ITEM: Three million children in the United States under the age of fourteen years are in programs guided by no national standards reflecting current knowledge obtained by research in child development. Licensed day-care facilities currently account for only 17 percent of out-of-home care for children who spend at least ten hours per week in child care. The rest of the children are in non-licensed, family-run day-care homes.

ITEM: Although more employers are providing child care at work, in 1986, these rep-

continued at top of next page

APPLICATIONS

resented less than one-tenth of one percent of the nation's employers. The private sector is not stepping in and picking up the responsibility.

ITEM: The situation is bad all around, but it is considerably worse for black families, who suffer from a lack of public policies for the adequate protection of their children's health, education, and welfare. Although most of the children in day care are white, blacks are disproportionately represented. Of children in day care, 28 percent are black and 9 percent are from other minority groups. Only 17 percent of the U. S. population under 17 years of age is from minority groups.

These disturbing statistics (Klein, 1985; Magid & McKelvey, 1987; Nelson, 1982; Ruopp & Travers, 1982; Slaughter, 1980; Weintraub & Furman, 1987) testify to the large gap between children's needs and the willingness of our leaders to provide adequately for them. We know that high-quality child care is correlated with successful outcomes for children, especially for children under the age of one year. We also know what is necessary to create high-quality care (see Table 9.2 on page 338). So, why have we been so slow to create a national policy?

Slaughter (1980) gives three reasons for the lack of effective policies for child care. The first is the myth that the modern family can be independent and self-sufficient. In spite of growing evidence to the contrary, people tend to think they are the masters of their own destiny. Hence, there is a strong resistance to the idea of social policy and social legislation (Bennett, 1987). Recent studies on the ecology of child development (see Bronfenbrenner, 1979; Belsky, 1981) have shown that what happens to the child and the family depends, to a large measure, on the exosystem, mesosystem, and macrosystem of the surrounding society (see Chapter 2). Although a parent may believe that day-care services should be found close to or in the home, the reality

for many parents is that their children are left to fend for themselves in situations that are often inadequate and unregulated by state and federal laws.

A second reason given by Slaughter is the fragmentation of social services that exist for families, especially for high-risk families with low incomes. Support services are scattered among many different agencies, making it difficult for parents to obtain necessary services and nearly impossible for the government to exert reasonably efficient regulatory controls. Efforts to unify and streamline these services typically meet with strong political opposition, since many of them fall under the authority of different branches and departments of government (Weintraub & Furman, 1987).

The final reason for lack of clear policy is a public disaffection toward research in general and behavioral science research in particular. The Title XX program has not even availed itself of the skills of social scientists in determining its own effectiveness. Title XX cannot report how many children it serves under what forms of care, how many handicapped children it serves, and a list of other unanswered questions (Beck, 1982).

Currently the most effective resources for the implementation of research-based, informed social policy on children and the family are the professional organizations for behavioral scientists—in particular, the American Psychological Association, the American Psychological Society, and the Society for Research in Child Development. These groups have representatives in Washington, D.C., to act as eyes and ears for the welfare of the child and family. In addition, the Society for Research in Child Development has a Social Policy Committee. Because of the group's wide representation among researchers as well as practitioners in the area of child development, it may have a greater impact on governmental policy than would the individual scientist.

■ TABLE 9.2   Accepted Standards of High-Quality Child Care*

FACTOR	NEEDED TO MAINTAIN EFFECTIVE DEVELOPMENT
Group size	Care giver-child ratio between 1:4 and 1:10 over three years of age; between 1:3 and 1:8 under three years; and 1:3 under age one year.
Care givers	Trained in specialized, formal teacher training programs that emphasize early childhood education and experienced in working in child care settings. Care givers should be nurturant and supportive; they should talk to, hug, and smile at children and enjoy their company. Also, they should be willing to firmly and appropriately enforce guidelines for behaviors that affect the rights and safety of others, as well as have respect for parents' points of view and concerns.
Staffing	Low staff turnover, staff support, and low burnout; only one or two care givers should be responsible for the same child.
Curriculum	Planned in advance, emphasis on development. Age-appropriate and safe toys, flexible program with special events and outside trips. Curriculum adapted to needs of the individual child. Opportunities for diverse activities and movement.
Parents	Should be informed daily about child's day and any special problems or special achievements; should be encouraged to visit at any time and to participate if desired.
Facility	Clean, bright, safe, lots of room for toddlers to move about. Nap times and quiet areas, access to a fenced outside play area. Emergency essentials available. Food safe and nutritious.

*Applicable to day-care centers and family day care.

SOURCE: Magid & McKelvey, 1987; Provence, 1982; Scarr, 1984; Weintraub & Furman, 1987.

The data suggests that substitute care for infants under the age of one year is indeed a different experience for the infants than if they are placed in such care after the age of one year. Under the age of one year, infants appear to be more sensitive to the effects of child-care quality and to the availability of nonparental attachment figures within the child-care setting. These factors are less important for infants older than one year, who have already formed a strong attachment to one or both parents.

Does this mean that one should not place children under the age of one year in child care for more than a few hours a week and that mothers or fathers should plan to stay home with infants for at least one year? Some observers make a strong case for this position on the following grounds. First, this early experience outside the home reduces somewhat the importance of the parental role. Second, and more importantly, it may not be possible in the United States today to guarantee high-quality child care for more than a handful of children (see the Applications section of this chapter). If this is true, one may be justified in supporting home care for infants under a year (Barglow, 1987b; Belsky & Rovine, 1988; Magid & McKelvey, 1987).

On the other hand, parents may not be disturbed by a change in their parental role. The findings do not mean that parents are unimportant, only that they have a different type of relationship and provide different sorts of needs for their children than parents who chose to stay at home. In many countries, such as Israel, China, and the Soviet Union, extensive out-of-home child care is an accepted part of the culture. Advocates of child care in the United States argue that if child care were made more of a national priority, we could guarantee high-quality care for all infants. In the meantime, these advocates provide guidelines for parents to use in evaluating the quality of care in order to assure a good setting for their infants (Howes, 1988; Phillips et al., 1987; Scarr, 1984). We take up these issues at the interface between research, practice, and policy-making in the Applications section on page 336. ■

POINTS OF CONTACT

In some ways, babies of this age seem quite fearless, walking into the street, putting screwdrivers into electrical outlets, sticking fingers into their eyes, and perching precariously at the top of a flight of stairs. Care givers need to limit the child's access to certain dangerous or precarious areas or objects. This is best accomplished by physical barriers, such as a baby fence across the entrance to basement stairs, or by offering the baby some alternatives for exploration. Although babies of this age learn to understand the meaning of "no" and even come to use it on their own, overuse of negative language by parents ultimately may dilute its effectiveness. Of course, parents don't have to walk around saying "no" all the time. Other common and important prohibitive words include "yukky," "hot," or "that's Mommy's."

The major attractions of the baby's world at this age are adults and containers. Babies want to try out everything the adult does. This may mean trying to talk on the telephone, eat from Dad's plate, sit in Mom's chair at the table instead of the usual high chair, smoke Dad's pipe, or "read" the newspaper. While these things may seem cute at first, they often get in the way of household routines and stretch the limits of health and safety. Adults can offer alternatives like toy telephones or pipes, feeding the baby first before the adults eat, or just spending time with the baby and allowing the child to play at being grown up.

At this age, babies love to pull things out of and put things into containers. Unfortunately, this could mean kitchen cabinets, fish bowls, soap boxes, ears, mouths, and eyes. Some parents try to arrange the house so the baby has his or her own drawer, stocked with an array of harmless kitchen gadgets and plastic cups and dishes. The situation is not as easy to handle when the baby decides to tear the pages out of an older brother's favorite book. Toddlers' natural urges to test the limits of their environment are not intentionally negative or malicious in any way. Nevertheless, babies must learn the effects their actions have on

continued at top of next page

people around them. The older sibling's angry responses and the adult's prohibitions are part of that learning process. So are the tears and tantrums that often result.

Babies do not restrict their exploratory activities to inanimate objects. Parts of others' bodies are also fair game. Babies will recklessly pull off your glasses, twist your nose, pull your hair, pull on your necklace, pat you, and even hit you. Toward the end of this developmental period, at fifteen to eighteen months, babies will do some of these things just to get your attention. Showing off, which we already discussed, and putting on performances for admiring audiences are also part of trying to attract the attention and laughter of others.

To some extent, babies need to know that you recognize and appreciate them and that you are willing and able to share a laugh with them. It is also important to impose and enforce reasonable limits on what you consider to be overexuberance. This may be particularly true when attention getting begins to look downright mischievous, as in hitting, throwing food, or pulling and tugging.

Social games are still important to the baby, such as peek-a-boo or "give and take." Babies of this age like to sit on an adult's lap and identify mutual body parts, like touching their own nose and then the adult's. Looking at pictures and books, talking on the telephone with the baby, playing with puppets, and action rhymes like "Pop Goes the Weasel" and "This Little Piggy" are all best sellers. Babies love it when you act as a tour guide to the world of the adult. This could involve holding their hands and walking places where they could not go on their own, like up and down stairs or outside. You can pick them up and let them see things that are not visually accessible from their normal viewing height, let them be a "helper" and carry a pot or utensil, or let them listen to your watch ticking (or sounding its alarm, if you have an electronic watch).

Babies are learning and laughing, giving and sharing, and beginning to communicate via the spoken word. Although they are starting to test the limits of their world, they have not yet fully discovered their own unique individuality, something that occurs in the next stage of development. For these reasons, many parents think that twelve to eighteen months is the "best" age for a baby. The next stage, however, brings with it the mastery of the *symbol*, a genuine turning point in the child's development: the transition from action to thought.

■ SUMMARY

Physical and Motor Development

■ At this age, infants can adjust their locomotor movements to the characteristics of the surface. They won't cross a wavy surface or a downward sloping surface while standing. They perform different actions on objects when the table is hard compared to soft.

■ Spoon use becomes more efficient during this period, including corrections for the amount of food on the spoon and entering the mouth.

Cognitive Development

■ Infants are experimenting to find new ways to cause similar effects, such as trying alternate strategies to reach goals through trial-and-error exploration.
■ Infants can now conceive of higher order categories, such as animals and vehicles.

Emotional Development

■ Infants are getting better at making good feelings last and controlling negative feelings.
■ Infants know how to tease adults by varying the patterns of normal routines or stopping just short of misbehavior and laughing.

Social and Language Development

■ Languages have properties that distinguish them from other forms of communication.
■ Functional theories of language are discussed at length, and most of the recent research is on how infants use language to communicate.
■ At this age, infants develop both linguistic and gestural referential communication, naming, gestural combinations, and the ability to coordinate their communications with those of the adult.
■ Infants typically comprehend more than they can produce, although the gap between comprehension and production is much larger for some infants than for others.
■ Particular forms of adult response seem more conducive to infant language development than others.
■ Linguistic communication is more likely in certain situations, and gestural communication is more likely in others.
■ Peer interaction is more focused on direct actions on objects, while adult-infant interaction has more referential communication about objects.
■ Peers are more likely to get along better when one of the parents is not around.

Family and Society

■ Family members face a difficult period of adapting to a handicapped infant.
■ The effect of a handicap on the parent-infant interaction depends on the severity of the handicap and how long it persists. In general, parents tend to adapt their behavior to suit the needs of the handicapped infant.
■ Families are encouraged to seek support services to help with coping and education.
■ Day care has different effects on infants and families, depending on the age of the child at entrance into day care, the parent's feelings about day care and returning to work, and the quality of care.

Applications: Social Policy and Day Care

■ There is a growing gap between the need for day care in the United States and public support for day care.
■ The role of the researcher in forming public policy has been limited for a number of social reasons.

■ GLOSSARY

Displacement   The property of language to express concrete and abstract ideas that are not physically present to the speaker.

Illocutionary   The phase of language development in which infants communicate intentionally.

Overextension   Applying a single word to refer to more objects and situations than are normally found in adult speech.

Perlocutionary   The phase of language development in which infants are not aware of their roles as communicators.

Pragmatics   The study of the functional uses of language, as opposed to the structural (grammatical) properties of language.

Productivity   The ability of language to express multiple meanings using a small number of words simply by rearranging the word order in novel ways.

Semanticity   The ability of language to carry meaning for both speaker and listener.

Situational constraints   Elements of the context of a stimulus or event that determine a child's response to that event. In interactions with other children, for example, the peer's age, sex, and familiarity to the infant; the infant's experience interacting with other children; and the care giver's location are all situational constraints that may determine the quality of the peer-infant interaction.

Syntax   The structure, or grammar, of a language; the rules that determine word order.

Tertiary circular reactions   New means invented to achieve goals by trial-and-error experimentation.

TEN

Conflict, Doubt, and Power

(EIGHTEEN TO TWENTY-FOUR MONTHS)

———

CHAPTER OUTLINE

Motor and Cognitive Development
Emotional Development
Social and Language
    Development
Family and Society

Applications: Poverty and Risk
Points of Contact
Summary
Glossary

In the realm of cognition, babies are beginning to think; they are able to plan things out before acting, thus eliminating much of the trial-and-error quality seen in the last stage. The ability to think without having to act is at the root of our capacity to plan, dream, solve complex problems, and know ourselves. As the title of this chapter suggests, infants of this age are beginning to establish a sense of their own potency and self-sufficiency; they learn to experience the feeling of pride for the first time. With this sense of new power comes the emotions of defiance and negativism, which bring the two-year-old into direct conflict with care givers, siblings, and peers. Self-awareness often can bring self-doubt, but this is what infants need to learn about at this stage of development: how to handle the new experience of personal autonomy and yet still maintain close and affectionate ties with the people around them.

    We'll see how language develops rapidly during this period, as infants now begin to express more complex ideas in sentences rather than single words and peer relationships become more complex and more verbal. Finally, we will discuss issues related to the family in society, including the effects of social supports on parenting and the effects of poverty on family and infant development.

■ MOTOR AND COGNITIVE DEVELOPMENT

Motor and cognitive development have been included in the same section in this chapter and the next, primarily because there is little concrete research from which to draw conclusions. We know, however, that a great many motor changes take place during this period. Some of these are discussed in the Points of Contact section at the end of the chapter. A few things will be mentioned here.

Motor Advances

Infants' locomotion is so stable that they now prefer to be independent walkers and may resist holding an adult's hand. It is not until the third year that infants can negotiate stairs on their own. Few eighteen-month-olds will not be able to feed themselves, and most prefer to manage their own food. This is another case in which infants seem to feel confident about their own motor abilities. Self-dressing is well underway by eighteen months, and many infants will be able to put on their own coats, shoes, and socks by age two years.

One of the big advances, from a parent's perspective, that is likely to occur at this age is toilet training. Based on findings from some African countries in which toilet training begins in the first month of life (see Chapter 6), it is likely that infants have the potential to regulate their bowels and bladders well before they are trained in most Western countries. So why should we wait so long? The reason is that in these African societies, there is almost constant physical contact between the mother and infant, enabling mothers to detect the signs of impending elimination. In societies where physical contact is at a minimum, infants must learn to signal their intentions across a distance. Typically, this means by using words. So the trick in Western societies is to help the child associate the need to eliminate with a communication about being taken to the toilet. Toilet training is most likely to begin at between eighteen months and three years, although it may take up to a year to complete.

Another aspect of physical development about which parents are concerned is the child's sleep patterns. Most infants of this age are still napping during the afternoon and sleeping through most of the night. It is not uncommon, however, for infants between the age of one and three years to wake occasionally at night (Richards, 1977).

Out of seventy-seven babies in Richards's study, twenty-nine were waking during the night at one year. Richards found that the style of parental handling, such as how much the baby was encouraged to "cry it out," did not affect whether the baby woke at night. Families had tried different techniques to handle the problem: verbal battles with the babies; sleep deprivation by keeping the baby awake during the day; and, as a last resort, the modification of parental life-styles so the parents could spend several hours awake with the baby at 3 A.M.

Since none of these parental methods seemed to change the babies, what accounts for night waking? Richards found that babies who woke at night at one year had longer labors and they were more wakeful—but more fussy—during the first ten days of life. He also found that at three years, these same children had learned to sleep through the night, but they still were difficult to get to sleep. Similar findings have been reported by Blurton-Jones, Ferreira, Brown, and MacDonald (1978). The findings suggest that night waking may result from some biological predisposition: if parents have such babies, their best bet is to learn to live with them. It also helps parents to know that they do not have the only baby who can't sleep through the night and that they are probably not the cause of the problem.

Cognitive Development: Symbolic Play

Piaget has referred to the sixth and final stage of sensorimotor development as the *invention of new means through mental combinations*. In the previous stage, the infant could experiment with new ways of making things happen. However, all this trial and error happened in the sphere of real action. The child had to actually do all the alternatives to get to the goal. This is one reason why, in the last chapter, we remarked on the sheer energy of the toddler in Stage V.

All this changes in Stage VI, because children no longer have to physically carry out the actions: they can think about the possible paths to a goal, eliminate the most improbable ones, and only then act. According to Piaget (1952), the child's first thoughts are internalized action sequences. Babies now can find objects after any number of visible or invisible displacements; they can go around a detour to get at something.

At the heart of thinking is the *symbol*, a mental representation of a thing or event. Symbols appear only gradually in children's repertoires. At first, children represent objects by performing some action related to the objects and physically similar to the represented objects (Ungerer, Zelazo, Kearsley, & O'Leary, 1981). Gradually they begin to use abbreviated forms of action to represent objects, leading to the development of a set of idiosyncratic representations. Recall in the last chapter how the infant Carlotta began to use the word "bam" at first as a mere extension of her action and then later to symbolically represent a number of different things that made a crashing noise. See also the observations of symbol usage that Piaget made on his own children in the Observations Box below.

■ **OBSERVATIONS: Stage VI Behavior (Piaget, 1962, pp. 121 and 124)**

OBSERVATION 1

At 1;6(30) Jacqueline said *cry, cry* to her dog and herself imitated the sound of crying. On the following days she made her bear, a duck, etc., cry. At 1;7(1) she made her hat cry. . . .

OBSERVATION 2

At 1;8(30) Jacqueline stroked her mother's hair, saying *pussy, pussy*. At 1;9(0) she saw a shell and said *cup*. . . . The next day, seeing the same shell she said *glass*, then *cup*, then *hat* and finally *boat in the water*.

Exploring objects that are challenging to understand leads to a sense of mastery and personal competence. Exploratory play also contributes to cognitive development.

In Stage VI, the symbol becomes detached from its original context of meaning and becomes something that, like objects, can be manipulated and explored. Several researchers have developed systems for classifying different levels of symbolic play (see Table 10.1 and 10.2). Although there is no clear-cut age at which infants begin to display a particular level of play, at eighteen months, most babies are entering some of the early stages of pretend play. By the age of two years, most children can execute complex sequences of play requiring multiple symbols and advance planning, such as pretending to cook a whole meal using blocks and pegs to substitute for food and utensils (Belsky & Most, 1981; Nicolich, 1977; Ungerer et al., 1981).

One of the favorite forms of play of children this age involves containers. Children love to put things into containers, and they also enjoy nesting-cup

■ TABLE 10.1   Level of Symbolic Play

1. Presymbolic acts, such as combing one's own hair

2. Self-symbolic acts, such as pretending to be sleeping

3. Object-centered symbolic games, such as feeding a doll

4. Object-combination symbolic games, such as taking a baby doll and a teddy bear for a walk

5. Planned symbolic games, such as saying "let's cook dinner," before actually doing it

SOURCE: Nicolich, 1977.

toys, in which smaller cups are placed inside of successively larger cups. By the age of eighteen months, infants understand the concept of containment as shown by the following experiment. Infants were shown videotapes of sand being poured into cups and tubes. In some cases, the sand poured right through the container and came out the other side (violation condition). In other cases, the sand did not go through the container but filled it up to the rim (nonviolation condition). Only infants older than eighteen months looked longer at the violation condition, suggesting that they found it unusual (Caron, Caron, & Antell, 1988).

On the other hand, when actually presented with a set of nesting cups, children of this age period had trouble stacking them without errors. The infants might combine one or two cups correctly. Then the infants will take a small cup and place it at the large end of their stack. Typically, under twenty-four months, the infants will try to force the cup to fit, perhaps because they see that it might fit if the bottom cup were not in the way. At this point, most infants of this age will actually take the cups apart and start all over again or else just give up: the infants do not attempt alternative solutions, such as simply moving the cup to the other end of the stack (DeLoache et al., 1985).

These studies show that even though infants recognize what is necessary for containment, they have trouble organizing their actions when a series of containers is present. This is similar to the AB̄ error in Stage IV in which infants understand that objects exist when out of sight but persist in searching for them where they were last seen. If they fail, they give up the search. It is not until about two and a half years that infants are able to understand that two objects could have multiple relationships with each other: a cup that won't fit when placed on top of another might fit when placed under the other. When younger infants place one cup on top of another, they fail to realize that the order of placement of the same two cups could be reversed.

Categorization

Even during the first year of life, infants begin to organize the information they see and hear into meaningful groups of items or events. At first, this is done at the level of simple categories: faces, birds, cars and the like. Next, infants group items into higher-level categories, such as animals and vehicles.

■ TABLE 10.2   Levels of Exploratory and Pretend Play

1. Mouthing—indiscriminate mouthing of materials

2. Simple manipulation—visually guided manipulation (excluding indiscriminate banging and shaking) at least 5 seconds in duration that cannot be coded in any other category (e.g., turn over an object, touch and look at an object)

3. Functional—visually guided manipulation that is particularly appropriate for a certain object and involves the intentional extraction of some unique piece of information (e.g., turn dial on toy phone, squeeze piece of foam rubber, flip antenna of Buzy Bee toy, spin wheels on cart, roll cart on wheels)

4. Relational—bringing together and integrating two or more materials in an inappropriate manner, that is, in a manner not initially intended by the manufacturer (e.g., set cradle on phone, touch spoon to stick)

5. Functional-relational—bringing together and integrating two objects in an appropriate manner, that is, in a manner intended by the manufacturer (e.g., set cup on saucer, place peg in hole of pegboard, mount spool on shaft of cart)

6. Enactive naming—approximate pretense activity but without confirming evidence of actual pretense behavior (e.g., touch cup to lip without making drinking sounds, tilting head back, or tipping cup; raise phone receiver in proximity of ear without making talking sounds; touch brush to doll's hair without making combing motions)

7. Pretend self—pretense behavior directed toward self in which pretense is apparent (e.g., raise cup to lip; tip cup, make drinking sounds, or tilt head; stroke own hair with miniature brush; raise phone receiver to ear and vocalize)

8. Pretend other—pretense behavior directed away from child toward other (e.g., feed doll with spoon, bottle, or cup; brush doll's hair; push car on floor and make car noise)

9. Substitution—using a "meaningless" object in a creative or imaginative manner (e.g., drink from seashell; feed baby with stick as "bottle") or using an object in a pretense act in a way that differs from how it is previously used by the child (e.g., use hairbrush to brush teeth after already using it as a hairbrush on self or other)

10. Sequence pretend—repetition of a single pretense act with minor variation (e.g., drink from bottle, give doll drink; pour into cup, pour into plate) or linking together different pretense schemes (e.g., stir in cup, then drink; put doll in cradle, then kiss good night)

11. Sequence pretend substitution—same as sequence pretend except using an object substitution within sequence (e.g., put doll in cradle, cover with green felt piece as "blanket"; feed self with spoon, then with stick)

12. Double substitution—pretense play in which two materials are transformed, within a single act, into something they are not in reality (e.g., treat peg as doll and a piece of green felt as a blanket and cover peg with felt and say "night-night"; treat stick as person and seashell as cup and give stick a drink)

SOURCE: Belsky J. & Most, R., From exploration to play: A cross-sectional study of infant free play behavior, Developmental Psychology, 1981, 17, p. 635. American Psychological Association.

By eighteen months, another important principle of categorization emerges: categorization by sequential order, or by cause and effect. Infants at this age remember items and events better if they are organized into a sequence. For example, in a bath sequence with a teddy bear, the bear's shirt is removed, the bear is put into the tub, the bear is washed, and then it is dried. Infants remembered the exact sequences up to two weeks later whether they were familiar sequences, such as the bath, or unfamiliar, such as events related to a train ride. Some evidence suggests that even when events are not related naturally, infants will remember them by the sequence in which the events were observed (Bauer & Mandler, 1989).

It seems that concepts and memories are organized in terms of some ideas the infant has about how the events are related to each other in time. This kind of conceptual organization has been called a *script* (Nelson, 1978). Scripts become increasingly important as ways of representing complex aspects of reality, such as remembering to get dressed, eat, get in the car, get out of the car, walk inside the day-care center, take off one's coat, and go to one's assigned area. All of the separate events required to get from bed to the day-care center would be difficult to remember if they were not organized into expectable sequences of events. Thus, although two-year-olds cannot memorize long lists of new words or concepts, they can execute complex sequences of related actions.

The Emergence of a Sense of Self

With the advent of script-based conceptual memory, infants are now able to categorize and remember sequences of events that are most familiar to them. Among such sequences are the actions performed and the feelings experienced by the children themselves over time. The self is what emerges out of the conceptual unification of sequences of individual experiences. It is not surprising, therefore, that other measures of self-concept show dramatic changes between eighteen and twenty-four months.

One method that has been developed to study the emergence of the self is to observe infants' reactions to their own mirror images (Lewis & Brooks-Gunn, 1979). Initially, infants are put in front of the mirror for a few minutes. Even young infants will show interest in the mirror image, touching the mirror or parts of themselves, smiling and showing other emotions. After this period of free play with the mirror, the experimenter removes the infants and pretends to wipe their faces with a cloth. In actuality, the experimenter dabs a bit of red rouge on the infants' noses without the babies realizing it. Then, the babies are returned to the mirror. If the infants recognize that the mirror image is of themselves they will touch their own noses, but not the mirror image nose.

By twenty-four months, the majority of children will touch their own noses after seeing the red spot. Table 10.3 describes the steps in the infant's development of self-recognition. Researchers refer to this achievement of self-recognition as the *existential self,* the notion that the self can be recognized and can be distinguished from others. In the next chapter, we'll discuss the emergence of a more conceptual sense of self. The *categorical self,* or self-concept, emerges when children can identify their own membership in one or more categories, such as, "I am a boy," "I am a brother," "I am not a baby" (Harter, 1983).

Recall that babies during the first year are able to form simple mental categories: they can recognize male versus female faces and infants compared to older children and adults. It is curious that it takes until the third year for this conceptual skill to be applied to the self. One research study on the

■ TABLE 10.3   Stages in the Development of the Existential Self, the Ability to Recognize the Physical Features of the Self

BEHAVIORS	APPROXIMATE AGE IN MONTHS	INTERPRETATION
EMERGENCE OF SELF AS SUBJECT, AS ACTIVE, INDEPENDENT, CASUAL AGENT		
I. Interest in mirror image; regards, approaches, touches, smiles, vocalizes. Does not differentially respond to self vs. other in mirror, videotape, or pictorial representation.	5–8	No evidence that self is perceived as a casual agent, independent of others. No featural differentiation between self and other.
II. Understands nature of reflective surface: contingency play, imitation, rhythmic movements, bouncing, waving; can locate objects in space, attached to body. Differentiates between contingent and noncontingent videotape representations of self	9–12	Active agent in space emerges, awareness of cause-effect relationship between own body movements and moving visual image.
III. Uses mirror to locate people/objects in space. Reaches toward person, not image, and reaches toward object not attached to body. Distinguishes between self movement and movement of others on videotape.	12–15	Self-other differentiation with regard to agency. Appreciates self as an active, independent, agent separate from others, who can also cause their own movements in space.
EMERGENCE OF SELF AS AN OBJECT OF ONE'S KNOWLEDGE		
IV. In mirror and videotape, demonstrates mark-directed behavior, sees image and touches rouge on nose. Points to self. Distinguishes between self and other in pictorial representation and videotape.	15–18	Featural recognition of self; internal schema for own face that can be compared to external visual image.
V. Verbal labeling: infant can state name, attach appropriate personal pronoun to own image in mirror. Can distinguish self from same-gender infant in pictures and can label self.	18–24	Appreciation that one has unique featural attributes that can be verbally labeled as the self.

SOURCE: Harter, S. Developmental perspectives on the self-system. In E.M. Hetherington (Ed.) *Handbook of Child Psychology* (Vol. 4), 1983, p. 283. New York: Wiley.

application of such concepts to self and to mother gives some insight into why it takes babies so long to discover themselves.

In this study (Pipp et al., 1987), infants were given the standard rouge test on themselves and also on their mothers. A number of different self and other recognition tasks were given to the children as well (see Table 10.4). (As an aside, these tasks are great fun to do with babies of this age.) In addition to these recognition tasks, infants were asked to perform actions either on a doll, on themselves, or on their mothers. An example would be pretend feeding the doll or self or pretend feeding the mother.

The results show that before eighteen months, infants were able to correctly recognize their mothers and respond correctly to questions about mother at ages earlier than for themselves. This is consistent with studies of concept development done in the first year: infants are able to recognize the

■ TABLE 10.4   Self and Other Physical Feature Recognition Tasks

INFANT VERSION	MOTHER VERSION
Infant touches own nose with rouge after seeing self in mirror	Infant touches mother's nose with rouge after seeing mother in mirror
Where's (child's name)?	Where's mommy?
Who's that? (said while pointing to child)	Who's that? (said while pointing to mother)
Whose shoe is that? (said while pointing to child's shoe)	Whose shoe is that? (said while pointing to mother's shoe)
Are you a boy or a girl?	Is mommy a boy or a girl?

SOURCE: Pipp, et al., 1987.

common features of objects and group them into categories. Before eighteen months, on the other hand, infants were more successful at performing actions on themselves or the doll than on the mother.

This study suggests that there are different ways of knowing the self and knowing the other. Knowledge of action sequences is easier to conceptualize for the self, but knowledge of features is easier for the other. This may be because infants have more experience with their own actions than with images of themselves. As their cognitive ability to remember and conceptualize longer sequences of action emerges in the form of whole scripts, it may be that infants can then link this action knowledge with knowledge of their own features.

From this perspective, the emergence of the self-concept between eighteen and twenty-four months is the result of the linking of two different kinds of knowledge into a single unified representation. At the same time the infants come to realize that their own features go together with their own action, they also recognize that the same is true for their mothers. Thus, self-concept and other-concept achieve similar levels of consistency by the age of two years (Pipp et al., 1987).

■ EMOTIONAL DEVELOPMENT

These more complex event memories and concepts, and the ability to think symbolically, account for some of the changes in emotional development during this period of infancy.

How Does Symbolic Thought Affect the Child's Emotional Experiences?

The ability to form mental images and create symbols increases the range of the infant's emotional experiences. In the previous stage, fear, for example, could be triggered by a concrete event that might remind the infant of a related and unpleasant past event. Seeing someone in a white coat might remind the infant of a doctor and cause the infant to become frightened and cry.

In Stage VI, fear can be evoked by a symbolic mental image like a monster or the thought of being sucked down the drain of a sink. Starting at this age, children develop fears of the dark and of things that might lurk behind doors, refrigerators, and other unseen places (Sroufe, 1979). Dreams, which at this age begin to take on representational forms that can be remembered and talked about, also can be the source of fears, although nightmares do not seem to appear until after the second birthday (Piaget, 1962; see Chapter 11 of this book). Piaget reported observing instances of dreaming in one child as young as twenty-one months; she called out the names of several of her friends in the middle of the night and on one occasion said, "Pussy's hiding."

Symbolic skills also increase the probability that infants will talk about their emotions. Indeed by twenty months, about one-third of all children will talk about one or more of the following states: sleep/fatigue (tired), pain (ouch), distress (sad), disgust (yuk), affection (love mommy), and value (good/bad) (Bretherton et al., 1986; Ridgeway et al., 1985). By the age of twenty-four months, infants engage in conversations about their feelings, they talk about the causes of their feelings, and they play games with siblings in which they pretend to have certain kinds of feelings (Dunn et al., 1987). These types of conversations are illustrated in the Observation Box.

■ OBSERVATION:
Communicative
Behavior between
Siblings
(Dunn et al., 1987)

OBSERVATION 3

Family M., child 24 months: Baby sibling is crying after child knocked him (accidentally). Mother comes into room.
Child: Poor Thomas.
Mother: What?
Child: I banged his head.
Mother: You banged it?
Child: Yes.
Mother: Are you going to kiss it?
Child: Yes.
Mother: Kiss his head.

OBSERVATION 4

Family Th., child 24 months: Older sibling has been showing child a book with pictures of monsters. Child leaves sibling and goes to Mother.
Child: Mummy, Mummy. (whines)
Mother: What's wrong.
Child: Frighten.
Mother: The book?
Child: Yes.
Mother: It's not frightening you!
Child: Yes!
Mother: It did, did it?
Child: Yes.

How Does the Concept of the Self Affect Emotional Experience?

What kind of emotion might you expect infants to display when they finally begin to recognize themselves in the mirror and touch the rouge spot on their own noses? Lewis, Sullivan, Stanger, and Weiss (1989) found that the primary emotion experienced is embarrassment. They compared infants' reactions to the mirror with infants' reactions to an unfamiliar adult. To the adult, the predominant expression was wariness, defined as an attentive look, a sober facial expression, a cessation of ongoing action or vocalization, followed by a gaze aversion. To the mirror, infants were embarrassed, as shown by a smiling facial expression, followed by a gaze aversion and movement to touch the hair, hands, or face in a self-conscious manner.

Similar feelings of self-awareness are generated in a more positive way when infants see themselves as effective and competent individuals able to learn, achieve, and have an impact on others. The resultant positive emotion, based on a budding sense of self-awareness, is *pride*. In previous stages, children expressed enjoyment at being a cause, at being contingent, and at having an effect on others. In this stage, the feeling of pride is the result of meeting their own standards, as well as the awareness of having accomplished a personal goal.

At the end of the second year, the infants' predominant emotional expression is smiling and laughter (Malatesta et al., 1989). Some of these expressions are for the self, that is, they might occur in the absence of other people during toy play. Other smiles are clearly intended by infants to be communicative to other people. The babies will look around, and if someone is watching, they will smile at them. If someone is not watching, the infants will not smile (Jones & Raag, 1989).

In the realm of *anger*, a growing sense of independence and a feeling that the self is separate from others leads to feelings of *defiance, negativism,* and *aggression* (Sroufe, 1979). These feelings, which arise out of earlier feelings of anger provoked by frustration or the immediate situation, are due more to the *mental idea* that the self is and should be independent. Defiance of parents is one way infants experience themselves—one way in which they make a private declaration of self-sufficiency. Thus in Stage VI, anger is no longer a private response to an unyielding situation; it becomes a communication tool used willfully to affect other people. It is, therefore, one of the first signs of the child's sense of personal autonomy and signals the first break in the cycle of initial dependency.

How Do Infants of This Age Cope with Stress?

In this period, infants are better able to tolerate strong emotions by regulating their behavior. For example, an experimenter while talking with a child placed an attractive toy on the table. The experimenter then told the child that she (the experimenter) had to go out of the room to get something and asked the child to please wait and not to touch the toy. By age two years, children could wait on average for a full minute before being tempted to touch the toy, a long time for a two-year-old (Vaughn et al., 1984).

At this age, children come to rely on their teddy bears and favorite blankets to comfort themselves in stressful situations and when their parents are not around. Studies compared the behavior of children who were attached to a blanket with others who were not (Passman, 1977; Passman & Weisberg, 1975). The children ranged in age from twenty to forty months, and each was observed in a novel play situation with either their mother, their blanket, a favorite toy, or no available objects. There were no differences in exploratory behavior or in the amount of distress between children with their mothers present and blanket-attached children with their blankets. Children in these two situations performed considerably better (had more exploratory play and less distress) than either nonblanket-attached children with their blankets, all children with only a favorite toy, or children without any objects.

It seems that a two-year-old's attachment to a blanket may serve as an effective substitute for a mother, at least for brief periods. There are a number of reasons why this might be true. Blankets are soft and cuddly, and they also carry plenty of familiar smells that may remind the child of the comforts of home and impart an increased sense of security.

Some students of child development have suggested that children's reliance on blankets as sources of comfort comes at a time when they are becoming aware of their physical and psychological separateness from the care giver. Although this sense of self as an independent individual does not fully take hold until the third year of life (see Chapter 11), the end of the second year can be thought of as an important transitional phase in the growth of independence. The blanket and other such attachment objects therefore have been called *transitional objects* (Mahler et al., 1975; Winnicott, 1971), because they seem to serve as an intermediate bridge between a child's total reliance and dependence on the mother and the development of individuation.

Not all children develop blanket attachments. In countries where there is relatively more physical contact between infants and care givers, there is less likely to be a blanket attachment (Super, 1981). In a study of Italian children, only 4.9 percent of rural children had transitional object attachments, whereas 31.1 percent of urban children in Rome had them (Gaddini, 1970). Hong and Townes (1976) found that Korean infants used transitional objects less than a matched sample of U.S. infants; Caudill and Weinstein (1969; see also Chapter 6) reported less sucking on fingers and pacifiers in the relatively more indulged (compared with Americans) Japanese infants. It seems that in societies in which children have continued access to physical contact, there is little need for transitional objects.

What Happens to Children during Separations from Their Primary Care Givers?

We already know that when even very young infants are left in the company of substitute, familiar care givers, few problems are seen. Infants quickly adapt to the new situation, and they seem to be able to use the familiar substitute as a secure base for exploration, as well as a source of support and comfort. This is true even though infants almost always prefer their mothers when given the choice (see Chapter 9).

By the end of the second year, infants take their own initiatives in separating from the parents. Ley and Koepke (1982) found that infants of this age observed with their parents in a public park were not afraid to wander at some distance from the parents. Although males left the parents' side more often than females, there were no significant sex differences in how far the children went or how much total time they spent at a distance.

The situation is different, however, when it is the parents who initiate a separation. This could happen for many reasons. The parents may want to go out in the evening, or they may need to travel away from the child for several days. This is often the age when mothers go into the hospital to have a second child. Other separation occasions include a parents' business trips and even brief hospitalizations for a child who is ill or needs an operation.

Research suggests that separation episodes are more tolerable to the infant if the parent prepares the child for them beforehand. In one study (Weinraub & Lewis, 1977) children were least upset during the separation if the mother explained that she would be leaving and gave the child instructions on what to do in her absence. This was especially true for children who were more developmentally advanced and who could understand better the mother's instructions. It also seemed to help the child during the separation if the mother spent more time at a distance, and less time in close physical contact with the infant, in the three minutes just prior to the departure.

A somewhat contradictory finding was reported by Adams and Passman (1981). They found that the longer a mother spent in preparing a child for separation (seventy seconds versus ten seconds), the less content the child remained during the separation. It could be, however, that mothers in the Adams and Passman study who were assigned to the seventy-second preparation condition also spent more time in close contact with the infant before departure.

In a related study (Lollis, 1990), mothers were instructed to be extremely brief in separating from their infants. They were told to say only, "I'm going to leave for a little while. You stay here and play until I come back." These departures took only about twenty seconds. Another group of mothers was asked to take leave of the infants quickly, but no instructions were given about what the mothers should say. These uninstructed mothers took a bit longer but prepared the infants for the separation more thoroughly. The infants of the uninstructed mothers fared better during the separation, similar to those in the Weinraub and Lewis study. This suggests that it is not the duration of leave taking but rather how well the infant is prepared by the parent during this time that is the important factor.

Several other related findings are of interest here. Infants are more predisposed to separate from parents if they are dropped off at a familiar day-care setting or preschool, due primarily to the presence of peers already in the setting (Gunnar, Senior, & Hartup, 1984). This suggests that the environment in which the child is left is an important factor in regulating separation protest. Other research has shown that when infants are left at the preschool or day-care setting, they show more protest if their mothers dropped them off than if their fathers did. Mothers took longer to leave the children, compared to the fathers (Field, Gewirtz, Cohen, Garcia, Greenberg, & Collins, 1984).

The best way for parents to prepare their two-year-olds for a brief separation is to avoid close contact just before they leave, give the children some concrete suggestions about what they might do while the parents are gone, and try to tailor speech to the comprehension level of the infants. Even with this advice for parents, and even with the knowledge that children of this age do quite well in brief separations, it is still difficult for parents to leave their babies alone in a strange place with a new baby-sitter or to go out on their own for the first time. No matter how hard parents try to prepare themselves and their children, it is almost inevitable that the children will get upset as soon as they understand that their parents are *actually* leaving. There is little in the annals of parenthood that is more emotionally wrenching than the painful wails of a child being left behind.

One additional finding of the Weinraub and Lewis (1977) study should provide at least a small measure of comfort to parents or prospective parents. They discovered that the infant's immediate response to the parent's departure was not correlated with anything the parent said or did. Only after this initial response, when the infant finally calmed down, did the baby's behavior begin to reflect the efforts of the parent's work at preparation. Indeed, it seems common for babies of this age to protest loudly during the actual departure of the parent. As soon as it is clear that these protests are ineffective, the two-year-old generally is capable of quieting down and even enjoying the substitute care giver.

Perhaps the most striking demonstration of this was offered by Robertson and Robertson (1971) in their study of children left by their parents in a British residential nursery for several days. The children were provided with a warm and affectionate substitute care giver. Some of the younger children showed almost no signs of distress or despair, and they gradually became attached to the substitute. Some of the older children in their study—the four-year-olds—started off their stay with some sadness and a lowered tolerance for frustration, but they were able to use the foster parent to sustain their feelings, and their intimacy with her increased over time. All the children in the study greeted their parents warmly upon their return. The Robertsons found that it was not the separation *per se* that caused the problems but the psychosocial environment of the situation in which the child was left. Similar findings have been reported for infants institutionalized over the long term and infants in foster-care situations by Tizard and Rees (1974) and Tizard and Tizard (1971). The lack of social interaction in the institution was the most important factor accounting for the delayed or disturbed development of some institutionalized infants.

■ SOCIAL AND LANGUAGE DEVELOPMENT

The period between eighteen and twenty-four months is marked by a number of important changes in language, due in part to the child's more conceptual and symbolic forms of cognition. The main advance in language is the emergence of the sentence. Correlational studies show that sentences emerge at about the same age (on the average, about twenty months) when children begin to pursue objects after multiple hidings, when they use tools in deliberate ways, when they begin symbolic play, when they can combine symbolic objects and gestures in novel ways and classify objects by sorting, and when they can solve complex problems mentally without trial-and-error behavior (Bates et al., 1987; McCune-Nicolich, 1981; Piaget, 1962; Shore, 1986; Sugarman, 1982; Zachry, 1978).

The onset of sentences with a series of words parallels the emergence of the use of a series of related gestures to communicate meaning (Acredolo & Goodwin, 1988; Lock, 1980; McCune-Nicolich, 1981). An example would be pulling on mother's skirt, lifting one's arms up, looking distressed, and perhaps saying "Mommy up." The pragmatic view of language development, discussed in the last chapter, suggests that language serves one main purpose for young children: to communicate their intentions. As children develop cognitively, they discover better ways to get their point across to others. During the illocutionary stage, children relied on the context or situation, intonation patterns, and interpreting adults to communicate their meanings with single words.

In the *locutionary* phase, children discover they can create new meanings simply by changing *the order in which several words are spoken together*. When gestures and words first are used in intentional communication, they are a direct extension of some sensorimotor act of the child. These *idiosyncratic* gestures only gradually develop into *conventional* signs. We see a parallel development in the realm of grammar or syntax: the first two-word combinations are idiosyncratic usages that only later become conventionalized in the form of adult syntax (see Table 10.5).

The transition from single to multiword speech is not as abrupt as it might seem. Around the age of eighteen to twenty months, infants undergo a large burst of new word learning, a vocabulary spurt. Just before the spurt, a child may know as few as fifty words. A few weeks later, the same child might know as many as four hundred words! The interesting fact about this spurt is that many of the new words are not nouns used for naming, but they are adjectives (pretty, hot, dirty) and verbs (play, kiss, go) (Bates et al., 1987). When children use a verb or an adjective, it suggests that they are referring not simply to the word itself but to several words or things.

When children under eighteen months say "shoe," they may be referring to shoe in the form of simply naming. After eighteen months they may point to the shoe and say "dirty" or "mommy." This type of behavior could be paraphrased into multiword speech as "the shoe is dirty" or "this is mommy's shoe." It seems, therefore, that just before the acquisition of multiword speech, infants begin to use single words in more complex ways that suggest a subject and a predicate (Bates et al., 1987; Greenfield & Smith, 1976; Lock, 1980).

According to Braine (1976), the child's first multiword utterances are not as sophisticated as adult grammar. Apparently, children first learn to use word

■ **TABLE 10.5 Development of Conventionalized Semantics and Syntax**

AGE	SEMANTICS	SYNTAX
9 to 12 months	Sensorimotor gestures	
12 to 18 months	Idiosyncratic words (symbols)	
19 to 24 months	Conventional words (signs)	Idiosyncratic word order
Over 24 months		Conventional word order

order to express meanings by learning a fairly limited set of speech patterns. These speech patterns are better thought of as *formulas* than as sentences: children seem to learn a particular kind of word sequencing in which they can "fill in the blanks" to vary the meaning of the phrase. Table 10.6 gives these early formulas, along with their meanings and some examples of each.

Slobin (1970) reported formulas similar to those found in Table 10.6 for children from six different language groups. For example, "more milk" is found in Germany as "mehr Milch," in Russia as "yesche moloka," and in Finland as "lisaa kakkua." Similar patterns can be seen in the first word combinations of deaf children learning to use sign language. Dale (1976) found hand signs that could be interpreted as *daddy work* ("daddy is at work") and *Barry train* (referring to a brother's train) in a language-learning deaf child.

The speech examples in Table 10.6 are called *telegraphic speech*, because they usually seem to leave out small words such as prepositions and word endings such as *ing, -'s* and *ed*, which add additional refinements to the

■ TABLE 10.6   Early Two-Word Combinations

FUNCTION	FORMULA	EXAMPLE
Drawing attention to something	*see* + X *here* + X	see car here milk
Object's properties	*big/little* + X *hot* + X *old* + X	big house hot pipe old cookie
Possession	X + Y	doggy hold pig tail Kendall birthday
Plurality	number + X	two book
Recurrence	*more* + X *other* + X	more raisins other hand
Disappearance	*all gone* + X *all done* + X	all gone airplane all done juice
Negation	*no* + X *not* + X	no water not eat
Actor-action relations		sits doll sleeps baby Kendall break Mommy hit Kendall
Location	X + preposition	rock outside milk in there milk in cup
Request	*want* + X	want dessert want get down

SOURCE: Braine, M. Children's first word combinations. *Monographs of the Society for Research in Child Development*, 1976, 164, p. 56-57.

meaning of words and sentences. Usually, simpler endings such as *ing*, the plural -*s*, and the possessive -'*s* are learned first, followed by the relatively more difficult use of the verb *to be* with all its tenses, auxiliaries, and contractions (deVilliers & deVilliers, 1973).

Two Types of Speech Style

While these syntactic refinements are taking place, children continue to develop a vocabulary. This means increasing the number of conventional words they know how to use and learning to refine the meanings of the words that have been overextended or used incorrectly in the past. According to Nelson (1981), young children show two distinct styles of vocabulary acquisition: *referential speech* and *expressive speech*. Differences between referential and expressive word use are summed up in Table 10.7.

Some examples of expressive language are "I don't want it," "Don't do it," "I'll get it," and "I don't know where it is." These phrases have the characteristics of being spoken as a single word, since the individual words are poorly articulated. There is no evidence that the use of either of these styles of language acquisition relates to later behavior in any way. Indeed, they both may be used by the *same* child in different contexts, for example, in referential versus interpersonal situations (Nelson, 1981). Some studies have shown that as children get older, they tend to favor one style over another—a more social-oriented versus object-oriented approach—although the evidence is based almost entirely on case studies.

Children's use of one or the other style may reflect the speech spoken to them. If a care giver responds to questions by clearly labeling objects, the child may focus more on individual words. If the care giver uses social control language like "D'ya wanna go out" or "I dunno where it is," the child is likely to hear these as whole phrases rather than single words.

■ TABLE 10.7   Two Styles of Word Use in Infancy

ATTRIBUTE	REFERENTIAL SPEECH	EXPRESSIVE SPEECH
Word type	Object names	Social routines
Part of speech	Nouns	Pronouns
Syntax	Single words	Phrases
Size of vocabulary	Large	Small
Content	Substantive	Relational
Production	Original	Imitative
Articulation	Clear	Mumbled
Situational	Referential	Interpersonal
Context	As in reading books	As in free social play

SOURCE: Nelson, K. Individual differences in language development: Implications for development and language. *Developmental Psychology*, 1981, *17*, p. 170-187. Adapted American Psychological Association.

Relationship Between Language Development and the Social Environment

It is extremely rare for adults to directly correct children's language errors. What do adults actually say and do that might be conducive to the development of speech? One major trend that occurs is an increasing reliance on verbal suggestions and commands, as compared to nonverbal gestures, in the last half of the second year. When this happens, mothers tend to emphasize two basic verbal forms: requests and comments. A study done in Brazil found that requests may include asking for information through what and where questions (What's this? Where's the doggie?). Mothers also request the children to speak about something (Talk to daddy on the telephone. Tell me what you saw in the park.). Comments are responses to the children's utterances or attempts to initiate a conversation (Yes, that's an apple. The duck is swimming. This is the same car we saw the other day.) (Stella-Prorok, 1983).

Similar patterns were found in a study of picture book reading of middle-class mothers in Israel (Ninio, 1983). Mothers referred to pictures with simple labeling, with what questions (What's that? What does the doggie say?), and with elicitation of pointing by the children using where questions (Where's the kitty?). Mothers also imitated their infants' utterances. Imitation was most likely to occur when the child made an error of pronunciation. Rather than correct the child's speech, the mother simply imitated the correct pronunciation. (Bohannon & Stanowicz, 1988).

There is only indirect evidence that these methods actually promote speech development from research in which the total amount of maternal speech is measured, although it is generally the case that mothers who talk more to their infants have infants who are more advanced linguistically (Sigman et al., 1988; Tomasello et al., 1986). More to the point, if mothers time their verbal inputs to those instances in which the infants are looking at them or at an object, infants develop higher language production scores compared to situations in which the mothers first attract the children's attention to an object and then comment on it (Harris et al., 1985; Schachter, 1979; Tomasello & Farrar, 1986; Whitehurst et al., 1988).

In general, adult speech that is more responsive to the child's focus of interest and the use of the child's interest to achieve a joint focus of attention before talking lead to greater linguistic competence in the child (Hoff-Ginsberg, 1986; Hoff-Ginsberg & Shatz, 1982; Olson et al., 1984; Papousek et al., 1985; Snow, 1984). To the extent that maternal speech around the world shares some of the characteristics mentioned above, then it is likely to be the particular style of speaking to the child, rather than simply the amount of child-directed speech, that is the important factor.

The use of requests and comments as the primary mode of maternal speech may also be understood from the results of a study on infant imitation of adult actions during the period from eighteen to twenty-four months (Hay et al., 1985). Infants were shown how to use a party hat as a horn or as a shoe and how to use a string of beads as a telephone or as a comb. There was a much greater tendency to imitate adults' novel actions using these objects if the adults explained in words what they were doing (I think you need a new shoe. Here's a pretty new shoe!). Thus, verbal requests for action, when embedded into an action sequence, are more likely to be acted on by the child, thus providing more opportunities for direct learning experiences.

Guided Participation Between Infants and Adults

These studies on linguistic interaction reflect some more general patterns of adult-infant communication that emerge around this age. In most interactions, adult and infant are working on something together, but each has a different purpose. The adult is intent perhaps on instructing the child in the culturally appropriate uses of words and of objects. The child is perhaps more motivated by being a direct participant in the social world. The concept of *guided participation* reflects the active role that children take in observing and participating in the organized activities of the family and society in the company of adults (Rogoff, 1990). Although from the adult's perspective, the child is merely "playing games" or "playing at" cooking or taking care of a doll, from the child's perspective, the child is actually doing the task as an active participant.

Typically, in adult-child interactions, the children set the agenda for what they want to do and for how much they want to be involved. The more skilled partner collaborates in the child's goals by giving the child responsibility for certain actions that are part of the larger task but within the range of the child's competence. The adult also must constrain the child's participation for the sake of the child's, or of other's, safety or rights. Eventually, the adult transfers responsibility for larger segments of the task to the child, in relation to the growth of the child's competence as assessed by the adult (Bruner, 1983; Heckhausen, 1988; Kaye, 1982; Lock, 1980; Rogoff, 1990). These points are summarized in Table 10.8.

There are cultural differences in styles of guided participation. In one study (Rogoff et al., 1989), mothers from the United States were compared with Mayan Indian mothers from Guatemala on how they helped their twenty-month-old children to use a set of nesting dolls. The U.S. mothers acted more like peers, wanting to take turns in combining dolls and commenting on the process. These mothers took seriously their roles as teachers. The Mayan mothers retained more of an adult-child status differential. They assumed the children would eventually learn the task. They monitored the children's progress and gave verbal instructions, but they did not get very involved in the task.

■ TABLE 10.8   Components of Guided Participation between
                Adults and Young Children

Child sets the agenda according to interest and skill level

Adult adjusts level of child's participation according to child's skill

Adult constrains child's participation for the safety and rights of others

Adult transfers responsibility to child according to ongoing assessment of child's abilities

---

SOURCE: Rogoff, 1990.

Picture book reading is a particularly good setting for guided participation in language development.

One U.S. mother tried to play games with the dolls, then offered them to the child for "his turn." She gave instructions (Put the lid on) and then cheered when the child did this (Yeah! You're so smaaart!). This mother tried to change the agenda when she judged that the baby's attention waned. She commented on all the child's actions and made requests for actions through the task.

A typical Mayan mother demonstrated how the dolls come apart and go back together, using a few words to encourage the child to look. The baby wanted to handle the doll, but soon after, the mother took it back and again demonstrated how to do it. She pointed out the features of the task verbally as she performed the action. After that, she let the infant try for some time on his own, while she watched but did not intervene. When he ran into trouble, the mother would say something to help (Do this one first). When the child made a successful move, the mother would simply say "Okay" or "I see" in a quiet tone.

Both of these cases illustrate the general principles of guided participation listed in Table 10.8, but each is very different from the other. As for language, it is generally true that when adults become collaborators or participants in what children spontaneously seem interested in doing, children can achieve higher levels of play and cognitive development compared to when adults do not become involved (O'Connell & Bretherton, 1984; Slade, 1987a; Zukow, 1980).

The Development of Discipline and Compliance

As it turns out, these basic principles of guided participation and collaboration in infants' activities are the foundation for effective discipline of children at this age. These principles include adjusting one's actions to the child's agenda and providing clear guides to adult standards for the child to learn (Gordon, 1988; Rocissano et al., 1987).

Research suggests that the most effective forms of parental discipline combine both empathy and firmness (Baumrind, 1973). Care givers should be sensitive to the reasons for the child's behavior and to the natural negative reactions children are likely to have when restrictions are imposed. The most successful discipliners in Baumrind's studies were firm in their demands and appropriately expressive of their own angry or distressed reactions to the child's behavior. These kinds of parents, which Baumrind called *authoritative parents*, had children who showed purposive, independent behavior; were cooperative with adults; showed friendliness to peers; and were competent in their dealings with the environment. The key, therefore, seems to be a combination of both love and control.

Unfortunately, these studies offer few specific recommendations for how parents can get young children to comply with their wishes. In one of the few studies on compliance actually involving twenty-four-month-olds, Schaffer and Crook (1979, 1980) asked mothers to try to get their babies to play with *all* the toys that were set out in a laboratory free-play situation. They distinguished three types of compliance.

Orientation compliance refers to the mothers' ability to get infants to look where they wanted them to. Mothers succeeded in this about 50 percent of the time on the first try. It helped if they used a nonverbal gesture. Almost all the mothers succeeded in getting orientation compliance if they persisted long enough.

Contact compliance refers to getting children to touch a designated toy. First-time success rates ran at 33 percent. In this case, success was more likely if the children were already looking at the toy, either because of their own interest or as a result of orientation compliance.

Task compliance is shown when an infant manipulates a toy in an appropriate manner. It occurred only one-fourth of the time, and as you might expect, the likelihood of task compliance was higher if the infant was already looking at and touching the toy.

What conclusions can we draw about compliance from this research? First, it is important to get the child's attention; second, it helps if the child already is starting to do what is wanted. In other words, the mothers in Schaffer and Crook's research made their children look more compliant than they actually were by timing their requests for compliance to coincide with a behavior of the child that was most likely to lead to the desired response.

Benjamin Spock (1957) in *Baby and Child Care* advised control procedures like those found by Schaffer and Crook. If a baby is playing, for example, and you either want to go out, give her a bath, feed her dinner, or anything else, Spock suggest that you sit down on the floor next to the baby and start playing with her! If you only read this far, you would have to classify Spock as overly permissive. He continues to say, however, that the parent should become part of the baby's play for a few minutes to maneuver the game to a logical conclusion. An example would be to pick up the ball the baby is playing with, roll it back and forth with her a few times, tap it playfully on her stomach and nose, and then pick up the baby with a tickle, to be carried to the dinner table or bathtub. In this way, Spock argued, a parent can skillfully change the baby's goals without causing a confrontation.

The importance of these recommendations was confirmed in a study by Holden (1983). Unobtrusive observations were made of twenty-four middle-class mothers and their two-year-old infants in the supermarket. What were mothers' strategies in dealing with undesired behavior, such as asking for food, reaching for things, standing in the cart, and ignoring the mothers' requests? One group of mothers used "contingent" responses; that is, they scolded or reprimanded the infant after the transgression had occurred. The other group of mothers used "preventive" responses, such as talking to the child while shopping and giving the child something to eat. The mothers who used preventive measures had children who showed fewer instances of undesired behavior. When it comes to discipline and compliance in the second year, prevention is the best cure.

Holden (1985) suggests that preventive measures fall under the heading of *parental proactive behavior*, including any action that has the goal of a positive outcome for the child. Table 10.9 lists some examples of proactive behavior used by adults. This approach to discipline suggests that one may avoid potential problems in proactively controlling or regulating access to the environment. In a healthy, safe, and developmentally appropriate environment, infants have fewer opportunities to get into danger or out of control.

Finally, it is worth noting that even though infants of this age want to try things out for themselves and often resist parental requests that directly interfere with their own actions, the infants also have a strong desire to be part of the social group and to join in with whatever adults might be doing. Infants are attracted to objects that adults are handling and want to do the same, and they seem to think that most household tasks the adult is doing are

■ **TABLE 10.9   Examples of Parental Proactive Behavior**

TYPE	SHORT-TERM	LONG-TERM
Direct	Occupy with activities	Take child on an outing
	Divert attention	Train child to be wary of dangers
	Engage child in game	Organize peer groups
	Prepare verbally about upcoming situations	Select a day-care center
	Set limits in advance	
	Monitor child's action when danger is present	
Indirect	Place child in car seat	Buy a home in a neighborhood conducive to child's development
	Dress child appropriately for weather	Build a fence to keep child from danger
	Use night light	Keep poisons locked up
	Serve appropriate foods	Purchase safe toys and furniture

SOURCE: Holden, 1985.

fun and want to join in (Hay et al., 1985; Rheingold, 1982; Rheingold et al., 1987). Rather than ignoring or complaining about the children being nuisances for interfering in the adult's work, adults can encourage children to collaborate with the adults by giving them small tasks. This requires the adults to slow down and think about how to best include the children's efforts (Rogoff, 1990).

Compliance is more easily assured if it is clear to the infants that the expected behavior affects how they relate to others and how their behavior affects others. For this to happen, verbal skills are necessary, and indeed, compliance to requests is correlated with verbal development (McLaughlin, 1983; Schneider-Rosen & Wenz-Gross, 1990); Vaughn et al., 1984).

Peer Interactions

The last aspect of social development that we will discuss in this chapter is the change in the child's relationship to peers at this age. When given a choice of who to play with, infants almost always choose a peer—familiar or unfamiliar—over their mothers. They spend more time with the peer and make fewer bids for their mother's attention when a peer is present (Rubenstein, Howes, & Pedersen, 1982). In a day-care setting, a similar pattern can be seen: two-year-olds spend more time with one another than with teachers (Finkelstein, Dent, Gallacher, & Ramey, 1978).

When the tables are turned and the adult is with an adult peer while the child is not, the child increases the number of bids for attention and close contact. In fact, the child is more demanding of the mother's attention when she is with a friend than when the mother and child are home alone (Rubenstein et al., 1982). This finding should come as no surprise to any parent who has tried to carry on a conversation with a friend while the baby is around.

We saw in previous chapters that toddler-peer play is different in quality from toddler-parent play. Studies of nineteen-month-olds show that this same trend continues with age. Toddlers are more likely to play with, imitate, offer toys to, and talk to peers than to their mothers, although they touch both peers and mothers about the same amount of time (Rubenstein & Howes, 1976). When they play with their mothers, toddlers are more likely to have longer periods of sustained attention to single objects (Cohen & Tomlinson-Keasey, 1980).

Sometime between eighteen and twenty-four months, peer play begins to take on a more game-like quality. Children take simple turns involving complementary roles such as offering and accepting, throwing and catching, or simple verbal exchange (You're a sissy. No, I'm not). Words are used in such games, but not at the same level of elaboration as in adult-infant games. At this age also, there are few instances of actual collaboration on a task, as may be found during adult-infant interaction. Under twenty-four months, peer play seems to rest on the assumption that each child can influence the other, rather than on genuine cooperation (Brownell, 1986; Eckerman et al., 1989). Cooperation and complex verbal exchanges and pretend play with peers will be discussed in the next chapter.

Finally, the types of toys used in peer play influence the types of interactions between the children. Eighteen-month-old infants were observed

By this age, children can cooperate on a common activity and develop sophisticated social pretend games.

playing in pairs in four different play settings: a typical play setting, one with no play materials, one with only small portable toys, and one with only large nonportable play equipment (DeStefano & Mueller, 1982).

In the setting with the large play equipment (ladders, slides, and boxes), the researchers found more sophisticated social interaction and a greater expression of positive affect. With the small portable toys, more conflict and more negative affect was expressed. This is understandable, since children tend to fight over the possession of small toys. With only large toys, children tend to treat the environment as a space to be shared and enjoyed together.

Surprisingly, the children were most creative in the no-toy situation: they actually invented their own toys! The radiator became a "base," they took off articles of clothing to be used as play objects, and they even used each other as if they were toys. Parents tend to introduce toys and other play materials to keep the pace of play up or keep the toddlers out of their way. Perhaps peer interaction provides enough time for the child to be more inventive and develop independent initiatives.

■ FAMILY AND SOCIETY

We devote the Family and Society section of this chapter to some of the ways in which families with infants interface with their communities. Even well-functioning, middle-income families require support from their families and communities. In cases of poverty and other risks to parenting, community support is essential and makes a difference in the outcomes for both parents and children. We'll discuss both informal and formal supports for families with infants.

Informal support systems

Informal support systems are social networks that include friends, relatives, neighbors, co-workers, and other acquaintances, as well as community organizations that are not controlled by government agencies, such as churches, YWCAs, and community centers (Parke & Tinsley, 1987). One of the primary informal support systems is the marriage and extended family.

Research has shown that in two-parent families, the spouse is the most used and effective member of the social network. Spouses can provide relief from child care and consultation about child-rearing issues and can mediate when stresses on the partner predispose the partner toward impatience and harshness toward the children. Spouses can also provide needed encouragement and emotional support to each other (Levitt et al., 1986; Parke & Tinsley, 1987; Weinraub & Wolf, 1983).

Typically, the infant's maternal grandmother is the next most frequent source of support, and this is true for both two-parent and single-parent families. As we discussed in Chapter 8, grandparents who live nearby and spend time with the infants share secure attachments with the infants and provide similar types of support for the parents as a spouse does. The special value of spouses and grandparents is their embeddedness in the family and their willingness to intervene directly into the parent-child relationship. This may take the form of explaining child-rearing principles and mediating between the parent and the infant (Levitt et al., 1986; McLoyd, 1990; Stevens, 1988). Teenage single mothers, both black and white, are less punitive to their infants if the grandmother is involved (see the section in Chapter 3, on adolescent mothers). The teens say things like, "I would hit him more if it weren't for my parents" and "My parents won't let me spank him as often as I think he should be spanked" (McLoyd, 1990, p. 335).

As a general rule, emotional support is correlated with better parenting outcomes, regardless of where the support comes from. Parents, particularly mothers, who receive more support are less likely to be punitive in their child rearing (Colletta, 1981), more likely to play and be affectionate with their infants (Cotterell, 1986), respond more quickly to the babies' cries, and have more secure attachments (Crockenberg, 1987; Crockenberg & McCluskey, 1986), are more nurturant, have more positive attitudes about child rearing (Weinraub & Wolf, 1983), and abuse their infants less (Garbarino, 1976).

Factors mediating the impact of informal support systems

Social attitudes. Unfortunately, however, not all families benefit from social support systems. In some cases, this is due to social attitudes associated with certain types of families and children. For example, studies comparing social support for families with preterm and handicapped infants with families of normal infants find that the latter families receive more social support. Well-functioning, middle-class families with preterm infants report receiving fewer offers of support and gifts, such as clothing and furniture, compared to similar families with full-term infants (Feiring et al., 1987). Even when friends and family provide support to parents of preterm infants, the quality of that support may be diminished. With a preterm birth, network members may not know how to respond appropriately, and their attempts to help result in ambiguous or stressful communications, leading to a lessening of the impact of their support on the family (Zarling et al., 1988). In general, social networks are more supportive if the psychological stress of the parents is relatively low, during times of expected or understandable life transition (such as a temporary job loss or a death in the family), and when the source of stress is a single event rather than a long-term problem (Crnic & Greenberg, 1987; Crockenberg, 1987; Dressler, 1985).

Parental personality. A number of studies have shown that abusive parents have small social networks and an overall poorer quality of support. This may be due in part to the fact that the personality of the abusive parent keeps the child and the social network at a distance. These parents may actively discourage those who seek to help (Crittenden, 1985; Trickett & Susman, 1988). Some parents may have poor interpersonal skills that lead to an inability to seek help and maintain supportive social ties (Parke & Tinsley, 1987). On the other hand, seeking help from family and friends entails some cost in the form of obligations for friendly behavior and for doing favors in return. Some parents may prefer isolation to the burden of these obligations (McLoyd, 1990).

Cultural attitudes about seeking help. Finally, the effects of informal support networks may be lessened if parents distrust the sources of support. Blacks and whites differ in the types of supports that mothers find most useful. For example, black mothers tend to rely more on the extended family for support. They view professionals as unsympathetic and could not reconcile professional advice with family norms and values. White mothers were more likely to rely on professional sources of support (Colletta, 1981; Crockenberg, 1987; Stevens, 1988). These differences may be explained by the fact that most professionals are white and may not appreciate the differences in values between their culture and the minority family culture.

Formal support systems

Formal support systems are structured programs designed to meet the special needs of parents and infants. These include health care, education, counseling services, social services, housing, welfare, and recreational facilities (Parke & Tinsley, 1987). These services range from childbirth education (see Chapter 3) to well-baby care to parent training programs to early childhood education for disadvantaged toddlers. We do not have the space to review the variety of services available and their effects (see Parke & Tinsley, 1987, for a more complete review).

Generally, educational interventions for parents, even in small doses and when combined with health care and income support, can be enormously effective (see the Applications section in this chapter). For well-functioning families, short classes, films, and books can enrich their parenting experiences and give them needed confidence. For families at risk, a more comprehensive effort is most effective. Some of the more successful programs combine preschool education for the infants, a nurse/home visitor for home-based parent education, and an effort to link parents up with other formal and informal community supports (education, job training and placement, recreational facilities, etc.).

One example is the family support intervention program designed by Sally Provence (Provence & Naylor, 1983), and a similar program designed by Tiffany Field and colleagues (Field et al, 1980). The Provence project included a home visitor who served as a counselor and liaison with other agencies, pediatric care, day care, and developmental testing that the parents were able to observe. The families who participated were from a low-income inner-city area, the infants had no birth complications and were first-born, and the mothers had no history of serious psychological illness. A follow-up study of the children ten years after their participation in the program compared the children that were in the program to a matched sample of children who did not attend. The intervention children had better school attendance and required less welfare and special education programming. The mothers were more likely to be economically independent, had completed more years of school, and had fewer children than the control mothers (Seitz et al., 1985).

Head Start is a federally funded national program with goals similar to the other projects mentioned above. Recent long-term follow-up research comparing Head Start children with those who attended other day care or had no support show that Head Start children were more advanced educationally and cognitively; however, the differences between the Head Start and the other groups diminished with increasing age (Lee et al., 1988; 1990). Although the cognitive gains are not impressive, other research shows that fifteen years after Head Start the participating children had fewer teen pregnancies and a higher high school graduation rate, and they were more likely to be employed and less likely to have been arrested (Schweinhart & Weikart, 1979; Berreuta-Clement et al., 1984). Other research shows similar gains for Head Start as found for the Provence program (Lazar & Darlington, 1982). The problem is that these gains may only be true for the most high-quality Head Start programs in which the research is done. On the other hand, everyone agrees that Head Start children have a more enriched early childhood experience and do better in preschool and elementary school than controls. This, it can be argued, is sufficient reason to continue the program.

APPLICATIONS

Poverty and Risk

In 1960, one-quarter of all children in the United States were living in poverty. In 1980, this figure had fallen to 17 percent, and in 1990, it has risen to 20 percent of all children. An increasing proportion of these poor children live in female-headed single families, which today constitute the fastest growing poverty group in the United States (see Figure 10.1). These figures are shocking. They become a matter of national shame when compared to other wealthy nations. When our childhood poverty rate was the lowest, in 1980 at 17 percent, the childhood poverty rate was 10 percent in Canada, 8 percent in West Germany, 5 percent in Sweden, and 11 percent in the United Kingdom (Bane & Ellwood, 1989; Smeeding & Torrey, 1988).

What are some of the causes of these poverty rates and national differences?

Single parenthood

In all countries, as you might expect, single-parent families are poorer than two-parent families because of the reduced earning power of a single adult. In addition, due to the structure of most welfare systems, it is not advantageous for many single mothers to work outside the home because of the added costs and risks of child care.

For example, a single mother with two children in the United States in 1986 could collect $6,284 in welfare and food stamps if she were unemployed. If she worked full-time in a minimum wage job, she would earn a salary of $6,700 and could still collect $2,744 in welfare. By the time she paid for child care (about $3,000) and taxes ($373), her resulting income would be $6,817, only a little over

$500 more than if she were unemployed and stayed home with her children (Bane & Ellwood, 1989).

Diverse populations

In the United States, poverty level varies considerably as a function of race and ethnicity. The percentage of black children living in poverty (the number of poor black children divided by the total number of black children) is three times as high as for white children, and the rate for Hispanic children is twice as high as for white children. Even so, the poverty rate of white children alone (11 percent) is higher than in most other wealthy nations. Thus, not all poverty occurs in minority groups.

Public support for families

In the United States, welfare and other public benefits are given to individuals, not to families. One of the problems is that children do not have their own rights to such benefits. While the poverty rate among the elderly has dropped in recent years due to increased medical and Social Security benefits to individuals, the poverty rate for children has increased. At least 25 percent of families with children living below the poverty level in the United States receive no welfare or other forms of support. This is in comparison to almost 100 percent of poor families receiving benefits in Canada, Germany, Sweden, and the United Kingdom (Smeeding & Torrey, 1989). Contrary to popular belief, one or both parents work in over three-quarters of the poor families with children in the United States. Of the remaining 25 percent of families, 15 percent have parents who do not work because of illness or disability or they are past retirement

APPLICATIONS

age (Bane & Ellwood, 1988). Thus, the welfare system cannot be blamed for keeping families in poverty. Most parents work if they are able to.

The economic system

Since none of the above factors by itself—single parenthood, race and ethnicity, and welfare—can explain why so many families are poor, what does? The best explanation seems to be the economy as a whole. If the economy slows down, middle- and upper-income families fare better than those at the bottom. Lower-income families suffer more from a lack of an annual raise or a loss of a job, since they have no other resources on which to depend.

Analysts suggest some alternatives to welfare that might help these poor families. These alternatives include better tax credits for lower-income families (in the United States, higher-income families receive the most tax credits), a higher minimum wage, better child-care alternatives that are not based on how much money you can afford to pay, and better medical care to alleviate the chronic health problems associated with poverty. Nonwelfare options may also contribute to a better life for such families. These include enforcing child support payments from absent fathers, parent education and job training, and community support and intervention services (Bane & Ellwood, 1988).

How are children affected by living in poor families?

Stresses on adults

Poverty breeds mental and health risks due to an increased and continuous stream of stressful life events, including job loss, worry about bills, eviction, illness, alcoholism and drug dependency, marital discord, assault, arrest, and imprisonment. These factors feed off each other, leading to increasingly dismal cycles of loss, stress, and despair. When these factors are then compounded with racial prejudice and social-class prejudice, the risk to mental health is enormous (McLoyd, 1990).

Effects on children

Due to these stresses, poor parents have been shown to be less emotionally available for their children, less affectionate, harsher in their disciplinary styles, and more likely to respond punitively to relatively minor forms of child misbehavior. In addition, fathers seem particularly affected; they grow more harsh, and many leave the family entirely. On the positive side, however, some families report greater parent-child closeness following job loss and more family solidarity. Evidence from a variety of sources—including the effects of the Great Depression, the experience of inner-city black families and the results of job losses due to farm foreclosures and plant closings in white middle-class America—reveals a surprising pattern of individual variation in family response to poverty, ranging from renewed parent-child closeness to child abuse and neglect (Coles, 1971; Elder et al., 1985; McLoyd, 1990; Perrucci & Targ, 1988; Peterson & Peters, 1985; Portes et al., 1986). Some research even suggests that harsher parental discipline may better prepare children for the hardships they will face growing up in poverty (Sameroff & Seifer, 1983). In general, however, poverty has more negative than positive effects on parent-child relationships.

Children from poor families suffer more from depression, poor peer relations, social withdrawal, low self-esteem, deviant behavior patterns, aggressiveness (particularly in boys), and lowered aspirations (especially for girls).

continued at top of next page

APPLICATIONS

In addition, these children often contract more infectious diseases, they are less skilled verbally and interpersonally, and they do less well in school and on other indices of cognitive development (Bronfenbrenner, 1986; McLoyd, 1990; Patterson et al., 1990; Steinberg et al., 1981).

Conclusions

We have spoken in this section about children in general, but children under the age of three years are disproportionately represented in poverty rates. Because of their relative helplessness and vulnerability, infants may suffer more from the effects of poverty than older children (Bronfenbrenner, 1986).

Consider the following chain of events. A teenage girl or young woman has grown up in an inner-city culture of poverty. She has suffered from parental neglect and malnutrition. Even if she is lucky enough to have escaped physical or sexual abuse, she has been hardened against her own feelings and those of others. She gets sick often, she takes alcohol and drugs to excess, she eats mostly junk food, and she doesn't get exercise or fresh air.

She is likely to become pregnant before her twentieth birthday and is likely to bear and keep the child. She may not detect that she is pregnant until the second or third month, she may not see a doctor until near the end of her pregnancy, and she is unlikely to change any of her risky health behaviors. What would you predict is likely to happen to her child, based on what you know about the needs of a normally developing fetus?

It is statistically likely (see Chapter 3) that her baby will be born prematurely and in addition may suffer from a variety of prenatal and perinatal disorders, many of which will have lasting effects on the future development of the brain and body. The long-term follow-up data suggests that high-risk newborns who are raised in high-risk families are likely to develop problems in mental and physical health, behavior disorders, and intellectual deficits (see Chapter 12). When this child becomes a teenager, will she fare better than her mother? The conditions of poverty, acting through generational developmental cycles, perpetuate the suffering and widen the gap between rich and poor.

Earlier discussions in this text about child development and public policy suggest that it will be a long time before the United States government places the welfare of families and children high on the national agenda. The attitude of the government seems to be that the community will take care of itself and that private business, if it is given enough tax credits, will share the burden. This has not happened. Indeed, corporations and businesses spend millions of dollars to lobby against federal legislation for day care, parental leave, and raising the minimum wage. Businesses that support the family, in the community and for their own employees, make up a very small minority of all businesses.

Even small amounts of community support can have lasting positive effects on families and children living in poverty (see the Family and Society section in this chapter). One of the hopes fostered by the lessening of the superpower conflicts and the breakdown of the Soviet empire is that we can turn our national agenda away from defense and toward the family. For many, it may be too late. Some of the effects of early malnutrition, disease, abuse, and neglect may be irreversible. What kind of a future will deprived American children and their families face?

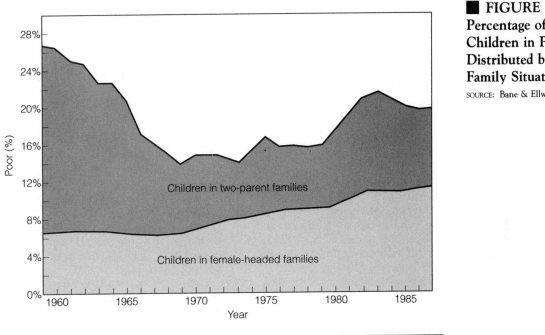

■ **FIGURE 10.1**
Percentage of Children in Poverty Distributed by Family Situation
SOURCE: Bane & Ellwood (1990)

The most striking and remarkable aspect of this stage of development is the emergence of the child's personality. For the first time, the baby no longer seems so much like a baby: the child begins to behave in more adult-like ways. Whole new realms of interpersonal communication are possible for those interested in taking advantage of them.

One of the most notable signs of the child's new grasp on personhood is the increasing use of negation. At first, this happens with an insistent *no!* Later, with improved language it becomes something like *I won't do it,* or *I don't want to.* Babies often say no just for the purpose of exploring its effect on others and, at other times, because they have a legitimate complaint or disagreement that needs attention.

This behavior signals a new recognition of personal bound-

aries and limitations. The difficulty during the *no* state comes when care givers and children are at odds on an issue or when the children insist on making up their own minds and then cannot handle the responsibility they seem to want to have for themselves.

It helps to give the children experience in making choices they can handle, for example, asking what kind of juice they would like or what color socks they'd like to wear. If the children have some things they know they can make responsible decisions about, it may be easier to discourage them from the ones they insist on making but that the care giver knows they cannot.

As in other aspects of dealing with children, a sense of humor is a good ally. You can some-

continued at top of next page

POINTS OF
CONTACT

times make *no* into a game by repeating it back in an obviously playful tone of voice as well as by suggesting obviously silly alternatives to the child's unreasonable request or to the care giver's snubbed demand. In this way, the toddler may learn that refusing to do something does not always have to end up in a fight with Mom or Dad.

It is not always possible to be so flexible, as when a child refuses to hold your hand when crossing the street. However, even this can be made into a kind of a game or *ritual*. Once you establish a pattern of doing things like crossing streets, changing diapers, putting the child to bed, reading a story, and so on, a child likes to stick to the initial routines faithfully. Although rituals can become downright boring and tedious for a care giver, it is important to realize that they are necessary ways of maintaining order, safety, and health in a generally peaceful manner. You may not understand why a sandwich cut in quarters tastes better than one cut in half, but if that's what it takes to get a meal down, then why not cut it that way?

One area in which children show self assertion is getting dressed. It is very difficult to know how much children need or want you to do for them and how much they can or want to do for themselves. Although babies of this age are just about able to put on their socks and shoes, for example, they still have some trouble getting socks over that inconvenient bend at the ankle or trying to figure out which shoe goes on which foot. You can be courteous as well as respectful by helping get things started and then letting the child finish. Some examples are putting on a sock partway, giving the child an over-sized sock to put on, or handing the child the proper shoe. Other situations include providing a step stool to reach the sink, turning on the faucet partway, pulling out the child's chair just enough for the child to climb up to the table on his or her own, and pushing the chair in once the child is settled.

Language helps all these problems immensely. Children are less likely to have a tantrum or cry when they are able to express their problems with words. Care givers can help this along by modeling words related to inner feelings, such as mad, tired, scared, happy, sad, or hurt.

Language also leads to new and interesting games and conversations with the child. Naming is one important kind of game at this age. Reading books becomes more fun, and at this age, children discover the fun of outdoor play and exploration, where there are many new things to name and explore. Car rides are usually a big treat, because children gradually come to recognize general categories of objects ("the cow like the cow in the book"); they also learn to recognize specific things like the brand of gasoline station their mothers always stop at. Every time that type of gasoline station is passed, children can pick it out, and they will happily search until they see another one. These kinds of discoveries almost always are accompanied by feelings of great pride on the children's part, and they want everyone else to appreciate the accomplishment.

As we've mentioned, pretending and tool using are important at this age. In the realm of object exploration, children are discovering how to make *towers* and *trains*, as well as how to destroy them in a flash. The following are traditional pastimes guaranteed to delight any child of one and a half years: riding a tricycle or scooter; playing catch; pushing and pulling large objects such as wagons or chairs; climbing on the sofa, chairs, and playground equipment; and playing a real game of hide-and-seek.

The second birthday is rather different from the first. Because of the ability to form mental representations, babies about to be two years old are able to look forward to their second birthdays, think about presents, get excited about the occasion, and ask whether they'll have cake. Although they still do not fully understand the concept of a birthday, they are aware that they are part of a special event that is somehow centered upon themselves. In the next chapter, we'll follow the development of that important sense of self-awareness as it unfolds in the third year of life.

■ SUMMARY

Motor and Cognitive Development

■ Motor advances include self-feeding, toilet training, and stable sleep patterns.

■ The ability to think about actions without actually performing them develops. Infants can solve some problems mentally, without trial and error.

■ Symbolic play develops by the combination of different types of symbols into complex event sequences. Infants still don't get all the connections between their own actions on objects.

■ Script-based memories allow for categorization of events according to the sequences in which they typically occur.

■ An existential sense of self emerges as the conceptual unification of sequences of actions performed by the subject.

Emotional Development

■ Fears originate in mental and symbolic images, and some dreaming begins. Infants develop new emotions, such as defiance, embarrassment, and pride.

■ Transitional objects serve to comfort infants when adults are unavailable.

■ Separations are easier for children if parents explain what will happen and when they will return, if the environment is one in which the infants feel comfortable, and if the infants have experience with separations.

Social and Language Development

■ Symbolic play and tool use correlate with the onset of multiword speech and the vocabulary spurt at around twenty months.

■ Infants combine words in flexible formulas that allow different meanings to be constructed but aren't as rigid as grammar.

■ Individual differences in style and amount of speech emerge at this age.

■ A linguistic environment conducive to infant language development is one in which adults are responsive to the infant's speech initiative by commenting and asking questions.

■ Guided participation is a general principle that applies to language, play, and discipline interactions.
■ Discipline can be achieved by guided participation and by proactively regulating the environment.

Family and Society

■ All families rely on both formal and informal sources of support during infancy.
■ Factors mediating the effectiveness of support include social attitudes about different types of infants, parental personality and its affect on support sources, and cultural attitudes about seeking help.
■ Early childhood intervention for disadvantaged families shows gains for infants in some areas but not in others.

Applications: Poverty and Risk

■ The poverty rate for children in the United States is among the highest of the wealthy countries.
■ There is a higher percentage of poverty among racial and ethnic minorities, but there are also many poor white children.
■ Poverty affects the psychological health of adults, which in turn affects how they interact with their children.
■ A variety of welfare and nonwelfare solutions to alleviate the effects of poverty on children have been proposed.

■ GLOSSARY

Authoritative parenting   A style of parenting containing both warmth and firmness.

Categorical self   A concept of self as belonging to one or more categories, such as baby or female.

Conventional communication   A communicative act that is used by all members of the same speaking community, such as a word.

Existential self   The ability to recognize one's own features as different from someone else's.

Expressive speech   Speech that is socially oriented and uses more but less well-articulated words per utterance.

Formal support systems   Community programs that are specifically designed to serve the needs of parents and infants, usually funded by the government.

Formulas   Flexible word orders that make up the first sentences of infants; not the same as mature grammar.

Guided participation   When a responsive adult collaborates on a task the infant is already doing, allowing the infant to take small, culturally appropriate roles.

Head Start   A federally funded program for enriched early childhood education and parent education for disadvantaged families.

Idiosyncratic communication   A form of communication that the individual makes up. It requires a familiar adult to interpret its meaning.

Informal support system A family's social network of relatives, friends, and community resources.

Locutionary The stage of speech development in which words are combined into sentences to create complex meanings.

Parental proactive behavior An approach to discipline in which the adult controls the child's environment by anticipating future problems.

Referential speech Speech that is object oriented and contains a few, clearly articulated words per utterance.

Script A form of conceptual organization in which events are remembered according to the sequences in which they usually occur.

Telegraphic speech Speech having two or more words per utterance but with endings and connecting words left out.

Transitional object An object to which the infant develops an attachment that may be used for comfort in the absence of the care giver.

ELEVEN

"I'm Not a Baby Anymore"

(TWENTY-FOUR TO THIRTY-SIX MONTHS)

This chapter is intended as a bridge between infancy and the preschool years. Although there is no clear demarcation between these two periods, a number of factors suggest that the infancy period is not completely over until late in the third year of life. At this time, infants can genuinely engage in linguistic and cooperative interactions with their peers, siblings, and parents. The three-year-old has a command of family relationships that the two-year-old does not have. By age three years, the child can nurture a younger sibling and take independent stands against older siblings. True grammatical speech does not emerge until the end of the third year, although this speech is still fairly simple in structure. A sense of categorical self and the emergence of self-understanding and gender identity is also a late third-year development.

In this chapter, we will attempt to describe these important transitions in the third year. We will not, however, have the space to give a complete account of preschool-age developmental changes. We will discuss such specific topics as the development of gender stereotyping, the differential treatment of boys and girls by parents, and sibling relationships in the family. The Applications section of this chapter covers the topic of child abuse and maltreatment as it affects infants.

■ MOTOR AND COGNITIVE DEVELOPMENT

Motor Development

The third year is an exciting developmental period from a motor perspective. Although we will be able to reference more research studies than in the last chapter, the study of motor development remains one of the least articulated areas of infant development. Recently, however, new research on motor development is appearing (Thelen, 1989), and a separate section on motor development was included for the first time in the program of the 1990 meetings of the International Conference of Infant Studies, held in Montreal, Canada.

Table 11.1 lists some of the motor achievements that occur in the third year. Age norms are not available for all these items, so we list them according to early and late in the third year. It is important to remember that there are wide individual differences in the age of acquisition of these skills, so that some children will not be doing all of these things by the end of the third year.

Most infants have developed their adult hand preference by the age of three years, although for some infants it takes until five years for a stable preference to finally emerge (Hardyck & Petrinovich, 1977; Ramsay, 1980). There is no evidence that left-handed children (about 12 percent of the population) have cognitive and motor deficits, and it is unjustified on normal developmental grounds to try to encourage children to switch their hand preference (Tan, 1985).

Whether right- or left-handed, by age three, children are drawing squiggles and making simple shapes on paper. Research shows that these early drawings

---

■ TABLE 11.1   Motor Achievements During the Third Year of Life

	SMALL MOTOR	LARGE MOTOR
First half of third year	Uses large crayons and pencils Uses hand gestures and sign language	Rides large-wheel toys Walks up and down stairs with both feet on each step Jumps with two-foot takeoff Throws a ball 4 to 5 feet Walks sideways and backward Runs Engages in free-ranging movement out of doors
Second half of third year	Uses building toys with many possible shapes (blocks, Legos, etc.) Uses paints and clay Hammers	Walks up and down stairs by alternating each foot Walks a line, heel-to-toe Hops 2 or 3 times Walks a short balance beam Throws a ball 10 feet Engages in rough-and-tumble play Finds route in unfamiliar spaces

are not mirrors of the child's emotional life but reflect the motor limitations of the arm and the hand (Golomb, 1974; Freeman, 1980). Once children begin to draw shapes, they prefer simple ones, such as circles and rectangles. Eventually these shapes are combined into more complex pictures (Goodnow, 1977). It is not developmentally appropriate to interpret the meaning or the subject of these early drawings. Rather, the child seems to be using the materials to explore the medium: what kinds of shapes, lines, and colors can be made with this brush or that crayon. Representational art is a later development.

One of the most interesting aspects of motor development at this age is that it is becoming integrated with conceptual abilities. In one study, three-year-olds were taken into a children's area in a natural history museum (Hazen, 1982). Some of the children were allowed to explore the area on their own, while others were led through the area by an adult. Those who went on their own had a more accurate spatial cognition of the layout of the area than those who were led. This study shows that self-produced movement involves active cognitive processing and that by their movement, children are increasing their knowledge of the environment.

Finally, in the realm of physical development, by age two years children are dreaming during sleep. These dreams often concern experiences the child has had, physical changes such as toileting, and strong emotions.

At 2;2(23) X. woke up crying: *"Poupette has come back."* Poupette was a little girl she had met the day before and who had obviously worried her by unceremoniously taking possession of all her toys. . . . At 2;8(11) X. woke with a loud scream: *"It was all dark, and I saw a lady over there* (pointing to her bed). *That's why I screamed."* Then she explained that it was a horrid lady who stood with her legs apart and played with her feces. *(Piaget, 1962, p. 177)*

These dreams are examples of some of the things reported by two-year-old children upon awakening. These dreams are classic nightmares, or dreams about fears that are still so fearful that the dream is unable to resolve them or make them better: in one case, the child's having her toys stolen and in another, the fear of her own feces. The latter is apparently a common problem in two- and three-year-old children who are becoming aware that their own bodies can manufacture these products. Children of this age are both fascinated by their feces and repelled and confused by them at the same time (see Chapter 2 and Erikson, 1950). Some children feel possessive about these products and may refuse toilet training for fear of losing part of themselves. Other children may show more curiosity and playfulness about their stools and urine than most parents are able to tolerate, and still others don't seem to be at all concerned with these matters.

Dreams other than nightmares may fulfill a wish, or they may take a painful event and finish it off with a happy ending. According to Freud (1900), dreams are the "guardians" of sleep. Without dreams to transform and sooth our minds, we might keep waking up with painful or troublesome thoughts.

Another common dream in very young children is the transposition of an organic stimulus (Piaget, 1962). A good example of this is when children dream about a watering can just when they feel like (or are in the process of) urinating.

Action and Attention

As we saw in the previous chapter, by age two, infants are beginning to organize their memories according to sequences of events. They can often remember complex sequences, and in some cases, they can remember sequences that happened some time ago. Researchers brought a group of two-and-a-half-year-old children back into a laboratory where they had been subjects in an auditory perception experiment at age one. Compared to a group of control children who had not taken part in the earlier study, the experimental children reproduced some of the behaviors they performed almost two years before in the experiment (Myers, Clifton & Clarkson, 1987). Paradoxically, even though they can remember complicated sequences of events, infants under two cannot produce such sequence in their action.

This changes between twenty-four and thirty months of age, as demonstrated by the following investigation (Bullock & Lutkenhaus, 1988). Researchers gave children three tasks. The first was to build a house from blocks in a particular fashion, modeled by the experimenter. The next was to clean a blackboard, and the last was to dress a doll so that it would not be cold. After age two, but not before, the children were able to regulate their actions in order to attain the standard set by the experimenter (the constructed house, the clean blackboard, and the dressed doll).

When the younger children made an error in putting the blocks together, they simply stopped or went on to another activity. The older children were able to correct the error and persist until the task was completed to a reasonable approximation of the standard. This ability to combine a series of actions together in a flexible way and persist until a standard or conventional goal is reached is a major cognitive achievement that is reflected in a variety of areas, including object play, pretend play, social play, peer play, self-control, and language (Brownell, 1988; Messer et al., 1987). Self-control is seen in the ability to wait as requested by an adult (Vaughn et al., 1986). In the realm of language, for example, children at this age are beginning to use grammatical syntax in which a number of words are combined into a flexible sequence and according to conventional usage.

What causes these changes to occur? Since attention span increases also around the same age, you might think that an increase in some kind of cognitive capacity allows the infant to process a longer series of actions. Some researchers believe, on the contrary, that longer attention is the result of more skilled actions sequences that require the child to spend more time following through with the details of completing a task (Ruff & Lawson, 1990). In related studies, it has been found that the more children comprehend of television programs, such as "Sesame Street," the longer they will watch and that TV watching shows a marked increase at thirty months, about the same time these other changes are happening (Anderson & Levin, 1976; Anderson & Lorch, 1983).

Action and Language

If attention increases as a result of more articulated action, that still leaves open the question of what causes action to develop. The explanation offered by Piaget (1952; 1962) is similar to the attention explanation: there is an increase in cognitive ability that cuts across a variety of domains of thought and action. Thought, according to Piaget, is internalized action, and the ability to perform thought allows the child to move beyond trial-and-error behavior and also to use language as a means of expressing thought.

Many scholars are unsatisfied with this explanation. Children's action is not perfect at any age. They still commit errors. The important developmental change is not the onset of an error-free performance but the ability to correct for errors of action in order to reach the goal. Children don't always think out the problem in advance, as Piaget suggests. Rather, they become more adept at correcting errors rapidly as part of their ongoing pursuit of the goal.

Then Piaget concluded that errors committed by children older than two years were errors of logical thinking: again assuming the primacy of cognition over action after age two years. He gave children problems, such as the following: "Bill is older than Tom. Tom is older than Steve. Who is older, Bill or Steve?" A typical three-year-old is likely not to know the answer or to be confused by the question. An alternative to the logical error hypothesis is that children have a difficult time comprehending the language used in such problems. Children often have difficulty understanding differences between similar words with different endings, such as the difference between *old* and *older*. Some research has shown that what children actually comprehend is something like this: "Bill is old; Tom is not old. Tom is old; Steve is not old." This seems like contradictory information. How can Tom be old and not old at the same time? Thus, it may be a linguistic problem, rather than a deficit in cognitive ability (Bryant & Trabasso, 1971; Riley & Trabasso, 1974).

There are two remarkable changes that happen at around thirty months. One is the ability to combine actions into complex sequences. The other is the ability to do it in socially accepted ways: to meet the standards set by the adult and to use speech that is conventionally accepted by the adult community. Piaget failed to realize that many of the experimental situations designed for children, although set up to test a cognitive capacity, are actually social situations.

Let's return to the original question, that is, what accounts for the development of complex action sequences? In the last chapter, we reviewed research showing that younger infants appeared more skilled in pretend play when in the company of adults. They are also more advanced linguistically with adults than with peers. The adult guidance and the adult language seems to regulate the infant's actions, providing a kind of external support system that the infant cannot maintain alone or with a peer. After thirty months, it seems, infants have begun to internalize this social-linguistic regulatory system, carrying it over into their activities in the absence of adults.

How do we know this? Beginning at thirty months, children begin to use language to regulate their behavior. For example, in one study, children were given a peg and hammer toy and told to hammer the pegs into the board in a particular order according to the color of the peg. If the children were allowed to say out loud the given order while hammering, they were more accurate than if told not to speak (Balamore & Wozniak, 1984).

At around thirty months, children begin, literally, to talk to themselves. *Private speech* is the use of language to regulate one's own behavior without the intention of a social communication. Private speech is different from the perlocutionary speech seen in the first year (such as saying "mmmmmm" while eating) because private speech uses both conventional words and conventional syntax. Private speech reflects the transition from social regulation to individual self-regulation.

Research has shown that private speech occurs in the following situations: the child talks about an intended action (I put that there); the child describes ongoing action (Banging it); a statement is made to inanimate objects (Get out of my way, chair!), and a question is asked and then answered (Why are you crying, dolly? Because I'm sad). In all cases, these words are said without looking at anyone else or seeking social confirmation (Berk, 1986; Furrow, 1984).

In conclusion, more complex action sequences are probably not the result of some increased cognitive power. Rather, they are the result of the regulatory effects of private speech on behavior. Since private speech is an internalized version of what had earlier occurred socially during the regulation of the infant's action by means of care-giver speech, the development of complex actions sequences has its origins in earlier social interaction. In a sense, babies turn dialogue into private monologue, social discourse into thought, and the result is the self-regulation of action (Vygotsky, 1978).

The World of Make-Believe

Because they say out loud (private speech) most of what they are thinking, children of this age are delightful to watch. Pretend play, discussed in the last chapter, is a kind of private speech that allows children to construct their own version of reality.

At the beginning of the third year, children develop more complex forms of pretending. The child begins to reconstruct whole scenes and experiences in play:

At 2;1(9) Jacqueline put her doll's head through the balcony railings with its face turned toward the street and began to tell it what she saw: "You see the lake and the trees. You see a carriage, a horse," etc. The same day she seated her doll on the sofa and told it what she herself had seen in the garden. (Piaget, 1962, p. 127)

In the previous example, the child tried to faithfully reproduce reality. In the following example, the child makes some attempt to change or correct reality to make it more to her own liking. These games are the beginning of *imaginative play*, or *fantasy play*, in which the child is able to invent whole new situations in make-believe:

At 2;4(8) Jacqueline, not being allowed to play with the water being used for washing, took an empty cup, went and stood by the forbidden tub and went through the actions, saying: "I'm pouring out the water." (Piaget, 1962, p. 131)

The final type of pretend play that occurs during the third year of life is what Piaget called *liquidating* play. This usually happens after the child experiences something unpleasant or threatening. Later, the child will try to relive the difficult situation in play as a way of coping with it. By removing it from its original unpleasantness, the child is more able to understand and assimilate what went on:

Pretend play is a common activity in the third year of life. Children pretend with adults, with other children, and often by themselves.

At 2;7(2) Jacqueline had fallen down and cut her lip. . . . She consoled herself by projecting it all on to "Cousin Andree," who took the form of a doll: *"Oh! It's Cousin Andree. They're washing her because she fell down and hurt her lip. She made a little hole in it. She cried."*

At 2;7(15) a friend of her mother went for a walk with them. Jacqueline, who did not care for the presence of the third person, expressed frankly what she felt: *"She's naughty . . . she can't talk . . . I don't like people to laugh"* . . . Then, as soon as the walk was over, Jacqueline accepted her, put her beside her in the bath, then in her bed, talked to her, and went for the walk again with her (all in imagination). *(Piaget, 1962, p. 133)*

These kinds of games allow the self to emerge victorious in the face of failure or to save face in the case of embarrassment.

Are There Individual Differences in Children's Styles of Pretend Play?

The last chapter showed that there are two different styles of language acquisition. Referential approaches emphasize single words, clear articulation, and the use of nouns. Expressive approaches use phrases, mumbled speech, and pronouns; they tend to refer to social situations (Nelson, 1981.

Similar styles have been found for symbolic play in the third year. Wolf and Gardner (1979) found that these patterns of individual difference cut across play, language, motor development, and problem-solving behavior.

Patterners are concerned with properties of objects, shape, and form. *Dramatists* are more involved in story telling, imagination, and social interaction. Children at age two were offered a set of sixteen items (four people, four animals, four small blocks, and four large blocks). They were asked to put the ones that were alike together. The patterners grouped objects according to their external forms, shapes, and colors. The dramatists grouped the objects by making a story out of them, such as a person in a house made of blocks (see Figure 11.1).

■ FIGURE 11.1
Patterner's and
Dramatist's Solutions
to the Classification
Task

SOURCE: From Wolf & Gardner,
1979. Reprinted by permission of
the publisher and the author.

(a) Patterner's solution

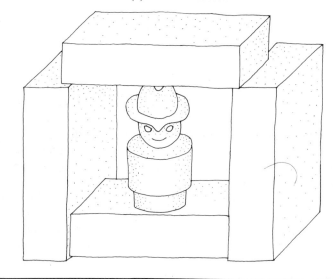

(b) Dramatist's solution

Piaget (1962) has suggested that dreams are very similar to symbolic play, since the dream images are purely egocentric. The images in dreams, however, are more vivid, more outlandish, more confused, and perhaps less directly connected to reality by the conscious mind.

▪ EMOTIONAL DEVELOPMENT

For children of this age, it is rather difficult to separate action, cognition, language, and emotion. The most important emotional developments are the ability to label and talk about emotions and the ability to understand the causes of emotional states in self and other. These are inherently linguistic, social, and cognitive achievements. Keep in mind, therefore, that the goal is to try to understand the child, rather than to make arbitrary distinctions between, say, cognition and emotion.

Developments in the Self-Concept

Because they now have the ability to take language out of it's immediate social context and use it to talk to the self and about the self, children's categorical self-concept improves during this period. By age three, children are able to describe themselves according to a number of physical characteristics (I am a boy. I am little. I have blue eyes.). Given a set of pictures of people of different sexes and ages, children of this age are quite accurate in labeling both age and sex differences in other people (Edwards, 1984; Keller et al., 1978). Thus, by the end of the second year, you might hear a child say, "I'm not a baby anymore!"

Children go through a series of stages in their understanding of gender, their identity as a biological male or female. The first stage is called gender labeling, when the child can identify self or other verbally as male or female. This begins about twenty months. Up until the age of three years, however, children don't understand that these labels reflect enduring characteristics of people. Two-year-olds will say correctly that they are a boy or a girl and will even engage in sex-stereotyped toy play (see discussion of sex roles in the section on Social Development below), but they don't understand that a boy will always grow up to be a man. Children believe that gender might be changed by changing one's appearance or dress, which might explain why they are fairly rigid in their adoption of sex-role stereotypes (Ladies can't wear pants. Boys don't play with dolls.) (Gelman et al., 1986; Slaby & Frey, 1975).

Interestingly, two- to three-year-old children who are more advanced in gender labeling (those who give the correct gender response to the question, "Who are you?") and who score higher on verbal intelligence tests are also more explicit about sex-role behaviors. That is, they will classify tasks and tools as male (car repair, shovels) or as female (cooking, irons). These children will also more readily adopt same-sex playmates in peer groups. Additionally, a number of studies have found that boys begin gender-labeling and sex-typing somewhat earlier than girls (Fagot et al., 1990; Fagot & Leinbach, 1989; McGuire, 1988; O'Brien & Huston, 1985; Weinraub et al., 1984).

■ TABLE 11.2   Statements of Emotion Made by Two-Year-Olds

Positive	I give a hug. Baby be happy.
	I laugh at funny man.
	I not cry now. I happy.
	Mommy exercise. Mommy having a good time.
Negative	Me fall down. Me cry.
	It's dark. I'm scared.
	No cry, Mama. It will be all right.
	I feel bad. My tummy hurts.
	Mommy, you went away. I was sad.
	He's sad. He'll be happy when his daddy comes home.
	I'm mad at you, Daddy. I'm going away, good-bye.
	If you go on vacation again, I'll cry.

SOURCE: Bretherton, 1986; Radke-Yarrow & Zahn-Waxler, 1973.

These studies of gender understanding suggest that cognitive and linguistic factors play some role because children who are more linguistically and cognitively advanced are also more stereotypic in their sex-role concepts. However, it may be that children who are more articulate about gender and sex-roles could have parents who talk more about such issues, so that we cannot rule out a possible social influence in such factors (see the Social Development section in this chapter).

Children of this age can also talk about their feelings and label emotional and physiological states accurately (Denham, 1986; Lewis & Michalson, 1983), they can talk about future and past emotions, and they can discuss the causes and consequences of emotions (Bretherton et al., 1986). By twenty-eight months, most children will have extensive emotion vocabularies for positive emotions (happy, fun, good time, funny, like, love, feel better) and negative ones (sad, scared, mad, yukky, messy, feel bad).

Perhaps more interesting from the perspective of self-understanding is that in the third year, children seem to have learned about emotional sequences in both themselves and in other people (Bretherton et al., 1986; Hoffman, 1975; Radke-Yarrow & Zahn-Waxler, 1984; see Table 11.2). In addition, two-year-olds are visibly affected by the emotions of others. In an experimental situation, children observed an experimenter having either an angry or a pleasant conversation with their mother. In the angry situation, the children expressed concern for their mother, sought her reassurance, and tried to comfort her (Cummings et al., 1989).

Development of Emotional Understanding

This research suggests that children are able to think about not only sequences of actions on objects but also sequences involving emotional and physiological states. Some researchers take these findings to imply that children of this age have a *theory of mind*, an appreciation of the psychological states of other people. Other findings also seem to support this view. Three-year-olds—both boys and girls—can modify their speech in the form of motherese when talking to a baby (Dunn & Kendrick, 1981; Shatz & Gelman, 1973).

Children as young as three years are able to describe the kinds of things you might do to take care of a baby (Melson, Fogel, & Toda, 1986). When asked to show a picture to another person three-year-olds turned the picture around to face that person (Lempers et al., 1977).

These studies, as interesting as they appear to be, don't demonstrate conclusively that three-year-olds have a theory of mind. A child can copy the parent's speech to a baby brother or sister or just describe what others do for a baby. If the children have had a lot of experience reading picture books with parents, they have learned that pictures must face adults in order for adults to talk about the pictures. Attempts to comfort a hurt adult have to be looked at not only with respect to what the child says (Table 11.2) but also what the child actually does. Two-year-olds often try to comfort adults with blankets, bottles, and pacifiers, suggesting that the children may be trying to calm their own upset by stopping the crying of the adult (Hoffman, 1975). The use of emotion language could refer to facial expressions and actions of other people that the children have come to label in a particular way, without realizing that others have feelings like themselves.

You don't have to presume that the child understands that other people have minds or have feelings, and some developmentalists suggest that genuine empathy for others does not begin to develop until four or five years of age (Hoffman, 1975; Selman, 1980). Similarly, adults can learn to operate computers just by following instructions, without having any notion at all of what makes a computer work. Just because the child uses an emotion word when talking about another person doesn't mean that the child realizes the other has emotions. I can talk about my computer as being "down" without knowing what that means from the computer's perspective. "My computer is down"; is a statement more about how the computer's behavior is affecting me than about a deep appreciation of the computer's inner workings.

On the other hand, evidence in favor of a rudimentary theory of mind comes from studies of the development of the ability to deceive others. Three-year-old children were left alone in a room with what they were told was a surprise toy. They were asked not to peek while the experimenter left the room. Observed from behind a one-way mirror, almost all of the children peeked, but when the experimenter returned and asked, "Did you peek?" only 38 percent of those who peeked admitted that they had done so. The ones who confessed showed little change in facial expression. The ones who actually peeked but said they had not peeked showed an increase in smiling, while the ones who peeked but refused to answer the question showed an increase in nervous self-touching (Lewis, Stranger, & Sullivan, 1989).

Do these differences in facial expression suggest that children may be aware of what adults are thinking, that is, they assume that the adult believes the children peeked, and they try to change the adult's beliefs? In a related study (Chandler et al., 1989), children were asked to hide a treasure from an experimenter. They could do this in a number of ways: by covering up the trail to the treasure, by creating false leads where the treasure was hidden if the experimenter asked for help, and by lying. Children as young as two and a half years used all three strategies, suggesting that they were acting to create a false belief in the adult. To create a false belief, you have to have a theory of mind, that is, you have to assume that others are capable of holding some beliefs. According to the authors, the children "not only slyly lied and disingenuously misled, but they did so with what often amounted to disarming delight in leading others astray" (Chandler et al., 1989, p. 1275).

The child's cognitive sophistication is revealed by the way in which emotion and action go together in these examples. Nevertheless, even though a case can be made that children of this age have a theory of mind, it is likely to be a rather simple theory, something like: "Adults will believe what I want them to believe, and they can't really tell that I'm trying to deceive them." In other words, children believe that adults are in some ways extensions of themselves and entirely in tune with their wishes.

According to Harris (1989), children need the following abilities in order to have a genuine theory of mind: self-awareness, the capacity for pretend, and the ability to distinguish reality from pretend. We know that by the beginning of the third year, most children have both self-awareness and the ability to pretend. These factors are necessary because, as Harris suggests, a theory of mind requires one to imagine that others have feelings like one's own feelings. Because we have no direct confirmation of the feelings of another, we have to imagine what someone might feel under certain circumstances.

What three-year-olds lack, however, is the ability to separate pretend from reality (see the discussion of pretend play above). Until children can do this, they will see others as mere extensions of their own desires. How do we know children of this age cannot always separate reality from fantasy? One study found that when adults entered into a child's pretend game, the child became confused about the difference. A mother pretended to hold up an umbrella and suggested to her thirty-month-old son that he hold out his hand to feel the rain. He did this and then very soberly looked at the palms of his hands to see if they were wet (DeLoache & Plaetzer, 1985). Another child while playing at cooking turned to a peer and said, "This is pretend, right?" (Slade, 1986). Another was pretending to be a monster by making growling noises. She became afraid of the noises she herself made, and she began to cry (DiLalla & Watson, 1988).

Of course, children in the third year can sometimes make the fantasy-reality distinction, but it would be more accurate to say that they are never really sure which is which. It is not until the age of four years that a greater feeling of certainty emerges, and therefore, it is not until this age that children solidify a theory of mind, an appreciation of the feelings and desires of others as independent from their own (Harris, 1989). In language, it is not until the fourth year that children produce words representing conditional or temporary states, such as *could* and *would* as opposed to *can* and *will* (Kuczaj & Maratsos, 1983). By four years, a child might say to a younger sibling, "You don't get it. It's just pretend. I could have fooled you!" On the other hand, at the beginning of the third year, it is fair to say that children begin to catch glimmers of the differences between self and other as part of their ongoing social interactions.

As you can see from this discussion of emotional development, it is difficult to separate it from its origins in the social relationship. Emotion becomes increasingly social as it is subject to labeling and explicit regulation by others. The ways in which adults respond to happy expressions versus temper tantrums ultimately impact on the child's own emotional understanding. In general, research suggests that adults should accept children's emotions as genuine expressions of feeling, while working toward changing the manner in which the emotion is expressed or talked about (I can see that you're angry, but I don't permit throwing things in the house). The general principles for dealing with emotions are the same as those discussed in the previous chapter for guided participation: accept the child's initiative (even if this is negative) and then find ways to encourage the child into culturally and socially acceptable forms of expression (Demos, 1982; Lewis & Michaelson, 1983; Rogoff, 1990).

■ SOCIAL AND LANGUAGE DEVELOPMENT

At the end of the second year, there is a vocabulary spurt that was discussed in the last chapter. Sometime during the third year, or later for some children, there is a spurt in the *mean length of utterance* (MLU). MLU is the average number of morphemes in each utterance spoken by the child. A morpheme is a meaningful unit of language, usually a syllable, but it can also be a word ending, such as *-ed, -s,* or *-ing.* Increases in MLU for three children are shown in Figure 11.2. Notice the wide range of individual variation. Eve has reached a peak in MLU development before Adam and Sarah have even begun to use more than one or two morphemes in an utterance (Brown, 1973).

These utterances are becoming less formula-like (see Chapter 10) and more like a flexible standard grammar for the language spoken in the home (Bates et al., 1987). To speak in a sentence, we must have at least two basic components: a subject and a verb. In a grammatical sentence, each of the components must agree with one another in number (and gender in gender-based languages, such as Spanish and French). In most cases, children learn verbs more slowly than nouns. For the two children studied by Greenfield and Smith (1976), the time between the first noun and the first verb (learned at about twenty months of age) was the same amount of time as between birth and the first spoken words.

Sentences do not truly emerge until children begin to use verbs in a systematic manner—near the end of the second year of life.

According to Gentner (1978), nouns and verbs are fundamentally different. Nouns represent the descriptions of things or objects; they serve a referential function. Nouns tend to refer to concrete things the child can see, touch, or feel. Verbs, in contrast, tell us about the relationship between things—between the subject and the object, for example. Verbs are relational rather than referential.

Because of this, verbs can express nontangible things. When you say "The ball rolls across the floor," the verb represents a transient action—one that relates the ball and the floor. The words *ball* and *floor,* in contrast, make fewer intellectual demands on the listener; these objects are there for all to see whenever they wish to. Verbs also can represent abstract properties that are difficult for a young child to appreciate, for example, *to think* and *to feel.*

When children first start to express action words, they often combine the action and its result in the same word. The word *up* can be used for a variety of situations, such as being lifted, being put down, asking to be picked up or

■ FIGURE 11.2

Average Length of Utterance in Morphemes at Different Ages for Three Children (Roman Numerals Indicate Stages of Development)

SOURCE: From Brown et al., Minnesota Symposium on Child Psychology, Vol. 2, edited by J. P. Hill, p. 29. © 1969 by the University of Minnesota Press. Reprinted by permission. Also reprinted by permission from p. 286 of *Child Development* by Alan Fogel and Gail Melson; Copyright © 1988 by West Publishing Company. All rights reserved.

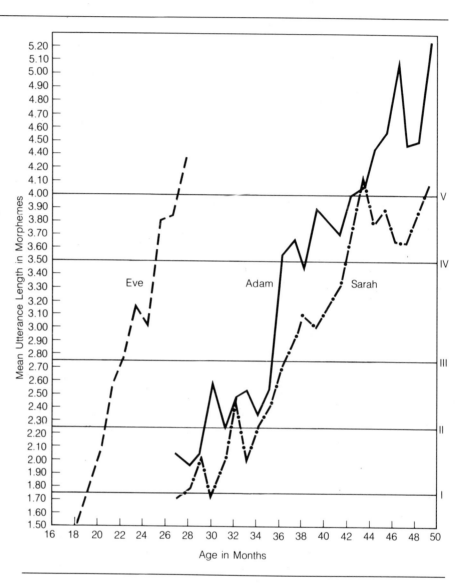

to climb on someone's lap, climbing up or down stairs, or even requesting out-of-reach objects (Clark, 1978). *Off, on, out,* and *open* can be used in similarly extended ways.

The next step in the development of action expression is the use of simple verbs, such as *do* and *make.* The initial use of these words is not always clear to the listener, since the child uses them in many different ways. Thus it is important to see the child speaking in the context of the ongoing activity (Table 11.3).

A final way in which children express actions is by using an object word to talk about the action (Clark, 1978). Some examples follow: "The man is keying the door" (opening the door with a key); "I'm souping" (eating soup); or "Pillow me!" (throw a pillow at me).

■ TABLE 11.3   Uses of *Do, Go,* and *Make* in the Third Year*

VERB	UTTERANCE	CONTEXT
Do	I do it again.	Said as knocks over blocks
	You . . . do . . . doing that	Said as watches O build blocks into a tower
	You do do it, OK?	Asking O to unroll some computer tape, after trying unsuccessfully to do it himself
	You do that!	Indicating which toy O should take out of a box
	Uh oh. I did.	Said as he turned off the tape recorder by pushing a knob
	The clown do!	Asking O to make the toy clown do what clowns do
Make	Make name!	Telling O to write his name
	I make a little doggie.	Said as cut a dog shape out of Play-Doh
	Make a dog	Telling O what to draw next
	Make it go in there.	Asking O to get a crayon back into its box
	Make that.	Said as pointed to the hand moving on a clock; seemed to be request for O to move the hand on
Go	It go there.	Talking about a block lying on the floor
	Red went boom.	Talking about a red block that fell on the floor
	They go in the car.	Talking about two storybook characters
	'N turn go up.	Said as turned a puzzle piece the right way up
	'N go like that.	Said as dropped puzzle pieces on the floor

*Examples cited come from the first month of recordings from S, a child taped at weekly intervals for 1 year from age 2–0. The utterances cited occurred without any immediately preceding use of the particular general purpose verb by either the observer (O) or the child's parents.

SOURCE: From Clark, E. Strategies for communicating. *Child Development,* 49, 1978, p. 957. Copyright by the Society for Research in Child Development. By permission of the publisher and the author.

In ways similar to the overextension of nouns, children of this age also make errors in the use of verbs. Some examples are given in Table 11.4. This usually happens after they learn to recognize the similarity in meaning between the verbs that they accidently substitute for each other (Bowerman, 1978). *Put* and *give,* for example, are both words in which a person makes an object move from one place to another. Bowerman argues that the substitution "errors" shown in Table 11.4 require that the child understand the basic relationship between *put* and *give,* since children rarely substitute words that have no semantic relationship to each other.

Adding the Proper Endings

Children still will have much to learn about verbs in the preschool years. This learning will relate to verb meaning and tense. Irregular verbs are the hardest to learn, since children want to extend regular verb endings to irregular verbs, as in *goed* and *maked* (Kuczaj, 1978). Regular and irregular endings are also a factor in learning the plural forms of nouns.

Children learn plurals in a way very similar to the way they learn verb tenses. Children first learn some irregular forms such as *men* and *children* almost without realizing that they are plurals of *man* and *child.* Once they learn the general rule of adding an *s,* they apply that rule to anything, even

■ **TABLE 11.4   Verb Substitution Errors***

A. *Put* substituted for *give*

E (2-2):	I go *put* it to Christy. (Starting off with a rubber band, then *gives* it to C.)
E (2-4):	Can I go *put* it to her? (Then takes juice and *gives* it to C.)
E (2-4):	M: It's all gone. (Re: C's juice.) E: Then *put* her some more.
E (2-4):	How come you're *putting* me that kind of juice? (As M prepares to *give* unfamiliar juice to E.)
E (2-4):	We're *putting* our things to you. (To D, after M has told children that it's time to *give* him their Father's Day presents.

B. *Give* substituted for *put*

E (2-7):	*Give* some ice in here, Mommy. *Put* some ice in here, Mommy. (Pointing to ice crusher.)
E (2-9):	*Give* those crayons right here. (Indicating to M spot on table near where she is sitting.)
E (2-10):	I'm gonna *give* your glasses right here. (M: Huh?) I'm gonna *put* your glasses right here.
E (2-10):	Don't *give* those next to me. (As C dumps things on couch near E's seat.)

*C = Christy, E = Eva, M = Mother, D = Daddy.

SOURCE: From Bowerman, M. Systematizing semantic knowledge. *Child Development, 49,* 1978, pp. 984–85. Copyright by the Society for Research in Child Development. By permission of the publisher and the author.

the things they previously had learned in the irregular plural forms: *mans* and *childs* (Berko, 1958).

Another type of meaningful word ending is negation. Although younger infants express negation by saying *no* or *not,* children of this age can create contractions, such as *can't* and *don't* (Clark & Clark, 1977). Although getting the proper endings on words is slow to be acquired, apparently children by age two years can understand the difference between words with different endings (Gerken et al., 1990).

When Do Children Begin to Ask Questions?

After children master the subject-verb-object composition of sentences, they usually move quickly beyond simple declarative sentences to form questions. Questions usually begin with *wh* words, and a definite developmental sequence in the order of acquisition of these words has been found (see Table 11.5). The ages listed in Table 11.5 are approximations, and we can expect individual differences in the age of acquisition.

The reason for this developmental sequence is that the *wh* questions differ in their complexity. *What, where,* and *who* all ask for single-word responses that usually are extracted simply from a situation: What did Bobby make? A tower. *Why, how,* and *when* require a more extended response giving a reason, process, or time.

The initial use of questions by two-year-olds also reflects a rudimentary ability to use them in a fully expressive manner. Most of the questions addressed by children of this age were not dependent upon the previous topic of discussion. Thus children used questions to start a conversation rather than

■ TABLE 11.5   Order of Acquisition of *wh* Questions

AGE	QUESTION
26 Months	Where and What
28 Months	Who
33 Months	How
35 Months	Why
36 Months	Which, Whose, and When (occurred rarely at this age)

SOURCE; Bloom, Merkin, & Wootten, 1982.

to continue one. The only exceptions to this rule are *why* questions (Bloom, Rocissano, & Hood, 1976; Bloom, Merkin, & Wootten, 1982).

Although some parents get annoyed with the constant *whys* of their young children, the ability to ask *why* reflects a growing linguistic sophistication that presages a more complex use of verbs and other *wh-* questions over the next few years.

Children's asking questions tells us that they have become aware of the importance of language for communication. When children ask *why* questions, they are not only requesting information but making a kind of statement as well. They are saying, "I know you know the answer," "I know I can use language to get a response from you," and possibly even "I have the right, duty, and privilege to ask you this question." These unstated forms of linguistic awareness, or awareness about the function of language and of the implicit relationship between speakers, are known as *meta-linguistic knowledge* (Kaye, 1982). Meta-linguistic means "above" or "outside of" language itself, and this kind of knowledge is akin to self-awareness. We will return to the topic of self-awareness in a later section.

In What Ways Is the Two-Year-Old's Language Limited?

In spite of the major accomplishments in the linguistic realm taking place during the third year of life, children still have a great deal to learn. They still make errors in pronunciation, fail to comprehend certain words and sentences, and have only rudimentary conversational skills.

Young children learning English have an endearing tendency to confuse *r* and *l* and to make them both sound like *w*. Kornfeld (1971) studied children who said *gwass* for both *glass* and *grass*. She found that a sound spectrograph (see Chapter 5) could detect differences between the child's pronunciation of the two words, even though the human ear could not.

A similar group of children who confused *r* with *w* was studied by Locke (1979). They all said *wake* to refer to the garden tool used to gather leaves. About two-thirds of the group, however, was able to tell the difference between an adult's pronunciation of *wake* and *rake*, and Miller (1964) found that children became annoyed when adults tried to mimic their mispronunciations.

The evidence suggests that comprehension continues to be ahead of production. Even though children can hear the difference, and even though they apparently are attempting to pronounce the words correctly, they are still unable to do this perfectly. This error tends to persist in the speech of some children until school age, whereas some children never have problems with the r - l distinction. All children, however, need a good deal of time to learn the correct pronunciations of most of the words they routinely use.

Some researchers have collected tape-recorded samples of children's private speech with a microphone hidden in their cribs. During these monologues, infants have been heard to practice their pronunciation. One child practiced the r in *story* as follows: "Stoly/Stoly here/ want a stoly/Dave, stoly/ story, story/ story's de hat/story's de big hat/store's a hat" (Weir, 1966).

Finally, children of this age have trouble comprehending unusual grammatical sequences. If you were told that the robin is being kissed by the bluejay, how would you answer the following questions? Who did the kissing? Who was the kisser? You're probably wishing all your test questions were this easy. However, two-year-olds studied by Bever (1970) could not get the right answer. Half the time they said the robin was the kisser, and half the time they said the bluejay did the deed.

They all got the right answer when they were told "The bluejay kisses the robin" or "It's the robin that the bluejay kisses." The first sentence—the one that confused the children—is a passive construction. Evidently, whenever the children hear a noun followed by a verb, they assume the noun represents the actor. Maratsos, Kuczaj, Fox, and Chalkley (1979) found that it wasn't until children were in elementary school that they could understand sentences such as "Donald Duck was liked by Goofy."

How Well Can a Two-Year-Old Carry On a Conversation?

The mother and child in Table 11.6 were reading a Richard Scarry picture book together. In the same study from which this conversation was taken, mothers and children also played with a set of toy teacups and plates, as well as with a Fisher-Price play family with a table, chairs, a dog, and a car, among other things (Kaye, 1982). The children were videotaped with their mothers

■ TABLE 11.6   A Conversation

MOTHER	CHILD (THIRTY MONTHS)
1. (Points to a picture) What is that one?	
	2. Kitty cat
3. Well what is it?	
	4. Kitty cat
5. Well, I know there's a kitty in it; what's he in?	
	6. Huh?
7. What's he riding in?	
	8. Airplane
9. Right.	
	10. (turns page)

SOURCE: From Kaye, K. *The mental and social life of babies.* Chicago: University of Chicago Press. 1982, p. 100. Reprinted by permission of the publisher and the author.

at twenty-six and again at thirty months doing these things (twenty-eight children in all).

What is the difference between this conversation and one you might hear between two adults? When adults talk to each other, the conversation is likely to continue because both partners are used to taking initiatives and starting new thoughts. In Table 11.6 the parent was more likely to get a response from the child if she asked the child a question or created a situation that required a response from the child. The parent, then, needs to keep prompting the child to continue the conversation. At this age, the child does not have a mature ability to carry on dialogue, even though the child may have mastered the words and phrases of the language. As an apprentice conversationalist, the child can respond to the adult, who makes the child look more capable than the child really is (Kaye, 1982; Shatz, 1978; Snow, 1977).

Aside from using prompts and questions in conversations, adults have other skills designed to make the infant a more active participant. Adults use a greater number of hand gestures and gestures of a more complex variety with their preschoolers than they do with their toddlers (Gutman & Turnure, 1979). These gestures are of three major types. From the beginning of the second year, parents use such gestures as pointing or otherwise specifying the location of something. As children learn meanings and become symbol users, parents employ gestures that copy or imitate the attributes of an object or situation (as in "Eensy, Weensy Spider"). Finally, parents use gestures, that add emphasis to speech, much like they would when talking to another adult.

No doubt these gestures aid the child in understanding more complex sentences, much like gestures aided the prelinguistic child to interpret the parent's meaning. Gestures function the same as the mother's speech in Table 11.6, since they help children maintain an active participation in a conversation that might otherwise be beyond their comprehension and production capacities.

Research has shown that by age two, social class differences in parent-child interaction emerge. One study in the United States found that middle-income dyads spend twice as much time in mutual play as lower-income dyads. Mothers in lower-income groups spend more time reading to themselves, and their children are observed more often in independent play (Farran & Haskins, 1980). Even within middle-income groups there seem to be individual differences. Parents with professional backgrounds—especially teachers—are more likely to read to and interact with their children than parents with blue- or white-collar jobs (Feiring & Lewis, 1981).

Lower- versus middle-income comparisons in Israel showed similar differences. Lower-income mothers thought infants were slower to acquire cognitive skills than did middle-income mothers. The tendency to see the infant as precocious, and therefore to create the "pseudodialogues" previously described, was found for middle-income parents only (Ninio, 1979). In observations of parents' reading picture books to their children, Ninio (1980) found that high-income Israeli mothers asked more questions, talked more during the reading session, and modeled more new words than the low-income mothers. The final chapter will discuss whether these differences in maternal behavior have any lasting impact on the child's social and intellectual development.

Peer Interactions

By the third year of life, children are capable of engaging in social interaction and of adapting to the messages and demands of the listener (Wellman & Lempers, 1977). Between twenty-two and thirty months, infants increase their rates of verbalizations to peers, learn to watch each other more, and increase their overall rates of social interaction (Mueller, Bleier, Krakow, Hegedus, & Cournoyer, 1977). Children also show a greater tendency to engage in mutual social play, and a decreasing amount of parallel play is seen near the end of the third year (Bakeman & Brownlee, 1980).

Important changes also are going on with respect to the kinds of interactions taking place, as well as the content of the interactions. Children gradually incorporate their symbolic play into peer interactions. No longer content to construct elaborate pretend sequences on their own, preschool children work together to elaborate a pretend game. At first, children's peer exchanges are simple copies or echoes of their partners. Later, they learn to provide complementary responses, and finally they learn to elaborate and embellish the others' responses (Garvey, 1974; Gunnar, Senior, & Hartup, 1989).

Eckerman and her colleagues have discovered some of the social processes that account for this development in the ability of peers to achieve and maintain coordinated action (see Table 11.7; Eckerman & Didow, 1989). One important change is that peers begin to imitate each other, first nonverbally and later verbally. Based on both naturalistic observations and observations in which adults acted like peers and imitated children, Eckerman found that the experience of being imitated is a powerful motivator of social behavior. If someone imitates me, it gives me immediate and recognizable feedback of my effect on the other person and inspires me to do the same (Eckerman et al., 1989; Eckerman & Stein, 1990).

Some examples of imitation that are specific to peer relationships in the third year are given in Table 11.8. A second component of increasing peer coordination, also shown in Table 11.8, is the emergence of complementary roles and alternative responses. In this case, the child makes a different, but appropriate response to the partner's overture. This might even occur as a slight variation in the context of imitation: one child might throw a ball and the other a bean bag. A third developmental change is the growing use of language as part of coordinated interaction. Instead of overt actions, the children begin to use words as directives, as requests, or as comments and responses.

Imitation, therefore, seems to serve as a social bridge between the simple kinds of uncoordinated peer play seen in the second year and the complex coordinated interactions seen later in the third year. One of the social functions of imitation is that it increases a feeling of closeness between two people (Uzgiris, 1983). Thus, we might expect similar feelings of interpersonal closeness to emerge between two-year-old peers.

Can Two-Year-Olds Make Friends?

Apparently two-year-olds can make friends. Research shows that social interaction is different between children who call themselves friends than between children who do not say that they are friends (Ross & Lollis, 1987).

■ TABLE 11.7 Developmental Model of Emerging Skills in Achieving Coordinated Action

AGE PERIOD	BEHAVIORAL SKILL	CHARACTERISTIC INTERACTION
Younger than 16 months	Assume and maintain complementary role in familiar, ritualized games	Sustained ritualized games, but little coordinated action in other contexts
16–24 months	Imitation of nonverbal acts as general strategy for coordinated action in nonritualized contexts; repeated imitation across turns of action	Widespread imitation of other's acts, resulting in imitation games and games with both imitative and complementary roles
28–32 months	Verbalizations coordinated to another's actions begin to occur with appreciable frequency; increasingly accompany nonverbal forms of coordinated action with verbal regulations, descriptions, and imitations	Words coordinated to partner's actions increasingly occur in context of games structured largely by nonverbal imitation; words begin to serve as turns in games
	Increasingly respond to another's overtures with alternative overtures composed of words and nonverbal actions or words alone	Games intermixed with periods of negotiation of topic for interactions
Older than 32 months	Use of overtures thematically related to ongoing activities to vary or elaborate on the ongoing coordinated action	Games less repetitive across turns; coordinated action sustained for longer periods of time, with changes in topic occurring during the bout

SOURCE: Eckerman, C. & Didow, S. Toddler's social coordinations. *Developmental Psychology, 25,* 1989, p. 803.

In one study, children were left in an unfamiliar room with either a familiar peer, an unfamiliar peer, or by themselves. The children with the familiar peer were the most comfortable, and the children left alone were the most upset (Ispa, 1981). In another study, children were asked to rank all their nursery school playmates according to how much they liked being with each

■ TABLE 11.8 Types of Imitative and Complementary Actions Seen in Peer Interactions During the Third Year

TYPE OF ACT	EXAMPLE
Imitative	Exchanging an object; playing catch, peek-a-boo; hitting each other; both running, copying sounds, laughing, screaming; faking laugh or cry; clapping; sticking out tongues; singing; jumping
Complementary	Finding a hidden peer; playing leader and follower; giving/following directives (Go jump. Come here.); answering a question

SOURCE; Eckerman et al., 1989; Kuczynski et al., 1987.

person. The children were paired off and taken to an unfamiliar place, where they played together. Half the pairs were made up of children who rated each other as preferred playmates, and half the pairs were made up of children who did not rate each other as preferred. At the end of ten minutes of play in the new setting, an experimenter took one of the children off to play a special game, leaving the other in the room alone. Children whose friends left them behind were more likely to be disturbed during the separation than children left behind by nonfriends. Thus, there is some indication that peer friendships show an attachment-like quality—that children are fond of their friends and like to be with them (Melson & Cohen, 1981).

Do Family Factors Affect Peer Relationships?

Family factors do affect peer relationships. One study found that children without siblings were more sociable with unfamiliar peers than were firstborns, and firstborns were more sociable than children born later. Children without siblings were the most outgoing of all. This could be because the children born later had the most nonpeers to play with or because they expected from peers the same kinds of aggressive rivalry they received from their siblings, and this made them more wary of peers (Snow, Jacklin, & Maccoby, 1981). Children who are more securely attached to their mothers also are more likely to show competence in peer encounters (Leiberman, 1977; Matas, Arend, & Sroufe, 1978).

Do Sociocultural Factors Affect Peer Relationships?

Sociocultural factors do affect peer relationships. For example, Israeli children who were brought up in farm cooperatives, or kibbutzim, showed more cooperative play with one another than Israeli children reared in an urban environment (Shapira & Madsen, 1969). The more a society is family oriented compared with peer-group oriented, the less the children will be encouraged to play in peer groups. This has been found in Mexico (Madsen & Shapira, 1970) and Switzerland (Boehm, 1977).

In smaller, agrarian societies, such as some African tribal societies, there are relatively few age-mates living in the same village. Children in these settings tend to play in mixed-age groups rather than peer groups (Konner, 1975). Mixed-age groupings are rare in modern, urbanized settings. They typically occur between siblings in the same family. Even preschools tend to be age segregated in Western countries. Although there is little research on the topic, we might suspect that some of the same benefits that exist in sibling relationships—such as the ability to lead and follow, to imitate and serve as role model, to learn and teach—would exist in mixed-age groupings of children outside the family. For example, Furman, Rahe, and Hartup (1979) found that if socially isolated preschool children were asked to interact with children younger than themselves, the older child became more sociable over time.

Societies differ in the amount adults supervise peer groups. In urban settings, young children are always under the watchful eyes of a care giver for

In many societies there are too few children in a group to form peer relationships. In these cases, mixed-age groupings are more common.

obvious ecological reasons. In rural and in smaller societies, children are relatively less supervised, even at a young age. The Fore people of New Guinea allow infants total freedom of movement as soon as they can walk (Sorenson, 1979). In the Marquesas Islands, starting at two years of age, children spend most of the day in unsupervised peer groups ranging in size from three to six children. They are allowed to play near the sea, in boathouses, on bridges, and near streams (Martini & Kirkpatrick, 1981). The authors of these two studies never observed children becoming lost or injured, but it is not clear why. These examples suggest that two-year-olds are indeed autonomous individuals, as well as that the social and physical ecology of the setting determines the manner in which that autonomy is expressed.

Social Mediation in the Development of Sex-Role Concepts in the Third Year

As we saw in the section on self-concept, children of this age adopt strong stands on sex-role stereotypes in the peer group. Children may actively discourage each other from playing with opposite sex-typed toys or even with members of the opposite sex. We also saw that boys typically acquire such attitudes earlier than girls and that boys tend to be more rigid in their sex-role beliefs (girls are more likely to play with opposite-sex toys than are boys). In this section, we examine the possible social influences over sex-role development.

One area that has been studied a great deal is parental influence over the child's choice of toys, specifically, parental reactions to traditional masculine toys (trucks, hammers, guns) and feminine toys (dolls, kitchen utensils) for their boys and girls. This is a difficult area in which to do research since one's reactions to a child's behavior regarding sex roles is highly culture-specific. Interpreting this research area is complicated because different studies use different measures (observations, questionnaires, parental reports) and because most of the research is done in white, middle-class American families. With these qualifications, the following conclusions can be reached.

Few parents will explicitly instruct their children in the sex-appropriate choice or use of toys. Sex-role stereotypes are communicated to children by the parents' emotional reactions to the children's choice of toys. First of all, when children are between eighteen and twenty-four months, parents have more emotional reactions, both positive and negative and not necessarily sex-typed, to any kind of gender-related toy. At this age, parents reacted less to toy choices that were not gender-related (such as blocks and nesting cups). Children who began gender labeling early had parents who evinced more emotional reactions to sex-typed toys during this early period (Fagot & Leinbach, 1989).

During the second year, as the children's toy choices became more sex-typed, some parents began to discourage sex-appropriate toys and encourage sex-inappropriate toys, again through emotional reactions rather than instruction (Caldera et al., 1989; Fagot & Leinbach, 1989; Weinraub et al., 1984). Parents also contributed to sex-role identity by discouraging aggression and encouraging prosocial behavior in girls and by encouraging responsibility in boys. In addition, most parents dress and cut their children's hair in sex-appropriate ways in order to avoid other peoples' incorrect identification of the children's gender (McGuire, 1988; Power & Parks, 1986).

Few studies have found parental sex differences in encouragement of sex-appropriate behavior. Mothers and fathers typically agree on the kinds of sex roles they want for their children (Fagot & Leinbach, 1989). Comparisons of the mother's versus father's behavior with their two-year-olds shows very few sex differences by parent. In a study of parental speech to infants, Golinkoff and Ames (1979) found that the types of speech, length of utterances, and number of questions and directives were the same for mothers and fathers when each interacted individually with the infant. They found, however, that when the mother, father, and child all were observed together, the fathers did less speaking. In a study of verbal and nonverbal behavior of mothers and fathers, Clarke-Stewart (1978) found no parental sex differences in responsiveness to the infant, use of stimulation, affection, or effectiveness. She found other differences, however. Mothers in her sample did relatively more verbalization, used more toy play, and held the babies more, whereas fathers did more physical/social play. She also found that the infants' attachments to mother and to father were similar.

Even though mothers and fathers are using similar behavior toward the children, the early onset of gender labeling and the frequency of sex-typed toy play in children is predicted by personality characteristics of the father rather than of the mother. Early labelers, both boys and girls, have fathers who are more traditional in their sex-role orientations and who at home engage in more masculine tasks (car washing, lawn mowing, carpentry) than feminine tasks (laundry, cooking, dish washing). Additionally, in homes in which mothers work outside the home or in which fathers are absent (single-parent mother-headed homes), children have less traditional sex-role stereotypes (Fagot & Leinbach, 1989; McGuire, 1988; Stevenson & Black, 1988; Weinraub et al., 1984).

This research is difficult to sort out. Why should sex-role development of children be correlated with the father's personality or absence, even though mothers and fathers in the same family are similar in their encouragement of sex-role behavior? Could it be that fathers are influencing the mothers' actions? Or, could it be that these women married men who had similar beliefs? Finally, it could be that both parents are being affected by the child's behavior. Although a parent-to-child socialization effect is the most plausible explanation, it is difficult to get unambiguous evidence in support of this position.

Other Gender-Related Differences in Parent-Child Relationships

The literature on sex typing shows that parents of both sexes treat boys and girls differently, from a young age, with respect to sex-appropriate toy choice. Are there any other differences in parental treatment of boys and girls? Again, the data are not clear on this issue, probably due to the large variability between families. One study found that both traditional and nontraditional (egalitarian) mothers talked to their two-and-a-half- to three-and-a-half-year-old sons differently than to daughters. To sons, mothers' speech had more *what* questions, more questions in general, contained more references to numbers, and had more explicit instructions during play tasks. There were no sex-differences in speech related to play or feelings (Weitzman et al., 1985). These speech behaviors directed to males are those believed to be most associated with cognitive development (see Chapter 10).

Other research has found that fathers focus more on play and instrumental behavior, and the father's involvement with the child is correlated with the child's problem-solving abilities. On the other hand, the mother's involvement is more strongly correlated with the child's security of attachment (Easterbrooks & Goldberg, 1984; Lamb, 1978c; Lamb et al., 1982; Lamb & Urberg, 1978).

Once again, we are faced with a difficult explanatory task with this research. There is really too little evidence and too much variability between studies and between families to make firm conclusions about parent-infant sex differences and their effects on development. More evidence exists for older children whose sex-role behavior is more obvious and salient, so it may be that before three years of age, these variations contribute little to the child's sex-role identity.

In earlier chapters, we discussed the infant in relationship to an older sibling. In this chapter, the infant will be discussed from the perspective of being both the older and the younger sibling. Sibling relationships in the family will be our main topic. We will cover types of interactions between siblings and interfamily differences in sibling interactions.

■ FAMILY AND SOCIETY

Types of sibling interactions

All sibling pairs share both positive and negative interactions. Furthermore, no matter what the interaction is, the children learn something specific from their siblings that they do not learn in other relationships.

If the two-year-old is a younger sibling, he or she will spend a lot of time paying attention to and following around the older sibling. Younger siblings have been observed to imitate older siblings more often than they are imitated by older siblings; younger siblings are more likely to follow older siblings' directions and suggestions and are more compliant in taking designated roles in games (Abramovitch et al., 1986; Brody et al., 1982; Lamb, 1978b; Stoneman et al., 1984).

In one study, twenty-three-month-old children were observed both with and without their older siblings (Samuels, 1980). When they were with the

Older children can be important as models and teachers for their younger siblings. The younger child seems to enjoy the company of the older, even if the younger one doesn't always understand what's going on.

siblings, the toddlers went farther from their mothers, left their mothers sooner, stayed away longer, and showed more independent exploratory behavior compared with toddlers without their siblings present. The increased boldness seems to be due almost entirely to following the older siblings around and imitating their behavior. In this way, younger children have the advantage of an older guide as they begin to explore the environment. This study does not suggest that the older sibling intentionally chooses to lead the way and teach the younger one but only that the younger one will follow what the older one does. Parents often remark that the younger child seems to learn to do things at a younger age than the firstborn, and this kind of imitative behavior may partially explain this observation.

On the other hand, older siblings are more likely to give directives, to orient the attention of the younger children, to command and prohibit, to support and to tease. Older siblings address infants in a form of motherese, except they rarely ask questions of the babies (Dunn & Kendrick, 1982; Ellis & Rogo, 1982; Jones & Adamson, 1987; Stewart, R. A. 1983). The Observation Box below shows representative directives of two-to-three-year-old siblings to their baby sisters.

OBSERVATION 1 (ENGLAND)

The younger sister, Robin, has just picked up a piece of candy from the floor and is licking it. The older brother, Duncan, tells Robin that the dog, Scottie, will eat it. When Robin doesn't listen, Duncan pushes her gently through the door.

　　Duncan: "No, don't you eat it. Scottie will eat it. Scottie will eat it. No, not you. Scottie will eat it. Not you. Scottie. Not you. Shall we go in door? Right, come on. Come on. In door, Robin. In door." (Dunn & Kendrick, 1982, p. 126).

OBSERVATION 2 (MEXICO)

Older sister Victoria and younger sister Lucha play in their courtyard with a small rabbit. Lucha is having some trouble keeping the rabbit in one place and is trying to do so by holding its ears.

　　Victoria: "Mira tu no sabes!" (Look, you don't know how!) Victoria then demonstrates how to hold the rabbit correctly (Zukow, 1990, p. 30).

■ OBSERVATION: Speech to Younger Siblings by Three-Year-Olds

The evidence suggests that after the birth of a new baby, older children become somewhat more dependent compared with firstborns of the same age without siblings. They tend to seek help more, seek proximity to their mothers more, and cry more. Research shows that the older child has good reason for behaving this way. The mother's behavior to the older child changes somewhat when the new baby is around: there is an increase in confrontation and a decrease in positive involvement with the firstborn. Even when the mother is not occupied with the baby, she tends to spend *less* time with the older child (Kendrick & Dunn, 1980; Stewart et al., 1987). Kendrick and Dunn also found that the increase in confrontations between mother and firstborn is due primarily to an increase in what they call "deliberate naughtiness" on the part of the older child. It seems that the older child's feelings of being displaced are met by the mother's increased work load in caring for two young children instead of only one.

On the other hand, two-year-olds are becoming more sensitive to the dynamics of the family environment. They are really very skilled at knowing just how to annoy the younger sibling (teasing, making disparaging remarks, showing a toy spider to a sibling who does not like spiders) on the one hand and enlisting the support of the mother during sibling conflicts on the other (Dunn & Munn, 1985). The older siblings also become adept at finding eloquent justifications to the mother for their disputes with the sibling. For example, after taking a toy away from a younger brother, the older child might say to mother, "He took it first!" or "But I needed that" (Dunn & Munn, 1987). They also become able to steer the direction of a mother-baby interaction toward their own needs or concerns (Dunn & Shatz, 1989).

Although older siblings don't shy away from causing conflict with the younger ones, when the conflict is between the mother and the younger sibling, the two-year-old older sibling might be the first to come to the rescue of the baby. Some of the strategies used by the older child to diffuse the conflict between mother and younger sibling include repeating the sibling's action that the other didn't like (drawing the mother's attention away from the younger one), giving the younger child a similar object to the one the mother had just taken away, prohibiting or scolding the mother for her punishment of the sibling, and comforting the sibling.

It is common in some societies for older siblings, even those as young as three years with adult supervision, to have some responsibilities for taking care of babies. Sibling caretakers for infants typically are found in societies that are relatively less complex and more traditional (Whiting & Whiting, 1975). If the division of labor in the family is such that the mother can't stay at home to take care of the infant, siblings are likely to take over this function. In simpler societies, all family members are called upon to do extra work. The children have more chores around the house than children in complex societies, and infant care is one of these tasks.

In Taira, a village in Okinawa, preschool girls patted, bounced, and talked to infants to calm them. If this didn't work, the girls returned them to mothers or grandmothers. Girls in Taira never bathed or fed infants, nor did they put them to bed. In Tarong, on the island of Luzon in the Philippines, child "nurses" were trained at age three to entertain, rock, and hold the baby, but adults continued to supervise them.

Among the Gusii living in Nyansongo, Kenya, child nurses were somewhat older (five to eight years), and they were given more responsibility. They were assigned the total care of an infant beginning when the infant was around two months of age. They fed, bathed, and cared for the infants while the mothers worked in nearby fields (Whiting & Whiting, 1975). In the Marquesan islands, two-year-olds become important as companions, instructors, and comforters of their infant siblings. These children were held in high esteem by the adults, who often asked the child to show off the baby. Children were relied upon to calm an infant if an adult failed (Martini & Kirkpatrick, 1981).

In summary, these studies reveal that siblings are important to each other's development. Younger siblings benefit from the guidance and protection of a role model, and they must also learn self-protective social skills and how to resolve conflicts. Older siblings benefit from being tutors and care givers by learning to focus their attention on the needs of others. When they get scolded for annoying the younger child, the older children learn the nature of codes of conduct and some complex social and emotional regulatory skills.

Interfamily differences in the types of sibling interactions

Why do some siblings fight more than others? What should parents do to help their children get along better with each other? A number of family and child factors have been associated with a higher incidence of both mother-older child and older child-younger child confrontations. We discuss the evidence for some of the factors in this section.

The older sibling's prior relationship with mother. Suppose you could divide mother-toddler pairs into two groups based on how much play and attention the toddlers got from their mothers as infants. One group of infants would be those who received a good deal of attention, whose mothers played with them often, and who received few prohibitions from their mothers. The other group of infants would be those who played less with their mothers and more on their own during the first year. Now suppose you were asked to predict which of these two groups of infants, at age two or three, responded more positively to their baby brothers or sisters when they were born.

Do you think the ones that got the most attention would be secure in their relationship with their mothers and therefore be more willing to extend their good graces to the new member of the family? Or do you think the extra attention these babies got would make them more "spoiled" and therefore less able to tolerate a new rival in their well-established and comfortable territory? Which group of firstborns, in other words, would be more jealous of the baby?

According to the findings of Dunn and Kendrick (1981), you would be right if you guessed the second hypothesis. They found that the infants who were most indulged were the most jealous: they showed little positive response to the new baby and received just as little positive response back. The effect was especially true of firstborn girls, but it was true to a limited extent with boys as well.

Related research shows that each sibling's attachment to the mother affects the quality of the sibling relationship. When the mother is present with the children, securely attached two-year-old younger siblings were less likely to be aggressive to the mother or to the older sibling when the mother played exclusively with the older sibling. Older siblings who are securely attached are more likely to respond to the needs and distress of the younger sibling in the mother's absence; older siblings who are not securely attached are less likely to do so (Teti & Ablard, 1989). A similar result has been found for twins (Vandell, Owen, Wilson, & Henderson, 1988). It is typical for both children in the same family to have similar attachment classifications (Ward et al., 1988).

Sex and age differences between the siblings. Another factor that may play a role in the incidence of positive-versus-negative sibling relationships is the sex composition of the sibling pair. Although there is a great deal of variability across families, same-sex pairs tend to have fewer instances of aggression than mixed-sex pairs, and parents are more likely to treat children in same-sex pairs equally than mixed-sex pairs (Corter et al., 1983; Stewart et al., 1987). Firstborn females are somewhat more prosocial, whereas firstborn males are somewhat more aggressive; however, these differences do not appear across all studies. Finally, the number of years between siblings does not seem to have any measurable effect on the amount of prosocial or aggressive behavior exchanged between them (Abramovitch, Corter, & Landau, 1979; Lamb, 1978c).

Temperamental differences between the siblings. Because the findings on age and sex differences between the siblings do not strongly predict the level of conflict between the siblings, some researchers have suggested that temperamental factors might be more important. Indeed, research shows that temperament is a better predictor. If one of the siblings is rated as having a generally negative mood and as being temperamentally nonadaptable, the siblings are less likely to engage in joint play. A mismatch in the temperament of the siblings is related to higher levels of conflict (Munn & Dunn, 1989).

One interpretation of these results is that the temperamental characteristics of the children affects the way that they relate to each other. Another interpretation is possible, however. As we'll see in the next chapter, one of the issues related to the measurement of infant temperament is that a parental rating of infant temperament is generally used. This introduces a possible bias in the parent's perception of the child, independent of the child's actual behavior.

The alternative interpretation related to differences in temperament between siblings is that these differences are created in part by the parents, who attempt to differentiate between siblings by viewing them as different individuals in a process called *sibling de-identification*. In this regard, research has shown that parents tend to rate the first two children in the family as having different temperaments, while temperaments for later-born children are rated more alike (Schachter & Stone, 1985). In a longitudinal study in which observers studied mother-infant interaction for the first two children in the family when each was twenty-four months, it was found that mothers expressed similar levels of affection and verbal responsiveness to both children, but there were differences in the amount of parental control of the children. Control was measured by the amount of direct interventions in the child's actions in the form of commands, rejections, and disciplinary actions (Dunn et al., 1986).

In summary, many factors are likely to play a role in how well siblings get along with each other. From a family systems perspective, it is difficult to say with certainty that a single factor taken in isolation is the cause of sibling aggression. Temperament, although it is strongly related to sibling conflict, could be multiply determined by parent-child and child-child interactions over the course of the first years of life. Is the child really difficult, or has the child come to be labeled as difficult? Or is difficult temperament a stance one takes in the face of a sibling who is constantly rejecting or ignoring? It may be some time before we can sort out the answers to these questions. ■

Infant and Child Abuse

Child abuse and neglect are problems that should concern anyone who cares about the welfare of children. The problem can take a number of forms that range in relative severity. "Abuse" typically refers to cases in which a child sustains a nonaccidental injury from a parent or other care giver. Estimates of the incidence of child abuse are not very satisfying due to deficiencies in reporting procedures. Referring to abuse only, there may be as many as several hundred thousand cases in the United States every year. Abuse and neglect combined may reach the one million mark (Fontana, 1973).

What are the causes and effects of child abuse?

No one knows for sure what causes child abuse, although certain factors have been implicated. The four most important are (1) child characteristics, (2) parental personality, (3) the history of the parent-child interaction, and (4) the relative level of social stress on the family (Belsky, 1980; Lamb, 1978b).

Some infants and children, by virtue of being endowed with undesirable characteristics, may contribute to their own abuse. Infants who are deformed, slow to develop, and relatively unresponsive place demands upon their care givers that normal infants do not. Research suggests that premature infants and infants with handicaps, Down's syndrome, and other illnesses are overrepresented in the abused population (Burgess, 1979; Sherrod et al., 1984). These babies are often expensive to care for and thus contribute to family stress. They require more effort and are more fussy and demanding than other infants. In addition, they show less positive affect and therefore provide fewer reinforcements for the care giver (see the Family and Society section in Chapter 9).

Parental factors play an important role in child abuse. Abusive parents showed less positive emotions, interacted with their babies less, and talked less to their babies than nonabusive parents in a study by Burgess and Conger (1978). Abusive parents were less adept at verbal skills in general, scored lower in abstract reasoning, and showed a reduced capacity for planning and control over impulses. Abusing fathers, in particular, were lower in parental warmth and interpersonal relationships, and they were more introverted than nonabusive fathers (Hyman & Mitchell, 1977). Child abusers have been found to be hypersensitive to their infants. Instead of adaptively tuning out a loud or piercing cry, the abusers were likely to get annoyed and aroused by the crying (Frodi & Lamb, 1980).

Abusers are less able to correctly identify emotion signals, and in some cases, they interpret negative emotion as positive (Kropp & Haynes, 1987). Compared to normal parents, child abusers view child rearing as less satisfactory and more difficult, and they and their children tend to live more isolated lives (Trickett & Susman, 1988). Some evidence suggests that parents who abuse their children were themselves abused as children (Parke & Collmer, 1975).

Parents who neglect their children but do not abuse them seem to be somewhat different. The overall picture of the abusing parent is of a hypersensitive and nonempathic person. The neglectful parent, in contrast, seems to be more apathetic and depressed (Polansky, 1976). Fortunately, none of these factors is conclusive evidence that parents actually are going to abuse or neglect their children. Many parents who suffer from these problems in

continued at top of next page

APPLICATIONS

their personality or personal histories never show signs of child maltreatment.

Another important factor in child abuse is family stress. Higher rates of child abuse has been recorded in lower social classes (Burgess, 1979; Garbarino, 1976; Garbarino & Crouter, 1978; Gil, 1970). The stress in lower-income families may be caused by a number of factors. Low income is one factor, but economic stress alone is not a major factor (Garbarino, 1976). More important factors seem to be the availability of social support systems and the stability and continuity of day-to-day existence. Families that are constantly changing in size, composition, and location are more at risk for abuse than others.

Maltreated children do not fare as well as children who have not been maltreated. They have been found to show more anxious than secure attachments at twelve and eighteen months than normal children (Lamb et al., 1985). At two years, the maltreated children showed more anger, frustration, and opposition, as well as a relative slowdown in developmental progress over the first year (Egeland & Sroufe, 1981). George and Main (1979) studied abused versus nonabused children in a day-care setting. They found that the abused children were less likely to seek comfort from the adult care givers, more likely to avoid contact with care givers and peers, and more likely to be aggressive.

Several studies have found that the attachment patterns of abused children do not fit into the typical three categories used in the Ainsworth Strange Situation Test. Resistant infants alternate between clinging and pulling away, while avoidant infants tend to ignore the presence of the mother and will reject her advances. Abused infants' response to the Strange Situation has been described as disorganized/disoriented, comprised of a strong proximity seeking of the mother on reunion, followed immediately by a strong avoidance of her or gaze aversion while approaching her (Carlson, et al., 1989; Main & Solomon, 1986). This pattern may be the result of a fear of the mother mixed with normal attachment motivations, creating a conflict between approach and withdrawal.

Other negative effects on infants of abuse include a lack of concern for the distress of peers and an often inappropriate response to distress, such as by physical aggression (Main & George, 1985). Abused infants compared to nonabused have shorter MLU, less speech related to their own emotional states, and less speech that is relevant to the ongoing topic of conversation (Coster et al., 1989).

Since the children in these studies are under the age of three years, the conclusions are very disturbing. They suggest that abusing parents can disrupt the normal developmental process by which infants come to seek help, comfort, and information from people around them. In other words, at as young as two years, abused children show behavior that is nonadaptive to the extent of avoiding those who might offer and extend support and encouragement.

What are the limitations of the research on child abuse?

All the factors previously mentioned probably are interrelated in their impact on child abuse. For example, there are higher rates of handicapped and premature births in mothers of lower social class. However, it is possible that the reporting rates are higher for lower-class children than for middle-class children. A more difficult problem is that the causes of child abuse are likely to be particularistic: some factors are more likely to operate with

APPLICATIONS

certain people than with others (Garbarino, 1982). Therefore, any research design that does not take into account the complex interactions between different types of people, circumstances, and infant characteristics will find few systematic effects.

Another problem with research on child abuse is that studies almost always begin with a sample of abused infants and abusing parents. The search for causes of child abuse then are limited to only those people who actually demonstrate the symptom. Usually researchers try to trace the abuser's or the abused infant's history back in time. Findings such as "Child abusers were abused as children" and "Handicapped infants are more likely to be abused" are typical conclusions from this kind of research.

When a target sample's history is traced backward through time, it is known as a *retrospective study*. Whereas it may be the case that, for example, most abusing parents were in fact abused as children, it is not true that being abused as a child always will lead to becoming an abusive parent. If we looked at the data prospectively, we would have to sample all children in a generation, follow them up until they became parents themselves, and then see which of them abused their children. Obviously, such a study cannot be done. If it were, however, we would probably find that only a very small percentage of abused children actually ended up abusing their own children.

What can be concluded from this evidence? A history of abuse in the family of origin is one factor that may contribute to a person's becoming an abusive parent, but other factors must operate on abused children to make them into abusing parents. We do not know what these factors are at present because of the difficulty of doing this kind of research.

Social and cultural influences are major factors likely to affect the outcomes of parents with a history of abuse or to lead other parents to become abusers. We live in a society in which violence is accepted. It occurs in the streets, and we are inundated with mass media violence (Gil, 1970).

Do these factors cause child abuse? It is hard to say and harder to do research that might establish a conclusive link between social values and the incidence of abuse and neglect. We might think of doing a cross-cultural study in which we would select societies that varied in the amount of value placed on violence and corporal punishment and then look to see if this dimension correlated with child abuse or neglect. The problem is that these societies are likely to differ on factors other than the value of violence, and we could not say whether violence alone, violence in combination with other factors, or those other factors alone were most responsible for the observed amount of child abuse.

It would not be totally unwarranted at this time, however, to say that abuse and neglect are social and family problems—not merely the result of individual factors in the parent. If this is true it suggests that we can act to prevent child abuse by strengthening community and neighborhood support systems for parents, providing human services for families as a whole rather than for single individuals, and taking preventive measures to strengthen the relationship between the family and the community support systems when the child is born. The birth of a child invariably brings parents into contact with community institutions. Action at this time is essential, since some parents may not contact other community institutions until the child is in school, and by then it may be too late (Garbarino, 1982; Hamilton, 1989; Wiehe, 1989).

POINTS OF CONTACT

In the second year of life, children discover the power of assertiveness over their parents. In the third year, children expand this personal sense of force to their own bodies and to other people. It is easier for parents to deal with a situation in which another child takes a toy from their child than a situation in which it is their own child that does the taking (or biting or pushing). These behaviors are natural developments of the child's growing self-awareness and the child's exploration of the limits of the self's power and ability. It helps to remain calm in such situations, to insure that the wronged child is properly attended, and not to overreact. Biting, however, needs to be dealt with firmly because of the risks to the health of the bitten child.

Parents may worry when they see their children manually exploring their genitals for the first time. A parent may want to distract the child by offering a toy, but reprimanding is not recommended. Self-exploration is a natural part of development, as are a child's curiosity about the sex organs of others, the origins of babies, and so on. It helps to keep your answers to sex-related questions simple, direct, and honest. The child does not treat these questions with any more prurient interest than questions about the moon, the grass, or the picture book, so why should you?

Genuine socialization begins at this age. Children need to be introduced to a wide range of experiences and places, but only gradually and at the pace that seems most comfortable to them. As children are learning self-help skills, it is easy to let them take greater responsibility for some of these tasks. Examples are picking out and putting on clothes, wiping themselves, washing and drying their own hands, and so on.

One of the most striking contradictions of this age is that the children's growing appreciation of reality and their own place in it is mixed with a growing fantasy life and a whole new crop of very unrealistic (at least to the adult) fears that come up in dreams and while awake. Remember that such fears are very real to children. They may arise because they begin to notice things they never noticed before, and they realize that there are things they do not understand.

Because a child's fears seem silly and inconsequential to an adult, there is a tendency to laugh at them or to tease the child about them. This does not help the child, who probably needs reassurance more than anything else. Two-year-olds are beginning to have worries just like anyone else. They may have nightmares, bite their nails, stutter, or show other signs of behavior disruption. It is important to try to understand the source of children's worries and help them to solve the problems.

Children also are becoming more active participants in the adult world. They may want to help out around the house, preschool, or day-care center. Even though this may mean getting work done more slowly or with some extra mess, it pays to encourage these budding signs of helpfulness, at least once in a while. It helps to talk about the next thing that is going to happen while you are engaged in a task. This aids in a child's understanding that one thing leads to another. Telling the child about expectable future events also may help alleviate some fears. Talking about a visit to the doctor, a new baby-sitter, or some other potentially disturbing situation can be a very effective means of avoiding trouble before it begins. Teaching good habits in staying clean, picking up toys, and putting away clothing can be started at this time, and the child's own initiatives are not to be ignored. You will have to take the role of a reminder and a coach for many years to come, so don't be discouraged if the child does not take over right away.

In the realm of play, two-year-old children enjoy such things as clay and fingerpainting. These materials are wonderful ways to let children creatively exercise their newfound fine motor skills. Children of this age also like sand and water, which go best with pails and shovels. Cars and pegboards are also of great interest. Be sure the toys you get are safe—nontoxic, not sharp or jagged, and having no parts that can be swallowed.

At this age, children get involved in many exciting things, and they want to have their own say about most things. The problem is that they have trouble striking a balance between alternatives and extremes. It is typical for two-year-olds to play too long and get overtired. It is hard for children to relax at bedtime; they may need a story, a talk with parents, or just some time to themselves before they can settle down.

It is common to see movement from one extreme to another at this age; for example staying dry all day and then suddenly wetting, or screaming for dinner and then turning it down when it finally appears. These swings can be frustrating for parents, but they are necessary steps on the path to autonomous self-regulation.

■ SUMMARY

Motor and Cognitive Development

■ Motor skills become more complex and adaptive during the third year, including running, jumping, constructing with blocks, and making art.

■ Motor skills become integrated with language and cognition, as language regulates the execution of a motor skill and self-produced movement enhances cognition.

■ Children are now able to execute complex sequences of action, work toward an adult standard, and correct their own errors. This leads to increases in attention span.

■ Language becomes internalized as private speech such that prior forms of social regulation now become self-regulatory.

■ Make-believe and pretend become complex and creative.

Emotional Development

■ A sense of categorical self emerges, including age and gender self-labeling.

■ Descriptions of emotional states of the self and others become elaborate.

■ Three-year-olds can act by taking the behavior of others into account, but they do not yet behave as if they have a clear theory of the other's mind.

■ Children of this age lack the ability to differentiate reality from make-believe in most cases.

Social and Language Development

■ Grammar emerges with the use of verbs and the ability to add the appropriate endings to words for tense and number.
■ Complex question asking emerges.
■ Limitations of language include pronunciation problems, inability to appreciate complex grammar, and lack of skill in maintaining conversations.
■ Peer interaction shows evidence of coordinated actions, imitative and complementary turn taking, and the emergence of friendships.
■ The acquisition of sex-role stereotypes is a complex developmental process involving cognitive understanding of gender and family role relationships.

Family and Society

■ Older and younger siblings derive different benefits from their mutual interactions. Younger siblings benefit from the guidance and protection of the older sibling and learn self-protection skills. Older siblings learn to pay attention to the needs of others and about the leadership role.
■ Interfamily differences in sibling conflict may depend on the children's prior relationships and attachments to parents, on the sex similarity of the pair, on the temperament of the children, and on sibling de-identification by the parents.

Applications: Infant and Child Abuse

■ Factors contributing to child abuse include child, parent, and societal influences. Child abuse is multicausal, and treatment approaches should recognize this.
■ Research on child abuse is problematic because of the way in which data is gathered and because of how the data is interpreted.

■ GLOSSARY

Dramatists   Children who classify objects based on a script or story in which the objects are embedded.

Imaginative play   Play in which the child invents make-believe situations.

Liquidating play   Play in which the child's make-believe situation alters reality to better suit the child's desires.

Metalinguistic knowledge   An understanding of the uses and functions of language, independent of knowledge of semantics and syntax.

Patterners   Children who classify objects based on similarities in their forms or functions.

Private speech   An internalized dialogue with the self in which children describe their thoughts and actions out loud.

Prospective study   A longitudinal research study in which data is gathered from subjects at periodic intervals, so that the subject's current behavior and ideas are being observed.

Retrospective study   A research study in which the past of a subject is recollected by the subject or in which the experimenter traces records of the subjects backward in time.

Sibling de-identification   The process by which parents differentiate between siblings.

Theory of mind   The idea that other people have independent beliefs and feelings.

TWELVE

The Effects of the Infancy Period on the Formation of Individual Differences

---

Is early experience important or critical for later development? Do traumatic experiences in infancy, such as extreme poverty or maternal deprivation, affect later cognitive or social functioning? Can we predict whether a child will be bright, average, or dull from scores on assessment tests done in early infancy? Can later developmental dysfunctions be diagnosed from early infant testing? What is the importance of infancy in the human life cycle?

These questions have been reserved for the last chapter of this book for several reasons. First, answering them requires one to examine individual stability and change across the entire age span of infancy and from infancy to later childhood and adulthood. This type of long-term approach is difficult to discuss in chapters focused on particular age periods. Second, answering these questions requires an examination of the concepts and methods used in longitudinal research. Although we have discussed findings of longitudinal studies—such as the relationships between attachment at twelve months and peer competence in the preschool—we have not addressed the potentials and problems unique to the interpretation of such studies.

There are no simple answers to the questions raised in the first paragraph. For some questions, we have no answers at all, aside from theoretical speculation. An appreciation of the research difficulties requires some familiarity with the way in which research in this area is carried out and the implicit and explicit theories that guide the work.

■ CONTINUITY BETWEEN EARLY AND LATER DEVELOPMENT

In order to make sense of the complexity of the infancy period, most scholars have adopted one or another perspective about the meaning of infancy and the ways in which infant experiences become transformed through interaction and development to contribute to the formation of individual differences. The author of this text is no exception (cf. Fogel, 1990), and my position is outlined in the section of this chapter entitled "Development as a Dynamic Process." The reader is referred to other detailed treatments of this problem: in the chapters comprising the final two sections (on risk factors and current issues) of the *Handbook of Infant Development,* second edition, edited by J. Osofsky (1987); in *Sensitive Periods in Development: Interdisciplinary Perspectives,* edited by M. Bornstein (1987); in *Individual Differences in Infancy: Reliability, Stability, and Predictions,* edited by J. Colombo and J. W. Fagen (1990); and in a variety of other works, many of which are cited throughout this text.

What makes children different from each other? The formation of individual differences is a complicated field of study about which we understand relatively little.

■ TABLE 12.1   Forms of Developmental Continuity

TYPE OF CONTINUITY	EXAMPLE
Absolute consistency	A lack of change during development. Once an ability is acquired, it is never lost or altered, such as the ability to form attachments or to think symbolically.
Consistent pattern of change	A particular ability has a predictable and invariant developmental course, for example, cooing, babbling, and single words precede the onset of language.
Consistent pattern of behavior	A predominant mode of behaving in spite of minor fluctuations. An infant who generally is withdrawn may show some instances of openness, but more usually, a pattern of withdrawal can be inferred across a variety of circumstances.
Consistent relation to the group	Even though developmental change occurs, individuals maintain their relative ranking within a group. For example, an infant gets taller but may always be short compared to other infants of the same age.
Consistency in process	Behavior is not consistent, but the underlying process may not be different across time. For example, a sensitive and warm social partner may be necessary at all ages, but the type of relationship will not be the same at each age (infant-mother, infant-teacher, infant-peer).
Consistency between early and later factors	Events and experiences early in infancy have an impact on some later outcome. For example, the security of early attachments predicts other social and cognitive abilities during the preschool years.

SOURCE: Rutter (1987).

Developmentalists generally talk about lasting individual differences in terms of developmental continuity. *Continuity* is the extent to which aspects of the individual are preserved from one age to another. The existence of developmental continuity would suggest that a particular sensitivity or ability acquired in infancy is likely to affect in some way the functioning of the individual at later ages. There are many forms of continuity, some of which are listed in Table 12.1.

Continuity has been investigated in many different areas, and we cannot cover them all in this chapter. In this text, we have already reviewed a considerable amount of research related to continuity, although we have not labeled it as continuity research. We begin with a brief review of these topics, including perinatal factors; motor development; maternal employment and day care; attachment; care-giving and disciplinary styles; risk, disadvantage, and parent-infant intervention programs; and gender-related behavior. The student is encouraged to reread the relevant sections in the text from the perspective of continuity. In addition, we will cover in more detail several continuity effects that have not been discussed earlier, including intellectual development and temperament.

Perinatal Factors

The long-term effects of heredity on later behavior were discussed in Chapters 2 and 3. The data suggests that the effects of one's heredity are nondeterministic. That is, not everyone with the same types of genes or chromosomes will inherit the phenotypic characteristic usually associated with those genes or chromosomes. Some genetic structures have a higher probability of being expressed in the phenotype, and these structures are typically associated with severe disorders. The genetic contributions to behavior, cognition, emotion, and personality have a much lower probability of being expressed in the phenotype because many genes are involved, and they require a specific set of environmental contingencies in order to be expressed.

Heredity influence is an example of continuity in which there is a consistency between early and later factors (Table 12.1), that is, an early factor (the genes) is consistently related to a later outcome (for example, PKU or temperament). Our discussion of heredity shows that a strict continuity is observed only in some cases. It is more typical for environmental mediating factors to influence the way in which those genes are expressed or not expressed in the individual.

Another topic we have already covered is premature birth and other perinatal factors (see Chapters 4 and 9). Newborns are susceptible to a wide range of perinatal problems ranging from oxygen deprivation to low birth weight. For all infants, the period immediately following birth is a time of adjustment from intrauterine to extrauterine life. An infant who suffers from one or more risk factors in the perinatal period may be unable to cope with the normal stresses of the first months of life and therefore may fall behind in developmental progress.

In general, research has found that many perinatal problems can be alleviated by a supportive environment. In a multiracial, multiclass sample of 670 infants born on the Hawaiian island of Kauai, all groups of children—regardless of race, social class, or age of mother—had about the same proportion of perinatal complications. In this sample, 13 percent suffered moderate complications, and 3 percent had severe complications. However, group membership predicted how well the infant recovered from the complication. Children born into lower-income families were less likely to recover fully by age two. By age ten, the effects of perinatal problems had all but disappeared for all the groups, but children from lower-income groups had lower scores on intelligence tests and were doing worse in school than children from middle-income groups (Werner, Bierman, & French, 1971).

Other research in this area has supported these conclusions. In general, the more stressful the environment and the more parents lack economic and social support systems, the more likely it will be that infants will not recover quickly from perinatal risk factors. The continuity with negative outcomes tends to be related to the total number of risk factors and/or traumas, which have an additive effect (Baker & Mednick, 1984; Breitmayer & Ramey, 1986; Crockenberg, 1981; Johnson et al., 1987; Rutter, 1987; Sameroff & Chandler, 1975; Sigman et al., 1981; Waters et al., 1980). However, if there are adequate economic resources, if the parents are not under psychosocial stress, and if the perinatal complications are not too severe, the effects are usually not continuous over a long term. Thus, continuity arises because of consistency in the environments to which the infant is exposed, environments that either alleviate or exacerbate the early risk factor.

Another general proposition to emerge from this research is that the more severe the perinatal disorder, the more likely that long-term effects will be continuous. For example, by the gestational age of two years, when most preterms have caught up with full-terms, infants who were very low birth weight (less than 1,500 grams) are more passive and less attentive than the full-terms of the same gestational age, and some very-low-birth-weight infants have continuing cognitive and attentional deficits at school age (Barrera et al., 1987; Vohr & Coll, 1985). Other extreme factors, such as auditory neurological deficits measured at birth that relate later to impaired auditory sensitivity (Murray, 1988) and other forms of severe brain damage at birth, have also been found to be related to later cognitive and sensory impairment (Stewart, A., 1983). Finally, particular types of early onset teratogens, especially those that occur during the periods of rapid growth of the limbs, organs, and brain, are generally continuous with later disorders, such as fetal alcohol syndrome.

These findings represent many of the types of continuity shown in Table 12.1. For example, the deformation of a limb or a disorder of auditory neurology reflects absolute consistencies in which the affected organ reaches a final state during early life and does not change later. The effects of very low birth weight could be part of an absolute consistency associated with brain damage, or it could reflect a general retardation of developmental progress and thus be an example of consistency in relation to the group (that is, these babies continue to score lower than full-terms even after many years).

If infants are not at risk, their behavior in the perinatal period seems not to predict any later aspects of infant functioning. Bell, Wéller, and Waldrop (1971) found virtually no perinatal behavior that predicted the behavior of children in the preschool years. Dunn (1975) found that the success (or lack of success) with which the mother and infant adjusted to each other during early feedings did not predict later mother-infant interaction patterns. These authors speak of the newborn's *buffering* against difficulties of early adjustment, whereas Sameroff and Chandler (1975) speak of the infant's having a *self-righting ability:* given an appropriately responsive environment, perinatal complications do not create any lasting organismic deficits.

Perhaps if mothers are not under stress and are predisposed to providing competent care, the infant at risk evokes more maternal attention and solicitude than normal infants (Bakeman & Brown, 1980; Beckwith & Cohen, 1978; Crawford, 1982). This increased solicitude may be a factor in alleviating the early deficits over the first year or two of life. Thus, in certain circumstances, the environment can *compensate* for individual variation in perinatal factors.

Motor Development

Environmental influence on normal motor development was discussed in Chapters 6 and 7. As a general rule, environmental stimulation of particular motor systems does advance the infant receiving that stimulation in the short-term, compared to other infants. We reviewed in particular the case of African infant motor development in which infants are given a rigorous program of exercises and stretches, leading to an earlier onset of sitting, standing, and walking than in Europe and North America. We also discussed the research on attempts to give babies practice in standing and walking. In general, these differences in environmental stimulation do not lead to long-term differences. Even though the exercised babies may sometimes achieve a motor milestone earlier, it does not mean that as preschoolers they will be superior in motor development to babies who achieved their milestone at a later date. Alternatively, in infants at risk, physical and motor stimulation can have an important remediative effect leading to catch-up growth.

At least as far as the evidence gleaned from normal variations of infant development shows, there does not seem to be any continuity between early motor practice and later outcome. As mentioned earlier, however, there is relatively little research in the area of motor development, so it would be incorrect to reach any general conclusions at this time. In the preschool and later years, practice with a motor skill does have a definite effect on later ability, as is seen in the teaching of sports and music to children.

What is unknown, however, is the extent to which very early exposure to music, art, or athletics will produce a later genius. Some children may have a particular facility and desire for one or another area of endeavor and with appropriate guidance may achieve high levels of skill (Sternberg & Davidson, 1985; Wallach, 1985). However, in the absence of the child's early desire and facility, early intensive skill testing and training is not advisable for the majority of young children. The provision of a preschool education program that is responsive to the needs of the individual child and that has the resources to challenge each child at his or her level of interest seems to be the most useful approach (Johnson, 1983).

Maternal Employment and Day Care

We discussed the effects of maternal employment in Chapter 7 and the effects of day care in Chapter 9. There does not appear to be a continuity between maternal employment or day care and later child developmental outcomes. Instead, the long-term effects are mediated by other factors. One of the major risks related to maternal employment is for the mother herself, especially if she has an economic need to work but would prefer to stay at home or if she is highly career motivated and suffers from role overload. In some, but not in all cases, these mothers may have some difficulty establishing a secure relationship with their infants. We know little, however, about the long-term effects of maternal employment during infancy on later child development.

The risks in day care lie primarily in the quality of care available. The risks are highest for infants under the age of six months who are in poor quality care, and some effects have been found in preschool and kindergarten for these children. The research, however, is difficult to interpret because of methodological problems and differences across studies. Infants under the age of six months in high-quality day care may develop different patterns of social and cognitive skills compared to their home-reared peers, although the long-term effects beyond the infancy period of these positive outcomes are unknown at the present time.

Attachment

Research on attachment has found consistency between early and later factors (Table 12.1), for example, in the relationship between parental sensitivity in the first year and later security of attachment and between security of attachment at age one year and later social and intellectual competence in preschool. Consistency of process is shown by the general stability of attachment security between one year and six years, even though the specific types of attachment behavior differ at each age (see Chapter 8). The current explanation for these types of continuity is the concept of the internal working model of attachment, suggesting that individuals acquire particular expectations from their early social relationships that they then carry over into other relationships. Because internal working models are relatively stable and only get changed very slowly, they may account for the long-term consistencies in attachment across time.

Care-giving and Disciplinary Styles

In Chapter 10, we discussed a style of parent-infant interaction called guided participation. This approach is based on following up the child's spontaneous interests and actions, structuring those actions in ways that enhance the child's competence and sense of participation, and then allowing the child to take increasing responsibility. This type of developmental strategy has been shown to be correlated with more advanced language and cognitive skills in infants and in older children.

Guided participation is also related to authoritative parenting styles that combine respect for the child's interests and points of view and parental firmness in the enforcement of rules. Such child outcomes as independence, cooperativeness, and social competence have been associated with authoritative parenting. We also noted that parental proactive behavior—preparing the environment or the child for anticipated positive outcomes—is part of guidance and authoritative disciplinary styles. Infant compliance is more readily assured if parents use proactive planning and guidance strategies, rather than confrontational approaches.

Research related to attachment (Chapter 9) has shown that maternal responsivity to infant behavior during the first year is correlated with secure attachment at twelve months. Cognitive and language development have been found to correlate with maternal vocalization, contingent responsiveness, and parenting involvement in the first two years and in the third year with parental proactive behavior, such as providing opportunities to interact with other people and to explore the environment (Bradley et al., 1979; Carew, 1980; Feiring & Lewis, 1981; Wachs & Gruen, 1982).

The research in this area is, however, not well developed. Global measures of parenting often are not sensitive to variations in disciplinary style that depend on the nature of the infraction and the responsivity of the child to adult interventions. Furthermore, there are cross-family and cross-cultural differences in care giving that are difficult to compare on any absolute scale of parental effectiveness. Finally, all of the findings in this area are based on correlations, which means two things. First, the parent's style could be shaped by the child's behavior, at least in part. Second, the correlations are typically positive but small, meaning that while there is a general association between care giving and child behavior, the association may not hold true for particular individuals.

The ultimate question is whether the continuity between care giving and child positive outcome is sustained by factors inherent in the child over time, by the consistency of adult care over time, or by an ongoing transaction between the adult and the child in which the interaction promotes consistent behaviors in both participants. Consistency could also derive from the influence of mediating factors on the parent-infant dyad, such as the effect of social supports (Chapter 10) and economic advantage and disadvantage (Chapter 10).

Risk, Disadvantage, and Parent-Infant Intervention Programs

As we saw in Chapter 10, economic disadvantage is a clear case in which consistency of negative outcomes can be maintained over long periods in the absence of any other mediating factors. Children from poor families are developmentally handicapped at all ages. They suffer more from depression, poor peer relationships, social withdrawal, low self-esteem, aggressiveness, and deviant behavior. They are more likely to have physical ailments, school problems, and language and cognitive deficits. In the Applications section of Chapter 10, we explored some of the cyclical processes that tend to maintain these negative outcomes over time. Stress, nutrition, health, and behavior interact to create increasingly negative patterns.

Another major risk factor in early development is severe stress on the infant and the family. Stress may be due to economic deprivation. It may also be due to disease, hospitalizations and other extended separations, parental psycho-pathology, family changes due to relocation or parental or sibling death, and extreme situations of social unrest, such as war, persecution, famine, migration, or being refugees. The research is complicated, detailed in some areas and not in others, and often dependent on case studies and personal recollections. Nevertheless, after extensive review of this literature, Rutter (1979) concluded that a single stressful incident in early infancy has negligible long-term effects. However, multiple stresses create cyclical patterns of increasing risk and deprivation and are more likely to be associated with long-term emotional or behavioral disorders in later childhood.

We also looked in Chapter 10 at the effects of early intervention programs, such as Head Start and other parent-infant programs. Although research on the long-term effectiveness of these programs is difficult to do, there is some evidence that such interventions do make a difference, especially for disadvantaged children and especially when the intervention contains some parent-educational component either in the home or at the program center (Burchinal et al., 1989; Lyons-Ruth et al., 1990).

Interventions involving nutritional supplementation when malnutrition is a factor are generally successful if they are accompanied by parent-child behavioral interventions (see Chapters 4 and 7; Cravioto & Arrieta, 1983; Stein & Susser, 1985; Winick et al., 1975). In a study done in Colombia, malnutrition was treated in one group with only food supplementation for the entire family and in another group with food supplementation plus parent education during home visits. The children in the group that received supplementation plus parent education were taller and heavier at the age of six years and had fewer cases of mental retardation than the food-only group (Super et al., 1990).

One problem with intervention research is that the populations of children served vary enormously between locations. In addition, even clearly outlined interventions will vary in their application according to location, staff training and interpretation, and the reactions of the children and their families. The Mother-Child Home Program, found to work well with disadvantaged children in the United States, was relatively ineffective in a broader-based population of children in Bermuda (Scarr & McCartney, 1988).

Thus, the best statement that can be made at the current time is that some programs work some of the time for some groups and that overall, intervention programs provide an important source of enrichment and encouragement for parents who are under social and economic stress. In this perspective, short-term relief from stress may be as valuable as any long-term developmental benefit. It could be that the long-term effects are present but that researchers have not been able to develop measures to assess them. Virtually all researchers and practitioners agree that early intervention is important and should continue for many years into the future. In supporting the continuation of Head Start at increased funding levels into the 1990s, the U.S. Congress and the president apparently concur with child-care professionals.

Gender-Related Behavior

We saw in Chapter 11 that by three years of age, children are beginning to express a gender identity, and they are beginning to adopt sex-role appropriate behavior. What has been difficult to establish is the extent to which individual differences in the sex-role orientations (that is, from traditional to egalitarian) of children are consistent with any factors in their prior history. So far, research has not yielded any strong conclusions. There are individual differences in sex-role orientations from a young age, but these differences do not possess a high degree of any form of continuity over time. The stability of sex-role orientation may not emerge until later childhood or young adulthood. For example, the sex-role socialization behavior of the parents (selecting sex-role-appropriate toys for children), especially that of the father, is strongly related to the father's prior history and beliefs about roles.

Gender differences during infancy have been related to factors other than sex role socialization. For example, males seem to be more vulnerable to the effects of environmental stress. When they grow up in homes that are overcrowded, noisy, or confusing, males show deficits in their cognitive development, while females growing up in similar environments do not. Environmental opportunities to explore large areas in the home were more beneficial for the long-term cognitive development of males compared to females. Females, but not males, who were provided with a great deal of stimulus variety (different colors, shapes, and textures in the home) showed higher levels of cognitive development (Rutter, 1979; Wachs & Gruen, 1982). Finally, higher levels of androgens (hormones associated with masculinity) at birth are correlated with lower scores on spatial ability for girls at six years, but variations of androgen level has no effect on variability of spatial ability in boys (Jacklin et al., 1988).

Although the reasons for these long-term continuities are not entirely clear, it may be that boys and girls process information differently or that they require different types of environmental inputs in order to maintain similar levels of cognitive growth. This has been called the environmental specificity of long-term effects (Wachs, 1982). *Environmental specificity* occurs when

Providing large numbers of toys to infants is no guarantee of advanced intellectual development. The toys must be chosen to match the inclinations of the child, and must be accompanied by sensitive social play and opportunities for individual exploration.

certain aspects of the environment are more effective in promoting specific types of competencies than others or when certain aspects of the environment are more effective in promoting development in some children but not in others.

Intellectual Development

Environmental specificity effects have been found in long-term continuity studies of factors in early infancy that promote cognitive and intellectual development.

For example, early exposure in the first year to a variety of inanimate objects and to contingently responsive inanimate objects has been shown to lead to a greater skill in problem solving and exploratory play in the second year (Yarrow et al., 1975). The provision of age-appropriate play materials during the first two years strongly predicts a child's Stanford-Binet IQ score at four and a half years (Bradley & Caldwell, 1976), as well as elementary school achievement test scores between five and nine years of age (VanDoorninck et al., 1981).

The development of spatial relations and perspective taking could be predicted best by the avoidance of noise, confusion, and environmental overcrowding during the first two years. In contrast, exploratory play skills in the second and third year were best enhanced by care givers' providing responsive objects and a variety of objects in the first year. These factors, plus a well-organized environment and the use of age-appropriate play materials, were the best predictors of a child's ability to invent new means and plan effective strategies (Wachs, 1982; Wachs & Gruen, 1982; Widmayer et al., 1990).

How specific factors may mediate the influence of other factors in development is shown in the following study. Siegal (1981) measured infants on the Bayley Mental Scale at four, eight, twelve, and eighteen months and then tested their performance on the Reynell Developmental Language Scales at two, three, and four years. Siegal also assessed the nature of infants' home environments in this longitudinal study involving 148 infants.

If we look at the Bayley scores as predictive of the language scores at two years, there was no relationship. Infants who scored low on the Bayley test could be developing normally at two years in the area of language, or they could be slower than average. The same two outcomes were possible for children who had normal scores on the Bayley test in the first year (see Figure 12.1).

Of the four groups of two-year-olds shown in Figure 12.1, two of them fit a simple-effects pattern. In Group 1, low Bayley scores led to low language scores; in Group 4, normal Bayley scores led to high language scores. Groups 2 and 3 do not fit. In each of these cases, the environment played a significant role (Siegal, 1981).

Infants in Group 2, who had low Bayley scores in the first year but who scored high on language at age two, had home environments that were significantly more enriched and stimulating than the home environments of Group 1 babies. Infants in Group 3, who had low language scores in spite of

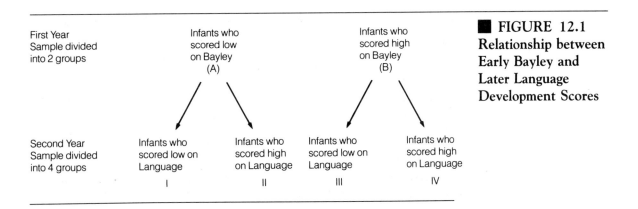

■ FIGURE 12.1
Relationship between Early Bayley and Later Language Development Scores

the fact that they were developing normally in the first year, had a less enriched environment than infants in Group 4. Similar results were also reported by Ungerer and Sigman (1984).

Another interpretation of this study is that the very early tendencies of the infant and the environment are less important in determining long-term intellectual outcomes than later experiences, those that occur after the second year of life. Family factors after the age of two years are better predictors of cognitive outcomes than similar family factors earlier in infancy (Bradley & Caldwell, 1984; Coll, 1990; Ramey et al., 1984).

In general, the results of these studies show that there are few consistent relationships between infant and family factors early in life and later cognitive developmental outcomes. In other words, there is little continuity of cognitive development across the infancy period. In most cases, these findings suggest that cognitive development is mediated by a number of factors, most of which occur after the second year of life.

In contrast to this perspective, a number of studies suggest that the reason for the lack of continuity is that investigators have used measures of cognitive development that are too global: the child's overall score on a developmental assessment or MLU. Research that has focused on particular ways in which infants directly process information have been more successful in uncovering continuities. In particular, infants in the first six months vary in their efficiency of information processing. In a habituation task, for example, some infants habituate rather quickly and require less looking time overall to process the visual stimulus. These efficient information processing strategies in early infancy are correlated with higher childhood standardized cognitive and language development test scores. Infants who at four months continued to fixate on an unchanging stimulus had lower intelligence test scores at eight years of age (Bornstein & Sigman, 1986; Rose et al., 1988; Rose et al., 1989; Sigman et al, 1986; Tamis-LeMonda & Bornstein, 1989).

In play tasks, some one-year-old infants are more focused on the particular toy and persist in exploring many of the toy's properties, while other infants show more variable attention spans. These inattentive infants will move rapidly from one toy to the next without spending much time investigating the individual properties of each. These babies seem to move restlessly between things without fully appreciating the properties of any one thing. Babies who are inattentive at one year also tend to be inattentive at age three and later score lower on intelligence tests (Heinicke et al., 1986; Heinicke & Lampl, 1988; Ruff et al., 1990; Wenckstern et al., 1984).

Both the mediated effects view and the direct continuity view could be correct. That is, some factors are more likely to be mediated by the current social and physical environment of the child. Other factors may be more permanently a part of the individual and less subject to environmental influence. Another interpretation of the direct continuity studies is that the continuity is due to constant social and physical factors that the investigator did not measure.

Temperament

Temperament refers to lasting individual differences in emotional expressiveness and general responsiveness to the environment. Researchers have identified a number of expressive and responsive dimensions along which infants vary. One list of temperamental dimensions, developed by Thomas & Chess (1977), is given in Table 12.2. On each dimension, some children are especially high or especially low, and such extreme cases have been referred to as "easy" or as "difficult" (see Table 12.2; Thomas & Chess, 1977).

■ TABLE 12.2 Temperamental Characteristics Crucial in Classifying Children as Easy or Difficult*

TEMPERAMENTAL QUALITY	2 MONTHS	2 YEARS
Activity level	Does not move when being dressed or during sleep.	Enjoys quiet play with puzzles. Can listen to records for hours.
	Moves often in sleep. Wriggles when diaper is changed.	**Climbs furniture. Explores. Gets in and out of bed while being put to sleep.**
Rhythmicity	Has been on four-hour feeding schedule since birth. Regular bowel movement.	Eats a big lunch each day. Always has a snack before bedtime.
	Awakes at a different time each morning. Size of feedings varies.	**Nap time changes from day to day. Toilet training is difficult because bowel movement is unpredictable.**
Approach/withdrawal	Smiles and licks washcloth. Has always liked bottle.	Slept well the first time he stayed overnight at grandparents' house.
	Rejected cereal the first time. Cries when strangers appear.	**Avoids strange children in the playground. Whimpers first time at beach. Will not go into water.**
Adaptability	Was passive during first bath, now enjoys bathing. Smiles at nurse.	Obeys quickly. Stayed contentedly with grandparents for a week.
	Still startled by sudden, sharp noises. Resists diapering.	**Cries and screams each time hair is cut. Disobeys persistently.**
Intensity of reaction	Does not cry when diapers are wet. Whimpers instead of crying when hungry.	When another child hit her, she looked surprised, did not hit back.
	Cries when diapers are wet. Rejects food vigorously when satisfied.	**Yells if he feels excitement or delight. Cries loudly if a toy is taken away.**
Quality of mood	Smacks lips when first tasting new food. Smiles at parents.	Plays with sister; laughs and giggles. Smiles when he succeeds in putting shoes on.
	Fusses after nursing. Cries when carriage is rocked.	**Cries and squirms when given haircut. Cries when mother leaves.**

*Bold-type rows highlight temperamental ratings and behaviors for difficult children; light-type rows describe easy children.

SOURCE: From Thomas, Chess, & Birch, 1970. Reprinted by permission from p. 209 of Child Development by Alan Fogel and Gail Melson; copyright © 1988 by West Publishing Company. All rights reserved.

■ TABLE 12.3   Dimensions of Infant Temperament according to Buss and Plomin (1984)

TEMPERAMENTAL QUALITY	DESCRIPTION
Emotionality	Emotional infants have strong fear, anger, or distress responses, as shown by high ANS activity. Emotional infants may also respond more to minimal aversive events and may be less easy to calm or to appease. Emotional infants tend to "specialize" in one emotion, showing for example, strong anger but not strong fear or distress.
Activity	Active infants tend to be busy and energetic. They move around a lot and prefer more active forms of play.
Sociability	Sociable infants tend to spend more time in the company of others. This concept refers more to frequent initiation of contact with a wide range of individuals rather than to intimate contact with attachment figures. Sociable infants prefer to be with people rather than alone and seem genuinely pleased by social contact.

SOURCE: Information from Buss & Plomin, 1984.

Considerably shorter lists of temperamental dimensions have been developed by other groups of researchers and are shown in Tables 12.3 and 12.4.

Aside from proposing different definitions of temperament, each research team has a slightly different view of the origins of stable temperaments. According to Thomas and Chess, temperament is a style of approach to the environment, and temperament may be affected by the situation. For Buss and Plomin (1984), temperament is stable because it is an inherited personality trait that appears early in life. While some traits are acquired, the three dimensions shown in Table 12.3 are believed to have some inherited basis (Goldsmith et al., 1987).

For both Rothbart (Rothbart & Derryberry, 1981) and Kagan (1987), temperament is rooted in biological processes, but it is not necessarily inherited. For these researchers, behavioral characteristics called temperamental must be associated with specific CNS and ANS activity (Kagan et al., 1987; Rothbart, 1986). A number of other researchers have found such physiological correlates for children rated as highly reactive, emotional, or inhibited (Fox, 1989; Gunnar et al., 1989; Healy, 1989).

One of the problems in the study of infant temperament is that researchers can't agree on what the important dimensions might be. Although there is some overlap between the different temperamental dimensions, there are also

■ TABLE 12.4   Temperamental Dimensions of Reactivity (Rothbart & Derryberry, 1981) and Inhibition (Kagan, 1987)

Reactivity	Includes brain activation, ANS processes, and hormonal processes. High reactivity includes both a rapid response and a high intensity response, and it may also include a slow recovery from the response.
Inhibition	Inhibited children are restrained, watchful, and gentle. They tend to experience uncertainty about how to respond or how to think about a situation. Inhibition can also be characterized by particular brain, ANS, and hormonal processes.

differences. Temperament is *by definition* characterized by developmental continuity; that is, temperamental dimensions are those aspects of infants that are consistent over time. A child who is sociable on a particular day is not necessarily temperamentally sociable unless there is a consistent pattern of such behavior over a long period. Because of this, the study of temperament is more difficult than other areas of research because the investigator has to identify that which stays the same when other things are changing. Because infants change in so many ways, it is difficult to capture their essence (Bates, 1987; Kagan, 1987).

Another problem is that of language. Even though we might have some strong intuition about the consistent temperament of a baby we know, it is hard to describe in words what that consistency is. Once a word is chosen, like inhibited, it cannot describe exactly what the temperamental quality is, and the word itself often distorts what is unique about the baby (Kagan, 1987). To call a baby "inhibited" does not do justice to the fact that the child may play, walk, and talk like most other children. However, under certain circumstances, such as in the presence of an unfamiliar person, this child may be especially shy.

Given the difficulties in identifying a commonsense concept of temperament, it should come as no surprise that researchers have found temperament to be a difficult construct to measure in a reliable and valid manner. Some attempts have been made by researchers to observe children over a long period in response to particular situations, such as reactions to distress and separation, or examining overall activity level. More typically, parents are used to rate their children's temperaments under the assumption that the parents have the most complete, long-term experiences with the children and can better assess any stable characteristics (Bates, 1987).

When mothers and fathers are asked to rate the same child, their reports agree only about half the time (Bates & Bayles, 1984; Goldsmith & Gottesman, 1981; Hubert et al., 1982). Similarly, there is only a moderate amount of agreement between mothers and outside observers (Bates, 1980), although there is more overall agreement about the difficulty of an infant than any other dimension of temperament. There is also some evidence that temperament is related to other measures of the infant's behavior. For example, infants rated as "distractable" by their parents at two weeks had lower scores on the Brazelton Neonatal Assessment Scale at one week and lower scores on the Bayley infant assessment test at ten weeks (Sostek & Anders, 1977). Infants who were rated as difficult had cries that were independently rated as more irritating and had longer pauses between cry sounds as revealed by sound spectrograph analysis (see Chapter 5), giving their cries a greater sense of urgency (Lounsbury & Bates, 1982). Mothers' ratings of infant temperamental fussiness correlated with direct observations of crying behavior at three months (Crockenberg & Acredolo, 1983). The correlation between parental reports and actual behavior is improved if infants are selected only from the extreme ends of the behavioral scale. Infants who were either extremely inhibited or extremely uninhibited in a laboratory situation had parents who also rated them in this manner (Garcia-Coll et al.; 1984). These findings suggest that there is some correspondence between parental reports and actual behavior but that in many cases, there is no correspondence.

It could be that each parent and each observer has a different experience with the child and thus a different data base from which to draw conclusions. Also, the child may actually behave differently across situations and in the company of different observers. It could also be that the questions asked on rating forms (ranging from general questions about the overall difficulty of the child to specific questions about the child's reaction to strangers) are not sufficiently sensitive to capture the individuality of the child.

Another possibility is that the parental reports reflect the parents' personalities more than the child's (Matheny et al., 1987; Vaughn et al., 1987) or something about the current psychological state of the parents. Mothers who were multiparous and extroverted were more likely to rate their infants as easy than other mothers (Bates et al., 1979). Other studies found that mothers from low-income groups who were black, had a history of mental illness, or scored high on tests of anxiety rated their infants' temperament in significantly different ways than mothers who did not fall into any of these groups (Sameroff et al., 1982; Vaughn et al., 1981).

Another way to test the validity of temperament measures is to study their consistency over repeated testings. On the whole, parental reports and observational measures are quite stable over the infancy period. In other words, children who are rated as fearful or inhibited or sociable at one year are likely to be rated the same way at three years (Bates, 1987).

This pattern is especially true if one selects the children who are at the extremes. According to one series of studies (Garcia-Coll et al., 1984; Kagan & Reznick, 1984; Kagan et al., 1984; Kagan et al., 1988; Reznick et al., 1986) about 10 to 15 percent of normal infants are either extremely inhibited or extremely uninhibited (see Table 12.4), and these children tend to persist in such behaviors over early childhood at least up to the age of seven and a half years. In addition, they can be detected even in the first few months of life (Woroby & Lewis, 1989).

Continuity does not always occur. Inhibited children, with appropriately sensitive child rearing, may eventually lose their extreme sensitivity. Normal children may become more inhibited in extremely stressful environments. While extreme fussiness at birth predicts later emotionality in normal infants (Worobey & Blajda, 1989), fussiness at birth is not related to later behavior in premature infants (Riese, 1987). The stress of premature birth may have made it impossible to assess the infant's temperament at the time of birth. If there is a biological predisposition toward inhibition or other temperamental factors, such as emotionality, it does not operate in the absence of environmental influences (Kagan, 1987; Wachs, 1988).

On the other hand, temperamental characteristics don't seem to influence strongly the ways in which parents interact with infants, and they don't seem to predict long-term personality characteristics or behavior disorders. Temperament may have short-term influences on cognitive information process-ing, as when an inhibited infant is unlikely to approach a novel stimulus, but there is less evidence that temperament contributes to longer-term cognitive deficit or enhancement (Bates, 1987; Kagan, 1987). One reason may be that parents adjust their short-term behavior to the child's reactivity. If parents respond cautiously to inhibited children and reduce the intensity of stimulation for highly active children, the parental behavior may attenuate the long-term effects of the early temperamental characteristic (Gandour, 1989; Kagan, 1987).

In summary, like intelligence and gender effects, temperament is continuous for some children under some conditions. In other cases, temperament may have some short-term consistency, but after several years, the child does not persist with the same characteristics. The study of temperament is confounded because of the inconsistencies in the definition of temperament and because of the problems of obtaining reliable and valid measures.

■ CONCLUSION: DEVELOPMENT AS A DYNAMIC PROCESS

Each of the domains of infant development reviewed in this chapter tell a somewhat different story about the existence of continuity over developmental time. The evidence is diverse, confusing, and subject to multiple interpretations even by seasoned researchers. There are also a wide variety of theoretical explanations for both the persistence of traits over time and their lack of persistence.

At this time, let us take a step backward from the research and ask what continuity and discontinuity mean to the child, the family, and the society. For example, how should we interpret strong evidence for continuity? We might be pleased to find an early marker for some later disorder or an early sign of intelligence or social adjustment. This logic, however, is somewhat contradictory, since strong continuity implies a lack of change. Perhaps what we hope is that evidence of strong continuity would lead us to discover ways to guarantee it, so it doesn't happen just by chance, or to break down its grip on negative outcomes by discovering new treatments or interventions.

Now, consider research that shows a lack of continuity. Should we take this research as having no value, in the sense that discontinuities tell us little or that discontinuities reveal that early experiences or predispositions are unimportant for later outcomes? Or should we use the findings of discontinuity as an incentive to discover the process by which the effect of the early disposition or environment was gradually attenuated? Taking the latter approach, we can learn just as much about development from discontinuity as we can from continuity. It is not that early experience is unimportant; rather, developmental changes arise from particular combinations of early experiences. What are those combinations, and do they lead to positive or to negative outcomes?

The important question underlying research on continuity and discontinuity, therefore, is to find out about the *process of formation of developmentally desirable and developmentally undesirable outcomes*. If we have a desirable tendency early in life, we would like to find ways to preserve it, and if we have an unfortunate circumstance early, we wish to bring the individual back to a closer approximation of healthy development and behavior. The goal of theory and research is the understanding of developmental processes, rather than the determination of continuity and discontinuity for its own sake.

In actuality, the phases of the life of an individual are never unconnected. Perhaps the most salient example of developmental discontinuity is in the life cycle of moths and butterflies. Here we have stages of development that are so radically different—larva, cocoon, and adult—that it seems almost certain that the experiences of the larva, for example, could not impact on the adult. And yet even here continuities are present because the olfactory (smell) experiences of the larva influence the food choices of the adult (Klopfer, 1988).

In humans, developmental processes of the infant are embedded in social dyadic and family systems, and families are embedded in the multiple and interconnecting social systems of the larger society and culture. There are several features of such complex systems that are worth mentioning again here (see Chapter 2) in the context of our discussion of continuity over time.

First, in complex systems, changes in one factor are likely to affect other factors in such a way that the system as a whole adapts to the change in any single part. We have seen countless examples of this kind of systems effect in this book, as infants and parents, siblings and peers, families and cultures affect each other in a variety of ways.

Second, when systems adapt to changes, the response of the whole system is not necessarily a change. In fact, quite often, the various interacting factors achieve a kind of dynamic balancing act in which the system as a whole returns to a stable mode of functioning. A good example of this is the case of premature infant development. Due to the compensatory actions of the parents to provide extra support and stimulation for their infant, the developmental course of the infant approaches that of full-terms, and the family system returns to a stable mode of functioning following an earlier period of stress and uncertainty.

System dynamics alternatively may progressively move a child and family off the normal developmental course. An example of a continuing cycle of negative effects that amplify each other is the cycle of persistent poverty, ill health, infant disadvantage, and maladaptive parental behavior.

An explanation for why some family systems achieve stable states of positive functioning, become self-righting after a trauma, or continue to suffer deprivations must lie in the dynamic interactions between family members and between the family and society. The overwhelming body of research on the development of all species of animals suggests that the more complex the system and the more alternatives (two functioning parents, formal and informal supports, economic resources) there are, the more likely it is that these multiple facets of the system will eventually absorb the initial trauma. The more the continued trauma depletes the system of multiple resources, the more likely that the child will develop some type of deviance (Klopfer, 1988).

As I interpret the complex fabric of research on continuity in early development, it seems that there are many possible pathways to desirable outcomes and fewer pathways to undesirable ones. Lack of resources constrains development and forces individuals into the limitations of their heredity and their early experiences. The availability of resources (home, family, nutrition, support, etc.) opens development up to a wider range of possibilities. In the research reviewed in this chapter, we have seen many examples in which early predispositions and risk factors were essentially eliminated as causal factors for later development. No one factor arose to claim the role of cause; instead, later outcome was determined to be a product of a complex set of events that were unique to the individual.

Suppose you were able to chart the developmental histories of many individual infants, recording all the relevant family and environmental factors that may affect their development. This can't be done, of course, because of the complexity of human individuals and their social systems. But if it could

Many complex factors must combine to ensure healthy development during the infancy period. Adults have an important responsibility to provide the best possible environments and care that bring out the highest potential of each child.

be done, do you think that you could find, ultimately, a reasonable explanation for everything that individual does and for how the individual develops over time? Many developmental researchers would say that, yes, given all the important data, they could predict in all cases the developmental outcomes of the person.

This view, while recognizing the complexity of the person-environment-family-social system in which the infant develops, is at bottom deterministic. *Determinism* is the view that all natural phenomena are the result of some specifiable cause or series of interlocking causes (see Chapter 2).

My own view is that while some aspects of developmental change are determined by specifiable sequences of events, many outcomes are nondeterministic (Fogel, 1985; Fogel, 1990a; Fogel & Thelen, 1987). It seems to me that individuals are continually open to opportunities that they do not plan and cannot predict. A baby may discover an important contingency between the child's own behavior and something in the environment merely by chance, because the baby happened to turn his or her head to see something and was ready to follow up the opportunity without fully understanding where this direction might ultimately lead. Sometimes the infant is able to make sense of this foray into the unknown and sometimes not. Sometimes the sense of meaning of the infant's attempt is clarified by an adult who "explains" to the child what he or she just did.

An individual whose developmental fate is determined by a predictable set of causes and effects cannot also be open to the opportunity for discovery, exploration, risk taking, and personal growth in the absence of predictable guarantees.

Part of the problem is that the debate about the causes of developmental outcomes is sketched in strokes that are too broad. Genes, environments, parents, attachments, and the like are concepts that are far from the daily life of the individual child. In this text, I have focused more on research that describes the actual behavior of infants in everyday contexts, what they do, what they see, what they think and feel. The puzzle of understanding why one child blossoms while another withers must be understood in terms of the daily, real, and meaningful transactions between the child and the surround.

Suppose you participated in a study of the academic development of college students. In the study, you were interviewed as a freshman and the research recorded your course grades that year. A similar interview was conducted when you were a senior and your senior year grades were noted. Perhaps the grade point averages of all the students in the study didn't change much. While you were a solid B student as a freshman and also as a senior, another classmate was consistently an A student. The researcher concludes that you didn't change much. This study does not give credit to the wealth of experiences you had in college and tells us almost nothing about the processes going on in your life.

Unfortunately, this is the type of continuity study that is most frequently done on infants. Few studies observe the process of development within individuals to determine how they solved daily problems and maintained their equilibrium to stay on course. Until there are more such studies, our conclusions about how to foster desirable development and how to remediate early risk factors are going to be oversimplified. This type of research is difficult to do, and there are relatively few researchers who are doing it. The problem is how to get sufficient detail about an individual's life and still have the time to study many individuals in order to make more general conclusions.

For the present, as you encounter infants and young children in personal and professional roles, you will have to piece together the general principles learned from the broad concepts of current research with your own personal experiences with real children in everyday settings. It will be up to you to bridge the gap between the abstract and the specific. In doing so, you will be rewarded with a deepening understanding of human life and human development with all its richness and surprises.

■ SUMMARY

Perinatal Factors

■ Outcomes for perinatal factors depend on the quality of the environment, and on the severity of the initial disorder.

Motor Development

■ In early infancy, motor skills can be enhanced in the short-term, but there seems to be little long-term benefit.

■ Motor skill enrichment programs show more lasting effects when they begin after the age of two years.

Maternal Employment and Day Care

■ Little is known about the long-term effects of maternal employment; however, few short-term effects have been found.
■ Different considerations must be applied to the effects of day care for children under six months of age.

Attachment

■ Attachment shows strong continuity with early mother-infant relationships and with later social and emotional competence.
■ The concept of the internal working model may best explain this continuity.

Care-giving and Disciplinary Styles

■ Guided participation and authoritative and proactive care-giving styles are associated with long-term patterns of child cognitive, social, and emotional competence.
■ Problems in the research make it difficult to determine whether the continuity is due to the parent, the child, or external mediating factors.

Risk, Disadvantage, and Parent-Infant Intervention Programs

■ Economic disadvantage has long-term effects on development, usually due to the increased stress on the family. Other stress-producing factors also create the opportunity for negative outcomes.
■ Intervention is typically helpful in alleviating the effects of risk and disadvantage if it includes both a child and a parent education component and, where necessary, nutrition and health care.

Gender-Related Behavior

■ Few long-term influences on sex-role behavior can be found during infancy.
■ Gender may mediate a child's response to the environment and the care giver's response to the child, creating the possibility of differential outcomes.

Intellectual Development

■ Specific aspects of the physical and social environment are linked to specific long-term cognitive developmental outcomes and only for specific groups of children.
■ Some information-processing factors, including habituation and attention, may show unmediated long-term consistency.

Temperament

■ There are many different definitions of temperament.
■ Temperament is difficult to measure and shows consistency for some but not all infants.

Conclusion: Development as a Dynamic Process

■ Research should focus on the process of the formation of desirable and undesirable developmental outcomes.

■ Human development in complex family and social systems is regulated by both deterministic and nondeterministic factors. Research has fewer ways to capture the nondeterministic effects. Research results should be integrated with personal experiences to achieve a well-rounded view of infancy.

■ GLOSSARY

Buffering   The ability of the environment to maintain infant development on a normal course in spite of deviations caused by early infant risk factors.

Compensation   The provision of additional environmental support for infants who suffer from early deficits.

Continuity   The preservation of individual characteristics across ages.

Determinism   The view that all natural phenomena are the result of some specifiable set of causes.

Environmental specificity   Continuities between the environment and the individual's development are found only for specific facets of the individual with specific features of the environment. Specific individuals are better able to profit from some environments and not others.

Self-righting   The ability of the infant organism to assimilate those aspects of the environment that serve to normalize development.

Temperament   Lasting individual differences in emotional expressiveness and general responsiveness to the environment.

APPENDICES

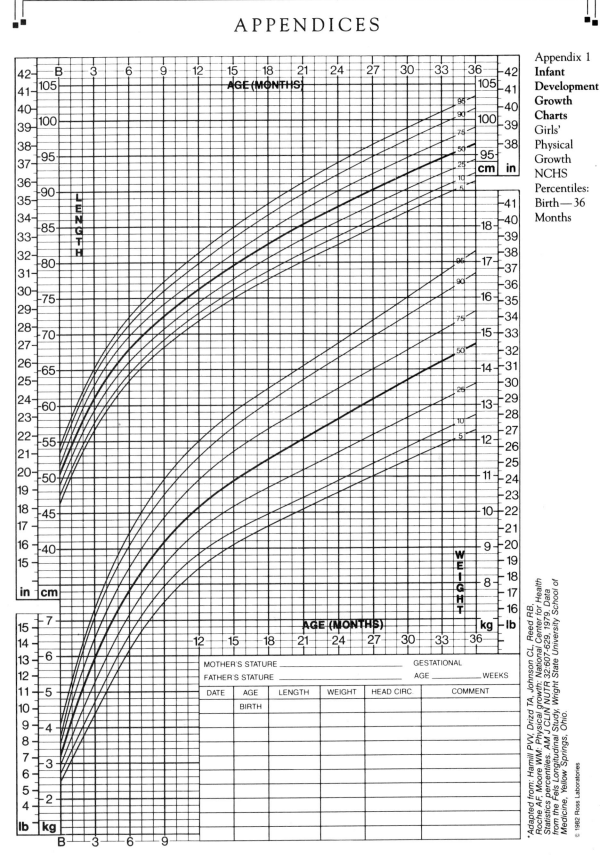

Appendix 1
Infant Development Growth Charts
Girls' Physical Growth NCHS Percentiles: Birth—36 Months

*Adapted from: Hamill PVV, Drizd TA, Johnson CL, Reed RB, Roche AF, Moore WM: Physical growth: National Center for Health Statistics percentiles. AM J CLIN NUTR 32:607-629, 1979. Data from the Fels Longitudinal Study, Wright State University School of Medicine, Yellow Springs, Ohio.

© 1982 Ross Laboratories

MOTHER'S STATURE _____ GESTATIONAL
FATHER'S STATURE _____ AGE _____ WEEKS

DATE	AGE	LENGTH	WEIGHT	HEAD CIRC.	COMMENT
	BIRTH				

Appendix 1
**Infant
Development
Growth
Charts**
Girls'
Physical
Growth
NCHS
Percentiles:
Birth—36
Months

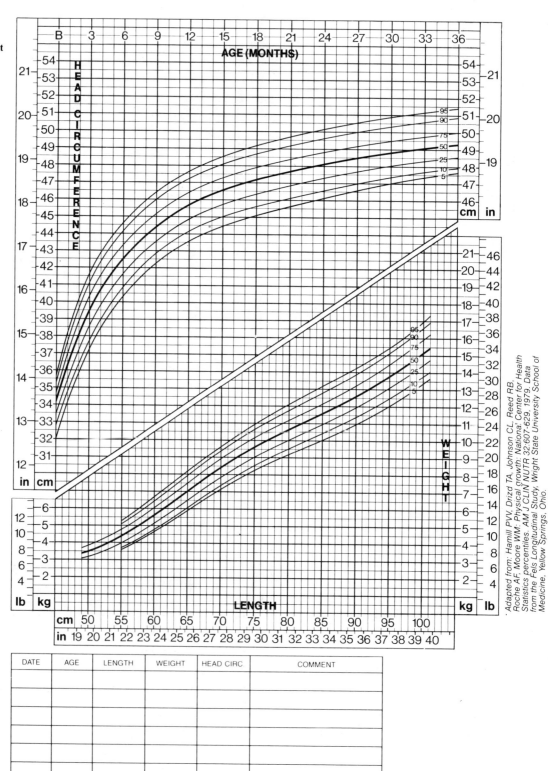

AGE (MONTHS)

HEAD CIRCUMFERENCE

WEIGHT

LENGTH

*Adapted from: Hamill PVV, Drizd TA, Johnson CL, Reed RB,
Roche AF, Moore WM: Physical growth: National Center for Health
Statistics percentiles. AM J CLIN NUTR 32:607-629, 1979. Data
from the Fels Longitudinal Study, Wright State University School of
Medicine, Yellow Springs, Ohio.

© 1982 Ross Laboratories

DATE	AGE	LENGTH	WEIGHT	HEAD CIRC	COMMENT

Reprinted with permission
of Ross Laboratories

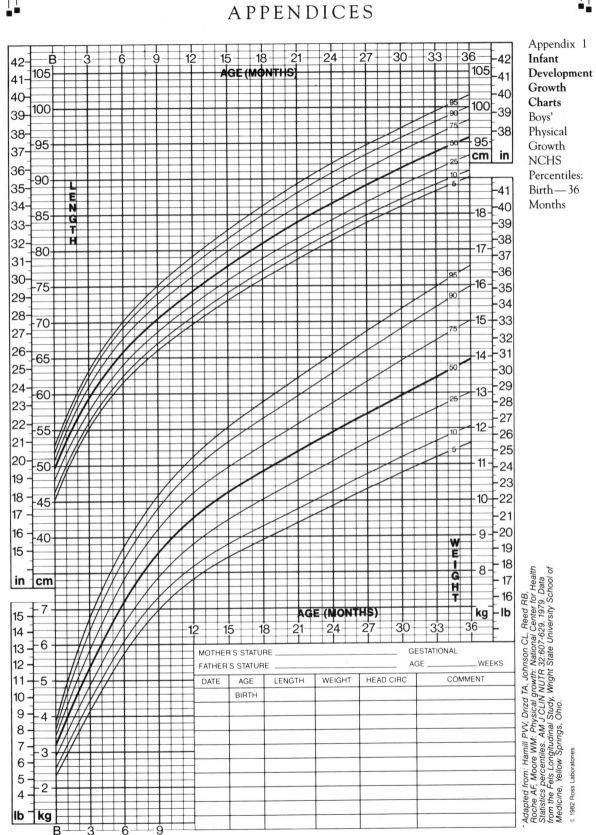

Appendix 1
**Infant
Development
Growth
Charts**
Boys'
Physical
Growth
NCHS
Percentiles:
Birth—36
Months

LENGTH

AGE (MONTHS)

WEIGHT

AGE (MONTHS)

MOTHER'S STATURE _____ GESTATIONAL

FATHER'S STATURE _____ AGE _____ WEEKS

DATE	AGE	LENGTH	WEIGHT	HEAD CIRC.	COMMENT
	BIRTH				

* Adapted from: Hamill PVV, Drizd TA, Johnson CL, Reed RB, Roche AF, Moore WM: Physical growth: National Center for Health Statistics percentiles. AM J CLIN NUTR 32:607-629, 1979. Data from the Fels Longitudinal Study, Wright State University School of Medicine, Yellow Springs, Ohio.

© 1982 Ross Laboratories

Appendix 1
Infant Development Growth Charts
Boys' Physical Growth NCHS Percentiles: Birth—36 Months

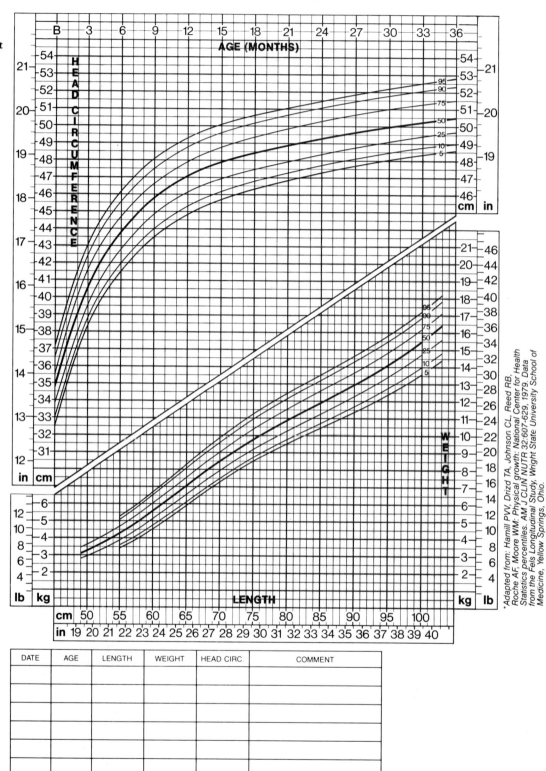

*Adapted from: Hamill PVV, Drizd TA, Johnson CL, Reed RB, Roche AF, Moore WM: Physical growth: National Center for Health Statistics percentiles. AM J CLIN NUTR 32:607-629, 1979. Data from the Fels Longitudinal Study, Wright State University School of Medicine, Yellow Springs, Ohio.

© 1982 Ross Laboratories

DATE	AGE	LENGTH	WEIGHT	HEAD CIRC.	COMMENT

Reprinted with permission of Ross Laboratories

HEALTH RELATED CAREERS

PEDIATRICS
  Pediatrician
  Neonatologist
  Infant intensive care worker

NURSING
  Women's health nursing
  Pediatric nursing
  Intensive care unit nursing
  Neonatal nursing

TECHNICAL
  Biomedical engineer
  Intensive care technician
  Designer/marketer of health and safety equipment

NUTRITIONAL
  Nutritionist
  Dietitian
  Baby food salesperson

EARLY INTERVENTION PROGRAMS
  Infant stimulation specialist
  Rehabilitation/special education worker
  Early intervention specialist, and program designer and assessor
  Placement and adoption/foster care worker
  Social worker/child protection worker
  Audiologist/speech therapist

PEDIATRIC PSYCHOLOGY
  Developmental tester
  Follow-up assessor and researcher
  Psychosomatic disorders specialist

EDUCATION-RELATED CAREERS

INFANT CARE
  Day-care teacher, supervisor, or administrator
  Infant/toddler nursery program teacher, supervisor, or administrator

PARENT EDUCATION
  Parent educator
  Family life educator
  Parent-child programmer
  Childbirth trainer
  Counselor for teenage parents
  Psychotherapist or psychiatrist for disturbed parents
  Marriage and family counselor

COLLEGE TEACHING AND RESEARCH
  Researcher
  College teacher
  Administrator of college programs in early childhood and child development

OTHER CAREERS WITH INFANTS

  Baby product salesperson, designer, or manufacturer
  Toy salesperson, designer, or manufacturer
  Baby clothing salesperson, designer, or manufacturer
  Environmental and furniture designer for nurseries and day-care centers
  Journalist
  Writer/producer of books and other media for young children

REFERENCES

Aadalen, S. (1980). Coping with sudden infant death syndrome: Intervention strategies and a case study. *Family Relations, 29,* 584–590.

Abel, E. L., Randall, C. L., & Riley, E. P. (1983). Alcohol consumption and prenatal development. In B. Tabakoff, P. B. Sutker, & C. L. Randall (Eds.), *Medical and social aspects of alcohol abuse.* New York: Plenum.

Abramovitch, R., Corter, C., & Landau, B. (1979). Sibling interaction in the home. *Child Development, 50,* 997–1003.

Abramovitch, R., Corter, C., Pepler, D. J., & Stanhope, L. (1986). Sibling and peer interaction: A final follow-up and a comparison. *Child Development, 57,* 217–229.

Acredolo, L., & Goodwyn, S. (1985). Symbolic gesturing in language development. *Human Development, 28,* 40–49.

Acredolo, L., & Goodwyn, S. (1988). Symbolic gesturing in normal infants. *Child Development, 59,* 450–466.

Adams, R. J. (1987). An evaluation of color preference in early infancy. *Infant Behavior and Development, 10,* 143–150.

Adams, R. J., & Passman, R. H. (1981). The effects of preparing two-year-olds for brief separations from their mothers. *Child Development, 52,* 1068–1070.

Adamson, L., & Bakeman, R. (1985). Affect and attention: Infants observed with mothers and peers. *Child Development, 56,* 582–593.

Adamson, L. B., Bakeman, R., Smith, C. B., & Walters, A. S. (1987). Adults' interpretation of infants' acts. *Developmental Psychology, 23,* 383–387.

Adinolfi, A. M. (1971). The postnatal development of synaptic contacts in the cerebral cortex. In M. B. Sterman, D. J. McGinty, & A. M. Adinolfi (Eds.), *Brain development and behavior.* New York: Academic Press.

Adolph, K. E., Gibson, E. J., & Eppler, M. A. (1990). Perceiving affordances of slopes: The ups and downs of toddler's locomotion. *Report of Emory Cognition Project.* Atlanta, GA: Emory University.

Affonso, D. (1977). "Missing pieces": A study of postpartum feelings. *Birth and the Family Journal, 4,* 159–164.

Agiobu-Kemmer, I. (1986). Cognitive and affective aspects of infant development. In H. V. Curran (Ed.), *Nigerian children: Developmental perspectives.* London: Routledge & Kegan Paul.

Agnew, B. (1990). States weigh new abortion curbs. *Journal of NIH Research, 2,* 26–28.

Ainsworth, M. (1979). Attachment as related to mother-infant interaction. In R. Hinde & J. Rosenblatt (Eds.), *Advances in the study of behavior.* New York: Academic Press.

Ainsworth, M., & Bell, S. (1970). Attachment, exploration, and separation: Illustrated by the behavior of one-year-olds in a strange situation. *Child Development, 41,* 49–67.

Ainsworth, M., Bell, S., & Stayton, D. (1971). Individual differences in strange situation behavior of one-year-olds. In H. R. Schaffer (Ed.), *The origins of human social relations.* London: Academic Press.

Ainsworth, M., Blehar, M. C., Waters, E., & Wall, S. (1978). *Patterns of attachment.* Hillsdale, NJ: Erlbaum.

Allen, D. A., Affleck, G., McGrade, B. J., & McQueeney, M. (1984). Effects of single-parent status on mothers and their high-risk infants. *Infant Behavior and Development, 7,* 347–359.

Als, H., Duffy, F. H., & McAnulty, G. B. (1988). Behavioral differences between preterm and full-term newborns as measured with the APIB system scores: I. *Infant Behavior and Development, 11,* 305–318.

Alvarez, W. F. (1985). The meaning of maternal employment for mothers and their perceptions of their three-year-old children. *Child Development, 56,* 350–360.

Ambrose, J. A. (1961). The development of the smiling response in early infancy. In B. M. Foss (Ed.), *Determinants of infant behavior* (Vol. 1). London: Methuen.

American Academy of Pediatrics, Committee on Nutrition. (1981). On the feeding of solid food to infants. *Pediatrics, 68,* 435–443.

Anderson, A. S., Purvis, G. A., & Chopra, J. G. (1979). The introduction of mixed feeding in infancy. In *Pediatric nutrition handbook.* Evanston, Ill.: American Academy of Pediatrics.

Anderson, D. R., & Levin, S. R. (1976). Young children's attention to "Sesame Street." *Child Development, 47,* 806–811.

Anderson, D. R., & Lorch, E. P. (1983). Looking at television: Action or reaction? In J. Bryant & D. R. Anderson (Eds.), *Children's understanding of television: Research on attention and comprehension* (pp. 1–33). New York: Academic Press.

Anderson, G. C., Burroughs, A. K., & Measel, C. P. (1983). Non-nutritive sucking opportunities: A safe and effective treatment for preterm neonates. In T. Field & A. Sostek (Eds.), *Infants born at risk.* New York: Grune & Stratton.

Anisfeld, M. (1979). Interpreting "imitative" responses in early infancy. *Science, 205,* 214–215.

Antonelli, P. L. (1985). *Mathematical essays on growth and the emergence of form.* Canada: University of Alberta Press.

Apgar, V. (1953). A proposal for a new method of evaluation in the newborn infant. *Current Research in Anesthesia and Analgesia, 32,* 260.

Arehart-Treichel, J. (1979, December 1). Down's syndrome: The father's role. *Science News,* 381–382.

Arend, R., Gove, F. L., & Sroufe, L. A. (1979). Continuity of individual adaptation from infancy to kindergarten: A predictive study of ego-resiliency and curiosity in preschoolers. *Child Development, 50,* 950–959.

Arterberry, M., Yonas, A., & Bensen, A. S. (1989). Self-produced locomotion and the development of responsiveness to linear perspective and texture gradients. *Developmental Psychology, 25*(6), 976–982.

Aslin, R. N. (1981). Development of smooth pursuit in human infants. In D. F. Fisher, R. A. Monty, & J. W. Sanders (Eds.), *Eye movements: Cognition and visual perception.* Hillsdale, NJ: Erlbaum.

Aslin, R. N. (1987). Visual and auditory development in infancy. In J. D. Osofsky (Ed.), *Handbook of infant development* (2nd ed.). New York: Wiley.

Atkinson, D. (1983). An evaluation of Apgar scores as predictors of infant mortality. *North Carolina Medical Journal, 44,* 45–54.

Bahrick, L. E. (1987). Infants' intermodal perception of two levels of temporal structure in natural events. *Infant Behavior and Development, 10,* 387–416.

Bahrick, L. E. (1988). Intermodal learning in infancy: Learning on the basis of two kinds of invariant relations in audible and visible events. *Child Development, 59,* 197–209.

Bahrick, L. E., & Pickens, J. N. (1988). Classification of bimodal English and Spanish language passages by infants. *Infant Behavior and Development, 11,* 277–296.

Baillargeon, R. (1987). Object permanence in 3 1/2- and 4 1/2-month-old infants. *Developmental Psychology, 23,* 655–664.

Baillargeon, R., & Graber, M. (1988). Evidence of location memory in 8-month-old infants in a nonsearch AB task. *Developmental Psychology, 24,* 502–511.

Bakeman, R., & Adamson, L. B. (1984). Coordinating attention to people and objects in mother-infant and peer-infant interaction. *Child Development, 55,* 1278–1289.

Bakeman, R., & Brown, J. (1980). Analyzing behavioral sequences: Differences between preterm and full-term infant-mother dyads during the first months of life. In D. Sawin (Ed.), *Psychosocial risks in infant-environment transactions.* New York: Brunner-Mazel.

Bakeman, R., & Brownlee, J. (1980). The strategic use of parallel play: A sequential analysis. *Child Development, 51,* 873–878.

Baker, T. L., & McGinty, D. J. (1979). Sleep apnea in hypoxic and normal kittens. *Developmental Psychobiology, 12,* 577–594.

Baker, R. L., & Mednick, B. R. (1984). *Influence on human development: A longitudinal perspective.* The Hague: Kluwer-Nijhoff.

Balamore, U., & Wozniak, R. H. (1984). Speech-action coordination in young children. *Developmental Psychology, 20,* 850–858.

Baldwin, D. A., & Markman, E. M. (1989). Establishing word-object relations: A first step. *Child Development, 60,* 381–398.

Ball, W., & Tronick, E. (1971). Infant responses to impending collisions: Optical and real. *Science, 171,* 818–820.

Balog, J. (1976). A new look at our infant mortality. *Birth and the Family Journal, 3,* 15–23.

Bandura, A. (1977). *Social learning theory.* Englewood Cliffs, NJ: Prentice-Hall.

Bandura, A. (1989). Human agency in social cognitive theory. *American Psychologist, 44*(9), 1175–1184.

Bane, M. J., & Ellwood, D. T. (1989). One fifth of the nation's children: Why are they poor? *Science, 245,* 1047–1053.

Barden, R. C., Ford, M. E., Jensen, A. G., Rogers-Salyer, M., & Salyer, K. E. (1989). Effects of craniofacial deformity in infancy on the quality of mother-infant interactions. *Child Development, 60,* 819–824.

Barglow, P. (1987a). Effect of maternal absence due to employment on the quality of infant-mother attachment in a low-risk sample. *Child Development, 58,* 945–954.

Barglow, P. (1987b). Some further comments about infant day-care research. *Zero to Three, 8,* 26–28.

Barnard, K. E., Bee, H. L., & Hammond, M. A. (1984). Developmental changes in maternal interactions with term and preterm infants. *Infant Behavior and Development, 7,* 101–113.

Barness, L. A. (1981). [Letter to the editor]. *Pediatrics, 67,* 166.

Barnett, R. C., & Baruch, G. K. (1987). *Journal of Marriage and the Family,* 29–39.

Barrera, M. E., & Maurer, D. (1981). Discrimination of strangers by the three-month-old. *Child Development, 52,* 558–563.

Barrera, M. E., Rosenbaum, P. L., & Cunningham, C. E. (1987). Corrected and uncorrected Bayley scores: Longitudinal developmental patterns in low and high birth weight preterm infants. *Infant Behavior and Development, 10,* 337–346.

Barrett, D. E., Radke-Yarrow, M., & Klein, R. E. (1982). Chronic malnutrition and child behavior: Effects of early caloric supplementation on social and emotional functioning at school age. *Developmental Psychology, 18,* 541–556.

Barrett, K. C., & Campos, J. J. (1987). Perspectives on emotional development II: A functionalist approach to emotions. In J. D. Osofsky (Ed.), *Handbook of infant development* (2nd ed.) (pp. 555–578). New York: Wiley.

Barss, V. A., Benacerraf, B. R., & Frigoletto, F. D. (1985). Ultrasonographic determination of chorion type in twin gestation. *Obstetrics Gynecology, 66,* 779–783.

Bass, M., Kravath, R. E., & Glass, L. (1986). Death scene investigation in sudden infant death. *New England Journal of Medicine, 315,* 100–105.

Bates, E., Benigni, L., Bretherton, I., Camaioni, L., & Volterra, V. (1978). From gesture to first word: On cognitive and social prerequisites. In M. Lewis & L. Rosenblum (Eds.), *Cognition, communication and language.* New York: Wiley.

Bates, E., Camaioni, L., & Volterra, V. (1975). The acquisition of performatives prior to speech. *Merrill-Palmer Quarterly, 21,* 205–226.

Bates, E., Carlson-Luden, V., & Bretherton, I. (1980). Perceptual aspects of tool using in infancy. *Infant Behavior and Development, 3,* 127–140.

Bates, E., O'Connell, B., & Shore, C. (1987). Language and communication in infancy. In J. D. Osofsky (Ed.), *Handbook of infant development* (2nd ed.) (pp. 149–203). New York: Wiley.

Bates, E., Thal, D., Whitesell, K., Fenson, L., & Oakes, L. (1989). Integrating language and gesture in infancy. *Developmental Psychology, 25,* 1104–1119.

Bates, J. E. (1980). The concept of difficult temperment. *Merrill-Palmer Quarterly, 26,* 299–319.

Bates, J. E. (1987). Temperament in infancy. In J. D. Osofsky (Ed.), *Handbook of infant development* (2nd ed.). NY: Wiley.

Bates, J. E., & Bayles, K. (1984). Objective and subjective components in mothers' perceptions of their children from age 6 months to 3 years. *Merrill-Palmer Quarterly, 30,* 111–130.

Bates, J. E., Freeland, C. A., & Lounsbury, M. L. (1979). Measurement of infant difficultness. *Child Development, 50,* 794–803.

Bates, J. E., Maslin, C. A., & Frankel, K. A. (1985). Attachment security, mother-child interaction, and temperament as predictors of behavior-problem ratings at age three years. *Monographs of the Society for Research in Child Development, 50*(Serial No. 209), 167–193.

Bates, J. E., Olson, S. L., Pettit, G. S., & Bayles, K. (1982). Dimensions of individuality in the mother-infant relationship at 6 months of age. *Child Development, 53,* 446–461.

Bateson, M. C. (1975). Mother-infant exchanges: The epigenesis of conversation interaction. *Annals of the New York Academy of Science, 263,* 101–113.

Bateson, P. P. G. (1966). The characteristics and context of imprinting. *Biological Review, 41,* 177–220.

Baumrind, D. (1973). The development of instrumental competence through socialization. In A. Pick (Ed.), *Minnesota symposia on child development.* Minneapolis: University of Minnesota Press.

Bayley, N. (1969). *The Bayley Scale of infant development.* (Manual). Stanford, CA: Psychological Corporation.

Beauchamp, G. K., Cowart, B. J., & Morgan, M. (1986). Developmental changes in salt acceptability in human infants. *Developmental Psychobiology, 19,* 17–25.

Beauchamp, G. K., & Maller, O. (1977). The development of flavor preference in humans: A review. In M. R. Kare & O. Maller (Eds.), *The chemical senses and nutrition.* New York: Academic Press.

Beck, R. (1982). Beyond the stalemate in childcare policy. In E. F. Zigler & E. W. Gordon (Eds.), *Day care: Scientific and social issues.* Boston: Auburn House.

Becker, J. (1977). A learning analysis of the development of peer oriented behavior in nine-month-old infants. *Developmental psychology, 13,* 481–491.

Beckwith, L., & Cohen, S. E. (1978). Preterm birth: Hazardous obstetrical and postnatal events as related to caregiver-infant behavior. *Infant Behavior and Development, 1,* 403–412.

Bell, R., Weller, G., & Waldrop, M. (1971). Newborn and preschooler: Organization of behavior and relations between periods. *Monographs of the Society for Research in Child Development, 36*(Serial No. 142).

Bell, R. Q., & Costello, N. S. (1964). Three tests for sex differences in tactile sensitivity in the newborn. *Biologia Neonatorum, 7,* 335–347.

Belsky, J. (1980). Child maltreatment: An ecological integration. *American Psychologist, 35,* 320–335.

Belsky, J. (1981). Early human experience: A family perspective. *Developmental Psychology, 17,* 3–23.

Belsky, J. (1984). The determinants of parenting: A process model. *Child Development, 55,* 83–96.

Belsky, J., Goode, M. K., & Most, R. K. (1980). Maternal stimulation and infant exploratory competence; Cross-sectional, correlational, and experimental analyses. *Child Development, 51,* 1168–1178.

Belsky, J., & Isabella, R. A. (1985). Marital and parent-child relationships in family of origin and marital change following the birth of a baby: A retrospective analysis. *Child Development, 56,* 342–349.

Belsky, J., & Most, R. K. (1981). From exploration to play: A cross-sectional study of infant free play behavior. *Developmental Psychology, 17,* 630–639.

Belsky, J., & Rovine, M. J. (1988). Nonmaternal care in the first year of life and the security of infant-parent attachment. *Child Development, 59,* 157–167.

Belsky, J., Rovine, M. J., & Taylor, D. G. (1984). The Pennsylvania infant and family development project, III: The origins of individual differences in infant-mother attachment: Maternal and infant contributions. *Child Development, 55,* 718–728.

Belsky, J., Steinberg, L. D., & Walker, A. (1982). The ecology of day care. In M. E. Lamb (Ed.), *Nontraditional families: Parenting and child development.* Hillsdale, NJ: Erlbaum.

Belsky, J., Ward, M. J., & Rovine, M. (1986). Prenatal expectations, postnatal experiences, and the transition to parenthood. In R. D. Ashmore & D. M. Brodzinsky (Eds.), *Thinking about the family: Views of parents and children.* Hillsdale, NJ: Erlbaum.

Benn, R. K. (1986). Factors promoting secure attachment relationships between employed mothers and their sons. *Child Development, 57,* 1224–1231.

Bennett, W. J. (1987). The role of the family in the nurture and protection of the young. *American Psychologist, 42,* 246–250.

Berg, W. K. (1975). Cardiac components of defense responses in infants. *Psychophysiology, 12,* 224.

Berg, W. K., & Berg, K. M. (1979). Psychophysiological development in infancy: State, sensory function, and attention. In J. D. Osofsky (Ed.), *Handbook of infant development.* (pp. 283–343). New York: Wiley.

Berg, W. K., & Berg, K. M. (1987). Psychophysiological development in infancy: State, startle, and attention. In J. D. Osofsky (Ed.), *Handbook of infant development* (2nd ed.). New York: Wiley.

Berger, J., & Cunningham, C. C. (1983). Development of early vocal behaviors & interactions in Down's syndrome and non-handicapped infant-mother pairs. *Developmental Psychology, 19,* 322–331.

Berk, L. E. (1986). Development of private speech among preschool children. *Early Child Development and Care, 24,* 113–136.

Berko, J. (1958). The child's learning of English morphology. *Word, 14,* 150–177.

Berman, P. W., Goodman, V., Sloan, V. L., & Fernandez, L. (1978). Preference for infants among black and white children: Sex and age differences. *Child Development, 49,* 917–919.

Berman, P. W., Monda, C. C., & Merscough, R. P. (1977). Sex differences in young children's responses to an infant: An observation within a day-care setting. *Child Development, 48,* 711–715.

Berrueta-Clement, J. R., Schweinhart, L. J., Barnett, W. S., Epstein, A. S., & Weikart, D. P. (1984). *Changed lives: The effects of the Perry Preschool Program on youths through age 19* (Monograph No. 8). Ypsilanti, MI: High Scope/Educational Research Foundation.

Bertenthal, B. I., & Bai, D. L. (1989). Infants' sensitivity to optical flow for controlling posture. *Developmental Psychology, 25,* 936–945.

Bertenthal, B. I., Campos, J. J., & Barrett, K. C. (1984). Self-produced locomotion: An organizer of emotional, cognitive, and social development in infancy. In R. N. Emde &

R. J. Harmon (Eds.), *Continuities and discontinuities in development* (pp. 175–210). New York: Plenum.

Bertenthal, B. I., Proffitt, D. R., & Cutting, J. E. (1984). Infant sensitivity to figural coherence in biomechanical motions. *Journal of Experimental Child Psychology, 37,* 213–230.

Bertenthal, B. I., Proffitt, D. R., Kramer, S. J., & Spetner, N. B. (1987). Infants' encoding of kinetic displays varying in relative coherence. *Developmental Psychology, 23*(2), 171–178.

Bettes, B. A. (1988). Maternal depression and motherese: Temporal and intonational features. *Child Development, 59,* 1089–1096.

Bever, T. G. (1970). The cognitive basis for linguistic structures. In J. R. Hayes (Ed.). *Cognition and the development of language.* New York: Wiley.

Bibring, G. L. (1959). Some considerations of the psychological process in pregnancy. In *The Psychoanalytic Study of the Child* (Vol. 16). New York: International Universities Press.

Bigelow, A., MacLean, J., Wood, C., & Smith, J. (1990). Infants' responses to child and adult strangers: An investigation of height and facial configuration variables. *Infant Behavior and Development, 13,* 21–32.

Bijou, S. W., & Baer, D. M. (1965). *Child development: Vol. 2. Universal stage of infancy.* New York: Appleton-Century-Crofts.

Birns, B., Blank, M., & Bridger, W. H. (1966). The effectiveness of various soothing techniques on the human neonate. *Psychosomatic Medicine, 28,* 216–221.

Black, L., Steinschneider, A., & Sheehe, P. R. (1979). Neonatal respiratory instability and infant development. *Child Development, 50,* 561–564.

Blackman, J. A., Lindgren, S. D., Hein, H. A., & Harper, D. C. (1987). Long-term surveillance of high-risk children. *American Journal of Diseases of Children, 141,* 1293–1299.

Blaikie, P. M. (1975). *Family planning in India.* New York: Holmes & Meier.

Blake, A., Stewart, A., & Turcan, D. (1975). Parents of babies of very low birth weight: Long-term follow-up. In Ciba Foundation (Ed.), *Parent-infant interaction.* New York: Elsevier.

Blake, P. M., & Scott, W. J. (1984). Determination of the proximate teratogen of the mouse fetal alcohol syndrome: 1. Teratogenicity of ethanol and acetaldehyde. *Toxicology and Applied Pharmacology, 72,* 355–363.

Blank, M., & Klig, S. (1982). The child and the school experience. In C. B. Kopp & J. B. Krakow (Eds.), *The child: Development in social context* (pp. 456–513). Reading, MA: Addison-Wesley.

Blass, E. M., Fillion, T. J., Rochat, P., Hoffmeyer, L. B., & Metzger, M. A. (1989). Sensorimotor and motivational determinants of hand-mouth coordination in 1- to 3-day-old human infants. *Developmental Psychology, 25,* 963–975.

Blass, E. M., Ganchrow, J. R., & Steiner, J. E. (1984). Classical conditioning in newborn humans 2 to 48 hours of age. *Infant Behavior & Development, 7,* 223–235.

Blehar, M. C., Lieberman, A., & Ainsworth, M. (1977). Early face-to-face interaction and its relation to later mother-infant attachment. *Child Development, 48,* 182–194.

Block, J. A., & Block, J. (1980). The role of ego-control and ego-resiliency in the organization of behavior. In W. A. Collins (Ed.), *Minnesota symposia on child psychology* (Vol. 13). Hillsdale, NJ: Erlbaum.

Bloom, L., & Beckwith, R. (1989). Talking with feeling: Integrating affective and linguistic expression in early language development. *Cognition and Emotion, 3*(4), 313–342.

Bloom, L., Merkin, S., & Wootten, J. (1982). *Wh*-questions: Linguistic factors that contribute to the sequence of acquisition. *Child Development, 53,* 1084–1092.

Bloom, L., Rocissano, L., & Hood, L. (1976). Adult-child discourse: Developmental interaction between information processing and linguistic knowledge. *Cognitive Psychology, 8,* 521–552.

Bluglass, K., & Hassall, C. (1979). Alternative forms of community support after sudden infant death. *Medicine, Science and the Law, 19,* 240–245.

Blurton-Jones, N., Ferreira, C., Brown, M., & MacDonald, L. (1978). The association between perinatal factors and later night waking. *Developmental Medicine and Child Neurology, 20,* 427–434.

Boehm, L. (1977). The development of independence: A comparative study. *Child Development, 28,* 85–92.

Bohannon, J. N., III, & Stanowicz, L. (1988). The issue of negative evidence: Adult responses to children's language errors. *Developmental Psychology, 24,* 684–689.

Bohlin, G., Hagekull, B., Germer, M., Anderson, K., & Lindberg, L. (1989). Avoidant and resistant reunion behaviors as predicted by maternal interactive behavior and infant temperament. *Infant Behavior and Development, 12,* 105–117.

Bornstein, M. H. (1981). Two kinds of perceptual organization near the beginning of life. In W. A. Collins (Ed.), *Aspects of the development of competence.* Hillsdale, NJ: Erlbaum.

Bornstein, M. H. (1985). Habituation of attention as a measure of visual information processing in human infants: Summary, systematization, and synthesis. In G. Gottlieb & N. A. Krasnegor (Eds.), *Measurement of audition and vision in the first year of postnatal life: A methodological overview.* Norwood, NJ: Ablex.

Bornstein, M. H., & Benasich, A. A. (1986). Infant habituation: Assessments of short-term reliability and individual differences at five months. *Child Development, 57,* 87–99.

Bornstein, M. H., & Krinsky, S. J. (1985). Perception of symmetry in infancy: The salience of vertical symmetry and the perception of pattern wholes. *Journal of Experimental Child Psychology, 39,* 1–19.

Bornstein, M. H., Krinsky, S. J., & Benasich, A. A. (1986). Fine orientation discrimination and shape constancy in infants. *Journal of Experimental Child Psychology, 41,* 49–60.

Bornstein, M. H., & Sigman, M. D. (1986). Continuity in mental development from infancy. *Child Development, 57,* 251–274.

Bower, T. G. R., Broughton, J., & Moore, M. (1970). The coordination of vision and touch in infancy. *Perception and Psychophysics, 8,* 51–53.

Bower, T. G. R., Broughton, J. M., & Moore, M. K. (1971). Infants' responses to approaching objects: An indicator of response to distal variables. *Perception & Psycho-physics, 9,* 193–196.

Bowerman, M. (1978). Systematizing semantic knowledge: Changes over time in the child's organization of word meaning. *Child Development, 49,* 977–987.

Bowlby, J. (1969). *Attachment and Loss: Vol. 1. Attachment.* New York: Basic Books.

Bowlby, J. (1980). *Attachment and Loss: Vol. 3. Loss, Sadness and Depression.* New York: Basic Books.

Boyd, P. A., & Scott, A. (1985). Quantitative structural studies on human placentas associated with pre-eclampsia: Essential hypertension and intrauterine growth retardation. *Obstetrics and Gynecology, 92,* 714–721.

Brackbill, Y. (1970). Acoustic variation and arousal level in infants. *Psychophysiology, 6,* 517–526.

Brackbill, Y. (1971). Cumulative effects of continuous stimulation on arousal level in infants. *Child Development, 42,* 17–26.

Brackbill, Y. (1975). Continuous stimulation and arousal levels in infancy: Effects of stimulus intensity and stress. *Child Development, 46,* 364–369.

Brackbill, Y. (1979). Obstetrical medication and infant behavior. In J. Osofsky (Ed.), *Handbook of infant development.* New York: Wiley.

Bradley, R. H., & Caldwell, B. M. (1976). The relation of infants' home environment to mental test performance at fifty-four months: A follow-up study. *Child Development, 47,* 1172–1173.

Bradley, R. H., & Caldwell, B. M. (1984). The relation of infants' home environment to achievement test performance in first grade: A follow-up study. *Child Development, 55,* 803–809.

Bradley, R. H., Caldwell, B. M., & Elardo, R. (1979). Home environment and cognitive development in the first two years: A cross-lagged panel analysis. *Developmental Psychology, 15,* 246–250.

Bradley, R. H., Caldwell, B. M., Rock, S. L., Ramey, C. T., Bernard, K. E., Gray, C., Hammond, M. A., Mitchell, S., Gottfried, A. W., Siegel, L., & Johnson, D. L. (1989). Home environment and cognitive development in the first 3 years of life: A collaborative study involving six sites and three ethnic groups in North America. *Developmental Psychology, 25,* 217–235.

Braine, M. D. S. (1976). Children's first word combinations. *Monographs of the Society for Research in Child Development, 164*(Serial No. 164).

Brake, S. C., Fifer, W. P., Alfasi, G., & Fleischman, A. (1988). The first nutritive sucking response of premature newborns. *Infant Behavior and Development, 11,* 1–19.

Branchfeld, S., Goldberg, S., & Sloman, J. (1980). Parent-infant interaction in free play at 8 and 12 months: Effects of prematurity and immaturity. *Infant Behavior and Development, 3,* 289–306.

Brazelton, T. B. (1977). Implications of infant development among the Mayan Indians of Mexico. In P. H. Liederman, S. R. Tulkin, & A. Rosenfeld (Eds.), *Culture and infancy.* New York: Academic Press.

Brazelton, T. B., Koslowski, B., & Main, M. (1974). The origins of reciprocity. In M. Lewis & L. Rosenblum (Eds.), *The effect of the infant on its caregiver.* New York: Wiley.

Brazelton, T. B., Nugent, J. K., & Lester, B. M. (1987). Neonatal behavioral assessment scale. In J. D. Osofsky (ed.), *Handbook of infant development* (2nd ed.). New York: Wiley.

Breitmayer, B. J., & Ramey, C. T. (1986). Biological nonoptimality and quality of postnatal environment as codeterminants of intellectual development. *Child Development, 57,* 1151–1165.

Bremmer, J. (1978). Egocentric vs. allocentric spatial coding in nine-month-old infants: Factors influencing choice of code. *Developmental Psychology, 14,* 346–355.

Bretherton, I. (1985). Attachment theory: Retrospect and prospect. *Monographs of the Society for Research in Child Development, 50*(Serial No. 209), 3–35.

Bretherton, I. (1987). New perspectives on attachment relations: Security, communication, and internal working models. In J. D. Osofsky (Ed.), *Handbook of infant development* (2nd ed.) (pp. 1061–1100). New York: Wiley.

Bretherton, I., & Bates, E. (1979). The emergence of intentional communication. In I. Uzgiris (Ed.), *New directions for child development* (Vol. 4) (pp. 81–100). San Francisco: Jossey-Bass.

Bretherton, I., Fritz, J., Zahn-Waxler, C., & Ridgeway, D. (1986). Learning to talk about emotions: A functionalist perspective. *Child Development, 57,* 529–548.

Bridges, K. M. B. (1932). Emotional development in early infancy. *Child Development, 3,* 324–341.

Bridges, K. M. B. (1933). A study of social development in early infancy. *Child Development, 4,* 36–49.

Bridges, L. J., Connell, J. P., & Belsky, J. (1988). Similarities and differences in infant-mother and infant-father interaction in the strange situation: A component process analysis. *Developmental Psychology, 24,* 92–100.

Bril, B., & Sabatier, C. (1986). The cultural context of motor development: Postural manipulations in the daily life of Bambara babies (Mali). *International Journal of Behavioral Development, 9,* 439–453.

Brody, G. H., Stoneman, Z., & MacKinnon, C. (1982). Role asymmetries among school-age children, their younger siblings, and their friends. *Child Development, 53,* 1364–1370.

Broerse, J., Peltola, C., & Crassini, B. (1983). Infants' reactions to perceptual paradox during mother-infant interaction, *Developmental Psychology, 19*, 310–316.

Broman, S. H. (1981). Risk factors for deficits in early cognitive development. In G. G. Berg & H. D. Maillie (Eds.), *Measurement of risk.* New York: Plenum.

Bromwich, R., & Parmalee, A. (1979). An intervention program for pre-term infants. In T. Field, A. Sostek, S. Goldberg, & H. Shuman (Eds.), *Infants born at risk: Behavior and development.* New York: Springer Medical and Scientific Books.

Bronfenbrenner, U. (1979). *The ecology of human development: Experiments by nature and design.* Cambridge: Harvard University Press.

Bronfenbrenner, U. (1986). Ecology of the family as a context for human development: Research perspectives. *Developmental Psychology, 22*(6), 723–742.

Bronson, G. W. (1972). Infants' reactions to unfamiliar persons and novel objects. *Monographs of the Society for Research in Child Development, 47*(Serial No. 148).

Brookhart, J., & Hock, E. (1976). The effects of experimental context and experiential background on infants' behavior toward their mothers and a stranger. *Child Development, 47*, 333–340.

Brooks, J., & Lewis, M. (1974). The effect of time on attachment as measured in a free-play situation. *Child Development, 45*, 311–316.

Brooks, J., & Lewis, M. (1976). Infants' responses to strangers: Midget, adult, and child. *Child Development, 47*, 323–332.

Brooks-Gunn, J., & Furstenberg, F. (1986). Antecedents and consequences of parenting: The case of adolescent motherhood. In A. Fogel & G. F. Melson (Eds.), *Origins of Nurturance.* Hillsdale, NJ: Erlbaum.

Brooks-Gunn, J., & Lewis, M. (1982). Affective exchanges between normal and handicapped infants and their mothers. In T. Field & A. Fogel (Eds.), *Emotion and early interaction.* Hillsdale, NJ: Erlbaum.

Brown, J., Bakeman, R., Snyder, P., Frederickson, W., Morgan, S., & Hepler, R. (1975). Interactions of black inner-city mothers with their newborn infants. *Child Development, 46*, 677–686.

Brown, R. (1966). Organ weight in malnutrition with special reference to brain weight. *Developmental Medicine and Child Neurology, 8*, 512–522.

Brown, R. (1973). *A first language: The early stages.* Cambridge: Harvard University Press.

Brownell, C. A. (1986). Convergent developments: Cognitive-developmental correlates of growth in infant/toddler peer skills. *Child Development, 57*, 275–286.

Brownell, C. A. (1988). Combinatorial skills: Converging developments over the second year. *Child Development, 59*, 675–685.

Bruner, J. (1983). *Child's talk: Learning to use language.* New York: Norton.

Bryant, P. E., & Trabasso, T. (1971). Transitive inferences and memory in young children. *Nature, 232*, 456–458.

Bryne, J. M., & Horowitz, F. D. (1979). Rocking as a soothing intervention: The influence of direction and type of movement. *Infant Behavior and Development, 2*, 209–214.

Buhler, C. (1930). *The first year of life.* New York: John Day.

Bullock, M., & Lutkenhaus, P. (1988). The development of volitional behavior in the toddler years. *Child Development, 59*, 664–674.

Burchinal, M., Lee, M., & Ramey, C. (1989). Type of day-care and preschool intellectual development in disadvantaged children. *Child Development, 60*, 128–137.

Burgess, R. L. (1979). Child abuse: A social interactional analysis. In B. B. Lakey & A. E. Kazdin (Eds.), *Advances in clinical child psychology.* New York: Plenum.

Burgess, R. L., & Conger, R. D. (1978). Family interaction in abusive, neglectful and normal families. *Child Development, 49*, 1163–1173.

Bushnell, E. W. (1982). Visual-tactual knowledge in 8- and 9 1/2- and 11-month-old infants. *Infant Behavior and Development, 5*, 63–75.

Buss, A. H., & Plomin, R. (1984). *Temperament: Early developing personality traits.* Hillsdale, NJ: Erlbaum.

Butler, J., & Rovee-Collier, C. (1989). Contextual gating of memory retrieval. *Developmental Psychobiology, 22,* 533–552.

Butler, N. (1974). Late postnatal consequences of fetal malnutrition. In M. Winick (Ed.), *Nutrition and fetal development.* New York: Wiley.

Butterworth, G. E. (1977). Object disappearance and error in Piaget's stage IV task. *Journal of Experimental Child Psychology, 23,* 391–401.

Butterworth, G. E., & Cochran, E. (1980). Towards a mechanism of joint visual attention in human infancy. *International Journal of Behavioral Development, 3,* 253–272.

Byers, T., Grahm, S., & Rzepka, T. (1985). Lactation and breast cancer: Evidence for a negative association in premenopausal women. *American Journal of Epidemiology, 121,* 664–674.

Cain, L. P., Kelly, D. H., & Shannon, D. C. (1980). Parents' perceptions of the psychological and social impact of home monitoring. *Pediatrics, 66,* 37–41.

Cairns, R. (1979). *Social development: The origins and plasticity of interchanges.* San Francisco: W. H. Freeman.

Caldera, Y. M., Huston, A. C., & O'Brien, M. (1989). Social interactions and play patterns of parents and toddlers with feminine, masculine, and neutral toys. *Child Development, 60,* 70–76.

Caldeyro-Barcia, R. (1981, October). *The scientific bases for preserving the normal physiology of labor and birth through non-intervention.* Paper presented at the Conference on Obstetrical Management and Infant Outcome, New York.

Caldwell, B. M. (1986). Day care and early environmental adequacy. In W. Fowler (Ed.), *Early experience and the development of competence. New Directions for Child Development, 32,* 11–30.

Callaghan, J. W. (1981). A comparison of Anglo, Hopi and Navajo mothers and infants. In T. M. Field, A. M. Sostek, P. Vietze, & P. H. Leiderman (Eds.), *Culture and early interactions.* Hillsdale, NJ: Erlbaum.

Campos, J. J. (1976). Heart rate: A sensitive tool for the study of emotional development in the infant. In L. P. Lipsitt (Ed.), *Developmental psychobiology: The significance of infancy.* Hillsdale, NJ: Erlbaum.

Campos, J. J., & Barrett, K. C. (1984). Toward a new understanding of emotions and their development. In C. E. Izard, J. Kagan, & R. B. Zajonc (Eds.), *Emotions, cognition, and behavior* (pp. 229–263). New York: Cambridge University Press.

Campos, J. J., Campos, R., & Barrett, K. (1989). Emergent themes in the study of emotional development and emotion regulation. *Developmental Psychology, 25*(3), 394–402.

Campos, J. J., Emde, R. N., Gaensbauer, T., & Henderson, C. (1975). Cardiac and behavioral interrelationships in the reactions of infants to strangers. *Developmental Psychology, 11,* 589–601.

Campos, J. J., Langer, A., & Krowitz, A. (1970). Cardiac responses on the visual cliff in prelocomotor human infants. *Science, 170,* 196–197.

Campos, R. G. (1989). Soothing pain-elicited distress in infants with swaddling and pacifiers. *Child Development, 60,* 781–792.

Carew, J. V. (1980). Experience and the development of intelligence in young children at home and in day care. *Monographs of the Society for Research in Child Development, 187*(Serial No. 187).

Carlile, K. S., & Holstrum, W. J. (1989). Parental involvement behaviors: A comparison of Chamorro and Caucasian parents. *Infant Behavior and Development, 12,* 479–494.

Carlson, V., Cicchetti, D., Barnett, D., & Braunwald, K. (1989). Disorganized/disoriented attachment relationships in maltreated infants. *Developmental Psychology, 25,* 525–531.

Carlsson, S. G., Fagerberg, H., Horneman, G., Hwang, C., Larsson, K., Rodholm, M., Schaller, J., Danielsson, B., & Gundewall, C. (1979). Effects of various amounts of contact between mother and child on the mother's nursing behavior: A follow-up study. *Infant Behavior and Development, 2,* 209–214.

Caron, A. J., Caron, R. F., & Antell, S. E. (1988). Infant understanding of containment: An affordance perceived or a relationship conceived? *Developmental Psychology, 24,* 620–627.

Caron, A. J., Caron, R. F., & Carlson, V. R. (1979). Infant perception of the invariant shape of objects varying in slant. *Child Development, 50,* 716–721.

Caron, A. J., Caron, R. F., & MacLean, D. J. (1988). Infant discrimination of naturalistic emotional expressions: The role of face and voice. *Child Development, 59,* 604–616.

Caron, R. F., Caron, A. J., & Myers, R. S. (1982). Abstraction of invariant face expressions in infancy. *Child Development, 53,* 1008–1015.

Caudill, W., & Weinstein, H. (1969). Maternal care and infant behavior in Japan and America. *Psychiatry, 32,* 12–43.

Cernoch, J. M., & Porter, R. H. (1985). Recognition of maternal axillary odors by infants. *Child Development, 56,* 1593–1598.

Chacon, M. A., & Tildon, J. T. (1981). Elevated values of triiodothyronine in victims of sudden infant death syndrome. *Journal of Pediatrics, 99,* 758–760.

Chandler, M., Fritz, A. S., & Hala, S. (1989). Small-scale deceit: Deception as a marker of two-, three-, and four-year-olds' early theories of mind. *Child Development, 60,* 1263–1277.

Chase-Lansdale, P. L., & Owen, M. T. (1987). Maternal employment in a family context: Effects on infant-mother and infant-father attachments. *Child Development, 58,* 1505–1512.

Cherlin, A. J., & Furstenberg, F. F., Jr. (1986). *The new American grandparent.* New York: Basic Books.

Chisholm, J. S. (1983). *Navajo infancy: An ethological study of child development.* New York: Aldine.

Chomsky, N. (1975). *Reflections on language.* New York: Pantheon.

Chubet, C. T. (1988). *Feeding your baby: Breast, bottle and baby foods.* Stamford, CT: Longmeadow Press.

Cicchetti, D., & Mans, L. (1976, September). *Down's syndrome and normal infants' responses to impending collision.* Paper presented at the meeting of the American Psychological Association, Washington, D.C.

Clark, E. V. (1978). Strategies for communicating. *Child Development, 49,* 953–959.

Clark, H. H., & Clark, E. V. (1977). *Psychology and language: An introduction to psycholinguistics.* New York: Harcourt, Brace, Jovanovich.

Clark, J. E., Whitall, J., & Phillips, S. J. (1988). Human interlimb coordination: The first 6 months of independent walking. *Developmental Psychobiology, 21,* 445–456.

Clarke-Stewart, A. (1978). And daddy makes three: The father's impact on mother and young child. *Child Development, 44,* 466–478.

Clarke-Stewart, A. (1984). Day care: A new context for research and development. In M. Perlmutter (Ed.), *Minnesota symposia on child psychology* (Vol. 17). Hillsdale, NJ: Erlbaum.

Clarkson, M. G., & Berg, W. K. (1983). Cardiac deceleration and vowel discrimination in newborns: Crucial parameters of acoustic stimuli. *Child Development, 54,* 162–171.

Clarkson, M. G., Clifton, R. K., Swain, I. U., & Perris, E. E. (1989). Stimulus duration and repetition rate influence newborns' head orientation toward sound. *Developmental Psychobiology, 22,* 683–705.

Clifton, R. K., & Nelson, M. N. (1976). Developmental study of habituation in infants: The importance of paradigm, response system and state. In T. J. Tighe & R. N. Leaton (Eds.), *Habituation: Perspectives from child development, animal behavior, and neurophysiology.* Hillsdale, NJ: Erlbaum.

Cohen, L., Zilkha, S., Middleton, J., & O'Donnohue, N. (1978). Perinatal mortality: Assisting parental affirmation. *American Journal of Orthopsychiatry, 48,* 727–731.

Cohen, L. B., DeLoache, J. S., & Strauss, M. S. (1979). Infant visual perception. In J. Osofsky (Ed.), *Handbook of infant development.* New York: Wiley.

Cohen, L. B., & Strauss, M. S. (1979). Concept acquisition in the human infant. *Child Development, 50,* 419–424.

Cohen, L. J., & Campos, J. J. (1974). Father, mother and stranger as elicitors of attachment behaviors in infancy. *Developmental Psychology, 10,* 146–154.

Cohen, N. L., & Tomlinson-Keasey, C. (1980). The effects of peers and mothers on toddlers' play. *Child Development, 51,* 921–924.

Cohen, R. (1981). Factors influencing maternal choice of childbirth alternatives. *Journal of the American Academy of Child Psychiatry, 20,* 1–15.

Cohen, S. E., & Beckwith, L. (1979). Preterm infant intervention with the caregiver in the first year of life and competence at age two. *Child Development, 50,* 767–776.

Cohler, B. J., & Grunebaum, H. V. (1981). *Mothers, grandmothers, and daughters: Personality and childcare in three-generation families.* New York: Wiley.

Cohn, J. F., Campbell, S. B., Matias, R., & Hopkins, J. (1990). Face-to-face interactions of postpartum depressed and nondepressed mother-infant pairs at 2 months. *Developmental Psychology, 26*(1), 15–23.

Cohn, J. F., & Elmore, M. (1988). Effect of contingent changes in mothers' affective expression on the organization of behavior in 3-month-old infants. *Infant Behavior and Development, 11,* 493–505.

Cohn, J. F., Matias, R., Tronick, E. Z., Lyons-Ruth, K., & Connell, D. (1986). Face-to-face interactions, spontaneous and structured, of mothers with depressive symptoms. In T. Field & E. Z. Tronick (Eds.), *Maternal depression and child development, New directions for child development* (pp. 31–46). San Francisco: Jossey-Bass.

Cohn, J. F., & Tronick, E. Z. (1983). Three-month-old infants' reaction to simulated maternal depression. *Child Development, 54,* 185–193.

Cohn, J. F., & Tronick, E. Z. (1987). Mother-infant face-to-face interaction: The sequence of dyadic states at 3, 6, and 9 months. *Developmental Psychology, 23,* 68–77.

Cohn, J. F., & Tronick, E. Z. (1988). Mother-infant face-to-face interaction: Influence is bidirectional and unrelated to periodic cycles in either partner's behavior. *Developmental Psychology, 24*(3), 386–392.

Coles, R. (1971). *The South Goes North.* Boston: Little-Brown.

Coll, C. T. G. (1990). Developmental outcome of minority infants: A process-oriented look into our beginnings. *Child Development, 61,* 270–289.

Colletta, N. D. (1981). Social support and the risk of maternal rejection by adolescent mothers. *Journal of Psychology, 109,* 191–197.

Colletta, N. D., & Lee, D. (1983). The impact of support for black adolescent mothers. *Journal of Family Issues, 4,* 127–143.

Collis, G. M., & Schaffer, H. R. (1975). Synchronization of visual attention in mother-infant pairs. *Journal of Child Psychology and Psychiatry, 16,* 315–320.

Colman, A., & Colman, L. (1977). *Pregnancy: The psychological experience.* New York: Bantam.

Colombo, J., Mitchell, D. W., O'Brien, M., & Horowitz, F. D. (1987). The stability of visual habituation during the first year of life. *Child Development, 58,* 474–487.

Colombo, J., Moss, M., & Horowitz, F. D. (1989). Neonatal state profiles: Reliability and short-term prediction of neurobehavioral status. *Child Development, 60,* 1102–1110.

Conel, J. L. (1939). *The postnatal development of the human cerebral cortex: Vol. 1. The cortex of the newborn.* Cambridge: Harvard University Press.

Conel, J. L. (1941). *The postnatal development of the human cerebral cortex: Vol. 2. The cortex of the one-month infant.* Cambridge: Harvard University Press.

Connell, J. P. (1985). A component process approach to the study of individual differences and developmental change in attachment system functioning. In M. E. Lamb, R. A. Thompson, W. Gardner, & E. L. Charnov, (Eds.), *Infant-mother attachment* (pp. 223–247). Hillsdale, NJ: Erlbaum.

Connolly, K., & Dalgleish, M. (1989). The emergence of a tool-using skill in infancy. *Developmental Psychology, 25,* 894–912.

Cornell, E. H. (1979). Infants' recognition memory, forgetting, and savings. *Journal of Experimental Child Psychology, 28,* 359–374.

Corter, C. (1977). Brief separation and communication between infant and mother. In T. Alloway, P. Pliner, & L. Krames (Eds.), *Attachment behavior.* New York: Plenum.

Corter, C., Abramovitch, R., & Pepler, D. J. (1983). The role of the mother in sibling interaction. *Child Development, 54,* 1599–1605.

Coster, W. J., Gersten, M. S., Beeghly, M., & Cicchetti, D. (1989). Communicative functioning in maltreated toddlers. *Developmental Psychology, 25*(6), 1020–1029.

Cotterell, J. L. (1986). Work and community influences on the quality of child rearing. *Child Development, 57,* 362–374.

Cottrell, B. H., & Shannahan, M. K. (1987). A comparison of fetal outcome in birth chair and delivery table births. *Research in Nursing and Health, 10,* 239–243.

Cowan, C. P., & Cowan, P. A. (1981). *Couple role arrangements and satisfaction during family formation.* Boston: Society for Research in Child Development.

Cox, M. C., Owen, M. T., Lewis, J. M., & Henderson, V. K. (1989). Marriage, adult adjustment, and early parenting. *Child Development, 60,* 1015–1024.

Cravioto, J., & Arrieta, R. (1983). Malnutrition in childhood. In M. Rutter (Ed.), *Developmental neuropsychiatry.* New York: Guilford.

Crawford, J. W. (1982). Mother-infant interaction in premature and full-term infants. *Child Development, 53,* 957–962.

Crittenden, P. M. (1985). Social networks, quality of child rearing, and child development. *Child Development, 56,* 1299–1313.

Crnic, K., & Greenberg, M. (1987). Maternal stress, social support, and coping: Influences on the early mother-child relationship. In C. Boukydis (Ed.), *Research on support for parents and infants in the postnatal period* (pp. 25–40). Norwood, NJ: Ablex.

Crockenberg, S. B. (1981). Infant irritability, mother responsiveness, and social support influences on the security of infant-mother attachment. *Child Development, 52,* 857–865.

Crockenberg, S. B. (1987). Support for adolescent mothers during the postnatal period: Theory and research. In C. Boukydis (Ed.), *Research on support for parents and infants in the postnatal period* (pp. 3–24). Norwood, NJ: Ablex.

Crockenberg, S. B., & Acredolo, C. (1983). Infant temperament ratings: A function of infants, of mothers, or both? *Infant Behavior and Development, 6,* 61–72.

Crockenberg, S. B., & McCluskey, K. (1986). Change in maternal behavior during the baby's first year of life. *Child Development, 57,* 746–753.

Crockenberg, S. B., & Smith, P. (1982). Antecedents of mother-infant interaction and infant irritability in the first three months of life. *Infant Behavior and Development, 6,* 61–72.

Crook, C. K. (1978). Taste perception in the newborn infant. *Infant Behavior and Development, 1,* 52–69.

Crouter, A. C., Perry-Jenkins, M., Huston, T. L., & McHale, S. M. (1987). Processes underlying father involvement in dual-earner and single-earner families. *Developmental Psychology, 23,* 431–440.

Crowley, P. H., Gulati, D. K., Hayden, T. L., Lopez, P., & Dyer, R. A. (1979). A chiasma-hormonal hypothesis relating Down's syndrome and maternal age. *Nature, 280,* 417–419.

Cummings, J. S., Pellegrini, D. S., Notarius, C. I., & Cummings, E. M. (1989). Children's responses to angry adult behavior as a function of marital distress and history of interparent hostility. *Child Development, 60,* 1035–1043.

Curry, M. (1979). Contact during the first hour with the wrapped or naked newborn: Effect on maternal attachment at 36 hours and three months. *Birth and the Family Journal, 6,* 227–235.

Curtiss, S. (1982). *Genie: A psycholinguistic study of a modern-day "wild child".* New York: Academic Press.

Dale, P. S. (1976). *Language development: Structure and function* (2nd ed.). New York: Holt, Rinehart and Winston.

Daly, M., & Wilson, M. I. (1981). Abuse and neglect of children in evolutionary perspective. In R. Alexander & D. Tinkle (Eds.) *Natural selection and social behavior: Recent research and new theory.* New York: Chiron Press.

Danforth, D. N. (Ed.) (1977). *Obstetrics and gynecology* (3rd ed.). New York: Harper & Row.

Daniels, D., Plomin, R., & Greenhalgh, J. (1984). Correlates of difficult temperament in infancy. *Child Development, 55,* 1184–1194.

Dannemiller, J. L., & Stephens, B. R. (1988). A critical test of infant pattern preference models. *Child Development, 59,* 210–216.

Darwin, C. R. (1859). *The Origins of Species.* New York: Modern Library.

Darwin, C. R. (1872). *The Expression of the Emotions in Man and Animals.* London: Murray.

Darwin, C. R. (1877). A biographical sketch of an infant. *Mind, 2,* 285–294.

Darwin, C. R. (unpublished). *Notebook on child development.* Cambridge University Library.

Davenport-Slack, B., & Boylan, C. H. (1974). Psychological correlates of childbirth pain. *Psychosomatic Medicine, 36,* 215–223.

Davis, D. (1967). Family process in mental retardation. *American Journal of Psychiatry, 124,* 340–350.

Davis, D. (1985). Infant car safety: The role of perinatal caregivers. *Birth, 12*(Supplement), 21–27.

Davis, H. (1978). A description of aspects of mother-infant vocal interaction. *Journal of Child Psychology and Psychiatry, 19,* 379–386.

DeBoysson-Bardies, B., Sagant, L., & Durand, C. (1984). Discernible differences in the babbling of infants according to target language. *Journal of Child Language, 11,* 1–15.

DeCasper, A. J., & Fifer, W. P. (1980). Of human bonding: Newborns prefer their mothers' voices. *Science, 208,* 1174–1176.

DeCasper, A. J., & Sigafoos, A. D. (1983). The intrauterine heartbeat: A potent reinforcer for newborns. *Infant Behavior and Development, 6,* 19–26.

DeCasper, A. J., & Spence, M. J. (1986). Prenatal maternal speech influences newborns' perception of speech sounds. *Infant Behavior and Development, 9,* 133–150.

DeChateau, P. (1987). Parent-infant socialization in several western European countries. In J. D. Osofsky (Ed.), *Handbook of infant development.* (2nd ed.). (pp. 642–668). NY: Wiley.

DeChateau, P. (1980). Early post-partum contact and later attitudes. *International Journal of Behavioral Development, 3,* 273–286.

DeLoache, J. S., & Plaetzer, B. (1975, April). *Tea for two: Joint mother-child symbolic play.* Presented at the meeting of the Society for Research in Child Development, Toronto.

DeLoache, J. S., Sugarman, S., & Brown, A. L. (1985). The development of error correction strategies in young children's manipulative play. *Child Development, 56,* 928–939.

DeMeis, D. K., Hock, E., & McBride, S. L. (1986). The balance of employment and motherhood: Longitudinal study of mothers' feelings about separation from their first-born infants. *Developmental Psychology, 22,* 627–632.

Demos, E. (1982). Facial expressions of infants and toddlers: A descriptive analysis. In T. Field & A. Fogel (Eds.), *Emotion and early interaction.* Hillsdale, NJ: Erlbaum.

Denham, S. (1986). Social cognition, prosocial behavior and emotion in preschoolers: contextual validation. *Child Development, 57,* 194–201.

Department of Health, Education, and Welfare, National Center for Health Statistics. (1981). *Vital statistics of the United States.* Washington, DC: U. S. Government Printing Office.

Desor, J. A., Greene, L. S., & Mauer, D. (1975). Preference for sweet and salty in 9- to 15-year-olds and adult humans. *Science, 190,* 686–687.

Desor, J. A., Miller, O., & Turner, R. (1973). Taste in acceptance of sugars by human infants. *Journal of Comparative and Physiological Psychology, 85,* 496–501.

DeStefano, C. T., & Mueller, E. (1982). Environmental determinants of peer social activity in 18-month-old males. *Infant Behavior and Development, 5,* 175–183.

deVilliers, J. C., & deVilliers, P. A. (1973). A cross-sectional study of the acquisition of grammatical morphemes in child speech. *Journal of Pyscholinguistic Research, 2,* 267–278.

Diamond, A., (1988). Abilities and neural mechanisms underlying AB performance. *Child Development, 59,* 523–527.

Diamond, A., & Doar, B. (1989). The performance of human infants on a measure of frontal cortex function, the delayed response task. *Developmental Psychobiology, 22*(3), 271–294.

Dick-Read, G. (1972). *Childbirth without fear: The original approach to natural childbirth* (Originally published 1933). (Rev. ed.). H. Wessel & H. Ellis (Eds.). New York: Harper & Row.

Dickstein, S., & Parke, R. D. (1988). Social referencing in infancy: A glance at fathers and marriage. *Child Development, 59,* 506–511.

DiLalla, L. F., & Watson, M. W. (1988). Differentiation of fantasy and reality: Preschoolers' reactions to interruptions in their play. *Developmental Psychology, 24,* 286–291.

DiPietro, J. A., Larson, S. K., & Porges, S. W. (1987). Behavioral and heart rate pattern differences between breast-fed and bottle-fed neonates. *Developmental Psychology, 23*(4), 467–474.

Dixon, S. D., LeVine, R. A., Richman, A., & Brazelton, T. B. (1984). Mother-child interaction around a teaching task: An African-American comparison. *Child Development, 55,* 1252–1264.

Donovan, W. L., & Leavitt, L. A. (1989). Maternal self-efficacy and infant attachment: Integrating physiology, perceptions, and behavior. *Child Development, 60,* 460–472.

Dow, K. E., & Reopelli, R. J. (1985). Ethanol neurotoxicity: Effects on neurite formation and neurotrophic factor production in vitro. *Science, 228,* 591–593.

Drachman, D. B., & Coulombre, A. J. (1962). Experimental clubfoot and arthorogryposis multiplex congenita. *Lancet, 2,* 523–536.

Dressler, W. (1985). Extended family relationships, social support, and mental health in a southern black community. *Journal of Health and Social Behavior, 26,* 39–48.

Drotar, D., & Irvin, N. (1979). Disturbed maternal bereavement following infant death. *Child Care, Health and Development, 5,* 239–247.

Dubowitz, L. M. S., Dubowitz, V., & Goldberg, C. (1970). Clinical assessment of gestational age in the newborn infant. *Journal of Pediatrics, 77,* 1–10.

Dunham, P., Dunham, F., Hurshman, A., & Alexander, T. (1989). Social contingency effects on subsequent perceptual-cognitive tasks in young infants. *Child Development, 60,* 1486–1496.

Dunn, J. (1975). Consistency and change in styles of mothering. In Ciba Foundation Symposium, *Parent-infant interaction.* New York: Elsevier.

Dunn, J., Bretherton, I., & Munn, P. (1987). Conversations about feeling states between mothers and their young children. *Developmental Psychology, 23,* 132–139.

Dunn, J., & Kendrick, C. (1979). Interactions between young siblings in the context of family relationships. In M. Lewis & L. Rosenblum (Eds.), *The child and its family.* New York: Plenum.

Dunn, J., & Kendrick, C. (1981). Social behavior of young siblings in the family context: Differences between same-sex and different-sex dyads. *Child Development, 52,* 1265–1273.

Dunn, J., & Kendrick, C. (1982). *Siblings: Love, Envy, and Understanding.* Cambridge: Harvard University Press.

Dunn, J., & Munn, P. (1985). Becoming a family member: Family conflict and the development of social understanding in the second year. *Child Development, 56,* 480–492.

Dunn, J., & Munn, P. (1987). Development of justification in disputes with mother and sibling. *Developmental Psychology, 23,* 791–798.

Dunn, J., Plomin, R., & Daniels, D. (1986). Consistency and change in mothers' behavior toward young siblings. *Child Development, 57,* 348–356.

Dunn, J., & Shatz, M. (1989). Becoming a conversationalist despite (or because of) having an older sibling. *Child Development, 60,* 399–410.

Dworetzsky, J. P. (1981). *Introduction to child development.* St. Paul: West.

Dyer, A. B., Lickliter, R., & Gottlieb, G. (1989). Maternal and peer imprinting in mallard ducklings under experimentally simulated natural social conditions. *Developmental Psychobiology, 22,* 463–475.

Dyregrov, A., & Matthiesen, S. B. (1987). Stillbirth, neonatal death and sudden infant death (SIDS): Parental reactions. *Scandinavian Journal of Psychology, 28,* 104–114.

Easterbrooks, M. A. (1989). Quality of attachment to mother and to father: Effects of perinatal risk status. *Child Development, 60,* 825–830.

Easterbrooks, M. A., & Goldberg, W. (1984). Toddler development in the family: Impact of father involvement and parenting characteristics. *Child Development, 55,* 740–752.

Easterbrooks, M. A., & Goldberg, W. (1985). Effects of early maternal employment on toddlers, mothers, and fathers. *Developmental Psychology, 21,* 774–783.

Ebaugh, H. R., & Haney, C. A. (1980). Shifts in abortion attitudes: 1972–1978. *Journal of Marriage and the Family, 42,* 491–499.

Ebert, J. D., & Sussex, I. M. (1970). *Interacting systems in development* (2nd ed.). New York: Holt, Rinehart and Winston.

Eckerman, C. O., Davis, C. C., & Didow, S. M. (1989). Toddlers' emerging ways of achieving social coordinations with a peer. *Child Development, 60,* 440–453.

Eckerman, C. O., & Didow, S. M. (1989). Toddlers' social coordinations: Changing responses to another's invitation to play. *Developmental Psychology, 25,* 794–804.

Eckerman, C. O., & Stein, M. R. (1990). How imitation begets imitation and toddlers' generation of games. *Developmental Psychology, 26,* 370–378.

Eckerman, C. O., & Whatley, J. L. (1975). Infants' reactions to unfamiliar adults varying in novelty. *Developmental Psychology, 11,* 562–566.

Eckerman, C. O., & Whatley, J. L. (1977). Toys and social interaction between infant peers. *Child Development, 48,* 1645–1656.

Eckerman, C. O., Whatley, J. L., & Kutz, S. (1975). Growth of social play with peers during the second year of life. *Developmental Psychology, 11,* 42–49.

Eckerman, C. O., Whatley, J. L., & McGehee, L. J. (1979). Approaching and contacting the object another manipulates: A social skill of the one-year-old. *Developmental Psychology, 15,* 585–593.

Edwards, C. P. (1984). The age group labels and categories of preschool children. *Child Development, 55,* 440–452.

Egeland, B., & Sroufe, L. A. (1981). Developmental sequelae of maltreatment in infancy. *New Directions for Child Development, 11,* 77–92.

Eilers, R. E., & Gavin, W. J. (1981). The evaluation of infant speech perception skills: Statistical techniques and theory development. In R. Stark (Ed.), *Language behavior in infancy and early childhood.* New York: Elsevier.

Eilers, R. E., Gavin, W., & Wilson, W. R. (1979). Linguistic experience and phonemic perception in infancy: A crosslinguistic study. *Child Development, 50,* 14–18.

Eimas, P. D., Siqueland, E. R., Jusczyk, P., & Vigorito, J. (1971). Speech perception in infants. *Science, 171,* 303–306.

Einspieler, C., Widder, J., Holzer, A., & Kenner, T. (1988). The predictive value of behavioral risk factors for sudden infant death. *Early Human Development, 18,* 101–109.

Eisenberg, R. B. (1976). *Auditory competence in early life.* Baltimore: University Park Press.

Ekman, P. (1984). Expression and the nature of emotion. In K. Scherer & P. Edman (Eds.), *Approaches to emotion* (pp. 329–343). Hillsdale, NJ: Erlbaum.

Elder, G., Nguyen, T., & Caspi, A. (1985). Linking family hardship to children's lives. *Child Development, 56,* 361–375.

Ellis, S., & Rogoff, B. (1982). The strategies and efficacy of child versus adult teachers. *Child Development, 53,* 730–735.

Emde, R. N., Gaensbauer, T. J., & Harmon, R. J. (1976). Emotional expression in infancy. *Psychological Issues, 10*(1).

Entwisle, D. R., & Alexander, K. L. (1987). Long-term effects of cesarean delivery on parents' beliefs and children's schooling. *Developmental Psychology, 23,* 676–682.

Entwisle, D. R., & Doering, S. (1981). *The first birth: A turning point.* Baltimore: John Hopkins University Press.

Erickson, M. F., Sroufe, L. A., & Egeland, B. (1985). Relationship between quality of attachment and behavior problems in preschool in a high-risk sample. In I. Bretherton & E. Waters (Eds.), *Growing points of attachment theory and research.* Monographs of the Society for Research in Child Development, *50*(Serial No. 209), 147–166.

Erikson, E. (1950). *Childhood and society.* New York: Norton.

Escalona, S. K., & Corman, H. H. (1968). *Albert Einstein Scales of Sensorimotor Development.* Unpublished manuscript.

Estok, R. N., & Lehman, A. (1983). Perinatal death: Grief support for families. *Birth, 10,* 17–25.

Fagan, J. F. (1979). The origins of facial pattern recognition. In M. H. Bornstein & W. Kessen (Eds.), *Psychological development from infancy: Image to intention.* Hillsdale, NJ: Erlbaum.

Fagard, J., & Jacquet, A. (1989). Onset of bimanual coordination and symmetry versus asymmetry of movement. *Infant Behavior and Development, 12,* 229–235.

Fagen, J. W., Ohr, P. S., Singer, J. M., & Klein, S. J. (1989). Crying and retrograde amnesia in young infants. *Infant Behavior and Development, 12,* 13–24.

Fagot, B. I., & Leinbach, M. D. (1989). The young child's gender schema: Environmental input, internal organization. *Child Development, 60,* 663–672.

Fagot, B. I., Leinbach, M. D., & Hagan, R. (1990). Gender labeling and the adoption of sex-typed behaviors. *Developmental Psychology, 22,* 440–443.

Falkner, F. (Ed.). (1985). *Prevention of infant mortality and morbidity.* Basel, NY: Karger.

Fantz, R. L. (1961). The origin of form perception. *Scientific American, 204,* 66–72.

Fantz, R. L., Fagan, J. F., & Miranda, S. B. (1975). Early visual selection. In L. B. Cohen & P. Salapatek (Eds.), *Infant perception: From sensation to cognition* (Vol. 1). New York: Academic Press.

Farran, D. C., & Haskins, R. (1980). Reciprocal influence in the social interactions of mothers and three-month-old children from different socioeconomic backgrounds. *Child Development, 51,* 780–791.

Fein, R. (1976). The first weeks of fathering. The importance of choices and supports for new parents. *Birth and the Family journal, 3,* 53–58.

Feiring, C., Fox, N. A., Jaskir, J., & Lewis, M. (1987). The relation between social support, infant risk status and mother-infant interaction. *Developmental Psychology, 23,* 400–405.

Feiring, C., & Lewis, M. (1981). Middle class differences in cognitive development. In T. M. Field, A. M. Sostek, P. Vietze, & P. H. Leiderman. (Eds.), *Culture and early interactions.* Hillsdale, NJ: Erlbaum.

Feiring, C., Lewis, M., & Starr, M. D. (1984). Indirect effects and infants' reactions to strangers. *Developmental Psychology, 20,* 485–491.

Feldman, S. S., & Nash, S. C. (1978). Interest in babies during young adulthood. *Child Development, 49,* 617–622.

Feldman, S. S., & Nash, S. C. (1979a). Changes in responsiveness to babies during adolescence. *Child Development, 50,* 942–949.

Feldman, S. S., & Nash, S. C. (1979b). Sex differences in responsiveness to babies among
　mature adults. *Developmental Psychology, 15,* 430–436.

Feldman, S. S., & Nash, S. C. (1986). Antecedents of early parenting. In A. Fogel &
　G. F. Melson (Eds.), *Origins of nurturance: Developmental, biological and cultural
　perspectives on caregiving.* Hillsdale, NJ: Erlbaum.

Fenson, C., Kagan, J., Kearsley, R. B., & Zelazo, P. R. (1976). The developmental
　progression of manipulative play in the first two years. *Child Development, 47,* 232–236.

Fenson, L., Sapper, V., & Minner, D. G. (1974). Attention and manipulative play in the
　one-year-old child. *Child Development, 45,* 757–764.

Ferland, M. B., & Mendelson, M. J. (1989). Infants' categorization of melodic contour.
　Infant Behavior and Development, 12, 341–355.

Fernald, A. (1985). Four-month-old infants prefer to listen to motherese. *Infant Behavior
　and Development, 8,* 181–195.

Fernald, A. (1989). Intonation and communicative intent in mothers' speech to infants:
　Is the melody the message? *Child Development, 60,* 1497–1510.

Fernald, A., & Kuhl, P. (1987). Acoustic determinants of infant preference for motherese
　speech. *Infant Behavior and Development, 10,* 279–293.

Fernald, A., & Simon, T. (1984). Expanded intonation contours in mothers' speech to
　newborns. *Developmental Psychology, 20,* 104–113.

Fernald, A., Taeschner, T., Dunn, J., Papousek, M., DeBoysson-Bardies, B., & Fukui, I.
　(1989). A cross-language study of prosodic modifications in mothers' and fathers' speech
　to preverbal infants. *Journal of Child Language, 16,* 477–501.

Field, T. (1979a). Differential behavioral and cardiac responses of 3-month-old infants to
　mirror and peer. *Infant Behavior and Development, 2,* 179–184.

Field, T. (1979b). Infant behaviors directed toward peers and adults in the presence and
　absence of mother. *Infant Behavior and Development, 2,* 47–54.

Field, T. (1981a). Interaction coaching for high-risk infants and their parents. In H. Moss
　(Ed.), *Prevention and human sciences.* New York: Haworth Press.

Field, T. (1981b). Infant arousal, attention and affect during early interactions. In L. P.
　Lipsitt & C. Rovee-Collier (Eds.), *Advances in Infancy Research* (Vol. 1). Norwood, NJ:
　Ablex.

Field, T. (1982). Affective and physiological changes during manipulated interactions of
　high-risk infants. In T. Field & A. Fogel (Eds.), *Emotion and early interaction.* NJ:
　Erlbaum.

Field, T. (1987). Affective and interactive disturbances in infants. In J. D. Osofsky (Ed.),
　Handbook of infant development (2nd ed.). New York: Wiley.

Field, T., Dempsey, J. R., Hatch, J., Ting, G., & Clifton, R. K. (1979). Cardiac and
　behavioral responses to repeated tactile and auditory stimulation by preterm and term
　neonates. *Developmental Psychology, 15,* 406–416.

Field, T., Healy, B., Goldstein, S., Perry, S., Bendell, D., Schanberg, S., Zimmerman,
　E. A., & Kuhn, C. (1988). Infants of depressed mothers show "depressed" behavior
　even with nondepressed adults. *Child Development, 59,* 1569–1579.

Field, T., Healy, B., & LeBlanc, W. G. (1989). Sharing and synchrony of behavior states
　and heart rate in nondepressed versus depressed mother-infant interactions. *Infant
　Behavior and Development, 12,* 357–376.

Field, T., Ignatoff, E., Stringer S., Brennan, J., Greenberg, R., Widmayer, S., &
　Anderson, G. (1982). Non-nutritive sucking during tube feedings: Effects on preterm
　neonates in an intensive care unit. *Pediatrics, 70,* 381–384.

Field, T., Gewirtz, J. L., Cohen, D., Garcia, R., Greenberg, R., & Collins, K. (1984).
　Leave-takings and reunions of infants, toddlers, preschoolers, and their parents. *Child
　Development, 55,* 628–635.

Field, T., Greenberg, R., Woodson, R., Cohen, D., & Garcia, R. (1984). A descriptive
　study on the facial expressions of infants during Brazelton neonatal assessments. *Infant
　Mental Health Journal, 5,* 61–71.

Field, T., Sandberg, D., Garcia, R., Vega-Lahr, N., Goldstein, S., & Guy, L. (1985). Pregnancy problems, postpartum depression and early mother-infant interactions. *Developmental Psychology, 21,* 1152–1156.

Field, T., & Sostek, A. (1983). *Infants born at risk: Physiological, perceptual and cognitive processes.* New York: Grune & Stratton.

Field, T., Vega-Lahr, N., & Jagadish, S. (1984). Separation stress of nursery school infants and toddlers graduating to new classes. *Infant Behavior and Development, 7,* 277–284.

Field, T., Vega-Lahr, N., Scafidi, F., & Goldstein, S. (1986). Effects of maternal unavailability on mother-infant interactions. *Infant Behavior and Development, 9,* 473–478.

Field, T., & Widmayer, S. M. (1980). Developmental follow-up on infants delivered by caesarean section and general anesthesia. *Infant Behavior and Development, 3,* 253–264.

Field, T., Widmayer, S. M., Stringer, S., & Ignatoff, E. (1980). Teenage, lower class, black mothers and their preterm infants: An intervention and developmental follow-up. *Child Development, 51,* 426–436.

Field, T., Woodson, R., Greenberg, R., & Cohen, D. (1982). *Discrimination and imitation of facial expressions by neonates.* Paper presented at the International Conference on Infant Studies, Austin.

Fifer, W. P. (1987). Neonatal preference for mother's voice. In N. S. Krasnegor, E. M. Blass, M. A. Hofer, & W. P. Smotherman (Eds.), *Perinatal development: A psychobiological perspective.* New York: Academic Press.

Fifth Special Report to the U. S. Congress on Alcohol and Health (1984). *Alcohol Health & Research World, 9,* 1–72.

Finkelstein, N., Dent, C., Gallacher, K., & Ramey, C. (1978). Social behavior of infants and toddlers in a day-care environment. *Developmental Psychology, 14,* 257–262.

Fiorentino, M. R. (1981). *A basis for sensorimotor development-normal and abnormal: The influence of primitive, postural reflexes on the development and distribution of tone.* Springfield, IL: Charles C. Thomas.

Fischer, K. W. (1987). Relations between brain and cognitive development. *Child Development, 58,* 623–632.

Fisher, C. B., Ferdinandsen K., & Bornstein, M. H. (1981). The role of symmetry in infant form perception. *Child Development, 52,* 457–462.

Fleming, A. S., & Orpen, G. (1986). Psychobiology of maternal behavior in rats, selected other species and humans. In A. Fogel & G. F. Melson (Eds.), *Origins of nurturance: Developmental, biological and cultural perspectives on caregiving.* Hillsdale, NJ: Erlbaum.

Fleming, A. S., Ruble, D. N., Flett, G. L., & Shaul, D. L. (1988). Postpartum adjustment in first-time mothers: Relations between mood, maternal attitudes, and mother-infant interactions. *Developmental Psychology, 24,* 71–81.

Fleming, A. S., Ruble, D. N., Flett, G. L., & Van Wagner, V. (1990). Adjustment in first-time mothers: Changes in mood and mood content during the early postpartum months. *Developmental Psychology, 26,* 137–143.

Fogel, A. (1977). Temporal organization in mother-infant face-to-face interaction. In H. R. Schaffer (Ed.), *Studies in mother-infant interaction* (pp. 119–152). New York: Academic Press.

Fogel, A. (1979). Peer vs. mother directed behavior in 1- to 3-month-old infants. *Infant Behavior and Development, 2,* 215–226.

Fogel, A. (1980). The effect of brief separations on two-month-old infants. *Infant Behavior and Development, 3,* 315–330.

Fogel, A. (1981). The ontogeny of gestural communication: The first six months. In R. Stark (Ed.), *Language behavior in infancy and early childhood* (pp. 17–44). New York: Elsevier.

Fogel, A. (1982a). Affect dynamics in early infancy: Affective tolerance. In T. Field & A. Fogel (Eds.), *Emotion and early interaction* (pp. 15–56). Hillsdale, NJ: Erlbaum.

Fogel, A. (1982b). Early adult-infant face-to-face interaction: Expectable sequences of behavior. *Journal of Pediatric Psychology, 7,* 1–22.

Fogel, A. (1982c). Emotional development. In H. Mitzel (Ed.), *Encyclopedia of educational research.* New York: Macmillan.

Fogel, A. (1985). Coordinative structures in the development of expressive behavior in early infancy. In G. Zivin (Ed.), *The development of expressive behavior: Biology-environment interactions* (pp. 249–267). New York: Academic Press.

Fogel, A. (1990a). The process of developmental change in infant communicative action: Using dynamic systems theory to study individual ontogenies. In J. Colombo & J. Fagen (Eds.), *Individual differences in infancy: Reliability, stability and prediction.* Hillsdale, NJ: Erlbaum.

Fogel, A. (1990b). Sensorimotor factors in communicative development. In H. Bloch & B. Bertenthal (Eds.), *Sensorimotor organization and development in infancy and early childhood.* NATO ASI Series. The Netherlands: Kluwer.

Fogel, A., Dedo, J. Y., & McEwen, I. (in press). Effect of postural position on the duration of gaze at mother during face-to-face interaction in 3- to 6-month-old infants. *Infant Behavior and Development.*

Fogel, A., Diamond, G., Langhorst, B., & Demos, V. (1981). Affective and cognitive aspects of the 2-month-olds' participation in face-to-face interaction with its mother. In E. Tronick (Ed.), *Joint regulation of behavior.* Baltimore: University Park Press.

Fogel, A., & Hannan, T. E. (1985). Manual actions of 2- to 3-month-old human infants during social interaction. *Child Development, 56,* 1271–1279.

Fogel, A., Karns, J., & Kawai, M. (1990). Lateral asymmetry in attention for 3-month-old human infants during face-to-face interaction with mother. *Developmental Psychology, 23,* 1–14.

Fogel, A., Melson, G. F., Toda, S., & Mistry, J. (1987). Young children's responses to unfamiliar infants: The effects of adult involvement. *International Journal of Behavioral Development, 10,* 37–50.

Fogel, A., & Reimers, M. (1989). On the psychobiology of emotions and their development. Commentary on Malatesta, et al. *Monographs of the Society for Research in Child Development, 54*(Serial No. 219), 105–113.

Fogel, A., Stevenson, M. B., & Messinger, D. (in press). A comparison of the parent-child relationship in Japan and the United States. In J. L. Roopnarine & D. B. Carter (Eds.), *Parent-child relations in diverse cultural settings.* Norwood, NJ: Ablex.

Fogel, A., & Thelen. E. (1987). Development of early expressive and communicative action: Reinterpreting the evidence from a dynamic systems perspective. *Developmental Psychology, 23,* 747–761.

Fogel, A., Toda, S., & Kawai, M. (1988). Mother-infant face-to-face interaction in Japan and the United States: A laboratory comparison using 3-month-old infants. *Developmental Psychology, 24,* 398–406.

Forestier, D. F., Kaplan, C., & Cox, W. (1988). Prenatal diagnosis and management of bleeding disorders with fetal blood sampling. *American Journal of Obstetrics Gynecology, 158,* 939–946.

Fox, N. A. (1977). Attachment of kibbutz infants to mother and metapelet. *Child Development, 48,* 1228–1239.

Fox, N. A. (1985). Sweet/sour—interest/disgust: The role of approach-withdrawal in the development of emotions. In T. Field & N. Fox (Eds.), *Social perception in infancy.* Norwood, NJ: Ablex.

Fox, N. A. (1989). Psychophysiological correlates of emotional reactivity during the first year of life. *Developmental Psychology, 25,* 364–372.

Fox, N. A., & Davidson, R. J. (1987). Electroencephalogram asymmetry in response to the approach of a stranger and maternal separation in 10-month-old infants. *Developmental Psychology, 23,* 233–240.

Fox, N. A., & Davidson, R. J. (1988). Patterns of brain electrical activity during the expression of discrete emotions in ten-month-old infants. *Developmental Psychology, 24*, 230–236.

Fox, N. A., & Gelles, M. (1984). Face-to-face interaction in term and preterm infants. *Infant Mental Health, 5*, 192–205.

Fox, R., Aslin, R. N., Shea, S. L., & Dumais, S. T. (1980). Stereopsis in human infants. *Science, 207*, 327–324.

Fox, R., & McDaniels, C. (1982). The perception of biological motion by human infants. *Science, 218*, 486–487.

Fraiberg, S. (1974). Gross motor development in infants blind from birth. *Child Development, 45*, 114–126.

Francis, P. L., Self, P. A., & Horowitz, F. D. (1987). The behavioral assessment of the neonate: An overview. In J. D. Osofsky (Ed.), *Handbook of infant development* (2nd ed.). New York: Wiley.

Frankenburg, W. K., Dodd, J. B., Fandal, A. W., Kuzuk, E., & Cohrs, M. (1975). *DDST: Reference manual* (Rev. ed.). Denver: Ladoka Project and Publication Foundation.

Freedman, D. G. (1974). *Human infancy: An evolutionary perspective.* Hillsdale, NJ: Erlbaum.

Freeman, N. H. (1980). *Strategies of representation in young children: Analysis of spatial skill and drawing processes.* London: Academic.

Freud, A. (1965). Normality and pathology in childhood. New York: International Universities Press.

Freud, S. (1900/1953). [*The interpretation of dreams.*] In J. Strachey (Ed. and trans.), *The standard edition of the complete works of Sigmund Freud* (Vol. 3). London: Hogarth. (Originally published 1900).

Freud, S. (1903/1953). [*Three essays on the theory of sexuality.*] In J. Strachey (Ed. and trans.), *The standard edition of the complete works of Sigmund Freud* (Vol. 7). London: Hogarth. (Originally published 1903).

Friedman, S. L., & Jacobs, B. S. (1981). Sex differences in neonates' behavioral responsiveness to repeated auditory stimulation. *Infant Behavior and Development, 4*, 175–183.

Frigoletto, F. D., Greene, M. F., Benacerraf, B. R., Barss, V. A., & Saltzman, D. H. (1986). Ultrasonographic fetal surveillance in the management of the isoimmunized pregnancy. *New England Journal of Medicine, 315*, 430–432.

Frodi, A. M., & Lamb, M. E. (1978). Sex differences in responsiveness to infants: A developmental study of psychophysiological and behavioral responses. *Child Development, 49*, 1182–1188.

Frodi, A. M., & Lamb, M. E. (1980). Child abuser's response to infant smiles and cries. *Child Development, 51*, 238–241.

Frodi, A. M., Lamb, M. E., Leavitt, L. A., & Donovan, W. L. (1978a). Father's and mother's responses to infant smiles and cries. *Infant Behavior and Development, 1*, 187–198.

Frodi, A. M., Lamb, M. E., Leavitt, L. A., Donovan, W. L., Neff, C., & Sherry, D. (1978b). Father's and mother's responses to the faces and cries of normal and premature infants. *Developmental Psychology, 14*, 490–498.

Furman, W., Rahe, D. F., & Hartup, W. W. (1979). Rehabilitation of socially withdrawn preschool children through mixed-age and same-age socialization. *Child Development, 50*, 915–922.

Furrow, D. (1984). Social and private speech at two years. *Child Development, 55*, 355–362.

Furstenberg, F. F., Jr., Brooks-Gunn, J., & Morgan, P. (1987). *Adolescent mothers in later life.* New York: Cambridge University Press.

Gaddini, R. (1970). Transitional objects and the process of individuation. *Journal of the American Academy of Child Psychiatry, 9,* 347–365.

Gallup, G. (1988, October 23). Opinion on abortion nearly the same as in 1973. *Los Angeles Times.*

Galvin, E. S. (1989). Children and child care in China: Some observations. *Children Today,* 19–23.

Gandour, M. J. (1989). Activity level as a dimension of temperament in toddlers: Its relevance for the organismic specificity hypothesis. *Child Development, 60,* 1092–1098.

Gandour, M. J., & Gardiner, H. W. (1981). *Child and adolescent development.* Boston: Little, Brown.

Garbarino, J. A. (1976). A preliminary study of some ecological correlates of child abuse: The impact of socioeconomic stress on mothers. *Child Development, 47,* 178–185.

Garbarino, J. A. (1977). The human ecology of child maltreatment: A conceptual model for research. *Journal of Marriage and the Family, 39,* 721–727.

Garbarino, J. A. (1982). Sociocultural risk: Dangers to competence. In C. Kopp & J. B. Krakow (Eds.), *The child: Development in a social context.* Reading, MA: Addison-Wesley.

Garbarino, J. A., & Crouter, A. (1978). Defining the community context for parent-child relations: The correlates of child maltreatment. *Child Development, 49,* 604–616.

Garcia-Coll, C., Kagan, J., & Reznick, J. S. (1984). Behavioral inhibition in young children. *Child Development, 55,* 1005–1019.

Gardner, C. A. (1989). Is an embryo a person? *The Nation,* 557–559.

Gardosi, J., Hutson, N., & Lynch, C. (1989). Randomized, controlled trial of squatting in the second stage of labor. *The Lancet, 2,* 74–77.

Garvey, C. (1974). Some properties of social play. *Merrill-Palmer Quarterly, 20,* 163–180.

Gelfand, D. M., & Teti, D. M. (in press). The effects of maternal depression on children. *Clinical Psychology Review.*

Gelles, R. (1978). Violence toward children in the United States. *American Journal of Orthopsychiatry, 48,* 580–592.

Gelman, S. A., Collman, P., & Maccoby, E. E. (1986). Inferring properties from categories vs. inferring categories from properties: The case of gender. *Child Development, 57,* 396–404.

Gentner, D. (1978). On relational meaning: The acquisition of verb meaning. *Child Development, 49,* 988–998.

George, C., & Main, M. (1979). Social interactions in young abused children: Approach, avoidance, and aggression. *Child Development, 50,* 306–318.

Gerken, L., Landau, B., & Remez, R. E. (1990). Function morphemes in young children's speech perception and production. *Developmental Psychology, 26,* 204–216.

Gesell, A. (1925). *The mental growth of the preschool child.* New York: Macmillan.

Gesell, A. (1928). *Infancy and human growth.* New York: Macmillan.

Gesell, A., & Ames, L. (1940). The ontogenetic organization of prone behavior in human infancy. *Journal of Genetic Psychology, 56,* 247–263.

Gewirtz, J. L. (1965). The course of infant smiling in four childrearing environments in Israel. In B. Foss (Ed.), *Determinants of infant behavior* (Vol. 3). New York: Wiley.

Gewirtz, J. L. (1972). *Attachment and dependency.* New York: Halsted Press.

Gianino, A., & Tronick, E. Z. (1988). The mutual regulation model: The infant's self and interactive regulation and coping and defensive capacities. In T. M. Field, P. M. McCabe, & N. Schneiderman (Eds.), *Stress and coping across development.* Hillsdale, NJ: Lawrence Erlbaum.

Gibbs, E. D., Teti, D. M., & Bond, L. A. (1987). Infant-sibling communication: Relationships to birth-spacing and cognitive and linguistic development. *Infant Behavior and Development, 10,* 307–323.

Gibson, E. J., Owsley, C. J., Walker, A., & Megaw-Nyce, J. (1979). Development of the perception of invariants: Substance and shape. *Perception, 8,* 609–619.

Gibson, E. J., Riccio, G., Schmuckler, M. A., Stoffregen, T. A., Rosenberg, D., & Taormina, J. (1987). Detection of the traversability of surfaces by crawling and walking infants. *Journal of Experimental Psychology: Human Perception and Performance, 13,* 533–544.

Gibson, E. J., & Walk, R. D. (1960). The "visual cliff." *Scientific American, 202,* 64–71.

Gibson, J. J. (1966). *The senses considered as perceptual systems.* Boston: Houghton Mifflin.

Gil, D. G. (1970). *Violence against children: Physical child abuse in the United States.* Cambridge: Harvard University Press.

Goldberg, S. (1983). Parent-to-infant bonding: Another look. *Child Development, 54,* 1355–1382.

Goldfield, E. C. (1989). Transition from rocking to crawling: Postural constraints on infant movement. *Developmental Psychology, 25,* 913–919.

Golding, J., & Peters, T. J. (1985). What else do SIDS risk prediction scores predict? *Early Human Development, 12,* 247–260.

Goldman-Rakic, P. S. (1987). Development of cortical circuitry and cognitive function. *Child Development, 58,* 601–622.

Goldsmith, H. H., Buss, A. H., Plomin, R., Rothbart, M. K., Thoman, A., Chess, S. Hinde, R. A., & McCall, R. B. (1987). Roundtable: What is temperament? Four approaches. *Child Development, 58,* 505–529.

Goldsmith, H. H., & Gottesman, I. I. (1981). Origins of variation in behavioral style: A longitudinal study of temperament in young twins. *Child Development, 52,* 91–103.

Golinkoff, R. M., & Ames, G. J. (1979). A comparison of fathers' and mothers' speech with their young children. *Child Development, 50,* 28–32.

Golomb, C. (1974). *Young children's sculpture and drawing: A study in representation development.* Cambridge: Harvard University Press.

Goodnow, J. (1977). *Children drawing.* Cambridge: Harvard University Press.

Goodson, B., & Greenfield, P. (1975). The search for structural principles in children's manipulative play: A parallel with linguistic development. *Child Development, 46,* 734–746.

Gopnik, A., & Meltzoff, A. (1987). The development of categorization in the second year and its relation to other cognitive and linguistic developments. *Child Development, 58,* 1523–1531.

Gordon, S. (1982). Teenage sexuality. In M. Schwarz (Ed.), *TV and Teens* (pp. 136–138). Reading, MA: Addison-Wesley.

Gordon, T. (1988). The case against disciplining children at home or in school. *Person-Centered Review, 3,* 59–85.

Gottfried, A. W., Rose, S. A., & Bridger, W. H. (1977). Cross-modal transfer in human infants. *Child Development, 48,* 118–123.

Gottlieb, G., Tomlinson, W. T., & Radell, P. L. (1989). Developmental intersensory interference: Premature visual experience suppresses auditory learning in ducklings. *Infant Behavior and Development, 12,* 1–12.

Graham, F. K., Anthony, B. J., & Zeigler, B. L. (1984). The orienting response and developmental processes. In D. Siddle (Ed.), *Orienting and habituation: Perspectives in human research.* New York: Wiley.

Graham, F. K., & Clifton, R. K. (1966). Heart-rate change as a component of the orienting response. *Psychological Bulletin, 65,* 305–320.

Graham, F. K., Leavitt, L., Strock, B., & Brown, H. (1978). Precocious cardiac orienting in a human anencephalic infant. *Science, 199,* 322–324.

Granrud, C. E., & Yonas, A. (1984). Infants' perception of pictorially specified interposition. *Journal of Experimental Child Psychology, 37,* 500–511.

Granrud, C. E., Yonas, A., & Opland, E. A. (1985). Infants' sensitivity to the depth cue of shading. *Perception and Psychophysics, 37,* 415–419.

Green, J. E., Dorfman, A., Jones, S. L., Bender, S., Patton, L., & Schulman, J. D. (1988). Chorionic villus sampling: Experience with an initial 940 cases. *Obstetrics and Gynecology, 71,* 208–212.

Greenfield, P., & Smith, J. H. (1976). *The structure of communication in early language development.* New York: Academic Press.

Greenleaf, P. (1978). *Children throughout the ages: A history of childhood.* New York: Barnes & Noble.

Greenough, W. T., Black, J. E., & Wallace, C. S. (1987). Experience and brain development. *Child Development, 58,* 539–559.

Gregg, C. L., Haffner, M. E., & Korner, A. F. (1976). The relative efficacy of vestibular-proprioceptive stimulation and the upright position in enhancing visual pursuit in neonates. *Child Development, 47,* 309–314.

Grieser, D. L., & Kuhl, P. K. (1988). Maternal speech to infants in a tonal language: Support for universal prosodic features in motherese. *Developmental Psychology, 24*(1), 14–20.

Grieser, D. L., & Kuhl, P. K. (1989). Categorization of speech by infants: Support for speech-sound prototypes. *Developmental Psychology, 25,* 577–588.

Grigoroiu-Serbanescu, M. (1981). Intellectual and emotional development in pre-mature children from 1 to 5 years. *International Journal of Behavioral Development, 4,* 183–200.

Grimm, E. (1967). Psychological and social factors in pregnancy, delivery and outcome. In S. Richardson & A. Guttmacher (Eds.), *Childbearing: Its social and psychological aspects.* Baltimore: Williams & Wilkins.

Grobstein, C. (1988). *Science and the unborn.* New York: Basic Books.

Grossman, K., Grossman, K. E., Spangler, G., Suess, G., & Unzner, L. (1985). Maternal sensitivity and newborns' orientation responses as related to quality of attachment in northern Germany. *Monographs of the Society for Research in Child Development, 50*(Serial No. 209), 233–256.

Gruen, A. (1987). The relationship of Sudden Infant Death and parental unconscious conflicts. *Pre and Peri Natal Psychology Journal, 2,* 50–56.

Gruendel, J. M. (1977). Referential extension in early language development. *Child Development, 48,* 1567–1576.

Grunwaldt, E., Bates, T., & Guthrie, D. (1960). The onset of sleeping through the night in infancy. *Pediatrics, 26,* 667–668.

Gunnar, M., Leighton, K., & Peleaux, R. (1984). Effects of temporal predictability on the reactions of 1-year-olds to potentially frightening toys. *Developmental Psychology, 20,* 449–458.

Gunnar, M., Mangelsdorf, S., Larson, M., & Hertsgaard, L. (1989). Attachment, temperament, and adrenocortical activity in infancy: A study of psychoendocrine regulation. *Developmental Psychology, 25,* 355–363.

Gunnar, M., Senior, K., & Hartup, W. W. (1984). Peer presence and the exploratory behavior of eighteen and thirty-month-old children. *Child Development, 55,* 1103–1109.

Gunnar, M., & Stone, C. (1984). The effects of positive maternal affect on infant responses to pleasant, ambiguous, and fear-provoking toys. *Child Development, 55,* 1231–1236.

Gunter, N., & LaBarbera, R. (1980). The consequences of adolescent childbearing on postnatal development. *International Journal of Behavioral Development, 3,* 191–214.

Gusella, J. L., Muir, D., & Tronick, E. Z. (1988). The effect of manipulating maternal behavior during an interaction on three- and six-month-olds' affect and attention. *Child Development, 59,* 1111–1124.

Gustafson, G. E. (1984). The effects of the ability to locomote on infants' social and exploratory behaviors: An experimental study. *Developmental Psychology, 20,* 397–405.

Gustafson, G. E., & Green, J. A. (1989). On the importance of fundamental frequency and other acoustic features in cry perception and infant development. *Child Development, 60,* 772–780.

Gustafson, G. E., Green, J. A., & West, M. J. (1979). The infant's changing role in mother-infant games: The growth of social skills. *Infant Behavior and Development, 2,* 301–308.

Gustafson, G. E., & Harris, K. L. (1990). Women's responses to young infants' cries. *Developmental Psychology, 26,* 144–152.

Guthrie, H. A. (1979). *Introduction to nutrition.* St. Louis: Mosby.

Gutman, A., & Turnure, J. (1979). Mothers' production of hand gestures while communicating with their pre-school children under various task conditions. *Developmental Psychology, 15,* 197–203.

Guttmacher, A. (1973). *Pregnancy, birth and family planning: A guide for expectant parents in the 1970s.* New York: Viking Press.

Guttmacher Institute. (1981). *Teenage pregnancy: The problem that hasn't gone away.* New York: Author.

Guttmacher Institute. (1989). *Demographics of abortion.* New York: Author.

Guys, J. M., Borella, F., & Monfort, G. (1988). Ureteropelvic junction obstructions: Prenatal diagnosis and neonatal surgery in 47 cases. *Journal of Pediatric Surgery, 23,* 156–158.

Haith, M. M. (1980). *Rules that babies look by: The organization of newborn visual activity.* Hillsdale, NJ: Erlbaum.

Haith, M. M., Bergman, T., & Moore, M. (1977). Eye contact and face scanning in early infancy. *Science, 198,* 853–855.

Hallock, M. B., Worobey, J., & Self, P. A. (1989). Behavioral development in chimpanzee (Pan troglodytes) and human newborns across the first month of life. *International Journal of Behavioral Development, 12,* 527–540.

Halonen, J. S., & Passman, R. (1978). Pacifier's effects upon play and separations from the mother for the one-year-old in a novel environment. *Infant Behavior and Development, 1,* 70–78.

Hamilton, L. R. (1989). Variables associated with child maltreatment and implications for prevention and treatment. *Early Child Development, 42,* 31–56.

Hann, D. M. (1989). A systems conceptualization of the quality of mother-infant interaction. *Infant Behavior and Development, 12,* 251–263.

Hannan, T. E. (1987). A cross-sequential assessment of the occurrences of pointing in three- to twelve-month-old infants. *Infant Behavior and Development, 10,* 11–22.

Harding, C. G., & Golinkoff, R. M. (1979). The origins of intentional vocalizations in prelinguistic infants. *Child Development, 50,* 33–40.

Hardyck, C., & Petrinovich, L. F. (1977). Left-handedness. *Psychological Bulletin, 84,* 385–404.

Hareven, T. K. (1982). *Family time and industrial time.* New York: Cambridge University Press.

Hareven, T. K. (1985). Historical changes in the family and the life course: Implications for child development. *Monographs of the Society for Research in Child Development, 50*(Serial No. 211), 8–23.

Harkins, D. A., & Michel, G. F. (1988). Evidence for a maternal effect on infant hand-use preferences. *Developmental Psychology, 21,* 535–541.

Harlow, H., & Harlow, M. (1965). The affectional systems. In A. Schrier, H. Harlow, & F. Stollnitz (Eds.), *Behavior of non-human primates* (Vol. 2). New York: Academic Press.

Harris, L. (1985). Louis Harris Poll. Associated Press, November 5.

Harris, M., Jones, D., & Grant, J. (1985). The social-interactional context of maternal speech to infants: An explanation for the event-bound nature of early word use? *First Language, 5,* 89–100.

Harris, P. L. (1989). *Children and emotion: The development of psychological understanding.* New York: Basil Blackwell.

Harter, S. (1983). Developmental perspectives on the self-system. In E. M. Hetherington (Ed.) (P. H. Mussen, General Editor), *Handbook of child psychology: Socialization, personality, and social development* (Vol. 4). New York: Wiley.

Hartmann, H. (1958). *Ego psychology and the problem of adaptation.* New York: International Universities Press.

Hartmann, H., & Molz, G. (1979). Unexpected death in infancy. In J. Howells (Ed.), *Modern perspectives in the psychiatry of infancy.* New York: Brunner-Mazel.

Hay, D. F., Murray, P., Cecire, S., & Nash, A. (1985). Social learning of social behavior in early life. *Child Development, 56,* 43–57.

Hayne, H., Rovee-Collier, C., Perris, E. E. (1987). Categorization and memory retrieval by three-month-olds. *Child Development, 58,* 750–767.

Hazell, L. (1975). A study of 300 elective home births. *Birth and the Family Journal, 2,* 11–18.

Hazen, N. (1982). Spatial exploration and spatial knowledge: Individual and developmental differences in very young children. *Child Development, 53,* 826–833.

Hazlewood, V. (1977). The role of auditory stimuli in crying inhibition in the neonate. *Journal of Audiology Research, 17,* 225–240.

Healy, B. T. (1989). Autonomic nervous system correlates of temperament. *Infant Behavior and Development, 12,* 289–304.

Hebb, D. O. (1949). *The organization of behavior.* New York: Oxford University Press.

Heckhausen, J. (1988). Becoming aware of one's competence in the second year: Developmental progression within the mother-child dyad. *International Journal of Behavioral Development, 11,* 305–326.

Heimann, M. (1989). Neonatal imitation, gaze aversion, and mother-infant interaction. *Infant Behavior and Development, 12,* 495–505.

Heinicke, C. M. (1984). Impact of pre-birth parent personality and marital functioning on family development: A framework and suggestions for further study. *Developmental Psychology, 20,* 1044–1053.

Heinicke, C. M., Diskin, S. D., Ramsey-Klee, D. M., & Oates, D. S. (1986). Pre- and post-birth antecedents of 2-year-old attention, capacity for relationships, and verbal expressiveness. *Developmental Psychology, 22,* 777–787.

Heinicke, C. M., & Lampl, E. (1988). Pre- and post-birth antecedents of 3- and 4-year-old attention, IQ, verbal expressiveness, task orientation, and capacity for relationships. *Infant Behavior and Development, 11,* 381–410.

Heinicke, C. M., & Westheimer, I. (1966). *Brief separations.* New York: Academic Press.

Heinonen, O., Sloane, D., & Shapiro, S. (1976). *Birth defects and drugs in pregnancy.* Littleton, MA: Publishing Sciences Group.

Held, R., Birch, E., & Gwiazda, J. (1980). Stereoacuity of human infants. *Proceedings of the National Academy of Sciences, 77,* 5572–5574.

Helmrath, T., & Steinitz, E. (1978). Death of an infant: Parental grieving and the failure of social support. *Journal of Family Practice, 6,* 785–790.

Hess, E. H. (1959). Imprinting. *Science, 130,* 133–141.

Hess, E. H. (1970). Ethology and developmental psychology. In P. H. Mussen (Ed.), *Charmichael's manual of child psychology* (3rd ed.). New York: Wiley.

Hildebrandt, K. A., & Fitzgerald, H. E. (1979). Facial feature determinants of perceived infant attractiveness. *Infant Behavior and Development, 2,* 329–340.

Hill, W. L., Borovsky, D., & Rovee-Collier, C. (1988). Continuities in infant memory development. *Developmental Psychobiology, 21,* 43–62.

Hock, E., & DeMeis, D. K. (1990). Depression in mothers of infants: The role of maternal employment. *Developmental Psychology, 26,* 285–291.

Hodapp, R. M., Goldfield, E. C., & Boyatzis, C. J. (1984). The use and effectiveness of maternal scaffolding in mother-infant games. *Child Development, 55,* 772–781.

Hofer, M. A. (1975). Infant separation responses and the maternal role. *Biological Psychiatry, 10,* 149–153.

Hofer, M. A. (1981). *The roots of human behavior: An introduction to the psychobiology of early development.* New York: Freeman.

Hofer, M. A. (1987). Early social relationships: A psychobiologist's view. *Child Development, 58,* 633–647.

Hoff-Ginsberg, E. (1986). Function and structure in maternal speech: Their relation to the child's development of syntax. *Developmental Psychology, 22,* 155–163.

Hoff-Ginsberg, E., & Shatz, M. (1982). Linguistic input and the child's acquisition of language. *Psychological Bulletin, 92*, 3–26.

Hoffman, M. (1975). Developmental synthesis of affect and cognition and its implications for altruistic motivation. *Developmental Psychology, 11*, 607–622.

Holden, C. (1988). Family planning: A growing gap. *Science, 242*, 370–371.

Holden, G. W. (1983). Avoiding conflict: Mothers as tacticians in the supermarket. *Child Development, 54*, 233–240.

Holden, G. W. (1985). How parents create a social environment via proactive behavior. In T. Garling & J. Valsiner (Eds.), *Children within environments: Towards a psychology of accident prevention.* New York: Plenum.

Holden, W. A., & Bosse, K. K. (1900). The order of development of color perception and color preference in the child. *Archives of Ophthalmology, 29*, 261–277.

Holland, R. L., & Smith, D. A. (1989). Management of the second stage of labor. A review (Part II). *South Dakota Journal of Medicine, 42*, 5–8.

Hollenbeck, A. R., Gewirtz, J. L., Seloris, S. L., & Scanlon, J. W. (1984). Labor and delivery medication influences parent-infant interaction in the first post-partum month. *Infant Behavior and Development, 7*, 201–210.

Hong, K., & Townes, B. (1976). Infant's attachment to inanimate objects: A cross-cultural study. *Journal of the American Academy of Child Psychiatry, 15*, 49–61.

Hooker, D. (1952). *The prenatal origin of behavior.* Lawrence: University of Kansas Press.

Hopkins, B., Janssen, B., Kardaun, O., & van der Schoot, T. (1988). Quieting during early infancy: Evidence for a developmental change? *Early Human Development, 18*, 111–124.

Hoppenbrouwers, T., Hodgman, J., Arakawa, K., McGinty, D., Mason, J., Harper, R., & Sterman, M. (1978). Sleep apnea as part of a sequence of events: A comparison of three-month-old infants at low and increased risk for sudden infant death syndrome (SIDS). *Neuropadiatrie, 9*, 320–337.

Hormann, E. (1977). Breast feeding the adopted baby. *Birth and the Family Journal, 4*, 165–173.

Hornik, R., & Gunnar, M. R. (1988). A descriptive analysis of infant social referencing. *Child Development, 59*, 626–634.

Hornik, R., Risenhoover, N., & Gunner, M. R. (1987). The effects of maternal positive, neutral and negative affective communications on infant responses to new toys. *Child Development, 58*, 937–944.

Howard, J. (1978). The influence of children's developmental dysfunctions on marital quality and family interaction. In R. M. Lerner & G. B. Spanier (Eds.), *Child influences on marital and family interaction.* New York: Academic Press.

Howe, N., & Ross, H. S. (1990). Socialization, perspective-taking, and the sibling relationship. *Developmental Psychology, 26*, 160–165.

Howes, C. (1988). Relations between early child care and schooling. *Developmental Psychology, 24*, 53–57.

Howes, C., & Stewart, P. (1987). Child's play with adults, toys, and peers: An examination of family and child-care influences. *Developmental Psychology, 23*, 423–430.

Hubert, N. C., Wachs, T. D., Peters-Martin, P., & Gandour, M. J. (1982). The study of early temperament: Measurement and conceptual issues. *Child Development, 53*, 571–600.

Hunter, F. T., McCarthy, M. E., MacTurk, R. H., & Vietze, P. M. (1987). Infants' social-constructive interactions with mothers and fathers. *Developmental Psychology, 23*, 249–254.

Hunter, R. S., Kilstrom, N., Kraybill, E. N., & Loda, F. (1978). Antecedents of child abuse and neglect in premature infants: A prospective study in a newborn intensive care unit. *Pediatrics, 61*, 629–635.

Hunziker, U. A., & Barr, R. G. (1986). Increased carrying reduces infant crying: A randomized controlled trial. *Pediatrics, 77*, 641–648.

Hyman, C. A., & Mitchell, R. (1977). A psychological study of child battering. *Health Visitor, 48,* 294–296.

Illingworth, R. S. (1966). *The development of the infant and young child: Normal and abnormal* (3rd ed.). London: E. & S. Livinstone.

Immunization Practices Advisory Committee. Public Health Service. (1983). General recommendations on immunization. *Morbidity and Mortality Weekly Report, 32,* 1–17.

Information Please Almanac (1987). Boston: Houghton Mifflin

Isabella, R. A., Belsky, J., & von Eye, A. (1989). Origins of infant-mother attachment: An examination of interactional synchrony during the infant's first year. *Developmental Psychology, 25*(1), 12–21.

Ispa, J. (1981). Peer support among Soviet day care toddlers. *International Journal of Behavioral Development, 4,* 255–270.

Izard, C. E. (1971). *The face of emotion.* New York: Appleton-Century-Crofts.

Izard, C. E. (1981, April). *The primacy of emotion in human development.* Paper presented at the meeting of the Society for Research in Child Development, Boston.

Izard, C. E., Hembree, E. A., & Huebner, R. R. (1987). Infants' emotion expressions to acute pain: Developmental change and stability of individual differences. *Developmental Psychology, 23,* 105–113.

Izard, C. E., & Malatesta, C. Z. (1987). Perspectives on emotional development I: Differential emotions theory of early emotional development. In J. D. Osofsky (Ed.), *Handbook of infant development* (2nd ed.) (pp. 494–554). New York: John Wiley & Sons.

Jacklin, C. N., Wilcox, K. T., & Maccoby, E. E. (1988). Neonatal sex-steroid hormones and cognitive abilities at six years. *Developmental Psychobiology, 21,* 567–574.

Jacobson, J. L. (1981). The role of inanimate objects in early peer interaction. *Child Development, 52,* 618–626.

Jacobson, J. L., Boersma, D. C., Fields, R. B., & Olson, K. L. (1983). Paralinguistic features of adult speech to infants and small children. *Child Development, 54,* 436–442.

Jacobson, S. W. (1979). Matching behavior in the young infant. *Child Development, 50,* 425–430.

Jacobson, S. W., Fein, G. G., Jacobson, J. L., Schwartz, P. M., & Dowler, J. K. (1985). The effect of intrauterine PCB exposure on visual recognition memory. *Child Development, 56,* 853–860.

Jaroszewicz, A. M., & Boyd, I. H. (1973). Clinical assessment of gestational age in the newborn. *South African Medical Journal, 47,* 2123–2124.

Jarvis, P. A., Myers, B. J., & Creasey, G. L. (1989). The effects of infants' illness on mothers' interactions with prematures at 4 and 8 months. *Infant Behavior and Development, 12,* 25–35.

Jelliffe, D. B., & Jelliffe, E. F. P. (1988). Breastfeeding: General review. In D. B. Jelliffe & E. F. P. Jelliffe (Eds.), *Programmes to promote breastfeeding* (pp. 3–11). Oxford: Oxford University Press.

Johnson, H., Glassman, M. B., Fiks, K. B., & Rosen, T. S. (1987). Path analysis of variables affecting 36-month outcome in a population of multi-risk children. *Infant Behavior and Development, 10,* 451–465.

Johnson, L. G. (1983). Giftedness in preschool: A better time for development than identification. *Roeper Review, 5,* 13–15.

Johnson, T. R. B., Besinger, R. E., & Thomas, R. L. (1989). The latest clues to fetal behavior and well-being. *Contemporary Pediatrics,* 66–84.

Jones, C. (1987). *Mind over labor.* New York: Viking.

Jones, C. P., & Adamson, L. B. (1987). Language use in mother-child and mother-child-sibling interactions. *Child Development, 58,* 356–366.

Jones, K. L. (1975). The fetal alcohol syndrome. In R. D. Harbison (Ed.), *Perinatal addiction.* New York: Halsted Press.

Jones, L. C., & Thomas, S. A. (1989). New fathers' blood pressure and heart rate: Relationships to interaction with their newborn infants. *Nursing Research, 38,* 237–241.

Jones, O. (1977). Mother-child communication with pre-linguistic Down's syndrome and normal infants. In H. R. Schaffer (Ed.), *Studies in mother-infant interaction.* London: Academic Press.

Jones, S. S., & Raag, T. (1989). Smile production in older infants: The importance of a social recipient for the facial signal. *Child Development, 60,* 811–818.

Judd, J. M. (1985). Assessing the newborn from head to toe. *Nursing '85, 15,* 34–41.

Jusczyk, P. W. (1985). The high-amplitude sucking technique as a methodological tool in speech perception research. In G. Gottlieb & N. A. Krasnegor (Eds.), *Measurement of audition and vision during the first year of postnatal life: a methodological overview.* Norwood, NJ: Ablex.

Jusczyk, P. W., & Derrah, C. (1987). Representation of speech sounds by young infants. *Developmental Psychology, 23,* 648–654.

Kagan, J. (1969). On the meaning of behavior: Illustrations from the infant. *Child Development, 40,* 1121–1134.

Kagan, J. (1971). *Change and continuity in infancy.* New York: Wiley.

Kagan, J. (1987). Perspectives on infancy. In J. D. Osofsky (Ed.), *Handbook of infant development* (2nd ed.) (pp. 1150–1198). NY: Wiley.

Kagan, J. (1989). *Unstable ideas.* Cambridge: Harvard University Press.

Kagan, J., Kearsley, R., & Zelazo, P. (1978). *Infancy: Its place in human development.* Cambridge: Harvard University Press.

Kagan, J., & Reznick, J. S. (1984). Cardiac reaction as an index of task involvement. *Australian Journal of Psychology, 36,* 135–147.

Kagan, J., Reznick, J. S., Clarke, C., Snidman, N., & Garcia-Coll, C. (1984). Behavioral inhibition to the unfamiliar. *Child Development, 55,* 2212–2225.

Kagan, J., Reznick, J. S., & Snidman, N. (1987). The physiology and psychology of behavioral inhibition in children. *Child Development, 58,* 1459–1473.

Kagan, J., Reznick, J. S., Snidman, N., Gibbons, J., & Johnson, M. O. (1988). Childhood derivatives of inhibition and lack of inhibition to the unfamiliar. *Child Development, 59,* 1580–1589.

Kaltenbach, K., Weinraub, M., & Fullard, W. (1980). Infant wariness toward strangers reconsidered: Infant's and mother's reactions to unfamiliar persons. *Child Development, 51,* 1197–1202.

Kaplan, H., & Dove, H. (1987). Infant development among the Ache of eastern Paraguay. *Developmental Psychology, 23,* 190–198.

Karmel, B. Z., & Maisel, E. B. (1975). A neuronal activity model for infant visual attention. In L. B. Cohen & P. Salapatek (Eds.), *Infant perception: From sensation to cognition: Vol 1. Basic Visual Processes.* New York: Academic.

Karmel, M. (1959). *Painless childbirth: Thank you Doctor Lamaze.* Philadelphia: Lippincott.

Karrer, R., & Ackles, P. (1988). Brain organization and perceptual-cognitive development in normal and Down's syndrome infants: A research program. In P. Vietze & H. G. Vaughan (Eds.), *Early identification of infants with developmental disabilities.* Orlando, FL: Grune & Stratton.

Karrer, R., Monti, L., & Ackles, P. K. (1989, October). *Late ERP's of one-month old infants in a visual oddball task.* Presented at the Society for Psychophysiological Research, New Orleans.

Karzon, R. G. (1985). Discrimination of polysyllabic sequences by one- to four-month-old infants. *Journal of Experimental Child Psychology, 39,* 326–342.

Kataria, S., Frutiger, A. D., Lanford, B., & Swanson, M. S. (1988). Anterior fontanel closure in healthy term infants. *Infant Behavior and Development, 11,* 229–233.

Kaufmann, R., & Kaufmann, F. (1980). The face schema in 3- and 4-month-old infants: The role of dynamic properties of the face. *Infant Behavior and Development, 3,* 331–339.

Kaye, K. (1977). Toward the origin of dialogue. In H. R. Schaffer (Ed.), *Studies in mother-infant interaction.* New York: Academic Press.

Kaye, K. (1982). *The mental and social life of babies.* Chicago: University of Chicago Press.

Kaye, K., & Fogel, A. (1980). The temporal structure of face-to-face communication between mothers and infants. *Developmental Psychology, 16,* 454–464.

Kaye, K., & Marcus, J. (1978). Imitation over a series of trials without feedback. *Infant Behavior and Development, 1,* 141–155.

Kaye, K., & Wells, A. J. (1980). Mother's jiggling and the burst-pause pattern of neonatal feeding. *Infant Behavior and Development, 3,* 29–46.

Keen, J. K. (1974). *Fixation and cardiac responses of four-month infants to repeated visual stimuli of varying complexities.* Unpublished master's thesis, University of Iowa, Iowa City.

Keith-Speigel, P. (1983). Children and consent to participate in research. In G. B. Melton & M. J. Saks (Eds.), *Children's competence to consent* (pp. 179–211). New York: Plenum.

Keller, A., Ford, L. H., & Meacham, J. A. (1978). Dimensions of self-concept in preschool children. *Developmental Psychology, 14,* 483–489.

Kellerman, P. J. (1984). Perception of three-dimensional form by human infants. *Perception and Psychophysics, 36,* 353–358.

Kellerman, P. J., & Spelke, E. S. (1983). Perception of partly occluded objects in infancy. *Cognitive Psychology, 15,* 483–524.

Kendrick, C., & Dunn, J. (1980). Caring for a second baby: Effects on interaction between mother and firstborn. *Developmental Psychology, 16,* 303–311.

Kent, R. D. (1981). Articulatory-acoustic perspectives on speech development. In R. Stark (Ed.), *Language development in infancy and early childhood* (pp. 105–106). New York: Elsevier.

Kermoian, R., & Campos, J. J. (1988). Locomotor experience: A facilitator of spatial cognitive development. *Child Development, 59,* 908–917.

Kessen, W., Haith, M., & Salapatek, P. (1970). Human infancy: A bibliography and guide. In P. H. Mussen (Ed.), *Charmichael's manual of child psychology* (3rd ed.). New York: Wiley.

Kilbride, H. W., Johnson, D. L., & Streissguth, A. P. (1977). Social class, birth order and newborn experience. *Child Development, 48,* 1686–1688.

Kisilevsky, B. S., & Muir, D. W. (1984). Neonatal habituation and dishabituation to tactile stimulation during sleep. *Developmental Psychology, 20,* 367–373.

Kitchen, W., & Murton, L. J. (1985). Survival rates of infants with birth weight between 501 and 1,000 g. *American Journal of Diseases of Children, 139,* 470–471.

Klaus, M. H., Jerauld, R., Kreger, N. C., McAlpine, W., Steffa, M., & Kennell, J. H. (1972). Maternal attachment importance of the first post-partum days. *New England Journal of Medicine, 46,* 187–192.

Klaus, M. H., Kennell, J. H., Plumb, N., & Zeuhlke, S. (1970). Human maternal behavior at the first contact with her young. *Pediatrics, 46,* 187–192.

Klein, B. P. (1985). Caregiving arrangements by employed women with children under a year of age. *Developmental Psychology, 21*(3), 403–406.

Klein, R. P., & Durfee, J. T. (1976). Effects of stress on attachment behavior in infants. *Journal of Genetic Psychology, 132,* 321–322.

Kleitman, N. (1963). *Sleep and wakefulness.* Chicago: University of Chicago Press.

Klinnert, M. (1984). The regulation of infant behavior by maternal facial expression. *Infant Behavior and Development, 7,* 447–465.

Klinnert, M. D., Emde, R. N., Butterfield, P., & Campos, J. J. (1986). Social referencing: The infant's use of emotional signals from a friendly adult with mother present. *Developmental Psychology, 22,* 427–432.

Klopfer, P. (1988). Metaphors for development: How important are experiences early in life? *Developmental Psychobiology, 21,* 671–678.

Koepke, J. E., Hamm, M., Legerstee, J., & Russell, M. (1983). Neonatal imitation: Two failures to replicate. *Infant Behavior and Development, 6,* 97–102.

Koester, L. S. (April, 1987). Multimodal, repetitive stimulation in parent-infant interactions: A look at micro-rhythms. Paper presented at Biennial Meetings of the Society for Research in Child Development, Baltimore, MD.

Kojima, H. (1986a). Becoming nurturant in Japan: Past and present. In A. Fogel & G. F. Melson (Eds.), *Origins of nurturance: Developmental, biological, and cultural perspectives on caregiving.* Hillsdale, NJ: Erlbaum.

Kojima, H. (1986b). The history of child development in Japan. In H. Azuma & H. Stevenson (Eds.), *Child development and education in Japan.* New York: Academic Press.

Konner, M. (1975). Relations among infants and juveniles in comparative perspective. In M. Lewis & L. A. Rosenblum (Eds.), *Friendship and peer relations.* New York: Wiley.

Konner, M. (1977). Infancy among the Kalahari Desert San. In P. H. Leiderman, S. R. Tulkin, & A. Rosenfeld (Eds.), *Culture and infancy.* New York: Academic Press.

Kontos, D. (1978). A study of the effects of extended mother-infant contact on maternal behavior at one and three months. *Birth and the Family Journal, 5,* 133–140.

Kopp, C. B. (1982). Antecedents of self-regulation: A developmental perspective. *Developmental Psychology, 18,* 199–214.

Kopp, C. B. (1989). Regulation of distress and negative emotions: A developmental view. *Developmental Psychology, 25,* 343–354.

Kopp, C. B., & Parmelee, A. (1979). Prenatal and perinatal influences on infant behavior. In J. Osofsky (Ed.), *Handbook of infant development.* New York: Wiley.

Kopp, C. B., & Vaughn, B. E. (1982). Sustained attention during exploratory manipulation as a predictor of cognitive competence in preterm infants. *Child Development, 53,* 174–182.

Korn, S. J., Chess, S., & Fernandez, P. (1978). The impact of children's physical handicaps on marital quality and family interaction. In R. M. Lerner & G. B. Spanier (Eds.), *Child influences on marital and family interaction.* New York: Academic Press.

Korner, A. (1987). Preventive intervention with high-risk newborns: Theoretical, conceptual, and methodological perspectives. In J. D. Osofsky (Ed.), *Handbook of infant development* (2nd ed.). New York: Wiley.

Korner, A., Brown, B. W., Reade, E. P., Stevenson, D. K., Fernbach, S. A., & Thom, V. A. (1988). State behavior of preterm infants as a function of development, individual and sex differences. *Infant Behavior and Development, 11,* 111–124.

Kornfeld, J. R. (1971). Theoretical issues in child phonology. *Proceedings of the Seventh Annual Meeting of the Chicago Linguistics Society* (pp. 454–468). Chicago: University of Chicago Press.

Kornhaber, A., & Woodward, K. L. (1981). *Grandparent/grandchild: The vital connection.* Garden City, NY: Anchor Press.

Kotch, J. B., & Cohen, S. R. (1986). SIDS counselors' reports of own and parents' reactions to reviewing the autopsy report. *Omega Journal of Death and Dying, 16,* 129–139.

Krafchuk, E. E., Tronick, E., & Clifton, R. K. (1983). Behavioral and cardiac responsiveness to sound in preterm neonates varying in risk status: A hypothesis of their paradoxical reactivity. In T. Field & A. Sostek (Eds.), *Infants born at risk.* New York: Grune & Stratton.

Kremenitzer, J. P., Vaughan, H. G., Jr., Kurtzberg, D., & Dowling, K. (1979). Smooth-pursuit eye movements in the newborn infant. *Child Development, 50,* 442–448.

Kropp, J. P., & Haynes, O. M. (1987). To identify general and specific emotion signals of infants. *Child Development, 58,* 187–190.

Kuchuk, A., Vibbert, M., & Bornstein, M. H. (1986). The perception of smiling and its experiential correlates in three-month-old infants. *Child Development, 57,* 1054–1061.

Kuczaj, S. A. (1978). Children's judgements of grammatical and ungrammatical irregular past-tense verbs. *Child Development, 49,* 319–326.

Kuczaj, S. A., & Maratsos, M. P. (1983). Initial verbs of yes-no questions: A different kind of general grammatical category. *Developmental Psychology, 19,* 440–444.

Kuczynski, L., Zahn-Waxler, C., & Radke-Yarrow, M. (1987). Development and content of imitation in the second and third years of life: A socialization perspective. *Developmental Psychology, 23,* 276–282.

Kuhl, P. K. (1981). Auditory category formation and developmental speech perception. In R. Stark (Ed.), *Language behavior in infancy and early childhood.* New York: Elsevier.

Kurzweil, S. R. (1988). Recognition of mother from multisensory interactions in early infancy. *Infant Behavior and Development, 11,* 235–243.

LaBarbera, J. D., Izard, C. E., Vietze, P., & Parisi, S. A. (1976). Four- and six-month old infants' visual responses to joy, anger, and neutral expressions. *Child Development, 47,* 535–538.

Lamb, M. E. (1977). The development of mother-infant and father-infant attachments in the second year of life. *Developmental Psychology, 13,* 637–648.

Lamb, M. E. (1978a). Influences of the child on marital quality and family interaction during the prenatal, perinatal and infancy periods. In R. M. Lerner & G. B. Spanier (Eds.), *Child influences on marital and family interaction.* New York: Academic Press.

Lamb, M. E. (1978b). Interactions between eighteen-month-olds and their preschool-aged siblings. *Child Development, 49,* 51–59.

Lamb, M. E. (1978c). Qualitative aspects of mother- and father-infant attachments. *Infant Behavior and Development, 1,* 265–277.

Lamb, M. E. (1982). The bonding phenomenon: Misinterpretations and their implications. *Journal of Pediatrics, 101,* 555–557.

Lamb, M. E., & Bornstein, M. H. (1987). *Development in infancy* (2nd ed.). New York: Random House.

Lamb, M. E., Frodi, A. M., Frodj, M., & Hwang, C. P. (1982). Characteristics of maternal and paternal behavior in traditional and nontraditional Swedish families. *International Journal of Behavior and Development, 5,* 131–141.

Lamb, M. E., Gaensbauer, T. J., Malkin, C. M., & Schultz, L. A. (1985). The effects of child maltreatment on security of infant-adult attachment. *Infant Behavior and Development, 8,* 35–45.

Lamb, M. E., Pleck, J. H., Charnov, E. L., & Levine, J. A. (1987). A biosocial perspective on paternal behavior and involvement. In J. B. Lancaster, A. Rossi, J. Altmann, & L. R. Sherrod (Eds.), *Parenting across the lifespan: Biosocial perspectives.* Chicago: Aldine.

Lamb, M. E., & Urberg, K. A. (1978). The development of gender role identity. In M. Lamb (Ed.), *Social and personality development.* New York: Holt, Rinehart and Winston.

Lampert, R. W., & Schochet, S. S. (1968). Demyelination and remyelination in lead neuropathy. *Journal of Neuropathology and Experimental Neurology, 27,* 527–545.

Landau, B., & Spelke, E. (1988). Geometric complexity and object search in infancy. *Developmental Psychology, 24,* 512–521.

Landau, R. (1976). Extent that the mother represents the social stimulation to which the infant is exposed: Findings from a cross-cultural study. *Developmental Psychology, 12,* 399–405.

Landesman-Dwyer, S. (1982). Maternal drinking and pregnancy outcome. *Applied Research in Mental Retardation, 3,* 241–263.

Landry, S. H., & Chapieski, M. L. (1989). Joint attention and infant toy exploration: Effects of Down's syndrome and prematurity. *Child Development, 60,* 103–118.

Landry, S. H., Chapieski, M. L., & Schmidt, M. (1986). Effects of maternal attention-directing strategies on preterms' response to toys. *Infant Behavior and Development, 9,* 257–269.

Langlois, J. H., Roggman, L. A., Casey, R. J., Ritter, J. M., Rieser-Danner, L. S., & Jenkins, V. Y. (1987). Infant preferences for attractive faces: Rudiments of a stereotype? *Developmental Psychology, 23,* 363–369.

Langlois, J. H., Roggman, L. A., & Rieser-Danner, L. A. (1990). Infants' differential social responses to attractive and unattractive faces. *Developmental Psychology, 26,* 153–159.

Lawson, K. R., & Ruff, H. A. (1984). Infants' visual following: The effects of size and sound. *Developmental Psychology, 20,* 427–434.

Lazar, I., & Darlington, R. (1982). Lasting effects of early education: A report from the Consortium for Longitudinal Studies. *Monographs of the Society for Research in Child Development, 47*(Serial No. 195), 1–151.

Leboyer, F. (1975). *Birth without violence.* New York: Knopf.

Lee, C., & Bates, J. (1985). Mother-child interaction at age two years and perceived difficult temperament. *Child Development, 56,* 1314–1325.

Lee, V. E., Brooks-Gunn, J., & Schnur, E. (1988). Does Head Start work? A 1-year follow-up comparison of disadvantaged children attending Head Start, no preschool, and other preschool programs. *Developmental Psychology, 24,* 210–222.

Lee, V. E., Brooks-Gunn, J., Schnur, E., & Liaw, F. R. (1990). Are Head Start effects sustained? A longitudinal follow-up comparison of disadvantaged children attending Head Start, no preschool, and other preschool programs. *Child Development, 61,* 495–507.

Lefebvre, F., Bard, H., Veilleux, A., & Martel, C. (1988). Outcome at school age of children with birth weights of 1000 grams or less. *Developmental Medicine and Child Neurology, 30*(2), 170–180.

Legerstee, M., & Bowman, T. G. (1989). The development of responses to people and a toy in infants with Down's syndrome. *Infant Behavior and Development, 12,* 465–477.

Legerstee, M., Pomerleau, A., Malcuit, G., & Feider, H. (1987). The development of infants' responses to people and a doll: Implications for research in communication. *Infant Behavior and Development, 10,* 81–95.

Leiberman, A. F. (1977). Preschoolers' competence with a peer: Relations with attachment and peer experience. *Child Development, 48,* 1277–1287.

Leifer, J. S., & Lewis, M. (1983). Maternal speech to normal and handicapped children: A look at question-asking behavior. *Infant Behavior and Development, 6,* 175–187.

Leifer, M. (1980). *Psychological effects of motherhood: A study of first pregnancy.* New York: Praeger.

Lemmer, C. M. (1987). Early discharge: Outcomes in primiparas and their infants. *Journal of Obstetric and Gynecological Nursing,* 230–236.

Lempers, J. D., Flavell, E. R., & Flavell, J. H. (1977). The development in very young children of tacit knowledge concerning visual perception. *Genetic Psychology Monographs, 95,* 3–53.

Lenington, S. (1981). Child abuse: The limits of sociobiology. *Ethology and Sociobiology, 2,* 17–29.

Lenneberg, E. H. (1969). On explaining language. *Science, 164,* 635–643.

Lester, B. M. (1976). Spectrum analysis of the sounds of well-nourished and malnourished infants. *Child Development, 47,* 237–241.

Lester, B. M., & Dreher, M. (1989). Effects of marijuana use during pregnancy on newborn cry. *Child Development, 60,* 765–771.

Lester, B. M., & Zeskind, P. S. (1978). Brazelton scale physical size correlates of neonatal cry features. *Infant Behavior and Development, 1,* 393–402.

Leung, E., & Rheingold, H. L. (1981). Development of pointing as a social gesture. *Developmental Psychology, 17,* 215–220.

LeVine, R. (1977). Childrearing as a cultural adaptation. In H. Leiderman, S. Tulkin, & A. Rosenfeld (Eds.), *Culture and infancy: Variations in the human experience.* New York: Academic Press.

Levitt, M. J., Weber, R. A., & Clark, M. C. (1986). Social network relationships as sources of maternal support and well-being. *Developmental Psychology, 22,* 310–316.

Levy, H. L., Karolkewicz, V., Houghton, S. A., & MacCready, R. A. (1970). Screening the "normal" population in Massachusetts for phenylketonuria. *New England Journal of Medicine, 282,* 1455–1458.

Levy-Shiff, R., Sharir, H., & Mogilner, M. B. (1989). Mother- and father-preterm infant relationship in the hospital preterm nursery. *Child Development, 60,* 93–102.

Lewis, M., & Feiring, C. (1978). The child's social world. In R. Lerner & G. Spanier (Eds.), *Child influences on marital and family interaction*. New York: Academic Press.

Lewis, M., & Feiring, C. (1989). Infant, mother, and mother-infant interaction behavior and subsequent attachment. *Child Development, 60*, 831–837.

Lewis, M., & Michalson, L. (1983). *Children's emotions and moods*. New York: Plenum.

Lewis, M., Stanger, C., & Sullivan, M. W. (1989). Deception in 3-year-olds. *Developmental Psychology, 25*, 439–443.

Lewis, M., Sullivan, M. W., Stanger, C., & Weiss, M. (1989). Self development and self-conscious emotions. *Child Development, 60*, 146–156.

Lewis, M., Young, G., Brooks, J., & Michalson, L. (1975). The beginning of friendship. In M. Lewis & L. Rosenblum (Eds.), *Friendship and peer relations*. New York: Wiley.

Lewkowicz, D. J. (1988). Sensory dominance in infants: 1. Six-month-old infants' response to auditory-visual compounds. *Developmental Psychology, 24*, 155–171.

Ley, R. G., & Koepke, J. E. (1982). Attachment behavior out of doors: Naturalistic observations of sex and age differences in the separation behavior of young children. *Infant Behavior and Development, 5*, 195–201.

Lifter, K., & Bloom, L. (1989). Object knowledge and the emergence of language. *Infant Behavior and Development, 12*, 395–423.

Lipsitt, L. P. (1979a). Infants at risk: Perinatal and neonatal factors. *International Journal of Behavioral Development, 2*, 23–42.

Lipsitt, L. P. (1979b). The pleasures and annoyances of infants: Approach and avoidance behavior. In E. Thoman (Ed.), *The origins of the infant's social responsiveness*. Hillsdale, NJ: Erlbaum.

Lipsitt, L. P. (1980). Conditioning the rage to live. *Psychology Today, 13*, 124.

Lipsitt, L. P. (1981). Infant learning. In T. Field, A. Huston, H. Quay, L. Troll, & G. Finley (Eds.), *Review of human development*. New York: Wiley.

Lipsitt, L. P., Engen, T., & Kaye, H. (1963). Developmental changes in the olfactory threshold of the neonate. *Child Development, 34*, 371–376.

Lipsitt, L. P., Sturges, W. Q., & Burke, P. (1979). Perinatal indicators and subsequent crib death. *Infant Behavior and Development, 2*, 325–328.

Liptak, G. S., Keller, B. B., Feldman, A. W., & Chamberlain, R. W. (1983). Enhancing infant development and parent practitioner interaction with the Brazelton Neonatal Behavioral Assessment Scale. *Pediatrics, 72*, 71–78.

Lock, A. (1980). *The guided reinvention of language*. New York: Academic Press.

Locke, J. L. (1979). The child's processing of phonology. In W. A. Collins (Ed.), *Minnesota symposia on child psychology: Vol. 12. Children's language and communication*. Hillsdale, NJ: Erlbaum.

Loehlin, J. C. (1989). Partitioning environmental and genetic contributions to behavioral development. *American Psychologist, 44* (10), 1285–1292.

Lollis, S. P. (1990). Effects of maternal behavior on toddler behavior during separation. *Child Development, 61*, 99–103.

Lorenz, K. Z. (1952). The comparative method in studying innate behavior. *Symposium of the Society for Experimental Biology, 41*, 221–268.

Lorenz, K. Z. (1965). *Evolution and modification of behavior*. Chicago: University of Chicago Press.

Lounsbury, M. L., & Bates, J. E. (1982). The cries of infants of differing levels of temperamental difficultness: Acoustic properties and effects on listeners. *Child Development, 53*, 677–686.

Ludemann, P. M., & Nelson, C. A. (1988). Categorical representation of facial expressions by 7-month-old infants. *Developmental Psychology, 24*, 492–501.

Lunt, R., & Law, D. (1974). A review of the chronology of eruption of deciduous teeth. *Journal of the American Dental Association, 89*, 872–879.

Lupe, P. J., & Gross, T. L. (1986). Maternal upright posture and mobility in labor: A review. *Obstetrics and Gynecology, 67* (5), 727–734.

Lyons-Ruth, K., Connell, D. B., Grunebaum, H. U., & Botein, S. (1990). Infants at social risk: Maternal depression and family support services as mediators of infant development and security of attachment. *Child Development, 61,* 85–98.

Lyra, M., & Ferreira, M. (1987, August). *Dialogue and the construction of the mother-infant dyad.* Paper presented at International Society for Behavioral Development Conference in Tokyo, Japan.

MacFarlane, A. (1975). Olfaction in the development of social preferences in the human neonate. In Ciba Foundation Symposium (Ed.), *Parent-infant interaction.* New York: Elsevier.

MacLean, D. J., & Schuler, M. (1989). Conceptual development in infancy: The understanding of containment. *Child Development, 60,* 1126–1137.

McTurk, R. H., McCarthy, M. E., Vietze, P. M., & Yarrow, L. J. (1987). Sequential analysis of mastery behavior in 6- and 12-month-old infants. *Developmental Psychology, 23,* 199–203.

Madsen, M. C., & Shapira, A. (1970). Cooperative and competitive behavior of urban Afro-American, Anglo-American, Mexican-American, and Mexican village children. *Developmental Psychology, 3,* 16–20.

Magid, K., & McKelvey, C. A. (1987). *High risk: Children without a conscience.* New York: Bantam.

Mahler, M., Pine, F., & Bergman, A. (1975). *The psychological birth of the human infant.* New York: Basic Books.

Main, M., & Cassidy, J. (1988). Categories of response to reunion with the parent at age 6: Predictable from infant attachment classifications and stable over a 1-month period. *Developmental Psychology, 24,* 415–426.

Main, M., & George, C. (1985). Responses of abused and disadvantaged toddlers to distress in agemates: A study in the day care setting. *Developmental Psychology, 21,* 407–412.

Main, M., Kaplan, N., & Cassidy, J. (1985). Security in infancy, childhood, and adulthood: A move to the level of representation. In I. Bretherton & E. Waters (Eds.), *Growing points of attachment theory and research. Monographs of the Society for Research in Child Development, 50*(Serial No. 209), 66–104.

Main, M., & Solomon, J. (1986). Discovery of an insecure disorganized/disoriented attachment pattern: Procedures, findings and implications for the classification of behavior. In M. Yogman & T. B. Brazelton (Eds.), *Affective development in infancy.* Norwood, NJ: Ablex.

Main, M., & Weston, D. R. (1981). The quality of the toddler's relationship to mother and father: Related to conflict behavior and the readiness to establish new relationships. *Child Development, 52,* 932–940.

Malatesta, C. Z., Culver, C., Tesman, J. R., & Shepard, B. (1989). The development of emotion expression during the first two years of life. *Monographs of the Society for Research in Child Development, 54*(Serial No. 219).

Malatesta, C. Z., Grigoryev, P., Lamb, C., Albin, M., & Culver, C. (1986). Emotion socialization and expressive development in preterm and full-term infants. *Child Development, 57,* 316–330.

Malatesta, C. Z., & Haviland, J. M. (1982). Learning display rules: The socialization of emotion expression in infancy. *Child Development, 53,* 991–1003.

Mandell, F., McAnulty, E., & Reece, R. M. (1980). Observations of paternal response to sudden unanticipated infant death. *Pediatrics, 65,* 221–225.

Maratsos, M., Kuczaj, S., Fox, D., & Chalkley, M. (1979). Some empirical studies in the acquisition of transformational relations: Passives, negatives, and the past tense. In W. A. Collins (Ed.), *Minnesota symposia on child psychology: Vol. 12. Children's language and communication.* Hillsdale, NJ: Erlbaum.

Marcos, H., & Verba, M. (1990, April). *Referential communication with adults and infants in the second year.* Paper presented at International Conference on Infant Studies, Montreal.

Marecek, J. (1987). Counseling adolescents with problem pregnancies. *American Psychologist, 42,* 89–93.

Markusen, E., Owen, G., Fulton, R., & Bendiksen, R. (1977). SIDS: Survivor as victim. *Omega, 8,* 277–284.

Marquis, D. P. (1931). Can conditioned responses be established in the newborn infant? *Journal of Genetic Psychology, 39,* 479–492.

Marquis, D. P. (1941). Learning in the neonate: The modification of behavior under three feeding schedules. *Journal of Experimental Psychology, 29,* 263–282.

Martini, M., & Kirkpatrick, J. (1981). Early interactions in Marquesas islands. In T. M. Field, A. M. Sostek, P. Vietze, & P. H. Leiderman (Eds.), *Culture and early interactions.* Hillsdale, NJ: Erlbaum.

Marx, J. L. (1978). Botulism in infants: A cause of sudden death? *Science, 201,* 799–801.

Matas, L., Arend, R. A., & Sroufe, L. A. (1978). Continuity of adaptation in the second year: The relationship between quality of attachment and later competence. *Child Development, 49,* 547–556.

Matheny, A. P., Jr., Wilson, R. S., & Thoben, A. S. (1987). Home and mother: Relations with infant temperament. *Developmental Psychology, 23,* 323–331.

Maurer, D. (1985). Infants' perception of facedness. In T. M. Field & N. A. Fox (Eds.), *Social perception in infants* (pp. 73–100). Norwood, NJ: Ablex.

Maurer, D., & Salapatek, P. (1976). Developmental changes in the scanning of faces by young infants. *Child Development, 47,* 523–527.

Mayes, L. C., & Kessen, M. (1989). Maturational changes in measures of habituation. *Infant Behavior and Development, 12,* 437–450.

McCauley, E., Kay, T., Ito, J., & Treder, R. (1987). The Turner syndrome: Cognitive deficits, affective discrimination, and behavior problems. *Child Development, 58,* 464–473.

McClearn, G. E. (1970). Genetic influences on behavior and development. In P. H. Mussen (Ed.), *Child psychology* (Vol. 1) (3rd ed.). New York: Wiley.

McCormick, C. M., & Maurer, D. M. (1988). Unimanual hand preferences in 6-month-olds: Consistency and relation familial-handedness. *Infant Behavior and Development, 11,* 21–29.

McCune, L. (1989, April). *Toward an integrative theory of early language acquisition: Evidence from longitudinal trends in vocal behavior.* Paper presented at the biennial meeting of the Society for Research in Child Development, Kansas City, MO.

McCune-Nicolich, L. (1981). Toward symbolic functioning: Structure of early pretend games and potential parallels with language. *Child Development, 52,* 785–797.

McDonald, D. (1978). Paternal behavior at first contact with the newborn in a birth environment without intrusions. *Birth and the Family Journal, 5,* 123–132.

McDonald, R., & Avery, D. (1983). *Dentistry for the child and adolescent* (4th ed.). St. Louis: Mosby.

McDonnell, P. M., Anderson, V. E. S., & Abraham, W. C. (1983). Asymmetry and orientation of arm movements in three- to eight-week-old infants. *Infant Behavior and Development, 6,* 287–298.

McGraw, M. B. (1935). *Growth: A study of Johnny and Jimmy.* New York: Appleton.

McGuire, J. (1988). Gender stereotypes of parents with two-year-olds and beliefs about gender differences in behavior. *Sex Roles, 19,* 233–240.

McIntosh, J. R., & Koonce, M. P. (1989). Mitosis. *Science, 246,* 622–628.

McIntosh, K. (1984). Viral infections of the fetus and newborn. In M. E. Avery & H. W. Taeusch, Jr. (Eds.), *Schaffer's diseases of the newborn* (5th ed.). Philadelphia: Saunders.

McKee, J. (1974). Selections from "Two legs to stand on." In J. Milgram & D. Sciarra (Eds.), *Childhood revisited.* New York: Macmillan (Originally published 1955).

McKenna, J. J. (1987). An anthropological perspective on the sudden infant death syndrome: A testable hypothesis of the possible role of parental breathing cues in promoting infant breathing stability: I. *Pre and Peri Natal Psychology Journal, 2,* 93–135.

McKenna, J. J. (1988). An anthropological perspective on the sudden infant death syndrome: The neurological and structural bases of speech breathing and why SIDS appears to be a species-specific malady: II. *Pre and Peri Natal Psychology Journal, 2,* 149–178.

McKenzie, B., & Over, R. (1983). Young infants fail to imitate facial and manual gestures. *Infant Behavior and Development, 6,* 85–95.

McKenzie, B. E., Tootell, H. E., & Day, R. H. (1980). Development of visual size constancy during the first year of human infancy. *Developmental Psychology, 16,* 163–174.

McKim, M. K. (1987). Transition to what? New parents' problems in the first year. *Family Relations Journal of Applied Family and Child Studies, 36,* 22–25.

McLaughlin, B. (1983). Child compliance to parental control techniques. *Developmental Psychology, 19,* 667–673.

McLoyd, V. C. (1990). The impact of economic hardship on black families and children: Psychological distress, parenting, and socioemotional development. *Child Development, 61,* 311–346.

McNeill, D. (1970). *The acquisition of language.* New York: Harper & Row.

McPherson, M. G. (1983). Improving services to infants and young children with handicapping conditions and their families: The Division of Maternal and Child Health as collaborator. *Zero to Three, 4,* 1–6.

Mead, M., & Newton, N. (1967). Cultural patterning of perinatal behavior. In S. Richardson & A. Guttmacher (Eds.), *Childbearing: Its social and psychological aspects.* Baltimore: Williams & Wilkins.

Meares, R., Grimwalde, J., & Wood, C. (1976). A possible relationship between anxiety in pregnancy and puerperal depression. *Journal of Psychosomatic Research, 20,* 605–610.

Mebert, C. J. (1989). Stability and change in parents' perceptions of infant temperament: Early pregnancy to 3-to-5 months postpartum. *Infant Behavior and Development, 12,* 237–244.

Meder, A. (1989). Effects of hand-rearing on the behavioral development of infant and juvenile gorillas. *Developmental Psychobiology, 22,* 357–376.

Mehl, L., Peterson, G., Sokolsky, W., & Whitt, M. (1976). Outcomes of early discharge after normal birth. *Birth and the Family Journal, 3,* 101–107.

Meicler, M., & Gratch, G. (1980). Do 5-month-olds show object conception in Piaget's sense? *Infant Behavior and Development, 3,* 265–282.

Melson, G. (1980). *The family as an ecosystem.* New York: Burgess.

Melson, G., & Cohen, A. (1981). Contextual influences on children's activity: Sex differences in effects of peer presence and interpersonal attraction. *Genetic Psychology Monographs, 103,* 243–260.

Melson, G., & Fogel, A. (1982). Young children's interest in unfamiliar infants. *Child Development, 53,* 693–700.

Melson, G., & Fogel, A. (1988, March). The development of nurturance in young children. *Young Children,* 57–65.

Melson, G., Fogel, A., & Toda, S. (1986). Children's ideas about infants and their care. *Child Development, 57,* 1519–1527.

Meltzoff, A. (1988). Infant imitation and memory: Nine-month-olds in immediate and deferred tests. *Child Development, 59,* 217–225.

Meltzoff, A., & Moore, M. K. (1989). Imitation in newborn infants: Exploring the range of gestures imitated and the underlying mechanisms. *Developmental Psychology, 25,* 954–962.

Meltzoff, A., & Moore, W. (1977). Imitation of facial and manual gestures by human neonates. *Science, 198,* 75–78.

Mendelson, M. J., & Ferland, M. B. (1982). Auditory-visual transfer in four-month-old infants. *Child Development, 53,* 1022–1027.

Mercer, R. T., Ferketich, S., May, K., DeJoseph, J., & Sollid, D. (1988). Further exploration of maternal and paternal fetal attachment. *Research in Nursing and Health, 11,* 83–95.

Meredith, H. (1975). Somatic changes during human pre-natal life. *Child Development, 46,* 603–610.

Messer, D. J., Rachford, D., McCarthy, M. E., & Yarrow, L. J. (1987). Assessment of mastery behavior at 30 months: Analysis of task-directed activities. *Developmental Psychology, 23*(6), 771–781.

Messinger, D., & Fogel, A. (1990, April). *The role of referential gazing in object exchange.* Paper presented at International Conference on Infant Studies, Montreal.

Michel, G. F., & Harkins, D. A. (1986). Postural and lateral asymmetries in the ontogeny of handedness during infancy. *Developmental Psychobiology, 19,* 247–258.

Michaelson, K. L., et al. (1988). *Childbirth in America: Anthropological perspectives.* South Hadley, MA: Bergin & Garvey.

Milewski, A. E. (1976). Infant's discrimination of internal and external pattern elements. *Journal of Experimental Child Psychology, 22,* 229–246.

Miller, W. R. (1964). The acquisition of formal features of language. *American Journal of Orthopsychiatry, 34,* 862–867.

Minkoff, H., Deepak, N., Menez, R., & Fikrig, S. (1987). Pregnancies resulting in infants with acquired immunodeficiency syndrome or AIDS-related complex: Follow-up of mothers, children, and subsequently born siblings. *Obstetrics and Gynecology, 69,* 288–291.

Mintzer, D., Als, H., Tronick, E. A., & Brazelton, T. B. (1985). Parenting an infant with a birth defect: The regulation of self-esteem. *Zero to Three, 5,* 1–7.

Miyake, K., Chen, S., & Campos, J. J. (1985). Infant temperament, mother's mode of interaction, and attachment in Japan: An interim report. In I. Bretherton & E. Waters (Eds.). *Growing points of attachment theory and research. Monographs of the Society for Research in Child Development, 50*(Serial No. 209), 276–297.

Molfese, V. J., & Thomson, B. (1985). Optimality versus complications: Assessing predictive values of perinatal scales. *Child Development, 56,* 810–823.

Molnar, G. E. (1978). Analysis of motor disorder in retarded infants and young children. *American Journal of Mental Deficiency, 83,* 213–222.

Moore, T. R., Sorg, J., Miller, L., Key, T. C., & Resnik, R. (1986). Hemodynamic effects of intravenous cocaine on the pregnant ewe and fetus. *American Journal of Obstetrics and Gynecology, 155,* 883–888.

Moran, G., Krupka, A., Tutton, A., & Symons, D. (1987). Patterns of maternal and infant imitation during play. *Infant Behavior and Development, 10,* 477–491.

Morrongiello, B. A., Fenwick, K. D., & Chance, G. (1990). Sound localization acuity in very young infants: An observer-based testing procedure. *Developmental Psychology, 26,* 75–84.

Morrongiello, B. A., & Rocca, P. T. (1987). Infants' localization of sounds in the horizontal plane: Effects of auditory and visual cues. *Child Development, 58,* 918–927.

Morse, J. M., & Park, C. (1988). Homebirth and hospital deliveries: A comparison of the perceived painfulness of parturition. *Research in Nursing and Health, 11,* 175–181.

Moss, A. J. (1985, October). *Prenatal smoking and childhood morbidity.* Paper presented at the International Conference on Smoking and Reproductive Health, San Francisco.

Moss, M., Colombo, J., Mitchell, D. W., & Horowitz, F. D. (1988). Neonatal behavioral organization and visual processing at three months. *Child Development, 59,* 1211–1220.

Mueller, E., Bleier, M., Krakow, J., Hegedus, K., & Cournoyer, P. (1977). The development of peer verbal interaction among two-year-old boys. *Child Development, 48,* 284–287.

Mueller, E., & Brenner, J. (1977). The growth of social interaction in a toddler play group: The role of peer experience. *Child Development, 48,* 854–861.

Mueller, E., & Lucas, T. (1975). A developmental analysis of peer interaction among toddlers. In M. Lewis & L. Rosenblum (Eds.), *Friendship and peer relations.* New York: Wiley.

Muir, D., & Field, J. (1979). Newborn infants orient to sounds. *Child Development, 50,* 431–436.

Muller, A. A., & Aslin, R. N. (1978). Visual tracking as an index of the object concept. *Infant Behavior and Development, 1,* 309–320.

Munn, P., & Dunn, J. (1989). Temperament and the developing relationship between siblings. *International Journal of Behavioral Development, 12,* 433–451.

Murai, N., Murai, N., & Takahashi, I. (1978). A study of moods in postpartum women. *Tohuku Psychologica Ioliak, 37,* 32–40.

Murphy, C. M. (1978). Pointing in the context of a shared activity. *Child Development, 49,* 371–380.

Murray, A. D. (1988). Newborn auditory brainstem evoked responses (ABRs): Longitudinal correlates in the first year. *Child Development, 59,* 1542–1554.

Myers, B. J. (1982). Early intervention using Brazelton training with middle-class mothers and fathers of newborns. *Child Development, 53,* 462–471.

Myers, B. J. (1987). Mother-infant bonding: The status of this critical-period hypothesis. In M. H. Bornstein (Ed.), *Sensitive periods in development: Interdisciplinary perspectives.* Hillsdale, NJ: Erlbaum.

Myers, B. J., Jarvis, P. A., & Creasey, G. L. (1987). Infants' behavior and their mothers and grandmothers. *Infant Behavior and Development, 10,* 245–259.

Myers, N. A., Clifton, R. K., & Clarkson, M. G. (1987). When they were very young: Almost-threes remember two years ago. *Infant Behavior and Development, 10,* 123–132.

Naeye, R. (1979). Underlying disorders responsible for the neonatal deaths associated with low Apgar scores. *Biology of the Neonate, 35,* 150–155.

Naeye, R. (1980). Suden infant death. *Scientific American, 242,* 56–62.

Naeye, R., Dienera, M., & Dellinger, W. (1969). Urban poverty: Effects of prenatal nutrition. *Science, 166,* 1206.

Nakazima, S. (1972). Phonemicization and symbolization in language development. In E. H. Lenneberg & E. Lenneberg (Eds.). *Foundations of language development: A multidisciplinary approach* (Vol. 1). New York: Academic Press.

Nanez, J. E. (1988). Perception of impending collision in 3- to 6-week-old human infants. *Infant Behavior and Development, 11,* 447–463.

National Center for Health Statistics. (1976). *Monthly Vital Statistics Report, 25* (3, Supplement [HRA]).

National Safety Council. (1987). *Accident facts.* Chicago: Author.

Nelson, C. A. (1985). The perception and recognition of facial expressions in infancy. In T. M. Field & N. A. Fox (Eds.), *Social perception in infants* (pp. 101–125). Norwood, NJ: Ablex.

Nelson, C. A. (1987). The recognition of facial expressions in the first two years of life: Mechanisms of development. *Child Development, 58,* 889–909.

Nelson, J. R., Jr. (1982). The politics of federal day care regulations. In E. Zigler & E. Gordon (Eds.). *Day care: Scientific and social policy issues.* Boston: Auburn House.

Nelson, K. (1973). Structure and strategy in learning to talk. *Monographs of the Society for Research in Child Development, 38* (Serial No. 149).

Nelson, K. (1978). How children represent knowledge of their world in and out of language: A preliminary report. In R. S. Siegler (Ed.), *Children's thinking: What develops?* Hillsdale, NJ: Earlbaum.

Nelson, K. (1981). Individual differences in language development: Implications for development and language. *Developmental Psychology, 17,* 170–187.

Nelson, K., Rescorla, L., Gruendel, J., & Benedict, H. (1978). Early lexicons: What do they mean? *Child Development, 49,* 960–968.

Nelson, N. M., Enkin, M. W., Saigel, S., Bennett, K. J., Milner, R., & Sackett, D. L. (1980). A randomized clinical trial of the Leboyer approach to childbirth. *New England Journal of Medicine, 299,* 655–660.

Nettlebladt, P. Fagerstrom, C., & Udderberg, N. (1976). The significance of reported childbirth pain. *Journal of Psychosomatic Research, 20,* 215–221.

Newell, K. M., Scully, D. M., McDonald, P. V., & Baillargeon, R. (1989). Task constraints and infant grip configurations. *Developmental Psychobiology, 22,* 817–832.

Newton, N. (1972). Childbearing in broad perspective. In Boston Children's Medical Center (Ed.), *Pregnancy, birth and the newborn*. Boston: Delacorte Press.

Nichols, F. H., & Humenick, S. S. (1988). *Childbirth education: Practice, research, and theory*. Philadelphia: W. B. Saunders.

Nicolich, L. M. (1977). Beyond sensorimotor intelligence: Assessment of symbolic maturity through analysis of pretend play. *Merrill-Palmer Quarterly, 23*, 89–100.

Ninio, A. (1979). The naive theory of the infant and other maternal attitudes in two subgroups in Israel. *Child Development, 50*, 976–980.

Ninio, A. (1980). Picture-book reading in mother-infant dyads belonging to two subgroups in Israel. *Child Development, 51*, 587–590.

Ninio, A. (1983). Joint book reading as a multiple vocabulary acquisition device. *Developmental Psychology, 19*, 445–451.

Nora, J., & Fraser, C. (1974). *Medical genetics: Principles and practice*. Philadelphia: Lea & Febiger.

Nwokah, E., & Fogel, A. (in press). Laughter in mother-infant emotional communication. *Humor*.

O'Brien, M., & Huston, A. C. (1985). Development of sex-typed play behavior in toddlers. *Developmental Psychology, 21*, 866–871.

O'Brien, T., & McManus, C. (1978). Drugs and the fetus: A consumer's guide by generic and brand name. *Birth and the Family Journal, 5*, 58–86.

O'Connell, B., & Bretherton, I. (1984). Toddler's play, alone and with mother: The role of maternal guidance. In I. Bretherton (Ed.), *Symbolic Play*, (pp. 337–366). Orlando, FL: Academic Press.

Oehler, J. M., & Eckerman, C. O. (1988, April). *Regulatory effects of human speech and touch in premature infants prior to term age*. Presentation at International Conference on Infant Studies, Washington, D.C.

Oehler, J. M., Eckerman, C. O., & Wilson, W. H. (1990). Social stimulation and the regulation of premature infants' state prior to term age. *Infant Behavior and Development, 11*, 333–351.

O'Hara, M. W., Zekoski, E. M., Philipps, L. H., & Wright, E. J. (1989). A controlled prospective study of postpartum mood disorders: Comparison of childbearing and nonchildbearing women. *Journal of Abnormal Psychology, 98*.

Olds, D. (1981). Improving formal services for mothers and children. In J. Garbarino & S. H. Stocking (Eds.), *Protecting children from abuse and neglect: Developing and maintaining effective support systems for families*. San Francisco: Jossey-Bass.

Olds, S. B., London, M. L., & Ladewig, P. A. (1984). Nursing assessment of the newborn. In *Maternal-newborn nursing: A family-centered approach* (pp. 660–707). Menlo Park, CA: Addison-Wesley.

Oller, D. K. (1980). The emergence of the sounds of speech in infancy. In G. Yeni-Komshian, J. Kavanagh, & C. Ferguson (Eds.), *Child phonology* (Vol. 1) (pp. 93–112). New York: Academic Press.

Oller, D. K., & Eilers, R. E. (1988). The role of audition in infant babbling. *Child Development, 59*, 441–449.

Olson, S. L., Bates, J. E., & Bayles, K. (1984). Mother-infant interaction and the development of individual differences in children's cognitive competence. *Developmental Psychology, 20*, 166–179.

Oppenheim, D., Sagi, A., & Lamb, M. E. (1988). Infant-adult attachments on the Kibbutz and their relation to socioemotional development 4 years later. *Developmental Psychology, 24*, 427–433.

Oster, H. (1978). Facial expression and affect development. In M. Lewis & L. A. Rosenblum (Eds.), *The development of affect* (pp. 43–75). New York: Plenum Press.

Otaki, M., Durrett, M., Richards, P., Nyquist, L., & Pennebaker, J. (1986). Maternal and infant behavior in Japan and America: A partial replication. *Journal of Cross-cultural Psychology, 17*, 251–268.

Oviatt, S. L. (1978, April). *Qualitative change in the language comprehension of 9- to 17-month-old infants: An experimental approach.* Paper presented at the International Conference on Infant Studies, Providence, RI.

Palkovitz, R. (1984). Parental attitude and fathers' interactions with their 5-month-old infants. *Developmental Psychology, 20,* 1054–1060.

Palkovitz, R. (1985). Fathers' birth attendance, early contact, and extended contact with their newborns: A critical review. *Child Development, 56,* 392–408.

Palmer, C. F. (1989). The discriminating nature of infants' exploratory actions. *Developmental Psychology, 25,* 885–893.

Panneton, R. K., & DeCasper, A. J. (1986, April). *Newborns' postnatal preference for a prenatally experienced melody.* Paper presented at the International Conference on Infant Studies, Los Angeles.

Papousek, H. (1967). Conditioning during early postnatal development. In Y. Brackbill & G. G. Thompson (Eds.), *Behavior in infancy and early childhood.* New York: Free Press.

Papousek, H., & Papousek, M. (1977). Mothering and the cognitive headstart: Psychobiological considerations. In H. R. Schaffer, (Ed.), *Studies in mother-infant Interaction* (pp. 63–88). London: Academic Press.

Papousek, H., & Papousek, M. (1987). Intuitive parenting: A dialectic counterpart of the infant's integrative competence. In J. D. Osofsky (Ed.), *Handbook of infant development* (2nd ed). New York: Wiley.

Papousek, M. (1989). Determinants of responsiveness to infant vocal expression of emotional state. *Infant Behavior and Development, 12,* 507–524.

Papousek, M., & Papousek, H. (1981). Musical elements in the infant's vocalization: Their significance for communication, cognition, and creativity. In L. P. Lipsitt & C. K. Rovee-Collier (Eds.), *Advances in infancy research* (Vol. 1). Norwood, NJ: Ablex.

Papousek, M., Papousek, H., & Bornstein, M. H. (1985). The naturalistic vocal environment of young infants: On the significance of homogeneity and variability in parental speech. In T. M. Field & N. A. Fox (Eds.), *Social perception in infants.* Norwood, NJ: Ablex.

Parfitt, R. R. (1977). *The birth primer.* Philadelpha: Running Press.

Park, K. A., & Waters, E. (1989). Security of attachment and preschool friendship. *Child Development, 60,* 1076–1081.

Parke, R., & Collmer, C. W. (1975). Child abuse: An interdisciplinary analysis. In E. Hetherington (Ed.), *Review of the child development research* (Vol. 5). Chicago: University of Chicago Press.

Parke, R. D., & Sawin, D. B. (1980). The family in early infancy: Social interactional and attitudinal analyses. In F. A. Pedersen (Ed.), *The father-infant relationship: Observational studies in the family setting.* New York: Praeger Special Studies.

Parke, R. D., & Tinsley, B. R. (1981). The father's role in infancy: Determinants of involvement in caregiving and play. In M. E. Lamb (Ed.), *The role of the father in child development* (2nd ed.). New York: Wiley.

Parke, R. D., & Tinsley, B. R. (1987). Family interaction in infancy. In J. D. Osofsky (Ed.), *Handbook of infant development* (2nd ed). New York: Wiley.

Parmelee, A. H., Jr., Schulz, H. R., & Disbrow, M. W. (1961). Sleep patterns of the newborn. *Journal of Pediatrics, 58,* 241–250.

Parrinello, R. M., & Ruff, H. A. (1988). The influence of adult intervention on infants' level of attention. *Child Development, 59,* 1125–1135.

Parten, M. B. (1932). Social participation among preschool children. *Journal of Abnormal and Social Psychology, 27,* 243–269.

Passman, R. H. (1977). Providing attachment objects to facilitate learning and reduce distress: Effects of mothers and security blankets. *Developmental Psychology, 13,* 25–28.

Passman, R. H., & Weisberg, P. (1975). Mothers and blankets as agents for promoting play and exploration by young children in a novel environment: The effects of social and non-social attachment objects. *Developmental Psychology, 11,* 170–177.

Patterson, C. J., Kupersmidt, J. B., & Vaden, N. A. (1990). Income level, gender, ethnicity, and household composition as predictors of children's school-based competence. *Child Development, 61,* 485–494.

Paulson, G., & Gottlieb, G. (1968). Developmental reflexes: The reappearance of foetal and neonatal reflexes in aged patients. *Brain, 91,* 37–52.

Pearson, J. L., Hunter, A. G., Ensminger, M. E., & Kellam, S. G. (1990). Black grandmothers in multigenerational households: Diversity in family structure and parenting involvement in Woodlawn community. *Child Development, 61,* 434–442.

Pedersen, F., Suwalsky, J. T., Cain, R. L., & Zaslow, M. J. (1987). Paternal care of infants during maternal separations: Associations with father-infant interaction at one year. *Psychiatry, 50,* 193–205.

Peiper, A. (1963). *Cerebral function in infancy and childhood.* New York: Consultants Bureau.

Pena, I. C., Teberg, A. J., & Hoppenbrouwers, T. (1987). The Gesell developmental schedule in Hispanic low-birth weight infants during the first year of life. *Infant Behavior and Development, 10,* 199–216.

Perris, E. E., & Clifton, R. K. (1988). Reaching in the dark toward sound as a measure of auditory localization in infants. *Infant Behavior and Development, 11,* 473–491.

Perrucci, C., & Targ, D. (1988). Effect of plant closing on marriage and family life. In P. Voydanoff & L. Majka (Eds.), *Families and economic distress.* Newbury Park, CA: Sage.

Peterson, G., & Peters, D. (1985). The socialization values of low-income Appalachian white and rural black mothers: A comparative study. *Journal of Comparative Family Studies, 16,* 75–91.

Petitto, L. (1985, October). *On the use of prelinguistic gestures in hearing and deaf children: Implications for theories of language acquisition.* Paper presented at the Tenth Annual Boston University Conference on Language Acquisition.

Pettit, G. S., & Bates, J. E. (1984). Continuity of individual differences in the mother-infant relationship from 6 to 13 months. *Child Development, 55,* 729–739.

Phillips, D., McCartney, K., & Scarr, S. (1987). Child-care quality and children's social development. *Developmental Psychology, 23,* 537–543.

Phillips, R. D., Wagner, S. H., Fells, C. A., & Lynch, M. (1990). Do infants recognize emotion in facial expressions?: Categorical and "metaphorical" evidence. *Infant Behavior and Development, 13,* 71–84.

Phipps-Yonas, S. (1980). Teenage pregnancy and motherhood: A review of the literature. *American Journal of Orthopsychiatry, 50,* 403–431.

Piaget, J. (1952). *The origins of intelligence in children.* New York: International Universities Press.

Piaget, J. (1954). *The construction of reality in the child.* New York: Ballantine Books.

Piaget, J. (1962). *Play, dreams and imitation in childhood.* New York: Norton.

Piaget, J., & Inhelder, B. (1969). *The psychology of the child.* New York: Basic.

Pipes, P. L. (1985). *Nutrition in infancy and early childhood* (2nd ed.). St. Louis: Mosby.

Pipp, S., Fischer, K. W., & Jennings, S. (1987). Acquisition of self- and mother knowledge in infancy. *Developmental Psychology, 23,* 86–96.

Pistrang, N. (1984). Women's work involvement and experience of new motherhood. *Journal of Marriage and the Family,* 433–446.

Pleck, J. H. (1983). Husbands' paid work and family roles: Current research issues. In H. Lopata & J. H. Pleck (Eds.), *Research in the interweave of social roles: Vol. 3. Families and jobs.* Greenwich, CT: JAI Press.

Pleck, J. H., & Rustad, M. (1980). *Husbands' and wives' time in family work and paid work in 1975–1976 study of time use.* Unpublished paper. Wellesley College Center for Research on Women.

Plomin, R. (1990). The role of inheritance in behavior. *Science, 248,* 183–188.

Plunkett, J. W., Klein, T., & Meisels, S. J. (1988). The relationship of preterm infant-mother attachment to stranger sociability at 3 years. *Infant Behavior and Development, 11,* 83–96.

Plutchik, R. (1980). *Emotion: A psychoevolutionary synthesis.* New York: Harper & Row.

Polansky, N. (1976). Analysis of research on child neglect: The social work viewpoint. In Herner and Co. (Eds.), *Four perspectives on the status of child abuse and neglect research.* Washington, D.C.: National Center on Child Abuse and Neglect.

Pollitt, E., Garza, C., & Leibel, R. L. (1984). Nutrition and public policy. In H. W. Stevenson & A. E. Siegel (Eds.), *Child development research and social policy* (pp. 421–470). Chicago: University of Chicago Press.

Pomerleau, A., & Malcuit, G. (1980). Development of cardiac and behavior responses to a three-dimensional toy stimulation in one- to six-month-old infants. *Child Development, 51,* 1187–1196.

Portes, P., Dunham, R., & Williams, S. (1986). Assessing child-rearing style in ecological settings: Its relation to culture, social class, early age intervention and scholastic achievement. *Adolescence, 21,* 723–735.

Power, T. G., Chapieski, M. L., & McGrath, M. P. (1985). Assessment of individual differences in infant exploration and play. *Developmental Psychology, 21,* 974–981.

Power, T. G., & Parke, R. D. (1986). Patterns of early socialization: Mother- and father-infant interaction in the home. *International Journal of Behavioral Development, 9,* 331–341.

Prechtl, H. F. R. (1977). *The neurological examination of the full term newborn infant* (2nd ed). London: Heinemann.

Provence, S. (1982). Infant day care: Relationships between theory and practice. In E. F. Zigler & E. W. Gordon (Eds.), *Day care: scientific and social policy issues* (pp. 33–35). Boston: Auburn House.

Provence, S., & Naylor, A. (1983). *Working with disadvantaged parents and children: Scientific issues and practice.* New Haven: Yale University Press.

Provins, K. A., Dalziel, F. R., & Higginbottom, G. (1987). Asymmetrical hand usage in infancy: An ethological approach. *Infant Behavior and Development, 10,* 165–172.

Puffer, R. R., & Serrano, C. V. (1973). *Patterns of mortality in childhood* (PAHO Scientific Publication No. 262). Washington, D.C.: Pan American Health Organization.

Quienan, J. T. (1980). *A new life: Pregnancy, birth and your child's first year.* New York: Van Nostrand Reinhold.

Radke-Yarrow, M., & Zahn-Waxler, C. (1973). *Developmental studies of altruism.* Washington, D.C.: NIMH. (NIMH Protocol, Clinical Project No. 73-M-02, J00.111).

Radke-Yarrow, M., & Zahn-Waxler, C. (1984). Roots, motives, and patterns in children's pro-social behavior. In E. Staub, D. Bartal, J. Karylowski, & J. Reykowski (Eds.), *The development and maintenance of pro-social behaviors.* New York: Plenum.

Ragozin, A. S., Bashan, R. B., Crnic, K. A., Greenberg, M. T., & Robinson, N. M. (1982). Effects of maternal age on parenting role. *Developmental Psychology, 18,* 627–634.

Ramey, C. T., Yeates, K. O., & Short, E. J. (1984). The plasticity of intellectual development: Insights from preventive intervention. *Child Development, 55,* 1913–1925.

Ramsay, D. S. (1980). Onset of unimanual handedness in infants. *Infant Behavior and Development, 3,* 377–386.

Ramsey, C. N., Abell, T. N., & Baker, L. C. (1986). The relationship between family functioning, life events, family structure, and the outcome of pregnancy. *The Journal of Family Practice, 22,* 521–527.

Rapoport, R., Rapoport, R. N., & Strelitz, A. (1977). *Fathers, mothers and society: Toward new alliances.* New York: Basic Books.

Rappoport, D. (1976). Pour une naissance sans violence: Resultats d'une premiere enquete. *Bulletin Psychologie, 29,* 552–560.

Reardon, P., & Bushnell, E. W. (1988). Infants' sensitivity to arbitrary pairings of color and taste. *Infant Behavior and Development, 11,* 245–250.

Rebelsky, F., & Hanks, S. C. (1971). Father's verbal interaction with infants in the first three months of life. *Child Development, 42,* 63–68.

Reeb, K. G., Graham, A. V., Zyzanski, S. J., & Kitson, G. C. (1987). Predicting low birthweight and complicated labor in urban black women: A biopsychosocial perspective. *Social Science and Medicine, 25,* 1321–1327.

Reed, G., & Leiderman, P. H. (1981). Age-related changes in attachment behavior in polymatrically reared infants: The Kenyan Gusii. In T. Field, T. M. Sostek, P. Vietze, & P. Leiderman, (Eds.), *Culture and early interactions.* Hillsdale, NJ: Erlbaum.

Reilly, J., McIntire, M., & Bellugi, U. (1985, October). *Faces: The relationship between language and affect.* Paper presented at the Tenth Annual Boston University Conference on Language Development.

Reissland, N. (1988). Neonatal imitation in the first hour of life: Observations in rural Nepal. *Developmental Psychology, 24,* 464–469.

Reite, M., Kaemingk, K., & Boccia, M. L. (1989). Maternal separation in bonnent monkey infants: Altered attachment and social support. *Child Development, 60,* 473–480.

Reznick, J. S., Kagan, J., Snidman, N., Gersten, M., Baak, K., & Rosenberg, A. (1986). Inhibited and uninhibited children: A follow-up study. *Child Development, 57,* 660–680.

Rheingold, H. L. (1982). Little children's participation in the work of adults, a nascent prosocial behavior. *Child Development, 53,* 114–125.

Rheingold, H. L., Cook, K. V., & Kolowitz, V. (1987). Commands activate the behavior and pleasure of 2-year-old children. *Developmental Psychology, 23,* 146–151.

Rheingold, H. L., Hay, D. F., & West, M. J. (1976). Sharing in the second year of life. *Child Development, 47,* 1148–1158.

Ricciuti, H. N. (1974). Fear and the development of social attachments in the first year of life. In M. Lewis & L. Rosenblum (Eds.), *The origins of fear.* New York: Wiley.

Riccuiti, H. N., & Poresky, R. H. (1972). Emotional behavior and development in the first year of life: An analysis of arousal, approach-withdrawal, and affective responses. In A. Pick (Ed.), *Minnesota symposia on child psychology* (Vol. 6). Minneapolis: University of Minnesota Press.

Richards, M. P. M. (1977). An ecological study of infant development in an urban setting in Britain. In P. Leiderman, S. Tulkin, & A. Rosenfeld (Eds.), *Culture and infancy: Variations in the human experience.* New York: Academic Press.

Richardson, G. A., Day, N. L., & Taylor, P. M. (1989). The effect of prenatal alcohol, marijuana, and tobacco exposure on neonatal behavior. *Infant Behavior and Development, 12,* 199–209.

Ricks, S. S. (1985). Father-infant interactions: a review of empirical research. *Family Relations, 34,* 505–511.

Ridgeway, D., Waters, E., & Kuczaj, S. A., II. (1985). Acquisition of emotion-descriptive language: Receptive and productive vocabulary norms for ages 18 months to 6 years. *Developmental Psychology, 21,* 901–908.

Riese, M. L. (1987). Longitudinal assessment of temperament from birth to 2 years: A comparison of full-term and preterm infants. *Infant Behavior and Development, 10,* 347–363.

Riley, C. A., & Trabasso, T. (1974). Comparatives, logical structures, and encoding in a transitive inference task. *Journal of Experimental Psychology, 17,* 187–203.

Roberts C., & Lowe, C. (1975). Where have all the conceptions gone? *Lancet, 1,* 498–499.

Roberts, K. (1988). Retrieval of a basic-level category in prelinguistic infants. *Developmental Psychology, 24,* 21–27.

Roberts, K., & Cuff, M. D. (1989). Categorization studies of 9- to 15-month-old infants: Evidence for superordinate categorization? *Infant Behavior and Development, 12,* 265–288.

Roberts, L. (1990). U.S. lags on birth control development. *Science, 247,* 909.

Robertson, J., & Robertson, J. (1971). Young children in brief separation: A fresh look. *Psychoanalytic Study of the Child, 26,* 264–315.

Robertson, S. S. (1987). Human cyclic motility: Fetal-newborn continuities and newborn state differences. *Developmental Psychobiology, 20*, 425–442.

Robinson, C. H. (1978). *Fundamentals of normal nutrition* (3rd ed.). New York: Macmillian.

Rochat, P. (1987). Mouthing and grasping in neonates: Evidence for early detection of what hard or soft substances afford for action. *Infant Behavior and Development, 10*, 435–449.

Rochat P. (1989). Object manipulation and exploration in 2- to 5-month-old infants. *Developmental Psychology, 25*, 871–884.

Rochat, P., Blass, E. M., & Hoffmeyer, L. B. (1988). Oropharyngeal control of hand-mouth coordination in newborn infants. *Developmental Psychology, 24*, 459–463.

Rochat, P., & Senders, S. J. (1990, April). *Sitting and reaching in infancy.* Paper presented at the Seventh International Conference on Infant Studies, Montreal.

Rocissano, L., Slade, A., & Lynch, V. (1987). Dyadic synchrony and toddler compliance. *Developmental Psychology, 23*, 698–704.

Rodholm, M., & Larsson, K. (1979). Father-infant interaction at the first contact after delivery. *Early Human Development, 3*, 21–27.

Rogoff, B. (1990). *Apprenticeship in thinking: Cognitive development in social context.* New York: Oxford University Press.

Rogoff, B., Mosier, C., Mistry, J., & Goncu, A. (1989). Toddlers' guided participation in cultural activity. *Cultural Dynamics, 2*, 209–237.

Rose, S. A., & Feldman, J. F. (1987). Infant visual attention: Stability of individual differences from 6 to 8 months. *Developmental Psychology, 23*, 490–498.

Rose, S. A., Feldman, J. F., & Wallace, I. F. (1988). Individual differences in infants' information processing: Reliability, stability, and prediction. *Child Development, 59*, 1177–1197.

Rose, S. A., Feldman, J. F., Wallace, I. F., & McCarton, C. (1989). Infant visual attention: Relation to birth status and developmental outcome during the first 5 years. *Developmental Psychology, 25*, 560–576.

Rose, S. A., & Ruff, H. A. (1987). Cross-modal abilities in human infants. In J. D. Osofsky (Ed.), *Handbook of infant development* (2nd ed.). New York: Wiley.

Rose, S. A., Schmidt, K., & Bridger, W. H. (1976). Cardiac and behavioral responsivity to tactile stimulation in premature and full-term infants. *Developmental Psychology, 12*, 311–320.

Rosenberg, A., & Kagan, J. (1987). Iris pigmentation and behavioral inhibition. *Developmental Psychobiology, 20*, 377–392.

Rosenberg, A., & Kagan, J. (1989). Physical and physiological correlates of behavioral inhibition. *Developmental Psychobiology, 22*, 753–770.

Rosenblatt, J. S. (1972). Learning in newborn kittens. *Scientific American, 277*, 18–25.

Rosenblith, J. R., & Sims-Knight, J. E. (1985). *In the beginning: Development in the first two years.* Belmont, CA: Brooks-Cole.

Rosenstein, D., & Oster, H. (1988). Differential facial responses to four basic tastes in newborns. *Child Development, 59*, 1555–1568.

Rosett, H. L. (1980). The effects of alcohol on the fetus and offspring. In O. J. Kalant (Ed.), Alcohol and drug problems in women. *Neurobehavioral Toxicology and Teratology, 6*, 379–385.

Ross, H. S., & Goldman, B. D. (1977a). Establishing new social relations in infancy. In T. Alloway, P. Pliner, & L. Krames (Eds.), *Attachment behavior.* New York: Plenum.

Ross, H. S., & Goldman, B. D. (1977b). Infant's sociability toward strangers. *Child Development, 48*, 638–642.

Ross, H. S., & Lollis, S. P. (1987). Communication within infant social games. *Developmental Psychology, 23*, 241–248.

Rossi, A. (1968). Transition to parenthood. *Journal of Marriage and the Family, 30*, 26–39.

Rothbart, M. K. (1986). Longitudinal observation of infant temperament. *Developmental Psychology, 22*, 356–365.

Rothbart, M. K. (1988). Temperament and the development of inhibited approach. *Child Development, 59,* 1241–1250.

Rothbart, M. K., & Derryberry, D. (1981). Development of individual differences in temperament. In M. E. Lamb (Ed.), *Advances in developmental psychology* (Vol. 1). Hillsdale, NJ: Erlbaum.

Rothbart, M. K., & Posner, M. I. (1985). Temperament and the development of self-regulation. In L. C. Hartlage & C. F. Telzrow (Eds.), *The neuropsychology of individual differences: A developmental perspective* (pp. 93–123). New York: Plenum.

Rovee-Collier, C. K. (1987). Learning and memory in infancy. In J. D. Osofsky (Ed.), *Handbook of infant development* (2nd ed.). New York: Wiley.

Rovee-Collier, C. K., Enright, M., Lucas, D., Fagan, J., & Gekoski, M. J. (1981). The forgetting of newly acquired and reactivated memories of 3-month-old infants. *Infant Behavior and Development, 4,* 317–331.

Rubenstein, J., & Howes, C. (1976). The effects of peers on toddler interaction with mother and toys. *Child Development, 47,* 597–605.

Rubenstein, J., Howes, C., & Pedersen, F. A. (1982). Second order effects of peers on mother-toddler interaction. *Infant Behavior and Development, 5,* 185–194.

Rubin, D. H., Krasilnikoff, B., Leventhal, J. M., Weile, B., & Berget, A. (1986). Effect of passive smoking on birth-weight. *Lancet, 2,* 415–417.

Ruff, H. A. (1978). Infant recognition of invariant forms of objects. *Child Development, 49,* 293–306.

Ruff, H. A. (1984). Infant's manipulative exploration of objects: Effects of age and object characteristics. *Developmental Psychology, 20,* 9–20.

Ruff, H. A. (1985). Detection of information specifying the motion of objects by 3- and 5-month-old infants. *Developmental Psychology, 21,* 295–305.

Ruff, H. A., & Kohler, C. J. (1978). Tactual-visual transfer in six-month-old infants. *Infant Behavior and Development, 1,* 259–264.

Ruff, H. A., & Lawson, K. R. (1990). Development of sustained, focused attention in young children during free play. *Developmental Psychology, 26,* 85–93.

Ruff, H. A., Lawson, K. R., Parrinello, R., & Weissberg, R. (1990). Long-term stability of individual differences in sustained attention in the early years. *Child Development, 61,* 60–75.

Ruffwarg, H. P., Muzio, J. N., & Dement, W. C. (1966). Ontogenetic development of the human sleep-dream cycle. *Science, 153,* 604–619.

Ruopp, R. R., & Travers, J. (1982). Janus faces of day care: Perspectives on quality and cost. In E. Zigler & E. Gordon (Eds.), *Day care: Scientific and social policy issues.* Boston: Auburn House.

Rutter, M. (1979). Maternal deprivation, 1972–1978: New findings, new concepts, new approaches. *Child Development, 50,* 283–305.

Rutter, M. (1987). Continuities and discontinuities from infancy. In J. D. Osofsky (Ed.), *Handbook of infant development* (2nd ed.). New York: Wiley.

Sachs, J., & Devin, J. (1976). Young children's use of age-appropriate speech styles in social interaction and role-playing. *Journal of Child Language, 3,* 81–98.

Sagi, A. (1981). Mother's and non-mother's identification of infant cries. *Infant Behavior and Development, 4,* 37–40.

Sagi, A., Lamb, M. E., Lewkowicz, K. S., Shoham, R., Dvir, R., & Estes, D. (1985). Security of infant-mother, -father, and -metapelet attachments among kibbutz-reared Israeli children. In I. Bretherton & E. Waters (Eds.), *Growing points of attachment theory and research. Monographs of the Society for Research in Child Development, 50*(Serial No. 209) 257–275.

Salapatek, P., & Banks, M. S. (1978). Infant sensory assessment: Vision. In F. D. Minifie & L. L. Lloyd (Eds.), *Communicative and cognitive abilities: Early behavioral assessment.* Baltimore: University Park Press.

Salk, L. (1973). The role of the heartbeat in relations between mother and infant. *Scientific American, 228,* 24–29.

Sameroff, A. J. (1984). Developmental systems: Contexts and evolution. In P. H. Mussen (Ed.), *Handbook of child psychology: Vol. I. History, theory, and methods* (4th ed.). (pp. 237–294). New York: Wiley.

Sameroff, A. J., & Chandler, M. (1975). Reproductive risk and the continuum of caretaking casualty. In F. Horowitz (Ed.), *Review of child development research.* Chicago: University of Chicago Press.

Sameroff, A. J., & Seifer, R. (1983). Familial risk and child competence. *Child Development, 54,* 1254–1268.

Sameroff, A. J., Seifer, R., & Elias, P. K. (1982). Sociocultural variability in infant temperament ratings. *Child Development, 53,* 164–173.

Samuels, C. A. (1985). Attention to eye contact opportunity and facial motion by three-month-old infants. *Journal of Experimental Child Psychology, 40,* 105–114.

Samuels, H. R. (1980). The effect of an older sibling on infant locomotor exploration of a new environment. *Child Development, 51,* 606–609.

Sander, L. W. (1962). Issues in early mother-child interaction. *Journal of the American Academy of Child Psychiatry, 1,* 141–166.

Sardana, R. (1985). Examining for defects. *Nursing Mirror, 160,* 38–42.

Sawin, D., & Parke, R. (1979). Fathers' affectionate stimulation and caregiving behaviors with newborn infants. *Family Coordinator, 28,* 509–513.

Scaife, M., & Bruner, J. S. (1975). The capacity for joint visual attention in the infant. *Nature, 253,* 265–266.

Scarr, S. (1984). *Mother care/other care.* New York: Basic Books.

Scarr, S., & McCartney, K. (1983). How people make their own environments: A theory of genotype-environment effects. *Child Development, 21,* 391–402.

Scarr, S., & McCartney, K. (1988). Far from home: An experimental evaluation of the mother-child home program in Bermuda. *Child Development, 59,* 531–543.

Schachter, F. F. (1979). *Everyday mother talk to toddlers: Early intervention.* New York: Academic Press.

Schachter, F. S., & Stone, R. K. (1985). Difficult sibling, easy sibling: Temperament and the within-family environment. *Child Development, 56,* 1335–1344.

Schaffer, H. R. (1984). *The child's entry into a social world.* New York: Academic Press.

Schaffer, H. R., & Crook, C. K. (1979). Maternal control techniques in a directed play situation. *Child Development, 50,* 989–996.

Schaffer, H. R., & Crook, C. K. (1980). Child compliance and maternal control techniques. *Developmental Psychology, 16,* 54–56.

Schaffer, H. R., & Emerson, P. (1964). Patterns of response to physical contact in early human development. *Journal of Child Psychiatry and Psychology, 5,* 1–13.

Schanberg, S., Bartolome, J., & Kuhn, C. (1987, January). *Touching and the brain.* Paper presented at the American College of Neuropsychopharmacology, San Juan, Puerto Rico.

Schaller, J., Carlsson, S. G., & Larsson, K. (1979). Effects of extended post-partum mother-child contact on the mother's behavior during nursing. *Infant Behavior and Development, 2,* 319–324.

Schiffman, P. C., Westlake, R. E., Santiago, T. V., & Edelman, N. H. (1980). Ventilatory control in parents of victims of sudden-infant-death syndrome. *New England Journal of Medicine, 302,* 486–491.

Schindler, P. J., Moely, B. E., & Frank, A. L. (1987). Time in day care and social participation of young children. *Developmental Psychology, 23,* 255–261.

Schneider-Rosen, K., & Wenz-Gross, M. (1990). Patterns of compliance from eighteen to thirty months of age. *Child Development, 61,* 104–112.

Schreiber, J. (1977). Birth, the family and the community: A southern Italian example. *Birth and the Family Journal, 4,* 153–157.

Schulman-Galambos, C., & Galambos, R. (1979). Brain stem evoked response audiometry in newborn hearing screening. *Archives of Otolaryngology, 105,* 86–90.

Schwartz, A., Campos, J., & Baisel, E. (1973). The visual cliff: Cardiac and behavioral correlates on the deep and shallow sides at 5 and 9 months of age. *Journal of Experimental Child Psychology, 15,* 85–99.

Schwartz, P. (1983). Length of daycare attendance and attachment behavior in eighteen-month-old infants. *Child Development, 54,* 1073–1078.

Schweinhart, L. J., & Weikart, D. P. (1979, April). *Perry preschool effects in adolescence.* Paper presented to the biennial meeting of the Society for Research in Child Development, San Francisco.

Seitz, V., Rosenbaum, L. K., & Apfel, N. H. (1985). Effects of family support intervention: A ten-year follow-up. *Child Development, 56,* 376–391.

Self, P., & Horowitz, F. D. (1979). The assessment of the newborn infant. In J. Osofsky (Ed.), *Handbook of infant development.* New York: Wiley.

Seligman, M. E. P., & Maier, S. (1967). Failure to escape traumatic shock. *Journal of Experimental Psychology, 74,* 1–9.

Selman, R. L. (1980). *The growth of interpersonal understanding: Developmental and clinical analyses.* NY: Academic Press.

Serifica, F. C. (1978). The development of attachment behaviors: An organismic-developmental perspective. *Human Development, 21,* 119–140.

Serunian, S. A., & Broman, S. H. (1975). Relationship of Apgar scores and Bayley Mental and Motor scores. *Child Development, 46,* 696–700.

Sewall, M. (1930). Some causes of jealousy in young children. *Smith College Studies in Social Work, 1,* 6–22.

Shand, N., & Kosawa, Y. (1985). Japanese and American behavior types at three months: Infants and infant-mother dyads. *Infant Behavior and Development, 8,* 225–240.

Shank, R. (1970). A chink in our armor. *Nutrition Today, 5,* 2–11.

Shapira, A., & Madsen, M. C. (1969). Cooperative and competitive behavior of kibbutz and urban children in Israel, *Child Development, 40,* 609–617.

Sharan, P. (1988). One view of the cultural context for the study of childrearing in India. *Newsletter of the International Society for the Study of Behavioral Development, 13,* 1–3.

Shatz, M. (1978). The relationship between cognitive processes and the development of communication skills. In C. B. Keasey (Ed.), *Nebraska symposium on motivation.* Lincoln: University of Nebraska Press.

Shatz, M., & Gelman, R. (1973). The development of communication skills: Modifications in the speech of young children as a function of listener. *Monographs of the Society for Research in Child Development, 38*(Serial No. 152).

Sheppard, J. J., & Mysak, E. D. (1984). Ontogeny of infantile oral reflexes and emerging chewing. *Child Development, 55,* 831–843.

Sherrod, K. B., Crawley, S., Petersen, G., & Bennett, P. (1978). Maternal language to prelinguistic infants: Semantic aspects. *Infant Behavior and Development, 1,* 335–346.

Sherrod, K. B., Friedman, S., Crawley, S., Drake, D., & Dervieux, J. (1977). Maternal language to prelinguistic infants: Syntactic aspects. *Child Development, 48,* 1662–1665.

Sherrod, K. B., O'Conner, S., Vietze, P. M., & Altemeier, W. A. (1984). Child health and maltreatment. *Child Development, 55,* 1174–1183.

Sherrod, L. R. (1979). Social cognition in infants: Attention to the human face. *Infant Behavior and Development, 2,* 279–294.

Shirley, M. M. (1931). *The first two years: A study of twenty-five babies: Vol. 1. Postural and locomotor development.* Minneapolis: University of Minnesota Press.

Shnider, S. (1981). Choice of anesthesia for labor and delivery. *Journal of Obstetrics and Gynecology, 58* (5 Suppl.), 24S–34S.

Shore, C. (1986). Combinatorial play: Conceptual development, and early multiword speech. *Developmental Psychology, 22*(2), 184–190.

Siegal, L. S. (1981). Infant tests as predictors of cognitive and language development at two years. *Child Development, 52,* 545–557.

Siegal, M., & Storey, R. M. (1985). Day care and children's conceptions of moral and social rules. *Child Development, 56,* 1001–1008.

Sigman, M., Cohen, S. E., Beckwith, L., & Parmelee, A. H. (1981). Social and familial influences on the development of preterm infants. *Journal of Pediatric Psychology, 6,* 1–13.

Sigman, M., Cohen, S. E., Beckwith, L., & Parmelee, A. H. (1986). Infant attention in relation to intellectual abilities in childhood. *Developmental Psychology, 22,* 788–792.

Sigman, M., Neumann, C., Carter, E., Cattle, D. J., D'Souza, S., & Bwibo, N. (1988). Home interactions and the development of Embu toddlers in Kenya. *Child Development, 59,* 1251–1261.

Silberner, J. (1986). Survival of the fetus. *Science News, 130,* 234–235.

Silver, M. (1985). Life after Tay-Sachs. *Jewish Monthly, 99,* 14–23.

Singer, L. M., Brodzinsky, D. M., Ramsay, D., Steir, M., & Waters, E. (1985). Mother-infant attachment in adoptive families. *Child Development, 56,* 1543–1551.

Siskind, V., Schofield, F., Rice, D., & Bain, C. (1989). Breast cancer and breastfeeding: Results from an Austrialian case-control study. *American Journal of Epidemiology, 130,* 229–236.

Skarin, K. (1977). Cognitive and contextual determinants of stranger fear in six- and eleven-month-old infants. *Child Development, 48,* 537–544.

Skeoch, C., Rosenberg, K., Turner, T., Skeoch, H., & McIlwaine, G. (1987). Very low birthweight survivors: Illness and readmission to hospital in the first 15 months of life. *British Medical Journal, 295,* 579–580.

Skinner, B. F. (1938). *The behavior of organisms.* Englewood Cliffs, NJ: Prentice-Hall.

Skinner, B. F. (1969). *Contingencies of reinforcement: A theoretical analysis.* Englewood Cliffs, NJ: Prentice-Hall.

Salby, R. G., & Frey, K. S. (1975). Development of gender constancy and selective attention to same-sex models. *Child Development, 46,* 849–856.

Slade, A. (1986). Symbolic play and separation-individuation: A naturalistic study. *Bulletin of the Menninger Clinic, 50,* 541–563.

Slade, A. (1987a). A longitudinal study of maternal involvement and symbolic play during the toddler period. *Child Development, 58,* 367–375.

Slade, A. (1987b). Quality of attachment and early symbolic play. *Developmental Psychology, 23,* 78–85.

Slater, A., Morison, V., & Rose, D. (1984). Habituation in the newborn. *Infant Behavior and Development, 7,* 183–200.

Slaughter, D. T. (1980). Social policy issues affecting infants. In B. Weissbourd & J. Musick (Eds.), *Infants: Their social environments.* National Association for the Education of Young Children. Chicago.

Slobin, D. (1970). Universals of grammatical development in children. In G. B. Flores d'Arcais & W. J. M. Levelt (Eds.), *Advances in psycholinguistics.* Amsterdam: North-Holland.

Smeeding, T. M., & Torrey, B. B. (1988). Poor children in rich countries. *Science, 242,* 873–877.

Smialek, A. (1978). Observations on immediate reactions of families to sudden infant death. *Pediatrics, 62,* 160–165.

Smidt-Jensen, S., & Hahnemann, N. (1988). Transabdominal chorionic villus sampling for fetal genetic diagnosis: Technical and obstetrical evaluation of 100 cases. *Prenatal Diagnosis, 8,* 7–17.

Smigel, K. L. (1988). Breast-feeding linked to decreased cancer risk for mother, child. *Journal of the National Cancer Institute, 80,* 1362–1363.

Smith, P. B., & Pederson, D. R. (1988). Maternal sensitivity and patterns of infant-mother attachment. *Child Development, 59,* 1097–1101.

Smith, R. J. (1978). Agency drags its feet on warning to pregnant women. *Science, 199,* 748–749.

Snow, C. E. (1977). The development of conversation between mothers and babies. *Journal of Child Language, 4,* 1–22.

Snow, C. E. (1984). Parent-child interaction and the development of communicative ability. In R. Schiefelbusch & J. Pickar (Eds.), *The acquisition of communicative competence*. Baltimore: University Park Press.

Snow, C. E., DeBlauw, A., & VanRoosmalen, G. (1979). Talking and playing with babies: The role of ideologies in child-rearing. In M. Bullowa (Ed.), *Before speech*. New York: Cambridge University Press.

Snow, M. E., Jacklin, C. N., & Maccoby, E. E. (1981). Birth-order differences in peer sociability at thirty-three months. *Child Development, 52*, 589–595.

Sollie, D., & Miller, B. (1980). The transition to parenthood as a critical time for building family strengths. In N. Stinnet & P. Knaub (Eds.), *Family strengths: Positive models of family life* (pp. 19–36). Lincoln: University of Nebraska Press.

Sorce, J., Emde, R., Campos, J., & Klinnert, M. (1985). Maternal emotional signaling: Its effect on the visual cliff behavior of 1-year-olds. *Developmental Psychology, 21*, 195–200.

Sorenson, E. R. (1979). Early tactile communication and the patterning of human organization: A New Guinea case study. In M. Bullowa (Ed.), *Before speech*. New York: Cambridge University Press.

Sostek, A. M., & Anders, T. F. (1977). Relationships among the Brazelton neonatal scale, Bayley infant scales and early temperament. *Child Development, 48*, 320–323.

Sostek, A. M., Smith, Y. F., Katz, K. S., & Grant, E. G. (1987). Developmental outcome of preterm infants with intraventricular hemorrhage at one and two years of age. *Child Development, 58*, 779–786.

Spelke, E. S., & Owsley, C. J. (1979). Intermodal exploration and knowledge in infancy. *Infant Behavior & Development, 2*, 13–27.

Spelke, E. S., von Hofsten, C., & Kestenbaum, R. (1989). Object perception in infancy: Interaction of spatial and kinetic information for object boundaries. *Developmental Psychology, 25*(2), 185–196.

Spemann, H. (1938). *Embryonic development and induction*. New Haven: Yale University Press.

Spitz, R. (1965). *The first year of life*. New York: International Universities Press.

Spock, B. (1957). *Baby and child care*. New York: Pocket Books.

Sprafkin, J., & Silverman, T. (1982). Sex on prime time. In M. Schwarz (Ed.), *TV and teens* (pp. 130–135). Reading, MA: Addison-Wesley.

Sroufe, L. A. (1979). Socioemotional development. In J. Osofsky (Ed.), *Handbook of infant development* (pp. 462–516). New York: Wiley.

Sroufe, L. A., & Waters, E. (1976). The ontogenesis of smiling and laughter: A perspective on the organization of development in infancy. *Psychological Review, 83*, 173–186.

Sroufe, L. A. (1983). Individual patterns of adaptation from infancy to preschool. In M. Perlmutter (Ed.), *Minnesota symposia on child psychology* (Vol. 16). Hillsdale, NJ: Lawrence Erlbaum.

Sroufe, L. A., & Wunsch, J. P. (1977). The development of laughter in the first year of life. *Child Development, 43*, 1326–1344.

Stanton, A. N., Scott, D. J., & Downhan, M. A. (1980). Is overheating a factor in some unexpected infant deaths? *Lancet*, 1054–1057.

Stark, R. E. (1978). Features of infant sounds: The emergence of cooing. *Journal of Child Language, 3*, 379–390.

Stark, R. E., Rose, S. N., & McLagen, M. (1975). Features of infant sounds: The first eight weeks of life. *Journal of Child Language, 2*, 205–222.

Starkey, D. (1981). The origins of concept formation: Object sorting and object preference in early infancy. *Child Development, 52*, 489–497.

Stayton, D. J., Ainsworth, M. D. S., & Main, M. B. (1973). The development of separation behavior in the first year of life: Protest, following, greeting. *Developmental Psychology, 9*, 213–225.

Stechler, G., & Halton, A. (1982). Prenatal influences on human development. In B. B. Wolman, G. Sticker, S. J. Ellman, P. Keith-Spiegel, & D. S. Palermo (Eds.), *Handbook of developmental psychology*. Englewood Cliffs, NJ: Prentice-Hall.

Stein, A., Cambell, E. A., Day, A., McPherson, K., & Cooper, P. J. (1987). Social adversity, low birth weight, and preterm delivery. *British Medical Journal, 295*, 291–293.

Stein, Z., & Susser, M. (1985). Effects of early nutrition on neurological and mental competence in human beings. *Psychological Medicine, 15*, 717–726.

Steinberg, L., Catalano, R., & Dooley, D. (1981). Economic antecedents of child abuse and neglect. *Child Development, 52*, 975–985.

Steiner, J. E. (1973). The gustofacial response: Observation on normal and anencephalic newborn infants. In J. F. Bosma (Ed.), *Fourth symposium on oral sensation and perception*. (DHEW Publication No. NIH 73–546). Bethesda, MD: Department of Health, Education, and Welfare.

Steiner, J. E. (1977). Facial expressions of the neonate infant indicating the hedonics of food-related chemical stimuli. In J. M. Weiffenbach (Ed.), *Taste and development*. Bethesda, MD: Department of Health, Education and Welfare.

Stella-Prorok, E. M. (1983). Mother-child language in the natural environment. In K. E. Nelson (Ed.), *Children's language*. Hillsdale, NJ: Erlbaum.

Stenberg, C., Campos, J. J., & Emde, R. N. (1983). The facial expression of anger in seven-month-old infants. *Child Development, 54*, 178–184.

Sterman, M. B., & Hoppenbrouwers, T. (1971). The development of sleep-waking and rest-activity patterns from fetus to adult in man. In M. B. Sterman, D. J. McGinty, & A. M. Adinolfi (Eds.), *Brain development and behavior* (pp. 203–228). New York: Academic Press.

Stern, D. N. (1977). *The first relationship*. Cambridge: Harvard University Press.

Stern, D. N. (1985). *The interpersonal world of the infant*. New York: Basic Books.

Stern, D. N., Jaffe, J., Beebe, B., & Bennett, S. J. (1975). Vocalizing in unison and in alteration: Two modes of communication within the mother-infant dyad. *Annals of the New York Academy of Science, 263*, 89–100.

Stern, D. N., Spieker, S., & MacKain, K. (1982). Intonation contours as signals in maternal speech to pre-linguistic infants. *Developmental Psychology, 18*, 727–735.

Sternberg, R. J., & Davidson, J. E. (1985). Cognitive development in the gifted and talented. In F. D. Horowitz & M. O'Brien (Eds.), *The gifted and talented: Developmental perspectives* (pp. 37–74). Washington, DC: American Psychological Association.

Stevens, J. H. (1984). Black grandmothers' & black adolescent mothers' knowledge about parenting. *Developmental Psychology, 20*, 1017–1025.

Stevens, J. H. (1988). Social support, locus of control, and parenting in three low-income groups of mothers: Black teenagers, black adults, and white adults. *Child Development, 59*, 635–642.

Stevenson, M. R., & Black, K. N. (1988). Paternal absence and sex-role development: A meta-analysis. *Child Development, 59*, 793–814.

Stevenson, M. B., Roach, M. A., Ver Hoeve, J. N., & Leavitt, L. A. (1990). Rhythms in the dialogue of infant feeding: Preterm and term infants. *Infant Behavior and Development, 13*, 51–70.

Stewart, A. (1983). Severe perinatal hazards. In M. Rutter (Ed.), *Developmental neuropsychiatry*. New York: Churchill Livingstone.

Stewart, R. A. (1981). Supplementary foods: Their nutritional role in infant feedings. In J. Bond, L. Filer, G. LeVeille, A. Thomson, & W. Weil, *Infant and child feeding*. New York: Academic Press.

Stewart, R. A. (1983). Sibling interaction: The role of the older child as teacher for the younger. *Merrill-Palmer Quarterly, 29*, 47–68.

Stewart, R. A., Mobley, L. A., Van Tuyl, S. S., & Salvador, M. A. (1987). The firstborn's adjustment to the birth of a sibling: A longitudinal assessment. *Child Development, 58*, 341–355.

Stiefel, G. S., Plunkett, J. W., & Meisels, S. J. (1987). Affective expression among preterm infants of varying levels of biological risk. *Infant Behavior and Development, 10,* 151–164.

Stifter, C. A., Fox, N. A., & Porges, S. W. (1989). Facial expressivity and vagal tone in 5- and 10-month-old infants. *Infant Behavior and Development, 12,* 127–137.

Stone, L. J., Smith, H., & Murphy, L. (1973). *The competent infant.* New York: Basic Books.

Stoneman, Z., Brody, G. H., & MacKinnon, C. (1984). Naturalistic observations of children's activities and roles while playing with their siblings and friends. *Child Development, 55,* 617–627.

Strauss, M. S., & Curtis, L. E. (1981). Infant's perception of numerosity. *Child Development, 52,* 1146–1152.

Streeter, L. (1976). Language perception of two-month-old infants shows effects of both innate mechanisms and experience. *Nature, 259,* 39–41.

Streissguth, A. P., Martin, D. C., Barr, H. M., Sandman, B. M., Kirchner, G. L., & Darby, B. L. (1984). Intrauterine alcohol and nicotine exposure. Attention and reaction time in 4-year-old children. *Developmental Psychology, 20,* 533–541.

Streri, A., & Spelke, E. S. (1989). Effects of motion and figural goodness on haptic object perception in infancy. *Child Development, 60,* 1111–1125.

Strobino, B. A., & Pantel-Silverman, J. (1987). First-trimester vaginal bleeding and the loss of chromosomally normal and abnormal conceptions. *American Journal of Obstetrics and Gynecology, 157,* 1150–1154.

Sugarman, S. (1982). The development of preverbal communication: Its contribution and limits in promoting the development of language. In R. Schiefelbusch & L. Pickar (Eds.), *Communicative competence: Acquisition and intervention.* Baltimore: University Park Press.

Sullivan, M. W., Rovee-Collier, C. K., & Tynes, D. M. (1979). A conditioning analysis of infant longterm memory. *Child Development, 50,* 152–162.

Suomi, S. J. (1987). Genetic and maternal contributions to individual differences in rhesus monkey biobehavioral development. In N. A. Krasnegor, E. M. Blass, M. A. Hofer, & W. P. Smotherman (Eds.), *Perinatal development: A psychobiological perspective* (pp. 397–420). New York: Academic Press.

Suomi. S. J., & Harlow, H. F. (1972). Social rehabilitation of isolate reared monkeys. *Developmental Psychology, 6,* 487–496.

Super, C. (1976). Environmental effects on motor development: The case of "African infant precocity." *Developmental Medicine and Child Neurology, 18,* 561–567.

Super, C. (1981). Behavioral development in infancy. In R. Munroe & B. Whiting (Eds.), *Handbook of cross-cultural human development.* New York: Garland.

Super, C., Herrera, M. G., & Mora, J. O. (1990). Long-term effects of food supplementation and psychosocial intervention on the physical growth of Colombian infants at risk of malnutrition. *Child Development, 61,* 29–49.

Suwalsky, J. T., & Klein, R. P. (1980). Effects of naturally occurring nontraumatic separations from mother. *Infant Mental Health Journal, 1,* 196–201.

Swets-Gronert, F. (1984, August). *Temperament in young children.* Paper presented at European Conference on Development Psychology, Groningen, the Netherlands.

Swoboda, P. J., Kass, J., Morse, P. A., & Leavitt, L. A. (1978). Memory factors in vowel discrimination of normal and at-risk infants. *Child Development, 49,* 332–339.

Symons, D. K., & Moran, G. (1987). The behavioral dynamics of mutual responsiveness in early face-to-face mother-infant interaction. *Child Development, 58,* 1488–1495.

Takahashi, K. (1986). Examining the strange-situation procedure with Japanese mothers and 12-month-old infants. *Developmental Psychology, 22,* 265–270.

Tamis-LeMonda, C. S., & Bornstein, M. H. (1989). Habituation and maternal encouragement of attention in infancy as predictors of toddler language, play, and representational competence. *Child Development, 60,* 738–751.

Tamis-LeMonda, C. S., & Bornstein, M. H. (1990). Language, play, and attention at one year. *Infant Behavior and Development, 13,* 85–98.

Tan, L. E. (1985). Laterality and motor-skills in four-year-olds. *Child Development, 56,* 119–124.

Tanner, J. M. (1970). Physical growth. In P. H. Mussen (Ed.), *Manual of child psychology* (3rd ed.) (pp. 77–156). New York: Wiley.

Taub, H. B., Goldstein, K. M., & Caputo, D. V. (1977). Indices of neonatal prematurity as discriminators of development in middle childhood. *Child Development, 48,* 797–805.

Taylor, R. (1989). Cracking cocaine's legacy in babies of drug abusers. *Journal of NIH Research, 1,* 29–32.

Terjesen, N. C., & Wilkins, L. P. (1979). A proposal for a model of a sudden infant death syndrome act: Help for the "other" victims of SIDS. *Family Law Quarterly, 12,* 285–308.

Termine, N. T., & Izard, C. E. (1988). Infants' responses to their mothers' expressions of joy and sadness. *Developmental Psychology, 24,* 223–229.

Teti, D. M., & Ablard, K. E. (1989). Security of attachment and infant-sibling relationships: A laboratory study. *Child Development, 60,* 1519–1528.

Teti, D. M., Bond, L. A., & Gibbs, E. D. (1988). Mothers, fathers, and siblings: A comparison of play styles and influence upon infant cognitive level. *International Journal of Behavioral Development, 11,* 415–432.

Tharapel, A. T., Tharapel, S. A., & Bannerman, R. M. (1985). Recurrent pregnancy losses and parental chromosome abnormalities: A review. *British Journal of Obstetrics and Gynecology, 92,* 899–914.

Thelen, E. (1989). The (re)discovery of motor development: Learning new things from an old field. *Developmental Psychology, 25,* 946–949.

Thelen, E., Bradshaw, G., & Ward, J. A. (1981). Spontaneous kicking in month-old infants: Manifestation of a human central locomotor program. *Behavioral and Neural Biology, 32,* 45–53.

Thelen, E., Fisher, D. M., & Ridley-Johnson, R. (1984). The relationship between physical growth and a newborn reflex. *Infant Behavior and Development, 7,* 479–493.

Thelen, E., & Fogel, A. (1989). Toward an action-based theory of infant development. In J. Lockman & N. Hazen (Eds.), *Action in social context: Perspectives on early development* (pp. 23–64). New York: Plenum.

Thelen, E., Skala, K. D., & Kelso, J. A. (1987). The dynamic nature of early coordination: Evidence from bilateral leg movements in young infants. *Developmental Psychology, 23,* 179–186.

Thoman, E., Barnett, C., & Leiderman, P. H. (1971). Feeding behaviors of newborn infants as a function of parity of the mother. *Child Development, 42,* 1471–1483.

Thoman, E., Leiderman, P. H., & Olson, J. P. (1972). Neonate-mother interactions during breast feeding. *Developmental Psychology, 6,* 110–118.

Thomas, A., & Chess, S. (1977). *Temperament and development.* New York: Brunner/Mazel.

Thompson, R. A., Connell, J. P., & Bridges, L. J. (1988). Temperament, emotion, and social interactive behavior in the strange situation: A component process analysis of attachment system functioning. *Child Development, 59,* 1102–1110.

Thompson, R. A., & Lamb, M. E. (1982). Stranger sociability and its relationships to temperament and social experiences during the second year. *Infant Behavior and Development, 5,* 277–287.

Thorpe, L. A. & Trehub, S. E. (1989). Duration illusion and auditory grouping in infancy. *Developmental Psychology, 25,* 122–127.

Tiedemann, D. (1927). Tiedemann's observations on the development of the mental faculties of children (S. Langer, Trans.). *Pedagogical Seminary and Journal of Genetic Psychology, 34,* 205–230.

Tinsley, B. R., & Parke, R. D. (1984). Grandparents as support and socialization agents. In M. Lewis (Ed.), *Beyond the dyad.* New York: Plenum.

Titus, S. L. (1976). Family photographs and transition to parenthood. *Journal of Marriage and the Family, 38*, 525–530.

Tizard, B., & Rees, J. (1974). A comparison of the effects of adoption, restoration to the natural mother, and continued institutionalization on the cognitive development of four-year-old children. *Child Development, 45*, 92–99.

Tizard, J., & Tizard, B. (1971). The social development of 2-year-old children in a residential nursery. In H. R. Schaffer (Ed.), *The origin of human social relations.* London: Academic Press.

Toda, S., & Fogel, A. (1989, April). *Infant behavior in the still-face situation at 3 and 6 months.* Paper presented at the Society for Research in Child Development, Kansas City, Missouri.

Toda, S., Fogel, A., & Kawai, M. (in press). Maternal speech to three-month old infants in the United States and Japan. *Journal of Child Language.*

Tomasello, M., & Farrar, M. J. (1986). Joint attention and early language. *Child Development, 57*, 1454–1463.

Tomasello, M., Mannle, S., & Kruger, A. C. (1986). Linguistic environment of 1- to 2-year-old twins. *Developmental Psychology, 22*, 169–176.

Tompkins, S. (1962). *Affect, imagery and consciousness: Vol. 1.* New York: Springer.

Trause, M. A. (1977). Stranger responses: Effects of familiarity, stranger's approach and sex of infant. *Child Development, 48*, 1657–1661.

Trause, M. A., Boslett, M., Voos, D., Rudd, C., Klaus, M., & Kennell, J. (1978). A birth in the hospital: The effect on the sibling. *Birth and the Family Journal, 5*, 207–210.

Trehub, S. E., Bull, D., & Thorpe, L. A. (1984). Infants' perception of melodies: The role of melodic contour. *Child Development, 55*, 821–830.

Trehub, S. E., Thorpe, L. A., & Morrongiello, B. A. (1987). Organizational processes in infants' perception of auditory patterns. *Child Development, 58*, 741–749.

Trevarthen, C. (1973). Behavioral embryology. In E. C. Carterette & M. P. Friedman (Eds.), *Handbook of perception: Vol. 3, Biology of perceptual systems.* New York: Academic Press.

Trevarthen, C. (1977). Descriptive analysis of infant communicative behavior. In H. R. Schaffer (Ed.), *Studies of mother-infant interaction* (pp. 227–270). London: Academic Press.

Trickett, P. K., & Susman, E. J. (1988). Parental perceptions of child-rearing practices in physically abusive and nonabusive families. *Developmental Psychology, 24*, 270–276.

Triseliotis, J. P. (1973). *In search of origins.* London: Kegan Paul.

Tronick, E., Als, H., Adamson, L., Weise, S., & Brazelton, T. B. (1978). The infant's response to entrapment between contradictory messages in face-to-face interaction. *Journal of Child Psychiatry, 17*, 1–13.

Tronick, E., & Cohn, J. F. (1989). Infant-mother face-to-face interactions: Age and gender differences in coordination and the occurrence of miscoordination. *Child Development, 60*, 85–92.

Trost, J. (1985, November-December). Swedish solutions. *Society*, 44–48.

Turkewitz, G., Birch, H., & Cooper, K. (1972). Responsiveness to simple and complex auditory stimuli in the human newborn. *Developmental Psychobiology, 5*, 7–19.

Turkewitz, G., & Kenny, P. A. (1985). The role of developmental limitation of sensory input on sensory/perceptual organization. *Journal of Developmental and Behavioral Pediatrics, 6*, 302–306.

Turkheimer, M., Bakeman, R., & Adamson, L. B. (1989). Do mothers support and peers inhibit skilled object play in infancy? *Infant Behavior and Development, 12*, 37–44.

Ungerer, J., Brody, L., & Zelazo, P. (1978). Long-term memory for speech in 2- to 4-week-old infants. *Infant Behavior and Development, 1*, 177–186.

Ungerer, J., & Sigman, M. (1984). The relation of play and sensorimotor behavior to language in the second year. *Child Development, 55*, 1448–1455.

Ungerer, J., Zelazo, P. R., Kearsley, R. D., & O'Leary, K. (1981). Developmental changes in the representation of objects in symbolic play from 18 to 34 months of age. *Child Development, 52,* 186–195.

United Nations Department of Economic and Social Affairs. (1986). *Demographic yearbook.* New York: United Nations.

Uzgiris, I. C. (1983). Imitation in infancy: Its interpersonal aspects. In M. Perlmutter (Ed.), *Minnesota symposia on child psychology* (Vol. 17) (pp. 1–32). Hillsdale, NJ: Erlbaum.

Uzgiris, I. C., & Hunt, J. M. (1975). *Toward ordinal scales of psychological development in infancy.* Champaign: University of Illinois.

Vandell, D. L. (1979). Effects of a playgroup experience on mother-son and father-son interaction. *Developmental Psychology, 15,* 379–385.

Vandell, D. L. (1980) Sociability with peer and mother during the first year. *Developmental Psychology, 16,* 335–361.

Vandell, D. L., Henderson, V. K., & Wilson, K. S. (1988). A longitudinal study of children with day-care experiences of varying quality. *Child Development, 59,* 1286–1292.

Vandell, D. L., Owen, M. T., Wilson, K. S., & Henderson, V. K. (1988). Social development in infant twins: Peer and mother-child relationships. *Child Development, 59,* 168–177.

Vandell, D. L., & Wilson, K. S. (1987). Infants' interactions with mother, sibling, and peer: Contrasts and relations between interaction systems. *Child Development, 58,* 176–186.

Vandell, D. L., Wilson, K. S., & Buchanan, N. R. (1980). Peer interaction in the first year of life: An examination of its structure, content, and sensitivity to toys. *Child Development, 51,* 481–488.

VanDoorninck, W. J., Caldwell, B. M., Wright, C., & Frankenburg, W. K. (1981). The relationship between twelve-month home stimulation and school achievement. *Child Development, 52,* 1080–1083.

Van Giffen, K., & Haith, M. H. (1984). Infant visual response to Gestalt geometric forms. *Infant Behavior and Development, 7,* 335–346.

Van IJzendoorn, M. H., & Kroonenberg, P. M. (1988). Cross-cultural patterns of attachment: A meta-analysis of the strange situation. *Child Development, 59,* 147–156.

Vaughn, B. E., Bradley, C. F., Joffe, L. S., Seifer, R., & Barglow, P. (1987). Maternal characteristics measured prenatally are predictive of ratings of temperamental "difficulty" on the Carey Infant Temperament Questionnaire. *Developmental Psychology, 23,* 152–161.

Vaughn, B. E., Deane, K. E., & Waters, E. (1985). The impact of out-of-home care on child-mother attachment quality: Another look at some enduring questions. In I. Bretherton & E. Waters (Eds.), *Growing points of attachment theory and research. Monographs of the Society for Research in Child Development, 50*(1–2, Whole No. 209).

Vaughn, B. E., Egeland, B., Sroufe, L. A., & Waters, E. (1979). Individual differences in infant-mother attachment at twelve and eighteen months: Stability and change in families under stress. *Child Development, 50,* 971–975.

Vaughn, B. E., Grove, F. L., & Egeland, B. (1980). The relationship between out-of-home care and the quality of infant-mother attachment in an economically disadvantaged population. *Child Development, 51,* 1203–1214.

Vaughn, B. E., Kopp, C. B., & Krakow, J. B. (1984). The emergence and consolidation of self-control from 18 to 30 months of age: Normative trends and individual differences. *Child Development, 55,* 990–1004.

Vaughn, B. E., Kopp, C. B., Krakow, J. B., Johnson, K., & Schwartz, S. S. (1986). Process analyses of the behavior of very young children in delay tasks. *Developmental Psychology, 22,* 752–759.

Vaughn, B. E., Taraldson, B. J., Crichton, L., & Egeland, B. (1981). The assessment of infant temperament: A critique of the Carey Infant Temperament Questionnaire. *Infant Behavior and Development, 4,* 1–18.

Vertes, R. P. (1986). A life-sustaining function for REM sleep: A theory. *Neuroscience and Biobehavioral Reviews, 10* (4), 371–376.

Vibbert, M., & Bornstein, M. H. (1989). Specific associations between domains of mother-child interaction and toddler referential language and pretense play. *Infant Behavior and Development, 12,* 163–184.

Vohr, B. R., & Coll, C. T. G. (1985). Neurodevelopmental and school performance of very low-birth-weight infants: A seven-year longitudinal study. *Pediatrics, 76,* 345–350.

Von Hemel, J. O., Majoor-Krakauer, D. F., Jahoda, M. G. J., & Sachs, E. S. (1986). First trimester diagnosis from chorionic villi of a der(15), t(9;15), (q33;Q14)mat identified by DA/DAPI staining. *Journal of Medical Genetics, 23,* 89–90.

Von Hofsten, C. (1984). Developmental changes in the organization of prereaching movements. *Developmental Psychology, 20,* 378–388.

Von Hofsten, C., & Spelke, E. S. (1985). Object perception and object-directed reaching in infancy. *Journal of Experimental Psychology: General, 114,* 198–212.

Vorhees, C. V., & Mollnow, E. (1987). Behavioral teratogenesis: Long-term influences on behavior from early exposure to environmental agents. In J. D. Osofsky (Ed.), *Handbook of infant development.* New York: Wiley.

Vygotsky, L. S. (1978). *Mind in society.* Cambridge, MA: Harvard University Press.

Wachs, T. D. (1982). Early experience and early cognitive development: The search for specificity. In I. Uzgiris & J. Hunt (Eds.), *Research with scales of psychological development in infancy.* Champaign: University of Illinois Press.

Wachs, T. D. (1987). Specificity of environmental action as manifest in environmental correlates of infant's mastery motivation. *Developmental Psychology, 23,* 782–790.

Wachs, T. D. (1988). Relevance of physical environment influences for toddler temperament. *Infant Behavior and Development, 11,* 431–445.

Wachs, T. D., & Gandour, M. J. (1983). Temperament, environment, and six-month cognitive-intellectual development: A test of the organismic specificity hypothesis. *International Journal of Behavioral Development, 6,* 135–152.

Wachs, T. D., & Gruen, G. E. (1982). *Early experience and human development.* New York: Plenum.

Waddington, C. H. (1966). *Principles of development and differentiation.* New York: Macmillan.

Walden, T. A., & Ogan, T. A. (1988). The development of social referencing. *Child Development, 59,* 1230–1240.

Waletzky, L. (1979). Husbands' problems with breast-feeding. *American Journal of Orthopsychiatry, 49,* 349–353.

Walker, B. E., & Quarles, J. (1976). Palate development in mouse foetuses after tongue removal. *Archives of Oral Biology, 21,* 405–412.

Wallach, M. A. (1985). Creativity testing and giftedness. In F. D. Horowitz & M. O'Brien (Eds.), *The gifted and talented: Developmental perspectives* (pp. 99–123). Washington, DC: American Psychological Association.

Ward, M. J., Vaughn, B. E., & Robb, M. D. (1988). Social-emotional adaptation and infant-mother attachment in siblings: Role of the mother in cross-sibling consistency. *Child Development, 59,* 643–651.

Wasserman, G. A., Allen, R., & Solomon, C. R. (1985). At-risk toddlers and their mothers: The special case of physical handicap. *Child Development, 56,* 73–83.

Waters, E. (1983). The stability of individual differences in infant attachment: Comments on the Thompson, Lamb, and Estes contributions. *Child Development, 54,* 516–520.

Waters, E., Vaughn, B., & Egeland, B. (1980). Individual differences in infant-mother attachment relationships at age one: Antecedents in neonatal behavior in an urban, economically disadvantaged sample. *Child Development, 51,* 208–216.

Watson, J. S. (1973). Smiling, cooing, and "the game." *Merrill-Palmer Quarterly, 18,* 323–339.

Wedenberg, E. (1956). Auditory tests on newborn infants. *Acta-Oto-laryngologica, 46,* 446–461.

Weinraub, M., Clements, L. P., Sockloff, A., Ethridge, T., Gracely, E., & Myers, B. (1984). The development of sex role stereotypes in the third year: Relations to gender labeling, sex-typed toy preference and family characteristics. *Child Development, 55,* 1493–1503.

Weinraub, M., & Lewis, M. (1977). The determinants of children's responses to separation. *Monographs of the Society for Research in Child Development, 42*(Serial No. 172).

Weinraub, M., & Putney, E. (1978). The effects of heights on infant's social responses to unfamiliar persons. *Child Development, 49,* 598–603.

Weinraub, M., & Wolf, B. M. (1983). Effects of stress and social supports on mother-child interactions in single- and two-parent families. *Child Development, 54,* 1297–1311.

Weintraub, K. S., & Furman, L. N. (1987). Child care: Quality, regulation, and research. *Social Policy Report: Society for Research in Child Development, 2.*

Weir, R. H . (1966). Questions on the learning of phonology. In F. Smith & G. A. Miller (Eds.), *The genesis of language: A psycholinguistic approach.* Cambridge: MIT Press.

Weir, R., & Feldman, W. (1975). A study of infant feeding practices. *Birth and the Family Journal, 2,* 63–64.

Weitzman, N., Birns, B., & Friend, R. (1985). Traditional and nontraditional mothers' communication with their daughters and sons. *Child Development, 56,* 894–898.

Wellman, H. M., Cross, D., & Bartsch, K. (1986). Infant search and object permanence: A meta-analysis of the A-not-B error. *Monographs of the Society for Research in Child Development, 51*(3, Serial No. 214).

Wellman, H. M., & Lempers, J. D. (1977). The naturalistic communicative abilities of two-year-olds. *Child Development, 48,* 1052–1057.

Wenckstern, S., Weizmann, F., & Leenaars, A. A. (1984). Temperament and tempos of play in eight-month-old infants. *Child Development, 55,* 1195–1199.

Wente, A., & Crockenberg, S. (1976). Transition to fatherhood: Pre-natal Lamaze preparation, adjustment difficulty and the adult husband-wife relationship. *Family Coordinator, 25,* 351–357.

Werker, J. F., & Lalonde, C. E. (1988). Cross-language speech perception: Initial capabilities and developmental change. *Developmental Psychology, 24,* 672–683.

Werker, J. F., & Tees, R. C. (1984). Cross-language speech perception: Evidence for perceptual reorganization during the first year of life. *Infant Behavior and Development, 7,* 49–63.

Werner, E. (1979). *Cross-cultural child development.* Monterey, CA: Brooks-Cole.

Werner, E. (1986, April). *The infant's view of planet earth.* Paper presented at International Conference on Infant Studies, Los Angeles.

Werner, E., Bierman, J., & French, F. (1971). *The children of Kauai.* Honolulu: University of Hawaii Press.

West, L., & Fogel, A. (April, 1990). *Maternal guidance of object interaction.* Paper presented at International Conference on Infant Studies, Montreal.

West, M. J., & Rheingold, H. L. (1978). Infant stimulation of maternal instruction. *Infant Behavior and Development, 1,* 205–215.

Westbrook, M. (1978). Analyzing affective responses to past events: Women's reactions to a childbearing year. *Journal of Clinical Psychology, 34,* 967–971.

Whitehurst, G. J., & Vasta, R. (1975). Is language acquired through imitation? *Journal of Psycholinguistic Research, 4,* 37–59.

Whitehurst, G. J., Falco, F. L., Lonigan, C. J., Fischel, J. E., DeBaryshe, B. D., Valdez-Menchaca, M. C., & Caulfield, M. (1988). Accelerating language development through picture book reading. *Developmental Psychology, 24,* 552–559.

Whiten, A., & Milner, P. (1986). The educational experiences of Nigerian infants. In H. V. Curran (Ed.), *Nigerian children: Developmental perspectives.* London: Routledge & Kegan Paul.

Whiting, B. (1974). Folk wisdom and child-rearing. *Merrill-Palmer Quarterly, 20,* 9–19.

Whiting, B., & Whiting, J . W. (1975). *Children of six cultures: A psychocultural analysis*. Cambridge: Harvard University Press.

Whiting, J. (1981). Environmental constraints on infant care practices. In R. Monroe, R. Monroe, & B. Whiting (Eds.), *Handbook of cross-cultural development*. New York: Garland Publishing.

Wideman, M. V., & Singer, J. E. (1984). The role of psychological mechanisms in preparation for childbirth. *American Psychologist, 39*, 1357–1371.

Widmayer, S. M., Peterson, L. M., Lerner, M., Carnahan, S., Calderon, A., Wingerd, J., & Marshall, R. (1990). Predictors of Haitian-American infant development at twelve months. *Child Development, 61*, 410–415.

Wiehe, V. R. (1989). Child abuse: An ecological perspective. *Early Child Development and Care, 42*, 141–149.

Wiesenfeld, A. R., Malatesta, C. Z., & DeLoache, L. (1981). Differential parental response to familiar and unfamiliar infant distress signals. *Infant Behavior and Development, 4*, 281–295.

Wilkie, C. F., & Ames, E. W. (1986). The relationship of infant crying to parental stress in the transition to parenthood. *Journal of Marriage and the Family, 48*, 545–550.

Williams, O. (1952). *Immortal poems of the English language*. New York: Washington Square Press.

Wilson, E. (1975). *Sociobiology*. New York: Wiley.

Wilson, M. N. (1986). The black extended family: An analytical consideration. *Developmental Psychology, 22*, 246–258.

Winick, M., Knarig, K., & Harris, R. (1975). Malnutrition and environmental enrichment by early adoption. *Science, 190*, 1173–1175.

Winnicott, D. (1971). *Playing and reality*. New York: Basic Books.

Wolf, D., & Gardner, H. (1979). Style and sequence in early symbolic play. In N. Smith & M. Franklin (Eds.), *Symbolic functioning in childhood*. Hillsdale, NJ: Erlbaum.

Wolff, P. H. (1966). The causes, controls and organization of behavior in the neonate. *Psychological Issues, 5*(Monograph No. 17).

Woodson, R., Drinkwin, J., & Hamilton, C. (1985). Effects of nonnutritive sucking on state and activity: Term-preterm comparisons. *Infant Behavior and Development, 8*, 435–441.

Woodson, R., & Hamilton, C. (1988). The effect of nonnutritive sucking on heart rate in preterm infants. *Developmental Psychobiology, 21* (3), 207–213.

World Health Organization. (1976). *New trends and approaches in the delivery of maternal and child care in health services*. (Tech. Rep. Series No. 600). Geneva: Author.

World Health Organization. (1985). *The quantity and quality of breast milk*. Geneva: Author.

Worobey, J., & Belsky, J. (1982). Employing the Brazelton scale to influence mothering: An experimental comparison of three strategies. *Developmental Psychology, 18*, 736–743.

Worobey, J., & Blajda, V. M. (1989). Temperament ratings at 2 weeks, 2 months, and 1 year: Differential stability of activity and emotionality. *Developmental Psychology, 25*, 257–262.

Worobey, J., & Lewis, M. (1989). Individual differences in the reactivity of young infants. *Developmental Psychology, 25*, 663–667.

Yale Bush Center Infant Care Leave Project. (1985). *Facts on parents in the workforce and infant care*. New Haven: Author.

Yalom, I. D. (1968). Postpartum blues syndrome. *Archives of General Psychiatry, 28*, 16–27.

Yarrow, L. J., Rubenstein, J. L., & Pedersen, F. A. (1975). *Infant and environment: Early cognitive and motivational development*. Washington, DC: Hemisphere Publishing.

Yates, D. J., & Bremner, J. G. (1988). Conditions for Piagetian stage IV search errors in a task using transparent occluders. *Infant Behavior and Development, 11*, 411–417.

Yoder, P. J. (1989). Maternal question use predicts later language development in specific-language-disordered children. *Journal of Speech and Hearing Disorders, 54,* 347–355.

Yonas, A., Arterberry, M. E., & Granrud, C. E. (1987). Four-month-old infants' sensitivity to binocular and kinetic information for three-dimensional-object shape. *Child Development, 58,* 910–917.

Yonas, A., Beachtold, A. G., Frankel, D., Gordon, F. R., McRoberts, G., Norcia, A., & Sternfels, S. (1977). Development of sensitivity to information for impending collision. *Perception and Psychophysics, 21,* 97–104.

Yonas, A., Pettersen, L., & Granrud, C. E. (1982). Infants' sensitivity to familiar size as information for distance. *Child Development, 53,* 1285–1290.

Yonas, A., Pettersen, L., & Lockman, J. (1979). Young infants' sensitivity to optical information for collision. *Canadian Journal of Psychology, 33,* 268–276.

Yonas, A., Pettersen, L., Lockman, J., & Eisenberg, P. (1980, April). *The perception of impending collision in 3-month-old infants.* Paper presented at the International Conference of Infant Studies, New Haven, CT.

Young, G., & Lewis, M. (1979). Effects of familiarity and maternal attention on infant peer relations. *Merrill-Palmer Quarterly, 25,* 105–120.

Young, G., Segalowitz, S. J., Misek, P., Alp, I. E., & Boulet, R. (1983). Is early reaching left handed? Review of manual specialization research. In G. Young, S. J. Segalowitz, C. M. Corter, & S. Trehub (Eds.), *Manual specialization and the developing brain.* New York: Academic Press.

Young, I. D., Rickett, A. B., & Clarke, M. (1986). Genetic analysis of malformations causing perinatal mortality. *Journal of Medical Genetics, 23,* 58–63.

Younger, B., & Gotlieb, S. (1988). Development of categorization skills: Changes in the nature or structure of infant form categories? *Developmental Psychology, 24,* 611–619.

Zachry, W. (1978). Ordinality and interdependence of representation and language development in infancy. *Child Development, 49,* 681–687.

Zahn-Waxler, C., Friedman, S. L., & Cummings, E. M. (1983). Children's emotions and behaviors in response to infants' cries. *Child Development, 54,* 1522–1528.

Zahn-Waxler, C., Iannotti, R., & Chapman, M. (1982). Peers and prosocial development. In K. H. Rubin & H. S. Ross (Eds.), *Peer relations and social skills in childhood.* New York: Springer-Verlag.

Zarbatany, L., & Lamb, M. (1985). Social referencing as a function of information source: Mothers versus strangers. *Infant Behavior and Development, 8,* 25–33.

Zarling, C. L., Hirsch, B. J., & Landry, S. (1988). Maternal social networks and mother-infant interactions in full-term and very low birthweight preterm infants. *Child Development, 59,* 178–185.

Zeitz, D. (1969). *Child welfare: Services and perspectives.* New York: Wiley.

Zelazo, P. R. (1976). From reflexive to instrumental behavior. In L. P. Lipsitt (Ed.), *Developmental psychobiology: The significance of infancy.* Hillsdale, NJ: Erlbaum.

Zelazo, P. R., Brody, L. R., & Chaikan, H. (1984). Neonatal habituation and dishabituation of head turning to rattle sounds. *Infant Behavior and Development, 7,* 311–321.

Zeskind, P. S. (1980). Adult responses to cries of low and high risk infants. *Infant Behavior and Development, 3,* 167–178.

Zeskind, P. S., & Iacino, R. (1984). Effects of maternal visitation to preterm infants in the neonatal intensive care unit. *Child Development, 55,* 1887–1893.

Zeskind, P. S., & Iacino, R. (1987). The relation between length of hospitalization and the mental and physical development of preterm infants. *Infant Behavior and Development, 10,* 217–221.

Zeskind, P. S., & Lester, B. M. (1978). Acoustic features of auditory perceptions of the cries of newborns with prenatal complications. *Child Development, 49,* 580–589.

Zeskind, P. S., & Lester, B. M. (1981). Analysis of cry features in newborns with differential fetal growth. *Child Development, 52,* 207–212.

Zeskind, P. S., & Marshall, T. R. (1988). The relation between variations in pitch and maternal perceptions of infant crying. *Child Development, 59,* 193–196.

Zlatin, M. A. (1973). Explorative mapping of the vocal tract and primitive syllabification in infancy: The first six months. *Purdue University Contributed Papers,* Fall.

Zukow, P. G. (1980). A microanalytic study of the role of the caregiver in the relationship between and language acquisition during the one word period (Doctoral dissertation, University of California, 1980). *Dissertation Abstracts International, 42,* 18.

Zukow, P. G. (1986). The relationship between interaction with the caregiver and the emergence of play activities during the one-word period. *British Journal of Developmental Psychology, 4,* 223–234.

Zukow, P. G. (1990). Siblings as effective socializing agents: Evidence from central Mexico. In P. G. Zukow (Ed.), *Sibling interaction across cultures: Theoretical and methodological issues.* Springer-Verlag.

SUBJECT INDEX

O

O'Brien, M. 212, 387
O'Connell, B. 362
O'Hara, M. W. 227
O'Leary, K. 345
Oehler, J. M. 136
Ogan, T. A. 290
Ohr, P. S. 213
Olds, S. B. 130
Oller, D. K. 252, 253
Olson, S. L. 163, 360
Olson, J. P. 190
Olson, K. L. 222
Oppenheim, D. 335
Orpen, G. 190
Osofsky, J. 57, 157, 416
Oster, H. 54, 180, 181, 186
Otaki, M. 224
Over, R. 186
Oviatt, S. L. 325
Owen, M. T. 230, 260, 334, 407
Owen, G. 233
Owsley, C. J. 207, 209, 211

P

Palkovitz, R. 193, 261
Palmer, C. F. 314
Panneton, R. K. 85
Papousek, H. 183, 203, 204, 222
Papousek, M. 203, 222, 226, 360
Parfitt, R. R. 116
Park, K. A. 302
Parke, R. 226, 409
Parke, R. D. 189, 226, 230, 260, 265, 290, 305, 367, 368, 402
Parmelee, A. H., Jr. 154
Parmelee, A. 131, 132, 134, 333
Parrinello, R. M. 281
Parten, M. 15, 24
Passman, R. 287
Passman, R. H. 354, 355
Patterson, C. J. 372
Paulson, G. 168
Pavlov, I. 39
Pearson, J. L. 305
Pedersen, F. 265, 305, 365
Pederson, D. R. 301
Peiper, A. 168, 217
Peleaux, R. 284
Peltola, C. 211
Pena, I. C. 134
Pennebaker, J. 224
Perris, E. E. 213, 245
Perruci, C. 371
Perry, S. 227
Peters, D. 371

Peters, T. J. 232
Peterson, G. 292, 371
Petitto, L. 325
Petrinovich, L. F. 380
Pettit, G. S. 163
Phillips, L. H. 227
Phillips, D. 335, 338
Phillips, J. J. 274
Phillips, R. D. 251
Phipps, Yonas, S. 96
Piaget, J. 345, 352, 356
Piaget, J. 12, 15, 16, 43, 44, 45, 46, 47, 56, 212, 214, 215, 216, 217, 247, 273, 276, 277, 278, 279, 280, 284, 317, 381, 382, 384, 385, 387
Pickens, J. N. 253
Pipes, P. L. 266, 267
Pipp, S. 350, 351
Pistrang, N. 261
Plaetzer, B. 390
Pleck, J. H. 189, 261
Plomin, R. 37, 428
Plumb, N. 192
Plunkett, J. W. 331
Plutchik, R. 53
Polansky, N. 409
Pollitt, E. 147
Pomerleau, A. 221
Poresky, R. H. 284, 288
Porges, S. W. 225
Porter, R. H. 180
Portes, P. 371
Posner, M. I. 280
Power, T. G. 280, 402
Prechtl, H. F. R. 166
Proffitt, D. 210
Profitt, D. R. 210
Provence, S. 339, 369
Puffer, R. R. 138
Purvis, G. A. 266
Putney, E. 285

Q

Quarles, J. 81

R

Raag, T. 353
Radell, P. L. 85
Radke-Yarrow, M. 388
Ragozin, A. S. 230
Rahe, D. F. 400
Ramey, C. T. 418, 426
Ramey, C. 365
Ramsay, D. S. 380
Ramsey, C. N. 133

Rapoport, R. 329
Rapoport, R. N. 329
Rappoport, D. 126
Reardon, P. 245
Rebelsky, F. 189
Reeb, K. G. 133
Reece, R. M. 233
Reed, G. 320
Rees, J. 356
Reilly, J. 325
Reimers, M. 55
Reissland, N. 186
Reite, M. 287
Reoppelli, R. J. 161
Reznick, J. S. 255, 430
Rheingold, H. L. 292, 322, 326, 365
Ricciuti, H. N. 284, 285, 287, 288
Richard, M. P. M. 344
Richards, P. 224
Richman, A. 226
Ricks, S. S. 265
Ridgeway, D. 352
Riese, M. L. 430
Rieser-Danner, L. A. 286
Rieser-Danner, L. S. 208
Riley, C. A. 383
Risenhoover, N. 290
Ritter, J. M. 208
Robert, C. 89
Roberts, K. 318
Robertson, J. 287
Robertson, J.(a) 356
Robertson, S. S. 84
Robinson, C. 85
Robinson, C. H. 146, 266, 267
Robinson, N. M. 230
Rocca, P. T. 211
Rochat, P. 171, 182, 203, 205, 212, 241
Rocissand, L. 395
Rocissano, L. 363
Rodholm, M. 192, 193
Roggman, L. A. 208, 286
Rogoff, B. 258, 361, 365, 391, 405
Rose, S. A. 182, 211, 226, 245, 275
Rose, S. N. 216
Rosenblatt, J. S. 187
Rosenblith, J. F. 124
Rosenblith, J. R. 116, 120, 121, 240, 314
Rosenblith, J. 201, 202
Rosenstein, D. 180, 181, 186
Ross, H. S. 286, 304, 326, 398
Rossi, A. 104, 105
Rothbart, M. K. 280, 428
Rousseau, J. 4, 5
Rovee-Collier, C. K. 213
Rovine, M. 229
Rovine, M. J. 334, 338
Rubenstein, J. 365
Ruble, D. N. 230